Colour impacts upon every aspect of our lives. It inspires and uplifts, and has the healing on all levels of the body, mind and spirit. Few modalities embody colour's much as Colour Mirrors, the power of which is made visible and accessible in this Colour Mirrors is a fascinating read and an invaluable reference for anyone interest this captivating, enchanting system. The book is a gift to the world, a tangible pathwa activating Heaven on Earth.

Suzanne Ellis - Journalist, Editor, Author of *Faces in the Forest*, Co-Author of *The Art of Reflexology* and *Sky-Traveller-in-Training*

As Ray McKimm's foreword so brilliantly elucidates, the wisdom of the ages travels on wings, as it were, of colour. His words set the scene for you to understand immediately and deeply why this book is so important. Melissie and Korani's work in the pages that follow will give you a bottomless supply of spiritual food and guidance, backed up by the luscious images which are the product of Melissie's years exploring colour in its every facet and gift. These pages take you on a journey through the bottles she has created, and which you can use to read about, talk with, bathe in and venture into on every level while they work quietly with you to change your life from the inside out. This book will release you to be the self you were always meant to be, to do what you came here to do. And as you travel through its pages, it will deliver you into your natural state of joy and power and love as it sets you free.

Philippa Merivale – Author, Founder of Metatronic Healing, www.metatronic-life.com

This book makes a perfect companion guide as you get to know better the heritage, purpose, philosophy and many varied teachings of Colour Mirrors. Written in a style that both new starter and experienced teacher can learn from, it is like the system itself: multi-layered and intended as something to go back to time and time again - always with the ability to reveal something new. The pages are full of wonderful human stories, personal testaments to the power of colour healing and of course the whole range of shiny bright bottles that make up its core.

Amanda Ellis - Spiritual Teacher, Angelic & Celestial Channel, Colour Intuitive, You Tube: Amanda Ellis, www.amandaellis.co.uk

As I read the flow of it all, my eyes filled with tears for the profound clarity, joy and love that is the Colour Mirrors system and community. I had this deep sense of gratitude for being given access to it all and for being part of the generosity that the circle provides.

Kath Roberts - Colour Teacher, Systems Coach, Creative Entrepreneur, Co-Author of *Colourful Boardrooms*, www.kath-roberts.com

What shines through every page of this book is the love that both authors and all those who have contributed stories have for the Colour Mirrors system. My fervent wish is that this book acts as a way to start more conversations amongst those who have yet to experience the benefits of colour therapy so that its impact can continue to expand.

Kate Griffiths - Colour Teacher, Systems Facilitator, Co-Author of *Colourful Boardrooms*, www.wholeselfleadership.com

As a fellow spiritual warrior who has been trying to navigate the crazy world both internally and externally around me over many years, I have found great safety, guidance, trust and empowerment from using the Colour Mirrors system. This book has been patiently waiting for us all to be truly ready to face our fears, release our old patterns in life, explore our shadows and bring them into the light of our conscious minds to fully love and accept all aspects of ourselves - the good, the bad and the ugly. Allow yourself to be gently held, gently awakened and gently transformed. After reading this book, life will never be the same again.

Sharon King, Creator and Director of Magical New Beginnings, Author of *Heal Your Birth, Heal Your Life*, www.magicalnewbeginnings.com

The Wisdom

of

Colour Mirrors

Korani Connolly and Melissie Jolly

If you enjoy this book please share these websites with others:
www.colourmirrors.com
www.korani.net

We would like to express our heartfelt thanks to Martha Van Der Westhuizen for the brilliant cover photography.
Email: marthavdw@gmail.com
Visit Martha Van Der Westhuizen Photography on Facebook
www.facebook.com/MarthavanderWesthuizenPhotography

ISBN: 978-0-9564394-1-3

Acknowledgements

We are beyond grateful to Moira Bush for all the time you took to read through the book and for your invaluable advice, input and suggestions. Another huge thank you to Katherine Louise Jones for your feedback, ideas, enthusiasm and the support you have given us all the way through. Thanks too to Lesley McDonald, Michael Kapp, Amanda Bradbury and Kathryn Marshall for your input. Grateful thanks for the sterling job done by our proof-readers Alka Dharam, Lesley-Ann Iveson, Penny Wing and Lisa Moore, with a special mention to Alka Dharam for grammatical expertise and helpful feedback.

To everyone who has contributed stories and/or testimonials for this book, they are gold. Thank you all so much. To the beautiful souls who have contributed endorsements, we are honoured and humbled. Thank you.

We are enormously grateful to Leila Summers of www.info@spread-the-word.co.za for all your time, dedication and patience in turning the manuscript into a book and to Ruby Jane for all your hard work! Huge gratitude to the wonderfully gifted Martha Van Der Westhuizen for 'group' shots of the oils, various individual essences, and Melissie's photo. Big thanks too to the lovely and talented Bev Hooper for the photo of Korani. (You can see more of her work at www.rubydelaneyspicturefactory.co.uk).

And, of course, to the wonderful women who actually make the Colour Mirrors bottles, Gilly Ball and Anna-the-Angel-Maker Tobias.

There are many, many people who have supported and assisted Colour Mirrors and taken a role in its history and evolution, and we are profoundly grateful to each and every one, including:

Philippa Merivale, Sharon King, Ray McKimm, Kath Roberts, Kate Griffiths, Clara Apollo, Priscilla Elliott, Anne Whitehouse, Caroline Buckle, Amanda Ellis, Jackie Tweedie, Renira Barclay, Claire Lawson, Tadeja Jere Jakulin, Marit Tessem, Lina Katrine Larsen, Rui Diogo, Anne Clark-Caya, Hayden Crawford, Sara di Felice, and Premjay and Ananya from the Inner Guide Centre in Seoul.

If we have not mentioned you by name, please know that as a member of the Colour Mirrors family you are in our hearts and we appreciate you deeply. We are grateful to the many folks who take courses and workshops, all those who train as Colour Mirrors practitioners and teachers – in fact, anyone who shares, works, plays with and enjoys Colour Mirrors in any form!

Contents

Foreword

Since I discovered Colour Mirrors in 2007, I have seen a magical interplay between this system and my work as a psychotherapist within the NHS, the voluntary sector and in private practice. Colour Mirrors gives my clients tender instruments with which they can discover themselves and activate their strengths and passions, enabling them to take on life in a whole new way.

Through my training in Jungian Psychology, and with over 30 years of clinical experience, I have seen how symbols can reach the deeper parts of the mind and how we can symbolically express the things we find in our unconscious mind more fluently through colour than we might using words. This is particularly the case when those thoughts and feelings are confusing or threatening. We all know what it is like to be lost for words when life feels too much, and it is my experience that the Colour Mirrors system gives us the ability to express ourselves even when the spoken word evades us.

Colour is relevant to everyone because it is not bound to language or particular cultural traditions and does not depend on a high level of essential skills such as reading and writing. It is also non-threatening because an individual's colour choices can be seen as a personal expression of their challenges and strengths. It is comprehensive, as it relates to all potential scenarios of a person's life. The Colour Mirrors bottles act as tools we can use to bring into our conscious thinking what we already innately know about ourselves. In short, the Colour Mirrors system is a language that enables us to connect with our imagination, our aspirations, our individuality and our unity.

Individual and Collective History in Colour

Our individual and collective histories are interwoven with stories of light. In the Christian/Hebrew tradition there is the story of a god who brought light to the world as a way of bringing harmony to all that existed. The Hindu, Muslim and Buddhist faiths also have symbolic representations of the role of light in bringing meaning and purpose to life.

So in the beginning there was light and with it, inherently, there was colour. And colour not only brought life but also enabled us to make sense of that life. Since the beginning of time we have marked milestones and transformations through the medium of colour. It has been a way of expressing our needs, our identity and our connectedness. You might say it is the language of both 'I AMness' and oneness.

From the times of our earliest ancestors we evolved using colour as a tool through which we could relate to the world around us. We used colour as a coding system that enabled us to survive and thrive in a very challenging environment. As we moved out of the darkest corners of the world and the deep jungles and caves, we adapted to the world of light and shade by reading patterns of black and white, light and dark. These patterns still define the deepest, most primal drives and impulses that we use to make sense of the world, and we see their use in ancient spiritual symbols such as the Yin/Yang.

Through the ages as we navigated life and evolved into more complex beings, we processed new experiences in colour rather than black and white. By observing the rhythm of the day we set down our earliest circadian rhythms – our internal clock – against the colourful backdrop of the glowing sky and thus developed the ability to perceive and recognise yellow and blue. By developing behaviours to determine sources of nutrition we learned the contrast between berry and leaf: red and green.

The journey of self-discovery that can be facilitated through colour applies just as much to our collective evolution as it does to our personal growth and development. On humanity's evolutionary pathway, colour became a means of distinguishing sameness and difference in ways that helped our ancestors navigate the challenges of life. For example, it was essential for our survival and our health and wellbeing to learn to distinguish subtle differences in skin, eye and hair colour between those who were our tribe and those who were not.

Colour: A Two Way Process

As our intricate relationship with the world around us evolved, we began to have a clearer understanding of how we perceive colour. We learned that what we see as colour is actually the atoms and molecules in any solid matter spinning and bouncing back the remnants of the original light they took in but did not need. Depending on the chemical compound of the natural matter, be that a leaf, a rock or the water in a river, the energy bounces back in a short, long or anything-in-between wave. Through a combination of perception and recognition, our brains translate those waves into frameworks that help us make sense of the world: a set of symbols that we refer to as colour.

Exploring our perception of colour and our relationship to it we see that it is the result of a complex interaction between us and the world around us. On the one hand, we can see that from the light source in the physical world (the atoms and molecules bouncing back energy) we derive a system to interpret the energy waves that engage with and sustain us. On the other hand, as we attempt to make sense of our lives emotionally and psychologically, colour interacts with our understanding of people, events and our own expectations. It creates a tool that summarises the complexity of these experiences in a straightforward language, which allows us not only to respond to the world around us but to thrive and flourish in it.

In pursuit of a way to explain the hidden processes which come into play when we see colour, I have developed and published an overarching theory called Colour Analytical Psychology (CAP). This draws extensively upon Jungian Analytical Psychology but also includes the major themes of Evolutionary and Social Psychology. It aims to show how we can use colour as a group of symbols through which we can understand ourselves and the world around us.

By drawing together accepted knowledge of how we live our lives individually and collectively, CAP puts in place the theory behind the practice of Colour Mirrors. Essentially it shows us that colour exists in a two-way process between us and the world around us. On the one hand, the world around us is projected onto our lives through colour, and on the other, we project back who we are by the thousands of colour choices we make and the meanings we attach to them.

The Language of Health and Well-Being

The simplest science books show that colour is a light wave being projected onto our bodies, so it is no surprise that we can receive the stimuli both retinally (through the eye) and cutaneously (through our bodies). The earliest records of our ancestors' pursuit of well-being reference the benefits of colour received through the body rather than the eyes. You will see in this book how Colour Mirrors has utilised this phenomena by recommending that we bathe in the coloured bottles that resonate with us.

Since the mid-1800's modern science has been experimenting with the benefits of receiving colour through this alternative (cutaneous) method. It has explored the physiological and psychological consequences of our bodies' exposure to colour through both light and pigment and the health benefits of such exposure. Colour Mirrors gives us the tools to bring these benefits into our own lives and the lives of our clients through the wonderful bottles of single and dual colours.

Colour is light speaking, not in patterns of sound as we conventionally understand language, but rather in patterns of symbols which enable us to rapidly understand ourselves, others and the world around us. When our ancestors first saw green, red or yellow it was pre-language, in the same way that a baby first sees colour. It was about an experience of the stimuli: it sat with them, it reminded them, it inspired them, it warned them. Colour was not about a sound or a word; it was an experience interpreted on many cognitive and emotional levels.

In my work as a psychotherapist I have seen over and over again the profound benefit to my clients of connecting the unconscious mind with the conscious. We might refer to this as things 'coming into the light' or coming to awareness. The act of being aware of ourselves and the nature of the challenges we face is by far the greatest part of the therapeutic process. Using colour as a therapeutic language truly facilitates this process, bringing ease to the therapeutic conversation and providing a means to externalise the internal conflicts we experience. The act of externalising enables the client to see themselves as separate from the problem – an observer – and in doing so, makes it less about their character and more about a process in which they can set goals and achieve and maintain tangible change.

In this book we see how the Colour Mirrors system takes us back beyond word and sound to explore what is laid down in our unconscious individual and collective memory about colour and how we can draw on that deep knowing and use it in the daily experiences of life. We might say that our colour perception is the internalising of an ancient dialogue to keep us safe and well. In our modern, evolved lives we might refer to it as the language of health and well-being.

Just as we metabolise energy from food, so we can, like plants, metabolise energy from light and colour. We have overtly developed our understanding of food to maximise the benefit we get from it. I believe our ancestors did the same with colour and that we have that knowledge, albeit tucked away in the deepest parts of our minds, waiting to be released so that we can live healthily and well.

We live in an age where our understanding of the influence of colour on our lives is expanding. In an attempt to pursue this unfolding even further, this book goes behind the scenes with colour. The authors have given us a tool that we can utilise for ourselves and our clients to create lives where we not only survive but thrive.

Colour Mirrors: Connecting the Dots

In the Colour Mirrors system instinct combines with object (colour) to create a fascinating and useful tool for self-discovery. We are able to relate our deep inner knowing and our feelings to people, places and expectations, making it easier to resolve conflicts that lay within the deepest parts of our minds. The use of bottles of colour to explore our thoughts and feelings powerfully connects the unconscious with the conscious. Working with these tangible objects can bring the many features of who we are into the light, into a comforting wholeness.

Colour Mirrors activates both the individual and the collective unconscious thinking processes, enabling us to bring to our conscious thinking the things that bother us and impede us from being the fullest versions of ourselves. It unifies us in our exploration to make sense of the world and our desire to draw the best from the experiences that we encounter together.

Colour is a simple tool that enables us to say who we are and who we are becoming. It spans borders and spoken languages and speaks our story symbolically, enabling us to draw upon our instincts and our knowing to recognise what our lives truly need in any given circumstance. This book gives us the knowledge to draw on these symbolic riches and empower us towards the life we desire. And it gives us access to that knowledge in a practical and clear format.

It introduces us to the vast array of colours that we can perceive. It gives us a system similar to the Dewey Decimal system used in a library to help us find what we need amongst the masses of information stored there. This book is the Dewey Decimal system for colour, the vast knowledge available to us from our ancestors and the collective consciousness. It could also be said that it is the Dewey Decimal system for the knowledge of another level of consciousness: the Akashic Records which are stored in light and presumably colour. Whichever way you describe it, Colour Mirrors is the record of a language that gets us in touch with ourselves and our true potential.

In his book *Theory of Colours* Goethe tells us that to demonstrate his theory of colour/light refraction he hung a crystal on a string in his window. The result was a breathtaking rainbow of beautiful colours spread across the room. In the same way, this book bounces colour across our lives into every imaginable situation that we might encounter and brings a sense of magic and possibility. It is with humble gratitude that I recommend this book to you and encourage you to indulge yourself in a colourful exploration of your greatness. It is with a grateful heart that I thank the authors for their part not only in my own colour journey but also for the light that is cast by this book upon our collective journey to wholeness. By delving into the riches of colour contained in this book, I wish for you a colourful and enlightening journey.

Ray McKimm
Green Therapy and Training
www.greentherapyandtraining.com

The Wisdom of Colour Mirrors

In November 2001 a light quietly dawned on the planet in the far reaches of South Africa. A woman in a dusty village in the Western Cape began a process that was birthed out of necessity yet bore all the hallmarks of magic and alchemy. It was a process that would bear fruit for many years to come, touching people all over the world, transforming lives and enlightening hearts and minds. It was a process that would lead to the creation of a set of brightly coloured oils and essences, and the birth of a system for healing that would bring about shift and change in ways that could not have been foreseen.

That woman, of course, is Melissie Jolly, and the system is Colour Mirrors.

"I fell in love with colour the way people fall in love with their soul mate. It was instantaneous and forever. There is no other way to describe my connection to colour, and over the years we have brought together a tribe of people who feel the same. I have loved the vibrancy of the colours of a sunset and a rainbow, and I have loved the colours of a grey day over the sea. I have loved art and fashion, and when I was young I thought that either of those might be the direction I would have to go in if I wanted to follow my love. Sadly, it turned out that I was not an artist or in any way a designer, but when I discovered colour as a therapy I knew instantly what I was going to do when I grew up, and in that moment my love affair blossomed into its current state of joyous ongoing exploration." — Melissie Jolly

Have you ever wondered how it would be if you could look into a mirror and see everything about yourself, all your fears, doubts and blocks, all your gifts, talents and possibilities? How it would be to have guidance, support and assistance for every challenge you experience and the tools to help you embrace a life of courage, resilience and joy?

Well, now you can: meet Colour Mirrors.

Colour Transforms

Colour Mirrors is a healing system that takes the energies of light and uses them to address the deeply buried thoughts and beliefs that reside within your cells. The light at the core of the Colour Mirrors system and the healing intention embodied in each of the coloured bottles travels swiftly into the core of your being, releasing old stored memories and dissolving what is no longer required. The information carried on the light waves of colour also opens you to questions: "What am I here for? What choices can I make? What is life really about?" When you find yourself stuck, overwhelmed or in difficulty, colour has the capacity to bring your deepest confusions and doubts to the surface, providing answers that work, answers that help you feel renewed, answers that point the way forward.

Colour has been used for centuries as a therapeutic tool, and there are a myriad of ways to work with it. What Colour Mirrors does that is perhaps unique is to reveal colour as the ultimate mirror. When you look at an array of colours or combinations of colours that have been created with healing intent, you see reflected in each of them an aspect of yourself. Intent is a powerful energy. When it is added to love, the creative force that builds worlds, and light – which is its expression – a power-pack is generated that is both healing and enlightening.

By bringing the earth energies of flowers, crystals, water and oil into a formula whose expression is colour, and by infusing that formula with the force of pure and conscious intent, Colour Mirrors transmits the voice of love not just to your mind but to the cells of your body. When your cells fully receive a message – any message – they log the information. They have an innate intelligence that can transmute or change a perception, so if they perceive what once appeared to be a threat as an ally, what was once ugly as beautiful, what was once scarcity as abundance, then so it is. Change becomes not only possible but inevitable.

The coloured oils and essences of Colour Mirrors are highly energised, and it is not only when you apply them to the surface of your skin or smell their delicious scents that these energies reach you. A conversation around them – or indeed with them – causes things to happen in your body as well as your mind. As you work with these potent coloured energies, you discover that colour frees your psyche from distorted and unhelpful patterning. Disharmony returns to ease. Purposelessness and stagnation return to fulfilment and flow. Cells shed old programming like a snake sheds its skin, and new information moves in to take its place. Colour speaks to the whole of you in ways that little else does, and it comes as no surprise that so many people when they encounter colour – and Colour Mirrors – feel a deep sense of coming home.

This Book

The Wisdom of Colour Mirrors has its genesis in Philippa Merivale's *Colour Works*, which was produced in 2006. This marvellous book is now out of print but was based around a series of conversations between Melissie and her dear friend Philippa about each of the bottles in the Colour Mirrors set at that time. Many years later the system has grown and evolved so much that we felt it was time to offer an expanded, updated exploration of the bottles.

We wish to pay tribute to the initial work undertaken by Philippa. We owe her an enormous debt of gratitude for starting the ball rolling back in Colour Mirrors' early days. A small amount of the material from *Colour Works* has been included in this book in adapted or modified form, with Philippa's permission. Once again, Philippa, we are grateful.

This book covers all the bottles in the Colour Mirrors system to date, both oils and essences. The first section of the book is dedicated to bottles 1-36, which are in many ways the foundation stones on which the whole system is built. We sometimes refer to these as the 'issue' bottles because they so clearly indicate the issues going on for the person choosing them. But Ray McKimm calls them 'The Wisdoms' and really, this perfectly describes these bottles. They reveal both the wisdom of colour and the wisdom you hold within as your inner guidance moves you to choose them.

The next section of the book explores the Chakra set of bottles. Traditionally there are seven main chakras in the human body and energy system, yet our set is made up of 15 bottles, two bottles relating to each of the seven main chakras of the human body and one that connects with the eighth chakra or soul star. In 'The Evolution of Colour Mirrors' (p.6) and in the section on the Chakra bottles (p.96) we explore why this is so.

From the Chakra set we delve into the expansive world of the Gaia bottles – 36 bottles divided into various subsets which together tell our individual and collective stories of life on earth, from the history of humankind on the planet into our future. We finish with the 39 Colour Mirrors essences in the system to date, each of which has a special message to share.

As you pick up this book you may notice that you can already feel it – and the Colour Mirrors bottles – working with you. This book and the bottles it describes are energy, and the words shared with you here may touch you in various ways. At times you may feel uplifted and connected. At others, you may find yourself in tears. It is not our intention that you should have to process your 'stuff' as you read this book, but be aware that it may happen anyway!

Colour Mirrors has the gift of both helping you to see your inner light and supporting you when you cannot. In this book we aim to create a balance. On the one hand, your bottle and colour choices reveal things you may need to honestly address in order to create change in your life. Some of the bottles deliver tough messages and ask you to face yourself in the mirror. If you wish to walk lightly into the future, there may first be some healing required for your past. This is where the 'Wisdom' bottles, 1-36, and the chakra bottles tend to come in.

On the other hand, many of the bottles and their messages – particularly the Gaia set – highlight the purest intention with which they were made and focus on the greatest possible expression of their light. They show you the fullest potential you hold within, holding up a huge mirror made of light and love, reflecting to you the beauty and brilliance of your soul.

We have included stories about the bottles, some from our own experiences, some we have heard about from students, friends and clients and some from first-hand accounts given to us. There are many, many more, as any Colour Mirrors practitioner or teacher will tell you, but they are often not recorded, and most have become lost in the mists of time. We hope that the stories we share with you here will serve as inspiration for your own journey and illustrate the multitude of possibilities colour presents.

Many of the stories we hear from people who connect with Colour Mirrors are about shifts they have experienced, insights they have received or healing that has occurred – and sometimes they happen almost instantaneously. At other times, transformation happens slowly, step by step, day by day, little by little. Life is rarely linear and healing can come in stages, growth may happen in waves.

As shifts take place integration is needed, so while at times you may appear to be moving fast and growing in leaps and bounds, at others you may seem to plateau or even go backwards. The latter is an illusion, however, as what you are really doing is re-visiting part of your journey that has not been fully healed or integrated so that you can learn and grow even more. This is the spiral of evolution: as a soul opens to each new piece of information, each new beam of light, each new sweep of the spiral, it gathers strength, courage, knowledge and wisdom. This is the route to true transformation.

Will your experience be exactly as you read about in these pages? That will depend on your unique history, background and degree of willingness to engage with your journey. Our wish for you, whatever has drawn you to this book, is that something in these words and this system will connect with you, inspire you and open you to the greatness you hold within.

Colour Mirrors appeals to many who are on a conscious spiritual path – in other words those who have an interest in exploring areas such as healing, spirituality, energy and the cosmic nature of the universe. There is a core set of spiritual principles that underpin and overlight Colour Mirrors – and life. These principles are explained in the section on the Chakra bottles titled 'The Chakra Colours and the Spiritual Principles of Colour' (p.97), but essentially they can all be found throughout the pages of this book. Each bottle taps into one or more of these guiding principles in some way and highlights it. We recommend you read Melissie's book *What the Seeker Found*, as it explains, explores and expands on many of these principles and the concepts touched on here.

For those who are just waking up to the idea of spirituality or those who have less interest in this side of life, some of the language we use may be unfamiliar or refer to things outside of what is generally considered 'normal' or usual human experience. To this end, we have included a glossary at the back of the book (p.256).

Beyond the language, however, the bottles in the Colour Mirrors system may open you to energies and experiences you have not come across before. Sometimes the Gaia bottles in particular may take you into territory that feels strange or even a little daunting. We – and the bottles – invite you to stay open. If anything you read does not resonate for you, feel free to move on. If, however, it touches something in you at some level, perhaps feels uncomfortable or unexpected, stay open to the experience and go with it if you will. You may find that your resistance to any of the material offered here is actually an invitation to recognise your blocks, face some fears, question what you have believed up until now and find out more about yourself and life in the process. You may just find it offers you something you have been waiting all your life to find.

This system and this book are not solely for the spiritual seeker, yet the energies of all the Colour Mirrors bottles have the power to touch your heart and soul as you read about them, and they will continually show you to yourself as a being of Divine light. Every bottle in the system essentially reminds you that you are love, that you are light, that you are part of the oneness of all life. Each will speak to you in different ways at different times and each has its own unique message, yet fundamentally they all say much the same thing: you are Divine and you are loved beyond measure. Again, if this is challenging for you on any level, be open and let the possibility that it might just be true enter your body and your mind.

Many of the bottles refer to the idea of 'heaven on earth'. This is not a religious reference but a state of being, a way of viewing life. It arises when you are connected to the Divine in your daily life and see it in everything and everyone. It is an internal state rather than a place to arrive at. It might be summed up as the bliss of being at peace with 'what is', loving and accepting every moment as it unfolds and knowing yourself to be utterly one with all life. Each of the Colour Mirrors bottles in some way assists you in recognising what blocks you from this state of Divine connection and helps you overcome it. Each bottle guides you out of third dimensional density towards a higher vibration where you can acknowledge what keeps you in limitation, learn what it has to teach you and integrate its lessons into your body and life, thereby creating your very own 'heaven on earth'.

As we individually create this state of lightness within ourselves, we collectively begin to see it arise on the earth so that more and more people begin to live from a place of love rather than judgement, joy rather than fear and peace rather than conflict. As each person follows their bliss, connects with their inner Divine and becomes aware of the oneness of all life, so earth, in turn, becomes 'heaven'.

It might seem on many levels that earth is very far from heaven indeed at this time of huge upheaval and apparent crisis and conflict. Yet now more than ever we are called to shift our focus from the problems to the solutions. By turning towards love, towards peace, towards unity, we bring more of these qualities to the earth. By opening to inspiration and new ways of moving forward, both for ourselves as individuals and for the collective, we create new possibilities on the earth. We can either get lost in the apparent hopelessness of the task facing humanity at this time, or we can embrace the higher truth of our Divine nature and set about creating a quiet revolution of love, peace and joy on the planet. What we focus on expands, and what Colour Mirrors shows us, clearly and with intent, is that we *can* change the earth as we walk upon it. We *can* make a better world for everyone. We have the capacity to create a more empowered, more enlightened reality and Colour Mirrors is one of the tools that will help us do so.

It is our wish that this book will open you to the powerful and positive impact colour can have in your life. We hope you will find wisdom in its pages, in the world of colour itself and, of course, in the astonishing oils and essences that make up the Colour Mirrors system. Most of all, however, we hope you will be empowered to tap into more of the true, vast, deep wisdom you hold within.

The majority of the actual writing in this book was done by Korani, but the ideas and information here come from our collaboration over many years. Our work together is a source of constant joy for us both, and we are profoundly grateful that we exist at the same time on the same planet. This book is an interweaving of our energies, our words and our voices, but more than anything it is the voice of the overlighting energy of this thing we call Colour Mirrors, which is a greater source of light and wisdom than either of us have ever known.

Korani & Melissie, 2019

For the Love of Colour: Melissie's Story

The true business of this lifetime began at the age of 33. I had married for the second time and had three children – a daughter and two sons, my teachers and the loves of my life – and it was becoming clear that there was something I had come into this world to do, although I had no idea what that might be. There followed 10 years of intense searching and studying, everything from psychology to art and many things in between, and it really was not clear sailing. Every time I thought I had found the 'thing' I was here for, every time I had a 'Eureka!' moment, it passed – and the disappointment was intense.

At the age of 43 it finally found a shape and a form and mainly a colour. The thing that used to drive me insane about the world was that it didn't make sense and no one could give me answers – certainly not school or the church. The biggest gift of colour was that it gave me the answers I was seeking. When I discovered colour it literally lit up my world and made sense of it for the very first time, and finally my life's work and my joy could begin.

I worked intensely with colour for almost five years, running workshops, doing readings, loving every minute of it, when suddenly my world was turned upside down and the most intense initiation began. Thank goodness my soul was in charge and not my poor fearful personality because although the journey continued in exactly the way my soul knew would be for my absolute highest good, I had to undergo the loss of everything I had built up as walls to hide my true soul self. My husband left, my mother died, my business went bankrupt, I lost my house, and my children had to leave because I could no longer afford to support them.

Those were nightmare years. I was literally living on the kindness of friends and strangers. It was such an important part of the lesson: to receive. Those generous people who arrived when the cupboard was completely bare, often with money – small and large amounts and always on time – their names are written in gold and are kept in a shatter-proof glass case in my heart. The most difficult thing about being completely penniless is that it is not easy to be generous. I missed that the most. But I learnt how to receive generosity with grace and immense gratitude.

I did everything I knew spiritually to try and change things. No one told me at the beginning that it would take 10 long years before it would be over. Things just started breaking down around me, and all I could do was watch in horror as everything disappeared. I meditated and processed and prayed. I went to psychologists and psychics and anyone who might be able to explain things or help me, but for 10 years nothing stopped the breakdown of everything that felt familiar. Eight years into this process I went to an astrologer who told me that it would be another two years before this was over, but that then things would just burst into joy for me. I thought: "Two years! I won't survive another two years."

Not long after this I was sitting on the beach one night when a whale who had been very close to the shore just about beached himself to get my attention. Eventually I asked: "What?" As clear as a bell, in the most mellifluous voice I had ever heard, the whale told me that eight years of a ten year initiation were done and that there were just two more years to go. I was knocked down flat on the sand in floods of tears, and when I finally picked myself up I thought: "OK, I can do two more years." And so it was, and the next level began. Another incarnation without dropping the body. But it was a kind of death and rebirth, and as in all births, one lands naked on the planet with very little to define one. This time it was my job to live differently, with my soul as the guide, not my mind or my personality or anything that is not the soul's truth.

Just before all of this occurred I knew I had to keep working – for my sanity and literally to survive – and through sheer Divine grace at this time I received the information on how to make bottles of coloured oil, and a system, which was to evolve into Colour Mirrors, was created.

Birthing Colour Mirrors

It was 22nd November 2001 and I had students booked for a workshop a day or two later. My time with a previous colour system had come to a sudden end and I literally had nothing to teach them with. A friend who made candles suggested we try to work out a formula together to make our own coloured oils. We found we could colour the water but not the oil. Then another friend who was a chemist came to help. With some basic ingredients and a small supply of glass containers in hand, he showed me how to colour the oils so they would hold.

Next my wonderful friend Silva arrived with a basket full of essential oils and said: "Let's play." Within 36 hours it was done – 33 colour bottles and all the notes for a manual – and a day later I ran the first workshop with this brand new system. What was interesting and surprising was that there were colours in there that I passionately do not like. You can imagine that after working with colour for years I had masses of colour combinations in my head, but they were all the nice ones. The temptation was to make only pretty bottles, yet some of the bottles that form the core set in Colour Mirrors are quite far from pretty – and still they had to be there. There was no way they could not be included.

It felt completely right to create a set of 33 bottles, and I had already started making them when a friend arrived with a gift of Linda Goodman's *Star Cards*. In this pack were 33 cards. Thirty-three is the age at which Jesus/Yeshua became the Christ, and the Christ light is an energy I have always been comfortable with. It has also always felt like one of the overlighting energies of the system. I had thought that I would like to connect the bottles with Astrology somehow and the first nine Star Cards all related to planets. The colours were so astonishingly like the colours I had made that it was with goose-bumpy excitement that I saw what the cards held. It felt like the most enormous confirmation that I was on the right track.

Silva held my hand through the first difficult year where I really had nothing and had to build up everything from scratch. She was the most wonderful, solid support who told me endlessly to 'unpanic'. The next huge step forward was meeting Moira Bush and Amanda Bradbury in England. Moira needed a new career and scooped up Colour Mirrors with her magnificent marketing skills and started to take us out into the world. Amanda invested money that was entirely life-saving. Through Moira I met Korani, and from that time on, Moira, Amanda, Korani and I really became the four cornerstones of Colour Mirrors. I believe that if any one of us were not there, the rest would not have been able to do the job.

At this time I also re-met my darling soul sister Philippa Merivale. From all the generosity I have met in my life, nothing comes close to the profound gift Philippa gave us. Out of her own pocket, heart and time, Philippa wrote the book *Colour Works,* so-called because at that time the system was named Colourworks. Now we had a system of coloured oils, a series of workshops that could be presented – and a book. We were finally grown-up and real!

The Evolution of Colour Mirrors

It is interesting that the numbers in Colour Mirrors have always been so full of information. Over the years several bottles were added to the initial 33 so that now there are now 36 'Wisdoms'. The numbers 3 + 6 added together make 9, and 9 is the number of completion, so no more will be added to this part of the system. To me it has always felt as if these 36 bottles add up to make one person. Together they show the permutations of all our personality traits and all our possibilities. They also show us where we limit ourselves and where we stop ourselves from actively being able to access the whole of who we are.

The next part of the system had to be something that would offer more physical support. It is all very well to be able to access our soul qualities and all the parts of our personality, but while we are in a physical body we also need to acknowledge that, so a set of Chakra bottles was added. Chakra means 'wheel of light' in Sanskrit and refers to the energy centres in our bodies. The seven main chakras relate to the colours of the rainbow, starting with red at the base of our spine and moving through orange, yellow, green, blue, indigo to violet at the crown of our head. Magenta relates to the eighth chakra, or 'soul star', above the crown.

The chakra bottles were created to serve as physical support and to acknowledge the body as the congealed and accessible part of the soul that it actually is. One of the most elegant pieces of information in the system came when I attended a workshop by Diana Cooper, who writes books about angels and Ascension among other things. She did a meditation with different chakra colours, explaining that our chakra colours are evolving and changing as we raise our vibration. At first glance I did not really get the new colours, but when I made bottles to match the colours she spoke about, they suddenly made the most beautiful sense and told the story of what is happening to our bodies in a way that nothing else could. So there were now 15 chakra bottles, seven to match the traditional chakra colours, seven to represent the new higher vibrational chakra colours and the one in the middle that remains unchanged, the magenta Soul Star bottle.

The next part of the system began when a friend asked me to make a bottle with a copper fraction, as she kept seeing that colour in her clients' energy fields. I made one bottle that was clear over copper and put it on my bottle table. Every single person who came in that day wanted one. At that point I realised that it might have to be part of the system and as that decision was made, six more asked to be made as well. These seven copper bottles were called the Gaia bottles, as each one had a copper fraction and looked to me like the brown earth of Africa. Gaia is the name of the consciousness of planet earth, and these copper bottles were made very specifically to anchor our experience and ground it. I realised that one of the main difficulties for people on a spiritual journey is to stay grounded, and the copper bottles are energised to do just that. We tend to think that getting grounded would stop us being close to our spirit, but these colours are about earthing our spirit rather than grounding us away from it. They help us bring all the aspects of ourselves into the right here, right now – the present moment of a spirit in a body, on the earth.

Somewhere around this time I realised that we needed something in the system that would facilitate a more instant, 'push-button' kind of healing than the oil bottles provide, and that is when the spritzers appeared. A clever, wordy friend suggested that they be called 'Scent by Angels' and so the Angel sprays joined the system. I really wanted them just to be little 'house angels' – something that could help me find my car keys (Green Angel) and make my hay fever go away (Blue Angel).

While running a channelling workshop around this time, a lot of the participants were feeling drawn to the energy of Archangel Metatron, and they asked me if I could make a spritzer that would help them connect with this being. What I made was a deep magenta colour with a sweet, flowery smell that was absolutely delicious. Typically, I thought that this was the end of the spritzers and that the set was now complete. What has happened again and again in the system, however, is that anything magenta has acted as a bridge and has brought something else completely new to be added on. After Metatron there was suddenly a need for Element spritzers. They started with Air, Earth, Fire and Water and then I was asked to add Metal and Wood. I had also been asked to make Dragon essences but had not felt connected to the idea of dragons and could not see how I would make the numbers work. At this point there were seven Angels and seven Elements (if Metatron was the Ether element), and I found that each of the Angels had a matching Element and that they supported and worked perfectly with each other.

A friend then told me she felt there would be 21 spritzers in all, and I realised that there had to be seven dragon sprays added to the set. But every time I thought I knew what was happening I was proved wrong, and it turned out that there were eight dragons created at that time. I must say that all these years into the system I have finally given up trying to control any of it and simply follow instructions!

Just when I really thought that the whole set was finished and done, however, the biggest surprise of the system arrived in the form of an almost entirely black bottle: G8. It was the eighth of the Gaia bottles and I thought that it was the black full stop at the end of the system. This bottle was the most dense magenta I am capable of creating, and as per usual, the magenta became a bridge for a whole new part of the story to burst into our reality.

Not long after this, in 2009, Korani and I were discussing past life links when I mentioned a gold and turquoise combination and what that might mean. It was near my birthday and I sometimes make myself a birthday bottle just to see what the year might hold for me. As I was thinking about that and feeling that this time it might have to be a turquoise/gold combination, I suddenly heard a voice say that there had to be seven bottles, each with a pale gold fraction, and that they were to be Golden Gaia bottles as we were moving rapidly into a new Golden Age on this earth. These bottles would give us the information and support we needed to make heaven on earth a reality. I am not the kind of person who hears voices or sees visions, but very occasionally this kind of thing happens to me. It is always so unexpected that I wonder if I have finally lost my mind – but I never ignore it. So the seven Golden Gaias were created, and Korani fell in love with them and wrote the most beautiful book about them – *The Language of Light: Golden Keys to Ascension*.

About a year later it seemed we were ready for the next level and the Platinum Gaias were born. Korani was clearly part of the instigation of the Golden Gaias and it felt so appropriate that Moira, another key pillar of Colour Mirrors, instigated the Platinum Gaias. These bottles are mirror images of the Golden Gaias, with each Platinum Gaia made up of the complementary colours to its Golden Gaia partner. The Platinum Gaias take us right up and out into the stars and remind us how vast we are. They stop us from thinking that we might just be small souls doing small things on a small planet and show us an infinite cosmos of unlimited light and potential.

A year after they arrived came five Coral Gaias. These new bottles brought together what we had seen in the Gold and Platinum Gaias, asking us to live all that great, glorious light here on earth in solid, real, physical bodies and to love and accept the entirety of ourselves. Another year on and six Silver Gaias arrived, just in time for the 'Shift of Ages' to commence in 2012. These silver energies were initially quite elusive but promised much to come and revealed the continuing evolution of our DNA. They are collectively called 'The Homecoming'.

In 2016 three Magenta Gaias were added. These magenta bottles are dense and dark and very, very powerful. They are called 'The Anchors' and are more about anchoring our light on the planet than any of the other bottles to date. They brought the total of the Gaias to 36, a perfect balance to the Wisdom set of 36.

Over the years I have been asked to make many different bottles for people to work with. There are Korani's Starlights, a set of oils called the Pearls and various sets used by Colour Mirrors teachers and practitioners to support their individual businesses and therapy work. There are also numerous spritzers which have proven to be hugely popular, including Dolphin, Moldavite and Bliss. Other bottles really just came in to do a bit of magic at a particular time on the planet. None of these have been added to the official Colour Mirrors system but they have appealed to various people at various times and it is always fun to see what wants to be created.

At the time of writing there are 87 oils in the system and 39 spritzers, making a total of 126 bottles – a far cry from the 33 with which it began, when, I have to say, I had absolutely no idea where this would take me. If I were remotely in charge, none of it would have worked the way it has. It has been a journey where faith has been the only way forward. The right person has always appeared at the right time, and the right place has always been created. It is only in hindsight that I can see exactly how each moment happened in the perfect way. All I have been asked to do is show up, and in reality that is all every one of us has been asked to do. Show up for the moment in which you find yourself. Be present in that precise moment and miracles will happen. They certainly did for me.

Colour Mirrors really has been one big miracle all the way down the line. I was the pair of hands involved in bringing the system into physical existence, but it has never felt as if I 'created' it. Rather, it felt as if the whole thing had been sitting wrapped around my heart, waiting and waiting for the right moment to spring into existence. It seemed as if it had always existed, and all that needed to happen was just for someone to be there with the right set of tools to make that happen. With the hugest gratitude, I got to be the one.

In truth the whole thing has been a group effort. It has also been totally organic. None of it was created with business plans or anything that would be considered the right way in the 'real' world. This is a business built on profoundly deep spiritual intent. It created itself and has kept itself going. The key figures were put in place and every time we thought we had a proper 'grown-up' plan it simply ignored us and went its own way. I can honestly say that Colour Mirrors has very little to do with any of us. It is entirely its own thing and no one can really claim that they were the one who created it – we really were only the straws for this luscious chocolate milkshake.

It has always been my intent that everyone who ever saw this system would fall in love with it and then realise that they were looking into a mirror and fall in love with their own image. What is reflected to them is their own beauty and magnificence, the complete rightness of who they are in the world. What we have in Colour Mirrors is something that can go into all those places where we still believe we are not enough – not good enough, not clever enough, not beautiful enough: not enough on any level. The system is energised to heal all of it.

When we look at and choose the most beautiful colours and realise that they reflect the deepest, most magnificent aspects of ourselves, we can no longer believe that there are missing pieces. Each colour reflects an aspect of the Divine, and as we choose our colours we connect with that aspect of us that is our own inner divinity – the most magnificent, exquisite aspect of who we really are. There is not one bottle in the system that does not reflect all the beauty of the Creator right back at us, and now we have to claim it. As a system Colour Mirrors acknowledges who we are. Every single bottle here is an acknowledgment of our divinity and our magnificence, and we cannot get away with anything less.

I wish for you, dear reader, that reading this book and experiencing and exploring the colours will bring you the same satisfaction and ultimate joy that colour has brought me.

Korani's Story

I had waited for Colour Mirrors my whole life, at least that is how it felt when I finally found it – or it found me. When I met Moira and the Colour Mirrors bottles for the first time in 2004 it felt as if something slotted into place inside my heart and my being, and when I got to know Melissie in 2005, an unbreakable bond was forged.

My first encounter with Colour Mirrors took place when I was writing for a small holistic magazine, and among our advertisers was Moira Bush. Her advertisements were eye-catching and the energy of the Colour Mirrors bottles felt different to anything else I'd come across. After seeing Moira display the bottles at a holistic fair we had organised, the editor of the magazine suggested one of us should go and interview Moira to find out what it was all about. My hand shot up, and before I knew it I was booked to have a reading with Moira at her home, which at the time was on the south coast of England. I went online to read up about Colour Mirrors and found the then fledgling Colour Mirrors website. As I looked at images of the colour bottles my heart began to beat very fast and then to sing as I 'recognised' the energies of the bottles in a way I had never experienced before. Something inside me was shouting an enormous "YES!!!" I could hardly wait for my reading.

When Moira sat me down in front of a huge array of gorgeous coloured oils and essences and asked me to choose the ones I was most drawn to, I was in heaven. Like a child in a sweet shop, I could hardly believe how much deliciousness surrounded me. I selected about a dozen bottles and laid them out on the table in front of me. From there Moira proceeded to give me precise information about my past, my present and what lay ahead for me. I was enthralled. How could bottles of colour tell so much about who I was, what I was struggling with, what my gifts were and the potential that was waiting inside to be brought out? Everything Moira said resonated on some level. Every bottle she talked about spoke to me, and by the time we had finished I was booked on her next course to train as a colour practitioner a few weeks later.

My first weekend of colour training was completely mind-blowing. I heard things I had never known before about energy, light, the universe and of course, colour, and yet everything made total sense to me. It was as if I was having my circuits re-opened after years (or lifetimes) of them being closed. All night after the first day's training my third eye was humming with bottles and colour and images. I dreamed vividly and at length, culminating in a dream just before I woke up where an enormous swan sailed into a harbour. The swan is a symbol of the soul, and the message was not lost on me: my soul was coming home.

By the time I had completed two weekends of training, which at that time qualified me as a Colour Mirrors practitioner, I was totally hooked. I bought as many bottles as I could and connected with them endlessly. I shared them with anyone and everyone who I thought might be slightly interested, and before long I started incorporating them into my holistic healing practice, offering readings and healing with the stunning array of bottles.

At the end of 2005 Melissie came to England to offer the first UK Colour Mirrors Teachers' course, and my week with her remains to this day one of the most profound experiences of my life. Every word she spoke rang like a bell of truth for me. I probably sat with my jaw hanging open for most of the week as one door after another opened in my heart and my head. I had truly been waiting for this all my life. After the teacher training, I immediately set a date to run my first colour practitioner course and gathered five intrepid souls to take part. To say I was in joy that first weekend is an understatement. I had literally never felt so alive, so inspired and so lit up inside. I slept barely at all yet felt totally energised. Words poured through me as I shared the wisdom of the colour bottles with those first students, and I watched in awe as they left after two days, each of them touched and transformed by the light and magic of Colour Mirrors.

I began to offer frequent Colour Mirrors practitioner courses as well as using the bottles in my healing sessions, and then in 2007, I received the huge honour of being asked to become one of the first Colour Mirrors teacher trainers, alongside Moira and Amanda. Teacher courses were added to my repertoire, and the journey continued to unfold in astonishing ways as more and more people learned about this system and what it had to offer.

That same year Melissie and I began exchanging emails about colour combinations and what various colours together might mean. When she messaged me and said: "Korani, there's a book here. Will you write it?" I thought I might faint with happiness! I had always enjoyed writing and had vaguely dreamed of writing a book, and now two of my passions were going to come together. The book – which became the e-book *Colour Conversations* – took many years to see the light of day, but that was in part because the universe had other plans which took precedence.

One morning I received an excited email from Melissie: "Korani, Korani! There are to be seven new Gaias, and they will be golden to represent the new Golden Age on the earth!" Pale gold is a shade I adore, and to have a whole set of seven arrive at once was cause enough for excitement. That they were to help us bring about the new golden era upon the earth we had been hearing about and longing for felt like a dream come true. Not least because I already had a plane ticket booked to visit Melissie just two weeks later, as we had planned to work on the *Colour Conversations* book. The story of how the Golden Gaias came to be and what they are about is fully documented in my book, *The Language of Light: Golden Keys to Ascension*, so I won't go into that here. Suffice to say it was a life-changing experience among so many life-changing experiences I have had with and through Colour Mirrors.

A small e-book about the Platinum Gaias, *A Book of Platinum Light,* followed some years later, and I also had the joy of assisting Melissie in the creation of her book, *What the Seeker Found*. For many years I continued to use the bottles in my healing practice and teach courses. I have always been in awe of the way the bottles touch people's lives with such love and grace. I have witnessed huge spiritual awakenings, seen people change their lives, been humbled by their courage, moved by their struggles and inspired by their greatness. I have had the joy of meeting many extraordinary people through Colour Mirrors and have seen time and again how the system opens hearts and minds and provides incredible spiritual nourishment.

Over the years my business has changed and I no longer offer one-to-one sessions or indeed run many practitioner or teacher courses these days, but I have come up with numerous courses of my own devising and all have included the Colour Mirrors bottles, for how could they not? They have become such a fundamental part of my life and who I am that I cannot imagine being without them in my daily life or indeed my work. I continually learn from them and from Melissie.

In 2012 I asked Melissie to create three 'Starlight' bottles for me so that I could run a series of workshops, and she kindly obliged. From those initial three bottles the Starlight set grew over the next four years to 24 bottles and Melissie supported me whole-heartedly in this little off-shoot of the system. One of the most extraordinary things about Melissie is her infinite generosity. When she told me and my fellow teacher trainees back in the day to "take the system and do what you will with it", I took her literally! She has held the space for me to do just that, something that is indeed rare in this world. The Starlights have brought me incredible joy and expansion, and they seem to touch people wherever they go. I love that they acknowledge and celebrate our 'starriness' and that they lay down a pathway to a life based on light.

I am constantly grateful that what I call my 'work' is so creative and brings joy, inspiration and support to myself and others. As we have worked on this book I have connected with each bottle intensively and this has brought more layers of insight, information, guidance and expansion. Again I have learned from the storehouse of wisdom that is Melissie, and again the bottles have taught me about life and about myself. I am eternally thankful to whatever forces of the universe brought me together with this system.

Colour in Your Life

Your Responses to Colour

Colour is part of life on a daily basis, yet if you are like many people you may take colour for granted, unaware of its effects and the potentially powerful impact it can have in your life. Almost everyone responds to colour on a purely instinctive level: think of the colours of a sunrise or sunset; the iridescent shimmer of a rainbow after rain; the beauty of a flower, forest or ocean; the luscious hues of ripe, juicy fruit.

How about the colour of the car you drive, the clothes you wear, the furnishings in your home: what is it about a certain shade of colour that makes you choose it over another? What makes a particular colour your 'favourite'? Is it just random, or is there a deeper meaning behind your choices?

When it comes to colour, we all have preferences. You may like some, be indifferent to others and positively dislike still others, yet your body responds to colour in a way that is not just based on like or dislike. Even if your conscious mind does not pay much attention to colour and its properties, your body does. Have you ever noticed that you immediately feel warmer in a red room than you do in a blue one?

You do not 'choose' to see colour, rather you automatically respond to it. Colour is perceived through the cones in your eyes, which respond to the wavelength of light emanating from the object you are looking at. A red tomato absorbs all the colours *except* red, so when you look at the tomato only the red is reflected back to you. You could say the tomato is 'doing' red rather than being red! When the light from the tomato hits the cones it stimulates them to varying degrees. The resulting signal is moved along the optic nerve to the visual cortex of the brain, which processes the information and returns with a colour: red.

Colour is not just perceived at a physical level, however – it can also affect you on a subliminal level. If the room where your parents told you they were getting a divorce was yellow, you may have an intense dislike of that colour. If your favourite grandparent always wore bright blue, you will likely have a fondness for that shade. Indeed your story with colour began to unfold even before you emerged into the world. A baby in the womb sees pink, the colour of the light that shows through the walls of the womb. If your mother was excited about being pregnant, sang to you and sent waves of love, you probably arrived in the world feeling safe and loved and will respond to pink as a favourite colour. If, on the other hand, your mother hated being pregnant and was angry about her circumstances, your arrival into the world and experience of it probably felt quite unsafe, and for you pink may be unpleasant or even nauseating.

As well as its impact on your physical body and your emotions, colour affects you in ways that are perhaps less obvious but that are real nonetheless. People with the skills to read energy have always seen that the energy field around the human body contains colours, and when Kirlian cameras are used to take photographs of the energy field, those colours are revealed. When you are presented with an array of colours, you see them through the filter of your own unique energy field and will always choose colours that are already present in that field. And because your energy field holds everything you have ever felt and experienced, the colours you choose provide a visual representation of it and all it contains. This makes it possible to see your motivations and desires, your conflicts and challenges – indeed much of your life story – simply through the colour choices you make.

Those of us who work with colour find it an astonishingly powerful and accurate tool. It not only reveals what is hidden in the depth of the psyche, it also helps bring about healing as the information becomes clear and available to the conscious mind. And because you respond to colour from your deepest self, it transcends the limitations of the mind altogether and reflects to you the greater truth of who you are.

The Meaning of Colour

When you become consciously aware of colour, you may begin to look at yourself and your colour choices more closely. As you do, you are tapping into the basic psychology of colour and discovering more about yourself and the world in the process. Every colour has qualities and attributes associated with it; in fact, colour is a language you can learn to understand and utilise in your daily life. When you learn this language and use colour as a tool, it can open you up to an enormous amount of information and insight and help you better understand everything in your life: your relationships, your career, your health, your finances and your connection to the spiritual world.

There is a whole field of study to be made of the psychology of colour and many individuals and organisations make use of this in their work. Restaurant owners know that red stimulates appetite; prison authorities know that green is a calming colour and pink a soothing one. Executives all over the world wear black to make themselves look and feel powerful. If we look at the humble beginnings of this field of study we see that much of our understanding of different colours originates from a time when we relied on our senses to tell us what things meant. To our ancestors, if blood was red then that was the colour of vitality and health, and because spilling it was clearly not good for us, red was also the colour of danger. If lying back and staring at the blue sky brought feelings of peace, then clearly blue was a calming colour. White was the colour of purity; black was the colour of mystery, night and death, and so on.

In language, colour is used to describe feelings and explain emotions: feeling blue, green with envy, seeing red. There are many examples of the use of colour in everyday language: in the pink, rose-coloured glasses, out of the blue, a grey area, a sunny character, the golden boy – or black sheep – of the family. From here it is an easy step to furnish colours with a set of meanings and use them to interpret various character and personality traits.

Ray McKimm describes colour as "the language of health and wellbeing", stating that it gives us "a means of both self-reflection and self-expression, as well as providing us with the means of interpreting quickly, easily and effectively the enormous amount of stimuli we encounter daily." (McKimm, 2017, p.219).

He goes on to say: "Colour is encoded in our psyche not only as a tangible physical property – as we understand from the study of the cognition and perception of colour, but also as a set of meanings which relate to our survival, our ability to thrive – our health and wellbeing. Colour acts like a series of arches (archetypes) – like rainbows you might say that bridge the gap between what we know and don't know…" (McKimm, 2017, p. 227).

Colour Therapy

Colour has always been recognised as a powerful form of therapy and was used in many ancient cultures. Ray McKimm has produced a fascinating timeline summary of how colour has been used in the pursuit of health and well-being across millennia, giving examples from Chinese Medicine, Ancient Egypt, Ayurvedic Medicine, Hippocrates, Goethe, and Steiner, among others (McKimm, 2017). Nowadays colour is used therapeutically throughout the world in a multitude of ways and can form a stand-alone practice or be combined with virtually any other form of healing or therapy to great effect.

With colour therapy, you are offered the opportunity to take what is buried in your subconscious mind and bring it to the surface. Colour can both help you resolve your past wounds and open doorways to positive change and growth for the future. Often you know what you would like to change or what is no longer working, but because there is still a missing link you cannot always get your mind, heart and body to align to make the changes happen. This is where colour therapy comes in. It takes your instinctive response to colour, adds meaning through the psychology and language of colour and then, with a system such as Colour Mirrors, combines it all with a touch of something 'other' that is perhaps hard to define but potent nonetheless!

Colour Mirrors

How Colour Mirrors Can Help You

When you select from the beautiful range of Colour Mirrors oils and essences you transmit a very clear picture of who you are – physically, emotionally, mentally and spiritually. Each colour choice holds up a mirror from your soul, revealing not only your programmes and patterns but also a reflection of the greatness you hold within. Colour Mirrors is so-called because colour 'mirrors' what is inside you. It mirrors your energy field, all the information stored in your body and being, your personality, the paths you have chosen to travel, every aspect of your soul. Each Colour Mirrors bottle you choose reflects your true self, your Divine self.

Numerous Colour Mirrors teachers and practitioners display the bottles on their websites for you to browse and select from, and you can also find them on the Colour Mirrors website, www.colourmirrors.com, and Korani's website, www.korani.net. Whenever you feel called to, browse through the images of the bottles to see which stand out for you and click on the images to read their messages. You may find it useful to go to the palette of bottles when you have a question in your mind or heart that you are unable to resolve and ask: "Which bottle would be most helpful for me regarding this issue?" Notice which 'leaps out' at you first, and read the message. If it speaks to you, you may wish to purchase the bottle and work with it. You might also like to consider having a session with a Colour Mirrors practitioner to enable you to explore further and take things to a deeper level.

During a session with a Colour Mirrors practitioner you will be asked to choose the bottles you are naturally drawn to. Some you may find intriguing, attractive or appealing. There may even be a particular bottle which so magnetises you that you cannot take your eyes off it. Sometimes you will choose bottles you do not actually like – but there will be something about them that calls to you and draws you in. Your practitioner may ask questions and have you choose bottles to represent your answers. By interpreting the language of your colour choices, your practitioner will help you uncover where your current challenges come from, and when you understand where a problem comes from – its root cause – it becomes much easier to confront and resolve it.

The colours you choose might show what is blocking you from finding your path, what is sitting unresolved in your heart or how and why a relationship is no longer working. They might reveal your judgements around money, your unresolved grief, your blocks to communicating freely or any other fears, issues and challenges you are experiencing. Your colour choices provide insights, information and guidance to help you find the patterns or beliefs that created your difficulties and ways to overcome them. They also highlight your gifts, skills and opportunities and indicate how to access them more easily. Even in the course of one session, as you and your practitioner discuss the colours and their meanings and spend time in the company of these energy and love-infused bottles, you will almost certainly find that things begin to shift for you.

Working with the bottles enables the healing messages of the colours to go to the very core of your being. It also enables your body to really 'get' what you and your practitioner have discussed during your session. Even when you know what you want to have or do or change, your body may experience fear and resistance – usually as a result of past trauma or challenges – and stop you from taking the steps you wish to take. With the help of the soothing, healing coloured oils and essences, your body starts to feel safe enough to make the changes. The joy of working with the Colour Mirrors bottles is that shift and change can often happen swiftly and with ease.

One of the gifts of this system is that it helps you bypass the conscious mind and get straight to the heart of what is really going on. The bottles and colours you choose reveal what is behind your behaviours, choices and challenges, help you gain clarity as to why you have been following a particular path and show you how to change course if that is what you truly desire. They also help free your mind from programming and patterning by showing you new possibilities and other ways to move forward.

The colour choices you make provide strong clues as to where your heart really lies and what you really wish to be doing. If you are working as an accountant and your heart yearns to be an artist, the palette of colours you choose will tell your truth. It will be plain to see – and even if you have suppressed your desire to break out and be more creative, the colours will tell the story! What you do with this information is, of course, entirely up to you, but once you have seen something graphically and in colour it becomes harder to hide from your truth.

The beauty of Colour Mirrors is that while it highlights your issues, and in some cases there might be a warning implied, what you have in your hands is quite literally a remedy for those issues. The bottles bring clarity and insight so that you feel empowered to move towards whatever you desire or require in your life, and using them on your body means that every part of you 'gets' the message.

Colour Mirrors practitioners are often told by clients that they have never felt so completely and tenderly seen, nor have they ever had their life story so beautifully displayed. Every bottle in the set is a reflection of the Divine light shining through the person choosing it. As a practitioner it is the most profound gift to be trusted with such insight into another person's true soul qualities.

Visit www.colourmirrors.com to find a practitioner for a session online or in person.

Using Colour Mirrors Oils and Essences

There are many ways to use the coloured oils and essences to infuse yourself with colour. Here are some of the most frequently used methods:

- Place a bottle of your choice on whichever part of your body is most calling for it and let the healing energies flow
- Choose a bottle to meditate with, allowing it to deepen and expand your meditative experience
- Place a bottle under your pillow or by your bed and let the energies of the bottle connect with you as you sleep
- Use as an after-shower body oil or massage oil
- Spray an essence into your hands and breathe in the aroma
- Spritz an essence onto your body, into your energy field or around your home

Perhaps the most powerful way to connect with the messages of the oils and essences, however, and one we always recommend after a colour therapy session or workshop, is to bathe in them.

Bathing in Colour

Colour baths can be powerfully transformational in their effects. Your bath experience might be profound, with Divine healing energies streaming in or other cosmic experiences that defy description. You may receive deep healing, with tears and huge emotional releases as your body finally gets the message that it is safe for you to feel your feelings. You may have wonderful insights and 'aha' moments, and we know of many people who have written reams of information received during or following a bath.

On the other hand, your colour bath may be quite uneventful – relaxing perhaps and enjoyable but beyond that, not earth-shattering. The shifts and insights might then come over a period of time, and it is often not until you look back days, weeks or even months later that you realise how much has changed. The intention for these bottles is so highly attuned to create healing that people's lives often change – sometimes dramatically, sometimes in subtle ways – and we have included stories throughout the book to this effect.

Colour and Scent

The Colour Mirrors bottles, particularly the essences, work with your sense of smell. Aromatherapy is well-documented as a powerful therapy in its own right. By combining it with colour, Colour Mirrors contains a unique formula for healing. By spraying the essences into your hands or around your body and breathing in their scent, you allow them to support your energy field, your body and your nervous system. You can also spritz them into a space such as your house, garden, office, car or wherever else you choose, and enjoy the benefits of their clearing, healing and blessing energies in that space. Find out more about how to work with and enjoy the essences on page 224.

Colour 'Mirrors'

As an energy system, Colour Mirrors bottles quite often behave in ways you may not expect from apparently inanimate objects. They may change colour, go murky or lose some or all of their colour, sometimes literally overnight. They might develop bubbles in them, fall off a shelf for no obvious reason or even explode! When any of these things occur it is as if they are trying to get your attention. As mirrors, they are showing you in tangible ways that things are shifting and changing for you and that their messages are now more relevant to you than ever. If this happens to you, it is definitely time to take a deeper look and work with those particular bottles, bathe in them and invite their loving energies into your life.

Resolving Challenges

If you find yourself having a strong response when reading about a particular bottle or you find the colours difficult to look at, the very best thing you can do is work with that bottle. If the colours or words of a bottle press your buttons, consider that this might just mean that there is a button somewhere within you to be pressed! Rather than judge yourself when this happens, you have an opportunity to explore your responses, notice what is triggering you and observe how it affects you.

The key is to begin to work gently with the bottle that is difficult for you, perhaps rubbing some of the oil or spraying some of the essence onto your body each morning and evening or just holding the bottle on your body and noticing any physical responses or emotions that arise. One of the most powerful ways to address whatever is going on is to pour some of the oil or essence into a bath and soak up its energies. With openness and intention, invite your higher self to show you what is asking to be seen, felt, healed and resolved. Every single bottle in the system is designed to bring you to the higher Divine perspective so that you can get clear on what is causing the difficulties, draw old programmes and patterns from the subconscious into conscious awareness, shift them out of your cells and love them back into the light.

Sometimes, however, you may need to work with a different bottle first. If you feel too triggered by a specific bottle, choose another one to help move things forward. Ask something like: "Which bottle would make me feel safe?" or "Which bottle would help me let go of this issue?" Notice which bottle you are drawn to and begin to work with it. At some point, usually fairly swiftly, you will begin to feel comfortable with the bottle you were challenged by before. Healing often happens in layers, and you may need to untangle a few threads before you get to the root of an issue. The joy of working with Colour Mirrors is that you are able to see tangible progress. When you no longer have a negative reaction to a bottle that previously you disliked, this is a sign that something has shifted.

If you are unsure, need some support or feel out of your depth, we recommend you contact a Colour Mirrors practitioner for guidance. Visit the Colour Mirrors website, www.colourmirrors.com, to find a practitioner to work with online or in person.

Going Deeper with Colour

Complementary Colours

On an artist's colour wheel, each colour is laid out in a circle, moving from red to orange to yellow and on through the rainbow to complete the circle in magenta. As such, every colour has an opposite or complementary colour. In colour therapy, complementary colours tell us much about the 'underbelly' of your story, what is hidden or buried in the subconscious. If you choose bottles that are all in the red spectrum, there is highly likely to be a green story sitting behind your choice. Yellow choices indicate a hidden violet story; blue sheds light on buried orange issues. Although we make only passing reference to complementary colours in this book, they are relevant to all colour choices, and as you learn the language of colour they offer additional insight and information. Colour Mirrors practitioner courses offer training in this topic for anyone who is interested in learning more.

Colour Combinations

In this book you will find occasional references to some of the many combinations of colours found in Colour Mirrors and how they relate to each other. This is such a huge topic and there is so much rich information to be gleaned from colour combinations that we have produced an entire book to explore it: a 400-plus page e-book called *Colour Conversations*. This e-book delves into the vast array of colour combinations featured in the Colour Mirrors system and provides detailed information on them to enrich your colour journey. To find out more and to purchase your copy of *Colour Conversations,* please visit Korani's website, www.korani.net.

Conscious/Subconscious

In each of the oil bottles, the top section refers to what is in the conscious mind, the aspects of a situation or issue of which you may already be aware. The bottom half relates to the subconscious, or that which is hidden from your conscious mind. If the colours are the same top and bottom, this is a powerful opportunity to bring balance and wholeness to the issue it addresses. If the colours are different, it can be an interesting exercise to look at how that reflects what is in your conscious awareness and the subconscious programmes and patterns vying for your attention. If bottles change colour or go cloudy or murky, notice whether both fractions have changed or only one, and what this might mean about how and where the shift within you is occurring. As always, the colours reveal what your higher self is calling you to recognise or remember, and light the way forward for shift, transformation and change.

Colour and Numerology

Numerology is the study of numbers and their meanings. Each of the Colour Mirrors bottles has a number that can be used to bring further insight into your bottle choices. Translating the numbers of your birthday and your full birthdate into bottles, for example, reveals information about your life path, your soul's mission and your purpose here on earth.

There is also useful information to be found when you 'reduce' a double digit down to a single one. If, for example, you are selecting bottle 16, by adding 1 + 6 you reach 7, so bottle 7 will also have information for you; bottle 9 will reveal more about your choice of bottle 18 (1 + 8 = 9); bottle 4 will reveal more on bottle 31 (3 + 1 = 4) and so on.

Another way to look at how numbers relate to the bottles is to take a bottle number, split it into its component parts and then look at the bottles related to those numbers. We have included an example of this with bottle 17, where we break down the number 17 to 1 and 7 and show how those bottles relate to it. You can apply this to any other bottle in the system, and we invite you to explore these connections whenever you feel called to do so.

If you would like to know more about how colour works with numerology, our Colour Mirrors teachers are happy to share this with you in sessions and on Colour and Numerology courses.

Colour and Astrology

Bottles 1-9 and 13 in the Colour Mirrors system are all named after planets, and the messages of these bottles reflect the meaning of the planets in Astrology. For example, the Sun sign in Astrology relates to your essence, and the yellow Sun bottle shows how and where you shine. The Moon in Astrology and the Moon bottle both reflect your emotional world. And in both Colour Mirrors and Astrology, Saturn indicates barriers and boundaries, and Mars is how you express your life force and energy. There are also links between the Colour Mirrors Element essences and the elements in Astrology.

Colour and Astrology complement each other beautifully: astrology provides further insights to the information revealed by the colour bottles, and the bottles add an extra dimension to an Astrology reading by anchoring the session in a tangible way. Combining colour with Astrology is a powerful way to refine and deepen your understanding of yourself and others. Amanda Bradbury is an expert in this field and runs workshops and courses for healing with Colour and Astrology. Visit www.amandabradbury.com to find out more.

Colour in Business

While much of the focus in this book is on the benefits of colour for personal and spiritual growth, the Colour Mirrors system is a tool which can be used in all areas of life to bring insight, understanding and expansion. Some of our teachers and practitioners use the colour bottles in business to help executives and employees become more conscious of how and where they fit within their organisation as well as exploring their inner potential, career choices and future opportunities.

Colour Mirrors teachers Kate Griffiths and Kath Roberts help senior leadership teams in organisations to develop a lasting culture by understanding in greater depth their own personal values and beliefs. Experts in their field, Kate and Kath use the core chakra colours, red through violet, to define organisational values based on the key qualities associated with each of those colours, as defined in the Colour Mirrors system. By adapting the names and messages of the Colour Mirrors bottles to a more business-oriented language, and using them alongside a variety of other tools such as constellation work, Kate and Kath are able to unearth issues within businesses and facilitate appropriate changes in culture, behaviour and ethos.

Once senior managers start to grasp that the combined energy of each individual's unconscious field playing out has an impact on the business as a whole, they begin to appreciate the importance of examining emotions and giving appropriate time for reflection. Businesses have traditionally been designed with masculine principles in mind and a preoccupation for doing at the expense of being. Creating more transparency and balance is the key to retaining highly connected, innovative and trusted teams that live up to their vision and work for the common good. Working with colour helps brings clarity, understanding, meaning and alignment to the organisation.

In the process, the business leaders themselves go through internal shifts, and this begins to permeate out into the wider team field. Employees begin to feel seen, heard and understood. As old, stagnant, unprocessed energy clears, the business as a whole begins to look ahead with renewed momentum, a higher vibration and a deeper understanding of itself. Visit www.colourfulboardrooms.com for further information.

Taking the Colour Mirrors Journey

We hope this book will provide plenty of insights and food for thought. There is nothing quite like experiencing the bottles in person, however, and we highly recommend having a session or attending an introductory workshop with one of the skilled Colour Mirrors teachers and practitioners around the world.

If you would like to really sky-rocket your personal growth, however, look no further than a Colour Mirrors practitioner course. This is where Colour Mirrors teachers bring the system to life through information, training, practical exercises and experiential learning. On this course you are taught a set of skills enabling you to offer sessions to clients using the Colour Mirrors bottles. You become familiar with the language of colour so that you can offer various types of readings based around clients' bottle choices. You also learn chakra balancing using the bottles and how to incorporate the bottles into healing and therapy sessions. Beyond that, your practitioner training is designed to immerse you in the energies of colour and the Colour Mirrors bottles, which in itself brings about huge shifts and offers many transformational experiences. It would be fair to say that no one who takes a Colour Mirrors practitioner course remains the same as when they began!

After your Colour Mirrors training you are free to explore how the bottles fit into any other healing modality or develop entirely new methods for using the bottles. We have seen many exciting developments arise from this flexible approach. Colour Mirrors teachers and practitioners around the world use the system to expand and enhance their offerings in coaching and counselling, and the bottles wonderfully support EFT (Emotional Freedom Technique) and any other form of therapy, whether 'talk' therapy or hands-on healing. You may also find Colour Mirrors bottles in organisations, schools and the occasional doctor's surgery around the globe, as this system finds its way into the hands of more and more people who are ready to receive and share its benefits.

The system is bigger than any one of us, and we encourage practitioners and teachers to find their own unique ways to engage with it, personally and professionally. The possibilities for using Colour Mirrors in the wider world are endless, and we are excited to see how it continues to push new boundaries, show us new levels and take us in new directions. If you are drawn to train as a Colour Mirrors practitioner, you can find further information on the Colour Mirrors website.

The Wisdoms

Bottles 1-36

This account of the first 36 bottles is told as a kind of narrative, moving from one to the next and witnessing the story that unfolds. You are welcome to turn straight to the bottles you are most drawn to or dip in and out as you feel guided, because that is exactly how this book is designed to work. Yet it is interesting to notice how the system takes us on an epic journey from its beginnings in the yellow No. 1 Sun bottle to the blue-lilac of No. 36, The Gateway. The bottles arrived in their own sequence and timing rather than being deliberately planned, yet we find a Divine perfection and order to the bottles, their colours, their numbers and their messages. We invite you to explore how and where each bottle touches you personally and how it illuminates the collective human experience.

These first 36 bottles are incredibly supportive on your travels, acting as guides to the varying landscapes of life on earth as well as being friends in times of need. They highlight your issues and blocks, your blind spots and challenges. They also offer another viewpoint and reveal the many possibilities that arise as you free yourself from limitations and open to the beauty of a life based on love, balance and connection. These first 36 bottles, the 'Wisdoms', are firm but loving task-masters. They show you clearly in the mirror where you have been restricting yourself or choosing smallness. They also show how much more is available to you and point the way forward.

As each bottle arrived into the system it came with a meaning and a message. These essentially summarise each bottle's key features, introducing you to its themes and opening you to receive its energies. These descriptions are included in italics at the beginning of each bottle's story, as they are the perfect starting point from which to explore further.

Bottle 1: The Sun – I AM (Yellow/Yellow)

This bottle vibrates to the energy of the sun – the light source and the life force of the world. It also resonates with the energy centre at the centre of your being, the solar plexus. This first bottle acknowledges your I AMness, that feeling of being totally connected with your highest aspect. This is true power – the recognition that the Divine is in everything and oneness is the natural state of the universe. This bottle clears confusion and fear and is helpful for SAD and depression. Yellow is the colour of intellect, brightness, light and joy. The Colour Mirrors system as a whole is a journey of Ascension, and as Ascension is a by-product of joy, the only way the system could really begin was with a bottle which reflects that joy.

Colour Mirrors begins with a pure hit of bright sunlight yellow, right into the solar plexus. This first bottle in the system infuses you with the pure radiance of the sun, lighting up your body and your world. It is an awakener, a sharp burst of light after the depths of sleep. As the number one bottle in the system, it calls your attention to beginnings and the expansive energy of the sun that greets each fresh new day, inspiring you with the qualities of leadership, courage and confidence. It pulls no punches, asking you right off the bat to recognise and remember that you are brilliant, light and powerful. It also invites you to realise from the outset that this system is not just a collection of pretty colours but, in a perfect mirroring of everything you are, a potent force to be reckoned with.

The bright, sparkling sunlight energy of this bottle often calls to people who are already sunny and joyous, mirroring their shimmering light right back to them. If, however, you find it difficult to see your own radiance, this bottle challenges you to see yourself as the Divine being you really are. Right from the very first bottle, Colour Mirrors reflects back to you the glorious glow of your inner shine. The question is: are you ready to accept and embrace it?

The sun is an absolute necessity for life on this planet. Without it all life here would wither and die in short order. This bottle asks you to look at what is of absolute necessity in your life and whether or not you allow yourself to have it. Do you give yourself the time and space to be creative and inspired? Do you allow for play and fun and laughter? Do you feed and nourish yourself at a core soul level? Or do you turn away from the light, depriving yourself of the very things that would most sustain, support and please you?

Your Sun sign, the astrological sign you were born under, reveals much about your true self. It describes your personality and desires, your tendencies and patterns. It also reveals your true soul essence. In much the same way, the Sun bottle asks you to recognise the truth of who you are. When you choose this bottle it is a perfect opportunity to look at what makes you tick and what brings sunshine into your life. It is a chance to look at everywhere you are pulling back out of fear, selling yourself short because of doubt or staying stuck because of confusion.

Bottle 1 is a great place to start when you are running around inside your head getting precisely nowhere. It says "I AM" – it does not say "I think I am", or "I might be", or "I have no idea who or what I am." It delivers a sharpish nudge into the light of clarity when you are dithering or doubting. It compels you to step out of mind games, and when fear is holding you prisoner, it helps you break free. This bottle and this colour are helpful when your thoughts run in circles or when you cannot stop going over and over an idea in your head. Despite the vivid brightness of the colour, this bottle often helps to calm overthinking and hyperactive tendencies. Yellow increases concentration and is a great help to children, especially those who have trouble focusing. It brings in the energy of fun and play, helping a child of any age to feel more relaxed and think more clearly.

If yellow is not an easy colour for you, however, rest assured that you are not alone. Many people struggle with this colour and this bottle. Yellow may trigger responses from the ego-based, childish parts of yourself, making you want to stamp your feet or throw tantrums. It taps into anxiety and fear and can have a scattering effect on the mind. It can bring up discomfort or even nausea as it connects with your solar plexus, the power centre of your being, particularly if there are power issues from this life or another which have yet to be resolved. The key is to address whatever is causing you to react, and by working gently with this bottle you may begin to draw to the surface whatever has been buried that is looking for healing and love. As you acknowledge the issues it has awoken in you and face them in the mirror, this bottle will become a guide and a friend rather than something to avoid.

Yellow is the beginning of the human journey to awakening. It is where you begin to expand your consciousness and discover that there is more to life than your mind can possibly understand. Yellow's complementary or opposite colour is violet, which relates to your spirit and the light you hold within. When you are lost in the shadow aspects of yellow – fear, ego, confusion or power struggles – you might forget that you even have a spirit. As you step into the true essence of yellow, you come to recognise that you exist as a specific and unique strand of light in a physical body. You are a huge, vast, unlimited spirit having an experience of being human. Bottle 1 reminds you that it was all meant to be fun!

The Sun bottle is a dazzling reflection of the greatness of spirit within every human, no matter how far from that greatness you may perceive yourself to be. It helps you let go of disempowering behaviours and limiting thought patterns and opens you to new thoughts, new ideas and new growth. It is a great support if you are trapped down a hole, particularly if you are giving your power away to the weakening thrall of addictions. It is particularly challenging to own up to addictions, to face them and release their hold upon you. In any addiction there is confusion, self-deception and denial. Ego, fed by fear, does its best to hide, contorting and deflecting attention away from the real issues. This bottle brings those issues right to the fore and though this may be deeply uncomfortable, it may also be the key to releasing them.

Yellow can bring a much-needed boost to self-esteem and self-worth when you are feeling despondent or unable to find things about yourself to love. This bright yellow bottle shows you the route to the deeper, more authentic power you hold within. As you embark on your spiritual journey, you begin to recognise and acknowledge your brilliance, your light, your bright and shiny self – and the world tends to call that ego. Yet what if it was actually the key to helping you access your true Divine self? It is essential to claim your own worth before you can take the next step; while you are beating up on yourself there is no way through. When the yellow of self-esteem is in place you will naturally be led onwards to the next level of authenticity and self-empowerment. This is represented by the colour gold, created by adding the pink of self-love to the yellow.

This bottle helps shore up and strengthen your solar plexus, the literal 'sun' centre of your being, so that you can remember who you really are and begin to enjoy life. It asks you to step out from behind the cloudy morass of your mind and start living with confidence and joy. It invites you to turn your back on the cold, rainy drabness of the collective beliefs of much of humanity ('life is hard and then you die') and turn your face to life's sunshine in all its radiant, Divine glory. The solar plexus is the seat of your ego and your will. It is also where you hold fear and anxiety and where you may contract under stress. If you find yourself being run by the false and fearful ego, bottle 1 is a wonderful tonic – a blast of sunshine, joy and laughter. It sweeps out stale old fears, making space for freedom, fun and empowerment. It stops you taking yourself so seriously and helps you open to a more authentic way of being, one that engages with your wholeness, your I AMness.

The sun brings the light and warmth required for growth and expansion, and when you are feeling small, contracted and lost in the dark, the Sun bottle plugs you back into life. It inspires you to get moving, claim back your power and kick-start new projects. The sun is a metaphor for life: how you feel about this bottle may well reflect how you feel about life. If you are ready to live in inspired and joyful creativity, feel your mind unlocking and expanding, give up old unhelpful beliefs and step into something sparkling and new, this bottle is your key-pass.

Bottle 1 Story: Nicky Batt, UK, www.facebook.com/ConsciousColourLiving

This bottle helped me immensely with depression, which I used to have on and off for several years. It is the bottle that 'flicked a switch' for me and brought me out of the dross. It triggers my inner sunshine! I still live with SAD from around October to February; the dull dark days just keep me feeling so lethargic and heavy. However, by regularly bathing in a little of this bottle and spritzing with the yellow essences in the daytime, I feel able to cope. Bathing in this bottle seems to light up my cells and recharge my battery so that my inner sunshine burns brightly and I'm less affected by the dullness around me. This is my go-to bottle for winter months and dull days.

Bottle 1 Story: Shirley Archibald, UK, www.shirleyarchibald.co.uk

When I bathed in the No.1 bottle, the following day quite out of the blue I received a phone call asking me to do an interview with a New York radio station about my EFT (Emotional Freedom Technique) practice. Public speaking is a sticking point for me, but I went ahead and did it – although I didn't tell anyone I was doing it, so maybe there is some more work to be done! Nevertheless, this was an absolutely massive breakthrough for me.

Bottle 2: The Moon – I Feel (Pale Blue/Royal Blue)

This bottle carries the energy of the moon and the tides, the seasons and cycles of existence. It relates to the throat, choice and taking responsibility for your word. It is helpful when you have difficulty communicating and making yourself heard. This bottle brings peace, connecting you with the angelic realms and enfolding you in a protective blue cloak. So far very few of your fears have manifested. Begin to have faith that what has kept you safe until now will continue to do so.

Bottle 2 takes you from the intense light and brightness of the sun into the deep, still, peaceful space of a moonlit night. Where bottle 1 (The Sun) asks you to shine your light into the world with all of the sun's bright radiance, bottle 2 invites you to melt into softness, releasing your need to do and achieve, slipping gently into a more intuitive and restful state. With this bottle you can relax and let go, stop and sigh, breathe a little more deeply. The Moon opens you to an intuitive and connected space where you can settle into peace, stillness and silence and let your mind and ego take a backseat. The moon's luminous serenity opens your receptive channels so that you can step out of thinking and doing and open instead to all the wonder, mystery and beauty of simply being.

In numerology the number two relates to partnerships, cooperation and balance. Astrologically the moon connects with your emotions, your deepest inner needs and how you process your feelings. It also relates to your initial connection with your mother and how this affects all subsequent relationships. Although blue is often associated with the masculine, here it has an intensely nurturing energy that is powerfully female. We tend to think of the feminine as pink, but pink can have a needy, dependent quality. The Moon bottle represents the female who has claimed her power and has no need of a man – or anyone – to define her. This bottle contains all the female power of the moon and the moon goddesses, Mother Mary and the Goddess Isis. Here blue is the power of the mother to give life and then cherish and sustain that life with love.

The energy of bottle 2 may be female and nurturing, but it is certainly not light-weight. It carries a gravitas and power that command respect. This is the High Priestess who knows, sees and understands. What sometimes limits her is a tendency to keep her counsel and retain her wisdom rather than sharing it freely. When you choose this bottle it suggests you have knowledge and wisdom from which to draw. In the past you may have felt the need to hold on to your knowledge – perhaps from fear, perhaps from a desire to retain power. In this age of information technology where everything is available to everyone, it is no longer appropriate to hold on to what you know out of fear that you will somehow be diminished if you pass it on to others. Bottle 2 says it is safe now to share your wisdom. True power has nothing to fear.

Blue is about communicating and expressing, and this bottle helps you speak out and speak up, say what has been buried inside or left unsaid. Feeling safe to speak is so often a key to healing the shocks, traumas and abuse represented by the complementary colour, orange. This bottle supports you in feeling safe to release what has been held in for too long. Its qualities of silence, deep inner listening and compassion invite you to pour out everything that has been damned up inside.

The moon is powerfully connected with the unconscious mind. It helps you tap into and draw to the surface patterns and blocks that may otherwise have remained hidden. This bottle holds a soft and loving space for you to be with your feelings, experience all your emotions, accept the whole of yourself. The Moon illuminates your inner darkness with love, showing you how to be gentle with yourself so that your feelings can arise and be expressed. If you have been denying your feelings or burying them in the hope that they will go away, the soft supportive blue in this bottle gently encourages you to explore what you have been holding inside. As you allow and release it, you free yourself in the process.

Bottle 2 not only helps you speak up but supports you in hearing others in their time of need. It is a profound gift to allow another to be heard, and if you resonate with this bottle you are likely to be a natural listener, creating a safe and quiet space for others while you listen with your ears, eyes and heart – indeed, with your whole being.

The colour blue is often related to authority. In this bottle it is not an inappropriate or harsh power but a loving authority which provides a space that is completely safe, completely held. As you learn to feel safe, you can begin to trust that wherever you are and whatever is going on is, in fact, perfect. You can begin to trust your feelings. You can begin to trust life.

This bottle reflects the seasons, cycles and tides. It encourages you to flow with life's rhythms rather than trying to push water uphill. It gifts you with the knowing that whatever difficulty you may be experiencing right now, it will not last forever. With the weight of worry lifted, you can relax and let go – and sleep. The Moon bottle is a balm that settles and soothes with its energy of safety, peaceful nurturing and angelic support, and it is often chosen by children or those in need of a healing sanctuary. It helps relieve subconscious fears and is deeply supportive for anyone who has nightmares. It invites you to be still, go into the quiet and nestle into tranquillity. This bottle's message is: "Be at peace. All is well."

Bottle 2 Story: Hayden Crawford, Australia, www.dreemtimeacademy.com.au

Following a period of intense lunar activity I had been feeling extremely emotional. I'm not normally someone who gets affected by these cycles, but this one hit me hard. I had recently become a Colour Mirrors practitioner, and after noticing my 'Moon' bottle had changed colour in the upper segment from blue to clear, I knew I was being guided to bathe in it.

Fundamentally, this bottle relates to our emotions, the way that we feel. Blue guides you to a place of trust where you begin to see all of life as part of the oneness and that there really is nothing and no one to fear. Combining this with my magenta Metatron essence and some Bottlebrush flower essence for 'letting go' and clearing mother/child issues, I was set for the transformation I desired.

After an hour of relaxing in a hot bath, I felt the blue waters seeping into my skin and clearing and transmuting the fears from my cellular memory. I ventured back into the past to the time of my birth and was able to clear the trauma from the event by recreating a more loving and protective version of events. Metatron offered me technicolour symbols as I went deeper into an alpha state. When the transformation was complete, I observed a beautiful red admiral butterfly ascending into the sky.

I am in love with these truly amazing vibrational remedies and am grateful for the support they offer as old memories resurface to be released like the peeling of the layers of an onion.

Bottle 2 Story: Jackie Tweedie, UK, www.jackietweedie.com

I once had a client who chose this bottle when she was experiencing a lack of balance in her household. She explained that as the main breadwinner she had become a go-getter and had lost touch with her softer, more feminine side. This bottle helped her feel safe enough to surrender all that 'trying' and gave her permission to trust that she could relax more into being a woman and a mother.

Bottle 3: Jupiter (Coral/Coral)

Jupiter is huge, expansive and powerful – and this bottle reminds you that you are too. The colour coral is made up of pink (love) and yellow (wisdom) and indicates a shift from old patterns of giving your power away, to fearlessly reclaiming who you are and what you are for. Now is the time to finally stand up and say: "This is who I am." When you are able to do that with conviction, you will feel the full support of the universe and Jupiter's beneficence in your life. This can be a time of great blessings if you are willing to unconditionally accept yourself with love and compassion.

Although it was not planned this way, it feels appropriate that the first three bottles of the Colour Mirrors system are essentially the three primary colours, the building blocks of all other hues. From the bright yellow sunshine of the Sun (bottle 1) and the deep blue of the Moon (bottle 2) we move now to the buoyant zest of red, or rather coral, which is a softer, illuminated version of red.

Coral is a multi-faceted colour. It is filled to overflowing with love and joy; it is beautiful, abundant and luscious. Yet this colour and this bottle are often chosen when you feel none of these things, when your self-esteem is low, when you see only lack, when you cannot perceive the value in what you do and who you are. Its nurturing, gently expansive power sweeps in to your cells to help you let go of issues of 'not enough' – not good enough, not rich enough, not successful enough, not loving enough – or any other form of self-criticism and self-judgement.

Bottle 3 is particularly supportive when you do not believe you deserve, when you truly think you are not enough, when you cannot accept love, when your inner critic is running your life. There is such a strong sense of victimhood and self-denial in coral that this can show up in desperate attention-seeking, filling your inner emptiness with illness, even unconsciously growing a potentially fatal disease. Bottle 3 helps stop that coral pattern in its tracks.

This bottle picks up deeply buried programmes and pours a stream of love through them, melting and diffusing them. It helps you become aware of old wounds and blocks. It highlights those aspects of yourself you have been unable to fully accept so that you can bring them into the light of love and integrate them as part of your wholeness. It taps into your beliefs about love and helps you see where you have been rejecting it due to a lack of self-worth.

It also helps you free yourself from the burden of unrequited love: loving without being loved in return or without being loved in the way you expect to be loved. If this is your story, it may have begun with a parent or parents who could not love in the way you wanted them to, or it could have been an early crush, a first love that was never reflected. Once the pattern was set, you may have found it playing itself out time and again. Bottle 3 can reveal your hidden expectations about love, show you any beliefs that are no longer serving you, and help you find a path to real love on the inside so that it can be reflected in your outer world.

Coral relates to deep-seated emotions. If you are harbouring unresolved childhood traumas in your body, if your self-esteem is at an all-time low, if your relationships are a mess or you find yourself in an abusive partnership, this colour and this bottle are keys to finding your way out of the mire. You cannot continue along the same road, hoping it will all just go away. You are asked to look deeply into your subconscious beliefs and bring them to light, turn destructive behaviours and self-sabotage around and find your way back to the joy and riches the universe is holding out to you. Bottle 3 can gently help you see through the illusion and reach the higher truth: the one who did not love you actually loved you enough to give you the opportunity to heal the unconscious pattern; the abusive partner was mirroring your own lack of self-worth; the parent who judged you as not good enough was offering you a space to find your inner strength, courage and self-respect.

Jupiter shines the clarity of truth upon you so that your relationships can evolve into something more beautiful and nurturing. When you love yourself, you need not depend on someone else to do it for you. When you love yourself – truly, deeply and without judgement – others see your inner light and reflect it back to you. Your soul knows that you are perfect, whole and way more than enough. When your ego insists that this cannot be true, Jupiter helps peel away the lie to reveal the shining, lovely, lovable truth about you so that you might really begin to know yourself as love, as Divine.

Coral illustrates what the whole Colour Mirrors system is about – that whatever is inside of you is reflected in your outside world. It holds up a perfect mirror. With Jupiter's guidance and love you can begin to accept all your experiences as opportunities to see what is in the mirror rather than spending your time and energy trying to fix the mirror. Jupiter asks you to recognise that you hold great creative power and that what you experience in your outer reality is essentially created by your inner reality. It reveals that you, like much of humanity, may be labouring under a fundamental misunderstanding that you are somehow powerless, helpless, a victim of 'fate'. This bottle offers a different way of looking at your experiences and a new perspective on your life and choices. It takes you out of the constricted, contracted space of victimhood and lack into a much more open, receptive and empowered place where you can see the perfection in everything.

Bottle 3 shows you the potential for how life might look if you were to surrender to total self-acceptance. Jupiter, being expansive and generous, desires only to shower you with gifts and benevolence, and the more you learn to love and fully accept yourself the more you will receive. If you are choosing this bottle it is because you are ready to let go of disempowering patterns and open to something much more authentic and joyful. Jupiter is your guide as you shuck off your small self and step into your huge, magnificent, bright and shiny self! Astrologically Jupiter is the 'lucky' planet. It indicates where you excel and where you connect with the beneficence of the universe. This can be a very exciting time if you are ready to take the leap into a different way of being based on loving and honouring yourself.

Coral is warm and bountiful and plays a foil to its complementary colour, turquoise. It brings dormant feelings back to life, thaws frozen emotions, softens your defences. The number three relates to creativity and self-expression, and with the help of bottle 3 you can open yourself to love and blossom into the abundant, beautiful being the Divine has created you to be. As you embrace your generous, loving nature you begin to show your true self to the world without fear of judgement, without holding back. You begin to know what it is to live without limitations and take your rightful place in the cosmos, just as Jupiter does: bold, unreserved, unafraid.

Both coral and turquoise relate to the Christ energy – specifically, what we call the new Christ Ray. Traditionally, the Christ energy was represented by red and white: the blood of Christ; blood and tears; sweat and sacrifice. When red and white are mixed together they make pink. To reach coral, yellow is added – and yellow is the joy-bringer. Suddenly we can see that the way of the 'Christ', or the Divine consciousness that is becoming available to everyone on the planet, is love and joy. We have had 2000 years of blood and tears on the earth. Turquoise is the colour of the new age we are entering, and its message is to have faith that new ways of being and living are now available to all.

Coral embraces both the difficulties and the joys of the human condition. It provides opportunities for the lowest and the highest experiences of earthly life, showing that none are 'better' than others but that all are simply signposts on the path to consciousness and a return to your Divine self. This bottle reveals the possibility of a shift towards a more peaceful, joyous and loving world. Here is a new version of 'red' for the new age we are rapidly moving into, with the potential for love, self-acceptance, celebration and joy. Coral shows us a world that is sweet, rich and delicious. Jupiter is vast, expansive and full of love. This bottle is a template for heaven, a blueprint for bliss – and it is all yours for the taking.

Bottle 3 Story: Melissie

A woman on a two-day workshop chose this bottle on the first day. Her stories were all about the difficult relationship she was in. After she bathed in it on the first night she came back and told us, with a coy look, that she had had very romantic dreams about her difficult husband. She went home full of confidence and self-acceptance and plans to woo him back to the state he was in when she fell in love with him, and apparently it worked out exactly like that. A year later they had a baby and were fully committed to staying happily together. This bottle is a lovely, gentle healer of relationships that run into difficulty when the coral person is so super-sensitive and needy that they alienate their partner. This bottle seems to strengthen them to be more self-sufficient.

Bottle 3 Story: Lesley McDonald, UK, www.lesleytara.com

When I bought a coral sweater with a dark red/coral heart on the front at the end of 2018, I had no idea that 2019 was a 'three' year in numerology and therefore a Jupiter year, a coral year. I wore the sweater over the holidays when I had some big decisions to make: would I leave Denmark where I had lived for many years and move home to Scotland? Would I stay with my partner in his home and trust in his love? This was not something that came easily, and my 'unrequited love' shadow nearly caused me to lose my mind as I projected every fear of relationships and love I had onto him.

It took a bath in bottle 3 to begin to allow me to discern between old patterns and a possibility of relating differently. It was a fight, a real battle with my shadow aspects. It was worth the ill-health, the stress, digestive issues, urinary tract inflammation and other symptoms my subconscious patterns threw at me to dissuade me from taking this step. I know that these patterns were indirectly fighting to keep me safe, but I let the expansive side of Jupiter come through. I am taking this chance on love. I believe whole-heartedly that this is the essence of the 'three' energy: moving through our shadow despite 'the fight' and opening our hearts to change, supported all the way on Jupiter's wings of expansion.

Bottle 4: Uranus (Yellow/Deep Turquoise)

This planet signifies change and disruption of the old order. It is time to clear everything that no longer serves you and let go of old beliefs, structures, people and places that are not in alignment with your truth. This is the planet of the future and is about clearing everything that will not fit into the Golden Age of Aquarius. Expect the unexpected.

The first three bottles of the system are like the building blocks or foundations, each one connecting with a primary colour. Together they feel quite balanced, stable and coherent. When bottle 4 appears, the world begins to tilt on its axis as instability, movement and change arrive. In life, order and disorder tend to follow each other in a never-ending sequence – from order, chaos; from chaos, order – and change is the natural course of events. Yet sometimes nothing appears to change. You get stuck, fall into stagnation, and growth slows or maybe even halts altogether. This is where Uranus comes in. It stirs everything up, moves it all around, transforms it – and when you feel incapable of doing it for yourself, Uranus will provide the impetus to make it happen.

Astrologically Uranus relates to change and the release of stuck energies, whereas the number four has an energy of structure and stability. Although this may seem like a paradox, with bottle 4 you are being asked to look at both sides: what feels true in your life and what no longer serves you? What brings you the greatest support when you are feeling unstable, and where do you let the need for stability and the status quo hold you back? Uranus helps with both sides of the structure equation, bringing grounded support when you require it and shaking things up when you have a tendency to stagnate.

Uranus often comes in with an element of surprise. You may find sudden and unexpected change showing up, even massive 'life or death' type change, yet with bottle 4 alongside it does not have to be completely shocking and can even be quite fun. There is a saying that if you're not growing, you're dead, and Uranus reminds you of this, helping you find change and disruption and growth something to embrace rather than resist. This bottle seems to say that if you want to be at the real cutting edge of life, right inside its complex mysteries, travelling its highs and lows, you will have to move out of your familiar old comfort zones. Uranus takes you into a moment by moment experience where you can manifest from a thought or respond in an instant to life's questions, and the ride becomes exciting and enthralling as you let go into the unknown.

While you are in the process of change, you may not always feel the joy. You might feel lost, vulnerable and scared as your world shifts and moves, yet this bottle promises that eventually you will emerge into clearer waters. The yellow in the top fraction of the bottle helps you step out of fear and resistance, offering a sense of fun and play so that you remember not to take it all too seriously. The deep inky turquoise in the bottom fraction shows that even if you do not have a clear sense of what is going on, you are actually plumbing the depths and creating a shift in the deepest reaches of your subconscious. This is a key to bringing about true, lasting change. Turquoise is about flow, and when you choose this bottle you know in your heart that you cannot cling to the edges any longer. Dive into the water instead. Step into your creative flow and let it take you forward. With Uranus by your side, you will find the support you need.

This is a bottle to call on when you are feeling low, stuck or resistant, but it is so much about movement and stirring things up that if you are drawn to it you are almost certainly ready to shift. Uranus pulls you out of the boggy soil of confusion and indecision and lifts you onto drier ground so that you can set out on the next part of your journey. Splintered aspects of your life begin to reform as part of the whole, and what was lost and confused can become clear and focused. Change becomes something to celebrate and enjoy.

For many, the colours of this bottle are not particularly easy and the message can seem quite forceful. There may be a tendency to think: "Uh-oh, better look out!" when this bottle comes up. Yet when you use it you may feel quite different afterwards, finding yourself doing things with ease, things you would have hesitated about before. It soothes and supports and just makes everything feel OK again. What is interesting is that although Uranus is about shift and change, it tends to hold you while you go through the process. Rather than warning of a tough road ahead, this bottle is a change agent, solidly yet gently supporting you as you navigate new territory.

Bottle 4 Story: Melissie

An artist friend noticed she had begun to paint in the colours of this bottle and wanted to know what they were about. I sent her a bottle by way of explanation. My friend's story for as long as I have known her – about 30 years – was always that she was about to leave her marriage. She bathed in the bottle and immediately all talk of leaving came to an end. She no longer felt the need to have an escape route. The bottle shook up her habitual story and showed her a deeper truth and a different perspective about her relationship, and this enabled her to stay in it.

Bottle 4 Story: Melissie

A gay man who came for a reading was in a relationship where he felt controlled and undermined. He chose this bottle, took it home, bathed in it and promptly left the relationship. It gave him the impetus to get going, quit a relationship that no longer served him and be true to himself.

If we look at these two stories, one person shifted and stayed in the relationship; the other shifted and left. The very essence of Uranus is change, and this bottle supports movement in the most appropriate way – whatever that might be – according to your own deepest truth. Its job is to break down the old to make way for the new, and it may be uncompromising in the way it proceeds. Some of the changes that take place may occur in the outer structures of your life when, for example, you set boundaries with a family member, take some long-needed action in your work life or end a relationship. When you allow your mental and emotional barriers to come down and your blind spots to be revealed, you may also notice a more subtle, inner change as you make space in your heart and mind for the new. This inner shift enables you to be more empowered, more inspired, more open – and often translates into positive change in your outer life too.

One of the keys to bottle 4 is its link with Atlantis. There are many interpretations as to what, where and when Atlantis was. Whatever your take on it, turquoise is the colour related to the energies of that time or place or dimension, and despite appearing to many as deep green, the bottom fraction of this bottle is actually a very deep turquoise. This bottle shows that things are not always what they seem, and what you believe may not always be so. It supports you whole-heartedly in seeing beyond what you think you know to a deeper truth.

The yellow in the top of this bottle brings the potential for seeing the sunny side of the whole Atlantean experience. For many, there has been residual and often hidden grief and guilt about Atlantis for lifetimes, yet this bottle hints at the sunshine of the age of Golden Atlantis. Maybe it is time to bring the joy of that time back into the collective consciousness as well as your own personal story. Perhaps it is time to let go of the judgements and grief about what you thought happened and remember that from the perspective of the Divine infinite being you really are, it all unfolded perfectly, just as everything always has and always will.

We will look at Atlantis further when we reach bottles 7 (Neptune), 14 (Movement) and G3 (Return from Atlantis), but Uranus provides an opportunity to touch in to the Atlantean energy and reclaim some of the profound joy of that time as you move out of old, stuck patterns and beliefs into something much more in alignment with your Divine self.

Bottle 4 Story: Moira Bush, Canada, www.moirabush.com

A friend of mine had never contemplated any kind of therapy, perhaps because he was a Scorpio birth sign and every conversation with him already tended to be deep and meaningful. He did, however, take note of the mysterious Uranus bottle on my shelf. I explained that this bottle had a tendency to lift heavy energies or stuck feelings from the body. He liked that idea, as he was going through a difficult time at work and felt stuck. He reported back that instead of doing a three-week bath therapy as suggested, he felt he had to soak in the whole bottle at once. He said that during his bath he felt free to release buried emotions and fear of change and that it looked like little grey entities were floating out of his body up onto the bathroom ceiling. Soon afterwards, not having heard from him for a while, I enquired if anyone knew what he had been up to. I was told that he had quit his job, fallen in love and moved with his new partner to work for a charity organisation in Africa.

Bottle 4 Story: Kathryn Marshall, South Africa, k.s.marshall@mweb.co.za

When I looked at this bottle it did not feel comfortable for me on many levels until a client walked right up to it and gushed how amazing it was. Initially during the session I just asked her what story it was telling. She was in need of confirmation, and the answer this bottle gave her was YES. It allowed her to gently connect with her yellow energy and her 'I AM' and internally recognise herself, claim part of herself back, and with the support of turquoise, it confirmed that now was the time to speak up. It enabled her to tap into a resource that is often lacking when we get stuck in our thinking patterns. It became clear that this is an action bottle.

What I have learned from this bottle is that we need to really look at our stuff from all angles and decide exactly what we want: what we wish to experience every day, who we want to be around, who grows us, who is part of the journey and who is not part of our personal growth anymore. It is a bottle that gently says it is time, because if you look really carefully there is the most beautiful, thin, liquid green line between the two colours that enables us to recognise the voice of our heart space. It brings us back to ourselves to check in and see what needs to be changed, what needs to be cleared out – not from the space of reaction or fear but by going deeper into the parts of ourselves that need to be voiced, the parts of ourselves that remind us that this is about us and the journey of the flow of our life.

As we remain steadfast and connected to our joy we draw on our heart space and speak that language. It might be a different language, and it may create an absolute storm or turn our world upside down. BUT we need moments like that to be able to choose, and this is a bottle that enables us to say YES, which can often be the hardest thing to utter when we know the journey we need to go on will be one that changes our life completely.

Bottle 5: Mercury (Green/Pale Green)

This bottle links to Gemini: movement, communication and versatility. It relates to those who are mercurial and quick-minded, with a sense of feeling that is swifter than logic. Begin to be the magician; the old pattern of being the trickster no longer serves you. All has to be upfront and clear in your dealings. The number five relates to issues of discipline and freedom, and the colour green signifies change and new beginnings. This bottle is about letting go of all the masks: everything you have used to hide behind has to be removed. The truth about your magnificence has to be told clearly, and if any part of you still wants to hide, it will make life quite difficult. The answer to the dilemma that this bottle presents is to be constantly aware of what makes you feel small and change that. This is your time. You can only be free by being honest with yourself.

The previous bottle, Uranus, stirred everything up and moved it all around. Mercury comes in now bringing the fresh green of a new space. There is a sense of hope for the future, an energy of life and growth and the abundant flourishing of nature. New things are possible, spring is in the air, and it is time to leave the difficult times behind – but there may be some work to do first.

Mercury calls when you are deeply in need of the soft, green, restful space of nature, a sanctuary where you can stop and just be. This bottle says you have been putting up masks in an effort simply to get by on this planet – and effort is the word: it takes huge energy to play games and pretend. It becomes exhausting and confusing to wear masks. You may even find yourself forgetting what is mask and what is truth.

A mask is any form of behaviour that is inauthentic or any attempt to cover up who you really are. It may be an unconscious but habitual role you have taken on such as martyr, victim or rescuer. It might represent a mythical ideal you would like others to hold about you such as 'perfect mother', 'life and soul of the party' or 'spiritual master'. A mask may appear in situations where you feel you have to conform to social pressures, such as pretending to have more money than you really have or taking on everyone else's problems because you want to be seen as kind and caring.

Whatever they are and however they were formed, masks mean not showing others who you truly are, and this taps into the fundamental insecurity beneath the behaviours: a fear that if others see who you really are they will find out you are fundamentally flawed, unlovable and unworthy. Perhaps you never risk being real or true in the hope that if you get good enough at the games, no one will ever know.

Both the planet Mercury and the number five relate to discipline and freedom. This bottle asks: do you allow yourself to be carried along by the wishes of others or do you have the strength to follow your own inner flow and your own Divine calling? Where are you fully true to yourself and therefore free, and where do you try to go along with others' expectations and ideas about who you should be, never really asserting your truth?

There was a time some years ago when this bottle underwent a global transformation. All over the place bottle 5's were turning blue on top, effectively turning into bottle 35 (The Inner Guide), which at that time was blue over pale green (it is now blue-lilac on top). Bottle 35 relates to sibling rivalry, and the link we see here with bottle 5 is that masked behaviour is often learned among siblings. If a sister slaps you down when she sees how bright and shiny you are, or a brother laughs at you when you show him something you have created, your instinctual response may be to cover up your true self in order to fit in, be accepted, feel safe. Siblings are often the closest members of your tribe and if you are too different, if you are rejected, you risk being ousted from the tribe. For the primitive part of you this means potential death, so fitting in or being appropriate according to others' opinions will generally feel much safer.

Masks are often created depending on where in the family you fit. Younger siblings may fall into manipulative behaviours or play the role of 'baby of the family' to get what they want. Older siblings may be reluctant to show weakness. They may take on a bossy or authoritative role, especially if parents are absent or unable to parent effectively. They may decide they are the 'saviour' of the family who has to solve the problems of every other sibling. Middle siblings may play younger and older siblings off against each other to get what they want or use their 'middle' status to disappear altogether in the family constellation, taking no real part in family dynamics. All siblings can fall into roles with relative ease, and it may be tricky to spot the patterns and change them. Mercury is a guide and support in helping each member of a family or group find their unique place without resorting to game-playing and masks.

Relationships with siblings often contribute to childhood wounds and the resulting masked behaviours. And if we are all God's children, then we are all siblings. Anyone who presses your buttons is effectively a 'sibling' with the potential to trigger you into creating a mask to hide your true self. This is one of the biggest challenges faced by all of humanity and one that must be brought to the light of awareness, love and compassion if we are to find oneness on this planet. We cannot come to a state of oneness and unity while in the midst of rivalry, of separation, of 'better than' or 'worse than' or 'wrong'. We cannot come to a state of oneness while in judgement, and judgement – along with anger – sits in red, the complementary colour to green.

In this green bottle you are given another opportunity to look at judgements – of others certainly, but mostly of yourself. If you cannot believe in or accept yourself, you may expend enormous amounts of energy trying to be someone else. As this is blatantly impossible you may become angry and frustrated instead, and if you are afraid to show your anger, chances are you will put on yet another mask. If taken to the extreme, this can lead to mask piling on top of mask until you are so weighed down that all you can do is go under – or surrender.

This bottle is about looking in the mirror and seeing the truth. It is time to stop pretending, time to stop putting up a front, time to stop lying to yourself and others. Mercury was the messenger of the Gods, but he was also quite a trickster. This bottle says it is no longer necessary to play that or indeed any role. Bottle 5 contains a wonderful energy of movement and flow and helps you move to a much more peaceful place where you no longer need to hide or pretend. It helps you feel safe enough to give up the facade and the games and find the courage to be authentically you. But if you are reluctant to peel away the masks yourself, be warned that this bottle may just do it for you.

Mercury asks you to face some of your biggest challenges: it asks you to be real, to come out of hiding, to set clear boundaries and to shed false beliefs about yourself. But the higher purpose of bottle 5 is to get you to acknowledge that you are so much more than any mask you have chosen to wear. It dares you to reveal who you really are and shows you the truth in the mirror – that you have a core of light, love and brilliance inside you that is just waiting to be recognised and allowed to shine.

This bottle contains a quiet strength. As a perfect mirror of exactly the thing it asks you to recognise in yourself, it displays a soft, calm, pretty exterior, while underneath lurks a powerful conduit to your most deeply buried truths. As a kind of cleansing agent for the soul, it takes the tarnished mirror you have learned to see yourself through and gently, firmly and relentlessly cuts through the grime. It takes the distorted fun-fair reflections and sets them to rights, allowing you to see again what you may have long forgotten: the beauty and wonder and truly awesome light of who you really are.

Bottle 5 Story: Korani

On a workshop one of the participants took this bottle home to bathe in on the first night and came in the next day having had a huge row with her partner and another with her best friend. This bottle had gone so deep that she could no longer hide and she realised she had been wearing a mask, even with those closest to her. After this green bath she showed her real self to them both and they reacted with shock and anger because they did not know who that was. They had only seen the mask before.

Bottle 5 Story: Kathryn Marshall, South Africa, k.s.marshall@mweb.co.za

To be an adventurer is to be a soul that is a seeker. I have been working with a courageous young man who so wants to be able to live totally free, a young rainbow warrior of the planet and its animals. Things changed when he met a young woman, so we did a session for the two of them as a couple and put bottle 5 in the middle of the table. With green pieces of paper and green pens we became fully immersed in the conversation and worked with the energy. Because it is a bottle that allows you to connect from your green heart space, I have found that using this bottle to set the tone and steer the direction in a session is phenomenal.

The whole process was beautiful. I had various questions to ask them and set the intention that no answer would be right or wrong. They longed for their connection to work, but they wanted to be very clear and upfront from the beginning about what it needed to look like for each of them. This bottle supports that so beautifully, as it gently removes the masks and allows you the freedom to create. The brainstorming they did together signalled that it was time for a new adventure. As they talked about how to bring balance and give each other a gentle space to grow individually so that the relationship wouldn't become a push-pull at any time, their honesty and integrity was inspiring. To create a base within your relationship with this bottle is amazing.

They are both now on a new adventure, travelling the world together, growing independently but in the same direction. The branches they climb and the route they take is so clear. They both bathed in the bottle just before they left but saved some to take with them. They told me later that when they needed to regroup and see what new beginning needed to be created, they would take out the bottle and both bathe in it before the conversation took place. They still travel to this day, pioneering and fighting for the rights of nature and animals in countries all over the world.

Bottle 6: Venus (Pink/Pink)

Venus relates to love, harmony and joy in relationships. She brings love into your life when you learn that love from the outside comes when you reach a place of deep self-acceptance. Pink is the colour of unconditional love, and its message is that the more you are able to love yourself, the more abundant your life will be. A feeling of 'not enough' inside will always lead to a reality reflection of 'not enough' outside. This colour relates to all things feminine, including mothering. Now is the time to treat yourself to some of your own nurturing energy.

A new green space has been offered by the previous bottle, Mercury, and now it is time to fill that space with something. What else but love? Green is the traditional colour of the heart chakra and pink is the new – the colour of unconditional love. There was no conscious decision made about the order in which the bottles would appear in the system, yet it seems entirely fitting that after green, comes pink. Now is the time for love to be the foundation on which this earth rests, and now is the time for the human heart to evolve from a love with conditions and limits to a love with the doors wide open, a love that encompasses all.

Bottle 6 holds the qualities of love, romance, grace, beauty and relationships. It is also gentle, harmonious and nourishing. When you choose this bottle it can indicate new love and new relationships, and you may be drawn to it when you are in the throes of a wonderful romance or when you are feeling 'in the pink' and life is rosy. Yet it is also the one you will choose when you have not an ounce of self-love, when you are desperate to feel loved but cannot find it within or without.

It is almost part of the human experience for self-love to be the very hardest love to find, and we have noticed that Venus is one of the most popular bottles in the system. It also frequently changes colour. Time and again people have reported taking one home only to find that fairly swiftly, sometimes within hours or days, it starts to lose its pink hue and turn very pale or even go clear altogether. When this happens you are literally drawing the pink inside, pulling it to you. Your soul is showing you in dramatic visible form how very much you are in need of love, of self-love. Both coral and pink relate to self-love and self-nurture, but while coral expands outwards, pink tends to look inwards and find itself wanting. With coral you seek for love from others, whereas with pink you may not seek it at all because you deem yourself undeserving.

Venus is a 'balm' bottle, supporting and assisting you when your self-love has deserted you, or you cannot even remember what self-worth might be. Its soft, nurturing warmth may be challenging if you are feeling unworthy, but this is a bottle that can release fountains of tears, touching in to childhood wounds and misconceptions and misunderstandings, wrapping them in a blanket of pink love. Bottle 6 asks you to treat yourself as if you are already in love, as if you are already loved, even if you feel right now as if that could not be further from the truth. Venus is the perfect bottle for pampering yourself. Poured lavishly into a bath, with a sprinkle of the Pink Angel essence and a host of pink candles, it creates a warm and love-filled experience. It is one to hug to your heart whenever you feel vulnerable or lost, to place under your pillow at night or to keep somewhere visible so that its gentle, loving light can flow to you and remind you of the higher truth: you are worthy of love.

This pink bottle is infused with the feminine energy of the goddess, Venus. It is a reminder of the power of love, the power of beauty, the power of grace. Venus is gentle, nurturing, generous and kind; she is also potent, powerful, dynamic and alive. The Venus bottle invites you – whether man or woman – to open to your creative feminine power, unlock your inner goddess and bring her out to play.

Pink can, however, be the disempowered female, the little girl who does not want to grow up or take responsibility, who would rather stay a perpetual victim, locked into blaming others. Pink can have narcissistic tendencies including manipulation, game-playing, arrogance masquerading as victimhood and an excessive need for attention or admiration. Bottle 6 asks you to look squarely in the mirror and face up to these damaging behaviours. It also shines love into your heart so that you can find compassion for yourself as you do so.

Pink relates to all aspects of the feminine, including the ability to nurture, and this bottle may crop up when you are experiencing challenges in your relationship with your mother or issues around how you were mothered. Perhaps you are feeling the need for mother's love or questioning your own role as a mother. Bottle 6 taps into the very heart of your connection with your mother and any vulnerability you are holding there. It brings a wave of soft healing energy for a heart that is hurting in any way, and if you have stored up old wounds from the way your mother (or indeed anyone) has spoken to you or treated you in the past, it gently infuses them with love. It also helps you see that each apparent wound or difficulty in your relationship with your mother is a powerful opportunity to shine light on any unhelpful beliefs you are holding.

With the loving support of Venus, you are guided to bring these beliefs into conscious awareness for healing. As you let them go, you no longer have to inflict them on other relationships, carry the past into the present or bring old childhood patterns into your adult relationships. From a higher perspective, every last one of those stories was a gift to enable you to find your own strength, your own power and the inextinguishable light that exists at your very core.

There is much to love about a person with a 'pink' heart – your affection, sensuality, playfulness and charm. You are a true friend to those in need, holding a compassionate space for whomever needs a dose of love. You have the ability to bring people together, create a warm loving space for them and help them feel safe and cherished.

If, however, your pink persona is founded on appearing kind and sweet and caring only about others, you may never show your true feelings – especially anger. The number six relates to being of service, and if you are someone who spends all your time looking after others but denying your own needs, you may find anger bubbling up and spilling over. Pink is actually red with extra light added, so it often manifests as intensified red – intensified anger, intensified frustration – most of it directed at yourself. Shame, blame and self-hatred are all uncovered by this bottle – low frequency emotions that disempower you, keeping you chained to self-destructive behaviours and caught in an ever-increasing spiral of negativity. Bottle 6 supports you in facing your anger so that it need no longer drive your behaviour or undermine your life.

This bottle encourages you to reclaim your feelings as valid. It reminds you that all feelings are acceptable and that being true to yourself is not about ignoring the needs of others or being selfish but is, in fact, essential for healthy relationships. Venus invites you to bring home to yourself all that you have been offering to others and become your own truest friend. The parts of yourself you have hated, rejected or denied are only unevolved aspects of your being looking for love. As you bring those aspects into the pink light of love, as you acknowledge them and listen to what they have to share with you, they can stop hijacking your happiness and instead become part of your ongoing learning and evolution.

The colour pink and the energy of Venus are closely linked with love, money and the ability – or inability – to receive. If you have been denying yourself love in any way, you may also find money issues arising in your life. This bottle assists you in opening to the possibility of receiving both. In her true power Venus is hugely abundant, creating flow for both herself and the greater good. When you open to the positive power of pink and welcome love, you also step into the Divine flow of creation that draws abundance into your life. Venus invites you to notice what happens to your finances as you begin to really love and honour yourself.

This bottle lights a quiet flame of hope. It says there *is* such a thing as love and you can hold it, literally, in your hands. It is about recognising that love in its truest sense is utterly unconditional. As humans the very concept of love has become distorted. Some of your experiences on the planet may have seemed the opposite of love, or perhaps they were called 'love' but came loaded with conditions. Yet your heart knows the truth of love and yearns for it because that is where heaven ignites earth, where soul joins with body, where Divine joins with human. As you heal your pink stories you hold the potential for loving relationships with yourself and others. This bottle is a beacon of light, showing what might be possible for all of humanity as we learn to trust love to lead the way.

Pink is also a pathway to the female face of the Divine. The Divine has been viewed by many as 'male' for too long, and Venus offers an opportunity to redress the balance, inviting you to take the love of the Divine female and the truth of real, unconditional love right into your body, your heart and your cells.

Bottle 6 Story: Korani

I woke one morning from a dream where my dear friend Clara Apollo was asking me: "What colour are you today, Korani?" "I am feeling very pink," I replied. I'd been working on the words for the pink/rose pink bottle 33 (Love and Magic) the night before, so that was not entirely surprising. When I woke from the dream and saw a changed bottle 6 sitting on my window-sill, its bottom fraction having gone very pale, it was a no-brainer to pour it into a bath.

As I did I found myself playing and splashing in the water like a child, and my six-year-old self was very present. I wrapped her up in all that gorgeous pink love and asked her if she was willing to receive it. She was. Next I connected with my six-month-old self and did the same, then at six days, six minutes and six seconds and right back through birth to conception. This felt quite blissful, as if I was being treasured and deeply loved. I could also feel the very strong presence of Mary Magdalene. As I had been connecting with the Christ light through bottle 33 the previous night and she is the female face of Christ, this was again no surprise, yet deeply moving all the same.

I posted this on Facebook and shortly afterwards, Clara added her story.

Bottle 6 Story: Clara Apollo, UK, www.claraapollo.com

Korani's post came in right on time. I'd checked my messages just before I was about to hop in a morning bath – not usual practice at this time, but I was being called into the water for meditation. I had several other bottles poised to choose from when up popped dear Korani with this inspiration. I had just discovered that I had two Venus bottles in waiting, so I gathered them both as I went upstairs and added them to the collection.

I thanked myself for all that I'd loved myself enough to do and be. Pouring the bottle of oil down into my heart in front and behind and gathering a pool on my palm, I began journeying back through the sixes as Korani had inspired... wow! A good hour later and a whole bottle gone, I emerged, having called back my power from each stage and acknowledged the messages. Particularly BIG was when my Dad first held me at six minutes old; oh wow, the LOVE. Oh, Oh, Oh! My eyes were leaking with tears of poignant joy from this love acknowledged from him to me, his firstborn.

Bottle 6 Story: Alka Dharam, UK, www.lifecentredhealing.co.uk

Bathing in this bottle was like bathing in an ocean of pink. There were clouds of pink, and I was enveloped in this colour. I saw myself curled up in the womb of Divine Mother. Love poured from me. My third eye enlarged and in the middle was a bright light within which a celestial being danced. I heard Divine Mother saying to me: "You are me."

The next day my journey to London took almost five hours instead of two. Whilst stuck in slow moving traffic I realised just how peaceful, grounded and at ease with life I felt. There was no irritation at the other drivers or the circumstances or that I 'only' had half an hour left to get to an important meeting. The beautiful feeling of unconditional love towards everyone, everything and myself continued for days and affected others. People I had never met before or interacted with visibly relaxed around me, and beaming smiles replaced the stressed faces.

Bottle 7: Neptune (Turquoise/Deep Turquoise)

Neptune was the Roman god of the sea, ruling spirituality and the depths of the unconscious. The colour turquoise relates to mystery, illusion, miracles and faith. If this is your bottle, you are always able to hear others' troubles. You are perceptive, intuitive and a great peace-bringer to those suffering difficulties, yet you tend to carry your burdens alone and may find it difficult to share your secrets with others. This is a time to trust that miracles can happen and that you are on the brink of something wonderful. Trust the process – it works.

The previous bottle (Venus) guided you gently into love, particularly self-love. With this next bottle you are asked to go deeper, to explore the full spectrum of the turquoise emotional realm. Bottle 7 relates to Neptune: mystery and mysticism and all that is hidden from the conscious mind.

Neptune is the planet of inspiration and dreams, receptivity and intuition, enlightenment and higher consciousness. It can also be contrary, bringing fog, illusion and confusion. Sometimes fog appears simply because the perfect timing for what you are seeking has not yet arrived. If it is not your time to know or to move forward, the fog keeps you contained and still as you await the perfect unfolding. At other times it prevents you from realising you have reached the shore, and you continue to thrash about, thinking you have to do more or be more to reach your destination. Neptune takes you by the hand and says: "Get out of the boat. You're there."

This bottle asks you to be completely conscious, stay on course and notice when your ego is trying to control you or keep you in fear. What is needed as you set out on your voyage is trust that something greater than your small, unconscious self is guiding the process and that out there somewhere is the destination, even if you cannot see it yet. The colour turquoise and the number seven both relate to trust, and this is a powerful key to your unfolding journey.

People with strong turquoise qualities have a tendency to avoid emotions. When you choose this bottle you may be hiding your true feelings, keeping your mind busy, drifting around in your thoughts, circling restlessly and aimlessly through the mire – and consequently finding it almost impossible to move forward. If you cannot admit to your feelings or feel your feelings at all, Neptune assists with its loving yet penetrating support. If you are ungrounded, lost or confused, this bottle helps you navigate towards clarity and understanding.

The deep turquoise in the bottom fraction has solidity, solemnity and weight. It asks you to truly face your emotional seascape rather than wriggling away, and it gently but firmly holds you there as you explore it. The deep waters of your emotions, although perhaps scary, are ultimately liberating. In facing your emotions you are shown the doorway to freedom from their bonds. As you recognise and acknowledge your feelings, as you let yourself *feel* all your feelings – fully and without judgement – you reach insight, acceptance and peace.

Once you have passed through the mist, Neptune is a willing guide for your ongoing journey. As you allow everything to be as it is, without necessarily knowing the how, what, when, where or why, you find yourself carried on the Divine tide where control and struggle are no longer necessary, where flow and ease are entirely possible. Bottle 7 enables you to know that you know. It encourages you to access your inner wisdom, trust what you instinctively feel and follow your own Divine flow.

Turquoise often calls when you have choices to make, particularly in relation to career or work, and this bottle can be an ally. Neptune brings waves of opportunity, taking you to the right place at the right moment, opening you to new possibilities. With the surging power and energy of the sea, its tides are ready to carry you to wherever you wish to go next.

Neptune's capacity for mystery extends to the deeper secrets of what was experienced in Atlantis. So much about Atlantis remains shrouded in mystery, myth and illusion: where it was, what it was, why it happened, what its role was and how it impacts on the planet and humanity now. The collective holds memories of Atlantis, and many people carry left-over Atlantean guilt, grief or burdens, much of it unconscious. Although the collective belief at the time of Atlantis was that it was entirely possible to raise the level of light on the planet, there can be an underlying sense of panic, fear and doubt that the light will prevail this time around. Despite your faith and despite holding the light, still that civilisation fell. Still, there was death and destruction. Still, your light wasn't enough. Or was it?

By the time Atlantis was destroyed, the energy was strongly masculine. More and more were doing rather than being. More and more attempted to exert ego power over others rather than living from the true power of love. When the doing became over-doing and the balance between masculine and feminine energies dissolved, things came adrift. But was it wrong? Or was it just another experience? Another opportunity for the Divine to know itself in all its complexities? An opportunity to see what happened when power became unbalanced?

Korani's Experience

I personally dragged guilt and grief around for many years, never fully aware of their source. I cleared out and healed as many of my personal issues as I could, but still these millstones remained around my neck – until I met Melissie. She took me back through regression to an Atlantean lifetime and allowed me to see the truth. What I saw was a kind of after-party. There we all were, floods and destruction behind us, glasses in hand, chatting: "So, what was it like for you?" None of it was a mistake. No one was 'guilty'. No one had had anything other than an experience from which they had learned and grown and evolved.

There were some who had lost everything – loved ones, power, knowledge, their lives. Others had played an active role in the causative factors that led to the 'fall'. Still others were teachers who had felt responsible for their students and guilty about what had happened to them. No matter their role and no matter the consequences, all were in awe of the depth of the experience and the lessons it contained. All were fully accepting that what was, simply was. But the thing we were most in awe of was our ability to manifest such creative outcomes. I never felt the same guilt or grief again. It lifted, as surely as the morning mist lifts when the sun shines through.

Can anyone ever know the 'truth' about Atlantis? Perhaps, essentially, Atlantis is whatever you require it to be. It may represent the downfall of a civilisation or remind you of the power you appeared to lose, if those are the experiences you choose to pin on it. It can be a re-awakening of the faith that led you there or the wonderment of a life based on knowing and perceiving a greater truth than your ego and mind would ever allow. It can be the way-shower to a more expansive view of yourself and your reality. The only real 'truth' of Atlantis is the one you touch into within yourself. Your experience of it and feeling for it will be different to that of another – and that is perfect.

Bottle 7 creates a space to tap into and reconnect with your Atlantean self, with the knowledge, wisdom, insight and power you held then, allowing you to access it in a new way for a new time on the earth. It invites you to integrate the aspects of your Atlantean experiences you have been unable to fully accept until now. It beckons you forth to a new age, the Age of Aquarius, the dawning of a new era on the earth. It asks you to be neither held back by the past nor beholden to it, for it is only another story and one you have the opportunity to re-write any time you choose.

This bottle holds a key to your deepest inner treasure. It asks you to be willing to plumb the depths of the ocean, to enter the darkest cave and retrieve the gems your soul has buried for you there, bringing them to the surface as you emerge into the light and allowing them to illuminate your path.

Neptune's gift for mystery makes this a perfect time to enter the dream state where anything is possible. Taking a bath in this bottle can soak away the bonds and emotional shackles of the past as you open to the vast potential that awaits. When you let go of the thinking mind, you open to the feeling heart and the deeper layers of faith within. When you dispense with what you 'think' you know, you may just find something entirely new and infinitely more creative awaiting you.

Bottle 7 Story: Client of Rui Diogo, Portugal, www.facebook.com/kaleidosol

I took this bottle home after an appointment with Rui Diogo and used it as a thirst quencher, a drink of fresh water. However, it plunged me into the dark night of the soul. In this place I lost my naivety about human beings and became attentive and intuitive. It made me see that someone in my life was not being honest with me, and I ended the relationship with my boyfriend whom I came to discover to be a violent aggressor. I can tell you that this bottle took off my illusory veils. I can only thank Colour Mirrors, this wonderful energy system.

Bottle 8: Saturn (Pale Violet/Deep Violet)

Saturn is old father time, stern and fair. He relates to destiny and what you have set up that is not negotiable. Time passes; you cannot stop its progress. Saturn helps you see that no one is judging you and that it is time to stop judging yourself. As you learn to create balance in your life, this bottle brings gifts of wisdom and a deeper understanding of who you truly are. It helps you overcome feelings of restriction and burden and find the gifts in your experiences. This is not a time to rush things. Saturn teaches the value of persistence and insists that any new structure must be built on a solid foundation.

With its turquoise Aquarian energies, the previous bottle, Neptune, has links with the future. Bottle 8, Saturn, on the other hand, is steeped in the past. This bottle relates to Catholic past lives and the energy of controlling religions, a power wielded as spirituality but which was often uncompromising, sometimes destructive and ultimately disempowering. These were the lifetimes where you could not access the Divine on your own, where you were beholden to a powerfully masculine authority such as the church, which denied you any sense of your own God-self and viewed everyone as sinners, most likely beyond redemption. This meant that bodies were less than important, lives were only of value if they were malleable, and there was one truth and one way only. If you are choosing this bottle you may relate quite strongly to feelings of suppression and repression, persecution and unworthiness, many of which stem from previous lives and some of which may have played out in this one too.

Saturn asks you to recognise that through your many lifetimes you have experienced both sides of the equation: suppressing and being suppressed, persecuting and being persecuted. It assists you in reviewing, releasing and healing those occasions when you were judged and found wanting. It also helps you let go of the times when you judged and persecuted others, and as this is often even more painful to face up to, it can take something of the might and magnitude of Saturn to help you do so.

Connecting with this bottle may reveal to you all the judges in your life, played out in a long line, stemming back through your life and into the distant past. Saturn asks: Who were your judges? Who judges you now? Or rather, whose judgements do you continue to play out in your life? Any time you feel judged you have an opportunity to see where your unresolved issues lie. Your wounded feelings or pressed buttons are a clue to guide you to the blocks, negative beliefs and inner judgements you continue to hold. Bottle 8 asks you to acknowledge the stories you have been telling yourself and the power they have wielded over you and finally let them go.

One of the keynotes of violet is that it is helpful for depression. Depression is very often linked with unspoken anger, particularly anger that has never been fully felt or acknowledged. Violet is made up of red (anger) and blue (expression), and we have seen time and again that when people work with violet they are able to get their voice back, express their anger and move beyond depression.

Astrologically Saturn is associated with restriction and limitation, law and order, rules and regulations. Saturn is a father figure, and where Saturn sits in your astrological chart connects to your relationship with your father. It carries a powerfully authoritative energy that asks you to look at how you view the masculine: your own masculine side, your earthly father, and the Divine – in the traditional masculine sense of 'God the father'. You are given the opportunity to delve deeply into these relationships and open your eyes to any judgements, preconceptions and hidden associations you hold with the masculine so that you can ultimately transcend them.

This bottle also relates to lifetimes when you were afraid to embrace your spirit and live by its guidance or when you believed on some level that you did not have the appropriate authority to shape your own spiritual journey. Perhaps you believed it would be impossible to access the Divine without an intermediary such as a guru, a spiritual teacher or the church. Violet represents your crown chakra, your opening to heaven, your own personal connection to the Divine. It gives you a hint of the spiritual power you contain within and asks you to claim it. Saturn's message is to free yourself from the past and from controlling influences in this or any other lifetime such as a domineering father or a rigid brand of religion. This bottle asks you to find a new way to relate to and access the Divine within so that you can bring your spirit to the fore in your life in a way that is personal and unique to you. You are a sovereign being, and your spirit is just waiting to guide you forwards. You have no need of another to tell you what to think, feel or believe.

Violet relates to control on all levels, however, and choosing this bottle means that rather than being controlled, it may be you who is doing the controlling. With the deep violet fraction at the bottom of this bottle there is a sense of digging your toes in, refusing to move, being unwilling or unable to see another's point of view, perhaps even manipulating others to achieve your desires. Saturn's task is to bring you face to face with such behaviours and their consequences and to draw to the surface any lingering subconscious beliefs from previous lifetimes which do not serve you in this one.

Violet is intimately linked with grief and the things you feel you cannot change, cannot stop, cannot control. If you look more deeply into grief you will usually see guilt sitting right by its side. It may be survivor guilt – feeling guilty for being the one who survived when others did not. It may be guilt that you did not do something you wished you had done. It may be guilt that your behaviour led to pain or difficulty for someone you love. Whatever its source and however irrational, guilt sits in very close relationship to grief in your body, and both are often bound up with anger and rage at not being able to control the outcome.

Bottle 8 helps you look at your feelings of grief and guilt in a new light. It assists you in clearing the past, relinquishing your need for control and accepting the perfection of whatever unfolds – without judgement. If this bottle is calling, it is because now is the time to look in the mirror, shift out-dated beliefs and re-attune to the true power you hold within. The benefit of doing this with Saturn's help is that although it may appear a hard task-master, it is also a great support as you go through the process. The number eight relates to abundance and power, which makes this the perfect time to step into a lighter and more empowered space. Bottle 8 asks you to surrender to the universe's wisdom and move towards freedom and wholeness. It helps you see that everything in your life is part of the unfolding perfection of spirit.

When you are able to do so, it brings the opportunity for a new structure, a new form within which to shape your life. Saturn helps you build deep, strong foundations so that whatever you create is solid, stable and built to last. Its message is to take time to feel for what it is you truly desire to set up. This is not the time to rush and bulldoze ahead without going deeply into the vision your spirit wishes to show you. It calls on you to be patient, and this can be challenging, yet the rewards of a solid foundation will be incredibly beneficial as you embark on the next stage of your journey, free of the past and ready to embrace the future.

This bottle may relate to judgement, but it also includes all the positive traits of a judge: someone who is wise and fair, just and true; someone who is able to use discernment; someone who is dedicated to working for the highest good of all. Violet relates to being of service, and this could be the perfect time to look at where and how you would most like to contribute to the world. Having been through some of the darker and more challenging aspects of life yourself, you are perfectly positioned to help others free themselves from their limiting beliefs and behaviours.

If Saturn is your bottle, you have the ability to make a real difference to people and situations. You are likely to hold both wisdom and authority as well as the potential for great organisational skills and a huge degree of competence. With your valuable expertise and your ability to see projects through to completion and understand what others cannot, you make a great asset to any organisation.

When this bottle is calling to you, trust that you are deeply supported by the power of your spirit, and use Saturn's authoritative power to highlight and transform the areas of your life that feel out of balance, uncomfortable or out-dated. The number eight connects with the flow of the infinity symbol, and with Saturn's guidance and support, you have everything you need to shift whatever feels stuck in your life with relative ease. Now you can pave the way for true abundance, power and success – all built to last.

Bottle 8 Story: Elaine Nuelle, UK, elainenuelle@gmail.com

Saturn is my life path bottle and one that I'd always avoided picking up. I really didn't like it. It brought up feelings of anger, depression and hopelessness, and it took me a long time before I was prepared to work with it. I always went to the lighter bottles such as the paler coloured Gaias to escape, but then one day I was ready and started holding it. I felt the loving softness of it and its safety. I really understood the need to build those strong foundations. My anger and frustration at my perceived slow development and progress started to melt away. I understood the need for right timing too.

Then, to my surprise, it felt right to bathe in it. I didn't write anything down about the bath, but what I experienced was so simple yet so profound and beautiful. I realised that my anger and frustration was with God or Source and that it was a two-way street – I was always wrong, so I was being punished. I was hurt and scared and my survival response was anger. My grandfather, a very harsh man, had taught me to fear God. The bath in Saturn melted that away and taught me to love God and that I was loved right back.

Bottle 8 Story: Jackie Tweedie, UK, www.jackietweedie.com

This bottle can feel serious and heavy to some but when I choose it, it's always a timely reminder for me to take stock of where I'm putting my attention and what I'm trying to create. If I'm rushing, it slows me down; if I'm procrastinating it gives me a helpful nudge to speed up. It feels reliable and solid.

A client once chose this bottle when she had become blind to her own talents and felt diminished by her comparison to other people whom she considered more gifted. Through the gentleness of the violet in this bottle she came to see how harsh her self-criticism had become and how it was preventing her from appreciating that her specific talents were unique to her and were therefore beyond comparison. When she realised this she was delighted and chose then to celebrate her life and skills, determined to make this realisation a daily practice.

Bottle 9: Mars (Red/Orange)

Powerful and warlike, Mars is the source of your fire energy. Use it wisely to change what needs changing rather than just being angry and frustrated. This bottle urges you not to spend your life being meek and angry. Say what needs saying rather than holding grudges that endlessly play in your head as "I should have said". Mars is a powerful ally when things need to be set in motion. Now is the moment for drastic action. This bottle energises you so that you can do and say what needs doing and saying.

Bottle 9 in the system is both a completion and a lifting-off point. This is Mars: a blast of red and orange rocket fuel, a potent pack of fire-power and the potential for explosive energy. This is Mars: an invitation to pay close attention to your anger.

In the violet energy of the previous bottle, Saturn, lies a tendency to either bury and suppress your anger or turn it in on yourself, which may give rise to depression. With Mars you now have the opportunity to really feel and express your anger, speak it out and release it from your cells. It is a fireball of energy, with the potency to move you out of sadness or despair into positive action.

The positioning of violet Saturn and red Mars next to each other in the system is significant. Violet is at the crown of your being, red at the base. Violet is deeply connected with spirit; red is matter, the body, the physical realm. We know that the world tends to see these as essentially polarised and separate: one above, one below; one 'good', one 'bad'; one ethereal, one solid. Appearing next to each other in the system, side by side but quite separate, these bottles are a perfect illustration of this polarity.

Violet and red together reveal the potential for heaven on earth (see bottle 12). On its own violet cannot fully experience heaven, even though it is the colour of the spirit, because it holds the separation energies of grief and depression. Red is too busy being angry and explosive to even contemplate heaven. Yet together they create the very real possibility of a Divine life in a human body. What is more, when violet and red are mixed they make magenta, and magenta says you have full access to the power of Divine love because you *are* Divine. When spirit and matter merge within you, the realisation comes that Divine love is your essence. In the melding of heaven and earth, you are able to recognise your body as a portal to spirit and a vehicle for evolution and expansion. These bottles are a key to your unfolding journey, and using either of them (or both) will support you in stepping out of polarity and moving towards inner harmony.

The planet Mars relates to how you express anger, energy, action and desire. It connects with your animal nature and what you believe you have to do to survive. The number nine relates to detachment, integrity and wisdom. The Mars bottle brings the potential to embrace your physicality, get 'real' with your spirituality and anchor it fully into your body.

There is no doubt that when Mars is calling, however, anger is nearby. If you are actively angry, bottle 9 helps you move through the anger more easily and swiftly than you might have done otherwise. If you have been denying or hiding your anger, Mars gives you the nudge – or push – to get it out and clear the air. It takes you firmly by the hand and shows you what you need to do or say to reclaim your power without letting the anger burn you up or burn you out.

Suppressing your anger can result in pain, discomfort or illness in the body, and Mars helps you break the destructive cycle of burying your anger and hurting yourself in the process. With orange sitting in the base of this bottle you may find yourself tapping into issues of abuse, and here you are given the courage and impetus to feel and express your anger so that it no longer needs to remain buried in your body and potentially generate disease.

This bottle is an energiser. It does not let the grass grow under your feet or allow your body to hold on to harmful patterns and blocks. If you are feeling stuck, running old programmes or locked into frustration, Mars is a great ally. Whether you perceive the problems to be coming from outside interference or from your own self-sabotaging behaviours, this bottle is the perfect tonic. If you are feeling sluggish and unmotivated, this bottle stokes your inner fire and gets you moving. It brings power and movement, shifting you out of lethargy, creating momentum and releasing clogged energy from your cells. It keeps you feeling energised and motivated when you might normally give up, and rubbing it on the soles of your feet can provide a great boost.

Bottle 9 is about seeing the bigger picture of the physical aspects of your life. Your body is a truly unique vessel for housing your spirit, and rather than judge or resent it, Mars encourages you to view it as a source of joy, pleasure and adventure. This bottle helps you transform your anger, frustration and rage – at the challenges and struggles of a physical existence, at being in a body that does not always behave as you would like it to, at being on the earth and all that entails – into passion and excitement for all the experiences and possibilities life offers.

'Red' people often have the energy of fireworks, firing off in all directions but not always focused or consistent. They are stimulating to be around but may be over-excitable and cause things around them to become unstable. If you relate strongly to Mars you will likely have the ambitious and dynamic qualities that make you successful in business and the confidence to drive forward in your chosen direction. You do tend to need the balancing that comes with the grounding and stabilising aspects of red, however, and thankfully Mars has both. If you are angry, over-energised or hyped up, bottle 9 brings quiet and calm to your emotions and your body. Alternatively, if you lack drive and confidence this bottle can be a tremendous support in helping you get on your feet and get going. It helps you feel safe to take your next steps or embark on new projects.

There is something of the perfectionist energy in Mars. If taken to extreme, you will use the fiery red energy to push and berate yourself, striving, trying and obsessing. In its pure form, however, this energy shows up when you are tired of living half-measures, of settling for second best, of damping down your natural enthusiasm and vitality in order to 'fit in' with those around you. The perfectionist streak in Mars can be a signal that you have gone too far, yet it can also be exactly the dynamic and potent power that lets you break out of restrictive, limiting behaviours and patterns and helps you reach for the stars.

Mars has the fearless and powerful energy of the warrior. It is fire in liquid form, a burst of bright, sizzling power and light that removes obstacles and blazes through your life, igniting, opening, expanding and clearing. Its fiery light relates to Pele, the Hawaiian Goddess of the Volcano, who invites you to ignite your Divine passion. As your spark turns into a flame, your experiences on earth are enlivened and you feel able to share with others everything you most love and most deeply embody. Mars lets you be passionate and gives you permission to bring out your fire power. It teaches you to use your anger as a creative force rather than a destructive one. The orange in the bottom fraction of this bottle signals the potential for the bliss and enlightenment that can surely come when you are empowered and fired-up with the potency of the creative force within you.

The number nine is about completion, and when you choose this bottle it signals that you are ready to let go of worn-out old stories about being a victim. Now is the time to clear up old grudges, lift yourself out of the red mist of anger and set yourself free. The journey is to bring heaven and earth together, and with this bottle everything comes back to the physical, making it real, anchoring it in to the earth, providing a solid, grounded platform from which you can prepare to launch yourself to the next level.

Bottle 9 Story: Korani

I was asked to give a talk about colour to a group of recovering addicts. Some were more open to the bottles than others, but all were intrigued. I asked everyone to choose a bottle they felt drawn to and hold it in their hands or place it on any part of their body that felt right. We went around the group, exploring how their bottles made them feel.

When I got to one particular woman, she cried as she held bottle 9 to her heart. She was confused about why she was feeling such strong emotion from a bottle of coloured liquid. When I explained that bottle 9 was to do with suppressed anger she cried even harder. She then began to tell the group that she had always thought she was just a hopeless addict, but hearing the words of Mars made her realise she was, in fact, incredibly angry about the abuse that had happened in her life. She said she had realised, sitting with Mars on her heart, that she had always kept her anger buried deeply inside as she was so afraid of what would happen if she allowed herself to feel it. The tears were a sign that she was getting in touch with emotions she had been battling all her life to feel and express. She was amazed that just holding a bottle could give expression to something she had never fully realised was within her.

Bottle 9 Story: Alka Dharam, UK, www.lifecentredhealing.co.uk

I had such resistance to this bottle that as I was choosing a bottle to bathe in I completely ignored it, looking at bottles 1-8 and then bottle 10 onwards. On recognising my resistance, this bottle became the obvious but uneasy choice. When I bathed in it, I could feel my pores opening and the movement of the cells in my body. There was heat on my skin and the energy of liquid fire permeating my cells. I felt a thumping noise like marching: the sound of movement. Within a few days of this bath I booked to teach my first solo workshop after months of procrastination. Interestingly, nine participants attended this workshop.

Bottle 9 Story: Jackie Tweedie, UK, www.jackietweedie.com

This bottle was a powerful help to a client who had recently been let down in a romantic relationship. She was tormented by replaying the various arguments and miscommunications that had led to the break-up, but underneath her sadness she was enraged. This outrage was draining her energy and keeping her stuck in a rut. In this bottle of fire and energy she discovered she could feel empowered again. She realised that her life was her business and her responsibility and that she was not going to feel better by looking backwards and replaying 'what might have been' images. Instead she chose to use this fiery anger energy to help herself. She found her voice again and reclaimed her power.

Bottle 10: Wheel of Fortune (Gold/Olive)

This bottle says that now is the time to access your inner wisdom (gold) and activate your feminine power (olive). Olive is the green of the heart mixed with the gold in the solar plexus – your power centre. When power is connected to love it can never be abused and will always be a soft, feminine power. This bottle relates to an Egyptian lifetime and asks you to remember who you were at that time. Your power can be reactivated now as you stand before great changes in your life. You can do it. The wheel has turned and you have everything you need to make it work. Trust your heart.

After the first nine bottles, which all relate to planets, bottle 10 is a 'one' energy (1 + 0 = 1) and signifies the beginning of a new phase: the wheel is turning and the next level is coming up. Just like the 10th card in the Tarot, this bottle represents the wheel of change, the Wheel of Fortune.

Bottle 10 has strong links with Egyptian lifetimes in which you were able to embody power, wisdom and wealth. It connects with the life-giving force of the Egyptian goddess Isis whose immense power and light shines upon you, reminding you that true power is loving, kind and wise. Its bright rich gold plugs you into the source of your power and inner wisdom, while its soft peaceful olive signals hope for the future. Together these colours are encouraging and optimistic, the warmth of golden sunshine on the new green buds of spring.

Bottle 10 is new growth, new life. It is change and expansion. It is the possibility of living in different ways. It is positivity and optimism and a shift into joy as you move away from old patterns of lack and fear. This bottle suggests you are ready for something new and exciting to be revealed. There is a freshness and vitality to the colours which indicate that you now have the ability to create and manifest with ease and joy. Now is the time to open your mind and heart to all kinds of wonderful possibilities and step into them with enthusiasm and a sense of fun. If the bottles preceding this one introduce the idea of heaven on earth, bottle 10 lets you feel how it might actually be to live it.

These colours also relate to a Cathar lifetime when earth seemed a very long way from heaven indeed, and when you choose this bottle the sense is that it is finally time to leave that energy behind. The Cathars were a deeply spiritual community who were able to manifest and generate gold, so their lives were both spiritually and materially abundant. They were not only persecuted for this but effectively wiped out, and the memory of such lifetimes sits deep within the cells of many who are travelling a conscious spiritual path. These cellular memories leave clinging traces of fear, which means that if you relate to these colours, to be spiritual and wealthy at the same time has, until now, been virtually impossible.

This bottle is not called Wheel of Fortune for nothing, however. Its message is that it is safe now for you to have abundance. If you have struggled to achieve financial freedom in this lifetime or you have consistently lost money every time you have made it, your Cathar experiences may have led you, on an unconscious level, to equate wealth with betrayal, persecution, even death. When this bottle calls you it signals an opportunity to wipe the slate clean, heal the traumatic cellular memories and return to your natural state of abundance on both inner and outer levels.

Bottle 10 often comes up when you are at the beginning of a new cycle and everything is about to change. And if you have had a really difficult time and *nothing* has been working, it can help you finally shift. Choosing this bottle indicates that you are now open to choices, options, possibilities and the creation of your very own heaven on earth. It asks you to remember your truth, remember your power, remember your ability to receive. This bottle reminds you that heaven was always right here on earth if only you could see it. It reminds you to trust. It reminds you that the point of enlightenment has always been to create and live heaven on earth and that this comes from within you, from your consciousness, not from anything or anyone outside of you.

There is a story about an old lama whose students asked him: "If you are enlightened, why are you still here? Why are you hanging on to this planet of pain and suffering?" And he said: "That's the point of enlightenment. If you were looking at the planet through my eyes, you would see the perfection and the preciousness of each moment and each incident." Heaven on earth is just a change of viewpoint away.

This bottle is a reminder that everything is always in a state of change and nothing is forever – neither the 'good' times, nor the 'bad'. As you open to the messages of this bottle you can begin to embrace every turn of the wheel. There will be times when you hit bumps in the road and there will be times of ease and flow, and neither is actually good or bad. Each is simply an experience, offered to you by your ever-loving soul to enable you to learn and grow and discover all the many aspects of life as part of the Allness.

Bottle 10 Story: Melissie

A friend had bathed in lots of different bottles and often had powerful physical responses to them, but when she tried this one she felt nothing. I was surprised by this, but later she told me she'd found the perfect house and her children had found the perfect school and she had a new job and had doubled her salary. I looked at my friend and said: "And all of this happened after you used bottle 10?" She stopped and thought and said: "Oh, of course! It was virtually the day after I bathed in this bottle that things started falling into place. I didn't have a physical response, it just completely changed the reality around me in the most positive way."

Bottle 10 Story: Raluca Rusu, Switzerland, www.facebook.com/RalucaRusu.colours

This bottle is in my birth chart and is still a complex notion for me. I bathed in it during the Colour Mirrors practitioner course with Moira in Canada. From my birth reading Moira had already mentioned that it was time for me to get back to my authentic feminine power. I have been working as Mechanical Engineer, following my father's activity field in the mining and construction industry. Taking the men in my family as a model, I had always maintained a masculine attitude in order to protect myself and keep up with the image of how I believed an engineer should be.

For several years I worked in mining, and from the very beginning the only projects I came across were in gold mining, with Canada being involved in one way or another. Canada also featured in my childhood as my parents intended to emigrate there from Romania, although this never actually happened. Later I was able to put the puzzle pieces together when I discovered the story of my great-grandfather's brother who worked in a gold mine in Canada between the two world wars. He got rich from this job, and in our family there are several versions about how his life unfolded.

I might have identified myself with him and his story, a phenomenon that easily comes to the surface in family constellations, for example, where it is shown how information is transmitted through generations until the cycle is completed. Taking a bath with this bottle, I felt this great-uncle energy very present along with the pattern transmitted through my father's line of hard labour, making money in harsh conditions and at all costs. I felt the masculine energy that often drove me at work and the tight identification with the men in my family.

The work of these bottles is very subtle. It is a multi-layered experience and I am not always able to quantify the healing process, but ever since my bath in this bottle the gold mine story is becoming less and less significant, and I feel I am moving towards a new, more feminine direction in my life.

Bottle 11: Duality (Deep Magenta/Clear)

The number 11 is a master number, and the hidden message in this bottle is that it is a last look at issues of separation (think of the twin towers on 11th September). It indicates a difficult life path as you struggle to bring together the light and the dark. Look deeper. The dark is deep magenta, the colour related to Divine love and healing. Hidden in these colours are the answers to all issues of separation. This is where you finally let go of your judgement of God who got you into the mess in the first place. This bottle helps you see that there has only ever been perfection in the imperfections of your life. Be willing to claim this level of mastery and fully accept the gift of Divine love that is available for you now and always.

The previous bottle indicated a turning of the wheel and a shift into something new. But the new and all its possibilities can mean being asked to step up to the next level, peel away the next layer, shake off the old – and that can feel quite challenging. Bottle 11 tends to appear when you are having difficulties. You might be feeling disconnected, separate, cut off from your inner knowing. Maybe you are experiencing conflict within yourself or with another. Perhaps you have been flowing along just fine, and now you have hit a dark spot and nothing seems to be going right.

This bottle provides a powerful opportunity to face your judgements in a very clear way. It is the closest in the system to a black and white bottle, so it highlights the splits and divisions in your life and your being. It helps you look at where you still experience life as separate and polarised rather than unified and connected. It taps into the grief, shock and despair you experience when you feel as if you have been abandoned by the Divine, when you feel unsupported and alone.

Separation is perhaps the core human wound. Since the physical separation from your mother's body at birth, your sense of yourself as separate from others, the world and the Divine has coloured your experiences of life. In a spiritual sense we can talk about 'oneness', but your body feels separate from every other body on the planet and your mind believes itself to be singular, belonging only to you, not to anyone else. If you are separate you must therefore be alone. If you are separate you have to pit yourself against everyone and everything else in a bid to survive. If you are separate you can hurt others and they can hurt you. If you are separate, life can be summed up as you versus everyone else.

With this bottle any and all of your judgements about separation may come to light so that you can take a good look at them. Are you still in thrall to better than/worse than or right versus wrong? Is your way of viewing the world the only correct one? Or conversely, does it feel as if everyone else somehow knows the secret to life and you are the only one left out, unable to join in? Much of humanity's conditioning and its belief systems lead directly to duality, and it is duality that keeps separation alive.

Magenta is the colour of the healer and bottle 11 relates to the wounded healer, represented in astrology by Chiron. A wounded healer wishes to help others because they themselves have suffered. They also find that supporting others becomes a way of understanding their own challenges. This bottle helps you connect with your 'wounded healer' and your own deepest wounds so that they can be brought out of the darkness and into the light to be loved, integrated and healed. It also helps you explore how you can use the valuable experiences and learning you have gathered along the way to be of service to others.

Guilt is an example of how this may play out. Magenta relates strongly to guilt, and if you are drawn to this bottle you may harbour a sense of being 'wrong' or hold a subconscious belief that you deserve to be punished. As you become conscious of this wound and seek for a way to resolve it and grow beyond it, you begin to realise that offering healing could be a key: assisting others, helping them grow and change, making a difference. And perhaps, in order to assist others, you first needed to know and experience the essential human condition, much of which is riddled with guilt.

Guilt is the fundamental misunderstanding that there could ever be something wrong – with you or with the world – when all of it is created by, through and for Divine perfection. This bottle invites you to explore how and why you have let guilt and suffering run your life. It shines the light of Divine love on your soul so that each time you experience a sense of separation you can begin to see the higher perspective. What if guilt is simply a part of the game you have set up to help you remember your divinity? What if your experiences of guilt actually enable you to move closer to mastery? As you recognise the guilt, accept it and lovingly integrate the part of you that has needed to hold on to it, you take a step closer to the Divine love that exists at the core of everything and everyone. In the process, you become a wonderful support to others as they too journey from separation to wholeness.

Despite its apparent difficulties, bottle 11 is actually a 'master number' bottle, the first in the Colour Mirrors system. Master numbers are those which contain a repeated digit such as 11, 22 and 33. When they come up in your bottle choices you are asked to take note – for these bottles are invitations to step out of limitation and into your own personal mastery. The colours of bottle 11 might appear to be black and white, but this bottle is actually magenta and white – and magenta is the colour of Divine love, lit up and amplified here by the clear white light.This bottle says it is time to consciously connect with magenta as the potential for true enlightenment. It offers the promise of mastery if you are willing to go through the dark night and recognise it as an integral part of the journey. This bottle shows you that the first steps to mastery lie in letting go of judgement and your belief that you could ever be separate in the first place.

Bottle 11 is a godsend for any kind of shocking experience. It helps you release judgement, pain and suffering and the belief that 'it shouldn't have happened'. It guides you towards seeing the perfection of the situation, no matter how it may at first appear. The gift of this bottle is to show you a Divine who loves you wholly and entirely, without conditions or constraints. When you can see and know what was dark and difficult as magenta and Divine, you come to understand that there was never anything wrong. You were not being punished or made to struggle. There was simply an opportunity to shift and transmute a judgement and step into the perfection of every experience, in true Divine love, as true Divine love. Bottle 11's message is that as soon as you stop judging a situation, it has no hold upon you.

This bottle is a huge key. It supports you in seeing separation and guilt for the illusions they are. When your perspective shifts from a focus on duality and separation to the realisation that all life is interconnected, everything changes. You are no longer weighed down by feelings of isolation, loneliness and mistrust. What appeared to be separate becomes an aspect of you. As you see yourself in another, judgement dissolves. This bottle offers a stepping stone on the lighted path out of the dense forest of guilt, sadness and disconnection you have wandered for many lifetimes. It reconnects you with your innate truth: you are and always have been a child of the Divine and therefore whole and perfect, *no matter what*. And if you are Divine, whole and perfect, so too is everyone and everything else. Nothing is left out of Divine love, nothing is separate from Divine love, nothing can exist outside the infinite love of the Allness.

Bottle 11 is a powerful reminder that what you have called duality is simply a misconception, a blindness or unwillingness to see clearly that what you have believed to be two is, in fact, one. If all life is love, all life is Divine, all life is one, then night and day, male and female, light and dark, up and down, heaven and earth – all are at their core the same thing, from the same source. There is no duality, no separation, nothing to feel guilty about, nothing left to judge. This indeed might be heaven on earth: the light and the dark coming together to form one sacred circle.

Bottle 11 Story: Melissie

A woman that I had been teaching went through the most intense experience imaginable. She found out on a Friday that she was pregnant, and on the Sunday her husband died in a car accident. As a Colour Mirrors practitioner, she said that all she could think of doing was to bathe in bottle 11, so she did. She then felt she needed more – so she did it again. She said suddenly the whole thing shifted. It moved her beyond the judgement that this was a bad thing that shouldn't have happened. She felt a sense of her husband, of his joyousness at being out and away and his complete commitment to go on supporting her. She opened the floodgates to the absolute knowledge that everything that happens is part of the plan and that it is not a bad thing, it is simply another thing.

Within two months she was married to her husband's best friend, who had completely stepped in to support her. She lived in a fairly small village where the response was shock and horror that she wasn't behaving like a grieving widow. She just said she deeply knew that it was all divinely led.

Bottle 11 Story: Renira Barclay, UK, www.abovemiddlec.com

Although I have two 11's in my birth numbers, this was initially my least favourite bottle in the whole system. As I bathed in bottle 11, I saw myself travelling through the galaxies, sailing on a little boat amongst other little boats, able to travel anywhere I chose in this beautiful sea of galaxies. When I look at or hold this bottle now I can tune into huge potential. I am able to accept the darkness and the light and know that it is all part of me. I have in the past ducked away from my potential – and this bottle represents potential and the ability to view the world from both sides. I can accept my Gemini-ness and my speed of ideas, always knowing that I have bottle G11's generosity to soften the edges of bottle 11. I now find No. 11 exciting!!

Bottle 12: Heaven on Earth (Violet/Red)

Number 12 in the Tarot is the Hangman, which shows an image of a man hanging upside down – but with this bottle the colours are the right way up: violet is above red, crown is above base and heaven is above earth, implying that everything in between is also in its proper place. Yet with this bottle you are asked to look at what you believe is not perfect about your world. What are you still judging as not heaven and therefore not Divine? Where do you judge yourself or the world as imperfect? What is keeping you from living in heaven on earth? Let this bottle show you the core beliefs that are keeping you from living your perfect life.

After taking a close look at what still holds you in duality in bottle 11, the next bottle in the sequence asks you to bring together what has always been considered separate: body and soul, spirit and matter, heaven and earth.

The concept of heaven on earth may feel at times like a pipe-dream; after all, the vast majority of humankind is not yet experiencing anything like heaven on earth. Collectively, humanity has carried judgements and beliefs about the separation of heaven and earth forever – heaven as an unreachable place of perfection, earth as a place of suffering and density. How could they ever be united? Where in the red could heaven ever be found?

Red connects with everything that is physical, tangible and of the earth, everything to do with the practicalities of daily life. Bodies, health, sex, money, work – the whole of the material world is far removed from what is generally perceived as 'spiritual'. In previous lives, and perhaps in this one too, red was sheer, fundamental survival. Violet – the realm of spirit, angels, the Divine, the holy and the pure – was a level of perfection that no mere human could attain. On a conscious level you may know this division to be false, but almost everyone has some version of separation playing out in their lives, and to place your faith in a kind of nirvana here on earth may feel misguided or even delusional. It may feel safer to continue to believe in separation, to stick with the status quo, to let go of any foolish dreams of paradise.

At some time or other in the long history of humanity, more or less everyone on the planet has experienced persecution for their spiritual beliefs, and this is held in the energy of violet. In red sits the bloodshed that has undoubtedly also been a part of one lifetime or another. There is plenty of shock in this combination of colours. You may think you can be wholly spiritual here in a material world, but your body says you can talk about heaven on earth all you like – it does not believe you for a second. Bodies remember the persecution, the fear, the shock.

Bottle 12, however, prises open this narrow view of the world and lets you start to envision the possibility that heaven on earth can – in fact, already does – exist. This powerful little package of violet and red gifts you with an opportunity to re-visit all your fears, doubts and conditioned beliefs. You are asked to review everything in a new light, to shed whatever false concepts you have retained in your cells, to look at apparent separation and see it for the illusion it is. Every difficulty you have in the 'real' world; every challenge with money, health or career; every experience of feeling persecuted or betrayed; every trauma – all are opportunities to learn, heal, grow and return to truth. Each is a light on the pathway leading specifically to your very own heaven on earth, the one that resides within you.

This bottle shows the pure potent life force of red you can experience when you stop viewing yourself as a victim and life as a game of survival and open to the absolute joy of being alive and physical on planet earth. Here you can know beauty, passion, sensuality and power. Here you can taste, see, hear, sense and touch the most wondrous of heaven's creations. Bottle 12 gives you all the potential for heaven on earth and shows you what it might look like. It says heaven on earth *can* be attained. It acts as a reminder and a flag of hope that once you are finally ready to release your patterns of victimhood, survival fear and separation you will come much closer to the mastery you hold within.

It also has the perfect combination of red base energy and violet crown energy to shift you back into balance if you are shocked, devastated or completely thrown off course. These colours are incredibly helpful if you are going through huge trauma. They give you back perspective and help you step out of the drama so that you can see the bigger picture and understand why the event happened. The massive support provided by this bottle is one of its great gifts. A shocking experience can send you right out of your body and these colours will pull you firmly back in, reuniting spirit and body.

Until 2011 this bottle was coral over red rather than violet over red, and its name was Victim/Sacrifice. As we moved into the changing times heralded by the year 2012, bottle 12 morphed into the colours of violet over red and began taking things up a gear. The old bottle asked you to look at your patterns of being a victim or martyr, to own up to them and accept them so that you could let them go, and with its soft coral top fraction, it supported you gently in the process. This later version of the bottle is tougher, less willing to suffer fools. It tells you that letting go of victimhood is not actually negotiable and that when you are stuck in victim mode, a kick up the proverbial from your spirit may be just the thing. It asks why you might be wasting time wallowing around in victimhood or martyrdom when heaven on earth is right here, right now, waiting for you to claim it.

This bottle is a wake-up call. One Colour Mirrors client reported that she felt it would have taken years of therapy to deal with the issues she reached and cleared by bathing in it. Bottle 12 shows that now is the time to get real – where 'real' means perceiving, knowing and living the truth of your divinity. This bold, vibrant bottle of colour brings you back to a deep and embodied sense of your own spirit, power and value. It reveals all the red and violet stories of the past that have stopped you from moving on, and says your time for playing the weak, limited, 'poor me' human is up. The stories are over, you have lived them and told them and they have run their course. Now it is time to acknowledge that, on a soul level, you created the stories so that you would be given the knowledge and experiences you needed: to learn about life, to better understand yourself and your patterns, to grow and evolve, to set yourself free.

This is the ultimate 'letting go of the story' bottle. Much like bottle 11 (Duality), it also shifts grief and anger about what 'shouldn't have happened'. It is easy to get lost inside the illusion of the story you have been telling – the grief, the guilt, the emotions – and forget what the higher truth really is. The story may be over, but when you repeat it and re-tell it to yourself or others, it holds you prisoner. This bottle is like a sigh of relief: it is exhausting to hang on to your stories! Without them there is a draught of new energy available to you. This bottle frees you up, brings you into balance and opens you to the real potential of heaven on earth where all is, and always has been, exactly as it needs to be.

With this bottle you have it all – the human, physical, powerful life force energy of red and the healing, spiritual, supportive power of violet. And if you mix red and violet you get magenta, which is Divine love. This bottle empowers you to explore and expand on what heaven on earth actually means, for you as a unique individual and for all of humanity. It says heaven on earth really might be within reach any time you choose, and that is perhaps its greatest gift. It returns you to the knowledge that heaven on earth ultimately resides within you. It is a choice – one you can have, live and be in a heartbeat.

Bottle 12 Story: Korani

When the Coral Gaia bottles were born in 2011, I had a dream that I went to Melissie and told her the system was now complete. She agreed and then said: "Yes, except there is just this one...." and held up a bottle of violet over red. In the dream I told her I had been waiting for this bottle all my life. It turns out Melissie had, in reality, also been waiting for this bottle and had always wanted it in the system. She made it and brought it to England when she came a few weeks later. I happened to be going through a strange and challenging time: I'd managed to take on someone else's stuff – something I rarely did. Not only that, I'd also managed to allow a difficult energy situation to impact me and was finding myself going down into a negative spiral from which I was finding it hard to claw my way back.

I bathed in this violet and red bottle and got huge insights into my core judgements about being on the planet. I reconnected with a past life as a priest whose deepest belief was that bodies had no value. To him, spirit was all. Souls were what mattered. Bodies – who cared? They could burn for all their value. And they did. It was not a shock to me to discover this lifetime, as I knew from previous past life work that I'd been on both sides of the persecutions – as most of us have. We came, after all, to experience every aspect of being human. The real revelation here was that I was still carrying a thread of that priest's beliefs within my cells.

The bath didn't entirely shift those deeply entrenched beliefs, but it did bring them utterly into consciousness. I could no longer pretend they weren't there, part of me, and in the weeks and months that followed I watched as they slowly and gently transformed. What did change from the bath in bottle 12 was my state of disconnection and powerlessness – immediately. I felt energy downloads going on all day after the bath and all that night. By the following morning I was truly and fully back in my power, back in my light. It restored me to my truth in a way that was quite breathtaking in its swiftness and power.

Bottle 12 Story: Jackie Tweedie, UK, www.jackietweedie.com

When people choose this bottle I often ask them who or what has disappointed them, and then it comes flooding out: all the judgements and stories, past and present, which get in the way of people being able to live here on earth as if it were heaven. Through a self-inquiry process I share with clients, they often come to see that what they thought had happened, didn't; it was simply their interpretation of the event or action that had taken them off track. Once seen in the light of truth, the stories fall away and the realisations are profound. Without the judgements, relationships can heal and people can love and accept themselves fully again. I believe we all have access to the promise of this bottle – to live here on earth as if in heaven.

Bottle 13: Transformation – Pluto (Dark Violet/Pale Violet)

The number 13 relates to Scorpio, the sign of death, regeneration and rebirth. This bottle relates to the scorpion and the phoenix and is about being able to go through the dark night of the soul and come out stronger. These colours signify the releasing of grief so that it might be used as service to the world. Stand up and let the world see the new you.

If you have journeyed through the bottles of colour in the system so far you will have begun to get the messages in your body, heart and mind. Bottle 13 comes in now with the promise of significant change and transformation at a spiritual level. It calls when you seem lost in the darkness, sunk deep in depression, heavy with loss or grief, burdened by the weight of your fears and unable to see beyond the long dark night of the soul. With a light and gentle touch belied by the depth of the colours, it reaches into your spirit, your essence, your very being and asks you not to give up. It says that you are poised to break through now, so dig deep – because you are very nearly there. You will only be drawn to this bottle when your soul already knows that the darkness you are in is preparing to make way for new light, new dawn.

Bottle 13 relates to Pluto, which in astrology is the ruler of Scorpio. Pluto represents the subconscious as well as renewal and rebirth, and this bottle is about regeneration, the phoenix rising and the attainment of spiritual transformation. Just as Pluto sits at the furthest point of the solar system, bottle 13 guides you to the places within you that have been furthest from your conscious mind – the deepest, most inaccessible aspects of your being. As it helps you bring what has been most shadowed within you into light, it offers a re-claiming of your spirit. Like the Violet Flame of transmutation, it helps you purify and burn off all that does not serve the highest Divine light of your true essence.

Bottle 13 supports you as you move out of the dark night and lifts you up to another level entirely, showing you a completely different view than the one you have been choosing. Yet this bottle goes deep, and it may take time for the transformation it heralds to unfold. You may not fully understand the process or immediately recognise the gifts it offers. But as 1 + 3 = 4 there is a quality of change similar to that of bottle 4 (Uranus), which means that the shift, when you are truly ready, can happen with speed. And with this bottle by your side, you do not have to do it alone.

Bottle 13 relates to the Death card in the Tarot and invites you to re-tell the story of death. In her book *Many Lifetimes* Joan Grant recounts how as a child she assumed everyone knew, as she did, that death is a beautiful experience. When she encountered a family friend one day she could 'see' that he was about to die, and as far as she was concerned that meant he was going to have the best day of his life. She knew he would go on to the wonderful place that greets souls in between lives, and she was so happy for him that she congratulated him on being about to have a truly happy birthday. The man was bemused because it was not his birthday, nor did he have any reason to believe he was about to die. The girl was severely chastised by her mother for her remark – but the man was indeed found dead the following morning.

Is it possible that what you have been conditioned to think is death and therefore terrible and difficult is actually the easiest transition? Could it be that death is simply a change in state from one thing to another, not a final and devastating conclusion? This bottle reminds you that you 'die' every day. It is a natural and intrinsic part of life. It is in every breath. With every out-breath you experience a kind of small death, and with every in-breath life is returned.

Bottle 13 helps you release your fears around dying; it also helps you look at how your fears of dying may prevent you from fully living. This bottle is particularly about dying to whatever is old and out-dated in your life, dying to all that has kept you from being who you really are, dying to who and what you have been that is no longer your truth. It is the death of any story you have been telling yourself about your life. It shows you what spirit sees when it looks at your story: it was never about martyrdom and suffering but about life, growth and evolution. It asks you to see how perfect the whole of your story has always been and reminds you that if you had not had the experiences you have had, you could not be who you are now, could not have evolved, could not have grown and learned and transmuted all that you have. Bottle 13 shows that you do not need to fear the darkness. The difficulties you are experiencing are a path to growth, and they are leading you to the next level.

This bottle is a return to spirit, a reconnection with soul, an opening to a higher view. It gifts you with the knowledge that a difficult time or challenging situation can be a path to deep and lasting change. It acts as a portal to transformation, holding your hand as it takes you into the apparent darkness and showing you that there is nothing to fear, nothing to run from. As you sit with your darkness, you learn to befriend it. And when the moment for transformation arrives, this bottle allows you to emerge with greater clarity, greater strength, greater wisdom and a profound sense of connection to your spirit and the Allness.

Bottle 13 Story: Melissie

A boy of about six or seven chose this bottle, and my feeling was that it was about a near death experience that had never been acknowledged. I very tentatively asked his mother if anything had happened to him and she told me about a time when he just collapsed. She rushed him to the doctor, who was setting a broken arm at the time and could not leave it even though this child looked near death. The nurse took the mother into one of the rooms and laid the boy down on the bed. He came to, sat up and said chirpily: "I'm all better now, thank you!"

By this time the doctor had come running in, but when he looked at the boy he could find nothing wrong. So the little boy got up and played with a toy and although they waited in case he took a turn for the worse, eventually his mother took him home. On the way she asked him what that had been about, and he said with a sweet smile: "Oh, I asked the angels if I could go with them, but they said no, I had to stay with you," and carried on playing with his toy. He loved bottle 13 and was, of course, a Scorpio.

Bottle 14: Movement (Pale Turquoise/Pale Turquoise)

The number 14 is ruled by Mercury, which relates to communication and movement. This bottle is about magnetic communication with the public: the media, publishing, television and the internet. The unexpected can happen at any moment. Travel is in the air; good fortune is yours. Soon you will find the sanctuary your spirit calls for.

The previous two bottles have revealed the potential for heaven on earth and the transformation required in order to claim it. And it is turquoise – trust, faith and flow – that brings the impetus to make it happen.

Bottle 14 softens and opens the heart chakra and lungs, allowing you to relax and breathe a little more deeply. At the same time it holds a sense of anticipation that something exciting is on the way. This bottle is about potential, possibility and opportunity. Its energy is fresh, fluid and new, and it has the impulsion and flow to get things moving. Its name – Movement – says it all. It indicates that things are falling into place and that the changes you are making are positive. Now is the time to trust the flow and let yourself be shown your next steps. Your spirit has always brought you to exactly where you need to be for your highest good, and there is no reason for that to change.

Turquoise, more than any other colour, guides you into the realms of faith and trust. It is about stepping into a more expansive, more creative aspect of who you have believed yourself to be and recognising that you have always been guided, always held, always moved on to the next step of the journey – even if sometimes you have resisted and fought, kicking and screaming. Bottle 14 asks what would happen if you stopped fighting, opened the door to trust and embraced the possibility that everything is exactly as it needs to be. This bottle asks you to own and acknowledge that your Divine self is in charge, guiding the boat, steering your course. It is your inner guidance that will always take you forward on your evolutionary journey – and keep you safe as you travel.

Evolution, movement, change: these are fundamentally who you are. You did not come to this earth to be stagnant, to get stuck, to fall down a hole and stay there. You came to grow, to learn, to experience, to teach, to share. When you are drawn to bottle 14 it says now is your time for all of this – and more. Be open to the new, to the unexpected, to change. Be willing to make connections, for they may just lead you in new and exciting directions.

Bottle 14 is like a hub of communication, overflowing with potential. It opens the door to your inner communicator and asks it to step out of hiding. Now is the time to express who you are, take action on your creative ideas, engage with the world from your heart and share with it what you know. Be willing to discover your inner writer and artist, open to your creative channels and take yourself out into the world with the information and creative expression that is uniquely yours. It is time to get your work noticed – and it might just be bigger than you realise. If that feels scary, bottle 14 reminds you how joyful and expansive you feel when you listen to the calling of your heart and follow the lighted pathway of your inner knowing. It encourages you to stay in the flow so that you know exactly where to go, who to connect with and what to do next.

This bottle relates to the new era, the Aquarian age, the technological revolution taking place on the planet. It is a great support if you struggle with new technology, helping you feel safe with it so that you might use its power to get your message out into the world. Bottle 14 is often chosen by star children, Indigos, kids who are born with an in-built 'microchip'. If you are one of these, this bottle will make you feel at home: here at last on the planet is your vibration, your frequency.

This bottle is a favourite of teenagers, especially those with skin problems, who often harbour a belief that that their face to the world is somehow not acceptable. Many teenagers do not feel seen for who they are, and bottle 14 is like a grounding cord or anchor, making them feel safe to be here and to share who they really are. It also connects to the incredible potential everyone holds at 14.

Turquoise spans the whole of the emotional spectrum, every emotional response, from the vibrant expression of pure heart-based love to the absolute shut-down of feelings. If you are a star child who came in with your heart wide open you may have had to swiftly close down your feelings because of the density of vibration on this planet. You might now find that you experience extreme sensitivity in a world that generally does not value or acknowledge it. You may also tend to feel absolutely everything that others are feeling, and as this quickly becomes simply too painful and overwhelming, the barriers go up and the feelings shut down.

Turquoise's complementary colour is coral, and coral is hugely sensitive. Pollution levels in the ocean are measured by the coral found there – and when it gets too high, the coral dies. If your feelings are completely overwhelmed, your coral sensitivity may also 'die', to the point that you lose the ability to feel anything much at all. When using turquoise, your soft coral inner self is activated so that feelings can be re-awakened. Bottle 14 is a wonderful support, creating a safe space for you to feel again. It can literally open the flood-gates, letting the tears come after years or even decades of damning them up.

It is not always just the density of vibration on the planet that causes feelings to shut off. For some it is a lingering sense of what happened in Atlantis. Whatever your beliefs or thoughts about what Atlantis was – a place, a dimension, a planet, a myth – what really matters is whatever is left over from it that affects you in this lifetime. Many people have (often unconscious) memories of Atlantis: a sense of something going 'wrong', of guilt, of times and situations where you 'messed up'. This is resonant of 'the fall' and the guilt that has lived inside the psyche of every human being since time began. This bottle brings fresh new light into your cellular memories, helping you release the guilt. It assists you to see beyond the apparent story to the truth and perfection of what happened – and trust that all was exactly as it needed to be, no matter how it appeared on the surface.

There is a wonderful youthfulness about this bottle, an energy and enthusiasm that restores you to the light and truth of who you know yourself to be. It is like a sparkling river of turquoise water, washing you clean, bringing a fresh new day, inviting you to leave the past behind. If you have allowed yourself to stagnate or have been unable to move forward out of fear, the job of this bottle is to put you back in the flow again. It acts as an 'unblocker', softening tired old defences and opening you to trust so that you can take the path that is beckoning to you. With your heart awakened and your creative energy activated, all you have to do now is follow the divinely orchestrated flow so that you are taken to the perfect place at the perfect time. Let the universe carry you on its tides, and enjoy the ripples of movement you create for yourself and others.

Bottle 14 Story: Lesley McDonald, UK, www.lesleytara.com

Feeling stuck and very much in my overthinking head, I decided to soak in a turquoise bath. The tension began to drain from my body, slowly at first, until I entered a state of deep relaxation. Suddenly I heard, or perhaps sensed, the word 'genie'. For a moment I didn't quite know where it came from because I actually felt like I heard it out loud, but immediately my eyes were drawn to the empty bottle, and I clearly 'felt' that by releasing the turquoise oils into the water I had set the genie free. In the story Aladdin symbolically sets the genie free, thereby freeing his own inner genie (creative spirit). The bath became energised, and in my mind's eye I saw a little being of liquid turquoise emerging from what looked (and felt) like a thick pool of dark turquoise liquid. At first it was an effort for him to separate himself from the liquid and he struggled to fully stand up and climb out, but he did. He then opened his arms and began to sing clearly, pitch perfect. The vibration rocked through me and I came to, realising I had been far away, riding on the turquoise ray.

Two days later: a tearful day with the return of multiple old wounds. Who was I kidding that I could open the flow using Movement without bringing the blocked 'stuff' into conscious awareness? The powerful turquoise ray, unblocker of blocks and melter of hearts, was doing what it does, and I could clearly feel how I had been so 'in my head' that I had lost the joy of the journey. Today I am leaning into the anxiety as it arises. It is no longer blocked. I am feeling everything. This bottle is absolutely the unblocker of blocks.

Bottle 14 Story: Jackie Tweedie, UK, www.jackietweedie.com

Anyone choosing this bottle is in for an exciting time! The 'double turquoise' feels a huge invitation to trust and let yourself be carried wherever the flow of life wants to take you. I met a student once who was about to go to university. He chose this bottle and as a result of its guidance he decided to defer his studies in order to travel. He swapped lectures for adventures and found opportunities everywhere. Kind strangers offered him free tickets to events he couldn't afford to see, synchronicity seemed to engineer meetings with the right people at the right time to open up yet more experiences, and it all felt effortless. This bottle is also a powerful invitation to follow the advice of my teacher and great friend Moira Bush whose motto is "say yes and turn up" – you just never know where it might lead you.

Bottle 15: Magician (Olive/Olive)

This bottle is about magic based on feminine power and hope for the future. Olive is made up of yellow and green, where green is the heart and yellow is the solar plexus, and this bottle combines them as love and power. The magician is the bringer of heaven to earth because he has owned his power to co-create. This is the pot of gold at the end of the rainbow. The number 15 reduces to 6 and relates to the planet Venus, which is about love and magic. All you have to remember is to include others in your magic and make sure you create for the good of the greater whole.

The previous bottle was about releasing yourself from stagnation and old bonds and finding the impetus to take yourself out into the world. Bottle 15 follows on perfectly as you flow now into a bright fresh new day. This is the energy of hope and sunshine as you emerge from the deeper waters of your transformative process. This is the green of spring: buds pushing through, new leaves, new life, new beginnings. When you choose this bottle you are opening to a new flow in your life, a new phase. Your path and your space are becoming clearer as you make way for magic and potential to enter your reality.

Olive is power that has been taken and softened and loved – and brought fully into the light of the feminine. It is where solar plexus conjoins with heart; it is the power of love to transform. If you are choosing this colour it is time to tap into the inner light of the feminine and experience power in a new way. Old forms of power based on control and personal gain at any cost begin to dissolve as you move into a more heart-based way of being. Bottle 15 says that the only power with any relevance now is love – and love is the only path to true, aligned, authentic power. This may be a new concept to take on board, but once your cells truly get the message you will never look back.

The colour olive relates to rejuvenation and detoxification. It is associated with the liver meridian and can assist in releasing both physical and emotional toxins stored in the body. As you clear out false beliefs around power and love, as you open to a new chapter in your life, you may find you have a desire to cleanse your body, your home, your space. Olive supports you by making way for the fresh and the light to replace what was heavy and dark. This might include feelings of envy, jealousy or 'not enough', especially in relation to your space. If you have been feeling constricted, craving more space or longing for greater freedom in any area of your life, olive opens everything up. It brings an inner sense of expansion so that you can feel at peace in your existing space or attract a new space that better suits who you are now becoming.

Bottle 15 smooths everything from your skin to your passage through the world and puts you back together when you feel out of sorts. It contains a similar nurturing energy to bottle 6, Venus (1 + 5 = 6), softening and opening your heart, gently returning you to balance after a shock or difficult time. This bottle blends the yellow of the solar plexus with the green of the heart to soothe and restore harmony to both these centres – and when your heart and solar plexus are in alignment, you are capable of anything.

This bottle reminds you that you are magical. It lifts you out of closed, limited, fearful patterns and shows you a bright, strong and empowered way to move through your life. It supports you as you release any lingering fears about how magical you might be – fears perhaps instilled in previous lifetimes, where to be magical was to be different and therefore 'wrong', unacceptable, even feared. Bottle 15 is about claiming your magic and your power and allowing yourself to shine. It says now you can be the magician, without fear that someone will see how magical you are and sell you down the river for it. If you are drawn to this bottle you may have had envy directed at you at some time or another and felt the disempowering effects of others' low self-esteem projected upon you. With the flick of a wand, your inner magician releases you from such stories and instils in you the knowledge of your own true power, free from the beliefs or limitations of anyone else.

This bottle is about knowing that your very essence is creative. It reminds you that you are the creator of your reality in every moment, whether you are conscious of it or not. It puts you in touch with the magical truth of yourself so that you can consciously create through love; and with love as the power in your life you have the ability to generate a new and very different reality. The Magician bottle asks what you truly desire to create – and then supports you in finding your power so that you can actually get on and do it.

When you access your inner magician you really can have the pot of gold at the end of the rainbow – or whatever else you desire. And when your magic is in alignment with the universe, you automatically weave that magic through your own life and those of others, creating a joyful, abundant, fabulous reality for you and everyone around you.

Bottle 15 Story: Korani

A friend had been going through a challenging time, and when I visited her I saw that her energy field was clearly out of kilter, and she just didn't seem her usual bright, bubbly self. She had become stuck in a downward spiral of negativity and couldn't pull herself out. She began to use this bottle, and when I saw her again a few days later her energy was shiny and strong and bright and she had her bounce back. This bottle pulled all the scattered parts of her being back together and took her into a positive space so that she could feel joyful and creative again.

Bottle 15 Story: Gilly Ball, South Africa, www.colourmirrors.com/jasper-oils

I bathed in this bottle when I had just moved house and was trying to buy a car. Within a day after the bath, after weeks of looking for something affordable and nice, a salesman came back with the exact car I had on my dream-board and in line with what I felt I could afford. It was a very dreamy Mercedes in the exact colour and make that I wanted but hadn't even tried to find as it I had deemed it out of my league financially.

Bottle 16: The Tower (Olive/Lilac)

The image of the Tarot card is of a tower struck by lightning and a body falling, which is the exact image we saw on September 11, 2001. We all seem to be on the path of the tower in some way or another. In your own situation it relates to the explosion of the structures you hold on to because you believe them to be your comfort zones, even though they are no longer serving you. The colours, olive and lilac, are a clear indication of this vibration. Olive is made up of green and yellow, and in this bottle the colours show that your spirit (lilac) is asking you to move for your greater good so that you might begin to function with love (green) rather than from fear (yellow). This bottle says you are now being taken seriously as a spiritual being having a human experience and you can trust that your spirit will never let you down. Wherever change takes you, it will always be perfect.

The soft olive green of hope and feminine power we saw in bottle 15 (The Magician) sits now in the upper fraction of bottle 16, bringing it firmly into your conscious mind. It rests upon the lilac of your spirit, your connection to the Divine, which sits in the base of the bottle and the depths of your being. On the face of it, this bottle has all the gentle beauty of a garden in springtime – but if The Tower is calling you, its message is potent and not to be ignored.

This is a bottle many people are drawn to and then invariably shrink from when told of its name and the associated Tarot card, with its connotations of falling, explosions and structures breaking down. There is almost universal fear around having a 'Tower' experience. Yet this bottle comes up again and again, and there is often a powerful pull towards it, especially for people following a conscious spiritual path.

Olive can have connotations of war and battles over land or territory. It speaks of lack of boundaries, lack of respect for others' boundaries, lack of direction, lack of space. But it can be precisely these feelings of conflict and lack that push you into jumping off the tower, getting out of situations that are no longer suiting or serving you. By choosing the Tower bottle you are acknowledging that something in your life needs to change. When this bottle calls, you are no longer able to pretend that things can remain as they are. You are going to have to jump or be pushed – and choosing this bottle often means the universe will move you if you cannot or will not move on your own.

The number 16 reduces to 7 (1 + 6 = 7), and bottle 7 (Neptune) is all about trusting the process and going with the flow – which is exactly what you need to remember when you are in the throes of a Tower experience. Any major event, situation or change in your life can be an opportunity to grow, heal, evolve and allow more light into your being and your life, yet fear may stop you from embracing the changes. You may go into resistance, trying desperately to keep everything as it was. You may truly wish to change, yet find your shadow whispering in your ear that you do not deserve anything more or that you are better off with the devil you know. This bottle asks you to follow the guidance of your heart and your spirit because if you do not, things could get difficult. It warns that if you insist on staying stuck or try to manipulate your way forward, the outcome could be very challenging.

Central to bottle 16 is the theme of freeing yourself from old beliefs and the structures you have put in place to stop you from moving forward. The Tower calls you to look at the breaking down of whatever you have been clinging to, the fears that have been so tightly interwoven with your notions of power and the explosion of everything you have believed power to be. This bottle gives you the opportunity to look within to find your power, your I AMness, your divinity, rather than seeking it outside yourself in the existing structures of society and religion. It helps you realise that the explosions and implosions in your life only ever happen for the highest good.

Sometimes the Tower comes along not when you feel stuck or unhappy with your present circumstances but when you are cruising comfortably along in your life. You are probably aware that there is more you could be experiencing or allowing, more learning and growing you could be doing, but it hardly seems worth the effort – after all, everything is 'fine' as it is. When you get to a certain place of familiarity and comfort in your life it can be tempting to believe that there is no need to move any further. Even if it is not where your soul wishes to be, your ego may persuade you that it is all perfectly OK and that there is nothing to be gained by stretching yourself.

Imagine you have been given 100 stairs to ascend in this lifetime and when you get to stair 60 you decide just to stay put. You figure that as you have already come a very long way, there is really no need for you to go any further. But then the universe, as a loving parent, shows you the truth: for your highest good you must take the next step. And the next. And the next.

The Tower shows you that there is so much more awaiting you if you will let yourself be taken to the next level, even – or especially – if you are afraid. Its great gift is that it helps you along the way and makes you feel safe so that you can take those steps without being overwhelmed by fear. It supports you as you take courage and move away from your comfort zones. It shows you that the love of your own spirit and indeed the love of the Divine is right there alongside you – and always has been. It allows you to move forward from a place of authenticity and love-based, spirit-based power.

Bottle 16 is one that often changes colour, the lilac in its bottom fraction becoming pale blue or turquoise. When this happens it is a signal from your spirit that change is on the way and that all will be well. Your job is to stay in the trust and faith that this colour change reflects and allow the flow to carry you. What is interesting is that people who use the Tower bottle often find it a very gentle support. As well as the hope and potential of a new space, it also suggests you will find rest and peace once you have taken the step. It is only fear and resistance that make it seem so difficult. The lilac in the bottom of this bottle is rather like the Lilac Angel, your guiding angel, holding, loving and supporting you. You may be afraid to jump because you feel as if you might die if you do, but the message here really is that you cannot go wrong if you just follow your spirit – because it is waiting at the bottom to catch you.

When you look beyond the obvious challenges of this bottle you will see that it has a truly positive message. It signifies huge possibilities ahead, and not only does it provide you with a soft landing when you take heart, take courage and leap, it also shows you where to place your feet when you land. It puts you firmly in the hands of your spirit, which promises to be with you every step of the way. This bottle guides you towards a blank canvas of pure potential and shows you that with the support of your spirit, you can manifest and create an extraordinary reality.

Bottle 16 Story: Melissie

One of the things that is fun to do with the bottles is to look at which bottle relates to the numbers of each year. The one that has had the most impact, certainly for me, was looking at bottle 16 for 2016. In the Tarot, 16 is 'The Tower', and the meaning of that card and the bottle is that it is a time of explosive change. The Tower and/or bottle 16 appear when we need a little shove to get us moving. If we are prepared to move and it is all easy, bottle 16 is a lovely bottle to work with to make the transitions smoothly. If we are resisting the changes, however, it is often a bit more difficult.

If we look at the colours in 16 – olive over lilac – we have yellow and blue to make the olive, over red and blue to make the lilac. If we subtract the blue from both fractions we end up with yellow over red, and this colour combination says: "I have to be in control". The blue that is masked by these colours is the peaceful flow that happens when we are in accordance with our soul's plan or will, so the energy of this bottle is all about the stress created when we dig our heels in and try to control the outcome instead of checking with our Divine soul's will or plan.

This bottle relaxes the muscle that locks in our jaw when we stick our chins out and say: "My will be done! I am not budging or bending to any other plan." So for a lot of people, 2016 was the year when they had all those patterns of control brought out to be rechecked. For many it was not an easy year, but it certainly brought about change and opened the way for things to move ahead more smoothly.

Bottle 17: The Wish (Coral/Royal Blue)

This bottle relates to the star card in the Tarot, which has always had a connotation of wishes granted. Choosing these colours indicates that you have come to a place of grace, and at this point you can wish with the full knowledge that your wishes will be fulfilled. This is a time for positive payback – all the good you have done is about to be returned tenfold. This bottle signifies huge new possibilities. It may indicate a different way of viewing yourself, a new phase in your life or a change in status such as marriage or a new career.

By the time you have launched yourself – or been pushed – off the Tower in bottle 16, you are ready for something new. And bottle 17 delivers. Its coral top fraction promises joy, warmth, love and wisdom and a powerful new level of connection with the Divine. The inky royal blue base signifies the depth of your intuitive knowing and creates the perfect foundation for the mystical and the sacred, helping bring your unconscious desires into conscious awareness.

When you choose bottle 17 it indicates that things are now in place and you can truly wish them into being, in the sense that 'wishing' is not fairy-tale, pie-in-the-sky dreaming but is about aligning with your soul's deepest and highest truths and allowing them to be made manifest. This is where you know that you are a conscious creator with every thought, wish and action. When you reach this level of consciousness you are ready to take full responsibility for the creation of your own reality on a moment-by-moment basis. This bottle says that every thought is a wish – so what do you truly desire, and are you willing to wish for it with the full realisation of your power to manifest it in your life? If you can do that with the force of love behind your wishes and intentions, you have the capacity to bring all you could wish for to fruition.

This bottle is about letting go of previous definitions of yourself, who you have believed yourself to be. It signifies new beginnings, change, new directions, new opportunities, and in particular, new ways of viewing yourself. Many parents will relate to the experience of having their children leave home and finding themselves empty-nesting. Bottle 17 can be particularly significant at this time, helping you see who you are outside of your parent role. It is about getting face to face with yourself after another layer has been unmasked. It offers a wonderful opportunity to throw out old labels, cast off limiting beliefs about who you think you might be and open to the vast possibilities of who you really are when you stop defining yourself in any particular way.

This bottle delights and challenges in equal measure. Most people love it or hate it, but either way, it tends to bring up a strong response. If you are resisting this bottle or repelled by it, you may have a childhood story lurking in the depths of your subconscious that wishes do not come true – at least for you. With coral in the top fraction of this bottle, issues of self-worth come to the fore. The colour combination of coral with deep royal blue signals that you may have had a fairly shocking experience in a previous lifetime that has prevented you from believing in any kind of 'happy ending'. This bottle helps draw out those wounds and blocks. With the light of your soul, it supports you in finding resolution and healing so that you too can share in the magic and promise of these colours.

If you are attracted to bottle 17 you may be on the point of a big shift or change in your life. A new house, job or marriage can be the best thing in the world, and you might be genuinely excited and happy about your new situation, but your body registers change as potential death. Even if it is positive change, fears may still arise. When you choose this bottle it asks you to let into your life all the new and wonderful things that are waiting for you. Its message is that any changes you go through are always, from your soul's perspective, designed to move you to a better place. If you bring the light of conscious awareness to these changes and view them as your soul's wishes being fulfilled, you might find the transition happening with surprising ease and grace.

If we look at 17 as 1 + 7 = 8, this bottle relates to bottle 8 (Saturn), whose message is to build whatever you are choosing to create upon deep, strong foundations. After all, if you are going to bring your wishes to life it makes sense to give them a solid base from which to grow. Additionally, if we split the number 17 into 1 and 7 and look at the colours and messages of bottles 1 and 7, there is potential for joy and laughter here (The Sun – yellow) as well as faith and trust (Neptune – turquoise). It is all about what you put out into the thought-field, the dream-field, the wish-field. You can truly have whatever your soul is fully aligned with – indeed you cannot *not* have it! In the past you may have tended to align unconsciously with hidden and often limiting beliefs. This bottle draws out what has prevented you from making your wishes come true and helps make your soul desires a reality.

Bottle 17 Story: Melissie

Bottle 17 has always been very close to my heart, as it was the first bottle I ever made. When I had, with deep heart-break, changed from the system that I had worked with before, I needed these colours so desperately that I tried to make the colours more or less out of baby oil and makeup. I had to, HAD to have them! When I finally had the wherewithal to make the bottles, this new creation sat to the side as a kind of overlighting energy for the system, as I was really not sure where it would fit.

After I started making the bottles and had got to about 25 bottles on my way to 33 (I deeply 'knew' that there had to be 33 bottles in the set at that point), someone gave me a set of Linda Goodman's Star Cards, and the colours of her cards were so spookily similar to my bottles that I could match them one by one. And there in the cards were the exact colours of bottle 17 in the card known as the 'wish card'. In reality that is a bit of a misnomer; it always turns out that it is the wish your soul has for your highest good rather than your wish for new boots...

In my case it was the complete and utter turn-around of my life. I have three children, and for many years I had done babies and school lifts and the all-absorbing stuff one does as a mother. I was such an over-parenter that something huge had to happen to make me stop. At that point my daughter had left home but lived close by. My two boys, who had been the total focus of my days, left to go and live with their father in England, and the entire point to my existence disappeared. I had wrapped my whole personality around being 'Uber Mum' and now I had none of that. My nest was empty.

It was the most alarming wake-up call. We are not our labels. We are not Mrs Smith or Mum or Dr. So-and-So. We are the magnificent soul that animates all those titles, and if we pretend otherwise, it needs to be taken away – and that is the entire point of bottle 17. It puts us back in touch with the wish our soul had for us before we arrived on the planet. We all came in on a contract to keep evolving and to leave the planet and the souls we encounter brighter than when we got here. That is why we exist, and bottle 17 highlights and then helps us remove anything which stops that evolution.

So when you are standing at the door of huge transformation and you choose this bottle, remember that the outcome of this story of change and drama in my life was the creation of Colour Mirrors, which is now a global healing system bringing joy to very many people. Trust that there is a magical, shiny future if you follow the path of your soul's wish for you.

Bottle 17 Story: Jackie Tweedie, UK, www.jackietweedie.com

This bottle never really caught my attention until three things happened with a synchronicity that ensured that I noticed it!

1) I joined a coaching course, and after an intention setting exercise it was suggested that maybe I had forgotten how to 'wish' for things beyond what I thought was possible. It rang true, and I could see how it was limiting both my life and the growth of my business, so I sought out this bottle and felt into its message. I discovered that a part of me had indeed stopped believing in dreams and possibilities, and instead I had developed a "don't wish because that way you won't be disappointed" mentality.

Using this bottle to clear that pattern allowed me to give myself permission to 'wish' again, without any attachment to the outcome or desire to control the result. It made me feel joyful and freely optimistic again.

2) When choosing colours for my new website, I asked my mentor and great friend Moira Bush for help with discovering the numerological significance of my name (which is also my business title). I smiled when she told me that the total score added up to 17 – the Wish bottle.

3) For my birthday, my sister gave me a scarf which I loved straight away and wanted to wear all the time. It was only later that I realised it was made up of the colours of The Wish bottle (coral and royal blue). She said: "It just told me I had to buy it for you."

I love how messages of wisdom and direction are to be found in all aspects of our lives (even when we're not looking for them). The signs we need to see are everywhere, and colour has a very special way of first getting our attention and then showing us what we need to learn or understand about a situation.

Bottle 18: Spiritual/Material Conflict (Red/Rose Pink)

This is a difficult vibration because it denotes confusion and a struggle. You may feel a sense of betrayal when this number comes up. Notice what blocks you from bringing heaven to earth and where you still betray yourself by not believing that you are Divine. These colours are about bringing heaven to earth, the earth being the red, the lowest vibration and what you consider 'real': your health, money and relationships. This is the last bit of illusion to overcome so that you might bring the rose pink of love into everything in your life and see it all as part of your spiritual journey and the way back to the Allness. This bottle indicates a lifetime as a nun or monk.

In bottle 17 (The Wish) you were offered the opportunity to have whatever you wished for, and in accordance with universal law, when you ask, you receive. Bottle 17 helps you ask for what you truly want and align yourself with it. At this point, however, sneaking fears, old patterns and limiting beliefs might arise: "What if I don't deserve it? What if it is 'wrong' to be this happy or abundant? What if I am going to have to pay the price for getting what I want? How much of what I am asking for am I actually willing to receive?" This is where bottle 18 comes in. This is where you get to see where, how and why you are stopping yourself from having it all.

As your journey unfolds you will discover that you are part of the oneness of life, that every aspect of the universe is interconnected and interwoven. If bottle 18 is calling, it asks you to look at where you are unable to acknowledge this as truth, where you are unable to accept that the Divine is in everything and everyone, including you. Red is the lowest vibration, everything you think is furthest removed from spirit, everything that is somehow removed from God: your overdraft, your sore knee, a fight with your partner. This bottle taps into all your beliefs about the separation of spirit from matter. It asks you to look at where and how spirit and body interconnect, where and how spirit and money fit together, how spirit and unity can be present in all the tangible and 'real' experiences that make up daily life here on earth. It asks you to consider that the everyday, practical, mundane elements of life could actually be 'spiritual' too.

Bottle 18 crops up fairly frequently. How many people do you know who have the whole spiritual/material connection fully present and functioning perfectly? Probably not so many. It is a key issue for most people on the planet and certainly for those on a conscious spiritual path. If the spiritual/material divide is a core challenge for you, it will come up again and again in myriad forms until you resolve the underlying conflict.

This bottle tends to call when you are in the throes of anger, martyrdom, deep frustration, buried rage, terrible self-loathing. You may be knee-deep in judgement, even questioning the point of life. Bottle 18 shows you that the answer lies in the rose pink of pure love that sits in its base. Its message is that only the light of love can transform your difficulties, your blocks, your inner and outer conflicts. This bottle brings love into everything that is 'real': your body, your health, your finances, your anger, your preconceived limitations. If you are stubbornly clinging to misfortune and misery, it takes you by the hand and invites you instead to dance into the rich, luscious abundance promised by these vibrant red and pink hues.

This bottle puts you in touch with your body and the physicality of human existence. It asks you to look at where you have not allowed yourself to have the fun and pleasure of being physical. It touches in to beliefs about poverty, celibacy or any other means you use to avoid 'earthly' life in the misguided belief that this somehow makes you more 'spiritual' or deserving. Bottle 18 is often chosen by people who are putting all their energy into their spiritual growth and have forgotten about the joys of being physical.

This bottle reflects where you run the nun or monk archetype in your life, where you cut yourself off from all the 'red' aspects of being human – sex, chocolates, money, abundance and the sheer enjoyment of being physical. It asks you to look at where you block things, where your ceiling is, what stops you from having everything you truly desire. The answers to these questions reveal your hidden limiting beliefs about deserving, about self-worth – and this bottle helps blow the lid right off them. As part of the Divine, as a beloved child of the universe, you were never meant to be poor or deprived in any way. This is simply an illusion, albeit one upon which much of human history has been built.

As befits a bottle with the title Spiritual/Material Conflict, this bottle also taps into the polar opposite of the nun archetype: the prostitute. It asks where you are prostituting yourself in your life, where you are selling yourself short or not trusting life so that you have to go out and 'prostitute' yourself in order to survive.

There are overtones in bottle 18 of possible sex addiction or at least muddy waters around sexual issues. It is also a particularly female bottle. It speaks to women of issues with body image, what you do with your body, how you share it, how you treat it. Once again it is rose pink that brings the love back into each and every aspect of your life, whether you have been doing nun or prostitute. On a side note, we have noticed that many who bathe in this bottle report back with stories of erotic dreams!

Bottle 18 calls you to take a look at your beliefs around money. For many who are drawn to it, there is a fairly powerful inner conflict between being spiritual and being financially abundant. If you have an unresolved past life experience as a nun or monk, you may find that you have a strong, irrational and possibly puzzling belief in this lifetime that you are unable to be truly spiritual unless you are materially poor. You may find that every time you start to become financially solvent, you lose what you have gained. Bottle 18 helps release those stories from your cellular memory so that you no longer have to see money as outside of the Divine. As you let go of old beliefs you may enter into a new and much more balanced relationship with money, finding respect for it and enjoyment of it.

Spiritual/material conflict can take many forms. Yours may show up when you are called to make your spiritual beliefs known to the outside world. Perhaps you have been harbouring an inner yogi or Reiki healer (or colour therapist!) but have been too afraid to let your friends and family know. Maybe you have become fascinated by all things spiritual and have started to understand that everything in the world is energy but find yourself running from conversations or situations in which you would be called upon to share this side of yourself, lest you be mocked – or worse. Perhaps you feel as if you are the only person in your entire workplace or group of friends who has any understanding of or interest in the more esoteric side of life. Maybe you feel as if you have no one to talk to about what you are discovering as you open to the spiritual realms.

Bottle 18 brings love into your beliefs, helping you realise that there is nothing to fear. It encourages you to open even more to your spirit and embrace your awakening to higher consciousness, and in so doing, gain the strength, courage and confidence to be who you truly are. This in turn leads you to more people with whom you can feel safe to express yourself and more situations in which you can open to the wonders your spirit has to share with you.

When you realise that everything is part of the vast, all-encompassing Divine, things begin to change quite significantly. You start to let go of your judgements on money, on sex, on bodies, on what it is to be physical – and on the earth herself. Then you get to feel the joy of all these things: the rich, wild, extraordinary ride of being human. Choosing this bottle says that you are ready to recognise and release the areas of your life where you have been hooked into spiritual/material separation and open instead to the full blossoming abundance and bliss of a spiritual life lived in a physical body.

Bottle 18 is a 9 (1 + 8 = 9) and as such, it signals that something in your life is now complete. When you truly know that there is no separation, when you have no judgement on any of part of life – including money, including other people, including your body – when you truly know that you are not guilty or sinful or separate from the Divine, that the universe is perfect and so too are you, therein lies the ending of the spiritual/material conflict and the invitation to a heavenly life right here on earth.

Bottle 18 Story: Lesley McDonald, UK, www.lesleytara.com

I was at a fair with the Colour Mirrors bottles and people were flocking around the stand, picking them up and asking questions. I was worked off my feet and by the end of the day, although I had had a wonderful time and had spoken to dozens of people, I had not charged for the consultations and was definitely running at a loss. The last 'client' of the day picked out a few bottles, and as I talked about them I remember a distinct feeling of being stuck and unable to make sense of her choices. This was quite odd because usually as soon as I connect with the colour and the client I receive a flow of impressions and intuitive connections. I remember she was an accountant and loved her job but was also interested in the alternative world. I managed to relay some useful colour information but was left with a feeling that I was missing something. It was the end of the day, however, so I put the 'difficult' reading down to exhaustion and packed up.

That evening, drained and unable to move past my perceived failure, I sat in front of my bottles and asked for assistance. My eye fell quickly on bottle 18 and I noticed that it was filled with bubbles as though it was 'cooking'. I picked it up, held it in my hands and instinctively knew it had a message I needed to hear. That night I bathed in the bottle and began to 'hear' the wisdom it held for me. I realised with a sense of astonishment that it was the same bottle as the accountant lady had chosen when I had gone blank. I knew at once that the reason for this was that it was my blind spot, and by choosing that bottle she had acted as my mirror (although at that point I was still unable to see my own reflection). She was financially successful and opening up to the alternative world. I, on the other hand, had spent my whole day offering my knowledge free of charge and feeling awkward and conflicted about asking for payment for it. I had been in such spiritual/material conflict I had literally been unable to see the bottle she had chosen right in front of my eyes.

I now think of this lady as my 'accountant angel' and am grateful for the wake-up call. Since my bath in bottle 18, old issues of guilt and shame connected to my value have rapidly been leaving my life and I am happy to report that charging for my services is no longer an issue.

Bottle 18 Story: Kathryn Dzsudzsak, Canada, www.thebluehairmentor.com

It all began during my Colour Mirrors training with Moira. I had been going through a difficult time with my grandchildren's stepmother and had received an extremely vile email from her, which I could not get out of my head. I woke one morning with my phone on the bedside table. It was shut off, and when I turned it on to check the time the first thing that popped up was 'that' vile email. I was confused as to why that had happened. It had been sent days before, so there was no reason for it to just pop open – or was there? When I read it, it sent me into a very angry mode and no matter what I did I could not get rid of it. I had thoughts running through my mind that I never, ever had before.

As the day's training began I told one of the other participants about it, and the anger coming from me was crazy! Moira overheard me speaking and told me to pick a bottle, and the one I chose was bottle 18. She had me hold the bottle and asked me a series of questions about what and how I was feeling. I vented on exactly how I felt about this stepmother, then Moira had me take one full giant step to the left and imagine I was stepping into the stepmother's body. Once I had done that, Moira asked me a series of questions such as: "What do you feel? Is this hers? Did she bring it on herself? Is it something that was learned?" After going through that exercise I realised that I had not looked at the entire picture. This woman was only doing what she was taught/learned/saw. Once we had completed that exercise Moira said to me: "You WILL bathe in this bottle today!"

Now the weird stuff begins. I began filling the bathtub with nice warm, almost hot water and proceeded to pour bottle 18 into the bath. I noticed the water itself was a beautiful, very light pink, and there were big beautiful islands of red oil floating on top. I swooshed the oil around to disperse it more evenly and stepped into the tub. It was at that moment that the oil literally flung itself to the sides of the bathtub. No matter what I did, I could not scrape it off the sides and put it onto my body. No matter how often I scraped it off the sides and smeared it onto my arms or legs or chest or belly the oil would immediately slide off, and it seemed that sometimes it almost jumped right off my skin and stuck itself back onto the tub.

As I was sitting in this beautiful, deep tub continually trying to put this red oil onto my body, I was becoming angrier, more agitated and just generally pissed off at everything and everyone! I was continually asking: "Why are you doing this? Why won't you come onto my body? Why are you sticking to the side of the tub?!"

This went on for quite some time and then I became so angry, so agitated, so frustrated, that I was saying words that I would never usually say and really letting it all out. All the while I kept saying: "This is not me. These are not my words and these feelings do not belong to me. I do not resonate with this at all because it is not me!!!" I released all of that crap and asked for it never to come back! The moment I had this realisation and this forgiveness, the oil literally released off the side of the tub and I could see it beginning to crawl up my legs, arms and belly. Sound a little bit like a sci-fi movie? Absolutely. But it's real and it happened.

When I told Moira about my experience she asked me what I thought it meant. I realised I was resisting letting go of something I had absolutely no control over. I also realised that I was trying to control situations, not just for me but also for my grandchildren. The next morning I grabbed my phone and there it was again – that email! I read the email again, only this time I felt absolutely nothing. To this day, no matter how hard I try to get to that point of anger, I can't do it.

Bottle 18 brought me to that point. It's having the balance between heaven and earth and knowing the difference and understanding it. I hadn't realised that my earth being was vibrating so low that I couldn't even see it or feel it. I was having a difficult time with my daughter's death, and I didn't really realise that I was refusing to allow myself to be in a physical body here on earth because it is too easy for me to stay in the spiritual world. This bottle opened a journey for me, and without it, I might still have been stuck back in that anger and in that phase of control, not realising what was going on.

Bottle 18 Story: Priscilla Elliott, UK, www.priscillaelliott.co.uk

As part of an exploration into bottle 18 I held a Material & Spiritual Unity workshop, which focused on clearing emotions and limiting beliefs around the subject of the material world and the spiritual world. This enabled people to unify those 'two worlds' into one and start to walk it, talk it and really live it. There were 12 of us in total, and at the end of the workshop we all bathed in bottle 18. It was an immense energy because there were also around 50 other people who joined in on the same day around the world, bathing in the same bottle. We could feel the energy flow of the dynamic red vibration but also of the pink, bringing love into the red. It was an amazing energy shift that was felt by everyone, and it was reported that peace was felt where there had previously been conflict. It was a real honour for me to facilitate the workshop with those beautiful souls.

Bottle 19: Buddhic Bliss (Pale Magenta/Gold)

This bottle is about resurrection and new beginnings. It is a most positive colour combination, as the magenta denotes Divine love lit up and shining upon you, and the gold underneath denotes a deep sense of your own power and beauty. You have come through the dark night of the soul and now it is time to own heaven's blessings of joy and love. You are the power in your life, and everyone would agree with you at this point. Enjoy this time of peace and plenty.

The previous bottle asked you to step out of spiritual/material conflict and clear your judgements around the physical aspects of your reality: your job, your body, your finances. As you free yourself from old beliefs and conditioning and open to the fun and joy of being human, you invite in the kind of light, power and wonder that this next bottle, No. 19, reveals. This bottle has absolutely no issues with being of both spirit *and* matter. In its gold and magenta glory, it shows you how to love being human, love being Divine, love the incredible game of life you have set up for yourself. As you release yourself from bonds of unworthiness, you begin to understand that you truly can have whatever you want, be whatever you want. Choosing this bottle indicates that the difficult times are over and there is freedom and joy awaiting you.

There is a kind of shine to everyone at the age of 19. You are no longer experiencing the dubious joys of adolescence, yet you do not have to be entirely grown-up and responsible. At 19 it often feels as if whatever you want can just land at your feet. It is a time of engaging with life, exploring, playing and partying. Bottle 19 says that, whatever your age, it is time to celebrate your life and who you are on every level and in every aspect.

This bottle's warmth and richness gifts you with the bodily knowing that you deserve every bit of goodness in your life simply because you exist. The love the Divine holds for you is not about anything you do or do not do. It is ever-present and overflowing, and when bottle 19 calls to you, it is time to remember this love and welcome it into your life. You have reached a point on your journey where the spiritual and the material can join together to create the Buddhic bliss of this bottle's title.

Bliss and unconditional love are often talked about in a spiritual context, but for many they are simply concepts, nice ideas, something to aspire to but impossible to attain as a human being on earth. When you choose bottle 19 it is a recognition that you are ready to let the Divine flow right the way through your life and receive its gifts of bliss and unconditional love. You have come to a place where you can really live your spirituality, loving and accepting life in all its colours and shades. Your power, love and Divine light can all shine through now because you are ready to claim them. This bottle feels like a pre-cursor to bottle G15 (Satori), one of the Golden Gaia set, a bottle of solid gold over magenta that reflects the blissful, authentic, spiritual love that you came to be, embodied right here on the planet.

As you discover the light of your own unique essence, you not only find bliss within, you radiate it out to others. This bottle is about being deeply connected with your own divinity and sharing your joy and brilliance wherever you go. You do not have to dance around to show how happy you are and you do not need to manipulate others to gain love or anything else. This is light, wisdom and power that emanates from your core. This is truth. This is also where you become aware that your very existence is interwoven with everyone and everything on the planet.

The colours of this bottle echo the robes of the Dalai Lama, a being whose religion is entirely based upon compassion. In Buddhism the saffron inner robe relates to the earth and the earthly existence, and the magenta outer robe, laid over the top of the saffron, represents spirit overcoming the earthly ego self. Bottle 19 reminds you that your small human self is held, protected and over-lit by the greatness of your Divine self. As you immerse yourself in the rich, vibrant colours of this bottle, let it take you into vast, deep compassion for yourself, for the earth, for all.

As you stand in your I AMness and claim your golden authentic power, everything you see reflected back to you becomes magenta Divine love. When your light is this strong, it colours everyone else in its glow. With this quality of Buddhic unconditional acceptance flowing through you, Divine love is unimpeded: Divine love becomes your reality. You no longer need old paradigms of victimhood, guilt, shame or any other illusion. You no longer let ego rule your life. You no longer think that for one person to be up another has to be down or that for one person to be big another has to feel small. This is "I AM, You AM, We AM" – all one, with no separation. This bottle inspires true compassion as you come to know that you are the other, and the other is you. With this knowledge deep and alive in your cells, bottle 19 sets you on the path to the true and lasting peaceful joy of Buddhic bliss.

Bottle 19 Story: Kath Roberts, UK, www.kath-roberts.com

I bathed in this bottle just before I was due to go off on holiday to Bhutan. The colours of magenta and gold, when combined, relate to a Tibetan Buddhist lifetime. During my time away with two close girlfriends I felt the full weight of judgement coming towards me from one of those friends, who was also a close neighbour of ours. She explained to me one evening that I appeared to be neglecting my care-giving responsibilities to my husband who, in her words, was in need of my full-time attention. She said that there were others within our small community who felt that what I was doing was wrong and selfish. It felt like a real 'dark night of the soul' moment.

It is worth pointing out that I live in a small community and my neighbours have witnessed my husband's deterioration in health due to a Parkinson's condition and more recently, cancer. Arrangements had been made for my sister-in-law to come and stay whilst I was travelling, as I had also booked time away to lead a spiritual retreat following my 10-day trip to Bhutan. Within our partnership my husband and I had agreed that as much as possible he wanted me to continue my work, which would mean occasional trips away. He was keen to ensure that happened, no matter what, so I set off with both the excitement of discovering a new country and naturally some general trepidation and concern regarding his overall well-being.

I believe that bathing in bottle 19 brought to the surface the conflict I was feeling on the inside between wanting to travel freely for my work (my second trip within the same month) and a healthy loving concern for his welfare. I hadn't consciously worried about or even entertained the idea of what people might think or say or how they might react, and I was really shocked at my friend's opinion. I should also say that on leaving within the month on my second trip, I was sent an email from another neighbour and friend suggesting I come home, as they were concerned about my husband's health. This seemed odd as I had been checking in with him, and he appeared to be doing OK. The trip in question was a spiritual trip where we were travelling to ancient Atlantean and Lemurian sites and working with a local shaman. As part of our trip we naturally sent healing energy to our families and communities and undertook plant spirit medicine ceremonies.

My husband connected with me numerous times whilst I was away to update me on how he was, on one occasion conveying to me that he had completely lost his voice due to a chest infection. I registered this as a healing crisis in action and held faith in the healing ability of the group and the work itself to affect positive change back at home. This marks quite a shift from conventional medical practice, and I could see how my own personal experience was mirroring the macro picture of the bottle and its complementary colours: magenta and gold have as their complementaries indigo and olive, and these colours together relate to persecution for one's views and being held up as a sacrifice. I began to appreciate how much attitudes still need to shift in our collective worldview with regard to the judgements we hold and the treatment of others who approach life differently.

The whole experience has reinforced my faith and the need to follow my own inner calling in spite of what others might think or say. What became apparent to me when reflecting on this whole incident is that people are inherently good and genuinely concerned for others. This shows up in different behaviours and worldviews. My friend has her own health issues, and my response to what my husband is going through had likely raised her own future fears. The ego always operates from fear so moves to try to control and contain, but when we have faith, anything is possible. I followed up the email in a spirit of connection and conveyed in my own way what I was aware of and how I felt about matters. This communication has served to grow us all as friends and has been the ultimate lesson in forgiveness for all concerned.

Bottle 20: Awakening (Magenta/Copper)

The awakening this bottle refers to is the soul awakening to its true self and understanding the essential truth that there is no separation. As you realise that the Divine is in everything, you begin to understand that where you are in this moment is where heaven is. You never left home in the first place. You are the Divine in a physical form, and with copper connected to magenta, you begin to understand that your physical form is the link between heaven and earth. Your soul and body are as one, and your awakening comes when you see that truth clearly. What seems furthest removed from spirit becomes Divine perfection unfolding when you see it all as Divine, all perfect.

The next bottle takes you beyond the glories and joys of bottle 19 (Buddhic Bliss) into something deeper. With bottle 19 you learned to fly and now, with bottle 20, you learn to land. This is the high magenta frequency of your 'soul star' uniting with deepest earthy copper. On the colour spectrum this bottle takes you higher and further, beyond violet and beneath red, bringing the next layers of your journey together and expanding your awareness, preparing you to awaken.

Bottle 20 carries a very big message. If you are drawn to it you are asked to stop and really consider what it is showing you: everything which appears physical – your body, the planet and everything you regard as 'real' – is simply energy. Everything is simply light that has been condensed into physical form, and this light – whether you call it God, the Divine, love, spirit or whatever else you choose – infuses everything and everyone. Nothing is left outside of its all-encompassing presence.

If you struggle with this message, you may find bottle 20 quite dark and impenetrable. If it is hard to see your body, the planet, other people and/or any of the circumstances in your life as anything remotely resembling Divine light, this bottle might seem murky and obscure. If, on the other hand, you view the whole idea of awakening as fully wondrous, understand that the process will be absolutely supported and know that your body is an intrinsic part of the Divine here on earth, this bottle will reflect that. Its depth, warmth and richness will flow to you as you connect with it, feeding that deeper part of your being that knows the truth of what bottle 20 has to share.

This bottle asks you to invite its message into your cells and feel for the implications of it in your life. For it asks: what if there really is no separation? What if you were to live as though every part of yourself, every bit of your life, every aspect of your being is Divine? Would that mean you could live your life differently, with a whole lot more freedom and joy? Would it allow you to let go of every last bit of judgement and fear? Would it enable you to awaken to the wondrousness of life and live in profound gratitude for the gift of life in a body on the earth? This bottle helps you receive the truth of this message, right down deep inside your cells and your bones. It is hugely supportive of your journey, and as the number 20 reduces to 2 (2 + 0 = 2), it has the same sense of holding and nurturing as the No. 2 bottle, The Moon.

Your soul knows that you are light and you are love. It chose the experience of condensing this light and love down into a package called a body so that you could know yourself as a combination of vastness and limitation, cosmos and matter, heaven and earth. When you truly get this in the core of your being, 'reality' changes completely. Nothing can be wrong, nothing can be outside of the Divine. Perhaps that really is awakening, perhaps that is consciousness and awareness – perhaps that is enlightenment.

This bottle says now is your time to awaken, now is your time to remember – although from a higher perspective, you have always been awake; there is simply a moment in 3D time when your awakening appears to happen. The physical and the spiritual have always been one, but because you came to do 3D 'reality' here on earth, you had to experience them as separate until that apparent moment in time when you could 'get it', when you could 'awaken'.

In the past it was only certain particularly 'special' beings who managed to awaken or attain highest consciousness. Now, of course, the game is on – this collective awakening on the planet is for everyone, as we see if we relate bottle 20 to the current millennium beginning with '20'. This is a time of global awakening consciousness, where humanity steps out of the limited awareness of each person as a separate and isolated individual and begins to learn how to bring heaven and earth together. It is a time to question belief systems which teach that heaven is a place you can only reach once you die and open instead to the possibility that it can exist right here on earth. As this new era dawns on the planet, many are now awakening as healers and lightworkers, learning how to bridge their own spiritual and material worlds so that they can pass on this knowledge to others.

What is curious about bottle 20 is that it tends to sit on the shelf and nobody chooses it, until suddenly everyone does. It seems to tap into a collective raising of consciousness, so that as humanity goes through another burst of awakening, this bottle fully supports the process.

Bottle 20 is magenta Divine love on the copper earth. It says that even when you feel separate, you are absolutely loved. As you awaken to Divine love in and on this planet, Divine love in and as everything, Divine love in all its vastness, now is the time for you to recognise that love as truth and bring it right into your body, right into your being and all the way through every aspect of your life.

Bottle 20 Story: Korani

In the early days of working on this book Melissie and I were discussing how magenta connects us with the 'now' moment and how, with this bottle's colours of magenta and copper, we are asked to bring ourselves fully into the 'here and now' on earth. As we were talking about this, I picked the bottle up and held it in front of me and felt everything in my energy field vertically align. It was a powerful sensation of being brought into a coherent state on both physical and spiritual levels, as if my whole being was plugging into the universe and connecting with the timelessness that happens when we live in the present moment.

Bottle 21: The Key (Gold/Yellow)

Traditionally at 21 you are given a key to the door. This is the end of a cycle and you have come of age. You are now fully responsible for what you create and how your life unfolds. Your courage has overcome many obstacles and you no longer doubt your abilities. Yellow brings joy, and gold is the colour of wisdom. This bottle says you can look forward to worldly gains and peace in your heart.

Bottle 20 (Awakening) brought your magenta spirit into land on the copper earth. With bottle 21's vivid gold and yellow, you now reach a new level of spiritual maturity. As you begin to anchor in and feel safe on earth you can open up to the brightness, joy and sunshine carried in this bottle's colours and fill your life with fun, play and laughter. Yet although bottle 21 is vibrant, shiny and gregarious, it is not entirely frivolous. It reminds you that you now have knowledge and experience you did not have before and asks you to recognise and own the deeper qualities of wisdom and authentic power you hold within.

Everything in your solar plexus is given a boost by using this bottle. Yellow relates to the power of your body and gold connects with the power of your spirit, so with this bottle you are aligning with power on all levels. With the brightness of yellow this bottle brings to light your fears, and with the power of gold it lifts them out of your unconscious and into the fires of transformation. If you have been feeling powerless or stuck in a limited mindset, struggling with addictions or giving your power away, bottle 21 strengthens your connection to your inner power source, inviting you to shed these limitations and move forward.

As with bottle 10 (Wheel of Fortune), this is the turning of the wheel, the completion of a cycle and the beginning of a new phase. The world is your oyster and you can have all the fun and excitement of being 21, no matter your actual age. At 21 you may have felt completely immortal, with a sense of your own power, magnificence and absolute potential. Or if you didn't, now is your opportunity. Whatever your age, this bottle invites you to experiment with your life, branch out, stretch yourself, try something new – and be amazed at the results! Choosing this bottle is a signal from your radiant higher self. It says life is yours for the taking and it is time to be, do and have it all.

This bottle is an enormously positive choice, signifying that you are ready to go out into the world and shine. You are coming of age and hold the key to the next level in your hands. As your spiritual journey becomes more central to your life, this bottle helps you experience it lightly and joyfully rather than turning it into some sort of duty or taking it all too seriously. You can play the game of being human, fully knowing that you are a spark of Divine light and that you created this game for your growth and expansion – and quite possibly just for your own entertainment!

Bottle 21 is a party and a celebration, but it also indicates strength, empowerment, courage and decisiveness. It is time to take life by the horns. This bottle, The Key, asks you to celebrate your life, play your way to authentic empowerment and enjoy this amazing ride – for that truly *is* the key. This bottle helps you realise that there are no limitations. Its light burns steadily and brightly like an eternal candle flame, reflecting the remarkable glow of your own inner radiance.

Bottle 21 Story: Melissie

Anna, who makes the Angel spritzers for Colour Mirrors, has been married for many years to an abusive and difficult man. Out of the blue one day he suddenly came to her workplace to deliver boxes and wanted to know about the bottles he saw on the shelves. At this point she had worked with me for over 12 years and this was the first time he had ever come to see her at work. I asked him to choose a bottle and he immediately chose bottle 21. He suffers terribly from all kinds of stress complaints, so the colours made complete sense for an overwhelmed solar plexus. I gave him the bottle and he used it two nights in a row – but sparingly as he was scared that it would run out. He said he felt that a great light had gone right through him and that for the first time in his life he could breathe fully. He never sleeps, but for the first time in years and years, he slept through the night.

Bottle 21 Story: Client of Rui Diogo, Portugal, www.facebook.com/kaleidosol

After my reading with the colours I decided to take this bottle home with me. I intuitively felt that what I carried inside me was an unresolved issue and that it was time for it to end. I filled the bathtub and poured all the contents of the bottle into it. I lay down in the water and felt as if years and years of burden left my cells. I closed my eyes and travelled through my mind, and it felt as if my problem was over. I was no longer the usual ant, the one who works but never enough. Today I'm only a little bit the ant – I am also the cicada who can finally dance to the music of life without criticising myself for it.

Bottle 21 Story: Jackie Tweedie, UK, www.jackietweedie.com

During one of my workshops a man chose this bottle. He had come to the session full of questions about a business he had recently started, seeking reassurance to overcome his doubts and fears about its success. He didn't know why he was drawn to this bottle, but he laughed when he saw the number ("hey, 21 – that's my birthday!"). He said the colour made him feel very optimistic and hopeful about his business and that he felt a renewed confidence in himself and his ideas. What was also interesting was that when he arrived, he seemed rather insecure: talking very quickly and being restless and fidgety. But after working with this bottle he became calmer, quieter and much more self-confident and mature in himself, like he'd grown up in that short space of time. Time to come of age?

Bottle 22: Forgiveness (Deep Magenta/Rose Pink)

This is a challenging number and relates to the Fool in the Tarot. The Fool has to start the journey again and again, but these colours hold the answers to the Fool's predicament. Magenta relates to Divine love: this is a time to let go and let God. Surrender to your own highest knowing and allow the perfection of what is unfolding. You are starting a new cycle, and the more you let go of fear and connect with Divine love, the easier your path will be. These colours are strongly indicative of a healer's journey and ask you to finally forgive God, and yourself as part of God. With forgiveness comes freedom and a sense of joyful expansion and creativity that ripples out to touch others. Remember what it is to be in faith and innocence and childlike awe. There is no other time than now.

The previous bottle, No. 21 (The Key), was a celebration of your coming of age, a joyful recognition of the game of life and your role in it. Bottle 22 comes in next with a sobering reminder that as you are all grown up now, it is time to be completely honest with yourself. If you are drawn to this bottle, it is clear that you may still hold yourself or someone else as wrong – as guilty. This bottle says the time has arrived to find it in your heart to forgive.

You may be harbouring resentment and anger towards another, feeling like a victim of their behaviour or beliefs and finding it hard to even contemplate forgiveness. Or perhaps it is yourself you are unable to forgive. There may be a specific event or situation you wish you had handled differently. Perhaps you are prone to feeling guilty for every 'mistake', big or small. Maybe you have always carried a nagging sense of guilt around although you do not really understand why.

Whatever the circumstances and whoever you feel is to blame, the first and biggest step is to forgive God (or the universe or whatever you wish to call it). Until you do that, you cannot forgive yourself or anyone else. Even if you outwardly blame yourself or another, lurking behind most guilt is the deep-seated belief that it is actually 'God' who is at fault. And as long as you hold God guilty – for messing up your life, for creating chaos, destruction or terrible life events, for the things that 'shouldn't have happened' – you are refusing to see the bigger picture.

The first thing to recognise is that you *are* God, and God is you! In a divinely created universe you are an aspect of all that exists, intricately interwoven with the very fabric of creation. You are not separate, you are not outside the Divine. As long as you continue to hold an outside force as responsible for your life, you give away all your power and renege on any personal responsibility. You stay small, helpless and disconnected. Bottle 22 asks you to realise that you are inherently part of the Divine and therefore already authentically empowered.

Secondly, nothing that 'happens' in life occurs randomly or in a vacuum. Every soul is sovereign, a powerful Divine being of light who has come to experience, learn, grow, heal and evolve. Your soul has requested various learning opportunities in this lifetime, and the experiences on your path that have led to guilt or lack of forgiveness have done so – at a soul level – so that you could learn from them, grow through them, discover forgiveness and become a more compassionate, evolved, enlightened human being. They may also have happened, in part, so that you could hold a loving space for others as they go through similar experiences.

If you continue to see yourself as victim of another and hold them responsible for your happiness or well-being; if you blame God or fate or a random unfeeling universe for your experiences; if you stay locked in the blame/shame/guilt game in any way – you recklessly throw away any and all power the Divine has given you for self-realisation. Will you really choose to stay in resentment, lack and poverty of spirit, or will you answer the challenge this bottle lays down for you and claim back your Divine authentic power, set yourself and everyone else free, and finally forgive?

As so often, the clue to this bottle lies in its name and its colours: forgiveness comes by letting love (rose pink) right into your cells and opening to the truth that the Divine (magenta) loves you utterly, eternally and exactly as you are. This bottle's message is simple yet profound: you are not guilty and you do not deserve to struggle; you are innocent and you are beloved.

The number 22 is a master number and this bottle is an invitation to mastery. One of the keys to mastery is to fully acknowledge and release your judgements. Why? Because more than anything it is your judgements that stop you from living a life of peace and joy. Your judgements and fears tend to manifest the very things you are judging and fearing, so as you let go of your judgements you attract less and less things to judge, less and less things to fear. You no longer attract them because it is the judgement itself that brings whatever you are judging into your reality. Every single judgement is an opportunity to see that you have attracted this situation, event or circumstance because you judge it – and then choose to stop judging. With this bottle you also get the opportunity to look at every judgement as an inner judgement: what part of yourself do you still believe is so awful that you have to have this experience to mirror it to you?

Bottle 22 is about being responsible for every aspect of your life. It is about being able to claim yourself as a Divine being in a physical body. It is about moving once and for all beyond judgement, to a place where you no longer need to fix what you or anyone else did wrong because you have moved beyond any concept of 'wrong'. From there you can begin to acknowledge the Divine in everything and everyone. This bottle calls when you are finally ready to see that the judgements, blame, guilt and anger you have been holding on to are simply not serving you in any way. This bottle is your gift from the universe, revealing a path to freedom.

Magenta is the colour of the healer, and this bottle's message is that being a healer is not about fixing anything but about recognising the Divine in yourself and in the other. Fixing still says there is something wrong; love says there never was.

Bottle 22 combines rose pink and magenta: the human perception of love (rose pink) taken to a Divine level of love (magenta). It challenges you to go beyond conditionality, to become the master that you are, to love as though it were the only thing that existed and to know that you are loved beyond any limited beliefs about what love might be.

This bottle shows up in your life when you become aware that your energy and your love really make a difference to the world and you start to walk that love around the planet. As you do so, you realise that love changes everything. You realise that where you – literally – set your foot on the planet, you change the planet. With love shining out from the core of you, an energy vibration is created that paves the way for a new reality here on earth, one based on love, harmony and freedom for all.

Bottle 22 Story: Melissie

Bottle 22, more than any other in the range, has been my 'go-to' bottle when I get stuck in old patterns like depression, tiredness and just common or garden despair. The first time I bathed in this bottle it really shook my world, as I heard a voice telling me to forgive God. Shock, horror! Hearing voices in the bath is not what one expects on a normal Monday morning. After that I crawled out of the bath and collapsed on my bed until the next day, when I woke up absolutely reborn. I felt like a completely different person, and the strongest feeling was that if God was not guilty then I was not guilty, and if I was not guilty then I did not deserve to suffer. This one got me out of the feeling that I was somehow guilty for everything. I believed I was guilty and so what I saw outside of me was the reflection of things to be guilty about.

The biggest lesson in magenta is that guilt is a misunderstanding. Since that initial visceral experience of this as truth I can honestly say that my life has changed in really big and many small ways. If I feel any of those old patterns beginning to surface, I immediately go back to bottle 22 and remind myself that I am innately innocent and so is everyone else. I remind myself that suffering of any kind is created through a misunderstanding of reality and truth.

Another side effect of bottle 22 is that I am much more aware of God's hand in my dealings. If I think one thing should happen and it does not, I now know that I am not supposed to push and shove and drive myself and all around me mad. I stop and know that it is the right thing that is happening, as that is all that can happen. Every moment of every day is God's moment, and in God's time all things work perfectly. My body knows that as truth, and the knowledge of this stops endless amounts of anguishing.

Every single bottle in the system is about bringing heaven to earth, and they will each do the bit you need them to do in any given moment. But ultimately, the first thing to see is how perfect it all is, and then you will only see the reflection of the perfection. And you start by claiming your own perfection with every breath you take: "I am this and it is perfect."

Bottle 22 Story: Korani

Some years ago my brother contacted me in shock. His wife had been drawn to bottle 22 and had placed it by her bed before she went to sleep. When she woke the next morning there was an incredibly clear image of a face inside the bottle. The oils had literally formed into a face – and not only that, the face was her own face at age 22! It was so extraordinary that my brother took a photo to send to me, and I too was shocked! This was an exact image of my sister-in-law's younger self, appearing in physical form inside a bottle of oil. Needless to say, she took notice of the message she was being sent and took heed of her 22-year-old self who was asking for forgiveness.

Bottle 22 Story: Renira Barclay, UK, www.abovemiddlec.com

This bottle was huge for me. Whilst lying in the bath I got a sense of Jesus standing beside me. He asked me if I could forgive him. I remember thinking: "Hang on a minute, isn't it supposed to be the other way round?" And he said: "No, I am asking for YOUR forgiveness – for everything that has been done in my name that has hurt people." Well, I felt it would be impolite to say no – and so I said yes.

From that moment I was not scared of the deep magenta colour, and I know that my bath in No. 22 was a stepping stone along the way to co-creating the 'Heart to Heart Process' with my dear friend, Denny Ellis. This is a simple yet profound way of sharing heart energy with another person, tuning into the individual heart colours and observing how the colours change and merge to reveal emotions, life lessons and understanding between two people. Huge shifts can occur, and the main side effect would seem to be forgiveness. In a nutshell, it is a gentle path to love and forgiveness. Forgiveness is such an important door!

Bottle 23: Initiation (Royal Blue/Royal Blue)

This bottle indicates an initiation successfully completed. What was so difficult in this last cycle of events has now passed on and you can be at peace. Royal Blue relates to the third eye, and this colour says that your insight can be trusted and it is safe to say what you see. It might be that you find it easier to write than to speak, but it is necessary that your wisdom is shared. It is time to step out of the darkness and back into the light, where all that you have learned can be used to teach others.

Bottle 23 tends to show up when you have been through a challenging experience and have come out the other side. It literally says: "It is done." You can breathe a sigh of relief – the test has been passed. And it is not just "done", it is "well done". This is a pat on the back, a welcome respite after the rigours of bottle 22's journey towards mastery.

Choosing this deep royal blue bottle indicates that you have reached new levels of insight, wisdom and understanding and can now bask in a time of peace. This bottle acts as a confirmation of what you have been through and the journey you have been on. The difficulties are past and now it is time to pause and rest in order to integrate what you have learned. It is also time to enjoy the fruits of what has gone before as you emerge clearer, stronger and more enlightened about the path you have been on. Something significant has shifted in your world and everything can now unfold with greater ease.

All initiations are opportunities to go to the next level and each will take you into a new space, a new sense of resurrection. There are many small and large initiations in everyday life – the rites of passage, the testing times, the challenges and difficulties – and these are all part of your soul's growth. If you are choosing bottle 23 you are asked to recognise that whatever you have been going through was an initiation of some kind, and if you are reading this then you have survived! As each initiation is essentially a kind of death experience, so your 'survival' is a signal from the universe that you have grown, learned and evolved – which, at a soul level, is the purpose of every initiation. If at times you get lost inside an initiatory experience and find it difficult to see your way through, this bottle connects you with your inner wisdom and your inner vision so that you might see the higher view and find your way forward.

Bottle 23 has a particular connection with Egypt, and the highest Egyptian initiation in ancient times was to transmute death. This is also what Christ came to teach: if you are love then death cannot touch you. If you are love, if you are part of the Divine, then you are eternal, limitless, infinite. Death is an illusion that conjures fear and superstition, yet when you know yourself as life, as love, it has no substance. Yes, the physical body will eventually release its life force, but it will only change form, returning to dust, returning to the earth. Your soul will go on eternally, and as you fully open to this realisation bottle 23 acts as an initiation into a different way of seeing the world. If transmutation of death is the highest initiation a human can experience, perhaps the secret this bottle holds is to show you how to do it: to move beyond what you thought you knew and go beyond who you have believed yourself to be; to transcend your known boundaries and rise above the limitations of human ego and fear.

This bottle taps into a lifetime where you knew and saw things beyond your physical senses and where your highest desire was to know God, to know life, to know yourself as part of the infinite. You were willing to go through any experience and endure any hardship if it led to your ultimate goal of oneness with the Divine. Bottle 23's message is that you do not have to go through this intense kind of initiation again because the path to spiritual growth can now be found in your everyday life. Every time you let go of a judgement, every time you forgive yourself or another, every time you stand in your truth and claim your authentic power, every time you open to love – each of these is a kind of 'initiation' and naturally takes you closer to the Divine.

Royal blue relates to the ancient mystery schools, esoteric institutions whose teachings were designed to bring initiates to spiritual mastery. As the name suggests, much of what was taught in these mystery schools was shrouded in secrecy. Royal blue has connotations of the High Priestess who keeps information to herself until she deems an initiate fit to receive it. There is also a hint of past spiritual persecution, and if this is your colour you may have a tendency to keep your truth, your wisdom and your knowledge to yourself. With bottle 23 you no longer need to hide. It awakens your inner knowing and activates your Divine vision. It helps you recognise that the Divine is in everything and everyone and that no one is superior or inferior to another. You are safe now to be who you are and to share what you know.

This bottle carries an energy of powerful authority – and it helps you claim *your* inner authority. As you tap into the vast storehouse of wisdom and love that your essence self contains, you naturally desire to share this with others. People with strong royal blue tendencies have a gift for expressing their knowledge and expertise in writing, and if you are drawn to this bottle you may have a book inside you waiting to be freed. It is time to acknowledge your skills and recognise that you have something of value to offer the world.

However you choose to share your wisdom, now is your time to be seen and heard, and in this way, bottle 23 echoes the message of its numerological 'mirror', bottle 32 (Communication). It also links with bottle 5 (Mercury), as the number 23 reduces to 5 (2 + 3 = 5). Mercury is about taking off the masks you have been using to hide behind, and this reinforces bottle 23's message that it is time for you to come out of the shadows.

This bottle helps you open to a higher vision of life, an inclusive, expansive view that goes beyond previous limiting notions and fears. There is something inherently magical and mystical about this colour and this bottle. It is the colour of psychics and visionaries, those who see beyond the ordinary to the subtler, less opaque frequencies of the unseen world.

Whether you are aware of your innate intuitive capacities or not, this bottle helps you go beyond the veil of illusion that surrounds so much of third-dimensional life and see with a different sort of vision, a far-seeing vision that encompasses so much more than you might ordinarily experience. It opens you to magic, potential and the truth that absolutely anything is possible. With this knowledge deeply embedded in your heart and bones, your inner wisdom and clear vision guide you beyond initiation to the higher and greater levels that await you.

Bottle 23 Story: Melissie

This bottle feels like the one that holds the whole of the Colour Mirrors system in its being. When I started working with colour I really did not know that I had put down the ways of the child and had started to play with the grown-ups – spiritual grown-ups that is – and that I would have to go to a whole different level of training.

Bottle 23 has always had an Egyptian feel for me. Gold and yellow, especially when combined with royal blue or violet, are often connected with Egyptian lifetimes. In this case a solid royal blue bottle means that gold is the complementary colour, and we often say that the complementary colour sits within or 'underneath' any given colour. So in a way, this bottle is completely Egyptian.

In my journey with colour my soul knew that I was ready for the biggest shift, and I now understand that my life has a very clearly demarcated 'before' and 'after' time. In the first 50 or so years of my life, everything I did was the training to remember what it is to be human, and in that time I really took it seriously: every human condition and tragedy and drama was part of my experience. But then again, how else could I bring through a system that would explain and be a remedy for almost all human conditions? And so for many years I experienced, and then I did a full 10 years of initiation – and in that time all the structures I had built up had to crumble and be chipped off so that the true gold underneath the deep dark royal blue exterior could be revealed.

Everything I had created to hide my true self behind was removed, and as a stubborn Capricorn I did not flow with any of it. I resisted and resisted and was pretty much flattened in the process. But once the initiation was done it was done, and I didn't have to do anything more. I could rest and trust and watch in awe as my whole life changed from fear to love, from panic to peace and from control to faith. I can now look back with huge compassion at that part of me that was so small and so panicked and breathe and sigh and give grateful thanks for the other side of that experience, which is what I am living now. Now I am in faith and flow and ease and grace, and every day is filled with gratitude and best of all, with colour.

Bottle 23 Story: Raluca Rusu, Switzerland, www.facebook.com/RalucaRusu.colours

This colour makes me think of the engineering school I attended in France, which was in an old Benedictine abbey at Cluny. Our uniforms were royal blue, inspired from the French navy, and we had to go through an initiation process. The graduates' society has a secret, authoritative quality, like a mystery school.

Bottle 23 Story: Priscilla Elliott, UK, www.priscillaelliott.co.uk

This is my birthday bottle, and I recall that before bathing in it I was strongly drawn to rub some of the oil onto my third eye chakra, face and wrists. I happened to be looking in the mirror at the time and noticed that I was applying the oil to my right temple then left wrist. Afterwards, I applied it to my left temple then right wrist. As I was doing this it occurred to me that I had entered into some sort of a ritual… an Egyptian initiation… in a 'temple'! It made me laugh when I realised that bottle 23 is called 'Initiation' and has strong connections with Egypt and the third eye chakra where I had applied the oil. At that moment I glanced at the label on the towel which said 'Egyptian cotton'. A very amusing evening that was!

Bottle 23 Story: Sarah Impey, UK, www.sarahimpey.com

As I connected with this bottle I could feel a deep 'heartbeat' in my stomach like the earth's heartbeat, and I had a vision of myself surrounded by wild horses. I'd been seeing and connecting to wild horses over recent months, bringing me to tears, as if they were calling me home. In this vision two horses stepped forward and started coming towards me: a beautiful female horse to my left who I connected to on a deep level, to her heartbeat, to her soul; a beautiful male horse to my right, slightly holding back, tentative, not wanting to come closer. I stood there in my truth, my hands in prayer, my head bowed with my eyes closed, sending love to him, holding my space, standing in my sovereignty.

He reared up, angry, kicking up the dirt with his hooves, making a statement, standing his ground. I got a real sense of his rage, his anger. Was this my anger? Was he mirroring to me that sense of anger from the hundreds and hundreds of lifetimes of persecution? Was this the anger creating the fuel, the fire in my body, in my very soul, to fire me up? This was the energy to keep my soul coming back over and over and over, so many lifetimes of persecution, injustice and judgement. Standing his ground to speak up, with fire, motivation and determination.

The horse could feel my solidity, standing in my sovereignty, continuing to send out love to him, bowing down, still holding my hands in prayer. He slowly fell to his knees, onto his front legs as they buckled beneath him, kneeling to the floor. I stroked his magnificent mane, with his face close to mine. I saw his huge eye and his huge sadness deep within. I had a real sense he could no longer hold that energy within him. I got a sense of his surrender and of him completely letting go, a release from his bowels, from the depth within.

I realised that all the energy I could feel in the left side of my stomach was my soul's past echoes of all of my soul's lifetimes. Huge, huge suffering that has been endured, attracting suffering like a moth to a flame which I've held on to, to keep me fired up, to keep me going, like a fuel, reigniting that fire within, to come back again and again and again over thousands of lifetimes.

With his huge release, I called on the Egyptian scarab dung beetle to push and roll it away, to push up the sun, for the sun to rise. As the sun began to rise up I could feel my attention being pulled towards the sun, Divine Masculine, God, Source. I sat and bathed under the sun's rays like a connection, like electricity surging through my veins. Huge power, lighting up a spark within. And I realised: "It's time." It's time for those lifetimes to be healed, to be honoured, released from the suffering, released from my body, to allow the healing for Mother Earth, for this planet. It's time to step forward and into my power. With the energy of the sun I no longer need this fire in my belly. It's time now to embrace my light, to mirror and reflect to others the light within themselves. Each day, each sunrise helps to power up my light, to light the spark within, increase my energy and relight my passion and Divine power.

Bottle 24: Love, Money and Creativity (Pale Magenta/Pale Olive)

This is a time when it seems appropriate to look at the tapestry of your life and recognise that all the stitches were perfect – the light ones and the dark ones. The design you have woven is so cosmically, profoundly perfect that it leaves you breathless. You have to acknowledge that your conscious mind could not have worked out such a perfect design. You have always been taken to the perfect place at the perfect time to get to exactly this point in time, with all the gifts and understanding you have now. Well done. You are the master weaver, and your work is a work of art. Begin to acknowledge that the main part of the design is love and that where love shows in the design is where there is a glow that attracts others. Look at how the threads of love were woven through the design and what an important part of the picture that is. Now is the time to own the blessings of love, money and creativity in your life and the gifts of the past that brought you here. This is your heritage from past lifetimes. You have earned it all.

Having come through a testing time in bottle 23 (Initiation), you are now ready for something altogether more abundant and joyful. Bottle 24 holds it up before you and says: "Here it is: do you want it? And if you are not claiming all of it – the love, the money *and* the creativity – what is stopping you?"

This bottle asks you to look at your beliefs around lack and limitation and decide if they are serving you. Its message is that withholding from yourself, whether consciously or unconsciously, means you are stuck in a limitation mindset, and while this may be a common human trait, it is the opposite of Divine. The Divine is unlimited in every way, and as part of the Divine, so too are you. Why then would you cut yourself off from all the love, money and creativity the universe has to share with you?

Bottle 24 suggests that by holding back from yourself you are also limiting what is available to others, and this can have knock-on effects in your life, career and relationships. This bottle asks you to consider that it might just be a kind of arrogance to limit what you allow yourself, and it is most certainly a form of judgement. Might it even be that what is restricting you in your life, what is keeping you poor – whether in love, money or creativity – is a fundamental belief in limitation and lack? If you are subscribing to poverty consciousness on any level, this bottle invites you to take a look at what you are creating in your life with your beliefs and judgements.

Judgements around money are well-known and well-practised on this planet. Judgements around love – finding it and keeping it – are also common. Even creativity can come under fire if you are the only 'creative' one among your family, friends or colleagues. Most judgements around love, money and creativity, however, tend to be the judgements you heap upon yourself. These will usually take the form of 'not enough': not good enough, not wise enough, not beautiful enough, not talented enough, et cetera, et cetera, et cetera. Almost the whole of humanity struggles with lack of self-worth on some level; the high degree of struggle around money and love on this planet is evidence of that. The collective belief in 'not enough' is deeply entrenched. Even the damage inflicted on the earth is, in part, a result of humanity's fundamental belief in 'not enough'.

It is logical then that bottle 24 tends to come calling when you seem to be *lacking* in love, money and/or creativity: when you are going through financial difficulties, experiencing a relationship breakdown, struggling to manifest the relationship you are seeking, or finding your creative well has run dry. But the good news is that your choice of this bottle indicates you are now set to break the pattern.

The combination of magenta and olive in bottle 24 is a tonic for whatever has kept you in limitation. As magenta and olive are complementary colours, in their most positive aspects the two colours together represent balance and wholeness. Magenta says you are loved, divinely and entirely; olive creates hope and has the energy of putting you back together after difficulties. The message this bottle delivers is that you are not being punished. You may have hit a rough spot, but only because on some level you have chosen this particular experience as an opportunity to learn and grow. You are still connected to the love of the universe. It has not abandoned you and it never will. Divine love is eternal and ever-present. You may not be able to see it or feel it right now, but it is waiting patiently for you to drop the mantle of restriction and weariness you have been carrying and step into something altogether lighter, something much more aligned with your essence, your soul and your inner truth. The love, money and creativity are simply being blocked by something that is out of alignment, rather like a cloud blocking the sun, and connecting with bottle 24 might just be the means to bring that block to consciousness and transform it.

Have you ever noticed that when everything works out you can happily claim that it is Divine will or that it was 'meant to be', but when things do not work the way you think they should, you cannot see the same perfection? This bottle invites you to see everything as part of the Divine flow and come to peace with 'what is'. Many people who choose this bottle and read its message are deeply moved by it and sometimes even shed tears. When you are in a place where things appear not to be working out, hearing that everything is actually unfolding as it is meant to can be both empowering and deeply soothing. This bottle gifts you with a huge key to happiness: knowing that no matter how it looks, it is all exactly as it needs to be. You may forget sometimes that you only have some pieces of the puzzle, that there is a much higher picture unfolding that you may not have access to on a conscious level. This bottle holds that bigger picture up for you to see.

Bottle 24 shifts the 'I can't have' story out of your cells and restores you to your divinity. Magenta helps you remember that you are Divine and that you can have anything you desire, and olive brings in the new. With your inner power restored, love, money and creativity can now begin to flow.

Here is where you can have it all. This bottle offers a wonderful trinity of goods, but it also says you need to be willing to have them all because love and money without creativity will leave you bored; money and creativity on their own will leave you hankering for love; love and creativity without money will leave you feeling insecure – so take the whole package on offer!

The numbers of this bottle added together make 6 (2 + 4 = 6), and bottle 6 is Venus, which is about love and self-love – and this can now be reflected back in your life and relationships. As you open more to love, you open to the richness of life. As love filters into your being, your creative channels open and you find yourself basking in the 'having it all' state of joy and fulfilment that is your Divine birthright. There is an abundance of love, money and creativity to own, enjoy and share. This bottle returns you to a state of trust in the perfection of the universe. Which is rather apt, since Trust is the name of the next bottle in the system.

Bottle 24 Story: Alka Dharam, UK, www.lifecentredhealing.co.uk

The first bottle I ever bathed in was bottle 24, which was also the first bottle I picked on the Colour Mirrors practitioner training course when I knew nothing about Colour Mirrors. During the bath that evening I had an out-of-body experience. I could see my body in the water and I could sense being one with everything and everyone. I saw myself in and as everyone on the course. There was a sense of timelessness, lightness, space and oneness. The rest of the course felt exciting and empowering.

Since this bath I have increasingly been able to look past personalities to the essence and wholeness of the person before me, and at times I have felt such overwhelming love that it cannot be contained. I have also begun to recognise and feel gratitude for the abundance that is around me, knowing that I have help from the universe and have always been provided for. Consequently, financial insecurities and fears for the future have loosened their hold as I appreciate the present moment. Abundance has taken on an expansive meaning, not limited to money, which has opened me up to seeing the blessings around me and loving what is.

Bottle 24 Story: Jackie Tweedie, UK, www.jackietweedie.com

I love this bottle. It puts to bed all my past beliefs that spiritual people shouldn't be wealthy (what a crazy myth!) and allows me to flourish in both the heavenly and the material realms. It also shows me that wealth is so much more than money: it's that moment when you can't stop the ideas from flowing, or you feel such love you think you'll burst, or you raise your face to the sunshine after a downpour.

Bottle 25: Trust (Turquoise/Yellow)

This is the time to move beyond judgement. Begin to see how the flow and your faith have always taken you to exactly where you are meant to be. Use your intuition, trust your inner knowing and begin to be at peace with life. You have been given the ability to analyse so that you might understand the differences between things without labelling them as good or bad, and the gift of discernment to enable you to see clearly and make decisions from a basis of strength rather than fear. At the deepest level, use these gifts and follow your bliss, which is the easiest way to be in the flow. This has all the potential for new planet living.

The previous bottle offered you the key to having more love, money and creativity in your life. Bottle 25 comes in now to help you weigh your options, discern what it is you *really* desire to have or experience, and trust that it is absolutely available to you. This bottle is about consciously choosing the bright sparkling turquoise of trust and faith rather than the yellow fear that lies in the depths of your subconscious. It asks you to bring all the yellow sun energy of your mind to meet and merge with the flowing, intuitive, turquoise dreaminess of your emotional self. When these come together, you have a potent force for reality creation. You can play with the idea of life as a game, one to be explored and enjoyed to the full.

Any time you have a battle going on between intellect and intuition, this bottle is a tonic. How often do you instinctively and intuitively 'know' something, yet your head insists on arguing the point? This bottle helps bring these aspects of yourself together so that instead of a war, you have a peaceful union. People who choose it are often very bright intellectually and may have tremendous flashes of insight, but their intellect questions their intuitive knowing and they end up confused and unclear. When you are choosing this bottle you are asked to trust that both your bright intelligence and your intuition are valid, that indeed your intuition is *based* on your brightness and is not flaky or imaginary but rather a true source of wisdom.

Bottle 25 is about discernment. It helps you see the options and opportunities ahead of you clearly and reminds you to listen to both your rational mind and your inner knowing to show you the way forward. It is not about blindly trusting anything that shows up. Rather, it encourages the expansive higher view that discernment brings.

This bottle also taps into wisdom and knowing from other lifetimes, wisdom stored in your DNA that is waiting to be accessed and received again now. As befits the nature of this bottle, you may not yet 'know' on a conscious level what that wisdom and information is, but if you can trust it is there, it will reveal itself at the perfect moment.

Choosing this bottle says you are ready to take things to another level. If you will allow it all to unfold and be willing to trust every step of the way, you can find positive new solutions to challenges and shift your perspective so that you are more aware of the higher truth in any situation. You might also open to heightened perceptions of the world and the reality you are choosing to live in and find that it is possible to make different, more empowered choices.

This bottle asks you to let go of stories about why you cannot trust yourself, others or the universe. Look deeply at your fears around trust and the situations you have attracted in which you have believed your trust to be misplaced or betrayed. Were they not, at the deepest level, about tapping into your subconscious blocks and bringing them to the light of day so that they could be transformed? Were they not the most incredible opportunities to release judgement, transmute old wounds and step into a more empowered connection with life? Were they not gifts from the Divine to assist you on your path to mastery?

Lack of trust implies a fundamental disconnection from the flow of life itself. You may have had frightening or even horrific experiences in this or previous lifetimes that have created barriers to trust, yet you are asked now to remember that you are so much bigger than anything that has 'happened' to you. You are a Divine being who has come to experience, and through your experiences, to learn, grow and evolve. The shift from yellow fear to turquoise faith is huge and profound, and it is being held out to you now in the form of this bottle that your mighty soul has chosen for you. Will you heed its call?

The whole of life as a human on planet earth is a game of trust. Most people have, at best, a very limited understanding of how and why life is the way it is. A huge part of the human journey is to discover life in all its many facets, and your trust in the process is key to how the game unfolds: do you view your path as a nightmare of twists, turns and blind corners or as an exciting adventure to be relished?

Bottle 25 is a kind of instruction manual, one you may have wished you had when you were born. It is a guide to how to 'do' life in a way that engages both your thinking mind and your feeling heart. It challenges you to feel into your deepest self and ask whether the road you are travelling is the path to joy, flow and expansion. If it is not, you are absolutely free to choose again. When you are in trust, you can do this with the full understanding that you will be shown the way forward and supported as you open to new options and possibilities. This bottle encourages you to live from faith and trust, step into joy and let the flow take you to your bliss.

Bottle 25 Story: Korani

This was the first Colour Mirrors bottle I ever bathed in many years ago and it was so 'me' at that time. I knew I was reasonably intuitive but I had a very busy mind and came from a background which valued the intellect, so I wasn't always willing to trust the intuitive flashes I was increasingly experiencing. After this bottle I knew I finally could. My path really accelerated as I opened the doors to my intuition and began to balance it with my intellectual understanding. This was completely the 'next level' for me as I found a peace within myself that I hadn't known before.

Bottle 25 Story: Client of Rui Diogo, Portugal, www.facebook.com/kaleidosol

When I received this bottle I felt very powerful energy but also a lot of resistance. It took me some time to actually use it. With this bottle I learned to calm myself, to be observant, to put myself in another's place and to understand his point of view. Tolerance is the word. It was exactly what I had been running away from. I also applied some of the oil from this bottle to my skin where I had a cyst, and it disappeared from one day to the next. It's been six months since then and I have been told that surgery is not going to be necessary. Miracle? Maybe pure energy!

Bottle 25 Story: Jackie Tweedie, UK, www.jackietweedie.com

This colour combination is one of my favourites: turquoise, which I love to wear, lifts my spirits and makes me want to shine in the world; yellow stimulates my mind (solar plexus) and brings me joy. I don't often wear yellow, but when I choose this bottle it provides a wonderful affirmation of my mental strength and clarity. It allows me to relax and trust both myself and the universe. This bottle often gets chosen by the clients who come to me for clarity coaching. They come feeling lost, confused, needing to make a decision or find a new direction. They seek help because as a result of their life experiences they have stopped believing in themselves or their own 'knowing'. By bathing in bottle 25 they re-discover their ability to have faith in themselves again, to tune in to their own intuition and to trust it. From there they feel clear, back 'on track' as they often call it, and they know exactly what to do next, with confidence. I call it 'following the breadcrumbs' on their life path. They only need to trust that their next step will be revealed to them, not the whole path.

This bottle also helps people to realise that their power to trust that inner wisdom was never lost, they had simply lost faith in it and so could no longer feel it. The only thing ever lost is awareness. Once restored, they come to see how life has always served them just as they needed and that they can trust that. This brings them great peace.

Bottle 26: Partnerships (Magenta/Olive)

The number 26 reduces to 8 and relates to Saturn. This is not an easy vibration, and the main lesson is to stand on your own two feet. There is no room for co-dependency: you are God in a body and cannot be in a space where someone else does it for you. It is time to stand up and be counted so that you no longer have to face challenging personal, business or financial situations. Let go of anger and resentment; this is a time for love and radical forgiveness. The magenta in this bottle relates to Divine love and the olive to feminine leadership. These colours relate to Father God and Mother Earth, and as you make peace with them both, balance follows in all your dealings. As you find the balance of masculine and feminine within you, it becomes possible to attract a partner who reflects that balance.

From the space of faith and flow in bottle 25 (Trust), this next bottle may come as something of a shock because it highlights difficulties and areas of concern, particularly in your relationships. It could be your love relationship or a business partnership, your connection with the Divine, even the balance between your own inner male and female, but choosing this bottle means you are being called to look more deeply at relationships in general, or one relationship in particular.

Bottle 26 is frequently chosen by those seeking a love relationship who have been unable to find one. It often comes up when there are challenges in an existing relationship. It might call to those who feel cut off from the Divine, unable to connect with the love of the universe, or those who feel betrayed or abandoned either by a human partner or by God – or both. It is sometimes chosen by those who feel as if they are in the wrong body or gender entirely.

This bottle can be quite uncomfortable, even for those who are actively drawn to it. It contains the same colours as bottle 24 (Love, Money and Creativity), but they are deepened and tightened and have a tendency to go cloudy or murky. Magenta and olive are close in shade to red and green – and as red and green together spell separation, so too do the colours of bottle 26. At its core this bottle is about addressing and healing any issues of separation, whatever their source and however they present themselves.

Bottle 26 may feel somewhat unkind at first glance, as it seems to strip away your illusions. Yet that is precisely what needs to happen in order for you to reclaim yourself as the sovereign being you are. Whatever your relationship story, this bottle quite specifically and categorically asks you to stop looking for another to complete you. Partnerships based on demands or expectations that the other will somehow fulfil you are destined to founder. Seeking outside of yourself for someone to make you whole is a denial of your Divine essence, which already contains everything. It may also lead to co-dependency: "I will do this for you, but only if you will do that for me." This sets up perfect grounds for manipulation, martyrdom and approval-seeking, and often leads to conflict, denial and blame.

If you have been expecting your partner – or perhaps the universe – to somehow make everything better for you, this bottle shows you that it is time to take charge of your own life. It acknowledges that although life on earth can be tough, you do have the inner strength to stand on your own two feet. You can no longer expect your partner, or the idea of some mythical perfect partner, to enable you in your neediness.

A partner in the true sense of the word is someone who complements you and accompanies you through life rather than someone you cling to in desperation. Real, grounded partnership comes when two individuals each stand firmly and clearly in their own divinity and reflect to each other that steady light of truth. Then the dance of masculine with feminine, partner with partner, human with Divine can be one of joy, spontaneity and trust, based upon love that does not seek to divide or control but instead fully honours, respects and enjoys the other as an expression of Divine truth and love.

Bottle 26 carries both masculine and feminine in its colours. Magenta asks you to look at how your relationship with your father may be reflected in your relationship with God. With an angry father, God becomes the vengeful old man in the sky and something to be feared. An absent father usually means that God is also absent, and you may feel as if there is no one and nothing there to support you. This bottle is about enabling you to see the truth of the Divine masculine as a father who has allowed you every single experience in every incarnation out of the most profound love, in order to lead you back to the true understanding of who you are.

The olive in bottle 26 acknowledges the wisdom and light of feminine love and power and the truth of a loving Divine Mother. It helps you recognise where in your life you have felt unsupported by the feminine – whether that be your mother or other prominent females in your life.

Together, magenta and olive light the way for your own inner female and male to come together in perfect harmony. They show you how to be open, receptive, intuitive and connected, while also able to take guided positive action and create the foundation and structure for your visions to become real.

This bottle supports you as you let go of the fears and tears you have been holding inside, ushering you into a much more empowered state. It helps you understand at a bodily level that you are safe and loved. The magenta in this bottle says you are loved simply for existing. You do not need to behave in a particular way or do good deeds or manipulate your way to safety. The message here is that the love the Divine has for you is so huge that once you really take it in, you can stand in your own true power. If you let yourself feel the divinity of magenta right inside your consciousness and lay that on a peaceful olive foundation of hope and the wisdom of love, you will find your *own* deepest inner truth rather than one belonging to someone else.

The gift of bottle 26 is that it enables you to see the perfection of everything in life rather than viewing anything as a mistake, or choosing to believe in a misunderstanding or clinging to a distortion of the truth. What might look like abandonment, betrayal, separation, strife or relationship turmoil are all just further opportunities to look more closely in the mirror, to see beyond the illusions and right to the heart of your own deepest truth. You cannot attract the perfect loving relationship – Divine or human – if you are separate and split within. This bottle reminds you of your innate perfection and helps you heal and integrate the fractured aspects of yourself that you have brought to relationships in the past so that they might now become whole. We know of many people who have found their ideal partner after bathing in this bottle!

Bottle 26 Story: Moira Bush, Canada, www.moirabush.com

*Some years ago I had just moved into a new apartment and was unpacking my bottles and displaying them. As I touched this one it exploded in my hands. I rushed it to the shower and proceeded to pour the oil over my body. As I did that, I just knew that I was going to meet the love of my life. I actually swore out loud: "Oh ****, he is here." So sure that this bottle had intuited to me a future event, I started to refuse all invitations to go out and took myself off the dating website my friend had put me on, not feeling ready at all for the real thing.*

Three weeks later I accepted a dinner invitation to a client's home, thinking that it would be safe to say yes and turn up, and at the door was greeted with: "Hello, hope you don't mind, we asked our Canadian friend Paul to join us for dinner." Those seeking love, after hearing this story and seeing how happy Paul and I are together, often buy this bottle. We have heard of several success stories!

Bottle 26 Story: Kath Roberts, UK, www.kath-roberts.com

I had a client with a soul path which included bottles 26 and 8, and the theme of forgiveness came up in our conversations. She thought she had met the 'one' and they were trying for a child with IVF when out of the blue he ended their relationship, leaving her shocked and sad after being together for two years. She also had bottles 31 and 4 in her soul path and had just committed to bathing in her soul path bottles and doing the work with me. Previous to this relationship she had been on her own for eight long years and couldn't really understand why she seemed destined not to meet anyone, until she met this guy and he decided to leave his wife for her.

Whilst she was insistent that she had nothing to forgive, I suggested that her body might be holding on to something, even though intellectually she felt she had let go. I suggested that after bathing in bottle 26 this might present itself more strongly. It transpired that after 15 years of no contact, her ex-husband phoned her to suggest they reconnect over a drink. When they met he said that he had reconnected to tell her that he forgave her for walking out on him 15 years prior, and that he understood. Needless to say, she was flabbergasted at the clarity of the message and the precision of the healing effectiveness of bottle 26 and the information from her soul path notes generally.

Bottle 27: Harvest (Orange/Gold)

This bottle symbolises power and wholeness. It blesses you with courage and promises huge rewards gained through several lifetimes. Having sown in the most positive sense, you can now bring in the harvest. You and your higher self are becoming one and co-creating a magical reality. The number 27 reduces to 9 and relates to Mars. Use your power and energy wisely. Orange is the colour of bliss and enlightenment, and gold is wisdom and authentic power. This is your time.

With bottle 26 (Partnerships), you learned to stand on your own two feet and remember your wholeness. Now, with bottle 27, you can begin to claim the joyous bliss and promise of all that is awaiting you. This bottle says you have passed through an initiation of sorts, and now the happiness, light and expansive potential available to you is truly vast. This combination of orange and gold relates to optimism, joy, alchemy and creativity. It is time to reap the harvest.

The orange in the top 'conscious' fraction of this bottle reflects conscious creativity, conscious manifestation, conscious bliss. With the empowered energy of gold sitting underneath, you are activating your capacity to create a wondrous reality. Though not specifically a master number, bottle 27 does reveal a kind of mastery. It says you can trust that you know exactly what you are doing and exactly what you are about. This bottle is unapologetically bright and dazzling. It opens the doorway for you to step right into the shining radiance of your true self and love every bit of the journey. It is a festive celebration, a gathering and reaping of all that you have sown along the way: the learning, understanding, wisdom and sheer richness of the experiences that have brought you to where you are now. Your path may not always have been easy and there have undoubtedly been challenges, but this bottle says it is time now to drink from the over-flowing cup of life, to honour yourself and your journey and the very fact of existence itself, with all its highs and lows and all its complexity and brilliance.

The name of bottle 27 was once 'Sceptre', and there is a connotation here of royalty – in the sense of knowing yourself to be utterly worthy and deserving of every good thing. This bottle speaks of sovereignty and the birthright of everyone on the planet – including you – to be loved, celebrated and cherished.

As 27 reduces to 9 (2 + 7 = 9), this bottle says you have come to the end of a cycle – and this ending can be a joy-filled one, a celebratory one, a gift from on high. Where bottle 9 (Mars) warned of destructive tendencies, in bottle 27 you have transformed these into creative ones. There is a kind of Leo energy about this bottle that relates to an empowered core, the might of the lion, the light-force that emanates from the centre of your being. It says you are not to be trifled with. You have courage and strength now to enjoy as you travel your path with confidence. Gone are the shocks and traumas so often associated with orange. Now you can bask in the sunshine, free of the burdens you have carried in the past. This bottle shows you that it is possible to transmute all you have been through and gain the benefits of all you have learned. It takes you to a place where you can stand on a platform of solid gold and shine your creative light out for all to see, transcend your previous limitations, and reawaken to the intensely joyful light that is the very essence of your being.

Bottle 27 Story: Melissie

A friend of a friend borrowed a set of bottles for her child who lay dying of cancer. The bottles were set up in her room, and every day she chose the one that called to her. She would hold it while her mother read the words, and then she would keep it under her pillow where it brought peace to them both. The day before she died, she woke up and said she could only see one bottle: No. 27. This bottle says that finally your time for reaping the harvest has come. Everything you have sowed is now coming to fruition. It might seem a strange choice for a dying child, but the little girl was completely sure about it. With a beaming smile she said to her mother: "Look Mum, it says my time has come. Finally, my time has come!" And everything in both the mother and the child knew that the next event would be joyous and on-purpose, exactly as it was meant to be. The next day she died very peacefully, still clutching the bottle.

Bottle 27 Story: Joanne Arjoon, Canada, joannearjoon@gmail.com

I had issues with my menstrual cycle for over 20 years. Using birth control to regulate my cycle was a 'normal' way of life. I tried multiple times to stop using birth control and allow it to happen naturally but I was never successful. Being new to Colour Mirrors, I decided to get into a bath and resolve it. For my second bath ever, I selected the Harvest bottle to work through this block. I slept with the bottle for two days and was overwhelmed with feelings of bliss, power and bounty.

Within seven days of my bath I came to the realisation that with all the external facets of my life that I had tried to control I had 'failed'. I had internalised it all and punished myself. Shock, traumas, low self-esteem and addictions all kept coming up. Forgiveness was the heart of the matter. I felt such a huge sense of peace once I started my journey of forgiveness. In turn my menstrual cycle got back on track. I now have a regular cycle and have been medication-free for over two and a half years. My body loves it. More importantly, I love my body.

Bottle 28: New Beginnings (Yellow/Pale Turquoise)

More than any other, this bottle is about a new beginning. These colours indicate that the door is finally opening in a very real and accessible way to a new era of happiness and sunshine. This bottle relates to the goddess Lakshmi who brings good fortune in her wake and whose message is to love your life right. You cannot fight or panic it into being better, you can only love it into joy. These colours bring trust, laughter and a sense of fun, and as there is nothing that will bring about a new beginning faster than joy, this bottle will help you create the reality that serves you best. Stop worrying – everything is going to be fine.

Bottle 27 (Harvest) is about completing a cycle and reaping the rewards of all you have sown. The bright, sparkling energy of this next bottle, No. 28, signals doors and windows being thrown open, spring and sunshine entering your life, a new phase, a new beginning. You can start afresh now with the knowledge that everything is working out. This bottle is the harbinger of good times ahead and the potential for peace and pleasure in your life.

Bottle 28 has the joyful, laughing, summery quality of holidays, sunlight on water, children playing on the beach, fun times. With these colours you cannot help but acknowledge that happiness is what makes the world go around, that indeed happiness is the energy with which you can move mountains – because you no longer perceive them as mountains! The goddess Lakshmi overlights this bottle. She blesses you with abundance and the knowledge that every possible good thing is available to you. All you have to do now is be open to receive it.

This bottle asks you to play, have fun, laugh and enjoy – and not take anything too seriously. With its yellow top fraction, joy is clearly in evidence, while the turquoise underneath says you can trust that all is unfolding perfectly. This bottle brings ease and lightness and a truly refreshing sense of letting go of the past. It says now is the perfect time to move into a new space, a new place, a new job, a new relationship, a new way of being – any or all of the above – with a quick and light step.

Bottle 28 often acts as a confirmation. You may already know that you are in or approaching a time of new beginnings, and when bottle 28 calls and you connect with its name and its meaning, this knowledge begins to feel solid, reliable and real. These colours bring a sense of peace and contentment, clarity and connection. Now you can watch things really start to fall into place. Yet although a new beginning is often exactly what you desire, it may still call up your demons and engage your fears: "Will I be asked to change? Will I have to stop hiding? Will I be able to move into this new phase in my life and not fall back into my old patterns?" This gentle bottle of love, sunshine and flow helps ease your fears and bring back the joy and excitement of the new.

Bottle 28 adds a boost of light and energy to your journey back towards the light. Ascension, or spiritual evolution, is about lifting yourself out of 3D's heavy, dense, low vibration into the lightness and brightness of a higher frequency. We tend to say that Ascension is a by-product of joy – because when you are in a state of blissful love for every moment, you cannot help but lift the energy for yourself and for everyone. This bottle is a tangible key to Ascension, as it shifts your vibration out of fear and into joy – which has to be one of the biggest and best 'new beginnings' anyone could have!

This bottle relates to a new beginning for you on a personal level, but it also reflects the sun shining on Atlantis – a reconnection with the Golden Age of Atlantis when all knew themselves to be Divine beings of love and joy. This bottle signifies that it is time to reclaim your power from those lifetimes and remember that in your essence you are creative Divine light.

There is a new beginning happening on earth now as humanity summons the energy of a Golden Age once more. Whether you are consciously aware of it or not, you are part of that. You may have a specific role to play in teaching others how to lighten their vibration and live more joyful lives. You may be a way-shower, demonstrating through your actions, words and energy how to live in the flow of Divine faith and trust. You may facilitate new beginnings for people through your creative gifts and talents. You may simply light up a room when you enter it, or leave a wave of peace and light in your wake as you pass someone on the street. However it emerges through you, know that you have the capacity to touch people as you open to a new, more aware, more present and connected state of being.

One of the core gifts of this bottle is to remind you that you can have a fresh start every day and every moment if you choose. It calls you to stand on the golden sand, feel the sun on your skin, take a big breath and enter the waters. Whether you tentatively dip your toes or dive in without hesitation, this bottle assures you of the full knowing and faith that it will be an amazing ride. It also promises to hold your hand until you get to that point of readiness and stay beside you as you enter this exciting new time in your life.

Bottle 28 Story: Shirley Archibald, UK, www.shirleyarchibald.co.uk

When I used the New Beginnings bottle I had a violent reaction, developing food poisoning, but within a week the house move I'd been waiting for went through. It also kick-started a major new personal way of living. It shook things up and made me look at my life differently. It gave me a new sense of liberation and a growing sense of oneness with myself.

Bottle 28 Story: Alka Dharam, UK, www. www.lifecentredhealing.co.uk

This is what came for me as I bathed in bottle 28: I feel as if I am deep in the sea, swimming, sun above and water below. I am flowing. Lord Krishna appears and says: "Be like the reed, the flute, so that spirit can breathe through you. See how I blow." He blows through and I am pummelled way over, and then he blows softly and I am floating easily. I feel as if the past does not exist and has never existed. There is only the now, only the experience. The feeling is to go with the flow, wherever I am taken, being hollow like the flute so that life can breathe through me.

Bottle 28 Story: Clara Apollo, UK, www.claraapollo.com

Bottle 28 has been a favourite for many years, as turquoise and yellow is a colour combination that I love. I recently noticed something in my bottle 28 on the surface between the colours. There was a blob – of tiny proportions, but nevertheless a blob. Looking through a handy magnifying glass, I became enthralled with the structure of this blob. What was it illustrating to me?

Initially it was shaped like a plastic bag in water, or a jellyfish, then the shading and vein-like patterns revealed a shrouded/veiled head, a sacred face. Was this Mary, with such peace and such calm, accepting love? Wow! I communed with her for several breaths. What would she look like from the other side of the bottle? Here the shape looked more veiny and had a snout, like a micro-anteater. I felt strange looking at it. Turning the bottle to view from the side, the light hit the colours and they turned reddish as the shape began to move. All of a sudden it popped and shocked me. What?? I tipped the bottle back a bit and yes, there it still was, a beautiful explosion of tiny patterns, fronds and shapes, parting company until they disappeared. Yes, gone; no trace at all.

I gazed down through the magnifying glass, wondering what that was all about. It seemed that my observation and curiosity really had affected the process. I then read up on bottle 28 from the website and smiled as the goddess Lakshmi had the final word: I had just chosen a Lakshmi card at random from an oracle card deck. Boom! I knew then that new beginnings of abundance were afoot.

Six months later this astonishing magic was revealed when a place that I was house-sitting at then became my home for a much longer spell. A year on, I am deeply into reading the wisdom of Mary Magdalene and her call for me to come home to my own heart, my truth, my innate wisdom. Externally, all the main areas of my life are on the rise, for which I am ever great-full.

Bottle 29: Grace Under Pressure (Deep Turquoise/Deep Magenta)

This vibration carries the heaviest lessons of all. This is the path of the master. You will only do life in this way if you have chosen a path of accelerated healing and learning. This is the choice of the Olympic spiritual athlete. The way has been immeasurably difficult, but the outcome will be as magnificent as the journey was hard. Only those who are serious about their spiritual service and their journey towards the light will choose this path. You are back to help humanity so that it does not make the same mistakes again. Clear the past, which is based on self-judgement, and release yourself. It is time to turn the corner, stop the suffering and reap the rewards of this incredible journey. Your higher self and your angels know who you are, and you are deeply loved and supported. Honour yourself for your choices. This has been a difficult path, as you have had to lose everything to gain everything and more. Step into grace. All the debts are paid and you are free.

The light touch we saw in bottle 28 (New Beginnings), the skipping, joyous play-time of sunshine and laughter, settles in bottle 29 into something much deeper and more serious. This bottle has gravitas, weight and depth. It speaks of a battle hard-won, a path littered with obstacles, a journey to the very edge of yourself and beyond. Even its turquoise top fraction is dense, almost impenetrable. The faith is there all right, but this bottle suggests it has been one hell of a journey to reach it. If you are choosing this bottle you know what it means to be overwhelmed with challenges and difficulties, and while you have worked hard to hold on to your light and your God-given grace, the pressure has at times been intense.

The choice of bottle 29 is often a recognition of what has gone before, and part of the 'grace' of this bottle is to help you realise that it is time to put the struggle down, let it go and move on. Struggle is the energy of resistance and fight – an 'anti' energy. Bottle 29 offers you a chance to move from 'against' and struggle, to 'for' and flow. This bottle often comes like the lifting of a huge weight. It shows you how to smooth out the path and find a simpler route. It stops you from treading old, worn-out, unhelpful tracks. Now you no longer have to toil and tussle but can truly step into grace.

This bottle has helped so many people give up old and heavy ways of doing life, and it is surprisingly often chosen by young people, who find its message and its colours deeply reassuring. It lightens the load and relieves you of the pressure you have allowed to be your companion, making way instead for realisations, insights and a new and wiser self so that you can continue the journey with an altogether lighter step. It brings relief when you are tired of the stress and strain of holding on and supports you in letting go of endless effort and exertion.

Magenta is the colour of your inner Divine light, and turquoise relates to expression from the heart. Together they shine with artistic brilliance and power. When this bottle finds its way into your hands, you are ready to take yourself seriously as a spiritual being and become the artist and creator of your life. You are willing to recognise that every step along the way was perfect and that there really were no mistakes. You begin to realise that your soul brought you the exact experiences required to match your inner calls for growth. You discover that you were loved, seen, acknowledged and held by the Divine all along.

The difficulties of the journey have shaped and formed you into who you are – have, in fact, been a necessary part of your path towards mastery. This is reflected in the bottle's numbers, 2 + 9, which add up to 11, a master number. Like bottle 11 (Duality), bottle 29 relates to Chiron, the wounded healer, which indicates that a huge part of your journey has been to gain courage, strength and wisdom so that you might share it with others. Bottle 29 is the bottle of the spiritual teacher, one who has 'been there' and can hold a space of love and compassion for those who are facing obstacles and difficulties. If this is your bottle, you have much to offer the world. Your greatest gift to humanity is to have been through the dark times and come through them with your light intact.

The turquoise in bottle 29 helps you trust in Divine love so that you can forge ahead on your path, knowing that whatever lies ahead, you will be guided, loved and supported. In this bottle, magenta – which has been in the top 'conscious' fraction of various bottles in the system up to now – comes to sit solidly in the depths. This smoky, melting, mesmerising hue asks you to recognise that the Divine loves every bit of you, all the way down to your toes. It dares you to finally immerse yourself in Divine love, pour its message into and onto your body, claim it as who you are, and let it infuse deeply into your cells, your heart and your bones. No matter how difficult the story of your life, no matter how relentless the trials of the journey, Divine is who you are, right to your very core. You cannot *not* be Divine, for you are made up of the same particles of love with which the universe was woven. This bottle's message is that there is no separation – and there never was.

The depth of Divine love the universe holds for you is beyond question. It is solid, real, a foundation on which to base your life. Bottle 29 says you can count on Divine love; in fact, the more you do so, the more it can show up in every aspect of your life. Grace is ever-present, is indeed the universe's gift to you in every moment. This bottle asks you to recognise that every second of your life is quite literally filled with grace and that it cannot be otherwise. This bottle is your acknowledgement that the Divine has been with you – and within you – every step of the way.

Bottle 29 Story: Melissie

A young girl of 13 had been handed around her mum's druggy boyfriends and didn't know if she was pregnant or had AIDS. She chose one magenta bottle after another, but bottle 29 was the one she wanted to hold on to more than any of the others. These were really heavy bottles for a young person, but I felt I would just carry on and explain her choices anyway. So I told this child what magenta was about – that it was Divine love, that it was the energy of a healer, that it was about giving service and supporting others, that it was bringing spirit and truth into the things we do, that it was changing pain into love and happiness.

At the end of it all I looked at her and asked if she'd understood any of it. To my astonishment she replied: "I absolutely understood it. I know more than anybody my age because of the journey I've had. I am a healer and I am a spiritual person, and if you want to get fit you walk around the block, but if you want to be an Olympic athlete you train for 10 hours a day."

Bottle 29 Story: Korani

A woman came to a Colour Mirrors workshop when she was at a crossroads in every way in her life and unclear about everything. She chose this bottle to take home and bathe in, and when she came back to the workshop the next day she described herself as feeling like a newborn baby, clear and light, free of the burdens she had been carrying. Even her skin was like that of a young child and she said she felt immeasurably softer both inside and outside than she had before.

Bottle 29 Story: Irena, Slovenia

After the Colour Mirrors gathering in Slovenia in 2010 I chose bottle 29, as it attracted me the most. In my childhood I had a problem with my father's absence and my mother's lack of understanding. Bottle 29 brought an enlightenment to me. When I took a bath, I felt the presence of an unknown energy in the bathroom. It protected me, and today I know that this was the energy which helped my emotional healing process. The next day Moira explained to me that bottle 29 was the energy of Chiron. In astrology Chiron represents the area connected with great suffering, vulnerability and emotional traumas. I cut the karmic ties of suffering (with the help of bottle 7, Neptune, also).

At that time Melissie told me that my new journey would begin, towards the light and full of love, and this still lasts now. I cleared my mind with the wisdom which my Colour Mirrors teacher, Tadeja, shared with me: only a person who has suffered a lot can appreciate light and become a light. And when this person receives love, he/she recognises it, acknowledges it and shares it further.

Bottle 30: Creativity (Deep Turquoise/Pale Turquoise)

This bottle is related to writers and artists who need time by themselves to let their creativity grow. Give yourself the space to let your imagination expand and flourish, and become the creator of your own life. You are gifted in the arts and a wise counsellor. Unfortunately people often want too much from you, so make space for yourself. Learn to fill your own cup so that it might overflow into the world. Set boundaries to your space and time and do something creative, for that is how you feed your soul. Do not let yourself get over-stressed or you will be flirting with burnout.

Bottle 30 is a gleaming, glowing power-ball. It is a step up and out from the deeply sombre energy of bottle 29 (Grace Under Pressure), and it invites you to open your heart and your being to let the creative tide flow through you. Turquoise is the blue of the throat chakra, your communicative centre, married to the green of your heart centre. This is where you can express what you feel, and trust that you are safe to do so. Bottle 30's shiny turquoise light glides in to wherever you need it most, prising open your tightly shut defences and softening you in the process.

Turquoise is the colour of the higher heart chakra, which is a more refined energy than is associated with the physical or emotional heart. The higher heart is located in the space between your throat chakra and your heart chakra and refers to the sacred or spiritual heart. It is where you connect with unity consciousness and know yourself to be an integral part of all life. It is where you 'feel' your connection with the sacred and the Divine.

The higher heart connects who you are with how you present yourself to others. As this centre opens and expands, you become more willing to show your face to the world, and we have noticed that bottle 30 can be especially helpful for skin problems, particularly for those who dislike being seen. The number 30 reduces to 3 (3 + 0 = 3), and there is an echo here of the message in bottle 3 (Jupiter) that it is time to stand up and let the world see the real you. With the help of these bottles, the barriers you have put up can now come down.

Bottle 30 surges with life and mirrors the creative life force within you. It is a clarion call from your precious heart, inviting you to sing or dance, wander or play, doodle or draw, idle or dream. It beckons you to a waiting canvas, a pen and paper, a musical instrument, a walk in nature. It originally carried the name of 'Loner' and suggests the type of alone time that will feed your creative soul, such as long solitary walks by the sea or time spent in places of peace and tranquillity. It calls you to steep yourself in the kind of solitude and connection to Source that cracks your creative heart wide open. The loner here is not lonely. This bottle is about choosing to take time on your own to find the truth of your connection with spirit, love, nature and your creative potential.

This turquoise bottle combines brilliance with coolness and brings incisive clarity, insight and thought. It is a great friend when your creative well has run dry. This is the bottle for unblocking the dam, opening the channel, rooting out the doubts, releasing the flow. Turquoise is the colour of feelings – and what enables you to allow, express and actually feel all your feelings more than your creativity?

As you tune in ever more deeply with your creative soul, you are able to bring forth into the physical that which was only ever in spirit, heart or mind before. This is not just the joy of the creative flow for its own sake – although it can be exactly that. It is also the power to bring into tangible form your ideas, dreams and inspirations. This bottle encourages you to be a visionary, to live your creativity, to form, shape and mould your desires in whichever ways most appeal to you. This flow is not just for the artist, writer or musician. It is for everyone, gathering the collective creative force and opening the door to new ideas to help take humanity forward. Bottle 30 enables you to find your unique place within the greater tapestry as you discover your talents and your ability to innovate, invent and inspire.

There is, however, a strong warning in this bottle's message. It is a reminder that when you long for space and time to do what you most love in the world, such longing is a heart-call, a soul-call – perhaps even a wake-up call. It warns that you may be in danger of going under if you carry on as you are and asks you to stop, lift your head up, look around, get clear on who you are and discover what is most important to you. It asks you to recognise that you are a creative being first and foremost and that space and time just to be, to feed your creativity, is no longer a nicety – it is a necessity.

The complementary colour to turquoise is coral, and coral reflects all the ways you find it hard to love, honour and accept yourself. You may block up your creative flow out of a misguided belief that it is 'selfish'. You may constantly feel there is no time for you to get creative because you are so busy taking care of everyone else's needs. You may hide from your creative calling because you know deep down that it is going to bring buried feelings to the fore. Whatever the reason, if you are prone to putting everything ahead of your own desire to create, this bottle will pull you up short and put you on notice: this is going to have to change.

Bottle 30 is a balm whenever you let your creative light become smothered by shoulds, musts and oughts or the busyness of daily life. It calls you to down tools and walk away from life as you know it, even for a day, even for an hour – but to do it often. It asks you to take time to listen to the pure current of creativity that is always running through the cosmos and through your soul. The message of this bottle is to let that current in and immerse yourself in it. By filling yourself with the sustaining life-giving potency of your creativity you access a well-spring of life, love and generosity which can then overflow to others. As you replenish and nourish your own creative light, it brings you the space, time and energy to share what you have and who you are. This beautiful cycle of creativity then contributes to those around you and adds more light to the planet in the process.

Bottle 30 Story: Anne, UK

The first time I met the bottles was at a Colour and Chi Kung weekend retreat run by Clara Apollo and Korani. As they introduced themselves and the workshop, my attention was slowly drawn to the rows of coloured bottles lined up in front of a large bay window. I found my eyes opening wide, as if needing to absorb as much of these intense colours as possible. Being asked to choose one bottle, I felt awkward, stripped of any logic to help me decide. I picked, almost at random, a turquoise bottle whose colour combination intrigued me.

Korani went round the group explaining the meaning behind the bottles we had each chosen. I listened with interest. She explained that my bottle was No. 30, Creativity. When she described why people choose this bottle and what it was about, I felt as if I had been punched in the heart. How had this woman, whom I had only just met, been able to look into my life, my soul and draw out my story to voice back to me? I struggled to deal with the bare, beautiful truth I had been confronted with. In the meditation that followed, tears began to roll down my face. I left to go to my room. I cried and cried. I was crying from shock. I was crying from anger at having the rug of superficial contentment pulled from under my feet. I cried with gratitude and relief as my true self was being acknowledged and allowed. I also cried because finally I knew that what had happened could not be a coincidence. It was time to acknowledge the Divine.

It is still sometimes a struggle to express my creativity, but the difference now is that I am aware of the importance of my inner voice, and I know it is worth the fight to express it. As a busy mum I have had to broaden my definition of being creative. As a college student my work was about self-expression, but I was also there to pass my degree. As a designer, I may have been hoping to brighten up people's homes, but the goal was to make a profit. Nowadays no one is going to give me marks out of 10 for brightly coloured curtains or pay me to put decorated pebbles on a beach for strangers to find, but the sense of fulfilment in my heart is reward enough.

The balance between family life and time for myself is always seeking to be redefined and sometimes delightfully overlaps. Thank you bottle No. 30 for reminding me of who I am and accompanying me on the discovery of what it means to be creative.

Bottle 31: The Hermit (Pale Green/Deep Green)

This bottle relates to the Hermit in the Tarot and is about badly needing your own space and boundaries. It indicates that you are overwhelmed with life's responsibilities and need time out to rest and reflect. When life has presented you with challenges, it helps you stop and go within so that you can integrate the lessons you have learned. This bottle is about being able to function at the deepest levels from your heart, in the sense of making a difference in the world. If this gift is blocked or unexpressed, however, it could easily turn into martyrdom. Learn to be at peace in your own space rather than craving what others appear to have. No one has more than you. Green relates to the earth as well as the human heart chakra. As you heal your heart, you heal the earth. You have a deep connection with the earth and the devic realms. Everything you touch will grow.

Bottle 31 is about giving yourself space: space to be, space to stop and rest, space to attune to your inner light. It is about taking the opportunity to integrate what has gone before, and allowing the creativity that began to flower in the previous bottle to come to fruition. But where bottle 30 (Creativity) was a warning to take time out to feed your creative soul, bottle 31 says you have already pushed yourself beyond your limits. You are in desperate need of space and time for yourself. Green is to do with boundaries, and this bottle says yours may have been stretched almost beyond endurance. When bottle 31 calls it is often because there are too many demands on your time or too many people who want too much from you. Its message is that you cannot carry on indefinitely or you will be heading for overwhelm.

This is where you close the door, switch off your phone, unplug from the collective insanity of the 'real world' and open up to a deep connection with your heart. It is time for tapping into the silence, for embracing the stillness, and this is no longer just something to wish for – it is essential.

When choosing this bottle you may feel weighed down by the heaviness of duty, responsibilities and obligations. There is often disquiet, unease and a sense of inner conflict. This arises when what you love to be and do is at odds with what you *think* you should be and do, or when the way you are conducting your life is at variance with your deep inner truth. There is more than a hint of martyr energy in bottle 31. Martyrdom essentially means being inauthentic, living according to someone else's truth – and although this makes you angry, as a martyr you will suppress and bury that anger. This can lead to depression or passive-aggressive behaviour as you try to come to terms with being someone or something you are not. Bottle 31 indicates that over-giving to others has left your well dried-up. When you give from a place of 'having to' or duty rather than a heart-felt call to service, this may leave you feeling numb, tired and resentful.

Green's complementary colour is red, and the deep green of this bottle reflects some deep red issues, which is why the victim/martyr pattern often shows up. As you tune in to this green bottle, be willing to explore red issues such as anger and frustration as they come to the surface. There may have been difficult, even hideous experiences in your past, and indeed this bottle can indicate a past life of being burnt as a witch. Your body holds fear, anger and martyrdom from that lifetime when you were massively misunderstood and punished for being 'different'. This may explain, at least in part, why in this current lifetime you have chosen to hide yourself away or deny the true 'you'. Bottle 31 now asks if you will let your past define you, or if is it time to finally make peace with your experiences. This bottle gives you a fresh space to find out what makes you who you are, beyond anything that has 'happened' to you in this lifetime or any other.

Choosing bottle 31 means that you are quite possibly exhausted, craving for peace, longing for space. You may be desperate for respite from the unrelenting busyness and stress of your life and the clamouring thoughts in your head. This bottle asks you to look at why you might be unwilling to allow yourself the space and rest you so wish for. It asks you to consider what would happen if you were to stop and take stock, stop and spend time with yourself, stop and simply be.

Might you be faced with aspects of yourself you have been hiding from? Might you discover that while you have been so busy and concerned with everyone else and so over-ridden by others' needs, you have neglected to find out who you really are? Might you realise that others do not actually 'need' you as you have always assumed they do? Might you send the whole flimsy house of cards you have been basing your life upon tumbling down? Is it any wonder you have been avoiding asking yourself these questions?!

This forest green bottle is an opportunity to find sanctuary, a safe space to stop and go within and actually face a few of these fears. Beyond the immediate need for rest, for time out, this bottle asks you to take in the wider implications of its message. You are being given a clear and powerful opportunity to reassess your life and everything in it. It is time to address the fundamental who, what, where, when, how and why questions of your life. This bottle's name is the Hermit, and if we look at the archetype of the hermit, he is the one who goes into the silence of the cave and opens himself to the truth he holds within. The Tarot card with this name shows a man with a lamp emerging from a cave.

The hermit's message is to give yourself space and time to go deeply into your inner landscape and unearth the wisdom and insights that await you there. When you are willing to do this you can emerge into the world, just like the hermit, with an inner light that is so much brighter than you could access before. You can then share with others what you have learned and be of true service because your offerings come from a full and replenished heart. When you give to and honour yourself you pave the way to give to and honour others from a place of authentic truth. This rich green bottle holds the space for you to discover your inner wholeness. It offers you the possibility of finding a way to live that feeds and nurtures the real you. It enables you to share your gifts with others from a heart-space that feels entirely natural, easy and joyful. When you emerge from your cave after the inner transformation has taken place, you may just find new and exciting paths opening before you.

Because it relates to Uranus and bottle 4 (3 + 1 = 4), bottle 31 supports you in leaving behind what no longer fits. It nudges you to find out who you are when all the roles, responsibilities and 'musts' have been weeded out. It helps you decide what in your life is working and what is not. It aids you in discovering a space to live and be that truly works for you. It guides you to tune into the truth of your ever-loving, ever-waiting heart.

When you fully live from your heart, red and green come into balance. Your energy levels soar and you are totally *in* your life, joyously engaging with it, all the while listening to and honouring your inner truth. If this is your bottle, you have a beautiful loving heart and a desire to help others. As you learn to live from your truth you will find you can give and support from a place of balance and integrity – without giving yourself away too.

While we recommend bathing in any bottle that you are particularly drawn to, when bottle 31 is calling your name, a long relaxing bath in its calming green oils is almost mandatory. Its message is so much about taking time to give something loving to yourself that not to do so is really to miss the point entirely! As the messages of this bottle travel right into your cells, your body will thank you for it, your mind will be given permission to let go and your soul will be overjoyed that you are willing to open to its greater wisdom.

In times of stress and overwhelm this lovely soothing bottle spreads its cool green energy through your being like a refreshing breeze, softening, widening and opening your heart. It often appeals to gardeners and those who find sanctuary, peace and contentment among the plant kingdom and the natural world. It is an invitation to take time out in nature, to go into the deep green forest – both physically and metaphorically – and find the stillness there.

This bottle reminds you that if you are willing to listen, the gentle, quiet, but insistent voice of your heart always guides you out of the maze of restriction and overwhelm onto the path of tranquillity, freedom and peace.

Bottle 31 Story: Melissie

Several times I have seen this bottle chosen by Indian women, all of whom were living with their in-laws, desperate for their own space. Each had a similar story: her mother-in-law was tormenting her mercilessly, just as she had been tormented by HER mother-in-law, in a relentless wheel of pressure, expectations, duty and obligation. This bottle says you have choices. Even if your society, family or culture would not approve, you can step off the wheel of your past programming and move into a much more authentic space.

Bottle 31 Story: Korani

Bottle 31 always reminds me of a lovely woman I knew who was the ultimate carer. She was the primary care-giver for an elderly relative who was in a wheelchair. She cared for her own elderly parents and had a couple of grown-up children who she was still caring for in many ways too. She also worked as a therapist, and her days were entirely filled with looking after others. Her habitual patterning and conditioning meant she always put others' needs before her own. She had a strong sense of duty, fed by the environment she lived in, and the conflict between who she knew herself to be – free, vast, light, an embodiment of love – and who she felt she 'ought' to be – the dutiful wife, daughter, carer, mother – sometimes overwhelmed her.

She became conscious of her patterns and beliefs, indeed she began to see them very clearly. She diligently set about overcoming them, but sadly not in time before she developed cancer and died. The sense for her was that she could only truly find the space and peace she required in this lifetime by leaving her body, but bottle 31 was a huge blessing to her and helped her immensely in the final part of her journey.

Bottle 31 Story: Lina Katrine Larsen, Denmark, www.behandler.morrayah.dk

I bathed in this bottle when I was on a course with Korani in England. It was a wonderful experience, but what I noticed was that it was difficult for me to say yes to the colour, aroma and energy it was offering me. When I lay in the bath, I felt that I had not earned the healing that was waiting for me. Then my body let go and I felt an intense energy flowing in. Before this bath I had been going through a process in my life where I had burned myself out. I did not set limits for myself, and now I had to build myself up again. This bottle helped me a lot in my healing process. When I came home to Denmark to my husband and children, I felt that I had made a healthy and loving boundary for myself. I was no longer a pleaser for all the people around me. Now I could take care of myself.

Bottle 31 Story: Amanda Ellis, UK, www.amandaellis.co.uk

This is a bottle that I come back to time and time again, whose steady presence and energy never changes. Having experienced physical, mental and emotional burnout twice in my life, this bottle is now my gauge as to whether I am approaching another dose of over-giving, over-doing and stretching myself too far. When I notice and feel its deep green, velvety richness calling me, I know I am being told to slow down, breathe, let go, unburden and stop for a while.

I will always battle workaholic tendencies – they have been with me since I was a little girl. What I have learnt over the years is that rather than trying to change basic personality traits, it is better to learn to MANAGE them. For me bottle 31 is an aid in this respect. When I have been pushing the red energy of 'go, go, go', bottle 31 reminds me to seek refuge within, recharge, take stock, listen to my body and find the more gentle, loving rhythm of life again. It never judges me or reprimands me for again over-doing it – instead its green hues say: "Come sit with me a while. Let me replenish you. Rest, and then rest again. Everything else can wait. It is you who matters now."

This is a master bottle that teaches us how to stop when we don't know how. It balances out many aspects of our being, including male and female aspects, light and dark, giving and receiving. There is safety in its green embrace, an earthiness and robustness that commands attention – and when nothing else gets you to pause, bottle 31 will. This is a lifesaver bottle that sits beside me always.

Bottle 32: Communication (Royal Blue/Olive)

This is the culmination of a difficult journey, one which began long ago. It has now come to a point where you are able to make sense of it, recognise what it has taught you and let go of the persecution you have carried from previous lifetimes. You are safe now and need no longer fear that your words will be misunderstood. Your time of being 'seen and not heard' is over – now you can speak your truth. Your viewpoint is valid, and whatever you wish to express will be received. Royal Blue is the colour of the third eye and the ability to communicate your vision, so this is the perfect time to manifest your plans. The colour olive in the depths allows you to base your decisions on the feminine wisdom you hold within. Everything you touch is turning out positively at this time.

Bottle 31 (The Hermit) took you into the cave, your inner refuge, so that you might find your truth and your light beyond roles and duties and others' expectations of you. As you emerge now, having taken stock, it is time to share your authentic voice with the world.

Bottle 32 is about communication. With its olive top fraction, it is especially linked to the communication of feminine wisdom and intuited knowledge, and it supports you in getting in touch with your true feminine power and deep inner knowing. There is a strong rational and masculine energy in royal blue, however, so here is a bottle which highlights the potential for balancing your inner, powerful, masculine authority with the softness of feminine insight and understanding.

Bottle 32's key message is that you have something valid to share and now is the time to do it. This might be a creative endeavour such as a book, poem or song. It may be a business you have dreamed of starting, where you can use your skills to share what you know and what you do best. It may be that your voice needs to be heard in a social or political arena. Perhaps you have unique knowledge, experience and wisdom to offer, or perhaps it is simply time now to share with your family, friends and colleagues who you *really* are.

For many people, particularly women, it has often felt unsafe to share who you are or what you know. It has been said that knowledge is power, but for so many women throughout so many lifetimes it has not felt safe to share knowledge or to show genuine power. If this is your bottle, whether you are male or female, you will know what it means to feel unsafe to express yourself and your wisdom, especially if you have psychic, intuitive or healing abilities. If you are drawn to this bottle, it says that the energy of persecution and suppression from past lifetimes sits buried in your cells and embedded in your psyche – and is quite likely to have shown up in some form in this lifetime too.

Bottle 32 relates to all the times you have been in trouble for what you said or saw or knew – or what others *thought* you said or saw or knew, even if this were not true. Perhaps you have been bullied for being 'different'. Perhaps as a child you picked up on unspoken feelings or were aware of energies in a way your parents were not, but when you spoke about what you could see and perceive, you were told to shut up or not to be stupid. There is a sense of betrayal of your very being in these colours. Your body holds the fear of not being believed, of being denied for your intuitive wisdom. There is a whole tapestry of fear and persecution woven into the stories revealed by this bottle: stories of 'us against them'; separation and rivalry; treachery and discrimination – and fear about what it means to be a powerful, sensitive, insightful, intuitive being.

This bottle has a strong connection to the witch hunts and the persecution of women that occurred over a long period of history. It also holds the guilt of the times you spoke up and others suffered because of it – and the guilt, buried in your cells, of the times you were not persecuted, but persecutor. As a soul learning about every aspect of life and the universe, you have been on both sides of every story. If you have been on the receiving end of persecution in this lifetime or another, you can be sure you have also been the one doing the persecuting at some point in the course of your many lifetimes – and that can leave a powerful imprint.

When bottle 32 shows up, it is time to see the higher view more clearly. It is time to bring to light all the unconscious beliefs that have kept you from feeling safe. It is time to be genuine, frank, honest and true; it is time to stop hiding and fearing. If you have been engaging in conspiracy theories about who or what is against you, now is the time to drop them. Life is *for* you and always has been. Every single person and circumstance in every lifetime was only ever there to bring you closer to your true Divine self and to love.

With its royal blue top fraction, bottle 32 has an association with its numerological 'mirror', bottle 23 (Initiation). Could it be that if you have experienced persecution in any form, it was actually a kind of initiation? Initiations are always part of the journey to get you back to your light, back to your truth, back to a place of authentic power so that you might stand up to be seen and share who you are. On a human level this might be hard to take in, especially when you are in fear. Yet what if any form of persecution was an experience chosen by your soul – that aspect of yourself which has always known that you are Divine – in order to learn and evolve?

Any initiatory experience is a pathway designed to help you discover more of yourself and open you to qualities you may not have known you possessed, such as courage, resilience and compassion. What if the experience that felt so painful was actually a means of experiencing the opposite of your truth, so that you might come to know exactly what your truth is and claim it more consciously and fully? Part of any soul's growth is to have an experience, learn from it and share what you have learned. If you have been through the terrors of persecution, does this not enable you to be deeply supportive of others when they too experience it?

Bottle 32 helps you stand on equal terms with everyone and everything in your life, and the gift in this bottle is that it shows you that the time for persecution is over. You can now choose to know and express yourself without the need to have such experiences. This bottle helps you get the message, right into your cells, that it is safe to speak your truth and share your love and your light. Now is the time to tap into all the wisdom and knowledge you hold and take your message out into the world. Royal blue is protective, and olive is soft and nurturing. Olive is also hope for the future and brings in the new and the energy of spring. Together these colours provide a potent antidote to all that has gone before. It is time for your wise, intuitive self to emerge into the bright light of day.

The complementary colours to royal blue and olive are gold and magenta, and because complementary colours often reveal a deeper truth, what this bottle demonstrates is the potential for Buddhic Bliss (bottle 19 – solid gold/magenta). When you reclaim your intuition and feminine power and finally let go of any shame, blame or guilt about being the powerful, insightful and wise being you are, the bliss and light of a new golden era becomes available to you.

Those on a spiritual path often speak about the necessity of being open to receive; this bottle shows you what might be possible if you were to open to being received. Where fear and past experiences may have shut down your willingness to be visible on the planet, now you can communicate the truth and the light of all that you are and know that it – and you – will be received.

Bottle 32 Story: Lesley McDonald, UK, www.lesleytara.com

In my experience, bottle 32 is very often chosen by those who do not yet quite trust their own truth. This bottle is always such lovely confirmation that they can just open their mouths and trust what comes out because they are speaking from the heart. I always feel it is such a practical, honest combination.

I remember a lady chose it who was having a real fear of applying for a promotion, as she did not always agree with her boss or the way he made decisions. When we looked into it, she realised that she did not trust her own truth. She was afraid that if she spoke up at the interview as herself – rather than adhere to the strategy of the corporate model they wanted her to go along with – she might not get the job. These colours empowered her to speak up anyway, to trust her own truth and vision for the future of the company. Her vision came from her heart and yet was very practical and sensible.

I don't know if she got the job, and in the end she told me she didn't care whether she did or not. Her joy came from realising that she could trust her heart's knowing and speak up with confidence and trust in her own vision.

Bottle 32 Story: Catherine Ashworth, UK

This is an 'aaah!!!' bottle. The green is from the heart, solid, dense, very grounding – and there's no messing with the two colours together. This bottle is really what I needed to ground me solidly into my whole being, knowing that everything would be taken care of. It feels like new shoots are appearing now, offering gifts of lots of surprises that have been waiting in the undergrowth.

It feels like I am clearing away all the dead foliage, all the rubbish that was heaped on me for years and years, thus leaving me feeling strong enough to show the world who I really am. I know that there are still dark areas of the undergrowth to be cleared that will be dissolved with the colours as I go along.

I take absolute pride in myself for taking all the steps in assuring that the darkness will have to come out into the light, no matter what, however long it takes. I am no longer prepared to carry the garbage of the past and I want my body, mind and spirit to hear this. I am no longer my past. My future is the light, wherever I go or whatever I do for the rest of my life.

I thank my parents for all that happened, for I have learnt so much and it has made me into the person that I am today. I also thank my sibling and all the relationships that I have been in. Everything that has happened had to happen the way it did in order to get to where I am today. And if I can take the responsibility to ensure that I deal with my issues so that I can be free from the shackles of the past, so can others. I wanted so badly to be free that I went the extra mile to get it. And even though I am so sensitive and get triggered, I know that I have the strength, courage and will to do this work that was handed to me even before I was born, in order to break the cycle for future generations.

Colour Mirrors has revealed so much to me. How can anyone not want to know themselves, be authentic, speak their truth and let out what is in their heart? This bottle has opened a part of me that was so fearful of speaking up as a child that it was like a mouse. I had to say YES, knowing full well that I meant NO, otherwise I would be beaten up, and I had to save my own skin from further damage.

I can now look back, and see how far I have come and the future looks brighter and lighter. Thank you.

Bottle 33: Love and Magic (Pale Pink/Rose Pink)

Venus watches over this bottle and comes in bringing gifts of love, magic, money and creativity. The number 33 is a master number that carries the vibration of harmony, romance and success. This is a divinely blessed time for you. Pink is the colour of unconditional love and self-acceptance, and your ability to love yourself is your greatest gift or lesson. Everything you experience is only a reflection of what you believe you deserve. Change your mind about yourself and your whole reality will change. Love yourself and your whole universe will conspire to prove how right you are. In the pink you will find the road to tranquility and harmony in body, mind and soul.

The previous few bottles in the system are quite tough. Their messages are uncompromising, especially if you have been resisting life, resisting love, resisting the universe. Bottle 33 helps you slip gently into the love and magic of life again, restoring you to happiness, harmony and wonder. It helps you remember that you are a vessel of love, and as you relax into this truth, all manner of things become available: love in relationship, loving friendships, the love of the universe, sweet abundant love – all there ready and waiting for you the moment you look in the mirror and truly, deeply love who you see.

With its rose pink base, this bottle offers a divinely loving foundation from which to create a life of magic. Its message is that everything is part of the perfection of the Divine – including you – and if you are not yet ready to hear this, it will support you until you are. Bottle 33 is the one we call the Christ bottle, as it refers to Jesus/Yeshua who became 'Christed' at the age of 33. The number 33 is a master number, inviting you to open to the possibility of the same level of mastery that Christ attained. It holds the promise of the Divine love that every being on the planet carries within and asks you to be willing to fully feel it, experience it, be it and share it. This is Divine mastery embodied by the soft yet potent divinity of the rose. It is love, love and more love, and it gently encourages you to remember the beauty of your heart and find that love within.

This bottle is like a pair of rose-tinted glasses: when you embrace all the love it has to offer, suddenly the world seems more beautiful, more loving, more gentle, more magical. Yet this is no illusion: it is the love of the universe making itself known. Step into the glowing, rosy light this bottle shines on you and really feel it – the love that knows no limitations or boundaries. Let your body get the message right to the tips of your toes, into every cell and atom of your being. As you do so, you may just find that you become that love – and attract it right back to you. If you have been seeking a loving partnership, this bottle shows you that it is just a perceptual shift away. New relationships may materialise, or the relationships you already have may subtly change into something altogether more harmonious and supportive.

Pink not only relates to how much love you are willing to receive but also to how much money you are able to welcome into your life. This bottle can help you take your relationship with money to another level: *"Change your mind about yourself and your whole reality will change."* This bottle holds no space for denial, limitation or rules. It shows you where you have been holding back and denying yourself rather than giving to and celebrating yourself. Bottle 33 is entirely about love – abundant, unconditional, all-encompassing love. It asks what would happen if you dared to change your mind about life, about money, about love, about giving, about receiving. What would happen if you were willing to have it all? Be it all?

This bottle reminds you that to have anything, you must first be aligned with it. When you welcome love, you receive it bountifully. The same applies to just about anything else you might care to mention, including money – which is just the energy of love by a different name. This bottle also brings a sparkling element of magic into your life, which means that seemingly impossible things can happen. The more you let yourself fall into the love and magic held in this potent bottle, the more the universe can shower you with its blessings.

In fulsome, unapologetic pink, this bottle relates strongly to babies, children and mothers. It helps you connect with your inner child and your inner mother, inviting you to explore your feelings about both. It provides wonderful support to anyone who is pregnant or wishing for a child. It creates a love-filled environment for those going through a birthing process, whether of an actual child or a project. It also brings love and support to those who are holding on to trauma about being adopted.

Sharon King is a specialist in helping people change and heal their birth story. Sharon has always related to this bottle on a personal level and it has also been highly influential in her work, as so much of what she does is about bringing both love and magic back into people's lives. Even her business is called Magical New Beginnings. (See Sharon's bottle 33 story below). What Sharon has found over and over again is that as the birth story changes, lives change. A baby in the womb is a conscious being, experiencing all that its mother goes through as she adjusts to the idea of becoming a mother. The baby – wide open, innocent and highly receptive – picks up on all her fears and joys, all her feelings, thoughts and beliefs. Bottle 33 can be hugely supportive, helping you release these imprints and creating a shift in perception. What appeared to be traumatic or difficult can be revealed as the gift of love between souls that it always was.

It is in the womb where the love and the magic that create new life are found. This bottle is about all the potential and possibility you held as you entered into life. It is a kind of re-birth, where you come face to face with the truth of your divinely loving and beloved essence and begin to find, feel and experience that love for yourself, perhaps for the first time. It is about allowing the love and magic of who you really are – the perfect expression of love – to flow through your entire life: past, present and future.

Bottle 33 is a big one because when you finally get its message, you realise that who you are has always been based on love. You realise that you are the power in your own life – and that power *is* love.

Bottle 33 Story: Melissie

Many years ago when Colour Mirrors had just begun, I was living at a friend's house and making bottles from the boot of my car when another friend called in. Amazed by the bottles, she asked me what they were, so I gave her a reading and she ended up taking bottle 33 home with her. She worked freelance and was suffering all kinds of financial problems – the flow kept blocking up.

A few weeks later she phoned me and asked to go out for a walk, so off we went, and I asked her if she had used her bottle. She said yes, she'd used it a while back, and started talking about all the business that had been pouring in ever since. I said something to her about how there seems to be a funny thing that happens with pink and money. As I said this we both looked up, and the whole sky turned the pinkest pink that either of us had ever seen – little fluffy clouds which all turned shimmering pink. We walked round the whole of the village under this bright pink sky and both felt that this was the beginning of something huge.

From that moment onwards, everything started to change for both of us. Colour Mirrors began to grow and find its feet, and for my friend, business bloomed to the point where she became quite blasé about not needing to do what she was doing any more and began to pursue some of the things she really wanted to do.

At certain times of the year I again see sunsets in those exact colours, and when I do it is always a sign of something shifting and that magic is afoot. Every time, a magical event happens in my life. I love and totally trust the colours of bottle 33 wherever they show themselves.

Bottle 33 Story: Sharon King, UK, www.magicalnewbeginnings.com

On the day I finished creating the website for my business, the bottom fraction of my bottle 33 changed colour to turquoise (the same turquoise as bottle 28, New Beginnings). The turquoise not only helped me confirm the name for my business but also gave me confidence about stepping out as a teacher. It was a very powerful confirmation, especially as I was still a little unsure whether to use the full name 'Magical New Beginnings' instead of just 'New Beginnings'. It was as if bottle 33 was saying "you need the love and magic in there" – and at the time I was signing off my emails 'love and magic' too.

Bottle 33 Story: Lucy Byng, UK, www.lucybyng.com

I bathed in bottle 33, Love and Magic. Whilst running the bath I couldn't decide whether to put on music or not but eventually decided to bathe in silence. Just as I was about to place my foot into the bath I heard music from my adjoining bedroom. Curious, I returned to the bedroom; the music was simple single notes. Not the radio, not the TV not my iPad… What was it? As I approached my dressing table I realised that it had come from my jewellery box, a box with a music key which could be wound from underneath, a box that I had not wound up for years – so long, in fact, that I had forgotten that it had ever played.

Feeling amazed and amused, I decided to turn on the music on my iPad, as I presumed that I had been instructed to do so. I then stepped into my bath. As I lay there I listened to my 'Om' playlist through all 6 tracks. As the playlist ended I made to leave the bath when another track began to play, one I had never heard before – one that took me by surprise. I lay there, too shocked to move, and listened. The words were so beautiful and deeply touching. Remembering some of the words, I was able to find the song by searching the internet – it is called 'In Dreams' by Jai-Jagdeesh, and the lyrics were so perfect and so apt for bottle 33 that I could hardly believe it.

Bottle 34: The Whale (Deep Turquoise/Blue)

When you choose this bottle it signifies that the difficulties are coming to an end. It is a fresh start and the birth of something new and precious. There may even be something of a surprise in store. These colours are about a shift in consciousness where you are asked to finally have complete faith that you are on purpose, in line with the greater will and perfectly on track. It is time to take stock of the past and only take with you that which will serve you in the future. There is no time for blaming or resenting. If you open instead to gratitude, this will activate your higher heart centre and connect you to the information and wisdom of everything that exists. Turquoise is faith and blue is peace, and in these colours you can find all the answers to follow your true calling with ease and grace. At the time this bottle was created, Melissie saw a baby whale being born so close to her that she could have touched it.

From bottle 33's light-infused and joyful love, bottle 34 now takes you into the deeper realms of the ocean and the cetacean kingdom: the wisdom, light and power of the whales and dolphins. With the turquoise of the sea in the top of this bottle and its deep royal blue base, there is a sense of mystery, power and potential, inviting you to enter the unknown in a state of innocence and open awareness. This is where possibilities abound. If you have been closing yourself off, shuttering your consciousness, blocking your capacity to receive the wisdom and blessings of the universe, the Whale bottle asks you to remember that you are vast and powerful, unlimited by space, time and third-dimensional versions of 'reality'. It asks you not to resist but to allow, not to struggle but to flow, not to fight but to surrender.

This bottle is very much about the new time we are in on the planet, this time of expansion and awakening and global connection. Royal blue relates to the communication and expression of your visions and to your perceptive centre, the third eye. Turquoise is about communication, the internet, knowledge and flow and it is centred in the higher heart, the chakra located between the blue of the throat and the green of the heart. This is where you open to receiving and communicating essential spiritual information for this new era on the earth, and bottle 34 allows you to expand your awareness beyond perceived limits and move into a vaster vision for yourself and the greater whole. This is where the Golden Age on earth reveals itself as you envision it.

In a powerful meditation during their training, Colour Mirrors practitioners are taken to meet a whale right up close and look into her eye. For many, this is profound. Whales hold incredible wisdom and unconditional love, and one of their great blessings is to transmit those energies to you when you are ready to receive them. If you are fortunate enough to spend time in the presence of whales you will find that they communicate their energy and love in a very tangible way. It is as though they speak directly to your heart, inviting you to make the shift into a higher level of consciousness. Of course you do not need to be in their physical presence to feel their power. You can tap into their energy any time – and this bottle invites you to do just that.

Whales and dolphins also transmit frequencies that you may not necessarily understand with your conscious mind but which tap into the Akashic Records – the etheric records of everything that ever was, is now and ever will be. The cetaceans are record keepers, holding ancient and future information until such time as humanity is ready to hold their own true light. Now is that time. By choosing this bottle you are signalling your intention to be part of the conscious awakening on the planet, and it will help you find your own unique part to play in this evolutionary process.

Bottle 34 holds the depth and tranquillity of the ocean and a spacious, timeless serenity. It relates to Neptune, bottle 7 (3 + 4 = 7) and invites you to swim out into the deep blue sea and float there, letting the water soothe and calm you, bringing you to stillness, bringing you to surrender, bringing you to peace. This is a time for pause and reflection before you move ahead on your path. This bottle offers you the space to decide what you will take with you and what you are ready to leave behind, what will serve you and what is no longer necessary or useful. There is a sense of taking stock, taking time out to get clear, setting yourself free and then, when the time is right, watching your path unfurl before you in complete faith and trust.

The colours of royal blue and turquoise together indicate that you have an ability with words, especially in written form, but whales also remind you of how to communicate without words. This bottle is about being able to tune in with currents and vibrations and the essence of what is being communicated, and to receive without thinking or analysing. It also connects you with the traumas and shocks that happened when you were pre-verbal, before you had language to speak about them. This bottle helps you heal these issues and release them from your system. One of our Colour Mirrors practitioners reported taking this bottle into a regression healing session that she received from a fellow therapist. She found herself making noises not unlike whale song as the traumas were released from her body.

Bottle 34 has a strong connection with the healing of wounds. Whatever type of wound you believe you have – physical, emotional or spiritual – this bottle helps because it goes beyond any kind of story about what might have happened or been done 'to' you. It taps you into the pure power of love, wisdom and compassion that the whales hold. It reminds you that you too hold these qualities and that no story has more power than you do. It shows you that every wound is simply another opportunity to heal the story, bring love into your body and being, and open your heart to the Divine grace and serenity that is being held out to you.

This bottle is a great support for people going through taxing times. It says yes, the climb has been tough, but you are nearly there. If you take one more step you will be at the top, and the view will make it all worthwhile.

Bottle 34 Story: Korani

I remember a man who came to a talk I gave about Colour Mirrors. He had not experienced energy or healing or anything overtly 'spiritual' before and wasn't sure why he had come to the talk. Interestingly, when I asked if anyone wanted to choose a bottle he was the first to raise his hand. He went to the display of bottles and chose bottle 34 without hesitation. I asked him how he felt about it, and his response was that he just really liked it, he didn't know why. I explained a little about the bottle, that it related to the ending of a difficult time and that there was hope on the horizon. He was visibly touched by this, and it turned out he had been struggling with serious addictions and had recently started attending a rehabilitation programme. He was also shocked and delighted when he realised that it was number 34, as that was his age at the time.

Bottle 34 Story: Moira Bush, Canada, www.moirabush.com

This bottle of faith and life purpose came after I had been through an arduous journey of many years of darkness yet sensed I had a light switch in me somewhere. After leaving South Africa financially wiped out, I returned to visit after three years and arrived at Melissie's house. Feeling the old emotional bruises, I said: "I have to have a blue bottle – now." She tried to give me a few of the blue bottles in the system and I kept saying: "No, not that one, it is something else." She disappeared into her laboratory and came out with a specially made bottle, a combination of blue and turquoise – I literally grabbed it and ran upstairs to the shower and poured the entire contents over me. I knew I would never be the same again; something had switched on inside of me.

At the end of my stay, after dropping me at the airport, Melissie happened to stop by the coast. She joined a group of three people who told her that three whales had just dived. Soon a baby whale popped up. Melissie said she got that my blue bottle had to be part of the system: there were three people then she made four; there were three whales and baby made four – and this was to be bottle number 34. This bottle is also the number of my soul path, 34/7.

Bottle 35: The Inner Guide (Blue-Lilac/Pale Green)

This bottle is a peace-bringer, gently sending its harmonious light into any area of your life that is calling for it, from your relationships to your home to your work. It gifts your communications with the energy of peace and helps clear any issues of sibling rivalry. Its message is that when sibling rivalry has ended, when there are no more internal conflicts playing out as external battles, then there will be peace on this planet. This bottle's name is 'The Inner Guide' because peace has always been the inner guidance of each human. If you stay still long enough you will hear the inner guidance that leads you to peace on all levels.

Bottle 34 (The Whale) signalled the ending of a difficult time and re-attuned you to your inner flow so that you might move forward with greater ease. Bottle 35 comes in now offering a sense of gentle freedom, spacious awareness and stillness from which new possibilities can arise. It draws you into a state of peaceful calm, a resting place after your toils. It ushers in change on an inner level, helping you shift hardened beliefs and fixed, rigid viewpoints into something much softer, more simple and expansive.

Bottle 35 emerged after a Colour Mirrors workshop in South Korea where almost everyone in the group chose bottle 32 (Communication) at some point. Bottle 32's colours are darker, deeper versions of the pale and gentle colours of bottle 35, and it is strongly linked with the theme of persecution. Issues of persecution and rivalry have always loomed large in Korea, with a strong North/South divide and a history of being caught in the middle of other country's wars. As they taught the workshop Melissie and Moira experienced the energy of sibling rivalry, with each student trying to out-do and out-shine the other. As if to highlight the issue there was even another colour system being taught in the room next door to their workshop!

Bottle 35 was created in loving response to the energy of sibling rivalry. It was named 'The Inner Guide' after the Colour Mirrors centre belonging to Premjay and Ananya, who hosted the workshop in Korea. This bottle opens up the possibility of a different way forward for humanity. Extreme sibling rivalry can only happen when we forget that we are all one family on this earth. Wars and persecution can only happen when we forget that we are all brothers and sisters. It will come as no surprise then, that when you choose this bottle it asks you to look closely at any unresolved issues you may have with a sibling. This might be an actual sibling, anyone in your life who plays a 'sibling' role, such as a colleague or friend, or anyone who presses your buttons.

Bottle 35 offers resolution to the energy of conflict, whether that conflict is with another or with warring aspects of yourself. Internal conflict often shows up as difficulties with another person, as the outer world reflects the inner plane. This bottle shines light into any discord, dispute or rivalry you may be experiencing. It helps you root out any circumstance or situation in which you feel invalidated for who you are and what you stand for. Bottle 35 helps you begin to see it all from a higher perspective, to see it all as perfection unfolding rather than as something being wrong. You come to understand that your 'sibling' is simply showing you something that is unresolved within you and that this is an opportunity to learn and grow.

This bottle was born out of conflict and rivalry, yet it is the very balm that will help heal those aspects within yourself. It highlights where you continue to commit to struggle, to fighting, to frustration and envy, and guides you gently into the still waters of peace, where none of these things make sense any more. Bottle 35 helps you let go of your points of view about not being or having enough, about superiority and inferiority, about mine versus yours – all of which are ultimately based in fear. When you live in struggle and confusion, everyone and everything becomes a potential threat, a potential enemy, a potential challenge. When you move into peace, that heightened state of tension begins to dissolve. When you fight with your inner knowing you may end up in conflict, chaos and difficulty. When you follow it, your own innate guidance will always lead you towards expansion, greater possibilities, enhanced opportunities – and peace.

This bottle can show up if you are experiencing serious money challenges. The number 35 reduces to 8 (3 + 5 = 8), which relates to the violet No. 8 bottle (Saturn). Violet is the colour of spirituality, whereas the colour most often associated with money is red. These two colours are at opposite ends of the colour spectrum and highlight the illusion of separation between spirit and matter. Bottle 35, as a number 8, can bring up old fears and conditioning about having money while also being spiritual. One of the blessings of this bottle is that it helps you go beyond apparent separation to a higher, more expanded view. As you realise that matter and money are simply energy, you find a loosening of your fears and blocks taking place. Money becomes part of the oneness, no longer separate from spirit. As 8 is also the number of infinity, power and abundance, there is the potential here to completely shift your perspective and your financial reality.

Bottle 35 invites you to sink into its quiet embrace where all is one and differences are part of the beauty of life rather than something to be afraid of. Holding this bottle in your hands, you may feel time slowing down as everything becomes concentrated into a ball of pure, still, potential. Feel as your heartbeat also slows down, and your body responds to the call to go within and find there the space and peace you have been seeking. From this place there is no desire for battle, no heart for division and separation. From this space you can attune to your inner guide, that part of you that has never known separation, that has always been 'plugged in' to the universe. Your inner guide has been with you since time began and is with you still. When this bottle comes calling, it is a clear message to tap into that source of inner wisdom and follow where it leads.

The Transformation of Bottle 35

In 2007 bottle 35 underwent a change in colour after Premjay came to South Africa from Korea, and told Melissie: "Since you made that bottle, we have not stopped struggling." In an effort to understand this and to clear the issue, Melissie told him to go and pour three bottle 35's out on Table Mountain – seen by some as the base chakra of the planet. By the time he came down from the mountain, all the bottle 35's Melissie had left in her house had changed colour: the top fraction had gone from pale blue to a soft blue-lilac. At the same time, several Colour Mirrors teachers and practitioners around the globe reported this same colour change in their bottle No. 35.

The original colours of blue and green still held some of the conflict and separation energy seen in bottle 32. As the light was shone upon those issues, the struggle Premjay and his colleagues had experienced was brought to the surface. As he symbolically released the struggle the energy changed and lilac came to join the blue, bringing the light of spirit to transform and enlighten the blockages and difficulties.

What is fascinating, beyond the fact that this colour change happened at all, is that the next bottle to arrive in the system, bottle 36 (The Gateway), is exactly the blue-lilac colour that the upper fraction of bottle 35 turned into. Perhaps bottle 35 is in some way a key to entering the gateway. Perhaps as each finds peace and stillness within, this is in itself a gateway to a new reality on the earth where peace is the foundation upon which all life is based.

Bottle 35 Story: Dr Anne Whitehouse, UK, www.feminineconfidence.com

I had gone to a healing fair with the intention of having a colour reading. When I got there I saw all the Colour Mirrors bottles laid out on the table, but really I could only see bottle 35. I couldn't take my eyes off it. I remember walking up and down as an excuse to keep passing the table to see that bottle. I had the reading – which was amazing – and went home, then found myself going back to the fair to ask for the bottle to be ordered for me. I simply had to have it.

A few days later, my bottle 35 arrived. My whole life I had been fighting with myself to such an extent that there really were two voices in my head: the scientific, logical side and the musician, artist, healer side. There was a constant struggle for control, and I was always arguing with myself. There was huge conflict inside. I used the bottle in the bath, and to my amazement felt what I can only describe as a pinpoint of energy like a spark inside my brain. It started whizzing backwards and forwards, zig-zagging between the two hemispheres of my brain, over and over again at lightning speed for several minutes. I was very surprised by this but didn't at the time see what it had done.

The next day, however, I was walking down the street when I suddenly realised that the two voices in my head had gone and had been replaced with one voice. It was not until that moment that I truly realised I had really been two people all my life. From that day onwards, the internal battle has just evaporated and I am one. It was also at that point that my life purpose and direction became crystal clear. I have had a number of life-changing experiences with the bottles since then, but I can honestly say that this first experience with bottle 35 was the most profound.

Bottle 35 Story: Raluca Rusu, Switzerland, www.facebook.com/RalucaRusu.colours

During a very conflictual period with my twin sister she used to wear these colours. Visiting friends one day who have a nephew and a niece, these colours came out again: the boy was very jealous for the attention given almost exclusively to his sister. He was wearing these colours.

Bottle 35 Story: Client of Rui Diogo, Portugal, www.facebook.com/kaleidosol

My whole life was lived with the feeling that I was not good enough, a feeling that no matter how hard I tried I would never be able to satisfy ... but who? Myself? During the reading with Rui Diogo this bottle appeared, and I realised that I was in permanent competitiveness with my only brother because he was older than I was, as if I needed to prove to my parents that I deserved my place and that I too was perfect. This bottle helped me understand that he was just my brother and that my parents loved me and that the lesson was to know how to love rather than fight.

Bottle 36: The Gateway (Blue-Lilac/Blue-Lilac)

The number 36 reduces to 9, which carries the energy of completion. This bottle symbolises the ending of a cycle in your life. It is time to step through the gateway into a new way of being and doing. This gateway leads to a new landscape where your old fears and negativities no longer exist. The pale blue-lilac of this bottle helps you speak your soul's truth. It taps into the 'peace that passes all understanding' and helps you find that peace within you. Whatever chaos is going on around you, you will know it as an illusion and not need to be part of it. Once you have stepped through the gateway the old world will never look the same again.

Life is full of gateways. Every day you face them as you make choices in your life – to do this rather than that, go here rather than there, say this rather than that, be yourself or play a role. Some gateways are obvious: every birth or death you encounter, every relationship that begins or ends, every time you move house, every new job or career change you make. Each opportunity that presents itself does so as a form of gateway. Others are less apparent – you simply have the sense that you are in transition, about to move from one space in your life to another or embark on a journey of some sort, and you know that things are in the process of changing.

Especially with the 'big' gateways in your life, you may not always willingly go through the door – sometimes you are pushed, sometimes pulled – but when you do, you can be sure that change will come with you. Going through gateways can be utterly exhilarating and empowering, and it can also bring up your fears: "What will it be like? Do I have what it takes? What will be expected of me? Who will I be once I cross that threshold? Will I survive?"

When you are facing challenges and feel unsure which way to turn, this bottle can soften the sharp edges of your apparent dilemma. It invites you to drop any judgement about whatever is happening in your life and let it be just as it is. As you relax and come into stillness, you begin to see your choices laid out more clearly. Bottle 36 helps you surrender, enabling you to let go and flow to where your Divine self takes you rather than battling your way through the gates. It reminds you of easier ways to do things and the possibility of peace as you travel your path. Struggle can be released, simplicity embraced. You are shown that every experience in life is about choices and that every choice is simply an experience, neither right nor wrong.

The Gateway bottle reminds you of the cyclical nature of life, inviting you through new doors even as old ones close behind you. It guides you to move forward with curiosity and openness rather than fear, to enter the gateway willingly with eyes open and heart engaged, ready for whatever awaits you on the other side. As you do so, this bottle supports you in your transition and helps you enjoy the ride.

Bottle 36 is the culmination of the journey laid out by the first 35 bottles in the system. It heralds the possibility of total transformation as you move through the gateway to find a new world awaiting you. The colour of this bottle embraces you in its soft, pearly tranquillity, dissolving your fears and leading you gently into peace.

The unique blue-lilac of bottle 36 has no exact complementary colour, yet it feels closely aligned with the gold of authentic power. What you may discover with this Gateway bottle is that it works both ways – it may help you claim your true Divine power so that you are ready to venture through the gateway, or it might help you pass through the gateway so that, as a result, you discover your true power. Either way, this bottle signals completion and change and is an empowering ally for both.

The Gateway is a bottle of alchemical magic that is, for many people, an experience beyond words. It takes you by the hand and leads you past your mind and into your heart, into your spirit, into the wide blue-lilac yonder. It is so peace-filled that you cannot remain turbulent around it for long. Spending time with this bottle can downshift your mind into quiet mode, opening you to the softer, more expansive awareness of a meditative state. As your mind quietens, your Divine self is more able to transmit its light and energy to you. New possibilities arise. New information can be absorbed. You may even feel a desire to slumber as you hold this bottle or sit with it. If you do drift into sleep or deep meditation, as you awaken or come back to conscious awareness of your surroundings, you may notice that your fears, doubts and struggles have melted away. You may find that you have already slipped gently through the gateway in the easiest possible way.

Pre-Platinum Portal

Though we could not know it at the time, bottle 36 pre-figured the Platinum Gaia range that would arrive some years later. Its message is somewhat different, yet it has a similar colour and energy to bottle G19 (Om), which is platinum top and bottom. With its soft, smoky glow, this Gateway bottle invites you in, draws you to its utterly peaceful blue-lilac haze. And almost before you know it, you are offered a doorway to something that is altogether new and yet seems the most natural thing in the world.

While bottle 36 can be utterly practical, acting as a support and guide through the transitions and changes that feature in your life, its kinship with the Platinums shows most in this bottle's other-worldly, almost ethereal nature. It seems to offer a path 'home', to guide you towards a serenity and expansiveness that is not often experienced on this planet, opening you to something much greater than the limitations your mind would have you believe in. If you are ready, this Gateway bottle can act as an inter-dimensional portal, taking you beyond the world of your senses into the rich vastness of your cosmic self. It can be a gateway to awareness, an opening to the limitlessness of all life and a doorway to possibilities. It facilitates the expression of you as part of the Divine, helping you recognise that you are both unique and infinite, and that you are intimately connected with everything and everyone in the cosmos.

Bottle 36 Story: Melissie

More than any other in the system – apart from bottle G19 – this bottle represents me. It is beyond anything my favourite colour, and when I made it I suddenly looked at the rest of the bottles and thought: "Why do they have to exist?!" For me this one really was perfection.

At the time it was created I was being asked about legal contracts and recipes for the bottles and what would happen if I died. I suddenly realised that if I did die there was nothing in the system that actually reflected me, and I realised that I had to be in it. This bottle and the platinums really are me – these are my colours.

I have always had a very powerful connection with the being known as Melchizedek, and every time I see him in meditation I see him as this blue-lilac colour, but I never really spoke about my connection with him until just after bottle 36 was born. Korani, Moira and Amanda were with me at the time, and Korani asked me where the system came from, what its source was. I was astonished because no one had ever asked me that before. I thought for a minute and then I said: "Feel this," and I tuned into the light that is Melchizedek. They were all nearly knocked out by the energy! When I connect with that energy it fills me with profound, flowing power. When I look with that energy I can see the soul quality of others, and it is always so gloriously beautiful that it takes my breath away. It was only after I made this bottle that I began to really acknowledge the profound connection the Melchizedek energy has with me and with the system.

Bottle 36 Story: Jackie Tweedie, UK, www.jackietweedie.com

For me this bottle is like an experience of pure peace: the calm after the storm, the sunshine after the rain, that delicious feeling of relaxation just before you fall asleep. The blue-lilac speaks to me of a bliss into which my body wants to melt and swim away.

As the name implies, this peace is available when you step into a new behaviour or habit and leave an old one behind. Moving from the familiar into the unknown is never easy, but this bottle provides all the support required to guide you on that journey. Once through the gateway there is no turning back – but why would we want to? The peace on the other side is the prize we earn by recognising the end of that cycle and releasing all the old stories and drama. And if we can't identify what we need to move on from, the colours will always show us the way.

For me it was when I discovered that my Gateway bottle had changed colour that I became curious. The blue-lilac colour had changed to light turquoise, signifying that the red had been drained out of it. I asked: "What pattern/habit in my life has been using up that 'red' energy? What cycle needs to end and what new life am I being called to step into?" It didn't take long for me see it.

When both of my aged parents developed dementia, I stepped in to take care of them so they could stay in their own home. As the only self-employed relative, I told myself I had no choice and that I was the best person for the job. But after three years that sacrifice made me feel first like a martyr and then a victim – unsupported and exhausted.

Fortunately the turquoise colour I was left with in this bottle had a message of its own: to learn to speak from my heart, be easier on myself, listen to my intuition and trust. So I did all that, took a deep breath, and asked this bottle to guide me. I found I was able to voice my feelings to the family, and instead of resentment, I felt a resourcefulness coming through that helped me research other options.

I selected a professional live-in carer to take my place and did the necessary work (soul-searching) to finally let go. I took a deep breath and stepped through the gateway. The real exhaustion I had been suppressing out of necessity then came out fully, but the peace that I gained as a result was delicious and supportive.

Finally an end to an ancient victim/rescuer/persecutor cycle and a new beginning for me to explore my new role as a full time Clarity/Colour coach. Interestingly, thanks to this bottle's powerful message and my inspired action, I find I am actually more available to love and nurture my parents from this new place because I can also now love and nurture myself.

The Chakra Set: Introduction

Bottles C1-C15

The first 36 bottles take you on a powerful journey into your psyche, your emotions, your experiences, the stuff of your life – all of it mirrored and revealed by the colours and colour combinations in the bottles. The next set of bottles in the Colour Mirrors system explores how your physical body interacts with your mind, emotions and spirit.

Our ancient eastern forbears divided the body into specific centres called chakras. The Sanskrit word chakra translates as 'wheel of light', which perfectly describes the spinning vortices of energy running down the central column of the body. Although chakras are essentially energy, they each connect to a specific area of your physical body. They also each have particular emotions, characteristics, qualities – and colours – associated with them.

The seven main chakras relate to the colours of the rainbow, with red at the base of the spine, orange at the sacrum, yellow at the solar plexus, green at the heart, blue at the throat, indigo between the eyebrows and violet at the crown of the head. The eighth chakra, or 'soul star', is located above the crown and is magenta in colour. This chakra is the link between your physical self and your soul or higher self.

Colour Mirrors has 15 chakra bottles to support you in healing and balancing your body and each of your energy centres. The first seven bottles (C1-C7) contain the traditional colours associated with each chakra and address the key issues and patterns that may arise in that chakra during life on earth. Each bottle also contains the next colour on the colour wheel, so the red bottle has coral in the top fraction, the orange has gold, the yellow has olive and so on. This is a way of visually representing the idea that on humanity's journey to higher levels of consciousness the chakra colours are changing, with each chakra becoming a rainbow, capable of holding every colour. The colours of these bottles therefore help you prepare for a time when there will no longer be a need to differentiate separate chakras and separate chakra colours, a time when body and soul will act in unison and all aspects of your being will be harmoniously integrated.

The Colour Mirrors system contains further chakra bottles designed to help your entire body and being evolve as you move closer to this capacity to hold every colour in every energy centre. While the system acknowledges the traditional chakra colours and contains a bottle for each one, it also has a second bottle, a second set of colours for each of the seven main chakras. These more 'enlightened' versions of each of the chakra colours provide a hugely powerful and graphic colour representation of your journey, from unconscious patterning to conscious awareness and choice. Bottles C9-C15 show what is possible when you have cleared, healed and released the blocks from the main chakras, revealing your potential as an awakened being.

When you identify an issue in any given chakra, it may serve you to read about and work with both of the chakra bottles that relate to it. You can support yourself further by using the Colour Mirrors essences in the same colours as the chakra bottles. Together they will take you on an empowering journey out of struggle into a greater level of awareness and freedom.

The only chakra bottle in the range that is not one of a pair is bottle C8, the central bottle of the chakra set. This is the Soul Star bottle, the magenta energy that emanates from the eighth chakra located above the crown. This is where your soul guides you lovingly and ceaselessly at all times from a state of pure Divine love. It has no need of a transitional colour, connecting as it already does right into the Source of all light.

The Chakra Colours and the Spiritual Principles of Colour

Chakras and Colour

Dividing the body into specific colours means that it is very easy to see which areas of the body your colour choices relate to. If your bottle choices contain a lot of green, for example, you are likely to be experiencing heart issues. These might be physical heart problems or emotional challenges such as a relationship causing difficulties. Looking at each chakra through the lens of colour helps you find what you are holding on to in your body and where those blocks are presenting themselves. Colour helps you identify and then begin to shift the psychological, emotional and physical aspects of those challenges so that you can free yourself from the patterns and issues that have been keeping you stuck.

In the Colour Mirrors system, however, colour is not just about helping you release your blockages and heal your issues. It is also a potent tool to guide you towards a life of greater consciousness and joy. The teachings of Colour Mirrors encompass powerful spiritual insights, and we find it is this information that draws many to the system. Colour Mirrors offers the possibility of exploring, explaining and embracing life in ways that are simple, straightforward and clear, yet incredibly expansive and liberating. Colour can be used to bring your body and your spirit together, to free one while engaging with the other. Colour Mirrors teaches, above all, that body and spirit are not separate but intricately interwoven as part of a greater whole.

Eight Spiritual Principles

Overlighting the Colour Mirrors system are eight key spiritual principles linked with eight core colours, one for each of the seven major chakras and an eighth for the soul star chakra above the crown. Although none of these principles is necessarily unique to Colour Mirrors, what is perhaps distinctive is the way in which colour illuminates them. Connecting spiritual principles to colour makes them accessible and heartfelt rather than just intellectual concepts. With colour you are given the opportunity to experience them in your body, in ways that are physical and 'real' and incredibly powerful for both your spiritual journey and your everyday life. Many healing techniques and energy products offer shifts at a mental, emotional and spiritual level, yet it is in the physical aspect of your being – your body – that so many issues are housed and stuck. With actual physical substances that you can see, smell, touch and immerse your body in, Colour Mirrors bottles offer potent and tangible tools to support you in embodying your spirit.

The spiritual principles that overlight the Colour Mirrors system are:

1. Judge nothing
2. Forgive everyone
3. Claim your authentic power
4. Love (everyone including yourself)
5. Everything is perfect
6. Hold a clear vision of perfection
7. You are God in a body
8. Guilt is the biggest misunderstanding of all

The order of the eight spiritual principles is deliberate. The first principle leads directly to the second, which leads to the third and so on. The first principle asks you to 'judge nothing'. Judgements sit in the colour red and the base chakra, also known as the root chakra. Judgements truly are the 'root' of all other issues you may face in life. It is impossible to fully move into higher frequencies while you are mired in the low vibration of judgement. All of the chakras and their corresponding spiritual principles, however, give you opportunities to find your way back to the infinite being you really are. When you are truly able to 'live' any one of the principles, everything else will follow. If you cease to be in judgement, forgiveness is natural. If you know that you are God in a body, love automatically flows from you to everyone. If you claim your authentic power, you have no need of guilt and see the perfection in everything. And so it goes.

Because most on this planet are still playing at being human and therefore limited in some way or another, there are not many souls who have fully managed this – yet. But as you get clearer, free yourself from your issues and awaken more and more to your Divine potential, you will find that this powerful system and its principles are a key to immense happiness, peace, fulfilment, wonder, joy and possibility.

The chakra bottles, their colours and their spiritual messages offer a simple system for helping you identify where you are preventing yourself from living heaven on earth in your body and your reality – and the tools to help you change that. The spiritual principles all essentially guide you to the same place, where you can look at everything and say "this is perfect" – no matter how it presents itself. As you recognise that everything in your life has taken you to this moment, to being exactly who you are, with all the wisdom and learning you now hold, you begin to appreciate that every bit of it was perfection unfolding.

Chakra Balancing

The move from the traditional chakra colours represented by bottles C1-C7 to the higher vibrational colours of bottles C9-C15 is a progression from old, limiting behaviours and thought patterns to a new state of awareness, expanded consciousness, open-heartedness and possibility.

One powerful and effective method for using the Chakra set of Colour Mirrors bottles is chakra balancing. In this process, which is demonstrated and taught in the Colour Mirrors practitioner training course, the traditional coloured chakra bottles (C1-C7) are placed on the corresponding chakra of the body, one after another, with pauses between each bottle for any responses to arise. Sometimes this first set of bottles can bring up big emotions and fear, even shaking and trembling, as shock and trauma arise from the body and are released.

When the person's body has settled, these bottles are then replaced one by one with the newer, higher vibrational colours (C9-C15). The magenta Soul Star bottle, C8, remains in place above the crown throughout the process, anchoring the soul's energy. We also recommend a copper Gaia bottle at the feet to hold a safe and grounded space and to anchor the person's energy firmly into the earth while this powerful process unfolds. Colour Mirrors essences can also be used to great effect in helping to move stuck energies and generally facilitate the balancing process.

It is always astonishing to witness what happens during chakra balancing. We have noticed time and again that as the higher vibrational bottles are placed on the person's body they inevitably relax, and their energy field softens and expands. Many sigh or smile. Some go into altered states of consciousness or even receive visions. A comment we often hear when people experience these bottles is how 'natural' they feel, how light, how blissful. Your body has been waiting for you to catch up with it. It has always known that you are light in a physical form and that the old, dense stories revealed by the traditional colours are simply that – stories. They were all just experiences that have enabled you to play at being limited and small. All the while, your body has held the truth buried within. These higher vibrational colours allow you to remember that truth and integrate it, by reconnecting body, heart and soul and opening you to an expanded awareness of the powerful being of light you really are.

Chakra Balancing Story: Carol Hastings, UK, www.colourvibes.co.uk

The first time I met the chakra bottles was at a Colour Mirrors workshop where my teacher placed the bottles on my body. I knew roughly where my problems were and in which chakras, but I did not expect what happened! The bottles placed on my solar plexus and sacral chakras started vibrating, so much so that it became uncomfortable. As my teacher moved bottles around and sprayed me with the Metatron essence, it gradually subsided. As to what was going on in those chakras, the bottles were spot on! I was grieving, had food intolerances and fear of being on my own.

I have since learnt how these colours can indicate digestive imbalances or eating disorders. I worked with a lady who always wore orange, yellow or green, often all together. I suspected an eating disorder and later found out that she had anorexia and had suffered sexual abuse. Looking at the complementary colours [in this case, blue, violet and red] can become the key to unlocking the blocks. These incredible bottles help so many unlock their most painful emotions and work through their issues.

Chakra Balancing Story: Stephanie B, client of Debra Hubers-Paradis, USA, www.DebrasEnergyPoints.com

After my chakra balancing I felt like I just had a deep eight-hour sleep! I felt so balanced, with a productive and focused energy flowing through me. Prior to my remote session with Debra I had a draining type of fatigue, and all I wanted to do was go to sleep. Afterwards I felt really grounded and in my body, which for me is when flow occurs, and in a flow state I can accomplish anything. During the session I experienced all kinds of sensations that weren't there prior (lots of gurgling in the stomach area). Certainly an indication that energy was moving. I felt vitalised and ready to go. How cool is that?!

The Chakra Bottles

C1-C15

Base Chakra: Bottles C1, C9 and the First Spiritual Principle – Judge Nothing

C1: Base Chakra (Coral/Red)

This bottle supports the base chakra, balancing your energies. It helps unblock this chakra from survival issues, feelings of victimhood and patterns of martyrdom. Coral is supportive when you are experiencing relationship difficulties, and red brings calm when you are angry and frustrated. This bottle can be used to boost your energy, get grounded and step into action.

The traditional colour of the base chakra is red – a colour to ground, anchor and support you as you engage with everyday life on earth. Bottle C1 is a powerful tool to assist you in connecting with your physicality so that you remember the power and positivity of being in a body. The blood red of this base chakra bottle contains all the vitality and power of a pulsating heart, vibrant with life and energy. It surges with life force and encourages motion, action and dynamism. It is also the one you may connect with when you are feeling none of these things, when you are lethargic, uninspired, weak or exhausted. This bottle can be a tonic for a tired body or a boost to flagging spirits. It re-energises you, asking you to let go of the patterns that are keeping you disconnected from life.

It is in red that you find zest for life, passion and power, ambition and action, and it is here that you begin to use your gifts and skills and your light in real, practical ways. Bottle C1 helps you claim the power of red in all its positive, fiery dynamism and vibrancy. If you are feeling floaty, ungrounded, weak-willed or unable to stay present, this bottle will help you feel strong and focused again, bringing you back into your body and setting your feet on the ground.

In the red is where you meet issues of money and your ability – or otherwise – to receive. It is where you focus on your health, body, career and finances, your place in the world and your relationships with others – all the stuff of being human. If you are struggling with any of these areas of your life, bottle C1 helps you bring conscious awareness to whatever is causing difficulties and find ways to overcome them. It can be a powerful aid to clearing financial worries and blocks, as it assists you in releasing programming that might have been installed in your subconscious for many lifetimes. After using this bottle, numerous people we know of have received unexpected financial support or the exact material resources they required as their blocks to receiving were removed.

Survival fears are often buried in the base chakra. When asked for a colour to represent safety, many people choose red. Bottle C1 relates to fundamental human survival issues such as having enough money to pay your bills, enough food and clean water to sustain your body, somewhere warm and comfortable to live and someone to love and care for you.

Even if you currently have all that you need and more, you may retain cellular memories of actual physical threat to your survival during war, famine or tyranny in this or previous lives. In addition, all your many lifetimes of *not* surviving remain deeply embedded in your body's cells. Even if you live in relative luxury this time around, you may still feel as if you always have to be careful, as if it could all be taken from you at any moment. Or you may continually worry about not having enough and thereby attract situations and events which prove that to be the case. When these fears and worries affect your everyday life, bottle C1 is a friend and support, helping you step into the deep sense of security and safety that comes from knowing you are divinely loved.

The coral in the top fraction of this bottle softens the potential violence of red, bringing compassion and gentleness into the intense red issues it addresses. It supports you in rooting out beliefs that you are somehow a victim, powerless in the face of situations, events or other people. It may stir up or bring to light buried anger and passive-aggressive tendencies. Bottle C1 asks you not to judge yourself but to see these behaviours and beliefs for the coping mechanisms they are. It helps you recognise that there are more empowered ways to behave. This bottle allows you to engage with your anger rather than hiding it. It helps you remember that you are not a victim but a powerful being of light having an experience – an experience that encourages you to grow and expand rather than fall into the small, helpless role of victim.

The First Spiritual Principle: Judge Nothing

This bottle supports your base chakra and helps you resolve your base chakra stories – loss of power, victimhood, anger, money problems, survival issues, separation – by bringing you face to face with the thing that most binds you to those stories and maintains their hold on you: your judgements.

The first spiritual principle asks you to look at your life and notice everything and everyone you are judging – yourself, others, the universe – and then notice the effects. Judgements all ultimately come from fear, and they all keep you in separation and limitation. They prevent you from recognising and knowing the Divine perfection in yourself and your life. They shut you down and keep you from loving and receiving. Judgements are also exhausting to maintain, taking up huge amounts of energy that could instead be directed towards peace, love and happiness. One of bottle C1's key gifts is to help you shift your judgements and anger so that you have energy in your body and your life once more and can discover the freedom of truly living rather than simply surviving.

When you become aware of your judgements you can bring the light of consciousness to them rather than having them control you. When you notice that it is not events, situations or people that are causing you to go into judgement but your thoughts and beliefs about them, you have the awareness required to step out of judgement and into peace. When your programmed mind tells you what to think and feel about someone or something, when your judgements make them 'wrong', you cut yourself off from the bigger – Divine – picture.

If, instead, you allow that each and every human is a powerful being of light having an experience of playing at being limited, you will swiftly find that there is simply nothing to judge. If you can recognise the Divine in yourself and every other being on the planet, and if you are willing to see through the eyes of love rather than fear, judgement becomes irrelevant. You are able to experience life in pure, present awareness – without a story attached. This brings incredible freedom and a sense of lightness to your life, where being in judgement keeps everything heavy, difficult and dark.

In truth, you are unlikely to let go of all your judgements in one fell swoop, and the key is not to judge yourself for having judgements! Notice them instead, and remember that they are simply thoughts and beliefs, not truths. When you do this, judgements can have no hold over you. If they arise, you can simply move into awareness and choose to let them go. And as your consciousness expands and your connection with your spirit grows stronger you will find that judgements take up less and less space in your life.

It is worth recognising that there is a difference between judgement and discernment. You are given the ability to discern so that you can feel whether something resonates for you or aligns with your personal truth. This is a very different energy to that of judgement, which essentially blames, shames or makes wrong. In discernment, you observe and accept 'what is', without making up a story. You are still free to take action if you feel guided to. You can still choose one path over another. You simply do so from a place of love and clarity rather than the limited viewpoint of a judgement.

You might feel there are certain things you could never stop judging, things you deeply believe to be 'wrong'. If you are able to actively look for the bigger picture in these situations and also notice how and where they trigger you, you may just find you can stop the judgement in its tracks and make a more peaceful, enlightened choice. Perhaps you can seek compassion in those instances and recognise that there is always more to any situation than you can possibly be aware of. Maybe you can choose to focus love into the experience, knowing that what you project out into the ether not only affects you but also feeds into the very matrix of the planet. Does this mean you stop yourself from feeling your feelings or suppress any emotions that arise? Definitely not. But once you have felt and acknowledged them fully, you can still choose to act from a place of higher awareness and love.

This principle holds out the shining possibility of freeing yourself from the effects of judgement. In bottle C1 you have a potent physical tool with which to immerse your body so that you can literally resolve and release your judgements right at the cellular level where they have taken root. This bottle reminds you – as every bottle in the Colour Mirrors range ultimately does – that you are an infinite Divine being who has nothing at all to fear.

Bottle C1 and this first spiritual principle ask you to look at what would happen if you truly stopped judging. Could it be that you would free yourself of survival fears, anger, blaming and disconnection? Could it be that the illusion of separation would dissolve? Could there be the potential for all to live in oneness on this planet? Is it possible that choosing to let go of your judgements could be one of the most powerful things you could ever do?

When you are drawn to bottle C1, we invite you also to read about its 'partner' bottle, C9, for further insights and information.

Bottle C1 Story: Penny Wing, Spain, www.pennywing.com

A client who was in the middle of an unpleasant divorce came for a reading. She immediately picked bottle C1, and I took her through a short meditation whilst she held the bottle and breathed in the energies. Bottle C1 can be about letting go of anger and frustration and difficulties in relationships, so I was not surprised she picked it. When we had finished the session the client told me that she had been feeling sick before we started, but as soon as she began to connect with the bottle the feeling had passed. When we looked at bottle C1 we could both see cloudy formations floating around in the top fraction of the bottle. Later that day when I looked at the bottle again it had gone back to normal!

Bottle C1 Story: Park Youngsuk, Republic of Korea, www.instagram.com/suk_colorstory

I love people and have a passion for endless study and new things that spark my curiosity, but there is a difference between learning new things and making things happen. In the past when I started something it would cause me a lot of trouble and effort. I always had a lot of difficulty starting a new job. I was the one who always had an idea but didn't act on it because of fear. Everything was a matter of my mind – fear, anxiety, avoidance. When I had difficulty with a new challenge I used bottle C1 and it got me moving. After using this bottle I began to shift. I challenged myself in a new environment, started a new area of study as well as a new job, and met new people.

Bottle C9: Base Chakra – The Lightbody (Clear/Clear)

This bottle indicates a need to make a decision in your life. It asks you to take complete responsibility for the creation of your reality. The more you do so, the more choice you will experience and the more you will discover that life can be based on joy. This bottle helps bring the light of clarity into any situation, including the struggles and suffering you have experienced. Begin to see those experiences as catalysts on your path. Let them awaken your compassion and a deeper understanding of yourself and others. When you are free of judgement you are open to joy, and it is joy that raises your vibration. This bottle helps your body understand that it is simply condensed light and that death and aging are just another set of beliefs that can be changed. This bottle is a gift to show you that you are the light and always have been. When you truly get this message in your cells, survival issues become a thing of the past. Step into the light and feel the joy.

Bottle C9 is the second of the two base chakra bottles. The first, bottle C1, holds the qualities traditionally associated with the base chakra. It asks you to look in the mirror, face your judgements and open your eyes to the places in your life where you have been feeling separate, unsafe or victimised. Now, with bottle C9, you have the opportunity to shed every 'red' issue that was highlighted in bottle C1, literally bringing the white light of the Divine right down into your body – the densest, slowest vibrating aspect of your being. Now you can shine the light upon whatever has been stored deep in your base: every bit of judgement, everywhere you have bought into separation, every last survival fear. As you move from the red of bottle C1 into the clear white light of bottle C9, you are shown what it is to be the embodiment of Divine light, a light that has congealed itself into density and physical form but which remains light nonetheless.

This bottle shifts you out of the tight spaces you inhabited in bottle C1. It helps you move from just trying to survive, to a place where you can relax into the knowing that you are completely held by the Divine and there is nothing you have to 'do' to be worthy of the universe's support. Bottle C1 is about believing you have to do it all yourself, that you are alone and life is an ongoing struggle. With bottle C9 you can fully surrender to the truth that you are part of the Allness, utterly loved and filled with the light of the Divine and therefore never alone, never apart, never shut out. Begin now to create your life from a place of joy and presence rather than fear and absence. You are ready to choose something new – and choice is exactly what this bottle is about.

Bottle C9 acts as an amplifier, intensifying whatever you are facing up to in your life and asking you to get very clear on what you have been doing that has not been serving you. It illuminates your options and helps you clear the space for new choices to emerge. It will often call when you are faced with making a key decision in your life about which way to go, which path to choose, which action to take. This bottle may seek you out when you are trying to hide the truth from yourself. Perhaps you are immersing yourself in the world of spirit and light to avoid having to make an earthly decision you would rather not face. Maybe you are running around busily so that you do not have time or space to think about the challenges ahead of you. Bottle C9 gently takes you by the hand and guides you into clarity so that you can reconnect with what is true for you and make the best decision for the situation you are in with the knowledge you have. It also reminds you that no choice is 'wrong' but simply a choice that will lead to an experience – and this is precisely what your soul came to do: experience. How you respond to the experience is up to you. As a Divine, infinite soul you are free to make new choices, have different experiences and learn from each and every one.

In its clear white light this bottle carries the entire rainbow spectrum, offering you the choice of any and every colour. Here is life in all its potential, the light that life can be based upon, the clean slate from which you can begin every moment when you loosen the bonds that your judgements have placed upon you. As you step into the light of your true beingness, you are free to ask: "What do I choose in this moment?" Each new moment is a blank canvas of white, enabling you to choose the colours you would paint upon it. With the clear light of consciousness shining into your life, you get to see clearly, choose with clarity, open to possibility. You are free to choose again and again and again to be who you really are.

As you know yourself to be Divine, right down to the very cells of your body and all the way out into the vastness of your soul, the illusions of separation that have kept you in judgement can no longer hold sway over you. In the bright clear light of true choice in every moment, all that is illusory falls away. This white light in a bottle shows that if you are willing to look in the mirror and see everyone and everything in your reality reflected there, you have the potential to literally free yourself entirely from separation. When the red and white of the two base chakra bottles are mixed together they make pink – the colour of unconditional love. When no judgement remains, you can look in the mirror and love every bit of what you see: self, other, human, Divine – all one, all perfect.

There is a wonderful sense of simplicity in bottle C9. It empties out all that you no longer require, opens up a clear new space, brings light into any murkiness you may have been experiencing and calls you back to what is core for you, what is true, what is essential. Holding or bathing in this bottle may bring stillness and a sense of timeless ease and flow, where none of the stories you saw coming to the surface in bottle C1 make sense any more. Here all is light, all is perfection, all is Divine and you are returned to the knowing of your innate innocence.

This bottle is a gift to help you remember that you are light and always have been. It reconnects you with your lightbody, the energy blueprint from which you condensed into physical form. Your lightbody is both an extension of your physical body and intricately connected with it. It is formed of the electro-magnetic matrices that feed into and support your chakra system and your body. The lightbody is just what it says: a body made of light. As you reconnect with your lightbody, you remember who you are – light made manifest in physical form. As you remember who you are, your lightbody re-ignites and grows brighter. And as you move from survival mode into light, as you move from fear of death into the joy of life, you are free to embrace clarity, simplicity and peace.

When you are drawn to bottle C9, we invite you also to read about its 'partner' bottle, C1, and the first spiritual principle: Judge nothing.

Bottle C9 Story: Melissie

A dear friend who had suffered with cancer for a long time bought a whole set of bottles and went through them one by one. Her husband looked a bit bewildered that she had spent so much on bottles, but her argument was that it was still a lot cheaper than even the cheapest chemotherapy and that it did not cause her hair to fall out or make her nauseous. Thinking that she was feeling better and that the tests would show this, she went to the doctor and found that her white blood cell count was up again, which was not a good thing. She thought that as we had said about the colour red that 'like cures like', maybe the white bottle would sort out the white blood cell count. She used three bottle C9's over the next three weeks, and when she went for another test a month later her white blood cell count had stabilised and she was fully into remission.

Bottle C9 Story: Katherine Louise Jones, UK, www.katherinelouisejones.com

I chose bottles C1 and C9 as I looked at all the fears of survival that I'd held on to. I'd been thinking about money, the pattern of 'not enough' (money) and taking responsibility for my choices rather than relying on someone else, in a childlike way, to support me. It was the victim mentality of bottle C1 that I'd been feeling trapped in. It was also a family pattern, hearing from both parents the story of 'there's not enough', and I knew I was finally ready to face this on a personal and ancestral level. I was drawn to bathe in C9 rather than C1, as it represented the age I was the year before, though I hadn't been ready to let go of this pattern at the time. By instinctively choosing C9 I was acknowledging a 'coming of age'.

[Authors' Note: The Colour Mirrors Chakra and Gaia bottles can all be linked to a number. As the first bottle following on from bottle 36, bottle C1 becomes 37, bottle C2 is 38 and so on. These can then be linked to your age. It is a fascinating exercise to work with your 'age' bottle during any given year.]

As I sat in the bath I could feel my body relaxing, gently releasing, and a deep sense of peace and stillness. I felt humble just 'being', and as the water wrapped me in a warm embrace, everything became clear! I often record what comes through, writing up the insights I receive, and this is how I experienced the energy of bottle C9:

"I can allow my body to feel the vibration of bottle C9 by simply letting go of all the fears around how to live or be physical in a third dimensional experience and shift those survival/security fears into a clearer picture: into the lightbody. This feels like a welcoming of a new way of being, into a giving and receiving way, a loving, compassionate way. I can step into that lightbody and know that the pattern and the story is just a vibration that can be released with intention.

As bottle C1 transitions into bottle C9 and we release all the fears, judgements, beliefs and patterns, we move from the inner child that 'needs' nurturing into the clarity of crystalline experience. In this place there is no sense of 'needing' anything. There is no need to 'do'. I can 'be' in this experience. I can be in this place of lovingly, gently, compassionately handing over, with a humbleness that feels very real, knowing that the support is always there, as opposed to the fear of survival where I 'think' I have to survive by myself. It's separation versus unity, duality versus oneness.

With bottle C9 it's about holding the intention and vibration with a real clear sense of completion because it's already here now. There's no going back to survival. There's no going back to fear. There's no going back to the past. It's about being present. It's about being creative in the moment and owning it. And it's absolutely coming back to knowing that I am the universe, I am creation."

What changed for me after the bath was the understanding of victim versus choice. I have found that if any survival fears come up I instantly recognise my ownership and the fact that I have a choice to shift the story. Before the bath in bottle C9 I could easily wallow in 'why is this happening to me' and the machinations of the mind. Although it is still a 'work in progress', the shift since my bottle C9 bath is to be present, reclaim my power, drop the story and understand that I have chosen the experience and continue to have a choice as my creator self.

Bottle C2: Sacral Chakra (Gold/Orange)

This bottle is beneficial for trauma, loss of power and anywhere you are feeling abused. It can also help release any challenges you are facing around sexuality. This bottle soothes fears, settles emotions and is very calming after a shock. The colours of orange and gold together help ignite your creativity and boost ideas for artistic and writing endeavours.

The sacral chakra is the seat of your creativity, your emotions, your sexual energy, your sociability and your relationship with the world. This is where you connect with others. This is your hara, a place of immense power and potential if you are willing to fully claim it in your body. Orange is the colour of pure joyful existence, expansive body bliss and potent creativity. But orange is a colour of extremes, and it also refers to every bit of shock, trauma and abuse you have ever experienced.

It is in the sacral chakra, the soft yet ultimately powerful belly of your being, that you store many of your wounds, and it is here that deeply buried traumas can wreak havoc with your emotional and physical health. The belly area of the body is deeply interconnected with your experiences of life. It is where your 'gut' feelings are housed and where vast numbers of people have physical issues such as lower back pain, digestive challenges and reproductive issues. Much of human life is traumatic on some level, from the first shock of birth, through every unpleasant or difficult experience of infancy and childhood and on into adulthood. Is it any wonder that the sacral chakra of so many people is out of balance, that there is so much dysfunction around relationships and sexuality on this planet, that so many people feel blocked creatively and emotionally?

Bottle C2 assists in the release of past traumas from your body, and its healing love can be of great comfort and support. It is helpful for any experience or situation that shocks, traumatises or otherwise jolts you out of your awareness of yourself as infinite and Divine. Shock and trauma disconnect you from your life force, your sense of security and your fundamental beingness. This orange bottle helps bring you back to your body, to the warmth and softness that lies at the core of your belly, allowing you to feel safe to be vulnerable and to be strong within that vulnerability. It helps you re-engage, reconnect, come back to yourself. Bottle C2's healing messages go directly to the root of buried traumas, bringing them to the light of awareness and surrounding them with love and acceptance. This bottle holds and nurtures you so that you feel safe enough to process your experiences and release them. It supports you in integrating all that these experiences have to share with you so that you can move forward in your life, free from the burdens of the past.

This bottle can be a huge support for children. We have heard stories of parents rubbing some onto their child's sacral area each night, to great effect. Even just having it by the bedside can be helpful. Whatever the child has perceived as shocking or traumatic, no matter how great or small, this orange oil can act as a wonderful healing balm, soothing their sacral centre and helping them feel safe. We have also found this bottle particularly helpful with animals, who often hold shock or trauma in their bodies just as humans do.

The Second Spiritual Principle: Forgive Everyone

This bottle and this colour relate to the second spiritual principle: Forgive everyone. The second spiritual principle follows directly on from the first, which asks you to 'judge nothing'. If you are a fully enlightened being who has absolutely no judgement about anything or anyone, you have no need of the second principle. Forgiveness says there is something to forgive; without judgement, there is nothing to forgive in the first place. Until you reach that nirvana, however, you will find huge freedom and release from actively forgiving those you perceive to have harmed, damaged or hurt you in any way.

When you experience any form of shock, trauma or abuse in your life, a natural tendency is to ask why you are being subjected to such things. The human perspective is that these experiences are all 'wrong' and bad. The Divine perspective is that they are all opportunities to heal, let go of judgement, free yourself from the bonds of anger and powerlessness – and learn to forgive.

The second spiritual principle asks you to observe your thoughts and feelings, to notice the stories you are telling yourself about the situations or events you have experienced as shocking or traumatic. As you do so, you will come to realise that as the observer of your thoughts and feelings, you are not your thoughts and feelings. You are, in fact, much greater than any thought, feeling or belief. As you recognise that the pain you have been experiencing is as much a result of your thoughts and beliefs as the situation or event itself, therein lies empowerment. Now you are free to choose love, acceptance and forgiveness instead of suffering. You are free to remember that there is always a higher truth to every situation. You are free to take the enlightened path by offering forgiveness to everyone. As you do so, you liberate your spirit, strengthen your light and open more fully to the clarity and wisdom of your soul. In the process, you become much more grounded in your body and your life.

When you forgive, you actively open your heart and free up your sacral chakra energy. When your relationships are healthy, your hara can be open, your creative light and your sexual energy in balance. You become clear, strong, whole and freely able to express the Divine light that you are, right here on earth. If, on the other hand, you cannot or will not forgive, if you persist in holding on to blame, judgement, rage or vengeance, this slowly dries you out, shrivels you up, cuts you off from life. Orange is the colour of fire, and the energy of fire offers you a choice: you can let it expand your light, your creativity and your passion – or you can let it consume you.

Forgiving others is not always easy, yet it is often less of a challenge than forgiving yourself. If you find you can forgive anyone but yourself, the question becomes: if all is Divine, if all is part of the interconnected web of life, how could you remain outside of it? Did you somehow get to be bigger than God?! As you come to know yourself as part of the oneness of the universe, you will realise that nothing you did or said could ever be wrong. If you triggered someone by your words or actions, you gave them an opportunity to forgive – and to grow, heal and evolve. If you did something that led to harm coming to another, what was their soul's role in the situation? Did they not also, from a higher viewpoint, agree to be part of the scenario for which you are now unable to forgive yourself? Did your soul somehow get to be bigger than theirs? No, indeed. From the Divine perspective, everything is always exactly as it is meant to be, and each soul has precisely the experiences it has requested, with the perfect opportunities to grow.

As you forgive others you set yourself free, but if all is one then just as all judgement is essentially self-judgement, all forgiveness is essentially self-forgiveness. As you forgive yourself, you reclaim your true light. As you forgive yourself, you no longer limit what you have to share with others and the world. As you forgive yourself, you are able to fully *be* yourself.

So what does it take to forgive? For most, forgiveness needs to be active. It requires a visceral, tangible shift in your body and your heart. You need to feel it in your body, know it in your mind, get it in your cells. One of the keys to forgiveness is allowing yourself to truly feel and fully express your feelings about the event, situation or person. As you actively invite those feelings to emerge and you express them, ideally in a safe and supported environment, you loosen their hold on your body and your psyche. Blue, which is the complementary colour to orange, relates to communication and expression, so there is a natural link between the shocks and traumas of the orange sacral chakra and the release of them through the blue throat chakra.

There are many powerful paths to forgiveness, and bottle C2 is one of them. For here you have a remedy that the body can see, smell and touch. As you crack open the protective shell of whatever has been keeping you bound – fear, hurt, anger, resentment – bottle C2 is there to soften the iron grip of your emotions and help you release them from your body. As you express and let go of the pent-up emotions you have been holding inside, you are free to move to a place of peace and freedom – which is the ultimate result of forgiveness.

The second spiritual principle invites you to see yourself as a powerful being of light who has chosen a specific journey and particular experiences in order to remember that you are infinite and Divine. As a Divine soul, is it possible that you have chosen difficult experiences, not because you are weak and helpless and without power, but because you are, in fact, unbelievably powerful? As you evolve on your spiritual journey, you come to see that every shock and trauma played its part in shaping and forming a pathway that can ultimately lead to bliss and potential enlightenment. As you bring awareness and true forgiveness to every experience, no matter how distressing it was at the time, as you learn to forgive yourself as much as others, as you become willing to view every situation without judgement, then you are guided ever closer to peace and wholeness. You become more accepting of life in all its fullness. You resist less, and open more to the limitless possibilities all around you. As you forgive, you let go; as you let go, you surrender; as you surrender, you fly.

When you are drawn to bottle C2, we invite you also to read about its 'partner' bottle, C10, for further insights and information.

Bottle C2 Story: Melissie

A woman had a huge fight with her son, which ended with him virtually throwing her out of his house. The woman came to me shivering and in tears, and I immediately applied some oil from bottle C2 to her feet. The result was instantaneous – the energy flowed up from her feet in a wave of extreme relaxation, moving up her legs and into her body. She started to breathe properly and then giggled as the tension left her body. She phoned her son and apologised, and he laughed, saying that in her whole life she had never apologised – and with that, the fight was over.

Bottle C2 Story: Louise K. Shaw, UK, www.louisekshaw.com

As I was sitting listening to Korani on my Colour Mirrors practitioner training course, I started to see only a hazy figure against a sea of colour coming from the bottles, which were placed in front of the window. I began to feel queasy, and it was difficult to focus on her face. Her words started to sound muffled. As my own observer of what was going on, I was confused. Perhaps I was coming down with something? Then I heard the words: "Now come and pick a bottle, and place it on your body wherever you feel it needs to be." I watched as the five other ladies in the room got up and chose their bottles. For me it felt like it was happening in slow motion. When I reached the table I was drawn to bottle C2 – the sacral chakra bottle.

As I returned to the comfort of the sofa, what followed next was anything but comfortable. As I intuitively placed the bottle on my sacral point it felt like it was burning a hole in my skin, and almost as soon as I placed it there I threw it off. What happened next I don't really know, all I remember was hearing Korani's soothing voice telling me to breathe. This striking bottle with gold above orange had opened the doorway to an event that had been so buried in my subconscious that I wasn't even aware it had happened. Yet this was the second abreaction I'd had in the past 10 months, and it was confirming what I was just piecing together.

When your body has been traumatised, for whatever reason, this will remain in your cells until you enable it to be released. I have no idea how such an innocent-looking bottle could release so much shock and pain. That's the magic of the Colour Mirrors system. It needs no explanation. It requires no scientific research to prove its effectiveness. The reaction to and subsequent healing that it produces is evidence enough.

Bottle C2 is described as being 'beneficial for trauma, loss of power and anywhere you are feeling abused'. It had called me that day because my soul knew that I was ready to face what I had unknowingly suppressed for over 40 years. This bottle allowed my body to talk to me, and now I was equipped to listen. In that moment it was like bottle C2 had given me permission to feel – because only in feeling, truly being able to connect with our emotions, are we able to heal. The Colour Mirrors system has enabled me to understand the reason for events happening in my life and to release disempowering beliefs that are no longer serving me. This is the enormous gift that each of the bottles has continually provided me with, and I'm so grateful that I'm now able to share it with my clients.

Bottle C2 Story: Jackie Tweedie, UK, www.jackietweedie.com

For me this bottle holds the key to so much that keeps us stuck. When we choose this bottle it is often a sign that there is a blockage somewhere in our life that stops the energy flowing. It's like trying to water your garden with your foot on the hose – nothing comes out!

One of my clients was an actress who literally lost her voice halfway through a play. She croaked her way to the end, but the following day she couldn't make a sound and her understudy had to step in. This was an important role for her professionally, so she came to me in search of a solution. With the guidance from this bottle she uncovered a very old memory of abuse that had been triggered by a line in the play, the revelation of which came as a complete shock. She worked through it, and within two days was back on stage in full voice, feeling stronger and more confident than ever before. The gold in the top of this bottle pointed to her authentic expression of herself and not only helped her to overcome the fear but also gave her back her power.

Bottle C10: Sacral Chakra – Suchness (Orange/Rose Pink)

Rose pink brings love into the issues of abuse to which orange relates. It puts you in a state of alignment with your soul. Your soul never thought you were abused – it knew you were in a process of learning and healing. This bottle supports creative ideas and opens you to bliss and enlightenment. Here is where you can finally be at peace with the suchness of life.

Bottle C10 is the second of the two sacral chakra bottles. The first, bottle C2, gives you the opportunity to draw out the shocks and hidden traumas that lie deeply buried inside your body and psyche, offering them up to the light of consciousness so that they might be transformed.

With warmth, vibrancy and potency, bottle C10 brings you back now to joy, openness and the wonder of life. As you let the rose pink of love soften and support you through every orange shock or trauma you have stored in your body, you begin to see them all through the lens of love. As you open to forgiveness, love and a higher perspective, you are able to look at what you have perceived as traumatic from a very different point of view. You begin to loosen your fearful grip on the stories and dramas of your life – the ones you have held on to in some measure because they have defined you, even while they have bound you up and limited you.

When you are drawn to bottle C10, it is an indicator of a profound healing shift taking place. Particularly if you have been in a dark place, this bottle offers a bold ray of hope. This powerful combination of orange and rose pink says you are now ready to move into a space of forgiveness and love rather than shock. When you are able to see every shock, difficult experience and incident of abuse as an incredible opportunity to grow, then you are claiming your true power. When you are able to see the person who abused, traumatised or shocked you as the one who loved you enough, at a soul level, to give you the opportunity to heal and evolve, then you live life from an entirely different energy altogether. Then you live from a higher, wider, broader, deeper perspective. You are not locked into a limited viewpoint or defined by an experience. Instead you are firmly grounded in your sense of yourself as an infinite being of light who can never be damaged, never be broken, never have anything 'done' to you.

When you are able to take this on board and extrapolate it to every person on the planet so that all you can see is another's light rather than their story, you pave the way for a life of extraordinary peace and joy and a profound level of mastery. You recognise again your wholeness – and that of everyone else. As you let the shocks and ordeals of your life open your sacral centre of creative life force rather than closing it down, you not only grow in your light, you also offer hope and inspiration to others. You become expansive, balanced, filled with joy and love – and radiate that out into the world.

As you forgive yourself and others, you begin to claim and love every aspect of your reality as your own creation and as you do so, your creative power surges, unleashed by your ability to love and forgive. When you choose this bottle it shows that you are ready now to take your life experiences and create from them. You are ready to claim your ability to communicate and express your own unique style in your own individual way. The creative fire of orange is now lit from the transformational power of rose pink love. When your creative passion is inspired and fuelled by love, the world becomes your oyster.

With your creative centre fully open you become an expression of love and joy through your very beingness. This is the 'suchness' to which this bottle refers. As you come to peace with everything that has gone before and open to each moment as a new moment – not one based on a previous moment, not one based on a moment that is yet to come but THIS moment, with all its unique possibilities – you become one with life. You do not seek to change the moment but to be in it, embrace it and celebrate it. There is nothing for you to do but simply *be* love, joy and creativity. And now you can share all of it with the world and live as the light that you are. Orange is the colour of bliss, and rose pink is Divine love. Together they reveal you as a being both divinely loved and divinely loving, able to take part in the dance of creation with the joy of an open heart and the peace of a balanced mind.

When you are drawn to bottle C10, we invite you also to read about its partner bottle, C2, and the second spiritual principle: Forgive everyone.

Bottle C10 Story: Penny Wing, Spain, www.pennywing.com

A client came to me for a chakra balancing session. She chose which chakra bottle to place on each chakra rather than following the regular routine of placing the base chakra bottle on the base chakra and so on. When it came to her heart chakra she chose bottle C10 – a bottle about being ready to forgive. It came to light she had left her husband years ago and also left her young son. All these years she had carried guilt about this. She started to cry and continued to do so throughout the session. Before she left we agreed she needed to forgive herself.

I did not see her again until more than a year later when she came back with her son whom she had booked in for a chakra balancing. She told me that she had cried and cried after the session but had then felt so much lighter, as if a big burden had been released. She had brought her son along for a chakra balancing as the bottles had helped her so much, and she hoped they would do the same for him. It goes without saying that they did!

Bottle C10 Story: Jackie Tweedie, UK, www.jackietweedie.com

I have worked with many survivors of abuse and they often choose this bottle (as well as C2). One lady I worked with who had experienced this kind of trauma found enormous comfort in bottle C10. Despite her young age and innocence she had blamed herself for years and saw her experience as a blight on her life. After our work together she came to see that there are no mistakes. She valued the lessons she'd learnt and the gifts of insight she had received as a result. To me bottle C10 carries such hope and possibility – a chance for healing, a future free from old trauma and a rekindling of love for the self.

Solar Plexus Chakra: Bottles C3, C11 and the Third Spiritual Principle – Claim Your Authentic Power

Bottle C3: Solar Plexus (Olive/Yellow)

This bottle is beneficial if you are experiencing fear, anxiety or confusion. It helps with focus when studying and calms your nerves in testing situations such as exams. It is supportive when you are in need of a boost or your spirits are low. This bottle helps you see where you have been giving your personal power away so that you can claim it back.

The solar plexus is the power centre of your being, a place of potent energy and light. It is also where anxiety, worry and power struggles arise. Your solar plexus is right at your core, and when it is in balance you feel clear, strong and confident. When it is out of balance for any reason, fear and stress can easily take over. When this chakra requires support, signs tend to show up in your body: you may feel a sense of constriction in the solar plexus region or anxiety and tension in your stomach; your whole body may feel tightly wound up and unable to relax. You may also feel off-kilter or even out of control in your life, and bottle C3 is deeply soothing and supportive in any of these circumstances, helping you come back to your centre.

Yellow is the colour of the intellect and the logical, rational mind, yet it is also the colour of panic and confusion. When you are 'doing' yellow you may find yourself running around in circles inside your head, and here bottle C3 can be very helpful, calming your over-thinking mind and bringing you back to a more peaceful space.

Yellow is also the colour of the ego and will, and it tends to show up when your ego is shouting loudly, when you are quick to judge, when you are stubbornly fixed on getting your own way or when you are refusing to listen to others. By the time your ego has taken hold, you will probably find stress, confusion and fear close behind. Bottle C3 can assist you in accessing whatever you need to get back on track again, whether that is information, ideas, inspiration or an openness to others' opinions. It moves you out of ego and back into a sense of your true power, where you can think without being confused and make decisions without going into fear. It is a great support for stress, anxiety and nervousness, helping you ease into a more harmonious space from which you can find the fun and joy in life again.

Bottle C3 addresses issues of control. It asks you to look at who or what you are allowing to control you – the people, behaviours, beliefs, addictions or illnesses to which you are leaking your power. It also supports you in looking at where you feel the need to control – and your fears of what will happen if you let go. When you are truly empowered – light, free and open in your solar plexus – you have no need to be 'in control'. This bottle helps you align with your soul's deeper knowing and move into trust so that you do not need to resort to addictive or controlling behaviours or allow your power to be drained by others. It supports you in finding a deeper place of self-awareness so that you can claim your own light and power.

This bottle is a guide, showing you the way back to the solar power of your being, to the lightness, joy and strength of the true solar plexus energy. It is a friend when your spirits are low. When feelings of powerlessness send you spiralling down into despair and dejection, it lifts you up and out into the light of the sun. It helps you find the brightness in your life and in yourself again, re-attuning your inner dial to self-respect. We know of people whose lives have literally changed from one thing to another after using this bottle.

Yellow relates to digestion and what you are able to take in and assimilate on all levels – physically, mentally and emotionally. Bottle C3 is a powerful support for those with eating disorders, issues around food or any kind of addiction. It reminds you of your own sense of power so that you are not as inclined to give it away to a substance, person or limiting belief. Olive relates to the liver and detoxification, and the combination of olive with yellow makes this bottle a real tonic for your body and being. It helps you look at what you are no longer able to 'stomach', both physically and emotionally, and assists you in clearing from your life whatever is detrimental to your health and well-being.

This bottle also taps in to a Cathar lifetime. Cathars were highly spiritual beings who were true alchemists, literally able to make gold. They were tortured and killed for the gold itself and quite probably for their alchemical abilities too. If you are choosing this bottle it is highly likely that you hold cellular past life memories of this particular story. Anyone who has made a lot of money and then lost it carries this imprint somewhere in their cellular memory bank, as do those who have never been able to accept that material wealth could be part of a spiritual life. If you are called to these colours of olive and yellow – or indeed if they make you feel uncomfortable – you may find that the cellular memories begin to loosen their hold after using this bottle. As you release the Cathar lifetimes from your body, the fear of being materially abundant may begin to fall away so that you can enjoy money without subconsciously pushing it away.

Whatever your struggles, bottle C3 can be a godsend when you are drifting in uncertainty, confusion, fear or unhappiness. When you have veered off course or become lost, it guides you back towards the solid ground of your true self. When you have given away or misplaced your power, this bottle helps restore your inner strength. It returns you to a sense of balanced, stable peace and gently reminds you to connect with the light you hold inside.

There is also a greater gift in bottle C3 because yellow is where Ascension begins. Ascension is the raising of your frequency to a more enlightened state, an awakening of your inner divinity and the dawning of higher consciousness. It is a process of lifting yourself beyond your perceived limitations to the absolute joy of Divine knowing. Ascension begins in yellow because it reminds you to be child-like and to engage with life in awe, wonder and innocence – which is the easiest way to raise your vibration. Bottle C3 shows you that instead of basing your life on fear, doubt and confusion, you can live from joy, truth and authentic power. By connecting with bottle C3, you begin the process of opening to a much more empowered state of being, and from there the doors open wide to all the light and wonder that the universe has to offer you.

The Third Spiritual Principle: Claim Your Authentic Power

The solar plexus is about power and what you have chosen to do with it, in this and previous lifetimes. It relates to any form of power struggle, any time you have felt powerless or given your power away, any time you have used power over others or abused your power. Power is a word with many connotations, most of them negative. It tends to be associated with manipulation, aggression, control, dominance and fear. Yet so much of what has been called 'power' is the very opposite and is actually based on fear and a *lack* of authentic power. Truly powerful people have no need to bully, manipulate or dominate another, because they are complete and whole within themselves.

When you are in the presence of someone who is genuinely empowered, someone who has fully claimed and embodied their light, there is often an incredible softness to their energy. Ego is nowhere to be found. You do not feel manipulated or overpowered, instead you feel true power as it emanates from their being in the form of love. With its olive upper fraction, bottle C3 reveals the softness of authentic power and shows you how it looks to bring your heart to your sense of power. This is feminine power – whether you are male or female. This is access to a power that is based on love and authenticity. True power comes from being yourself in the world, without pretence, without shame, without games, without masks.

As you embrace the truth of who you are, your power becomes a natural energy that supports and guides you in living a balanced, peaceful, harmonious life. This third spiritual principle asks you to claim your authentic power, to stand unafraid in the light of your truth. It invites you to leave behind ego games and false pretences and step into a world of light, clarity, balance, openness and strength.

As you begin to claim your authentic power, you will be ready to dive into the second solar plexus chakra bottle, C11 (Wisdom). This bottle takes the yellow joy of bottle C3 and adds to it the pink of love, to make gold. This is the next step on the pathway to true, authentic power.

When you are drawn to bottle C3, we invite you also to read about its 'partner' bottle, C11, for further information and insights.

Bottle C3 Story: Moira Bush, Canada, www.moirabush.com

My initial response to this bottle was very negative. I was deeply in depression and Melissie suggested I bathe in it. The bath turned a putrid yellow, and I put one foot in and promptly got vertigo and an upset tummy. I had to pull out and pull the plug; I could not get my body into that bath. The vibration of the bottle did the work anyway as a few days later I got my energy back, took control of the depressive state and made a decision to relocate to a new area.

This bottle has supported many people preparing to start a business or become financially independent. When I moved home I essentially had to re-launch my business and felt drawn to bathe in this bottle. After the bath I felt inspired to offer a free talk on colour. I set a date, and 40 people turned up. The yellow gave me confidence and the olive helped me to step up as a female leader in my field. In the past I would tend to get stage-fright when doing talks, but this time I was calm and all went well.

Bottle C3 Story: Lesley McDonald, UK, www.lesleytara.com

When someone innocently nominated me for something on Facebook, instead of joining in the fun, my immediate reaction was of irritation (fury, actually) and a feeling of violation. I felt familiar feelings of panic as an old programme of being subjugated, controlled and victimised screamed out to be freed. This time instead of squashing it down I listened and asked what it needed. The answer came in the form of the olive and yellow bottle, C3. It was time to release that tired old control programme.

Underneath the frustration there was a great deal of fear so I took it slowly, using the oils on my solar plexus each night. It felt old, like past life stuff, as I let the fears surface and spill out. At first I could feel the panic gripping tighter as if terrified to let go, but slowly as the days passed and I continued to use the oil, the band of fear around my solar plexus began to loosen. A kaleidoscope of images flooded my dream states, always the same: imprisonment, enslavement, powerlessness. The images flashed by, different scenarios, but always a young woman with no way out.

I continued to use this olive and yellow oil, and then one day, sitting in my living room, I glanced out of the window and was drawn to the greenery, not just drawn but mesmerised by the olive green of the new spring foliage everywhere. I craved this colour. It was resuscitating me and re-empowering me – the young lady stepping back into her own worth, taking her power back softly and gently, drinking in the olive energy and becoming lighter, brighter. The pendulum was swinging from fear and enslavement to a gentle sense of empowerment. There was a way out now, a way forward.

Bottle C3 Story: Rui Diogo, Portugal, www.facebook.com/kaleidosol

The first time I put this bottle on my third chakra, I felt like it burned me. I was completely agonised and could not even eat dinner. When I got home I bathed in the oils and it was as if I jumped in time. With my eyes closed, I felt that I lived a past life, but I saw it as clearly as if I were watching a movie on television: Lisbon after the earthquake of 1755. I felt powerful because I was someone in politics and helped in the reconstruction of Lisbon. I also felt that perhaps I abused that same power, exploiting the poor for my own benefit. I suddenly found myself being tried for these same crimes, being condemned to hang, with a hood on my head. Suddenly I felt the force of an angel that pulled the rope from my neck and whispered in my ear: "Who never sinned? This life is no longer part of you. I hope you have learned."

After this bottle I was never the same. Now I feel secure in my power because it is used for good, without hurting others. This bottle has brought back to my consciousness the reasons why in this life I did not use my personal power before.

Bottle C11: Solar Plexus Chakra – Wisdom (Gold/Gold)

This bottle is an incredible support for fear, panic attacks and phobias. It helps you step into your authentic power and claim your wisdom. It is alchemical, guiding you towards inner transformation and helping you move beyond ego. Let it assist you in activating your I AMness, and remember that you are not small and limited but powerful and Divine.

When you are in need of the first solar plexus chakra bottle, C3, you are likely to be experiencing confusion, fear, doubt, worry or anxiety. If you are choosing its partner, the higher vibrational solar plexus chakra bottle, C11, this is a sign that you are ready to move on. The confusion is diminishing, you are making significant progress, heading towards empowerment and being more and more authentically yourself in the world. There is still room for some ego here – it is a kind of transition between the ego-based yellow of bottle C3 and the pale gold authenticity of true I AMness we find in bottle G12 (I AM). But this is a healthy, positive ego with the self-esteem and oomph to get things moving and happening.

Bottle C11 is a bridge, taking your fearful, limited self by the hand and guiding it towards the bright light of your authentic and powerful self. It says you can now be out in the world, shining, attracting, doing. It invites you to engage and connect, to share your gifts and abilities. There is an accessibility about this bottle that makes stepping into your wisdom and power do-able. It helps you become accustomed to being in your I AMness and says you do not have to do it all at once because there are steps along the way. You can play with your authentic power, allowing yourself to experience it without getting hung up on always getting it 'right'.

There is a lightness and brightness to this bottle which suggests that the whole of life can be a great adventure when you are willing to simply enjoy all it has to offer. There is something about bottle C11 that makes you want to laugh at things you thought were so terribly important before. You start to see that all your fears and limiting beliefs were mainly cooked up by your mind and your ego and have very little to do with what is true and 'real'. Rather than trying to think your way through life, this bottle encourages you to connect with your inner wisdom so that you can simply know.

This bottle often has a powerfully transformational effect. The shift from the yellow of fear into the gold of power happens through the addition of pink, which is the colour of unconditional love. In gold you are able to view the world from a place of love and allowance rather than fear and suspicion. In gold you step into wisdom rather than continue play-acting. In gold you open to the power of transformation, transmutation and transcendence. Your light becomes brighter; your willingness to be who you truly are, grows. Stress and tension dissipate as you move deeply into the warm golden glow of your true power, a power that nothing can diminish.

With bottle C11 you take a step closer to really claiming this power. As you do so your solar plexus lights up and expands so that you can breathe in more of life, in every sense. Your body opens up, you take in more oxygen, your breath becomes deeper, fuller and richer. Now you can breathe life into your projects, your work, your business, your creativity and your relationships. Your nervous system calms, your posture straightens, your stress levels drop and your life expands into new possibilities.

When you are truly powerful you do not need to over-analyse, rationalise, or attempt to think your way out of a situation. You can respond rather than react, allow rather than resist, open up rather than close down. You begin to experience a harmonious flow as you take your rightful place at the centre of your own life once more, firmly connected to the radiant light and love of the Divine. With your feet on the ground and your head in the sky, everything in between naturally falls into place.

Bottle C11 is a potent energiser, with just a hint of rocket fuel. It opens you to excitement, fun, joy and laughter as you stop taking life so seriously. At the same time it enables you to take on life – and yourself – in ways you may never have dared to before. In its golden light you awaken ever more fully to the Divine presence within, that God-spark inside that has been waiting to be ignited. This bottle helps you see, feel and know yourself as Divine all the way through. And the moment you do, you see it in everyone else too. As the golden warmth of this bottle wraps itself around you, take some time to bask in its glow and draw it into your body and being. Let your inner light take you out of the story, out of separation, out of 'me versus you', into wholeness, into unity, into wisdom.

When you are drawn to bottle C11, we invite you also to read about its 'partner' bottle, C3, and the third spiritual principle: Claim your authentic power.

Bottle C11 Story: Melissie

A woman on a workshop who was scared of absolutely everything chose this bottle, and suddenly she wasn't scared at all any more. When I've seen people using this bottle it has cleared fears and phobias – but completely. It has helped people who couldn't fly or travel, people who were terrified of spiders, people who were paranoid about locking their doors over and over. It seems to release those fears magically and instantaneously. I think the key is that you can't have God and fear in the same place: they're mutually exclusive.

I remember this bottle was chosen by a participant on a workshop in England many years ago. She wanted something to help her deal with her husband who suffered from severe agoraphobia to the point that he had not been able to leave the house for years on end. After sharing this bottle with him, he managed to leave the house and take the train to London on his own without any kind of panic.

Bottle C11 Story: Korani

This bottle was one of the first I ever bathed in, at a time when I was just trying out what it felt like to be authentically empowered. I experienced huge waves of energy wash over me and what seemed like an entire reconfiguration of my energy field taking place. I literally shook for about half an hour and came out of the bath feeling utterly transformed, ready to be me more fully than ever before.

Heart Chakra: Bottles C4, C12 and the Fourth Spiritual Principle – Love (Everyone Including Yourself)

Bottle C4: Heart Chakra (Turquoise/Green)

This bottle helps when suffering from heartache and relationship difficulties. It is useful when you need to express your feelings and get in touch with your heart. It may bring to the surface buried emotional trauma that you have not yet dealt with and gently help you release it – without having to re-visit the traumatic experience. This bottle is a wonderful tonic for self-care, inviting you to treat yourself with loving-kindness.

The green of the heart chakra explores the territory of love relationships, partnerships and emotions, complete with all their joys, conflicts and challenges. Bottle C4 will call to you any time you are having issues around the heart. You may be mourning the loss of a relationship or struggling to share your feelings with the ones you love. Maybe you are feeling stifled and smothered in a relationship or going through a calamitous break-up. Perhaps you are struggling with wounds you have been unable to resolve or feeling stuck in the past. This bottle brings healing love and support into any situation or circumstance in which your emotional heart is in difficulty. It also relates to physical heart conditions, which are often outward manifestations of inner struggles. It is a balm for any hurts of the heart, bringing you back to a place of connection with yourself, with love, with life.

There are as many stories of the heart as there are people on earth and a plethora of reasons for it to feel wounded. Many of these stories begin in childhood, and bottle C4 will touch into unresolved issues you are holding around love or lack of it. Perhaps your parents' hearts were closed and you never felt good enough, even blaming yourself deep down for being unable to earn their affection. Perhaps you experienced loss and grief at a young age and never fully recovered. You may have attracted difficulty or pain in your romantic relationships – or no relationship at all. You may have become hardened to love, your heart frozen, blocked up, closed off. Perhaps you feel that it is not safe to give or receive love. Whatever your heart story, and however big or small a role it has played in your life, bottle C4 can help relieve your wounds and restore your heart, preparing it once more for love.

This bottle is a great support for heartbreak. When you are in intense emotional pain it can feel as if your heart has literally shattered into pieces. If it had, of course, you would die – and this is where your biology and your biography become one thing. The story you carry in your heart becomes so real that you may literally feel it as a physical force with the potential to kill you. Bottle C4 eases the pain, pours soothing love onto the turbulent waters of your emotions and gently opens your heart so that you are able to believe that you will, in fact, survive. It offers hope of new possibilities and ultimately peace as you release the tangled emotions from your heart.

Family relationship patterns often play out from generation to generation, and this heart chakra bottle may call to you if you are struggling with parenting in some way. Perhaps you have been taking over-responsibility for your children, especially as they grow to adulthood. Maybe you feel as if your relationships with your children are less than 'perfect'. You may be watching your children struggle or suffer, perhaps seeing them repeat your own difficulties with relationships. This bottle offers you the opportunity to reassess all your family relationships – children, parents, partners and close relatives. If you have been playing a role that does not serve you, in your family or indeed any relationship, bottle C4 will invite you to take a good long look at how your heart feels about that.

Green is the colour traditionally associated with the heart. As we saw with the green No. 5 bottle (Mercury), it is also about hiding your true self – even if you are only doing so in an attempt to stay safe. If love equals pain in your experience, then the vulnerability required of true love is likely to feel very unsafe indeed. If your experiences of relationships have left you believing that you are not enough on some level, why would you risk showing who you really are? The turquoise upper fraction of this bottle relates to feelings, particularly feelings that have been put on ice.

Together, the green and turquoise of bottle C4 clearly spell out the patterns and games you have been playing, possibly throughout your life, in an effort to keep your heart from being hurt. It can be a tremendous relief to look in the mirror held up by this bottle and see clearly what you have been hiding from. There is nowhere to run to when the heart holds out its love to you. Now is the moment to face the pain, and in so doing, finally let it go.

This bottle relates to the judgements you hold about being here on the planet. Green is about borders and boundaries, space or lack of it, overwhelm, jealousy and envy. It holds everything that keeps 'you' versus 'me' or 'yours' versus 'mine' in place. If pain, separation and hurt have been your experience of life, if earth has been a place of suffering for you, if your heart has struggled here in any way, this bottle helps you step out of the drama. As you let go of the story and the judgements that keep it in place, you reconnect with the wisdom and love that is the true light of the heart chakra.

This bottle helps calm your body, soothe your battered nerves, replenish your tired heart and re-balance your emotions so that you can find peace and harmony in your space on this planet. The turquoise in the upper fraction of this bottle asks you to have faith that from a higher perspective, everything is unfolding perfectly, no matter how it might appear. The green in the bottom fraction indicates that a new space is now opening up for you.

Bottle C4 is a powerful healer of hurts and an incredible tonic to anyone struggling with relationship pain. It lightens and lifts the burdens you have carried in your heart, enabling you to expand this centre of your being. It frees up your lungs, helps you breathe, brings you into awareness, opens doorways and supports you in creating a new and expanded vision for yourself. Its soft, nurturing energy makes it safe to open to love – love for yourself as well as love for and from others.

The Fourth Spiritual Principle: Love (Everyone Including Yourself)

The fourth spiritual principle, just like the name of bottle C4's partner, bottle C12, is simply 'Love'. Simple to say, perhaps not so simple to do – certainly not all the time, in every situation, with every person. Yet that is what you are being called towards, that is what your heart already knows as truth. Your ego may battle it at every turn, yet as you awaken more fully, as you recognise yourself as a Divine being, it becomes more difficult to turn away from love than to embrace it.

With the help of the heart chakra bottles, C4 and C12, and the fourth spiritual principle, you can begin to find the strength, freedom and clarity to remove the masks and open the shuttered doors to your heart. This means you can come to relationships as who you are rather than as who you think you should be. When you are authentic, empowered and open with yourself and others, love follows. Love attracts more love. As you shine out into the world the light of the greatest power you hold – the love you have and the love you are – so it returns to you many times over.

When you love and value yourself there is space for life to reflect that back to you. With an open heart you can say "yes" when life offers itself to you. When you honour and respect yourself you can also say "no" when it is appropriate to do so. When you value yourself, your boundaries can be clear and strong, leaving no room for victimhood or martyrdom. Jealousy and envy wither and die when held up to the flame of love. In love there is no room for battles and territories. In love's embrace you know that there is always enough, that you are always enough.

When you live from love you have space to find out what you really want to generate and create in your life, who you have the potential to be, which direction you would like to flow in, who you would like to share your life with. You begin to see where you can expand and open to new possibilities.

The universe is made from love, with love, for love. Love is the very reason you exist and the greatest power you hold. Love is the current of energy that created the world and everything in it. It is the force that supports and sustains every single being in existence. Love is the key to every challenge, every illness, every dark and difficult situation. There is not a single thing, event, person or situation that cannot be transformed by the extraordinary power of love.

The fourth spiritual principle relates to the heart chakra, and it is in your heart that your greatest capacity to love resides. Yet it is also one of the most vulnerable areas of your being and one that is most prone to harbour the very emotions that disconnect you from love. Bottle C4 relates to your physical heart, the beating organ that distributes blood around your body. It also relates to your emotional heart, which processes all your feelings, emotions and experiences. Bottle C4's partner, bottle C12, relates to your true Divine spiritual heart, which is neither wounded nor afraid. Your Divine heart is only ever filled with love, connected with love, open to love. Your Divine heart gives and receives freely in equal measure. The fourth spiritual principle asks you to open to this expansive, enlightened aspect of yourself and begin to view the world through its lens rather than through the painful distortions of your emotional heart.

As you open to love in all its forms – human love, Divine love, relationship love, familial love and most importantly, self-love – your experience of the world changes. You stop feeling betrayed and start feeling compassion. You stop blaming and shaming and start understanding. You stop feeling separate and cut-off and start making connections. When love becomes your guiding light your heart begins to heal, and as your heart becomes whole again, you can view your past in an entirely new way. Your life becomes the path to making you strong, wise and complete. It is no longer a catalogue of terrible events and difficult relationships but an incredible journey to self-realisation. Love has always been the only way and now, as you let go of the stories you have been telling yourself, you can truly begin to claim it. As you grow in love, you become who you have always known yourself to be in your core and in your heart.

When you are drawn to bottle C4, we invite you also to read about its 'partner' bottle, C12, for further insights and information.

Bottle C4 Story: Melissie

I met a woman who had given up her daughter for adoption and who had always felt as if her heart was actually broken. Gradually over her life, her physical heart began to deteriorate. By the time I met her she was at death's door, and her doctors said they didn't think she had much time left. She used bottle C4 and is not only still alive and thriving years later, but she has also met with the daughter she adopted out and has formed a relationship with her.

Bottle C4 Story: Melissie

When a friend had a heart attack I gave her several bottles of C4. She used them all, one after the other. When she subsequently went for a scan, her bemused doctors could find nothing wrong with her heart.

Bottle C4 Story: Katherine Louise Jones, UK, www.katherinelouisejones.com

I give a lot of talks with the Colour Mirrors system and encourage participants to choose a bottle they are drawn to in order to explain how we work with the system. At one talk, as I went round each person saying what the Colour Mirrors bottle could be mirroring for them, I landed upon a lady with bottle C4. I explained to her the colours and offered the message that the heart chakra bottle is about love and relationships, to which she replied rather defiantly that hers were all good and that the bottle therefore didn't really resonate with her. She felt quite pleased with herself until I heard her say that all she really wanted to do was go on holiday, lie on a beach and rest. I asked her where she took care of herself and suggested that loving had to start with ourselves. I asked her if perhaps she invested in relationships with others whilst not looking after herself. She visibly shifted and quietened, and it was clear that the message of bottle C4 was not lost on her.

Bottle C4 Story: Elaine Nuelle, UK, elainenuelle@gmail.com

I went through an incredibly difficult period of about two years when my husband was very ill and then left the planet. I would often wake up in the night with heart palpitations. Putting bottle C4 on my heart calmed it all down, which meant I felt safe and could often sleep. During this time I went through three bottles of C4, as they all changed colour, which we know is a sign that they are working intensely with us. It's one of my 'go-to' bottles when the energies are intense or my adrenals start kicking off.

Bottle C12: Heart Chakra – Love (Lilac/Pink)

This bottle unites your heart with your spirit and relates to oneness and unconditional love. It connects you with the heartbeat of your soul and your true Divine loving light. This bottle reflects all the inner beauty you hold and asks you to share it with the world. Now is the time to recognise that you are one with all of humanity. This bottle may indicate grief over the loss of a mother or deep transformation of mother issues.

The shift from the green of the first heart chakra bottle, C4, to the pink of the second, bottle C12, is a reflection of one of humanity's core transitions – from emotional heart to spiritual heart. It shows the path from separation, division and the belief that another can hurt you, to wholeness, interconnection and the joy of the ever-expanding love that is at your core. Although the heart chakra has traditionally been associated with the colour green, for many years those with the vision to see it have witnessed pink around people's hearts. This was the first of the chakra colours to begin to shift, perhaps indicating its importance to humanity's spiritual evolution.

At this time of huge change on the planet, the move into the Divine heart is a key to the unfolding of a new era of awakened consciousness. Bottle C12, lilac over pink, marries spirit and heart in a union of divinely loving light. Its name is Love, and it speaks of the transformation of the heart from an emotional centre to a spirit-based one. It asks you to acknowledge that love is at the core of every atom of life and every cell of every being. This bottle invites you to embrace the love that has always been yours, the love that is who you are, and bring to it the grace and purity of your spirit so that you might live in communion, harmony and peace.

Any time you are struggling to see your own light, bottle C12 radiates it to you with full force. When you are choosing this bottle it says: "Look in the mirror. This is how beautiful you are!" It is a powerful reminder of the truth of your inner light and the love you carry within. Lilac is the colour of a clear connection to spirit, unhindered by ego's demands. Pink relates to self-love and self-acceptance and takes you into a space of generous open-heartedness from which you can offer your love freely to others without fear of causing or receiving hurt. Together these colours are softly, powerfully enabling. When you struggle to claim love for yourself, it is your spirit that shows you the way. When you find it a challenge to love yourself unconditionally, your spirit remembers the truth of your Divine perfection.

This bottle is linked with abundance and asks how much you are willing to receive. It supports you in opening to the abundance of love, money and everything else the universe has to offer. If you are experiencing money struggles, the likelihood is that you are struggling to love yourself. When you deeply and truly love and honour yourself, money tends to show up. When you are willing to open your heart fully to love for yourself and others, you can powerfully plug in to all the abundance of the planet that is available to you. People who select this bottle are often in the midst of both money and love challenges, and we have noticed that as one shifts, so does the other.

Bottle C12, like its partner, bottle C4, may come up when you are experiencing issues around parenting. It offers great support, teaching that the utmost gift you can give your children is to love and accept them for who they are. This bottle may also reflect your feelings about your mother, particularly if you are grieving her loss or are unhappy about your relationship with her. Bottle C12 says you are looking for love, looking for mother – looking, in fact, for perfect mother love – and connecting with this bottle may just give you a sense of the love you have been seeking. It brings healing to the wounds of your inner child so that instead of seeking love from the outside, you are taken deep inside your own Divine heart to the well-spring of love that awaits you there. And when self-love takes root and becomes deeply anchored in place, then there is space to welcome love from others.

This bottle shows that it is safe to have feelings. As you begin to view what has happened in your life from the perspective of your spirit, you gain a deeper understanding of why it occurred. If your heart has been frozen, it can thaw; if broken, it can mend. As you allow yourself to have feelings again, you no longer need to automatically shut them down or dive into painful emotions.

Emotions carry the energy of drama, trauma, pain and suffering; feelings are simply feelings – they let you know that you are experiencing. Feelings are also often a guidance system to let you know when something is out of alignment with your truth. When you perceive something in your energy or environment as uncomfortable, it is a gift from your higher self to show you that it is time to make a course correction. It is your opportunity to make a change, do something differently, learn from your experience and move forward. With bottle C12, you become more able to simply feel, perceive and experience, and less likely to fall into emotional drama.

When you have been over-giving, over-caring or over-doing, this bottle will remind you to stop and take care of yourself first. If you have been giving too much of yourself out of a misguided sense of duty or obligation – or perhaps because you wish to be seen as nice, good, caring, loving, kind etc. – bottle C12 supports you in honouring and loving yourself enough to let go of this pattern and find a more empowering way to relate to others.

There is great softness and gentleness to this bottle. It is a powerful healer, helping you find the deeper spiritual truth behind your relationships. It is about love across borders, boundaries, time and space. It is love that is unlimited, unbounded and unconditional. It takes exquisite care of you and as it does so, reminds you how to be tender with yourself and others. No matter the battering it has taken throughout your life, your heart can be completely renewed when you are ready – and choosing this bottle says that you *are* ready. This is the healing of the grieving heart that enables you to move gently towards joy.

Bottle C12 is effectively a lighter version of bottle 12, 'Heaven on Earth', which is violet over red. Both these bottles indicate that, as a species, humanity is finally preparing to release victim mentality and choose another reality, a new heaven, one that can be found right here on earth. When enough people leave victimhood completely behind, that surely will contribute to the creation of a totally new paradigm on this planet, one based on love.

The combination of lilac with pink in this bottle reflects the transformation and spiritualisation of the heart. It acknowledges the heart as the place where humanity makes the shift from being lost, limited and ego-based, to being loving, expansive and Divine. This shift is created by the ability to truly love one another, to see the Divine in the other, to see all as one. Bottle C12's message is that when you live from love, you can free yourself from any belief in victimhood and acknowledge that everything in your reality is unfolding exactly as it is meant to.

This bottle shows how life can be when your heart is restored to its true function as a creative and loving transmitter and receiver. Your spiritual heart is a fountain of infinite wisdom, infinite compassion and infinite love. Let it guide you towards fulfilment, wonder and plenty, and return home to the oneness of a truly loving relationship with yourself and all of life.

When you are drawn to bottle C12, we invite you also to read about its 'partner' bottle, C4, and the fourth spiritual principle: Love everyone including yourself.

Bottle C12 Story: Moira Bush, Canada, www.moirabush.com

There are two instances when this bottle gets picked all the time in my practice: either the client desires a new romance or to reignite romance in their old relationship, or they serve by caring for others and are busy burning out from over-giving. This bottle literally soothes a sore heart and any emotional trauma. It tops up the exhausted hearts of those who constantly offer unconditional love in the fields of nursing, hospice work and caring for people with disabilities. To do unconditional work you have to be connected to your spirit because often those industries are a calling, as indicated by the lilac spiritual colour in this bottle. I personally had relief from a broken heart when my mother passed away, and at the time I mentioned to Melissie that this bottle should be called Perfection. My mother was a nurse.

Bottle C12 Story: Amanda Bradbury, UK, www.amandabradbury.com

Bottle C12 is comprised of pink – which relates to the planet Venus, and lilac – which relates to Pluto. A student was drawn to bottle C12 when she was going through a divorce and was having to be heart-centred, unconditional and forgiving. She was dealing with extreme financial challenges including the loss of their lovely cottage, and her husband was also experiencing mental health challenges. Astrologically she was experiencing a connection between Venus and Pluto at the time, as transiting Pluto was forming a conjunction to Venus in her birth chart. Pluto was literally on top of Venus in the same way as the lilac in bottle C12 'presses down' on the pink.

Bottle C12 Story: Amanda Ellis, UK, www.amandaellis.co.uk

Bottle C12 has always been my favourite colour combination since I first found Colour Mirrors in 2005. Why do I love this one above all others? Well, its soft lilac and pink tones are soothing for sure. They carry such grace and gentleness and give a warm hug to all who place it to their heart. But I have also noticed that it holds its colour – for me anyway. Like most of us in spiritual service, I am so used to giving that I have to work hard on receiving. Bottle 6 (Venus – pink over pink) has always been my reminder of when I am overdoing it. I will suck out the pink energetically very quickly – it turns clear white – and then I'm drawn back to realising my life is out of balance: too much work and not enough play and light-heartedness. Yet bottle C12 never changes. It remains pure, it holds its tone – both lilac and pink. It seems able to anchor in the highest vision of me living and loving unconditionally – and most importantly, in balance.

As human beings, do we ever really live by unconditional love? We may have fleeting moments when we step into it and embody it, but day to day, hour by hour, it is a high goal to try and achieve. And yet of course achievement implies struggle and trial to get there, and I guess unconditional love is about ease and flowing into it as naturally as breathing should be. Maybe we as a species haven't yet arrived in that place of pure unconditional love, but bottle C12 reminds us that it is possible here on earth, not just in the heavens above. It holds that beacon for all of us, to highlight that unconditional love IS alive on this planet. It is seeded in each of us, and these colours help us to remember that. I can't see a time when it will ever be replaced in my affections by anything else.

Bottle C12 Story: Constance Schaap-van Zoelen, The Netherlands, www.powerfulhearts.nl

Bathing in this bottle made me feel peaceful to the level of meditation. The peaceful feeling was instant after stepping into the bath, when I had been feeling quite restless before. My body felt deeply relaxed, and even my digestive system seemed to relax. I also felt a deep love for my own body and felt like moving it in graceful movements, like a dolphin. I felt held in Divine love and care and saw beautiful pink and lilac colours with my third eye. I felt so open to surrendering to what is. I felt in bliss for three days after taking this bath.

Throat Chakra: Bottles C5, C13 and the Fifth Spiritual Principle – Everything is Perfect

Bottle C5: Throat Chakra (Royal Blue/Blue)

This bottle relates to communication and trust and is helpful for stress, sleeping issues and nightmares. It supports you in speaking up and being heard and is useful when you are battling to say what you need to say. If you have ever felt 'second best', this bottle helps you recognise your worth. Acknowledge your intuitive abilities and let your higher self guide your communications so that they are clear and true.

Blue is the colour of expression and communication. It is about sharing with others everything you are: your essence and divinity as well as your human-ness. Blue allows you to tell your stories, express your wisdom and share your voice. It helps you give of yourself through the medium of words and language as well as the many subtle forms of communication that have no words.

Bottle C5 relates to the throat chakra and communication in all its forms, helping you speak up, speak out and express yourself with clarity and precision. It supports you in communicating from a place of self-belief and self-worth so that you can speak truly, freely and with authority. It helps you learn to trust so that you can stand up and say what you need to say, whether at work, in business, at home or in family situations. With its royal blue top fraction, it also connects you with your inner knowing, and helps you perceive what is not being said or what is being conveyed beyond the words you hear. In this way, it assists you in listening with your body and your heart as well as your mind.

Blue's complementary or opposite colour is orange, the colour of shocks, traumas and unacknowledged wounds – and blue will help pacify, heal, settle and soothe the distress and pain these have caused. This bottle has the protective, loving and supportive energies of the angelic realm. As it guides you into peace, bottle C5 helps you begin to feel safe to speak up about what has tormented and troubled you, and in the process, release it from your body and your energy field.

Blue relates to the masculine, and when this bottle shows up you are asked to explore any stories you are holding about the male energy, especially with regard to your father or other male figures of authority. Bottle C5 raises to the surface the subconscious male stories you have been holding inside so that they may be spoken about and brought to peace. It relates to all stories of father relationships that have been less than 'perfect': the dad who could not love you for who you were or who did not see, acknowledge or value you; the father who dominated and controlled you; the father who ignored or belittled you. It taps into all the times you felt subdued, suppressed or smothered by the males in your life; any situations where you were unable to speak up in the presence of authority; past lifetimes when you were punished for speaking out; every time your voice was not heard. Bottle C5 supports you in releasing these stories from your throat chakra so that you might clearly, powerfully and authentically express who you are and what you have to say. In situations where you find yourself giving your authority away to someone else, this bottle assists you in reclaiming it.

One of the stories quite often revealed by this bottle is of women whose father wanted a boy and got a girl instead, or men who have been unable to live up to their father's expectations. There is an energy of 'second best', of not quite making the grade, of disappointed expectations and failed hopes. If this is your story and you have never felt fully seen or heard, you may also find yourself in relationships where you feel as if you are never 'enough'. Sadly it is a fairly common scenario to which many women, in particular, will relate.

Living this story can have a powerfully distorting effect on the throat chakra. If you are never enough you learn fairly quickly that anything you say will not be valued, so you keep the truth of who you are carefully hidden and your true voice locked away. Alternatively, you might over-compensate for your perceived shortcomings by becoming the expert, the authority, the teacher, the one who knows it all. Either way, if you have not felt valued, it is likely that you in turn will tend not to hear what others have to say. Think here of a certain prominent US politician who rather plays out the complementary colour (orange) by being larger than life and very keen on being seen. His underlying story is that all he is really trying to do is get his father to acknowledge him...

This bottle is a solid support if you relate in some way to the 'second best' scenario. It helps you learn to honour yourself, reclaim your voice and trust that who you are and what you have to say is valid. It enables you to step out of the role of 'little brother' or 'just a girl' or someone who views themselves as having nothing of value to say. It helps put you back on the path to knowing and expressing your worth in the world. When you open to the truth at the core of this colour you begin to understand that everything – *everything* – is perfect exactly as it is. You realise that there are no mistakes and that no one is at fault. You come to understand that *you* were never a mistake.

Children who select bottle C5 have often taken on a belief that they are responsible for keeping everyone in the family safe. They often also feel different from other children and may be picked on or bullied. This bottle has been found to stop nightmares and bed-wetting and has helped countless children feel safe and secure as they sleep. With this bottle's support, children realise they do not have to hold everything together for the family but can just be themselves. In the process, walls and blocks often come down, creating a more harmonious environment for all.

Blue is the colour of rules, regulations and analytical thinking. When you feel unsafe you may choose to immerse yourself in order and discipline in an attempt to maintain control. You may feel you have to try to take charge of everything or make sure that everyone is looked after. This bottle is often chosen by people who hold managerial positions, particularly in the service or hospitality industries, where they believe that their entire job is to keep everyone happy – and their stress levels are typically through the roof. This bottle helps when you tend to over-control or feel obliged to make everything 'right'.

Bottle C5 takes you into the steady waters of trust and lets you be at peace with the unfolding of your life. It helps you hand everything over to the universe and open to the serenity of letting go. It moves you into the tranquillity and peaceful depths of the moon and the bright expansive vastness of the sky. This bottle is a peace-bringer when your mind is over-active or when you fall into 'stuck record' repetitive thinking. It helps you see beyond what is stressing you so that you can move into a quieter place, a more relaxed state. From here you can come back to your truth, trusting and knowing that all is well.

The Fifth Spiritual Principle: Everything is Perfect

The fifth spiritual principle is about seeing and knowing the perfection in everything. When you are truly at peace with life and all it offers, you know that everything that has happened in the past was perfect and everything that will happen in the future will be perfect. You know that everything that is, is perfect. When you live in that state of perfection, all you see and experience and know is perfection – and there lies a very clear path to peace.

"Perfect?" you might ask. "What is perfect about my illness or my divorce or my child who is being bullied? What is perfect about war and famine and the devastation of the earth?" It might seem a tall order indeed to find any of these things 'perfect'. Yet what if they are? Not perfect as in 'good', but perfect as in offering incredible opportunities for growth – which is, after all, what each and every one of us came here for.

What if that illness was your wake-up call to living a healthier and more joyful life? What if your divorce was the beginning of infinite possibilities you would never have considered if you had stayed in the marriage? What if your child being bullied was an opportunity for you and your child to discover inner strength, compassion and authentic power? What if war was just an expression of the collective warring that goes on within each and every person on this planet and a mirror to show what is inside? An opportunity for humanity to change and heal those patterns and conflicts?

When you look at anything as 'negative', as 'wrong', as 'shouldn't have happened', you are viewing it through various lenses of distortion put in place by your ego and societal conditioning. This type of thinking also reflects the disconnection of the vast majority of humanity from the source of all life and beingness. Living your life from a human ego/mind perspective keeps you locked in judgement and limitation, especially if you insist on being right and finding others wrong. When you seek to control or judge, you automatically cut off much of what is available to you. The universe always gives itself to you fully, utterly and unconditionally, so why would you choose to turn away? Would you prefer to play out your dramas and stories rather than stopping to look up and see the truth? Would you rather choose to remain in righteous anger or misery than look beyond the walls that a limited human perspective has created?

The fifth spiritual principle shows you that is it possible to see everything from a different place, a higher viewpoint. One of the challenges and joys of life on earth is to come back to awareness in every moment so that you might choose to see its perfection instead of its imperfection. In returning to awareness of your true nature as a Divine being created from love, you can choose to know life as love, view life through love, experience life in love.

Admittedly, with humanity's history of judgement first, awareness later – if at all – it may take time to remember that you have a choice about how you view or perceive anything. Yet as you learn to claim the perfection of every single thing, you will find that you no longer have the desire to label, judge or control. Instead you can allow – and in your allowing, you open to more of the universe's love and bounty. When you allow, life flows to you, through you and with you. By allowing the perfection of an experience or situation, you attract – quite simply – more perfection.

When you are drawn to bottle C5, we invite you also to read about its 'partner' bottle, C13, for further insights and information.

Bottle C5 Story: Korani

During the initial writing of this book, as I wrote about each bottle I would place it on my desk so that I could look at it and hold it to receive its energies and messages. Sometimes I would be busy with other tasks for some days or even weeks as I was writing about a particular bottle and so it would sit on my desk, quietly working away with me, even if I was not consciously engaging with it.

When I got to bottle C5, I wrote prolifically. A writing project that had been waiting to be completed for months was completed swiftly. I re-wrote whole sections of my website in a short space of time. I wrote newsletters, worked with Melissie on various Colour Mirrors projects, found myself writing creatively again after a long period of not writing at all – and on and on it went. As a writer, blue has always been part of my make-up, but with this bottle I suddenly had great clarity and connection and a clear 'channel' to my writing muse.

Bottle C5 Story: Jackie Tweedie, UK, www.jackietweedie.com

Communication isn't just about speaking, it's also about listening deeply to others and to ourselves. It is so easy to put the needs of other people in front of our own (often mistaken for being of service), and to me this bottle is about noticing where and how we put ourselves last.

I had a client who chose this bottle when he found himself in busy meetings at work where he couldn't get a word in edgeways. His colleagues were loud and opinionated and he chose to just let them 'get on with it' rather than fight for his turn to speak. The sad part was that he actually had a great deal to contribute, but he was waiting for them to realise this and invite him to speak. They didn't. When he used this bottle it helped him to understand and clear the beliefs he held about his right to speak and be heard. He also saw that by not speaking he was actually letting the team down as well as himself, as he often 'just knew' the right way to get a good result, and withholding it wasn't serving him or the business.

Bottle C13: Throat Chakra – I Speak My Spirit (Blue-Violet/Blue-Violet)

This bottle is a mixture of the blue of communication and the violet of spirituality. Its message is that once you awaken to your spirit you automatically begin to communicate from a higher perspective. Become aware of what you say and how you say it because you have the power to manifest what you speak. This bottle connects you with your intuition and helps you appreciate the perfection of each moment.

The second throat chakra bottle, C13, moves from the throat's traditional blue of bottle C5 to a rich, deep blue-violet, the colour of the precious gem, tanzanite. This is where violet infuses blue, bringing the light of spirit into your communications. This is where you discover that you can speak your spirit and express your light through your words. This is your innate power to be a vehicle for Divine energy and love.

Bottle C13 is about claiming your inner authority. It is incredibly supportive for situations where you are challenged to speak up, particularly with regard to your spirituality. If what you say or do or is mocked or belittled, you might find yourself closing down or shutting up. If you are afraid of what others think, you may struggle to take your light out into the world. Deep down you know that what you have to say has value, and with the support of this bottle you can begin to trust that it is safe for you to share it. You can also trust the universe to bring you exactly what you need in any given moment, and this bottle helps you feel safe to ask others for help without worrying about what they might think of you.

If you have always feared speaking out, your body may be holding cellular memories of previous lives when you died for it. If, for example, your head was chopped off for 'speaking your spirit' in a previous lifetime, you may understandably be reluctant to speak up in this one! The throat is a place of infinite power, yet you may not have been able to fully own it as such because of the many deaths you have experienced there. If your throat is quite literally shut down for a long enough period of time you will die, so on some level you have always known that your words carry power and your throat holds life and death within it. This bottle is about releasing the deaths from your throat, releasing the fear that you might die for your beliefs and your words, releasing the trauma that comes from believing in death as obliteration. This is about relaxing instead into the perfection of every lifetime *and* every death, with the knowledge that you, as spirit, will endure eternally.

This bottle is the next step on from the healing offered by bottle C5. In bottle C13 the colours and energies deepen. They show you that this most vulnerable part of your body is also a seat of incredible power. Blue-violet asks you to take full responsibility for what you speak, for the language you use, for the energy generated by your words. It helps unite your words with your spirit so that your communications arise from your Divine self rather than your ego. Now is your time to be visible. You are asked to stand up and be seen and to communicate in a way that is genuine. Bottle C13 helps clear the blocks from your throat and your being so that you can live and speak peacefully and authentically. When you speak from your spirit your voice carries truth, and the perfect words appear at the perfect moment.

With the understanding that your throat is a power source for your spirit, you can begin to create on a whole new level. You are always creating with your very words and thoughts; this bottle asks you to do so consciously. It also asks you to be mindful when something 'happens' and to ask: "What is my spirit saying here?" To be aware when someone says something that triggers you and ask: "What is the Divine saying here?" This has the ability to change your perceptions and your life in ways that are both liberating and empowering.

Bottle C13 links with the fifth spiritual principle, and its message is that when you are completely free of judgement on an experience and can say with absolute authenticity that it is perfect, it can have no further hold upon you. When you judge something, you attract more of whatever you are judging. Without judgement, you no longer need the experience.

If, for example, you are having a difficult time and you judge the situation as bad, horrible or wrong, you keep the energy of difficulty in place and might find that you attract further challenging experiences. It may well feel horrible, and it is perfectly OK to feel and express all your feelings about it. The issue arises when you make a story out of it and repeat the story to yourself and others over and over again, building emotions and layers of meaning, creating a monster in your mind. Every experience is, at its core, simply an experience. It is what you choose to think, say and do with the experience that affects how things play out next. Every situation or experience is an opportunity to notice whatever triggers you and find the root cause of it so that you can resolve it, step out of judgement and set yourself free rather than staying locked in the prison of your thoughts and emotions.

Every judgement is simply an indicator of where you still have buttons to be pressed, and by acknowledging them as triggers to deeper, often buried issues, you have the opportunity to bring these areas of your life to resolution and move forward. When you can see that there is learning and growth to be gained from the experience; when you can see from the perspective of your spirit, which says that the situation or person is your teacher and has gifts for you if you are willing to recognise them; when the judgement is gone – then you no longer need to attract that behaviour or experience, as you have nothing left to learn from it. You are free to live your life from the peace of your spirit, which is entirely without judgement and sees only through the eyes of love.

This bottle is a key to opening to higher Divine energies, to the beings of light who are waiting to connect with you. It opens a gateway to your higher self and the light of Divine perception where you can speak with the angels and archangels as equals, knowing your true self to be ancient and wise, free and light, connected and inspired. It takes you into the starry realms of the night sky and the potent knowing within you of a much vaster world than you can experience through your senses. Bottle C13 is a portal to a life of expansion and peace. It opens you to the limitless ocean of communication that exists on levels far beyond your mind. And it is not only about speaking your spirit. It is about living, knowing and experiencing it, and in so doing, claiming the Divine perfection of yourself and your life in every moment.

When you are drawn to bottle C13, we invite you also to read about its 'partner' bottle, C5, and the fifth spiritual principle: Everything is perfect.

Bottle C13 Story: Lesley McDonald, UK, www.lesleytara.com

It was on my Colour Mirrors practitioner course that I finally found my voice. Plagued with sore throats as a child and an absolute terror of public speaking that had followed me through my adult years, I was aware that I had a throat chakra issue, but I had not consciously intended to face the root cause right there and then. I guess my subconscious knew that here, in this safe and supported environment, the time was right. We were asked to bathe in a bottle as a kind of homework assignment, and I was immediately drawn to bottle C13.

New to the system, I had no idea that it was a throat chakra bottle, but I was intrigued that it had the same number as my birthday: 13. That night I bathed in the dark blue-violet liquid, and mostly what struck me was how quickly my body seemed to soak up the oil, leaving next to no trace of it in the water. Otherwise, it was a peaceful experience – the night, however, not so much! I was gripped with an overpowering sense of fear of the dark and fear that there was an intruder in the house. I slept little and kept the lights on as waves of terror washed through my body.

In class the next day I pretty much huddled in a corner, sleepless, tearful and washed out. Shock and trauma surfacing, I was in safe hands as the group let me be, holding me in a loving space. When we did a chakra exercise, Korani (knowingly) asked me to volunteer to have the chakra bottles laid on my body. When I felt the throat chakra bottle on my throat I wanted to scream, and the tears flowed freely down my face. I was unable to utter a sound as panic gripped me. The group gathered round and offered to be my voice. If they screamed for me, perhaps I could join in. They did. I did. I screamed out loud, releasing in that moment the terrors of a lifetime – or lifetimes.

I had given up on my lifelong dream of being a teacher when I left school and found out I had to do a practical experience in front of a class. I knew that this was not possible due to my terror of being 'on show'. My heart wanted to teach, but my body dared not. I had a wealth of spiritual and colour knowledge but could never have dreamed of holding a workshop. Now, I teach courses, hold workshops – I even sing in the shower (I did not sing as a child). This bottle was a very powerful key for me. It was the marking point to a new phase of healing and thriving. Such a breakthrough after many lifetimes – and what a team of soul sisters who were there for it with me!

Bottle C13 Story: Jackie Tweedie, UK, www.jackietweedie.com

The deep blue-violet of this bottle speaks of a connection to a higher realm and reminds me to be aware of my power and my responsibility around my words and even my thoughts. It encourages me to stand back and notice where my own words might be putting me down or where I might hold back from expressing my truth for fear of what others might say, think or do. But mostly I find this bottle connects me to the wisdom with which to respond to any situation I'm in.

My yoga students often tell me that something I've said in a class has really helped them. One said: "It's like you can hear my thoughts, and then you speak the answer before I've even asked the question! How do you do that?" Well, the simple answer is that I don't. I just relax and allow whatever needs to be spoken or heard to come through me. I just trust that inner knowing now.

Third Eye Chakra: Bottles C6, C14 and the Sixth Spiritual Principle – Hold a Clear Vision of Perfection

Bottle C6: Third Eye Chakra (Violet/Royal Blue)

This bottle puts you in touch with your inner knowing and is helpful when you have difficulty trusting your intuition. It is supportive in overcoming grief and loss and useful for relieving panic attacks. It relates to a lifetime when you withheld your knowledge and spiritual insight out of fear and helps you trust that it is safe now to share these gifts with the world. This bottle carries the energy of initiation and shows you that the difficulties you have been facing are a path to greater awareness and wisdom. Use your inner knowing to see the bigger picture.

Bottle C6 brings us now to the rich, cool depths of royal blue with its qualities of authority, knowledge and power and the sense of royalty to which its name relates. It has a specific connection to spiritual authority and those who are able to impart wisdom to others, those who know and understand things beyond the ordinary range of the human mind. It comes into your life when you are ready to transcend the mundane and lower vibratory energies that make up much of human life and awaken your intuitive, spiritual and mystical gifts.

This bottle connects with the sacred energy of the third eye, the seat of your wisdom and insight. It helps you see beyond what is available through your limited thinking mind and realise that whatever you require is right at your fingertips. It is particularly supportive when you feel overwhelmed with fear and panic and cannot see a way forward, helping you open to a higher vision and expand your awareness so that you can gain clarity on your path.

This bottle also relates to fears around being psychic or intuitive. Experiences in this or previous lifetimes may have led you to believe that it is unsafe to see and to know what others cannot. Bottle C6 opens you to a much richer level of understanding. It awakens your perception beyond the ordinary human senses. It also helps you understand that everyone on the planet actually has such abilities and that most have simply shut them down through fear. When you recognise that your intuition is an innate and natural part of who you are, you can stop denying its place in your life and begin to acknowledge it as a wonderful guide and friend.

Intuition is a skill like any other – and just like a muscle, the more you exercise it the stronger it becomes. Bottle C6 calls you to practice listening to your intuition so that you become adept at tuning in to the deeper, higher messages of the world around you rather than taking everything in your life at face value. It invites you to see the greater truth in any event or situation rather than limiting yourself to ego/mind understanding. It lights up your intuition and supports you in trusting your inner guidance and inner vision. It guides you to realise that you already know – that you already hold answers to all your questions within.

Royal blue connects with Egyptian lifetimes and the energy of initiation. Initiations test and strengthen your knowledge, wisdom, courage and power, taking you to ever higher levels of evolution. Through the many ages of humankind, initiations have been part of every soul's journey. Each initiation or testing time you go through is an opportunity to sharpen your skills, widen your scope and awaken to a higher truth. Royal blue helps you reach into your deeper intuitive senses and find the courage and wisdom to engage with your initiations from a place of wonder and curiosity rather than fear. If you are able to see any 'test' in your life as a gift rather than something to dread or suffer through, you open to even greater possibilities as you move beyond it. Initiations sometimes come in the form of apparent betrayal, and part of the initiation is to look further than the seeming betrayal to a higher viewpoint. Is it possible that the one who 'betrayed' you actually offered you an incredible invitation to let go of smallness and step into mastery?

More than any other colour, royal blue carries a sense of secrets, mystery and all that is hidden. It says you will only share what you know when you believe that others are ready to receive the information. This 'High Priest/Priestess' energy is a carry-over from lifetimes in the ancient mystery schools to which this colour relates. In these places of spiritual learning and initiation there were strict hierarchies, and knowledge was only passed on when an initiate was deemed ready.

If you still hold remnants of these memories in your cells you may have a tendency to keep your distance from others, harbouring a sense of yourself as somehow 'special' or more wise and knowledgeable than others. Bottle C6 can help you release the influence of such lifetimes so that you are able to share freely what you know, without fear that doing so will undermine your power and authority. When you recognise that all is one, you know there is nothing that ever truly belongs to you and that the more you share and the less you withhold of yourself, the greater your authenticity and the richer your life becomes.

With its violet top fraction this bottle also taps into the energy of grief and helps you move beyond suffering. Painful as loss may be from a human perspective, there is now another possibility open to you: to see your experience from a higher view. Bottle C6 supports you in releasing the grief and sadness you have been holding on to and helps you connect with the Divine truth of the situation and the greater gift to be found there. If you have been closing yourself off because of pain and grief, this bottle can help you open again to the mystery and wonder of life and the knowing that what happened was part of the perfect unfolding of a higher plan.

Bottle C6 is not only about releasing emotional pain. Many people have also experienced relief from physical pain by using this bottle. When you open your spiritual eyes and connect with the truth of who you are, the need for pain falls away. Pain is only ever your infinite self calling you to wake up, to listen, to see, to learn. When you claim your authentic authority as a being of Divine love and you respond to the messages you are being sent, you no longer need pain to act as a reminder. When you release the darkness and pain of grief and fear, you are free to discover an empowering new vision. Now you can embrace life with eyes and intuition wide open, ready to receive, share, see and know.

The Sixth Spiritual Principle: Hold a Clear Vision of Perfection

Humanity is in a time of evolution on this planet where many are beginning to understand that life is a moment by moment creation and each person is the creator of their 'reality'. This means that whatever vision you truly connect with becomes a part of that reality. If you believe that what you can see, touch or hear with your physical senses is all that exists, you are missing whole realms of beingness that are available to you. If your inner vision is clear, you are open to every nuance of Divine light and can create a reality of 'perfection' based upon it.

The sixth spiritual principle encourages you to use your insight, spiritual connection and Divine knowing to create a vision for your life and the earth that feels perfect to you. Not everyone finds it easy to visualise, so be aware that your 'vision' may not necessarily be something you see – rather you may feel it, sense it, even hear it. The key is to activate a knowing inside of what it is you desire to create and let that energy permeate your body and being. Some believe that it is necessary to see or imagine in great detail whatever it is you wish to create. Others suggest that it is actually more powerful simply to allow yourself to feel how it would be to have your desired result and to infuse yourself with those positive feelings. However you choose to go about it, if you are willing to hold your golden vision, nurture it and know that it is real – even if it has not yet transpired – it cannot help but become a reality. Allow yourself to dream, to imagine, to be inspired. Open yourself up to the vast possibilities ahead.

When your inner vision is clear you are not beholden to the illusions of 3D 'reality'. You do not need to get tangled up in drama, stories or other people's versions of the world. Instead you hold open a doorway to unlimited possibilities and infinite wonder, to a true era of peace and joy on this planet. Bottle C6's partner, bottle C14 (Vision), will escort you there.

When you are drawn to bottle C6, we invite you also to read about its 'partner' bottle, C14, for further insights and information.

Bottle C6 Story: Melissie

This is just a silly story but a situation I think we all find ourselves in from time to time. I was at home with a cough and a tremendously sore throat. I was just tired and kind of knew that I was holding on to words that needed to be said, hence the sore throat. While I was mooching around at home and feeling sorry for myself, my very outspoken friend arrived. I was making tea and having a little whinge about all the stuff going on and she said, sarcasm dripping: "I know this woman who makes these amazing healing oils... Shall I try and find you a blue one for your sore throat??" I literally said: "Oh yes! That might help..." and went and got bottle C6 off my table – not the throat chakra but certainly the painkiller. I rubbed it on my throat and instantly felt deep relief, as if a muscle that had been clenched suddenly relaxed. My throat immediately stopped being sore, and I also realised that all the stuff I was holding on to and not saying had nothing to do with the other person and was just my own projection. My friend laughed and laughed.

Bottle C6 Story: Moira Bush, Canada, www.moirabush.com

Whenever anyone arrives at my practice saying that they are dealing with a big issue such as cancer, a broken bone or some life-threatening situation, I always suggest that they try C6 in a bath first, then identify and take care of the causal factor by selecting the bottle that they are most drawn to. For me C6 is the rescue remedy bottle in the Colour Mirrors system, pulling you out of pain and panic. My husband Paul has been in several accidents and has two crushed vertebra in his neck that often seize up and cause him a lot of pain. The oil I massage him with is from bottle C6. It gives him instant relief and a peaceful night's sleep.

Bottle C14: Third Eye Chakra – Vision (Gold/Clear)

This bottle brings light into the energy centre of the third eye, clearing away fear and replacing it with clarity and truth. If there is chaos or discord unfolding around you, it asks you to keep your inner vision clear and stay in your truth and power so that you do not get pulled in by the dramas. This bottle connects you with your inner knowing and the wisdom of your higher self. Now is the time to create a clear and powerful vision for your own life and for the earth. This bottle says you came to be part of the co-creation of a Golden Age on this planet, and by holding the vision you help bring it into reality.

Bottle C14 is the second of the two third eye chakra bottles, and it is a significant shift from the first, bottle C6. When you as an individual move from a particular colour into its complementary or opposite colour, this is a sign of big changes taking place. The third eye is the seat of your vision, higher insight and ability to perceive. Its shift in colour from the deep royal blue and violet of bottle C6 to the brightness of gold and clear in bottle C14 signals that something monumental is happening, not just for you but for all humanity. Royal blue, the traditional colour of the third eye, is dark, dense, almost impenetrable, and you might wonder how you were you ever supposed to 'see' through that!

As an infinite being, as spirit, the one thing you never had to develop was faith. With the ability to clearly see the future and the past and everything in between, you had no need of faith. You knew. But on a quest to continually grow, evolve and discover more of the Allness of which you are part, you asked yourself what would happen if you were to blind yourself to the truth of the light that you really are. You wondered what would happen if you no longer knew you were a Divine being. If you sealed your third eye with this deep, dense colour, you would have to learn to take every step on faith.

This has been humanity's journey, and in the not knowing, not seeing, you have learned much – about yourself, about life, about faith, about the Divine. You have learned about your shadow, you have discovered what you are capable of, you have explored what it means to go deeply into the darkness. Now, in order to complete this game, you must learn to love it all and judge none of it. If you can do that, you can truly move back into the light of your knowing. As you shift into another level of consciousness you can now take the royal blue and transform it into its complementary colour, gold – one of the brightest of all colours. It is time for the release and clearing of the third eye. It is time to recognise and remember its true function, which is to bring light and clarity to your vision for yourself, for others and the planet. It is time to step out of the darkness and into the light.

Many people have commented that when they place this bottle on their third eye they have a sense of powerful energy, swirling like a vortex. For some it brings a sense of instant illumination, as if whatever feels dense or dark can suddenly become light. When placed on another chakra that seems blocked it has the same clearing effect, making space for a new vision for that chakra. It might also be a perfect remedy for artist's or writer's block, giving you back the clear vision with which to create.

The colour gold relates to addictions, and if you are drawn to this bottle you are asked to acknowledge where you are beholden to addictions of any kind. This bottle has a solid wall of gold in the top fraction with a clear fraction underneath in which lie tears and an absence of feeling. Addictions often suppress emotions, blocking out sadness, pain or despair. If you are stuck in addiction there is precious little room for a new vision for your life. Perhaps one of the reasons you have let addictions take hold is precisely because the vision you held has failed to materialise.

Perhaps you are absent from your own life, checked out, only going through the motions, in which case having a vision for the future feels redundant. Maybe you are putting off making decisions, getting lost in toxic instant gratification and a desperate desire for the pain to go away *now*, without stopping to question why it is there in the first place. You may find yourself doing whatever it takes to make the pain stop, at least temporarily, by using food, drugs, alcohol, shopping, sex, or anything else that prevents you from feeling.

This bottle is deeply empowering, shifting you back into the golden light of your authentic truth so that you no longer give your power away to anyone or anything. As you remember the truth about yourself – that you are Divine, that you are golden – you are able to connect with a clear vision for your future again. Inspiration hits, possibilities arise, ideas come calling and you can tap back into the excitement of knowing that *you* are responsible for your own life – no one else – and therefore have the power to make whatever changes your soul truly desires to make. This bottle supports you as you move from the limited viewpoint of one who is powerless and addicted to the expansive, clear-sighted vision of one who is divinely connected and on track.

As is so often the case, bottle C14 reveals both sides of an issue. Some choose this bottle because they are lost in addiction and unable to see the way forward. It appeals to others because they are already visionary, clear-sighted and focused on creating a powerful, positive future. Whatever your circumstances, this bottle invites you to discover what 'vision' might truly mean for you. It also reminds you that your vision can be felt and experienced as much as seen, arising from your entire being, not just your eyes or your mind.

You are part of a collective, conscious agreement that 'reality' is based on what you can hear, see, smell, touch and taste. Yet bottle C14 also tells you that vast realms exist beyond your sense perceptions, that life is unlimited, that you are so much more than your mind and your body. This bottle leaves little room for the smallness of human ego. It assists you in awakening to a much greater vision for yourself, your life and the future of all humanity. Now you can access the Akashic Records, which hold all the information of everything that ever was, is now and ever will be. This information does not exist 'out there' somewhere – it is right inside the infinite complexity of your cells, and now is the time to reconnect with it all, to see beyond borders and boundaries and restrictions to a Divine reality that is not limited in any way.

This bottle reflects the light of the Divine – bright and glorious – blazing a path to a new era on the planet. It offers the clarity to see the Golden Age, create the Golden Age, live the Golden Age – and it reminds you that your vision is instrumental in creating it, for you personally and for all. The knowledge of how to do this is built into your DNA, available in your cells. Bottle C14 brings a wave of excitement and possibility. It is a sunrise on the horizon, a tonic for a jaded soul. Here is your chance to create in inspiring and brilliant ways. Here is the potential for you to be anything you can imagine yourself to be. Here is the opportunity to discover what it means to live as the powerful being of light that you are.

Bottle C14 is a gift, encouraging you to wipe the fear and darkness of the past from your brow, illuminate your inner vision and connect with a golden future. It assists you in understanding that a huge part of why you incarnated in this lifetime was simply to hold the vision of a Golden Age. Anything else you experience along the way is designed to bring you to mastery so that you can take up your role in the unfolding of this vision.

When you are drawn to bottle C14, we invite you also to read about its 'partner' bottle, C6, and the sixth spiritual principle: Hold a clear vision of perfection.

Bottle C14 Story: Melissie

My daughter, Gilly, told me: "I am making decisions my future self would be proud of." That might just be the way to create a perfect Golden Age.

Bottle C14 Story: Korani

I remember a woman who came on a workshop and chose this bottle to take home at the end of the first day. She had felt blocked and stuck for years. She had issues with relationships, pain in her body, a job she disliked and various other things that meant she felt frustrated and powerless. She said that for many years she daren't even dream that anything else was possible. By the time she found Colour Mirrors she had begun to feel that she might just be able to start to change things, which was why she had come to the workshop in the first place. She bathed in this bottle and in the bath 'saw' so clearly that she had been blocking herself and that it was not about anyone or anything else. In that moment she chose to take back her own power. She realised that she could begin to envision a new life for herself.

The Crown Chakra: Bottles C7, C15 and the Seventh Spiritual Principle – You are God in a Body

Bottle C7: Crown Chakra (Magenta/Violet)

This bottle helps activate the gift of healing and asks you to own your power as a healer. It awakens your ability to accept Divine love and then bring that love into everything you are and everything you do. It relates to a position of power in the Catholic Church in a past life and indicates that you may still be holding on to some grief and guilt from that lifetime. This bottle helps clear the cellular memories so that you can find peace, compassion and understanding for yourself and others.

Your crown chakra is the seat of your spirit, that part of you which is eternal, the essence of who you are. It is where you are connected to the Divine, and its traditional colour is violet. Violet blends the pink of pure feminine Divine love and the blue of the perfect Divine masculine to create a whole that is greater than the sum of its parts. In this way, violet represents a balancing and a return to wholeness. It opens you to your spiritual connection so that you begin to recognise the divinity in yourself and in all. With its support, you become more interested in life and the wider world than in your own concerns and dramas. You feel the call to give something of yourself for the greater good. Your focus moves from your personal human story to a higher perspective – to the view from your spirit.

Bottle C7 relates to the judgements you hold that have stopped you from accessing that higher perspective. Judgements always limit your understanding and keep your focus on the human experience rather than the Divine one. The colours of this bottle help shed light on your judgements and root them out so that you can expand your viewpoint and open to greater possibilities for your life. As well as exploring the judgements you hold, this bottle particularly highlights the judgements you have received, whether they come from others or are self-inflicted. It calls your attention to the many ways in which you feel judged and the effects of those judgements on your life.

This bottle relates to Catholic lifetimes and the attendant grief, guilt, judgement and belief in original sin. It is a support when you are unable to forgive yourself, whether for events in this lifetime or for past life actions and deeds. It often signals a lifetime as a Catholic priest during the Inquisition – which may well require some self-forgiveness! In that lifetime the prevailing belief was in righteousness and the separation of the body from the soul. Your role as priest was to burn the bodies in order to save the souls and yet, as in every situation, as in every lifetime, there is always a higher truth.

This was a lifetime in which you played the role you came to play in order to bring you and others the experiences that each of your souls requested. From this lifetime you and everyone involved learned about power, judgement, guilt and abuse. You learned what it meant to hold someone's life in your hands and you learned what it meant to play God rather than being God. No doubt there were endless complexities to your beliefs, experiences and judgements, and nothing about such lifetimes is easy to reconcile. Yet as a Divine being who came to experience every aspect of life, you chose this role to enable you to discover more about yourself and life, to play out the various aspects of your soul, to learn, grow and evolve and to move beyond previous limitations.

This bottle often shows up when you are facing shadow issues of separation, grief and depression or when you feel helpless, powerless and unable to make decisions. Whether you are trapped in the past, filled with despair, grieving for the life you feel you 'should' have led or just feeling stuck, this bottle is a gift from your spirit to help you move forward with a lighter heart. It helps you see from the Divine perspective whatever is keeping you locked in the past so that you can move out of judgement and into compassion and in the process set yourself free from the cellular memories of grief and guilt.

As you step out of the violet depths you are able to move back towards the light, let go of confusion, take back your power and begin to make positive choices. Violet's complementary colour is yellow, and the complementary bottle to

C7 is bottle C3 (Solar Plexus). Just as bottle C3 helps clear confusion and bring back the joy, bottle C7 puts you in touch with your true self. It helps you bring light to unresolved feelings and release them so that you can shift into a lighter and more empowered state of being.

This bottle tends to come calling when you are just waking up to your true self, when you have an inner yearning to do something more, be something more. You might be drawn to train in the healing arts, take up a socially responsible position, become a volunteer or find other meaningful ways to be of service. You may be in the midst of huge spiritual development and discovering that you are not limited or powerless but an aspect of something much bigger than you had ever allowed yourself to realise. This phase of your awakening is often filled with dreams, 'signs' and symbols. It can be very exciting – and possibly a little daunting – as you become aware that you are going to have to let go of some of your old ways and beliefs.

You may be quite ungrounded, wanting to fly off into the exciting new dimensions you are beginning to explore rather than staying here with your feet on the ground. You are likely to be seeking – reading everything you can get your hands on, having healing sessions or learning how to facilitate healing for others. You may be attending workshops or classes and going for readings. Bottle C7 can help you during this time to clear blocks in your crown chakra so that you become an open, clear channel for the light of spirit to work with and through.

When you are drawn to this bottle it signals that you are awakening to the truth that you are a spiritual being first and foremost. You are energy and light and potential, and you have very real abilities in the realms of spiritual work. It is time to explore your healing abilities, and this is often best done with the help of a guide or mentor so that you can explore where your interests and capabilities lie.

Bottle C7 helps you open your spiritual channels, and you may find that you can begin to feel, sense, see or hear healing frequencies. Healing is not always about laying your hands on someone, however, or 'channelling' energy. Your healing ability may come through the art you create or the books you write or the food you make to share with others. Perhaps your healing talents lie in coaching, counselling or 'talk' therapies. There are as many paths to 'healing' as there are people on the planet, so whatever you feel drawn to explore, be assured that you will be guided and shown the way forward as you learn to listen to your spirit.

If you are new to the spiritual realms, you may find yourself waking up tired every morning, no matter how much sleep you are having. This can happen if you are spending large amounts of time in meditation or if you are astral travelling in your sleep. It is often a sign that you are doing 'rescue' work, helping souls cross into the light. For a body that is unused to doing this work it can cause fatigue, and by working with bottle C7, rubbing some oil into your skin each night or bathing in some of the oil before bed, you will offer up the burden of responsibility that you have unconsciously taken on out of a sense of duty or guilt, and allow the process to proceed without needing to drain you.

This bottle is frequently chosen by those with ME or Chronic Fatigue. If this is your story you are almost certainly a powerful healer and highly intuitive, but you may be refusing on some level to claim your spiritual abilities. Do you go on course after course and gain more and more qualifications but never quite take the plunge and begin to offer your skills out in the world? Perhaps you hold a belief that it is not until you yourself are completely 'healed' in every aspect of your life that you will be able to help others. This is a way of keeping your true power at bay and denying the truth of yourself as a perfectly imperfect Divine human with much to offer. This bottle can relate to commitment issues and not fully claiming your spiritual responsibility. It asks you to look at how committed you are to life. Will you stay locked in the self-imposed restriction and past life programming that keeps you small, or will you set yourself free and show up in your life as the powerful healer and spiritual being you are?

With its magenta top fraction, this bottle offers hope. Its message is that you do not have to become bogged down in personal or existential grief or remain beholden to your beliefs and conditioning. Magenta is a beacon, helping you recognise and remember the truth that you are already Divine – and that you, as much as anyone on the planet, deserve love.

This bottle facilitates your awareness of the light that is in every person and every being. It also helps you recognise that in a sense, everyone you meet is a healer. Every human being is here on earth to support the journey and help facilitate the spiritual awakening of every other human. Everyone on your path comes into your life so that they can 'walk you home', just as you show up in the lives of others to do the same for them.

132

The time for hiding your spiritual light is over. You are a powerful Divine being who just needs to remember that no experience in this lifetime or any other can dim your light or cause it to go out. Bottle C7 asks you to be your authentic self and realise that you do not have to 'know' everything before you go out into the world and shine your light. You are ready. Let your spirit guide the way.

The Seventh Spiritual Principle: You are God in a Body

The seventh spiritual principle teaches that you are God in a body. It says you never left home in the first place. You are the Divine and it is you, and there never was any separation between the two. Everything is as it should be, just as it always was and always will be.

You may initially struggle with this concept. Perhaps you believe that you were born in sin and that you are therefore fundamentally flawed. You might have been taught that the Divine is outside of you, that the force we call Source or God emanates from a figure or entity that is somehow distanced from you, separate from you and very much better or higher than you. You may believe that it is fundamentally wrong to say that you are God or Divine, that this is egotistical in the extreme. These have all been prevalent beliefs on the planet for millennia.

Yet have these beliefs contributed to a world of peace, love and harmony? Have they brought joy, wonderment, freedom and spiritual fulfilment to all of humanity? Have they led to compassion, self-realisation and higher levels of consciousness? At the dawning of a new era on the earth you are asked to really take this spiritual principle in and take it on – 'You are God in a body' – and bottle C7 and its partner, bottle C15 (Crystal Being), will support you in seeing the truth in this. For when you fully embrace the knowing that you *are* Divine – completely interconnected with the universe, absolutely an aspect of the Allness, one with God – you realise that this is the opposite of ego.

As you release any remaining stories of victimhood, blame and judgement, you open yourself to a state of perpetual consciousness and the flow that comes from being aligned with natural Divine order. Grief subsides, fears dissolve and you automatically take up your authentic power and assume authority for your life. If you are beholden to the past, to old ways of being, to the third-dimensional constructs of limitation, or if you continue to give your spiritual power to an outside authority – whether you call that God, religion, the universe or fate – you continue to live as your small, ego-driven human self. When you know yourself to be an aspect of the Divine, experiencing life in a body, exploring life as a spirit who is housed in a physical form; when you truly know that you are the creator of your life – then the heaviness falls away and you are free to step into the light and live as your essence, your glorious spirit. In so doing, you offer yourself in true service to the planet, to humanity and to the Divine.

When you are drawn to bottle C7, we invite you also to read about its 'partner' bottle, C15, for further insights and information.

Bottle C7 Story: Melissie

I remember a reading I did for a man with bi-polar disorder who chose this bottle and took it home to bathe in. He had taken himself off his medication a year before, and although he had had no wild episodes, he was deeply depressed. He came back a few weeks after the bath in bottle C7 feeling very much lighter in himself.

Bottle C7 Story: Moira Bush, Canada, www.moirabush.com

Without fail, every time someone picks this bottle who is newly awakened to the world of energy and spirituality and I tell them that this bottle says "you are a healer", they gasp or cry or have some sort of deep emotional reaction. Mostly the response is that they have always known that they have a special gift but thought it was wishful thinking or that they 'imagined' making a difference when they helped others by placing their hands on the area of pain or praying for them. On my Facebook TV show where I feature the Colour Mirrors system, a guest picked bottle C7 and could not keep her hands off it. After the show we took the conversation deeper, and she cried with relief that she was not imagining her healing abilities. She signed up to a course and has begun working with the bottles.

Bottle C15: Crown Chakra – Crystal Being (Clear/Lilac)

This bottle indicates that you have a clear connection to your spirit. Your gifts include lightness, clarity and the ability to emanate a high frequency of light wherever you go. You are truly ready to be of service. This bottle helps activate the crystalline grid that surrounds the earth and relates to the Crystal children who have come to support the process of conscious evolution on the planet. You have much to contribute to humanity's Ascension process simply by being the light that you are.

By the time you shift from the more traditional crown chakra colours offered by bottle C7 to the next level revealed by the second crown chakra bottle, C15, you are beginning to realise that you are actively connected in every moment to the light of your spirit. This bottle, in its quietly glowing other-worldliness, reflects your innate innocence and purity. It activates the light within so that your spirit begins to illuminate your life. While it is not always experienced in tangible, practical ways, this bottle often shifts things hugely on a spiritual level, bringing clarity of knowing and lightness of being. The density of bottle C7 can be left behind, with a much lighter space becoming available to you from which to live your life.

This bottle is about clearing your dependence on external structures and reclaiming your own light. Its message is that you do not need an outside authority to facilitate a direct, clear connection to the Divine. With the violet of spirit now lightened to lilac in the bottom fraction and the purity of clear in the top, this bottle shows that your true spiritual connection is already inside you, with nothing in the way of the light of Source.

Bottle C15 helps you release any remaining blocks in your crown chakra and any lingering guilt and grief, ushering in a new phase in your life where you can truly rely on your spirit to guide you. This bottle says you have a role to play in the spiritual evolution of humanity and the earth, and that the lighter you take yourself, the lighter your personal Ascension experience will be. After bottle C7's heaviness, bottle C15 shows that you have the ability to give of yourself in spiritual service with a soft and light touch. Like the clear bottles, C9 (Lightbody) and G27 (Unity), this bottle can put a spotlight on and amplify whichever other bottles you are choosing. If you look at whatever you place it next to in a reading, this will help you see where to access your spiritual gifts and how to use them.

Many members of our Colour Mirrors family have experienced this bottle turning turquoise in the bottom fraction. This often happens when first opening to a spiritual path or when undergoing huge spiritual transformation. This bottle says that as you embrace your inner light and step up to be visible in the world, you become a guide for others in creating a paradigm shift on the earth, communicating as much through your beingness as by what you do or say. This is reflected in the colour change to turquoise, which relates to teaching, communicating from the heart and the dawning of a Golden Age on the earth.

This bottle looks rather like a Brandberg crystal. These are crystals of clear quartz with amethyst inside, which come from Namibia and are of great purity and extremely high vibration. Bottle C15 relates to the 'Crystal' children who began to arrive from the 1980's onwards, the next wave of lightworkers to incarnate after the Indigo children. These children came in with the knowing of their spiritual connection already in place. They often choose this bottle, which is about the full acknowledgment of humanity's connection beyond this planet and this earthly existence. When you choose this bottle you are tapping into lifetimes on other realms so that you might receive information and knowledge for your personal evolution and to assist in the unfolding of the Ascension process on earth.

Bottle C15 has an affinity with the Platinum Gaia bottles and bottle 36, The Gateway, and a similar vibration. It awakens in you a cosmic consciousness, an awareness of yourself as a Divine spirit in an infinitely vast universe. It takes your awareness into levels of light that are beyond your earthly human existence and awakens in you the ability to experience other dimensions. It reminds you of the potential you hold and helps you open to your purpose here on earth. It can also be a gateway or portal to higher realms, offering a sense of connectedness with the Divine, the Allness, the light of spirit.

There is a crystalline grid surrounding the planet that draws information, light and energy to the earth and those who live upon her. Bottle C15 carries the light of this grid, and if this is your bottle, it indicates that you are part of the light matrix holding the grid in place. You are someone of high frequency and purity, valued by the light beings who oversee the Ascension process for humanity and the earth. The more you tune in with your spirit on a daily basis and work with light, colour, crystals, sound or other healing energies, the more you will access the beauty and peace of the spiritual realms and the more you will be of service, naturally and easily, just by being yourself.

Crystals act as a bridge between the physical and spiritual realms. They carry the physical energy of the earth and the spiritual energy of the stars and galaxies. This bottle says that as a light being in a physical body, you too are a bridge. You are someone who helps transmute darkness just by the very fact of your light. You touch people with your gentle, loving soul. Lilac taps into the ray of magic, and you are someone who has the capacity to weave magic into your life with both subtlety and surety. Your light is greatly treasured. Cultivate it well.

When you are drawn to bottle C15, we invite you also to read about its 'partner' bottle, C7, and the seventh spiritual principle: You are God in a body.

Bottle C15 Story: Debra Hubers-Paradis, USA, www.DebrasEnergyPoints.com

I attended an event where I was doing chakra balancing with the chakra bottles. One of the participants had a sore tailbone, so we had her lie face down on the table. She had jeans on, a sweatshirt and a blanket over her. I placed bottle C15 on her tailbone area and several bottles on the rest of her back and ran some Reiki energy. After 20 minutes we went to take off the bottles and discovered that bottle C15 on the tailbone had generated so much heat that the blanket, her shirt and jeans were soaked through from the heat that came off the bottle, yet the bottle was dry and warm to the touch. When she got off of the table, she said the tailbone pain was almost gone.

Bottle C15 Story: Katherine Louise Jones, UK, www.katherinelouisejones.com

When I started my Colour Mirrors training I'd wake up each day and choose a selection of bottles to help me gain clarity on a situation. The bottles have a funny way of getting our attention – ones to work with, messages within and so on. My animals are a great help – if my cat knocks one over I will pay attention to the message it holds for me! I've had many a bath and deepening through my journey. On one occasion I read something on Facebook about a school reunion of friends I had known for 20 years. I hadn't been invited. Immediately old memories of feeling 'left out' resurfaced. I could feel my body reacting to these triggers and the emotional pain of sadness coming up, even though in my mind I knew I wouldn't have gone if asked. I sent out a prayer to the universe for clarity on the situation and shortly afterwards heard a noise. Investigating, I found that bottle C15 had smashed, the only one on a shelf of over 100 bottles. It gave me an instant reconnection to my Divine mission and purpose and cleared any lingering memories of feelings left in my body, shifting my perspective and vibration. I scooped up what I could, rubbing the remains of the oil onto my body so my cells could feel the message of 'Crystal Being'.

Higher Crown Chakra: Bottle C8 and the Eighth Spiritual Principle – Guilt is the Biggest Misunderstanding of All

Bottle C8: Higher Crown Chakra – The Bridge (Pink/Magenta)

This bottle is about creating a deeper, stronger connection with your soul. It is helpful when experiencing existential grief and is a powerful support for your inner child. It is beneficial for creating a loving space for a new soul and is about giving birth to something new. This could mean welcoming a baby into the family, or it could be a new venture or creative project to be nurtured into being.

Bottle C8 is the only chakra bottle that has no 'partner' bottle in the Colour Mirrors system. The first seven chakras, from base to crown, are all in the process of undergoing colour changes as humanity evolves to a point where every chakra holds every colour of the rainbow, and the system reflects that shift. The soul star chakra has no need of a colour change as it is already intimately linked with the Divine, and this is reflected in its magenta colour.

At the centre of the 15 chakra bottles, C8 relates to your 'soul star', the seat of your soul. It stands firmly and clearly in the light of Divine perfection. Its job is to help you really understand yourself as a soul, a spark of Divine light, a spiritual being who is here on earth to experience life in a physical body. In soft, loving pink and magenta, this bottle invites you to embrace the greater 'you', the part of yourself that has never felt separate or abandoned, the eternal essence that makes you who you are. Your soul or higher self is always within you, always available to you and always, always loves you. If you tend to forget to connect with this part of yourself or have never really been able to feel it, bottle C8 helps bring you closer to your Divine self so that you can feel its truth and its loving guidance.

As you connect with bottle C8 you may feel it calling to your inner child. This bottle is a power pack of love when your inner child is still holding on to the belief that it was somehow a mistake to incarnate here. When you cannot remember why you came or the bigger purpose of your journey, bottle C8 guides you back to your soul's deep connection with the universe. It reminds your inner child of its beauty, light and magic, and its incredible courage in choosing to be part of the shift happening on earth at this time. It helps you know that you are fully supported, now and always, and assists you in knowing and experiencing the fullness of your soul's love. This bottle says you are beloved. You are and have always been a Divine child of the universe.

Magenta is the colour of the healer. It often attracts those who have a great desire to help others and make a difference in this world. Because life on earth can be painful, challenging and bewildering for so many people, as you wake up to your healing abilities you may find yourself thinking that you have to try and fix at least some of what the universe has 'messed up'. If you keep that up for any length of time it will not be long before you are very tired indeed, and this bottle is often chosen by healers who exhaust themselves by trying to find a solution to everything in their world – and everyone else's – sometimes ending up with ME or Chronic Fatigue.

This bottle asks you to walk away from all the fixing. It also asks you to stop fighting, because fighting is never the answer. Things will only truly begin to change when you let go of the battle, which really stems from your judgements, and choose instead to open to compassion and love. This bottle shows you that life is not so much about what you do, it is about the energy with which you do it. It says you cannot fight anything right – ever. Love is the only possible force for true change and healing. So relax and let go. No one needs you to fix anything. Let your soul take over and guide you every step of the way.

Bottle C8 can feel almost like a re-birth, an opening to more of your true self. Choosing this bottle indicates that you are ready to shift – you know you cannot remain in the same old space, hanging on to the same old 'stuff'. It is time for a new beginning, a new reality creation. With bottle C8, it is as if the new space has already been created; now you simply have to move forward and take the step. With the support of this bottle – and your soul – it can be very easy. There are no more hurdles in the way; it is all there waiting for you. Even if you cannot yet see what you are seeking, as you take the step it will appear. If this bottle is speaking to you, its message is that you are now ready for your soul to take the driving seat in your life.

This bottle connects you with the synchronicity, magic and Divine timing of magenta. It holds a sacred space where everything can unfold with ease and grace. Magenta guides you gently but firmly back into the now and asks you to experience it, be it, live it. It helps you let go of past concerns and future worries and recognise that now is all there is. This bottle takes away the 'how' questions such as: "How will I do this? How will it happen?" It reconnects you with the present moment so that you can allow everything to unfold without getting in your own way. Soul energy opens you to so much more than mind energy, and this bottle asks you to let go into the possibility of something much bigger, better and greater than you have so far imagined.

This Soul Star bottle is a great support whenever you are 'pregnant' with something – whether a baby, a book, a painting, a creative project, a business or an idea. It can take you into new creative spaces in your life, encouraging you to branch out, open up and explore new avenues of potential. Its beautiful creation energy enables you to bring the new into being as it aligns you with your soul. Whatever you create from that place of soul connection carries your true energy blueprint. When you create from your soul, you offer your gifts to the world in a unique and potent way. With the magenta of your soul star combined with the pink of your heart's love, your creations become powerful points of light that bring fulfilment, joy and expansion to yourself and others.

Bottle C8 is about potential becoming realised. The idea or project – or baby – is no longer just a concept but a real, living energy that will go into the world and find its own unique path. Part of any birthing process is the recognition that as the 'parent', you are only one element in the equation – a necessary one, it is true! Yet in some ways you are only a facilitator, a caretaker and a guardian for a time. The child or project being birthed has its own blueprint to follow, its own life path to live. Bottle C8 holds a beautiful space of love for the birth to happen, and because magenta is always a bridge, it is also about allowing your creations to grow – perhaps into something you could never have dreamed of. If you trust that the Divine is within everything and everyone, you can let go of needing your creations or children to be a certain way. You can enjoy the 'baby' for what it is and let it grow into a toddler, a child and eventually an adult.

Magenta is the bridge between old and new, heaven and earth, spirit and matter. This bottle shows you that the bridge is being built as you walk upon it and if you allow yourself to cross it, you will come to a new space. When you give birth to something your life always looks and feels very different. Creating anything of substance always helps you move to a new level, and bottle C8 leads you towards the next stage of your journey. It brings in new souls. It also helps the souls who are already here realise that they came out of love and a desire to grow and evolve. It makes it not just safe to be here on earth but actually desirable. The depth of Divine love in the magenta base holds you completely. With its pink fraction this bottle is also mother love, baby love, family love and relationship love; indeed, all the love in a human life. This bottle is truly uplifting, guiding you onwards and upwards into the realms of your soul star. It opens you to your highest truth. It asks you to know that truth and live it, as the expression of the Divine that you are.

The Eighth Spiritual Principle: Guilt is the Biggest Misunderstanding of All

Magenta is about Divine love, but it also relates to guilt, punishment and struggle, and the eighth spiritual principle says that it is guilt – often unconscious guilt – which creates much of the pain, suffering and discomfort of a human life. When you are on the wheel of guilt, pain and struggle may be your everyday companions. But if you really believe that what you do or who you are is wrong, this means you have somehow managed to be the only piece of a perfect creation that is bigger than God and therefore able to mess up the perfect Divine unfolding of the universe!

It is time to see the higher truth, and pain is often the only way to get your attention and make you stop long enough so that the misunderstanding can be sorted out. Pain is frequently misinterpreted as yet another reason to suffer when it is only ever there to show you something greater, to reveal to you a higher truth. When you believe that you are somehow wrong, that you have made a mistake or that indeed the very fact of your existence was a mistake, magenta shows you the path out of the tangled woods of guilt and shame. If you are not guilty, you do not deserve to suffer, and the minute you shift your consciousness into 'not guilty', into 'innocent', everything changes – and then the moment can be whatever is. If you are not guilty there is no longer a struggle, and then it is not "God hates me", it is just "well, this is interesting…"

This is such a powerful key to living a wonderful life. As long as you are hung up on 'wrong' and 'shouldn't have happened', you keep yourself locked into pain, struggle and guilt. You forget that you are perfect and that every situation is perfect. Bottle 22 (Forgiveness) is all about clearing guilt. Bottle C8 takes you a step further to where there is no concept of guilt. Your soul says: "Guilt? What guilt?"

As a powerful being of light, you always have been and always will be innocent, a perfect aspect of God who can create only perfection – and so it is for every single being in existence. Every being that you will ever encounter is on a contract that says: "No matter what it takes, I will help you heal". If that means pressing your buttons, challenging you in some way or offering you a difficult experience to grow through and from, the soul who offers that to you is the one who loves you enough to give you what your soul requested when it incarnated: an opportunity to expand and evolve.

If you take the next step from magenta on the colour wheel you will find yourself back in the red and the first spiritual principle: Judge nothing. If you can now see it all from the magenta perspective, there really is not a single thing to judge. You cannot judge perfection. How can anything created by a perfect universe not be perfect? There may be choices that you experience as optimal and others that feel the opposite, but essentially none are wrong or bad. They are all simply choices which lead to experiences. They are all threads in the tapestry of your life and there are an infinite number of patterns available to you. Magenta asks you to look at every little battle and crisis in your life as an opportunity to create something new, grow beyond the limitations to which you have believed yourself chained and expand your knowledge of yourself and the universe in the process.

Bottle C8, the colour magenta and the eighth spiritual principle all help you release whatever guilt you may be holding on any level and guide you through the process of forgiveness – of yourself, of others, of God. They lead you to a place where forgiveness is no longer necessary because you can see and know the perfection of everything that has ever been, is now and ever will be. They guide you steadfastly towards the knowing that you, the other and God are all part of the Oneness. And although your mind may try to tell you otherwise, your soul knows that the moment you embrace the perfection of each moment, you are free.

Bottle C8 Story: Melissie and Korani

It was when Melissie bathed in bottle C8 back in 2009 that the Golden Gaias and their vision of a new Golden Age upon the earth announced themselves as the next part of the Colour Mirrors system. At the same time, Korani's stock of C8 bottles all turned blue on the bottom and very soon afterwards she went on to 'birth' a book about these golden energies, The Language of Light: Golden Keys to Ascension.

Bottle C8 Story: Debra Hubers-Paradis, USA, www.DebrasEnergyPoints.com

I was doing a long distance session with one of my clients who was very upset and overwhelmed. We worked with a few of the spritzers, and she began to feel more grounded. She remembered she had bottle C8 in her medicine chest and pulled it out. She noticed that the line between the two colours was bubbling and churning – similar to what she was feeling inside. As we continued with the session the bubbles stopped and disappeared as she became calm inside herself.

Bottle C8 Story: Lesley McDonald, UK, www.lesleytara.com

When I was a teenager I fell in love with a magenta dress in a posh downtown department store. As often as I could I would slip away to the store, and in the privacy of the fitting room, would transform my shy 14-year-old self into an Eastern princess. In that beautiful dress with the mandarin collar and slender pencil skirt, I connected with my true essence, and my life force stirred.

At the time I knew little of colour rays, but as I was to discover, the magenta ray was to be my greatest teacher and would be traceable as a path to moments of exquisite beauty, lighting up my life in the darkest of times. I had always had an affinity for magenta, not at a conscious level, but with the frequency of Divine love. I felt everything acutely, loved deeply and fiercely, but understood nothing of the harshness into which I had incarnated. It seemed at the time that all around me were sadness, fear, and sharp, critical tongues. I forgot that I was Divine and bit by bit the memory of being wrapped in the magenta ray of love drifted further and further away.

Years later, magenta would alter the course of my life in one of those precious moments when I again connected with the true essence of my soul. I was in my late twenties, pushing my little baby in his pushchair through the cemetery close to our apartment in central Copenhagen, and tears flowed down my face as I wondered where my joy had gone. Was motherhood really meant to be this hard? The dark clouds reflected the drabness of my thoughts, and in that moment I uttered a silent cry for help. As if in answer a magenta wild rose caught my eye, and I was transfixed. I stared unblinkingly at the rose and drank in the magenta frequency. It was, in fact, this magenta rose that led me to first study colour all those years ago. It lifted my spirts long enough to open a window of hope. Magenta does this. It is a bridge, a Divine nudge and a loving hand, gently guiding us when we think we can take no more. Watch for the magenta bridge, that sacred moment in time which always appears when we most seem to require it.

Many years later when I met the Colour Mirrors system, I was ready to heal all of it, to finally face myself and gather up the magenta child, the magenta teenager and the magenta mother, all still carrying the pain of those difficult years. I knew the moment I saw it. Just like that defining moment with the rose, I stared transfixed: bottle C8 mirroring my very soul, urging me to dive right in and let the healing happen, providing a window of hope, a way out of the shadow of grief and invisibility, encouraging me to let my light shine. I loved that sacred, precious bottle. I stepped onto the bridge it offered and bathed in its fragrant hues. It wrapped me in Divine love and brought me home to my very essence.

We are all that magenta child, the very essence of Divine love, and this amazing bottle enables us to step in to our truth, heal our wounded parts and become the love we truly are and always have been.

More on the Eight Spiritual Principles

If you would like to explore the Spiritual Principles in more depth, we recommend Melissie's book *What the Seeker Found* and her webinar series *8 Spiritual Principles to Ascension*.

The e-book *Colour Conversations* also weaves many of the principles into its pages.

These resources provide further information and insight into how you can live the principles in your everyday life for your own peace, joy and well-being and to assist in the evolution of humanity.

What the Seeker Found: available on Amazon worldwide

8 Spiritual Principles to Ascension webinar: available at www.korani.net

Colour Conversations e-book: available at www.korani.net

Colour Mirrors Mini-Sets

The Colour Mirrors Mini-Chakra Set

The chakra bottles are a favourite of many people. In 2016 a mini-chakra set was developed to provide small, portable sets of the first eight chakra bottles (C1-C8) as a resource for support and healing. These 'mini' chakra bottles have a roll-top so that you can apply them with ease to the body. They are great for travelling or just to have on hand for everyday use. Each set contains eight mini-oils, one each of C1 (base) to C8 (soul star).

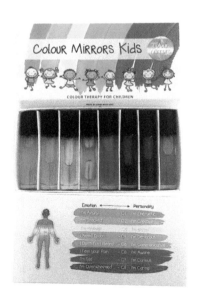

The Colour Mirrors Kids' Set

The mini-chakra set gave birth to another mini-set, this one designed specifically for kids. Using the same mini-set of oils, C1-C8, but with colourful packaging and an insert to show children how colours connect with their feelings, this set is a hit with kids young and old.

The Gaia Set: Introduction

Bottles G1-G36

The set of 36 'Wisdom' bottles takes you deeply into the human story on earth with all its joys, challenges and complexities. The 15 Chakra bottles help you see how you can take light and energy into all aspects of your being and evolve from a drama-based model of human living to the love-fuelled joy of living as a spiritual being in a physical body. Next in the Colour Mirrors system comes another set of 36 bottles, the Gaias, which illuminate the unfolding story of humanity's journey on earth. The Gaia set brings insight into how and why you personally have chosen to be part of this story and assists in laying to rest your ghosts and shadows from the past. Yet more than this, it lights the way for the future of this planet, revealing the potential that is waiting to emerge for the earth and all who live upon her.

Gaia is the name for the consciousness of the planet, the being who is Mother Earth. By naming these bottles 'Gaia' we are acknowledging the profound foundation of love, support and nourishment the earth provides to each and every human so that all might fulfil their Divine potential. One of the greatest blessings of Gaia is that she holds no judgement. Her contract with humanity is and always has been to provide a space for evolution and growth. As humanity has done its worst, as the planet has been used and abused, the being who is Gaia has held her steadfast love for each and every one of us. She is so clear, strong and empowered in her own light that nothing can 'damage' her. Her body definitely experiences the impact of our individual and collective decisions and actions, yet she judges none of it. Her covenant is to love us unconditionally and hold the light for us to grow. If we as a species evolve enough to make more enlightened choices, her body will recover and a new era will unfold on the earth. It is up to us, and the Gaia bottles encourage us to remember our part in the contract: to learn what it means to live from love, harmony and peace on an inner level so that we see this reflected all around us on the outer level.

Our job is to hold the vision for what is possible on this earth rather fall into blame or judgement about what has brought us to the current state of apparent chaos in much of the world. We must see beyond what our eyes show us to the truth in our hearts. The old 'reality' has to be dismantled so that a new one can arise, and much that appears to be difficult, dark and negative is simply coming to the fore now so that it can be transformed. If we get lost in the illusions placed before us, we will simply continue to create more of the same. If, on the other hand, we actively bring our consciousness to a higher, greater vision and take steps to create it, it cannot help but unfold.

The Gaia set pays homage to the planet and each being who has chosen to incarnate here to experience all that she has to teach and share. This part of the system invites you to explore your relationship with the earth, your feelings about her, your challenges with her. It also offers you a pathway as you raise your consciousness and vibration, and lights the way as you heal your past, fall in love with your present and embrace your future.

Like everything in Colour Mirrors, the Gaia set has evolved organically, from an initial seven Copper Gaias to a set of 36 that now stands in its own right. New Gaia bottles always arrived whenever they were needed, each time revealing another level of possibility for humanity to grow and expand into – or perhaps more accurately, for humanity to recognise and remember, for these Gaia bottles only reflect that which is already contained within the DNA of every human.

After the Copper Gaias, the rest of the Gaia set arrived over a period of several years in small subsets: the Golden Gaias (seven bottles), the Platinum Gaias (seven bottles), the Coral Gaias (five bottles), the Silver Gaias (six bottles) and finally the Magenta Gaias (three bottles). In this section we explore the intricate patterns of life on earth through these six colours and subsets of bottles, each with their own wisdom, light, energy and information to share, each building on the one before, each opening you to higher levels of light and consciousness.

There is a trail laid out by the Gaia bottles. The Copper Gaias show you how to be here, how to come to terms with life as a human being on a planet that has often provided as many challenges as gifts. The Golden Gaia set then helps you recognise a greater vision for life on earth and set about creating it. The Platinums light the journey with a remembrance of your cosmic connection to the universe, waking up your higher aspects and a deeper awareness of the expansive nature of all life. Next come the Coral Gaias, which encourage you to take action, get real with your spirituality and embody your light right here on earth in your everyday life. The Silvers gift you with an upgrade in spiritual awareness and an ability to tap into the higher frequencies of light that are required for you to live as a conscious creator of your reality. As you step into the pure power of the Magenta Gaias, you realise that you never left 'home' in the first place – and that the light of the Divine is the only thing that is actually real.

The Gaia set is a reflection of life on earth in all its facets and is profoundly supportive no matter where you are at on your journey. If you feel as if you have been hovering above the ground, unable to fully 'land' here in your body, it supports you in anchoring into the safety and love of Gaia. If you have not yet been able to free yourself from the demons of your past, it brings awareness of the purpose of your path and all that you have learned so that you can open to ease and joy. If you are ready to awaken to a much vaster, lighter, higher version of yourself than you have so far been able to experience, the Gaias will show you the way forward.

The Gaia bottles reflect the greatness you hold within, as do their words. In some regards, all the Gaia bottles share the same core messages: you are Divine light in a physical body, having an experience of limitation so that you might use it to evolve and grow; you are here on earth to assist in the transition of the planet to a higher frequency and to help guide humanity towards Divine consciousness; self-acceptance is a key foundation stone on which human evolution depends because it is only when you can find deep, honest love for yourself that you become able to spread that love to others – and it is each individual's capacity to love that will ultimately decide the fate of this planet. These messages are enormously relevant to life on earth at this time and each of the 36 Gaia bottles in some measure reflects and holds these core meanings.

Each Gaia bottle has its own distinctive qualities and nuances, however, and some will appeal to you more than others. Some will show you what is still waiting within you to be healed or resolved, others will reveal the power and potential you hold. All are infused with the love of the earth herself and the beautiful, steady light she holds for each and every one of us as we evolve.

The Gaia bottles are in many ways aspirational, showing you what is possible from the Divine perspective, holding up a mirror to let you see the bold and brilliant truth about yourself and all of life. Because of this, at times they may feel somewhat lofty, as if they refer to impossible dreams that the average human could never attain. Nothing could be further from the truth. Everything within the Colour Mirrors bottles themselves and within these pages is a mirror. None of it could even have begun to be created if it wasn't already in existence, within you, within everyone. Let the words and the colours of these bottles open your mind, expand your awareness, interact with your energy field and act like a tuning fork to bring you into resonance with them and the possibilities they offer. Some of what happens with Colour Mirrors goes beyond logic or conscious thought, and the words here are encoded with the same Divine light which infuses the bottles. We invite you to let their messages in to your cells as you read. All you have to 'do' to receive them is be open.

Numerology and the Gaia Set

In the introduction to this book (p.16) we shared how the numerology of the Colour Mirrors system adds to the information that can be discerned from each bottle. Now you are given a fascinating opportunity to look at the shifts that happen as you move from the energy of the Wisdom bottles, 1-36, to the more evolved qualities of the Gaia bottles, G1-G36, and how this reflects your own evolution and that of humanity. If, for example, your birth (soul) numbers are 27 and 9, bottles 27 and 9 will reveal information about who you are and what you came to experience in this lifetime. If you then explore the equivalent bottles from the Gaia range, G27 and G9, you will discover more of the potential now available to you as you move beyond your 'story' into greater possibilities, an expanded state of awareness, a more enlightened path.

Quite apart delving deeper into your birth number bottles and their messages, it can also be useful to look at both sides of the equation no matter which bottle you are connecting with at any given time. If, for example, you choose bottle G18, take a look at what bottle 18 has to say; when you are drawn to bottle 34, take a look at bottle G34. These comparisons may reveal the shift from an old pattern into something more empowered and enlightening, shedding light on where you have been, where you are heading now and just how far you have already come.

The Copper Gaia Set

Bottles G1-G8

The Copper Gaias arrived to fulfil a profound need. The system was running merrily along, supporting and empowering people everywhere, but there seemed to be something missing. Colour Mirrors was all about helping people with life on earth, yet prior to the arrival of the Copper Gaias there were no oil bottles in the system that represented the earth. When a friend asked Melissie to make a copper bottle to help anchor the copper light and energy she kept seeing in her clients' energy fields, a combination of clear over copper was created – and everyone who saw this bottle was stopped in their tracks. Suddenly people were lining up for copper bottles, and Melissie saw that it was time to embed the earthly energy deeply into the system. Six further copper bottles were created, and the Copper Gaia set of bottles was born.

In time an eighth bottle came to join the seven Copper Gaias. Bottle G8 is actually deep, dark magenta – so dark that it looks black. Although it is not copper, at that time Melissie thought it was the end of the system, and it seemed like a perfect 'full stop' with which to complete the Gaia set, so it took its place at the conclusion of the seven Copper Gaias. As it turned out, there would be many more Gaia bottles to follow, and just as the eighth bottle in the Chakra set is magenta – a bridge – this deep magenta bottle became the transition to the next set of bottles to be created, the Golden Gaias, which would herald the coming of a Golden Age on the earth.

The rich Copper Gaias have formed a unique core of Colour Mirrors from the start. Together these eight bottles build a solid foundation for you to engage deeply with your history, your programming and the collective and individual narratives about life on earth. These first Gaia bottles are strongly linked to the brown earth of Africa from where, after all, the system emerged. They share with her an unstoppable pulse, a beating heart of life, colour and energy, a rhythm and quality unlike anything else on the planet. There is nothing shy or vapid about the African sunshine, and these earthy bottles are infused with its light and the depth of the landscape's shadows. The Copper Gaias bring a powerful wave of energy that may not always be comfortable but is always, always founded in love. They have a deep connection to all that is nurturing and feminine within the human spirit. Their profound support draws out your own innate love for life and invites you to apply that love to everyone you meet, everything you see and everything you do.

The Copper Gaias present something of a paradox, however. For some, they are the richest, safest, warmest things on the planet. For many – especially for lightworkers – they can be deeply challenging. They seem to represent all that is dark, difficult and painful about life on earth. They invite you to meet yourself and your life in a physical body head-on, with all its highs and lows. They stare you in the face with their 'real' energy – asking you to feel and experience all of it rather than fly off to a metaphorical cloud. The spiritual journey, now perhaps more than at any other time in humanity's history, has become a profoundly physical one. It is no longer about removing yourself to a mountaintop or spending hours each day in meditation. The Copper Gaias remind you to 'be here now' – in your body, on the earth, as a spiritual being, as a human being – and show you that it is safe to do so.

The journey for many on a spiritual path has been to go up and out, into the star realms, into the wider cosmic landscape. This has been a necessary step, opening you to so much more than you might have discovered if you had remained focused on the purely material aspects of life. Yet it is not where the journey ends. 'Ascension' is not a one-time, one-direction process. What you discover as you continue to grow and evolve is that you cannot simply keep going up and out without simultaneously drawing what you have learned and experienced down and in. Many lightworkers on the planet have spent years or decades focusing on gaining knowledge and experiences in the spiritual realms but have been deeply challenged by applying what they have discovered to their everyday lives. Yet what use are spiritual principles, meditational practices or cosmic experiences unless you are able to live a life of harmony, joy, well-being and fulfilment in your body, your life, your work and your relationships?

The Copper Gaias are wonderful tools for grounding you enough that you can open to receive higher frequencies and utilise them effectively in your life. They are also ideal for channelling energy or information and lend themselves naturally to energy healing work. The love and support of these solid copper energies makes you feel safe even while connecting to the highest realms. This means you can receive clear spiritual insight and information and facilitate powerful healing without feeling ungrounded or burning yourself out. With your feet on the earth, safely anchored, you are free to explore the highs of the spiritual journey in a grounded, connected way, bringing the light of the universe through your body without overwhelming it.

Depending on your relationship with your earth mother – and your human mother – and your own personal history of life on earth, connecting with the Copper Gaias may make you feel nourished, held and embraced, or alienated, discombobulated and hugely resistant. If you experience the latter, take heart. We have found that for many people on their journey with Colour Mirrors there comes a moment when they no longer wish to run from the Copper Gaias but instead turn to meet them. Bathing in the Copper Gaia bottles can be an intense experience as the cells of your body and your nervous system respond to the grounding, earthing vibrations of copper, but if you are willing to let go of stubborn old patterns and dive into the bounty they hold, these bottles have many gifts to share with you.

When you let the copper energies in and really open to their messages and guidance, you are shown the possibility of releasing the past on all levels and finding a new relationship with Gaia. Numerous Colour Mirrors practitioners and clients have worked their way through the Copper Gaia set, bathing in each one in turn, and it would be fair to say that no one who has done this has remained untouched. Many have reported major shifts occurring and feelings of being much more present, much more able to be in their bodies and a sense of being planted and rooted here on the earth.

Spiritual teachers have always spoken of the need to be 'grounded', and the Coppers offer a bodily experience of what that means. They provide the safety to enable you to let go, sink into the loving support of your earth mother and know that you will always be held. Fears diminish, emotions subside; calm and peace prevail. When you truly embody the light of the earth within your cells, you can take your place in the world without fear, stand in your light, make a difference.

With the support of Gaia you can create for yourself a life that is blessed and beautiful rather than dark and dense – and hold a space for others to find that state too. You may require courage to take this step, but the rewards will be immense. You may even fall in love – with the bottles, with the earth, with yourself, with your life – and when you are in love, suddenly you cannot see the darkness or difficulty any more. You can see only the incredible beauty, lusciousness, vibrancy, intensity and joy of being part of life on earth. These copper energies come and sit inside you, beside you, within you, as part of you. As you recognise in them your fully earthed self, you will find you cannot imagine being here without them.

Copper Gaias Story: Renira Barclay, UK, www.abovemiddlec.com

When I was doing the Colour Mirrors practitioner training, I had the Copper Gaias placed on me as I was lying on the ground, and I felt as if I was a seed, safe in the ground and growing. It was a lovely experience. Not buried, but safe and growing!

Copper Gaias Story: Alka Dharam, UK, www.lifecentredhealing.co.uk

On the Colour Mirrors teacher training course in Canada we were asked to pick one bottle that we didn't like. I don't know what made me do it, but I picked three: G1, G2 and G4. Moira noted that they were all copper bottles and then proceeded to get to the root of the issue which, in effect, was that I did not want to be on planet earth, as I found it so painful here. In front of the bottles I was laid bare: my excuses, justifications and avoidance mechanisms clearly exposed. There was nowhere to run or hide. Being thus exposed was one of the most difficult times for me. I had hidden what was driving me, even from myself, although I don't doubt it was clear to those who had eyes to see. Now I had to face my shadows fully. One of the bottles I chose to represent a solution to this was G5, which was apt – healing copper issues with copper. Moira's prescription was that I bathe in the copper bottles on a daily basis, starting with bottle G1, so I began bathing in the bottles the day after my return to England.

The only one I had real resistance to was bottle G3, and as soon as I got into the bath, I wanted to get out. I persevered and forced myself to stay in the bath for 40 minutes, during which time I received valuable insights. I felt the physical sensations of morning sickness and felt my mother's feelings and thoughts during my time in utero. I felt her fears, her innocence, her vulnerability and her sacrifices and realised how I had acted out all of this in my life. My life began to make sense to me in a way that it had not before. Amidst tears, I honoured my mother for her love and sacrifices, promising that I would never forget her. I felt deep appreciation and love for her, which then extended to Ancient Mother and Gaia.

The remaining baths were much easier, showing me how totally loved and supported I am. I looked forward to the baths and felt safer, more grounded and stronger day by day. By the end of the week I felt totally grounded, very much present on earth. This was acknowledged by many who noticed the change in me and continues to be acknowledged by others I interact with. The benefits of doing the baths in quick succession is that the results are swift and long lasting. I still feel grounded, supported, grateful, stronger and happier and attribute this to those copper baths taken, at the time of writing, three years ago. I realise that the only place to be is where I am, and from here everything unfolds. Interestingly, I finished all the copper baths the day before I attended a workshop run by Melissie to ground the Magenta Gaias in England. I had felt the call to attend that workshop very strongly but obviously needed to be grounded to attend!

Bottle G1: Incarnating (Clear/Copper)

The message in this bottle is that you now have easy access to the wisdom of the earth. Having come from a place of being bitterly unhappy here, you can now feel deeply connected to Gaia and life on the planet. This bottle assists you in releasing difficult past lives and coming to terms with incarnation. In a certain light it shows a little flash of yellow on the centre line, which represents the joy you are now setting up for yourself.

The Gaia bottles tell the story of the human journey towards consciousness, towards a greater understanding of life, towards a higher level of light and awareness. Bottle G1 is the first chapter in the story and tells of a light condensing its energy into form and choosing to come to earth. Let its energy speak to your cells:

As light incarnate, you came to join the earthly realms. You sparkled and dazzled and glowed, overjoyed at the thought of encapsulating your Divine light in human form. You spun and wove and wound threads of light around you until you became denser and heavier and took on solid form. Embarking on a path previously unknown, you journeyed forth with joy. Your spirit led you forward without hesitation and you rallied to the call to aid the earth with your presence. You knew with certainty that you would bring great light, energy and power to a planet that was mired in its own density, to a people that was enmeshed in darkness, fear and struggle. There was never a moment when you wished to turn back.

Incarnating meant fully and truly 'embodying' all that you could be – literally 'incorporating' your light. This was not about squeezing an infinite being into a finite body. This was about expanding your light so much that it could literally take form. By making physical your intangible light, you could do and be so much more. You could be human and Divine, capable of seeing and knowing with your Divine soul while feeling and experiencing in ways that only a physical being can. This was what led you forward, what took you from your sweet slumber. This was the mission you embarked upon with great assurance, for you knew you could make a difference through your actions and your very beingness.

As you took the journey into density, you kept a silver thread of light firmly attached to your star-self and your cosmic home. You knew that one day, as part of this game, you would most likely forget the truth of your soul and your connection to the Allness, and you promised to keep the silver thread in place so that when density overtook you, as it might, you would have a light in the darkness to guide you back home.

And then you willingly and knowingly shut yourself off from that light in order to fully know and experience the human condition. You agreed, whole-heartedly, to turn away from your inner radiance and embrace life on earth in a physical body. Only in this way could you truly understand what humanity faced and what was needed in order to restore all to the truth of their own light. If you could do it, so too could everyone.

You took all your light and you buried it inside, and you joined the human race. You forgot that you were light and became more and more enmeshed in the 'real' world, losing sight of the beauty and bliss that you knew deep inside to be the truth. You felt and experienced and you hurt and you healed and gradually, over time, you awoke to the faintest of glimmers inside and began to remember that silver thread. You began to remember what it meant to be a Divine human instead of a victim. You began to see that the light and the dark are all part of the oneness, that there is nothing to judge and nothing was ever 'wrong'. You began to remember your purpose in incarnating in the first place, and you took up your light once more and began to spread it around the earth as you walked upon her.

Bottle G1 raises to the surface your fears, doubts and insecurities about having incarnated here on earth. It draws out your deepest judgements about humanity and the planet. It presents you with questions: Why did you come? What was the inner call that made you bring your light to the density of earth? What did you wish to experience and learn? How can you feel at ease here and not want to continually 'go home'? Could you consider the possibility that home is actually inside you and that you bring it with you wherever you go? This bottle invites you to get to the truth of what it means to have chosen to incarnate. It asks you to recognise that it was indeed a choice – a choice made by your soul so that you could learn, evolve and grow through the experiences you could have here on earth that you would not get anywhere else in the cosmos.

Like a delete key, this bottle offers the opportunity to erase any unhelpful programmes and beliefs you hold about incarnating. With its copper base, this bottle is your connection to the earth, and its clear top fraction is your connection to the light. These colours show that the whole point of the exercise was to discover what might be possible when light and density came together. Bottle G1 gives you a hint of the whole journey, as it earths and uplifts you simultaneously. Its purpose is to ground you, not by taking you away from spirit but by drawing spirit and matter together, anchoring your light so that you can easily manifest your dreams. If you float a foot above the planet trying to avoid the dense reality of earth you will find it tricky to manifest anything of value. For life here to work you have to keep your feet on the ground, even while you dream of heaven. Bottle G1 holds the space as you learn – or remember – how to do this.

Between the clear and copper fractions of this bottle, at the meniscus, is a little yellow line. This glint of yellow is a signal of hope, a sunrise on the planet and the promise of a new dawn. There will always be another day, and however lost you may feel at times in the dense vibration of the copper and the challenges of life on earth, this little band of yellow reminds you that while you might forget the light, the light will never forget you. It also reminds you of the joy of incarnating, the joy of discovery, the joy of a completely new experience for your soul: bringing the intensity of your light into a limited physical vehicle and learning how to harness and enjoy them both.

With its clear and copper fractions, this bottle shows you how to be a clear channel for Gaia, receiving information and wisdom from the earth while linking into your spirit so that you might join heaven with earth and see that they are, in fact, one.

Bottle G1 Story: Penny Wing, Spain, www.pennywing.com

I ran a 'Past Lives' workshop, which was attended by four people. The first exercise was to pick a bottle relating to a past life, which we then revisited, and bottle G1 was chosen by one of the group. The second exercise was to pick a bottle which would help to release any contracts or vows, and bottle G1 was chosen by another person in the group. The third exercise was to pick a bottle which would help to release karma, and bottle G1 was chosen yet again. At the end of the day bottle G1 was incredibly cloudy and misty in the top fraction, so it had worked its magic! I always find the Copper Gaias are picked when I run Past Lives workshops, but for three out of four participants to choose bottle G1 on this particular day was amazing, and the change in the energy of the bottle reflected that.

Bottle G1 Story: Stephanie Oliver, Canada, www.facebook.com/StephanieMuirRMT

My time with bottle G1 was a roller coaster. I am not generally a fan of the Copper Gaias. I've just never been attracted to them spiritually, emotionally or physically. I was trying to create my soul bottle, and at first I was thinking solid gold over magenta, but something didn't feel right. It felt ego-based and like I had a deeper lesson to learn before I could truly pick my 'soul' bottle. This led me to bottle G1. All of a sudden her copper tones were calling me. I quickly rushed home from class and dove into my bottle G1 experience. The bath itself was lovely, beautiful aromas, a calm meditative state, and my body felt heavy in a good way. I had an instant feeling of calm and grounding in a way I had never experienced before. I knew I was meant to do more and stop denying my passions.

The following weeks brought up all the fears and worries that were holding me back. All the things that I had made up in my mind as reasons why I could not move forward happened: my new staff member quit, expensive things came up at work and all the bills – I mean all of them – came in. My account was cleared and I had less help at work, even though I had just started yet another new venture. I couldn't stop it, all I could do was practice gratitude and know that all would be OK, as the universe knew my plans and knew I wasn't going to settle for less.

After a three week period almost all of my fears came to fruition, and I was grateful for them instead of fearing them. Now things are looking up, plans are getting into motion, and the universe knows I'm here to work with her for the long haul. Bottle G1 gave me the lesson that I have everything I need inside of myself to face anything in life. Her copper tones now make me smile, for I am reminded that I too have Gaia energy and can create the life I want. I am complete. I am worthy. Simply – I am.

Bottle G1 Story: Kate Griffiths, UK, www.wholeselfleadership.com

A few years after I become a Colour Mirrors practitioner I had a very powerful experience with bottle G1. I had a full set of bottles set up on stands in the spare bedroom, which was my therapy space, and one night there was a horrendous noise as all the Gaias bounced off the perspex stands and fell onto the carpeted floor. Only one broke and that was bottle G1. My hubby was furious because he couldn't get the copper out of the carpet, and he said it had happened because the stands were on a tilt on the chest of drawers. To me though it really felt as if my Akashic Records were opening up. There was a massive shift as all the hurt in this life, a reflection of past life pain, was being healed. Afterwards there was a sense of phenomenal growth as a result.

Bottle G2: The Core (Copper/Copper)

This bottle is powerfully healing for those who have been through birth trauma and a great support for those who have never felt at home on the earth. It nourishes even the most jaded soul and brings warmth, hope and healing when you cannot remember your reason for being here. It is wonderfully grounding for the star children who feel so disassociated from the planet and its energies, helping them feel safe and loved. This bottle is a tonic any time you feel lost, lonely or anxious, helping you receive the love of Gaia and in turn remember your love for her. This bottle is the real 'earth mother', representing the grounded earthiness of someone who loves to take care of others. If this is your bottle, you have the ability to help others connect with the earth and develop their innate love for the planet.

Bottle G2 is a deep dive into rich, warm copper, an immersion in the heart of the earth's love. All is safe here. You are held and loved. Relax and let go. This bottle may be the key to finally landing in your body and your life. It brings a strong sense of homecoming, of being able to feel at safe on the earth at last, possibly after lifetimes of feeling alienated, alone and disconnected.

This bottle addresses the very core of you and your relationship with Gaia. It brings tremendous stability, rooting you firmly into the heart of the earth and enabling you to draw up her riches into your body and being. It is the embrace of the warmest, most loving mother, nestling you into the cradle of her love. This bottle shows the truth of the love your earth mother has always held for you. Entirely grounded in her own strength, light and wisdom, she gives and receives without judgement or condition, singing to you, nurturing you, feeding and sustaining you.

Yet for many, this is not the story of life on earth at all. Perhaps for you the earth has been a place of intense judgement, separation and pain, with little love or nurturing to be found. In bottle G1 (Incarnating), you saw that your journey into the earth realm began with complete clarity about what you were taking on. You knew you were the light and could not imagine that you would ever *not* know. Yet to completely immerse yourself in the experience and gain the true value of the journey you had to fully take on your earth mantle, and so the next stage of the journey was to experience being only of the earth, to forget completely the light. Bottle G2 reminds you that you had to set aside the light for a time so that your experience would be all the more real. There is no white light here, no other colour to distract – only rich, coppery earth. The depth of the copper, top and bottom, depicts this stage of the journey.

In order to achieve what you set out to do, which was to forget that you were Divine and to experience separation and duality, you had to move into this reality on every level so that you could experience everything it had to teach you. You had to immerse yourself in the dense 'reality' of the earth completely. It was an opportunity to feel darkness and duality, to discover feelings, appetites and hungers. As spirit, you did not know what it was to run the gamut of emotion, trauma and darkness. On earth, you could experience joy and sadness, abundance and lack, rage and peaceful acceptance and everything in between. Although there were many times when you may have wondered, literally, why on earth you had to go through this, it was truly your brave pioneering spirit that gifted you this opportunity. It took you from knowing that you were completely part of the oneness to a place where you could experience the full range of emotions, the highs and lows of human life, the apparent darkness of life in a body on the earth.

Each human comes to experience life on the earth as a unique and distinctive strand of Divine light and in this way, adds to the Divine's knowledge of itself. As above, so below – and as you grow the Divine grows in its awareness of itself, and so the universe expands. With the help of bottle G2 you begin to remember why you came here, what you came for, what you can offer by being authentically who you are, what your particular piece of the puzzle is. Bottle G2 shows you that you can be both light and earth, both Divine and human. This rich copper bottle reminds you that no matter how much you may pretend you are other and separate, you are always intimately connected to the core of Divine love, indeed you are inherently a part of it, even – especially – while in a physical body.

When you connect with this bottle it can feel as if you are being laid bare. In the full gaze of the copper earth mother there is nowhere to hide. She sees you in all your greatness and despair, in all your truth and shadow. She sees you, loves you and holds you. For many, this bottle comes as the most welcome relief – a warm and soothing presence to make you feel at home where you may never have felt it before, an unconditional love that means you feel seen, loved and accepted for exactly who you are. Time and again we have witnessed people clutch this bottle like a lifeline, feeling – perhaps for the first time – what it means to know that the earth loves and understands them as she holds them reverently in her embrace.

This bottle is called 'The Core', and it is from deep within the core of the earth that this love emanates. As you let yourself connect with that core, Gaia gently and lovingly offers you all the beauty and richness available on this planet and invites you to sink into her luscious, glowing, melting softness and warmth. Her love is honey-sweet and kind, gifting you the delicious experience of pure earth energy. When you are in touch with this resonant earth love, it becomes a place of home, of 'enough'. Your sense of separation begins to dissolve and you feel more and more connected with life. You may find yourself wanting to take part in more physical activities, be out in nature, get your hands dirty, move your body and take pleasure from all the wonders of the earth. This bottle reveals all of Gaia's gifts. By immersing yourself in her limitless love, you open the doorway to a life overflowing with blessings.

Bottle G2 Experience: Katharine Bork, Canada, k.bork@hotmail.com

A 14-year-old girl came to see me for a session. When asked why she had come, she had three things she wanted to address: belonging, love and trust. She picked bottle G2 to represent her. As she held this bottle, and her story unfolded with information from other bottles, she began to understand. She had arrived on this planet and completely disconnected from her body. She described how she didn't feel physical pain and couldn't connect to emotions that other people were feeling around her. She was diagnosed with learning disabilities that didn't fit into the normal explanations. She was completely mute for two years and had recently been diagnosed with unexplained seizures. The list of physical symptoms went on (her body's way of trying to connect with her). She shared of her frequent thoughts around death and suicide.

As the session continued she started to feel physical sensations for the first time. She experienced goose-bumps on her skin. She felt a sensation in her chest and began to experience physical feelings moving around her body. This totally scared her as she had never felt this before.

Bottle G2 helped her to understand that she came from a place of belonging, love and trust and that she doesn't have to leave the planet to experience this again. She just has to connect with and value her body so she can experience it all here. She took bottle G2 home and bathed in it and later told me that it gave her a feeling of calm and comfort. As she continues to connect with her physical body and the feelings that go with that, I look forward to the joy and love she will experience and how it will overflow into her life so she can truly feel like she belongs. Thank you, Colour Mirrors!

Bottle G2 Experience: Lesley McDonald, UK, www.lesleytara.com

It was on my Colour Mirrors practitioner course that I really noticed the Copper Gaias for the first time. I was drawn like a magnet to their earthy hues, yet at the same time I was hesitant, avoiding the inevitable. Finally, after a particularly emotional day, having released a lifetime's worth of fear, I knew the time had come for that copper bath: I chose bottle G2.

I let my body relax in the delicious mixture of warm water and shimmering copper oil and let go of the tension. Gently but firmly held in the copper frequency, my body finally felt safe. I soon drifted off to that magical place beyond time and space, when from somewhere beyond the everyday, a little voice spoke. An image formed in my unencumbered mind, and I saw a little elven-like being, not quite a leprechaun or even an elf but a fine-featured little being. He looked like he may have been made out of liquid copper, yet he had form and substance and was almost human-like. He was watching me quizzically.

"So, you finally decided?" I wasn't sure if this was a statement or a question. "Good," he continued. "You'd better start to unpack." He was matter-of-fact – not rude exactly, just economical with his words. Beneath the sternness, however, I could feel a deep and unconditional love.

"Unpack?" I asked. Then I noticed he was sitting on top of a suitcase. "Oh, my goodness," I exclaimed loudly (inside my head), for this was not just any old suitcase, this was THE magenta suitcase! The one I had conjured forth as the sign of my date with destiny.

I lived in Denmark for over 30 years and for the latter part experienced a desperate longing to return home to my native Scotland. No matter how many plans I laid something always blocked me, and the magenta suitcase had been the sign I had asked for to let me know the time had come.

Yet here I was in a bathtub, communicating with a slightly disgruntled little being sitting on my imaginary suitcase and insisting I unpack before I had even gone anywhere. I can only assume that he knew, by virtue of me being emerged in a copper bath and by the 'she is at long last lodged fully into her earthly body' kind of resonance now singing in my cells, that I understood his message that home is not an external place but is about being present and connected and that while on our earth sojourn, this sense of connection involves a body. Home was not about Denmark or Scotland but about feeling at home on earth, at home in my body and fully connected to Gaia. As the magnitude of the moment dawned on me, I realised that my inability to find a true home was because I had never been 'home' in myself, not really – and my body had known it. Dressed in my pyjamas, I ran outside and planted my bare feet firmly and gratefully on our dear earth mother. As I stood there under my beloved stars, a new love burst forth, a love born of deep gratitude for the patience of the great mother and her elemental beings and for their unwavering love as they wait for us to finally unpack and plant our starry feet squarely and securely on this beautiful planet.

Bottle G3: Return from Atlantis (Copper/Turquoise)

This bottle relates to past lives in Atlantis. It indicates that there is information and healing from your Atlantean lifetimes available to support you with whatever you are going through now. It also helps you tap into the wisdom of that time and share it in a way that is grounded and easy to understand. This bottle helps heal the trauma of the sinking of Atlantis and the abuses of power which played out at that time. It also helps heal past life trauma through a death by drowning and is supportive for anyone who feels unsafe on the planet. This bottle is connected to water in every form, and those who are drawn to it have the capacity to receive the flowing wisdom and power found in all the waters of the earth. It also relates to the waters of your mother's womb and the programming you received in utero, and supports you in releasing the thoughts and feelings you took on from your mother during her pregnancy.

With its striking colour combination of copper and turquoise, bottle G3 balances the apparent solidity of matter, earth and body with the fluidity of mind, spirit and water. This is where you learn how to be in flow. It is where you unblock the stubborn patterning and behaviours you have been clinging to and let yourself be carried on the tides, knowing you will always come to shore exactly where you need to be. This bottle is about trust and faith and learning to ride the waves. It teaches that there is a time for everything and an intricate Divine template already in place. If you are willing to open to the universe's perfect design you will find that the flow of your spirit will weave it effortlessly for you, without trying, striving or pushing. This bottle reminds you that all is in Divine order.

As the name indicates, bottle G3 is strongly linked with Atlantean lifetimes. It holds memories and information from those times, and if you are called to this bottle it is an indication that there is something significant from Atlantis for you now, perhaps a memory to be released or a piece of information to be collected or a download of energy and light to be received. As you work with this bottle, let it help you access whatever is calling for your attention so that you can clear, allow and integrate as appropriate. You do not always need to know exactly what it is on a conscious level – simply let the energies do their work. If you are resistant to the idea that Atlantis was 'real' or that it has anything to do with you, you are free to look at it as an allegory as you explore its messages and their implications for your life. The fact that you have been drawn to this bottle says there is something here for you to discover if you will allow yourself to be open.

The civilisation known as Atlantis is believed to have been an experience or experiment for humans to see how evolved they could become. It allowed humanity to explore issues of power, expansion, spirituality and truth, reaching a pinnacle during an era known as Golden Atlantis. This was a period when all beings knew themselves to be part of the Divine. Humanity was highly evolved, with mind power, creativity and technological skills well developed and finely honed. As the concept of duality was still being explored, however, the darkness was able to bring its power to bear, and the golden times in Atlantis fell away as the power of light began to be misused. Those who stayed true to the initial intention for this experience realised it was necessary to bring it to an end when they saw that it would inevitably collapse into darkness as the power and knowledge of the light became corrupted. The story about Atlantis – whether it is myth, legend or fact – is that when its people were unable to sustain their light the civilisation 'fell', and the physical landmass known as Atlantis was submerged under the sea.

If you struggle with the idea of Atlantis and indeed with this bottle, you may well be holding unresolved and often unconscious memories and judgements from your Atlantean experiences. You may believe on some level that you did something 'wrong' and thereby contributed to the fall – or that others did, and should therefore have been held accountable. Perhaps you hold the universe responsible for 'messing things up'. Notice if there are echoes of these themes anywhere in your life. You may be carrying subconscious grief and guilt because lives were lost and the Golden Age of Atlantis came to an end, and this can play out in your life in various ways, including a sense of guilt or grief that has no logical basis but that seems to overshadow your life.

There has certainly been much collective anger and grief at a subconscious level over what happened in Atlantis. Yet what if nothing that happened was a mistake? What if it was all part of the Divine plan? It is time to let go of the judgements around what happened to 'perfect' Atlantis. The perfection was actually that it all worked exactly as it was meant to, and with the demise of Atlantis, numerous teachers left to found civilisations in Egypt, Greece and South America, taking their knowledge and wisdom with them. Atlantis rose and fell just like any other civilisation, of which the earth has seen many.

Whether you hold cellular memories of being an instigator in the process of the downfall or whether you tried valiantly to hold the light and stave off its demise, you were given an incredible opportunity to choose to see the higher picture as it unfolded. You were offered yet another chance to step out of judgement and claim your innate power and truth. And just as you learned from the experience, so the Divine added to its knowledge of itself through the many discoveries made by you and all who were part of the Atlantis experience.

Now that the vibration of the earth is rising once again, it is time to ensure that there is no residual resentment or blame that will prevent peace and plenty from becoming a reality for all earth's beings. When you choose this bottle it is because you are ready to put shame, blame and guilt behind you. You are ready to shuck off the mantle of past life fears and woes and any echoes from Atlantis still playing out in this lifetime. You are ready to embrace a whole new way of being. Water being what it is, tears may need to be shed in the process and grief may arise to be released. This bottle asks you to allow and embrace it all as the key to your freedom.

Whatever you experienced during the fall of Atlantis and whatever your feelings about it, much of what you learned in Atlantean times was about enlightened living. You knew how to communicate beyond your physical senses. You knew how to live in tune with nature and with Gaia herself. You knew how to tend to your garden and your body. You knew how to heal yourself and others and how to honour the Divine in everything. You knew how to create abundance and how to fully, deservedly enjoy it. None of that has been lost. It still resides in the water of your cells. The time has come now for you to access that wisdom and knowledge once more.

This bottle is intimately connected with your time in the waters of your mother's womb. All of the water on the planet is finite – there was never more nor less than there is now, and it is endlessly recycled. All water goes back to being part of the earth. When you die, the water from your body returns to the existing water of the earth. It seems that water might just carry an endless supply of information and memories. Is it possible that your Atlantean memories are also linked to memories of what happened when you were in the womb? This bottle connects with both, so it may be that when you clear, heal and release one, you do so for the other.

Many times we have seen this bottle have a profound effect on those who had taken on their mother's fears, feelings, emotions and patterns while in the womb. It seems to draw a line in the sand so that you no longer need to carry energies from your ancestral line that do not serve you. It establishes within you a deeper sense of your own Divine sovereignty so that you can unplug from the programming you picked up in utero and become more of who you really are rather than simply a product of your heritage.

Water is deeply, thoroughly cleansing. It has the ability to wash away all that is murky, stagnant or stuck. It can bring fresh new inspiration, energy and ideas to replace old thought patterns, habits and addictions. Water is one of the core elements of life, estimated at 70-80% of your body's cellular make-up. Your body has the ability to self-cleanse and self-heal, and you carry within you the ability to programme the water in your body to restore vibrant health and well-being. Bottle G3 can be an aid in reconnecting with your body so that you are able to find out what it truly has to say to you and how you can live peacefully and in tune with it.

Water teaches you to continually ebb and flow, to easily shift, transform and change, to endlessly grow and evolve. You are the water of life, you are the body of life, you are the flowing, magical stardust that takes form, disperses, and takes form again. Nothing is ever stuck. Every moment has the potential to be a new one, with renewed energy, insight and clarity. If you let it, this bottle can be your guide. Allow yourself to be washed clean of your past programming and open to a more enlightened path, a lighter journey, an inspired present and a clearer future.

Through this bottle you are invited to receive the wisdom that speaks from within the deep pools of your mind, heart and body. The water in your body contains all the memories of the light you held in Atlantis and long before, and all of it is now accessible – because it is inside you. If you take the time to connect with the water in your cells it will share with you vast information and energy about how to live your life in alignment with the Divine, the earth and the stars. This energy is both of the future and from the ancient past, coming together in the perfect 'now' moment.

Bottle G3 takes what you knew in Atlantean times, adds it to the vast infinite wisdom of the cosmos and the earth and gathers it all together for right here, right now. It reminds you that you are the bridge between past and future, heaven and earth, spirit and matter. It asks you to take a moment just to observe those connections, be with these colours and this bottle, and feel and remember it all.

Bottle G3 Story: Korani

A student on a Colour Mirrors teacher training course walked in on the first day of the course and could not take her eyes off bottle G3. As we went around the group the students all shared how they were feeling about taking their journey to the next level. When it came to her turn she said she was feeling incredibly excited about it but also quite scared of stepping up, of claiming herself as a 'teacher'. I asked her if the fear was hers or if it might have belonged to her mother. She was shocked because she could feel the truth of this.

Bottle G3 called to her all through the week of the course, so she took it home with her at the end of the training. She put it on a shelf in her bedroom as she thought she would bathe in it at some point. She knew it was key for her in leaving behind what she had taken on through her mother's lineage. She never quite got around to taking the bath until one day she walked into the room, saw it and knew it was time. When she did finally bathe in the bottle it was a peaceful experience, like a completion. She suddenly realised that it had been nine months since the course and that it had been literally working with her through a full gestation period so that by the time she came to bathe in it, the work was done. By then she was running courses and workshops with great joy and none of the fear she had felt nine months before remained.

Bottle G3 Story: Raluca Rusu, Switzerland, www.facebook.com/RalucaRusu.colours

This is one of the bottles I bathed in during the Colour Mirrors teacher training course in Canada. Before the course I had a family constellation on my masculine/control side. It came out that I had been adopting masculine behaviour so that my mother would see me as unique. She had had a miscarriage one month before getting pregnant with me and my twin sister, and it had come out in a previous constellation that it was a boy. From this last constellation it seemed that I wanted to take the place of this boy and did not want to let him go.

The constellation brought about a big breakthrough. I went through the birth moments (hardly breathing, a lot of emotions coming out, hardly seeing the people around me, almost fainting). During the teacher training course Moira told me that this boy was me in a first incarnating stage. My feeling now is that this bottle helped me finish this constellation, as before this there were moments when I saw myself as a transvestite (having makeup enhanced that feeling). Ever since, I see myself as a woman.

Bottle G3 Story: Ray McKimm, UK, www.greentherapyandtraining.com

A client came to me with a long history of difficulty in forming and maintaining close relationships. He had few friends as a child, and as an adult preferred not to attempt to get close to people. His relationship with his mother was distant, and he reported that as a child he had found her cold and uncaring. It was very difficult for him to express his emotions, and although he had gone to a counsellor some years before, he had stopped after two sessions as he could not find words for what he wanted to express.

In his first session with me he chose bottle G3. When I asked him about this bottle he was silent and seemed reluctant to engage. Although I would usually wait for a client to voice their feelings about their bottle choices, I decided to open up the dialogue in the hope that he would be drawn to speak. Because he had chosen this bottle, I asked him about his relationship with his mother and how she had felt during her pregnancy with him. Although he was initially startled by this, wondering how I 'knew', he began to open up and then shared at length his feelings of being unloved and unwanted. His mother had often told him as a child that she had planned to terminate her pregnancy.

After several further sessions using colour, my client found that he could begin to articulate his feelings more clearly and was more drawn to communicate with others. He began to experience an increased confidence in his relationships. Colour greatly assisted him in exploring and processing painful feelings and memories from his early life so that he could move forward in a more empowered way.

Bottle G4: Ancient Mother (Pink/Copper)

This bottle connects you with the Ancient Mother, mother of all. It helps release any issues you are holding about your own physical mother or Gaia, your earth mother. It is about accessing your own mothering ability and is especially supportive for those experiencing post-partum depression. This bottle connects you with your inner child and assists in healing old childhood wounds. It helps resolve issues about being on earth and feeling unsupported or alienated and reminds you of the deep and unconditional love that Gaia holds for you. Now you can feel safe and loved on the planet. In the system this is bottle number 55, a master number, and the colours reflect the teachings of Christ, the master who brought love (pink) to the earth (copper).

This bottle contains and reflects all the love of all the mothers of the world, all the love of Gaia for humanity, all the love of every woman – and every man – for every child of the earth. This is where you remember what it is to be a child who is loved, fully accepted, nurtured, cared for and adored. It is also where you release your memories of *not* being loved or looked after. This bottle may bring up for healing any stories you still hold about not being seen or heard or valued, particularly by your mother. It creates a space where you can feel all the feelings your child self did not get to fully feel or express. It is a warm, safe, gentle energy that enables you to face all that is left over from your childhood that you have not yet integrated, loved and accepted.

This bottle is a balm for any difficult relationship between mother and child. It may be chosen by anyone who has challenges with a mother, mother-in-law or mother figure in their life. It may also be chosen by mothers who are challenged by their role or questioning it. Bottle G4 asks you to look deeply at what you believe a mother is and to seek out your judgements, fears and demands around mothering. It goes to the core of your belief structures, your conditioning and any tendencies you may have to blame, shame and judge, particularly when it comes to mothers and indeed women in general. It challenges you to look deeply at your earth mother, your own mother, yourself as a mother – and to see there the Divine. If you are not yet able to do so, this bottle will support you while you take the journey.

The Ancient Mother is both earth mother and Divine mother. With this bottle she holds an unconditionally loving space for you to unravel all the tangled threads of your childhood feelings and memories so that you can fully embrace your adulthood. She particularly holds up a mirror to show you where you judge your mother for not being enough, loving enough, caring enough or doing enough to make you feel loved and worthy. She offers the light of redemption by opening you to forgiveness, acceptance, love and compassion, both as the child of your mother and where applicable, the mother of your children.

A mother's love, from the Divine level at which it was created, is the container for some of the most powerful growth on your human journey. Even when it manifests as an apparent lack of compassion or understanding, the love your mother's soul has for you is profound. Whatever the circumstances of your birth and childhood and whatever your relationship with your mother in adulthood, at a soul level, mother and child always choose each other. There are no accidents in the universe, and all mothers and children choose each other out of deep love and a commitment to come together so that both can heal and grow. You chose your mother to give you exactly the experiences and events that would lead to your soul's growth and evolution. She chose you to offer those experiences to, for your growth and her own. On a soul level your mother did everything you asked her to do for your highest good, just as you did and do for your children.

This is a bottle which, when it calls to you, is speaking directly to you and through you to your ancestral line. Many women express horror at the idea of turning into their mother. Yet half your genetic makeup comes from your mother, so if you reject her you effectively cut yourself in half. This bottle of pink over copper is your licence to take back the half of you that you inherited from your mother, with complete gratitude, acceptance and love. It sends out a thread of heart love and earth love to your mother and her mother and her mother and so on, offering healing all the way down the line. Part of your mission in being here at this time is to set your mother's line free. The more willing you are to love, forgive and accept your mother, the more fully that energy can flow into both past and future generations. When you are willing to acknowledge that the contract between you and your mother was always based on love, your mother wounds can heal and you can restore yourself to wholeness.

This bottle gives all the women in your family line permission to acknowledge themselves as sovereign beings. It invites them to enjoy the gift of their feminine wisdom and love as well as their bodies' astonishing power to create new life. It restores them to their rightful place as honoured, Divine beings. As your ancestral line is brought into harmony, you can create a space for your own family that is balanced, happy and whole, where your children do not need to cut themselves in half to deny the part of themselves that they cannot look at in the mirror.

This bottle of pure love sits in the centre – at the heart – of the Copper Gaia set. It is the warm embrace in which your earth mother has always held you, her beloved child. The earth – Gaia – is a living, sentient being with incredible love for everyone who lives upon her, and bottle G4 helps you reconnect with her and rediscover the love that brought you here in the first place.

As you learn to love and accept your mother, your earth mother and yourself, you bring healing to all aspects of creation and pave the way for a new era on the planet where love is both an anchor and a talisman. Bottle G4 shows you that with pink over copper, with love firmly rooted in the earth, everything becomes possible. With love you are safe to be who you are, to do what your heart calls you to do, to reach further and higher than you have dared before. With love you are free to embrace yourself and your life. With love as your guide, you can reclaim the Divine feminine light out of which every being was created and offer it into the world as a natural extension of who you are.

Bottle G4 Story: Amanda Bradbury, UK, www.amandabradbury.com

In August 2004 I went to Greece for a holiday with my husband and very lively three-year-old daughter. My husband and I had been going through some relationship challenges, and we hadn't been on a family holiday since our daughter was born. My mother had been experiencing some serious health issues and had needed a major operation. I took some Colour Mirrors bottles into hospital to support her, and she enjoyed looking at them while lying in her hospital bed. She particularly enjoyed the pink and copper bottle, G4, Ancient Mother, and spraying the olive Wood spritzer.

On the plane to Greece I was sitting next to someone working on a laptop, and to my delight, I noticed the laptop had a logo on it saying 'PowerBook G4'. We needed to spend a night in Athens on our way to the island, and I hadn't managed to find anywhere to stay because the Olympics were happening there at the time. I mentioned this to the owner of the apartments where we were staying on the island, and he immediately volunteered that his mother would be delighted to have us to stay. I remember his words: "She's very old." She was around 85. A real live 'Ancient Mother'.

This sweet, strong 'Ancient Mother' was an absolute joy. She insisted on giving us food when we arrived, reassuring me it was totally fine and natural that our daughter was letting off steam and running in rings round the sofa and glass coffee table in the sitting room.

This time represented a real turning point in terms of my close family relationships, and working with bottle G4 helped support this process. For me the synchronicities are reassurance and signs that the magic and healing are taking place.

Bottle G4 Story: Lisa Barry, UK, www.lisabarry.me

Please refer to Lisa's story on p. 156.

Bottle G5: Earth Wisdom (Gold/Copper)

This is a time for the masculine and feminine to come back into balance. As all beings reclaim their feminine power, the abuse of power we have experienced during a patriarchal rule will come to an end. Stop playing God and instead claim your ability to be God. Be everything you have come to be on this planet and claim it as your home. Find the golden wisdom in your connection with the earth, expand your creative capacities and awaken to the new golden era on the planet. It is here now.

Bottle G5 reminds you of your deep earth connection, all the way to the molten, golden core of her heart. It asks you to draw deeply from her well of honeyed love and bring that energy into your body and your life. By choosing this bottle you are acknowledging the earth and the gold at her centre as the core of your own life – a rich seam to be mined, explored and welcomed. This bottle provides a safe haven for you to anchor into when you are buffeted by the winds of change or challenging times. It opens a warm, deep, wide embrace from the earth mother and encourages you to put down roots, spread your toes and feel the rich, loamy soil beneath your feet.

This bottle reminds you of the many layers of gold you hold within. You may have to dig deep, and the process may not always be comfortable, but bottle G5 shows you that it will be worth the effort. You are asked to journey to the depths of yourself, and keep digging until you find a rich vein of gold – and then another, and another. You are asked to go below the surface of things, actively search for the gold, bring it to the surface, appreciate it, value it and use it – then share the riches you discover. In this way the gold becomes pure and valuable and ultimately creates beauty and value for yourself and others.

Wisdom is not gained by skimming over the surface of life. It is harvested from your many life experiences and your willingness to look at yourself in the mirror, to fully engage with every facet of yourself and your life. If you leave your true gold undiscovered, its value, wealth and preciousness remain hidden, of no use to you or anyone else. If you choose to live an 'unexamined life', all the treasures you hold inside perish with you. When you choose instead to embrace and celebrate the journey, despite its challenges, you are able to reap the rewards long into the future. The big question this bottle asks is: "If not now, then when?" Bottle G5 supports you in evolving beyond your perceived limitations to a more expanded and empowered state of being. It holds up your goldenness for all to see.

For much of the earth's history, power has been a 'masculine' energy – dominant, forceful and controlling – and Gaia has held the space for this to play out in power games of war, destruction, arrogance, violence and control. You have likely experienced every aspect of power throughout your many lifetimes, every form of abuse of power – as both receiver and perpetrator – and every opportunity to use power for good or ill. In order to know what true power is, you have had to experience all that it is not.

The earth is opening now to a different frequency. She knows there is another way. As you recognise the difference between ego power and authentic Divine power, you can no longer put male above female or one person above another. Now is the time to fully reclaim the truth of what power is and what it is for. Now is the time to move on from polarities and bring a greater force into being: the wholeness and oneness of all that exists.

The joining together of your own golden power with the gold in the earth creates a different space – a space where power, wisdom and abundance can come together and be expressed in new ways. True wisdom arises from the earth and the balance of male and female she holds within, and this bottle expresses the possibility of a new form of power for humanity based on love – a feminine power that joins with the masculine instead of being pitted against it.

The love-based feminine form of power softens the fears on which life on earth has been based for so long. It brings gentleness, intuition and receptivity into the power mix so that it becomes much broader, more grounded, more authentic. In the process, it dissolves the rigid and out-dated brand of power – based on judgement, separation and fear – which has held sway over humanity for much of its history.

Bottle G5 takes the gold of authentic power and anchors it firmly into the copper earth. In this bottle the gold from inside the earth is now visible and accessible, and what has been hidden inside you can come out to be seen and known. Here your light becomes valid, your worth is clear for all to see, and it is no longer necessary to hide it or believe you are only safe to show it when you are among your own tribe. This bottle says you are ready to shine right here on the earth in a real way, being true to yourself, taking your light to whatever you do, radiating it wherever you go. With this power you have the ability to create with love and bring your dreams to fruition. The whole point of the human experience is to merge heaven with earth right here in your body and to create with the richness, strength and joy of the golden light you truly are. Bottle G5 is a wonderful support on this quest.

If this bottle calls to you, its message is clear: you are golden and you are powerful. Yet because gold can have a tendency to trigger issues of lack and unworthiness, notice if any part of you still tries to reject this message. Bring attention to your ego self, your wounded or addicted self, and guide that part of you gently into the earth's warmly loving, copper-gold embrace. It is only asking for more love, more acceptance, more generosity of spirit. Let this bottle and these colours bring you whatever you require to claim their message once and for all. Bring that golden power into your life and create with it. Infuse everything you do with it. This is a light to be shared. Enjoy the fruits of your labours and the wisdom you have gathered and honed through all your many lifetimes and experiences and use them to bring light and empowerment to those around you. Change happens one person at a time, and each human awakening to their true power becomes a key to the shift now taking place on the earth.

The richness of sunlit love emanating from this bottle pours power into your bones, your psyche, your consciousness and your heart. Its leonine energy is an echo of the inner lion in your heart. This is the power of being in a body, on the earth, claiming your majesty, remembering your courage, relishing your strength. This is a power that knows itself as real and has no need for pretence. This is a power that flows from a foundation of love to create a life of joy and generosity. Bottle G5 invites you to step into a new and empowered connection with your Divine essence as you let go of ego games and embrace the earth's golden truth as your own.

Bottles G4 & G5 Story: Lisa Barry, UK, www.lisabarry.me

I bathed in bottles G4 and G5 together when I was on the last part of my Colour Mirrors practitioner training. It was a time in my life when all the past grief and loss experiences and patterns were being brought to the surface to enable me to 'really' let go. My daughter's boss/friend died tragically and unexpectedly and left a two-year-old daughter behind, and my partner's father died whilst I was away on the Colour Mirrors course. These were triggers for my own mother and father issues as well as the unresolved grief of everything that I had lost throughout my life, especially connected with being a mother. Experiencing and feeling it all again at a secondary level through others' experiences allowed me to really feel into it in a totally different way, which was deeper and more painful. The first time round it was too raw and too painful for me to allow myself to feel it, so I shut off and became numb. Now I had to do it again!

Prior to the Colour Mirrors course I had pneumonia, which added to my fear of death and loss, and whilst I was assisting on an EFT/Matrix course at this time, the theme of all the people I was working with was death, grief and loss – much of it to do with mothers and fathers. So many teachers were showing up in my life that year to help me let go and be free of this pattern! I was also tuning into the loss of my marriage and how that had affected my children, and the loss of mobility of my youngest son who became paralysed in a car accident and again, the effect of all the grief and loss on me as a mother.

At the end of that day I chose bottles G4 and G5, and I would say the huge message and experience of bathing in both bottles at the same time was to clear and transform everything to do with all mother and father issues in my childhood, loss of my mother and all the loss and grief I have experienced as a mother.

When I poured bottle G4 into the bath the pink disappeared, and I wished it had been able to remain! But my thoughts were about letting go of all the loss and grief and opening to unconditional love. I had the realisation that I have that unconditional love from Mother Earth and that it is always within me, and that I could therefore no longer feel separation or loss. I reflected on myself as a mother and how proud I am of myself for having been there for my children through my divorce and the time of separation from my son whilst he was in hospital and rehab. I have always shown them unconditional love to get them through all the darkness they have felt. This part of my journey has given me such wisdom and compassion to share with other mothers who are going through their 'Mother's Journey', and this is now the main focus of my work and the group/community I have formed.

Bottle G5 slipped into the bath easily and luxuriously, and with both bottles mixed, it looked like pale gold, authentic power! I recognised an old belief from my father that females are not as powerful as males and do not have the right to excel and lead in their chosen field. That was the belief I had taken on as a child, and I experienced many situations where I felt I didn't have a choice in my life and career and couldn't choose the path that was my passion and in true alignment with my soul. I felt controlled and that my father squashed my feminine powerful side – or was he just showing me how I needed to raise my vibration and be powerful?! I have gone through this all my life in my career, feeling unable to access my true passion – until NOW! With this new understanding, I realised that I would be able to finish my website, write blogs and run groups and workshops, which is exactly what I have gone on to do. Now I am no longer hiding my light. Now I am claiming my feminine power and sharing my wisdom with the world! Now I feel safe, powerful and confident to share unconditional love and compassion with other mothers.

Bottle G6: The Goddess Awakens (Copper/Olive)

This bottle celebrates the true power of the feminine, a very new concept on a planet where most power has been expressed as a destructive force. It indicates the coming of a time on earth when all beings will be held safely in the love of Gaia and the feminine will awaken to her power and strength once again. It is time to reconnect with your powerful inner female and bring her energy into your life. The main message in this bottle is that the difficult times are over. Begin to feel the joy – everything is working out just fine.

This bottle is similar to bottle 10 (Wheel of Fortune), with its joyfulness, its sense of spring and the hopefulness of new growth. Both have olive in the bottom fraction, but where bottle 10 has gold in the top fraction, bottle G6 has copper, indicating that your wisdom and light are now assured, deep and grounded. This bottle says you are ready to share your knowledge and gifts with the world. You are coming into a time of deeply rooted peace, balance, harmony and supported personal growth, and you have the ability to make a difference here on earth just by being your authentic self. What is more, you can no longer hide the wellspring of love that has been building inside you: it is time to let it out.

Olive is the colour of powerful feminine energy. It contains the yellow of the solar plexus mixed with the green of the heart – power blended with love. Bottle G6 is the awakening of the goddess energy within you and all of humanity. The Divine feminine is growing in strength on the earth as women begin to reclaim the inherent power of their femaleness and men begin to respect it. Although it might seem ludicrous now, it is not so long since women were denied the right to vote and had no real say in the running of their lives. It wasn't until the 1960's, when a new generation surprised their elders by insisting that it was time to "make love not war", that women began to be seen and heard and accepted as equals. The olive in the bottom fraction of this bottle indicates that this energy had to start in the depths of humanity, in the depths of each soul. It has been a slow movement that has taken centuries to come to fruition and now, at least in most of the world, we can hardly conceive of a time when women had no power and no say.

There is still some way to go before there is equal balance between male and female on the earth, but this bottle represents the end of masculine domination. Of course the masculine in and of itself is not 'wrong' at all, but many of the ways it has revealed itself have been unbalanced and extreme, a distorted version of the truth. As part of the game humanity has been playing, it has been the prevailing force on the planet for millennia. Now it is time for balance. As all on the planet come to understand that men and women are created equal, future generations will live from that balance and instead of competition between men and women there will be true partnership of souls. This bottle is about luxuriating in the power of the feminine, and it invites you to understand that now is the time for every man and woman to very deeply embrace that power, for it is the power of love, abundance, nature and nurture – the power of life itself. It is time to embrace wholeness in yourself and for that, you are called to draw on the power of the feminine so that it becomes an equal partner to the masculine.

Bottle G6 brings healing love and energy to unresolved relationship issues, particularly with your mother or the earth herself. It offers a double dose of healing: the olive supports and nourishes your heart, and the copper aids you in transforming your issues and moving into a more loving, integrated space. Together these colours help you come back to yourself so that you feel safe in your own skin and on the planet. As you resolve your feelings about your mother and/or your earth mother, you no longer need to deny or negate the feminine within. Energy can then begin to flow to creativity, expansion and learning. Your heart space opens up so that you can receive more love and joy and experience more freedom, movement and play in your world. In the process, you are able to move out of old, stagnant energy and replenish yourself with the fresh new zest of spring.

Bottle G6 is filled with hope for the earth and for humanity. Hope takes your present day activities and creates from them a positive future on and for the earth. As you plant seeds for yourself, you do so for future generations. This bottle reminds you to hold the vision of earth as a place of positive growth and abundance. As you open to your generous, expansive and compassionate nature, your own life improves exponentially and the projects you undertake and the decisions you make cannot help but have a positive impact on others.

Feel how you are an integral part of this world. You can never truly be separate or alone, even if you have felt this way at times. Everything in the universe is so intricately interwoven and interconnected that your choices *do* affect the world you live in. With this bottle you are given a powerful opportunity to feel into the heart of your truth and what you are about and make choices from that space.

Bottle G6 is deeply nurturing. It is a walk in a peaceful woodland on a beautiful spring day. It is a celebration of the joy of nature and the goddess within. It reminds you of all that is good about your life. The message for those who are drawn to this bottle is that your life is on track. Everything is happening exactly as it is meant to, and with your powerful inner female awake and ready to create with love, the path can now unfold before you with ease and grace.

Bottle G6 Story: Debra Hubers-Paradis, USA, www.DebrasEnergyPoints.com

I divided this bottle into two powerful baths. After the first bath I realised that the olive portion is all about new beginnings. This inspired deeper feelings within me, sparking new creative business ideas about how to share the message of loving yourself first and foremost and honouring your inner child (where creativity lies), which then overflows into all parts of your life, creating more joy and possibilities. The copper awoke within me the feeling that expressing my power and being female is not only OK, it is a must at this time. I felt more of an inner strength awakening within me and more confidence to share with others the importance of honouring and loving their inner child.

After the second half of the bath in bottle G6 I was inspired to create classes that married Colour Mirrors with other modalities. I floated the idea with a powerful teacher and found that we worked together really harmoniously. The experience of co-creating new classes was effortless and had us both in a flow state. Our first class blew us away with the impact it had on our attendees, and we have gone on to create further new offerings.

My soul's work is to inspire others to love, honour and play with their inner child. The baths in bottle G6 helped me discover a whole new way to express my own inner child and, wow, the classes we are offering are some of the most powerful work I have ever presented to support people to have clarity and follow inspired action.

Bottle G6 Story: Kath Roberts, UK, www.kath-roberts.com

A client came to me for a session, an old soul with a theme of giving away her power in past and current relationships. Her grandfather had been successful in the property business but her talent and passion lay in her singing, acting and creative abilities, and she had moved to the US many years earlier to pursue her dream. Whilst well connected in the film industry, she had failed to launch her career fully in the way that she wanted and had ironically found herself in a property role – managing commercial real estate – mainly to pay the bills, wondering whether she was in the right role/place. After bathing in bottle G6, and as a result of a recent promotion, she was invited into a senior meeting with three male partners, to broker an opportunity with a significant leading real estate partner to design creative state of the art co-working spaces with private membership facilities.

At the same time she was invited to another meeting for a partnered venture, including a leading world-renowned architect and innovative creative hotel brand who wanted to create a commercial office co-creative space of the future. Both these initiatives offered her the opportunity to use her feminine creative power to bring something new to the market, which over a two-year period would help her secure a strong material base to build from. The clients really bought her knowledge and creative flair. She told me it was like the universe was conspiring to bring her something that brought all her prior experience together and allowed her to use her intuitive intelligence to create magic.

Both these options delivered the practical, grounded earthiness of copper, allowing her concrete resources but still with the feel of the olive's fresh spring new beginnings. What is interesting in both cases are the names of the companies she partnered with. One had the word 'spring' in its title, and the other's name was all to do with intuition. These were very significant to my client and just go to show that you really can't make this stuff up!

Bottle G7: Gaia and the Elohim (Copper/Clear)

This is where you start to really live your spirituality on the planet. This bottle says you do not have to choose between being spiritual and materially abundant. You can be both. You are the vessel through which Gaia (earth) and the Elohim (heaven) are able to communicate, and holding both these energies may feel strange until you are able to integrate them within you. This bottle is often chosen by people who have gone through enormous spiritual growth and have battled to remain grounded in the process. The light of the Divine is within you. Begin now to see that light in all beings and in the earth herself. Claim your deep connection with Gaia, the mother who has always nurtured you. At this time of rapid shift she is lifting her frequency to a higher level and will be your guide as you take the journey with her.

Bottle G7 holds something of the mysterious, the unknown. There is nothing obvious about this bottle, and what you see is not necessarily what you get. The clear fraction in the base of the bottle relates to light in the depths and the subconscious rather than light that shines out for all the world to see. Your light is absolutely in place, but it may have been largely hidden from yourself as well as others. With its dark copper top fraction, this bottle indicates feelings of heaviness and contraction on a physical, emotional or spiritual level and a sense that your light has been hidden, squashed or simply unavailable to you. You may be someone who places extreme importance on outward appearances, yet rarely shows what goes on inside. You may have struggled to be seen, acknowledged and accepted and have chosen to keep your real light firmly locked inside. When you are drawn to bottle G7, it is a sign that this is about to change.

The name of this bottle refers to Gaia: the earth, all that is 'real', tangible and human – and the Elohim: celestial beings who overlight the angelic realm. The apparent difference between these two energies is huge, and there might seem to be a kind of duality showing up here, especially with this bottle's clearly delineated split between copper earth and clear white light – yet somehow it is the opposite. Although there is a stark contrast between the colours, in bottle G7 their energies blend and merge. This bottle's truth is that there was never any separation between heaven and earth; they always have been and always will be one thing.

Choosing this bottle means that two things, two aspects of your life, two energies that have been separate are now in the process of becoming unified. What has been seen as spirit versus matter, light versus dark, heaven versus earth – these polarities are now beginning to merge. Perhaps in the past you have felt a split between your 'spiritual' life and your everyday work and home life, or a disconnection between your true beliefs and the way you have been living. Perhaps you have been keeping your life separated out into neat divisions, never allowing the various aspects of it to overlap. Perhaps you have been aware of the spiritual light you carry within but have kept it largely submerged out of fear of what might happen if you were to reveal it.

If this is your bottle, you may already have done a lot of work to ground, anchor and earth the light within you. Bottle G7 speaks of a deep commitment to being here on the earth, to being part of the dance of Gaia and the Elohim and everything in between, to experiencing the fullness of earthly life in all its diamond-like facets. You may have had to compartmentalise your spirituality before, but now you can let it into every aspect of who you are and what you do, and share your light in a way that feels real and true. There is a strong energy of 'acceptance' with this bottle – acceptance for who you are on all levels. There is also a solidity to the light here. You may be light, you may be connected with the angelic realms, but you are also real. Choosing this bottle says you are now ready to weave all your threads together so that what you have to share is practical and grounded as well as inspiring and enlightening.

The message of this bottle is that you and all of humanity hold heaven inside. The earth is part of you and part of the universe and she connects you to everyone and everything else on the planet. With this bottle you are shown the truth of Gaia as a beautiful, sentient, spiritual being, lit up by the light of the Elohim, making her choices for the good of all humanity. Bottle G7 reveals the possibility of an earth where there is no more judgement, just an incredible light, grounded and made whole. It shows you that everyone – including you, including the earth – is part of the same essential oneness. Now is the time for you to embrace your own light and spirit and return to the full knowing of that unity.

You are deeply, richly human – flawed and complex. You are also perfectly, wonderfully Divine – clear and radiant. When you really begin to know this, play with it, explore and enjoy it, integration happens on every level of your being. This bottle points you to the true nature of your existence as a spiritual being in a physical body on the earth and supports and nurtures you as you learn to fully embrace and love the game of life.

Bottle G7 Story: Melissie

I remember when I very first made this bottle and included it in a workshop. One of the participants chose bottles and placed them in a flower pattern. There were so many of them all squashed up that you couldn't even really tell what she had chosen, but bottle G7 was in the mix. She was the first person to choose this bottle and she loved it, but I saw that for her it was all about not wanting to be seen or 'known'. She was always done up to the nines, with perfect hair, figure and outfit. She had absolutely no wrinkles, as if she had never expressed an emotion – and this was pre-botox. She sat upright with her knees tightly together, and as I was trying to read her bottles she seemed to freeze into position, so uncomfortable that I wondered what she was doing at a colour workshop where everyone was finding out about themselves. I suggested that she open up her tightly clenched group of bottles, but she could not. She did, however, take bottle G7 home to bathe in.

The next day she came in looking as nearly dishevelled as such a pristine person could. Less makeup, and hair not sprayed into a hard cap; in fact, everything about her looked softer, and she told us that in the bath it felt as if she had relaxed for the first time in her life. Her story was that her beloved mother had died young, and her military dad had brought her up with regimented precision. Her subconscious belief was that she had to make sure that everything was always perfect so that he wouldn't leave her too. Somehow bottle G7 unlocked all the tears and the light she had been holding inside, and she said that for the first time in her life she now felt safe on the planet.

Bottle G7 Story: Moira Bush, Canada, www.moirabush.com

Korani asked me to read the manuscript of this book to give feedback, and when I read the section about the Copper Gaias, the words hit me dead centre in my heart. Suddenly, even though I had been working intimately with this system since 2003, I 'got' what the Coppers meant. These words started a tangible, deep calling from my soul – an urging that stayed with me for weeks until I could no longer ignore it – to bathe in bottle G7 and make a conscious decision to let go of bottle 7 and its colour turquoise as my life path number and colour.

I was so attached to the watery turquoise of Neptune, bottle 7, as my spiritual identity – even the set of my TV spiritual talk show 'The 707 Show' was turquoise – that the thought of 'changing' my life path to bottle G7's copper and clear was deeply unsettling. I felt rocked to my core. Then one morning I woke up and knew it was time. This turned out to be one of the more profound dips into Melissie's bottles. The set of the show immediately changed to white and copper, and since then all the intern TV hosts working on this new set have made tangible shifts. Offers of new and different types of work opportunities are appearing – I was even surprisingly nominated for an entrepreneur award by my bank manager. Bottle G7 has given me a new solid foundation to build the next phase of my work and life on, and I no longer feel like I am treading water!

Bottle G7 Story: Alka Dharam, UK, www.lifecentredhealing.co.uk

I had a bath in bottle G7 after having a shocking experience when almost all my chakras went out of alignment, and I could feel that I was out of balance. In the bath the feeling transmitted was that Mother (Gaia) is happy to have me (us) from the stars and is looking after and providing for us. She is very happy we are here and wants us to spread our light to all other beings. The message I heard was: "Be the love that I AM. You are that love." The feeling I had was to BE here on earth and see all that she provides and be grateful. She has welcomed me with open arms, and now she asks me to love myself as she loves me and fall into her embrace. For the time I am here, love her as she loves me. I am a part of her. I am born of her and will return to her. I am her. After this bath I felt grounded and in a state of love.

Bottle G8: Illumination (Deep Magenta/Deep Magenta)

This bottle is the darkest of the entire range. It supports you as you go into the heart of darkness in your subconscious and begin to feel the warmth and depth of the love that exists there. This is the seat of all potential. It is the moment when sleep finally overtakes you. The void. The place of dreams. This bottle is called Illumination, as it is only by going into the darkness and embracing it that you have the potential to step into the light. As you accept your shadow, you release your fears and judgements about the unspeakable that you hold within.

This bottle brings to light the unhelpful beliefs and judgements you have been holding about your physical body and supports you in transforming them. It helps clear your genetic line of the physical, emotional and karmic patterns you have inherited. The 'sins' of the fathers can no longer be visited on the children once the past darkness has been illuminated. As you face your shadow, you can move beyond it to a place where you create a reality based on the light rather than the dark. Everything you have in your life exists because you created it, albeit unconsciously. Now is the time to become a conscious creator and focus on what you truly wish to create – and this bottle is the ultimate support. Let it help you clear unconscious blocks and return to clarity so that you can claim your absolute magnificence.

Bottle G8 is the perfect guide and companion when you are experiencing a dark night of the soul or when there is a decision to be faced that requires you to look deeply within. It brings you into the silence of the void so that you can take stock, confront what you have believed to be your inner demons and open to the truths that your soul has to share with you – which are often so much greater than you could imagine. Here is the opportunity to examine what you have kept hidden, to stand in the void and face yourself in all your darkness and all your light and know that you are held, guided, supported and totally loved. Bottle G8 is the final of the eight Copper Gaias and is an anomaly in that it is not copper at all but deepest, darkest magenta. Magenta is always a bridge from the old to the new, and for such a dark and apparently impenetrable bottle, G8 is surprisingly gentle as it leads you into a space where you can embrace the light and prepare to begin a new cycle.

If the idea of a void seems daunting or scary, this bottle reminds you that it is a place of potent creativity, incubation and germination. Here is a space to plant seeds, with the knowledge that they will, in time, begin to form and grow. When your life seems to be heading into a big black full-stop, when everything you have known is on the point of changing or when you are brought to a sudden halt through an apparently 'negative' incident or situation, bottle G8 reminds you that this is an incredible opportunity to reflect on your journey, release old wounds and let go for a time. It is an invitation to delve into what has brought you to this juncture, go deep, find what is no longer serving your heart and soul and get clear on what needs to change. From there a new space can emerge and with it, new light. In the darkness your soul can now lovingly illuminate what it is you really wish to create in your life, who you really desire to be, how you truly wish to live in the world.

This bottle is the most profound gift whenever you are lost in the shadows. It steers you back towards the light with love and gentleness, holding you as you travel. We have seen it chosen over and over again, as it taps into universal feelings such as despair, sadness, disgust, anger, pain and judgement. This is one of the Colour Mirrors bottles that speaks to almost everyone at some point on their journey. You may initially find it a little frightening, perhaps fearing that it will take you even further into the darkness or reveal too much that you are not ready to handle. Yet almost everyone who really connects with bottle G8 finds it to be deeply comforting. When you choose this bottle it holds you in such an incredibly safe and loving way that you do not need to fear your journey into the darkness. It provides a space of deep stillness and rest where you can simply let go.

This bottle, more perhaps than any other in the system, lightens the load of self-hatred, self-denial and self-torture that almost everyone experiences at some point, especially with regard to the body. As the physical container for much of your inner darkness, you may see your body as a source of anxiety, anger or frustration. You may judge it, blame it, even hate it. Bottle G8 is an extraordinary balm for both your body and your soul, peeling back the layers of ego-based judgement you have heaped upon your body and revealing the love that it has always held for you. As you illuminate the truth, you discover that your body has simply been doing and being what your thoughts and emotions have instructed it to do and be. Your body is not the darkness but simply the screen onto which you have projected your unconscious shadow. Bottle G8 restores you to a more loving connection, a partnership, where instead of abusing your body, your mind can begin to honour, acknowledge and love it. This bottle helps you view your body as ally, guide and teacher rather than enemy. It helps you befriend your body and see it in an entirely new light.

This bottle also reveals to you the family blueprints you have taken on that might have served you until now but that are no longer a necessary part of your story. It helps bring to light the deeply embedded programming and conditioning that has kept you imprisoned in shadow beliefs and behaviours – about your body, your 'reality', your life circumstances and what might or might not be possible. G8 is a guide out of the morass of complex family patterns that have kept you in limitation. It illuminates the power of your own innate and unique Divine truth so that you are no longer beholden to the past.

Black has always been the colour of night, mystery, the unknown, the hidden, the shadow. It touches in to all that is impenetrable and unknowable within you and in the world around you. Yet this bottle's name is Illumination, and its role is to shine Divine love into every corner of your soul and reveal the hidden gifts you might never have known had it not been for the darkness. When bottle G8 calls to you it is in truth a song from your depths, an opportunity to engage with yourself and your perceived darkness without fear or pretence. It is a mystery to be unravelled, a powerful and precious space to enter into and a chance to explore territories you may have previously shied away from or whose existence you may have denied. It is a black diamond: multi-faceted, glimmering and exquisitely powerful.

In the depths of this black bottle lie your darkest secrets. Here is where you have buried everything you deem 'not public property'. This is where your shadow holds everything about you that you have come to think is unacceptable. In your long human journey over many lifetimes you may have mistakenly bought into the belief that there is 'God' and 'not God'. You may have tried endlessly to bury all the darkness, all the 'not Godness' of yourself so that neither you nor anyone else would have to see it. What you may have forgotten is that in your essence you are light, and whatever you try to hide in the depths is simply another expression of that light – because there is nothing else that exists.

In this bottle lie possible answers to the mysteries of the darkness, for the black is not black at all but deep, luscious magenta. This spellbinding bottle of riches shows that what you have always believed to be the darkest aspects of yourself have, in fact, been just another expression of Divine love. There is dark and there is light but they are both love, and bottle G8 shows you very clearly that the dark and the light form one sacred circle. You may choose to embrace or deny this, just as you may choose whether to play in the light or the dark, whether to see the colour as black or magenta. The Divine judges none of it, and bottle G8 teaches you to judge none of it too. Instead it asks you to love, accept and honour yourself for all your many facets and embrace life in all its many shades.

In the darkness of bottle G8 lives the whole truth about why you exist. It is the invitation to love the unlovable, accept the unacceptable, retrieve the irretrievable and weave back together what has become separated, split or unravelled. It is the love that overrides everything and embraces all. When you open to its incredible truth, there can be no more turning away from the love of the Divine, no more pretending to be abandoned or rejected, no more fear of having to 'go it alone', no more expectation of being punished for your imagined transgressions. This is the love of the Divine shone into every cell of your body, every minute particle of your being, every cobwebbed corner of your consciousness. You are an infinite spark of divinity and you are part of the awakened earth. Embrace your magenta soul star, come out of the dark and step into the light of truth. Let all that has brought you to this point in your life be illuminated by the pure light of the Divine. Welcome your apparent darkness and remember that, at its core, it is only light by another name.

Bottle G8 Story: Lesley McDonald, UK, www.lesleytara.com

We all walk through a dark night of the soul from time to time when we are ready to let go of old patterns and embark on a new path. I had been ready to move forward for a long while but had been hesitant, held back by ancient fears. The universe in all its wisdom knew that if I was going to do it, it really needed to kick my butt!

I woke up one morning bathed in sweat after dreaming that someone was following me, and the feeling of fear lingered on day after day as a constant feeling of danger lurking close by. And prophetic it turned out to be, when the following weekend I missed my train home and arrived in my country town just in time to miss the last bus. There was nothing for it but to walk the 15 minutes home on unlit roads. I was nervous, as the dream had me spooked, so I stopped and fiddled with my phone until the flashlight function came on.

Suddenly a figure appeared from behind a hedgerow and began to follow me. I knew immediately something was wrong but kept going, plunging ahead into the darkness, calling for protection, and turning around to shine my flashlight (possibly my saving grace). Frantically I kept on, but knew I was coming to an area where the houses stopped and I would be plunged into absolute blackness. Walking as fast as I could, I made my way down a side road onto the main road where there were street lights, taking myself further from home. I thought he would not follow me there, but he did! Now it was worse, as the only way home was back into the absolute pitch dark. So, on reaching the end of the street-lit area, I abandoned flip flops, plunged into the inky blackness and ran for my life. I made it safely home.

When I got over the shock, I started to ponder the concept of everything we experience being a product of our own perceptions and a manifestation of our inner fears, and I started to figure out what had just happened from an energetic and 'bigger picture' perspective. Slowly, understanding began to dawn, and I realised that it was when I stopped trying to stick frantically to the street-lit area (my illusion of safety) and actually surrendered and plunged into the heart of the darkness that I was truly safe. At that point it was so dark it was impossible to know in which direction I had run, and without shoes it was silent too. So in the black silence of the 'void', I was safe.

With so much symbolism I began to cheer up and realise that the universe was sending me the perfect lesson in a way that would make me sit up and take notice. It was time to listen and to make the changes I have long needed to make. Finally ready, I grabbed the G8 bottle and plunged myself into the inky blackness of a warm, supportive bath, knowing that whatever it brought to the surface I was ready, I was supported and I was safe.

Bottle G8 Story: Victoria Pitt, UK, www.facebook.com/justvictoria.co.uk

It's no secret that I have an affinity with the darkness. It has been my biggest teacher and become a source of comfort and nourishment in ways I could never have imagined. Illumination, as it is so aptly named, was the first bottle I purchased whilst doing an 'Introduction to Colour' weekend in London. This bottle pulled me in by everything that was seemingly wrong with the world and therefore me, resonating so powerfully with the depths of my unfolding and experience. It slept under my pillow, sat on my shelf and generally accompanied me on much of my early journey with Colour Mirrors, reminding me often of its presence and inviting me to open more and more to the darkness that is within. Bottle G8 walked with me out of the depths of darkness and into the light whilst remaining solid in its message, which for me is that there is beauty in the darkness and without it there can be no light. As the saying goes, when you think you've been buried, you may well have been planted. The darkness houses rich, fertile, nourishing ground, and allowing it to envelop me with all its might was a journey well worth taking. Magenta, after all, is so very full of love.

Bottle G8 Story: Audrey Bossman, UK

The Colour Mirrors system helped me to articulate what was going on for me when I had no words. Bathing in the Illumination oil (bottle G8) changed everything for me, as I was able to admit to myself that the choices I made did not feed my soul. The depth and richness of bottle G8 also helped me realise that no matter how painful it may be at the time, each experience is an opportunity for growth.

The Golden Gaia Set

Bottles G9-G15

The Golden Gaias were the first of the higher vibrational Gaia bottles, and their arrival in 2009 signalled a paradigm shift on the planet. The glowing golden light with which they are infused is a tangible expression of the major changes unfolding on the earth, which continue to intensify as she lifts her vibration. Their lightness and ringing clarity is a powerful indicator of the growing awareness of humanity and the transition of the earth herself to a fifth-dimensional reality.

It has been foretold in almost every spiritual and religious tradition that there would come a time of great light and peace on earth, a new era of cooperation, harmony, unity and joy and a shifting of consciousness to Divine rather than ego-based living. This is what we refer to as Ascension, although it may also be referred to by various other names such as the Great Shift, the Awakening, and the Shift of Ages. The Golden Gaias reveal the possibilities of this new time in a very clear and tangible way. They herald a deeper knowing within you that you truly are a Divine being, here on earth to have an experience of being human so that you might add to the Divine's knowledge of itself. They offer a clear reconnection with your Divine heritage so that you can incorporate it into your daily life rather than simply understanding it at a mind level or feeling as if it might happen 'out there' somewhere.

When you are drawn to the Golden Gaias, it is because you are ready to look forward and leave the past behind. You are ready to live your spirituality more fully, live more lightly on the planet and express yourself with greater ease. You are preparing to embrace new ways of being that bring empowerment, expansion and Divine synchronicities into your life. You are willing to see the world from a higher, more expanded viewpoint, free of judgement and the weight of a third-dimensional perspective. More than this, you are ready to play your part in the monumental shift in consciousness that is taking place on the planet.

Korani's book *The Language of Light: Golden Keys to Ascension* shares the story of how and why the Golden Gaias came into being. It takes the reader on a journey through the set of seven Golden Gaia bottles, opening doors in a very real way to the new golden era upon the earth. The book devotes a full chapter to each of the seven Golden Gaias, with exercises and meditations sprinkled among the explorations of each bottle. Each chapter also contains stories about each bottle from those who have worked with the Golden Gaias and been through the Golden Keys experience. We recommend this book for anyone who is looking for more in-depth information and seeking to go deeper and higher on the golden Ascension journey.

As you travel through the Golden Gaia set you may encounter shadow aspects of yourself that are ready to be brought into the warm golden glow of love. You may also meet highly advanced aspects of yourself that are already immersed in the Divine frequencies of light and love. Their promise is that even if you have not yet been able to fully embody these higher frequencies, the knowledge of how to do so is already within. The Golden Gaias are a set of 'keys' to unlock the magnificent potential waiting inside you and assist you in opening to a simpler, clearer, more inspired way of living. If you choose to really embrace the golden journey in its fullness, you can be assured that your life will not remain the same. Each of the Golden Gaias on their own has the power to bring lasting change. As a set, they help to shape a new paradigm, for you and for the earth.

Bottle G9: Faith (Turquoise/Pale Gold)

After the darkness of bottle G8 comes a bright new vision, a shining light of turquoise and gold at the end of the dark tunnel. Now there is a new state available to you as you connect with your authentic, golden Divine power through your turquoise faith. It is faith that moved you through the dark tunnel back into the light. Without faith you would not have survived the dark night of the soul; in fact, you would not have needed to go into it. It was your faith that took you there, knowing that there was another level, closer to the Divine, closer to your true self.

The colours of this bottle reconnect you to the flow and the knowledge that everything is on track and part of the Divine plan. It takes you beyond trust and into the truth that you are Divine and that all experiences – past, present and future – are Divine and therefore perfect. This colour combination indicates that you are a teacher who can access ancient truths and share them in a new way so that all can begin to have faith in themselves, in life and in the dawning of a new golden era on the earth.

After the dense, dark and at times heavy quality of the Copper Gaias, bottle G9 comes in now with a blast of light. This bottle sparkles and dazzles with the energy of sunshine on the sea. It is about openings and possibilities, fresh new beginnings and stepping out of your comfort zone. It supports you in opening your heart to a brand new space, one where you can breathe and expand and reach out your arms to all that the universe has to offer.

Its gift is to show you what it means to be truly 'in faith', to be connected to the Allness in a way that defies logical thought or definition. When you are in doubt or turmoil it restores the sense of absolute safety that comes with knowing you are divinely loved and cared for, that all is well and will continue to be well. Faith is a golden key that, when slotted into your heart, unlocks a well-spring of optimism, hope, even wonderment. This shining bottle glows with light and life, daring you to look beyond cynicism, fear and resistance to a new world of opportunity and potential. It encourages you to see the world through new eyes: the eyes of faith.

Faith truly experienced can generate profound shifts in your life. It changes you from the inside out, inspiring confidence and courage and enabling you to walk out to meet life head-on rather than waiting fearfully for it to 'happen' to you. When you live in a state of faith your life unfolds in ways that can sometimes seem quite miraculous. You put aside thoughts of how you want things to turn out and let go of trying to make things happen. Instead you live in a flow where synchronicities abound, the right people, places and things turn up, and the universe dances with you in perfect tune and perfect rhythm.

Faith can certainly be tested, and at times you may find it difficult to access. When something you desire does not happen or a wish remains unfulfilled, you may begin to lose your sense of certainty and trust in life. This can lead to a downward spiral, and once you start doubting and fearing, you may find it increasingly difficult to attract the things and circumstances you most wish for.

The opposite is also true, however: faith is like a muscle that must be exercised in order to grow stronger. The more faith you have in life, the more life shows up for you. Once you have tasted true faith, even if it slips away for a time, it remains within you in some form, waiting only for you to rediscover and reconnect with it. Bottle G9 is a wonderful gift for anyone in the throes of doubt, anxiety, worry or fear. With joyful clarity it reminds you to lighten up, let go and enjoy life. When your faith is dwindling or you are lost and confused, this bottle is a tremendous support in setting you back on track again.

Bottle G9 is the perfect way to wipe the slate clean. It offers new hope, new light and a fresh page on which to write the next stages of your journey. Whenever life has become dull, clouded or cluttered, whenever you are unable to see the way forward, bottle G9 is like a window thrown open, with sunlight pouring into your soul and heart to ignite your inner light once more and guide you forward on your pathway.

As the first of the Golden Gaias, this bottle sets the tone for what is to come as you move into higher dimensional frequencies and higher states of consciousness. It opens a beautiful space for play, creativity and connections to occur. It shows you what a Golden Age on earth might look like, where your beingness is rooted in ease, flow and inspiration. In a state of clear-sighted faith you know when to take action, when to move forward and when to wait. You follow your inner guidance and trust it, always, to take you where you need to be. You do not have to be 'in control'. You can see the bigger picture. You do not let tests of faith knock you down but instead use them as opportunities to open to greater clarity, reconnect with your heart, listen to your soul's longings and if necessary, change course.

The colours of bottle G9 are reminiscent of bottle 28, New Beginnings. What is inspiring about this Faith bottle is that its message is not simply about new beginnings on a personal level but for the entire planet and all of humanity. As you embrace faith in all its depth and lightness and begin to create from this state of being, you not only experience greater flow and joy in your own life but you offer that into the matrix. You pour your empowered creative energies into the cosmos and breathe life into the new golden era on the earth. Faith becomes the foundation of life, and joy becomes a reality.

Faith – like the Divine – is ever-present and eternal, whether you choose to experience it or not. This bottle is an antidote for all that keeps you in fear and doubt, reminding you that in every second of every day you get another moment, another breath, another choice. There is something eternally new about this energy which means you also get to open to the new every time you connect with it. Bottle G9 is a physical symbol of the joyful faith energy, anchoring it for you while you learn – or remember – how to embody it. This bottle acts as a powerful reminder that you were always meant to soar, fly and be free.

There is an element of pure magic about faith that insists you remember what it is to be whole, utterly connected and in child-like awe of life and the universe. It reminds you of your innocence, your God-given grace, your pure innate radiance. Faith laughs in the face of cynicism and doubt and dances joyously even when you turn your back on it, waiting patiently and with love for you to turn around and hold your face to its sun-bright warmth once more.

Bottle G9 Story: Renira Barclay, UK, www.abovemiddlec.com

I took this bottle with me on holiday to Kefalonia in order to start the process of working my way through the Golden Gaias. Whether on my little balcony or on the beach, every time I held the bottle I cried and cried, sobbing coming from I know not where. For about three days I did this, giving up after about 15 minutes sobbing. On day four, in tears again, I decided to SIT on the bottle. As soon as I sat on bottle G9 the tears stopped, and I felt calm and composed! I then laughed out loud. Taking up the energy of Faith through my base chakra made all the difference! I have since advised clients to sit on their bottles, like hens.

Bottle G9 Story: Moira Bush, Canada, www.moirabush.com

When Korani's book The Language of Light: Golden Keys to Ascension *came out, she and Melissie created a training program that allowed us to guide groups of students through an eight-week Ascension course. Groups met every week for two hours, working their way through the Golden Gaia set. At the first meeting participants held bottle G9, talked about how it made them feel, did the harmonic meditation in Korani's book, then went home to bathe in the bottle over the next week – with the intention to share their experiences in the group at the next meeting. Well, every single student in my groups said that during the bottle G9 week they kept hearing the George Michael song, 'Faith', on the radio, in malls and on TV, and that his words: "You gotta have faith-a-faith-a-faith..." felt like a musical mantra confirming that their faith was being restored!*

Bottle G10: Impeccability (Pale Gold/Pale Blue-Lilac)

Impeccability means accepting and honouring every aspect of who you are and being clear and honest about both your shadow and your light. It is not about living up to a false standard of perfection, rather it is about seeing the perfection that already exists – in yourself, in others and the world. The colour blue-lilac is about communication (blue) from your spirit (lilac). It asks you to be vigilant with your words and speak with incredible integrity because you hold the power to manifest whatever you say. When you are impeccable, words can no longer be used as weapons or instruments of manipulation. Instead they become vehicles for love and connection. This bottle relates to the masculine side of creation and asks you to make peace with the masculine side of yourself and the males in your life. It takes you into a space of silence, simplicity and deep inner stillness from which you can access the voice of inspiration.

Bottle G10 shines softly, like a pale glimmer of sunshine on a peaceful lake, early morning on a beach before the sun becomes fully bright on the water, that time of stillness and quiet when anything seems possible. Its softness and freshness speak of the hope of a new day, a new dispensation, where all the shadows can dissolve and the truth can be brought to light. Impeccability shows up what is false and illusory and radiates such peaceful, loving acceptance that what you consider to be your flaws and your weaknesses are no longer something to deny or hide. This bottle shows them as simply another aspect of yourself calling for love. There is nothing here to fear.

This bottle is not swayed by the stories or fabrications you may tell about your life. It sees through them all to the heart of you and stays true to its course, serene and steady, unwavering in its total commitment to mirroring you to yourself. If you let it, bottle G10 will reflect back to you everything you have been hiding: your smallness, your self-doubt, your shadow; your greatness, your boldness, your brilliance. This bottle is about looking in the mirror and not looking away until you are willing to see the truth. It is unflinching in its honesty and asks you to be so too. It holds absolutely no judgement, only unconditionally loving acceptance. It asks you to be impeccable, yes, but not so that you meet others' standards or conform to some hypothetical ideal of perfection. Rather, it invites you to be impeccable with and for yourself. So what does that actually mean for your life?

It means that you honour yourself, backing yourself completely, saying yes to the things that light up your soul, saying no when something is not in alignment with who you are. It means that you trust in your own inner guidance and follow it. It means that you acknowledge and accept every aspect of yourself. It means that no matter what you think you have done that is unforgiveable, no matter how big or how small you believe yourself to be, no matter what you do or do not do, say or do not say – you look beyond the stories and love yourself for all that you are and for every piece of the journey.

Impeccability is where love can be practiced – true love, love without boundaries and conditions. This bottle asks you to love impeccably, to let the soft roundness of your love and your light encompass everything and everyone, most particularly yourself. You may not always succeed, and that too is part of impeccability. It is vast enough to hold every person and every experience in its embrace and allow all of it to be just as it is. Impeccability is where you speak from your heart and live from your essence and when you fail to do so, you love yourself anyway. It is the entirely benign love of the Divine father who accepts you completely, supports you utterly and is there for you unerringly. It is the next step on from Faith (bottle G9). In Faith, you believe in the love of the Divine and trust that it is there for you. In Impeccability, your life is based and founded upon that love – you *know* that it is eternally in place, always available to you, utterly without question.

The colours in bottle G10 relate to the masculine, and this bottle is a great support in helping you come to terms with the male energies in your life – your male partners, family members and friends, your own inner male and the Divine masculine or 'Father God'. If you have challenges with the masculine, this bottle assists you in recognising the issues and resolving them. Perhaps you are aware of imbalances in the way you relate to the men in your life. In its negative aspects, the masculine may be dominating, aggressive and unwilling to listen, and you may notice that you fear these qualities in yourself or others. Perhaps you find yourself pushing, striving and over-doing, or alternatively feeling lethargic, uninspired and powerless. Maybe you feel unsupported, reluctant to take action or unable to stand up for yourself.

This bottle helps you move on from such challenges by helping you get in touch with your empowered inner male qualities. The masculine is the aspect of yourself that supports you, taking action when needed. It is the dynamic part of you that is outward-looking, forward-moving, primed to respond when the moment is right. It protects, honours and holds you as you undertake your journey, providing a base of stability and safety from which you can move forward and out into the world. When your inner male is balanced and whole, when your connection with your Divine male is in place, you can go about your life with the steadiness of loving support behind you. You can explore and create, launch yourself into the great adventure of life, spread your wings and fly – all the while knowing that you have a safe haven to return to any time you choose.

'Impeccability' as a word may conjure up notions of rigidity, making you think you have to stand in line, follow the rules and measure up, especially in the light of its connection with the masculine. This soft round bottle is nothing to do with any of that – quite the opposite. It is a clear, calm, peaceful space filled with sunlight and stillness, where you are gently and lovingly welcomed home to yourself. It is a new kind of masculine, holding and honouring rather than forcing and judging. This is where you release expectations of yourself, where you forgo others' rules and dictates, where you follow your own natural rhythms and flow, where you dance to your own tune and let the song of your soul guide you. In impeccability you are free to hear the whispers of the universe and respond in the moment rather than being held back by the memories and burdens of the past. This bottle awakens in you a burgeoning sense of freedom as it guides you towards living impeccably, in alignment with yourself and your natural energy flows.

In his beautiful book *The Four Agreements* Don Miguel Ruiz writes about impeccability and what it means to be impeccable with your word. As you live in alignment with your Divine essence and honour your own inner wisdom and guidance, you discover that you no longer wish to speak with the voice of ego and falsehood. You do not wish to engage in gossip or speak ill of another. You recognise that the other *is* you, that you are the other, that all is one. As you claim impeccability for yourself, you naturally wish to extend that to everyone and everything. You open your eyes and heart to see the Divine standing before you in the form of your brother, your sister, your mother, your father, your children, your friends – and everyone you meet. You recognise that the words you speak are your Divine creative power made manifest and that to malign another or use your words as weapons creates a force field of negativity that not only affects the person you direct it towards but also comes powerfully back to you. Bottle G10 guides you to choose integrity, love and compassion instead.

As you open to the gentle, luminous light of stillness and silence at the heart of these colours, feel the purity of the note that sounds when you are in impeccability and the inspiration that arises as you tune into it. This bottle carries so much peace that it helps you let go of the racket of your over-thinking mind and step instead into tranquillity and calm. From there you can open to receive the loving guidance of the universe and your own Divine essence.

When you choose bottle G10 it is because it is time to let go of limiting behaviours and the decisions you have taken in the past that have kept you locked in a box – a box which can no longer contain you. It is time to stop trying to please others in order to be accepted and begin to accept yourself fully instead. It is time to cut loose from the self-imposed limitations you have been struggling against. You are ready now to go inside and access the wisdom that has always been there and hear what your higher self has to say. You are ready to start living authentically and with clarity. You are ready to start being impeccable with yourself – which, when all is said and done, really just means being your own truest friend.

Bottle G10 Story: Melissie

When the Golden Gaias first arrived, Korani and I created a new workshop where we studied one bottle a week for seven weeks, with an eighth week for integration at the end. My son David participated in the workshop and when we did the Impeccability bottle, the week's exercise was to really check our judgements. On the way to the evening meeting I told David that I had struggled with this bottle, as I realised how deeply judgemental I still was. And David, bless his beautiful heart, said: "Mum, why don't you stop judging your judgements??" It was the perfect comment, and I realised that this was the key: stop all of it, including judging my judgy-ness. If we stop judging everything about ourselves first, there is much more potential to stop judging everyone else.

Bottle G10 Story: Clara Apollo, UK, www.claraapollo.com

Back when the Golden Gaias were first shared with us I travelled to Spain, taking 'Impeccability' with me. Here I stayed a whole week, resting, integrating, drinking in the impeccable faith of my being, observing the impact of this approach as it rippled through each action and reflection. I began to find it easier and easier to maintain this raw honesty of self-truth, and now I notice that when I do, my vibration rises so that it jars when things come in that are not of a pristine quality. This G10 bottle was a golden wake-up call – along with the words on impeccability in Don Miguel Ruiz's book The Four Agreements.

Bottle G11: Generosity (Pale Coral/Pale Gold)

Coral is unconditional self-acceptance – I am perfect as I am – and pale gold is your connection to your authentic Divine self. This combination powerfully reconnects you to who you really are, a Divine creation, a magnificent human able to joyously dance your reality into being. If you are already perfect and aligned with your Divine self you can create anything, and this bottle opens you to harvest, abundance, love and joy. Now you can finally see yourself as part of the Divine's perfection. You deserve everything and more, and as you claim this you can access and generously share all of it. The love that you hold for your precious self is so magnetic that it can attract anything you focus on because you are in alignment with Divine truth. This bottle holds the softly loving power of the Divine feminine and invites you to connect with it as you explore and heal your relationship with the female energies in your life.

There is such warmth here, such open-hearted goodness, such pure delight. This bottle holds the promise of anything you could wish for, everything you could desire, gifted to you with joy and ease. This is a little bottle of sunshine. It lifts your mood, makes you smile, lightens your heart and opens you to receiving. It reminds you that generosity is about the whole cycle, that the more you open yourself to the universe's perfect generosity the more you can receive – and the joy you experience when receiving then translates into a natural desire to give. As you blossom in the light of bottle G11's warmth and abundance, your giving naturally flows from a place of oneness and connection that is effortless and often spontaneous.

The golden glow in the bottom fraction of this bottle reminds you of how fully and deeply you are held by the golden earth. As you let the gold permeate the very fibre of your being, it infuses and fills you so that you begin to radiate it out, effortlessly and easily. The gold becomes part of you and moves through you, being refilled and continually renewed as it does so. There is no end to the universe's love and what it is willing to give you. The only limits are the ones you place upon yourself. Bottle G11 asks you to stop withholding – from yourself and others – and instead open to the limitless flow of joy and abundance that is always available to you. The more you focus on and allow it, the more generosity can truly become your daily experience.

The coral top fraction of this bottle awakens you to the power of unconditional self-acceptance and helps you see that as you fully embrace who you are, you align with the universe and the unique role of your soul in the unfolding adventure of life. The Divine desires only for you to fall into its endless love and allow that love into all the cells of your body and the essence of your being. From there you cannot help but want to share what comes to you, and you do so in the full knowledge that the more you share and give, the more the universe brings right back to you. The energy of generosity, fully embodied, has the power to bring you the very situations, people, events and things you desire for yourself. It also assists you in taking your light and your message out into a world that welcomes what you have to share.

The challenge in this bottle is to allow yourself all the love, generosity and gifts that are waiting for you. There has never been any lack. The only lack you have experienced has been conjured up from your imaginings and your beliefs and made 'real' through your thoughts and feelings. Generosity asks you to hold those beliefs up to the light of the Divine's love, see them for the illusions they are and forgive yourself for having been fooled by them. Stepping into generosity is as much about surrender and letting go as it is about giving and receiving. It is time now to give up any remaining beliefs that you cannot or do not deserve or that you are not good enough. If the Divine could ever look at you with anything other than pure love (and it cannot), it would surely be bewildered that you are unable to fully love and accept yourself. How could one who is made from perfection, in perfect love, somehow be less than good enough?!

Sometimes what is called for is a mental shift, a willingness to see things from a different perspective, and bottle G11 helps bring to the fore those subconscious or hidden thought patterns and beliefs that have kept you from awakening to your true nature as a divinely loved and treasured being. It guides you to a greater awareness of where you have been holding back from yourself and others, and helps you heal the wounds that have led you into such a restricted, limited space.

The warm glow of Generosity invites you to expand, open up and create your life with joy and laughter. It encourages you to step into the gloriousness that the universe is gifting you. Its connection with the Divine feminine

169

means that this bottle has a powerful ability to hold you in the light of unconditional love while you let go of unworthiness, fear or doubt and open to the fullness of your divinely generous nature. Where bottle G10 connected you with the energy of the masculine, bottle G11 invites you to explore your connection with the feminine – your mother, your sisters, your female partners and friends, your own inner feminine and the energy of the Divine Mother.

Notice where you struggle with the feminine. Do you find the females in your life a challenge? Perhaps it is difficult for you to receive, to nurture, to be compassionate, to be sensitive to others. Maybe you nurture too much. Is your inner female suppressed by your dominant inner male wanting to run the show and be 'in control'? Do you default to 'negative' feminine qualities such as passivity, drama, manipulation or insecurity? Bottle G11 helps you remove the stories and get to the truth of the feminine as the blissful, warm, loving and generous light of the Divine Mother so that you can shine that light on yourself and others with no holds barred. It assists you in discovering how your inner female truly feels, how she wishes to express herself and how she behaves when she is fully empowered: creative, expansive and all-embracing.

This bottle asks you to look deeply at what you believe about abundance, flow, generosity and the cycle of giving and receiving. It challenges you to become a conscious creator in your own universe, to choose to put your awareness on the gifts that are available to you in any circumstance, in any situation, in every moment. This does not mean denying the difficulties and challenges you face, rather it means that you make the choice to focus on the abundance and generosity of the universe and that you continually return to gratitude. Gratitude is one of the most powerful keys to opening your generosity channels, and with bottle G11 you are given a beautiful opportunity to practice it. As you choose to consciously acknowledge the generous gifts life brings, the floodgates open and all the love and generosity of the Divine is free to pour through. And when you are swept up in that delicious flow, those around you become encompassed in it too, in an ever-widening and growing circle of generosity.

Bottle G11 Story: Katherine Louise Jones, UK, www.katherinelouisejones.com

As I lay immersed in the warmth of my bath with bottle G11, a candle flickering softly, I observed two flames – one big and a second, smaller one. In awe of this, I contemplated the message: mother/father, female/male, yin/yang, light/dark, higher self/shadow self, soul/ego. Then it dawned on me that the dance of the little flame was being mirrored by the big flame – a fluid movement of coming together then fluttering away. All the while the big flame patiently waited, loving the small flame, beckoning it to see its reflection in all its beauty and glory. I felt love for the little flame, excitedly dancing yet still hesitant, weaving in and out, connected and still growing. As I got out of the bath, still intoxicated by the message of two flames, I saw that there was, in fact, only one flame. What I had thought I had seen in the candle had simply been reflecting the illusion of separation.

Bottle G12: I AM (Pale Gold/Pale Gold)

Choosing this bottle means you are ready to release any beliefs which keep you small and limited and align instead with your 'I AMness', that greater part of you who is fearless, ancient and wise. Now is the time to claim yourself as part of the Divine: "The Divine is within me. I AM that." This bottle supports you in letting go of the separating influence of addictions, which only ever keep you feeling small and separate from your Divine self. When you claim back your true power, you can be free of addictions and deeply, authentically Divine.

On the surface this might appear to be a simple bottle – one colour top and bottom, pale and clean-looking, soft and smooth. There is wholeness here, clarity and acceptance, honesty and truth. Yet its messages are rather more complex than they might at first appear; in fact, this bottle holds in one small container almost everything Colour Mirrors teaches! Bottle G12's name is 'I AM', and there is perhaps no more powerful claim than this. 'I AM' – as a statement, a bottle, an energy – strips away layers of falsehood, leaving only essence, only truth. Any time you state "I AM", you claim your Divine inheritance – because 'I AM' is another name for God. When you fully embrace the light of your I AMness, your 'Godness', you open the gates to the pure potent light-force of the Divine to fill you right to the brim. You leave no space for doubt, fear or the falsehoods of ego.

This bottle reminds you that you are an alchemist, fully capable of creating and manifesting gold on an inner level and seeing the reflection of that gold showing up as abundance in your outer world. It connects you with the joy of claiming your I AMness. It exudes a subtle yet potent light of power and authenticity. It asks you to step fully into that light and let it in, all the way to your toes. This is the light of the 'new' earth, the golden earth, an earth whose vibration is clean and clear, soft and empowered, generous and gentle, strong and vibrant. On this new earth, Gaia asks you to match your vibration to hers, to be all that she is, to be all that you are. Here is an earth that nurtures and holds you and does so in partnership. You are no longer the child needing a mother to look after her or a father to take care of her problems. You are now a spiritual adult, walking a path of conscious awareness, co-creating your reality and your experiences.

At the same time, bottle G12 also reflects the fear that arises at being asked to step fully into the true and exquisite power of your I AMness. What is this fear that keeps you from being everything you really are? Mostly, it is memory. Mostly, it is past experiences. Mostly, it is a misunderstanding of life and what your experiences were about. It is the belief that you are somehow limited and helpless, at the mercy of forces completely outside of yourself. It is the belief that you are somehow *not* the 'I AM', that you are outside of the all-encompassing love of the Divine. For some, this bottle will bring up a sense of being far-removed from the Divine, from love, from light. It can be deeply uncomfortable when you are faced with your brilliance and your light, and you may find yourself diving into the shadows, scurrying back to limited versions of your life or the well-trodden paths of your addictions and stories, no matter how painful they may be.

In this bottle, Gaia holds up a very clear mirror for you to look into, a mirror that reflects back to you all the places you are unable to claim 'I AM', everywhere you are hiding from your light, anywhere you are choosing limitation and judgement over freedom and love. She invites you to be part of the ever-expanding energy of awakening and consciousness on the earth, and she also makes it clear that if you are not willing to claim your magnificent I AMness, if you are not willing to shed your stories and your 'stuff', you are free to remain part of the old 3D version of the earth and continue to play those games in the lower vibrational field. She holds no judgement on your choices. Free will allows you to choose what 'I AM' means to you. Does it mean "I am a victim"? "I am unworthy"? "I am unlovable"? "I am a slave to my addictions"? Or does it mean "I am free", "I am Divine light", "I am perfect just as I am"? Perhaps you simply choose "I am" – with no need for qualifiers, justifications or additions to your innate essential beingness.

A huge part of your human journey has been to forget the truth about the light you carry so that you could embark on a long voyage back to remembering that truth, with a myriad of experiences along the way. All of it is designed to help you personally grow and evolve while adding to the Divine's knowledge of itself in the process. This bottle helps clear out the cellular memories of lifetimes when you believed you could be the light and then had your light extinguished, or experiences of bravely claiming your I AMness and being shot down in flames – either metaphorically or literally. It reminds you of the essential truth of your divinity and your infinite soul that has never been diminished by any experience you have had. Your eternal soul remains completely aligned with and wholly loved by the Divine.

Bottle G12 calls when you are ready to stop the game-playing and let go of the habits, patterns and addictions that have kept you running around in circles. It comes when you are ready to stop pretending to be limited. It carries a similar energy to the Colour Mirrors Gold Dragon essence – fearless, bold and authentic. It supports you as you step off the wheel of self-perpetuated dramas, addictions and stories and shows you a new, lighter, vastly more empowered path to follow. If this bottle calls you, it is time. Time to stop hiding, time to stop the games. Time to stand up, face down your demons and BE who you really are. In the light of your true I AMness, your fears and worries reveal themselves as illusions. The power of the Divine within is, and always will be, far greater.

I am the light. I am the power of the Divine. I AM.

Bottle G12 Story: Nicky Batt, UK, www.facebook.com/ConsciousColourLiving

On my Colour Mirrors practitioner course we were looking at the colour pale gold, and I decided to take bottle G12 home to explore more overnight. Just before sleep I felt to meditate with the bottle, so I shut my eyes and gently held it to my heart whilst laying on my back. I must have fallen asleep pretty quickly because the next thing I knew I woke up around 2am with my bottle broken, my fingers inside the bottle and the gold 'elixir' all over my chest. I had had the bottle for only seven hours at that point! The number seven represents self and spiritual growth.

At the end of the course I felt pulled to the bottle again, so I bought another. I had it for a few days and then it too broke, so I bathed in the oils. I decided to buy a third bottle and take a really good look at this powerful colour. This one stayed intact and I recognised where I wasn't in my power, that I was a bit of a people-pleaser, saying yes when I wanted to say no. Now I'm confident and comfortable to speak my truth and say no when I need to. This bottle brought about one of my biggest shifts.

Bottle G13: Grace (Pale Gold/Pale Pink)

This delicate colour combination reminds you that only love exists and that everything you have experienced was chosen by you as an expression of Divine love. Step into grace and forgive yourself. You were never guilty, you were an expression of the Divine experiencing itself, and all of it was part of the plan. These colours indicate a rebirth, this time without the trauma of death. As you gently rebirth into your true self you remember that the Divine is love and therefore you are love. The true power that creates everything is love, love, love. This is the female face of divinity and it is beautiful – and so are you. While using this bottle it will serve you to take time every day to remember something fabulous about yourself, and if you write it down you will make it that much more real. Take time to honour your creative, intuitive vision.

Grace is like a wave that washes over you – gentle, subtle, soothing and soft. It carries you when you feel unable to go on. It nourishes you when you are tired and depleted. It eases your aches, bathes your wounds and loves you when you are unable to love yourself. Grace nudges you gently towards the light when you fall into despair and extends a loving hand when you are stuck. It opens doorways when you are ready to see that they are there. Grace is nothing more nor less than pure, sublime, Divine love. It is the most nurturing, holding energy you could ever envisage, and its love is infinite, timeless, limitless.

This bottle of liquid gold and pink love may call to you when you are feeling the opposite of grace – when you are fraught, scattered, disconnected or unable to receive love. It asks you to pause a moment and look up, reach out to the love of the universe and open to its blessings. It pulls together all the fragmented pieces of your soul and reconnects you with a cosmic wellspring of goodness that is just waiting for you to receive it. In its all-encompassing love, you can let go and know that everything is being taken care of.

Like bottle 6 (Venus), bottle G13 invites you to fall in love with yourself and to surrender up your stories of lack of love. It paves the way for you to see yourself in a new light and helps you recognise that struggle has simply become a habit and that there are different choices you can make now. In grace, effort and exertion are removed as you nestle into the loving arms of the Divine Mother. This is perhaps the ultimate surrender as you let go of the beliefs and stories that have kept you in limitation and darkness, as you remember again your innate innocence. There is a beautiful simplicity in grace. As you open fully to the love of the universe, you let go of all that is unnecessary and find gratitude for everything you already have. Grace is filled with light and blessings and restores you to a harmonious state of being so that ease and joy can be your everyday companions.

If bottle 13 (Transformation) was about death and rebirth, bottle G13 is purely a rebirth. Ascension, the transition into higher consciousness, is a form of rebirth without the need for physical death. With this bottle you are rebirthed into a new light, a new way of being, a new state – and that state is grace. In grace, you return to your original purity, your original innocence and bliss. Grace invites you to cherish, honour and love yourself, to cradle your newborn self in your arms, to awaken to the love of the Divine that is all around you. This is the heaven you brought with you when you incarnated so that you might offer that energy and all its love and blessings to the earth.

Grace gives you the opportunity to view life in a very different way. It reminds you that each moment is new and precious and that you do not need to remain beholden to the past or any beliefs that have kept you limited and small. You are free to explore different paths, open to new ideas and dance lightly through life with the love of the universe by your side. Bottle G13 is the culmination of the previous Golden Gaia bottles and the previous steps on the golden Ascension pathway: as you step into faith, begin to live impeccably, expand your sense of yourself and the world in generosity and claim your I AMness, the inevitable outcome is grace. This bottle's message is: let the love in.

Here you surrender to the heart. You let go of fixed notions and rigid thought patterns and flow easily into a beautiful state of peace. You remember that love is your true nature – the true nature of all life. Just like the air you breathe, grace is inherent in the very fabric of life and the universe itself. It is freely given at all times and you cannot earn it by trying harder or working for it or being 'good'. Grace is so deeply infused into life that you may not always realise it is there. You may have become immune to it or taken it for granted, yet it goes on giving of itself nonetheless. Your only task is to awaken to its presence in your life, your body and your being and open ever more fully to receive it. Bottle G13 is a golden bell that rings to remind you to turn your face towards the sun and restore yourself to the sacred state of grace.

Bottle G13 Story: Moira Bush, Canada, www.moirabush.com

Bottle 13, Transformation, can indicate someone who has attempted suicide or certainly had the thought. I once gave a numerology reading to a client whose daughter had two 13's in her birthdate. She said her daughter had tried twice to leave the planet. Knowing this about the number 13, I am always intrigued when those with 13 in their date of birth feel drawn to bottle G13 rather than bottle 13. What I have observed is that their shoulders drop as they gaze at this bottle, as if they put down ideas of leaving the planet in the presence of Grace.

My personal experience with Grace is that it brought into my bath the powerful energy of Mary Magdalene. At the time, I was not feeling empowered as a woman and a sense of futility was prevalent in my thoughts. After this bath I literally got off my self-pity train and changed everything, including where I lived and how I worked. I lost a lot of weight as I went dancing and joined a hiking club. Men started to notice me, and after five years of being single that was a welcome change.

Bottle G14: Ascension Light (Pale Gold/Clear)

This bottle intensifies the light you carry within and reminds you that you too can shine this brightly. With its clear light and radiance, this bottle attracts people who have a crystalline energy – those who are here to show humanity how to raise their vibration, how to live an enlightened life. Ascension happens when you remember that your body is made of light, that you are Divine light in physical form and that the density you perceive in your reality is an illusion. This bottle shines its light on everything that is illusionary, dispelling falsehood and leaving only the crystalline clarity of truth.

Bottle G14 is a place where you come to rest, where the quiet stillness enfolds you and brings you back 'home'. This is the light you connect with when you tap into your own divinity, when you are able to truly feel and know yourself as a light being, with a lightbody, beyond the boundaries of a limited self. The 'noise' of everyday life recedes as you welcome the soft clear light of your own deeper, higher, more expansive self – the true essence of your being.

This bottle invites you into openness, transparency and honesty with yourself. It awakens within you a dawning recognition of yourself *as* the light. As you remember that truth, you become aware of the ways you may have prevented yourself from fully accessing your light and the reasons why you may not have entirely embodied it in this lifetime as yet. With this awareness you are free to make new choices, take new paths and open to new behaviours and beliefs that support you in aligning more and more with joy. When you receive the gifts of this bottle, it paves the way for a lighter, happier, clearer life, with a greater sense of purpose and direction. It supports you in shucking off old, heavy, dense vibrations that keep you in limitation and helps you define a clearer vision for yourself and your life.

As with bottle C14 (Vision), however, which is also gold and clear, this bottle may indicate addictive behaviours, reluctance to earth yourself and resistance to being fully present in your life. It can represent escapist tendencies and the desire to float off into the ether, removing yourself from what you perceive as the harshness of life on earth. The star children who are often drawn to this bottle are generally high frequency, sensitive souls who long for 'home'. This bottle reminds you that home is within and helps you bring your starry qualities into balance so that you can be here on earth without wanting to disappear.

There is a purity and clarity reflected here which means that when you choose bottle G14, you are ready to step up to the next level of spiritual advancement. This bottle has a wonderful 'connecting' energy that makes it perfect for meditation, embracing the light of the Divine and opening to higher wisdom. It helps you experience the presence of the Divine more easily and activates frequencies within your DNA that support you in your quest to evolve as a spiritual being. It awakens your inner starlight, opening you to the glittering brilliance of your star lifetimes and the vast body of knowledge, wisdom and information you gained there. This bottle invites you to hold it, meditate with it or immerse your body in a bath of its soft pale gold and clear liquid light – consciously and with focus. As you do so, you open the door to the love, insights and support available to you from the light you hold within and the awe-inspiring wisdom of the universe.

This bottle's energy has the quality of a gift from the Divine, helping you tap into streams of information that may be beyond your mind's limited awareness and bringing them into consciousness so that you can share the energy through your words and creative projects. When the Golden Gaias first appeared in 2009, it was as we connected with this bottle that the book *The Language of Light: Golden Keys to Ascension* began to form. We know of several others who have selected this bottle and shortly afterwards found themselves writing books. It seems to make more accessible the light you hold inside, enabling you to bring that light into a form that can be shared with others. Your words become carriers of sacred Divine frequencies that may be experienced as transmissions or 'downloads' by those who read or hear them. Bottle G14 connects you with the 'language of light', a language that may or may not contain words but that speaks directly to your heart and your spirit; an ancient language of Divine creation, a language of love and joy.

The clear bottom fraction of this bottle indicates the potential to radiate your light up and out into the world and make it practical and real. What this bottle asks you to realise is that as you anchor your light on the earth, you not only light up your own life and contribute to the world, you also help to hold a clear vision of a Golden Age upon the earth for all. Bottle G14 is similar in colour to bottle C14: both are gold over clear. Yet where bottle C14 promises the vision of a golden era on the earth, bottle G14, with its gleaming pale golden top fraction, indicates that you are starting to embody the golden vision. Now you begin to see that it is by igniting the golden frequencies within yourself that the golden era on the earth is brought into being.

The process of Ascension is not just about the earth shifting into fifth dimensional reality and humanity following along, or vice versa. It is about a contract between Gaia and humanity: to do this together. This is where you recognise in your cells that you are light and the earth is light and there is no separation between you. Bottle G14's message is that balance occurs on all levels when you awaken to your inner light and willingly share it with others – on the earth and for the earth.

If you are drawn to the bottles in the system that are clear or have a clear fraction, this indicates nomadic tendencies and lifetimes of journeying rather than settling in any one place. When you choose bottle G14 there is a sense of travelling, either physically on the earth from one place to another to spread the light and frequencies of higher consciousness, or energetically – perhaps in dream states or meditation. With this energy illuminating your cells, you become a nomad of the light, joyfully sharing the glory of the Divine wherever you are and wherever you go.

Bottle G14 Story: Korani

When Melissie first realised she would be making a set of seven Golden Gaia bottles, she experimented with many different colour combinations to go with the pale gold, and together we looked at them to see which would make up the final set. Some were obvious from the start, such as the pale turquoise and gold combination that would become bottle G9, Faith. Others were beautiful, but we didn't feel they were going to be part of the set. We had more or less decided on six, but the seventh was proving elusive. Suddenly I got an inspiration and said to Melissie: "What about a gold and clear bottle?" She turned to me, pulled a face and said: "Korani, it will look like a raw egg!" We laughed, but I was not to be put off and encouraged her to make one.

I will never forget the look on her face when she held out the finished product to me for the first time, nor will I forget the bolt of light that shot into my heart when I first saw this bottle. It felt as if stars were exploding in my body and as if all the light of the galaxies was raining down upon me. It really was love at first sight. My feeling was that this bottle had to come and shine with the light of all the starry folk who inhabit the earth so that we could feel our vibration, remember our luminous light, hear our language being spoken. This bottle's alternative name could be 'The Language of Light', as it rings with the crystalline clarity of the stars.

Bottle G14 Story: Moira Bush, Canada, www.moirabush.com

A mother whose son was addicted to drugs and on the verge of self-destruction could not take her eyes off bottle G14 during her session. She had to have it, and took it home to bathe in. Some months later, I bumped into her and asked what had happened. She said her son had started to take stronger drugs and she feared the worst. I recommended she take into consideration the clear 'mirror' fraction of this bottle and to look at any addictive behaviours her son might see her engaging in, which would give him the excuse to not have to deal with his own addiction issue: if mom does it, why should he stop?

She was understandably a bit miffed at me for pointing out that she perhaps needed to look into the mirror of her own addictions, and I thought I would probably never see her again. The entire time I was speaking to her an image of bottle G14 was burning in my third eye, as if I was seeing her and her son through the glass and colours of this bottle. It felt like an energetic intervention for this family, and I have since learned that her son enrolled in a rehabilitation program.

Bottle G15: Satori (Solid Gold/Magenta)

This bottle makes your connection with your Divine self a solid reality. It no longer floats above you as a thought or a wish. This bottle settles the truth into your cells that you are Divine and that you can live heaven on earth in this moment. This is when you remember that you never left home in the first place. Heaven is where you are, and everything you see is Divine. It has always been so. This is the state of satori.

At the heart of the golden earth there is a pulse of perfect stillness inviting you into peace, into joy, into love, into oneness. The external world and your mind may fly around in busyness and doing, but the earth's true nature – and your own – is one of harmony and serenity, and the Divine holds you in complete love and total acceptance. Bottle G15 is a reflection of this heavenly love and earthly peace. It shows you that satori exists in the moments when you drop the veil of illusion and tap into the stunning light of the sacred Divine. In satori you are no longer beholden to thoughts or ideas about how life 'should' be. Instead you can embrace the wonder of the Divine that inhabits everything and everyone and be at peace with it all.

Satori is about coming home to who you are when you let go of limitations, ideals and preconceptions. It is the acknowledgement that there is nowhere to go and nothing to do. It is a moment of awakening and realisation, of deep soul-felt understanding and clarity. It may come as a perception shift or a sudden jolt. It may come in the midst of the most ordinary moment as you go about your day or it may arise from the depths of profound meditation. It may leave a lasting imprint on you or it may be a fleeting instant, but however it comes, it might just feel like the greatest gift you could possibly allow yourself to receive.

Satori is the bliss that comes from being completely connected to the Divine deep in your heart and your soul, and it is this connection that enables you to shine your golden light out in the world. It is as far removed from the limitations of ego as it is possible to be. It is the knowing that your magenta Divine self is perfectly mirrored by your golden earth connection. It is the deepest understanding that heaven and earth are one, Divine and human are one, and separation is merely an illusion.

In the state of satori you no longer focus solely on yourself and your own journey. You see life from a much bigger, wider, higher perspective as the universe's doors are flung open and you are shown the whole picture. You realise the interconnection of all life, you recognise the light network that links you to everything and everyone, and you are gifted the utterly transformational experience of knowing in the core of your bones that life is a blessing from the Divine and that you are an integral part of the oneness. In satori, this is no longer a concept or an idea but a reality you can fully grasp with your heart and in your body.

Bottle G15 is heaven in a bottle, champagne and roses, harmony and bounty, summer days and the sweet bliss of dreams. It is all that is wondrous, magical and magnificent in your world. Satori is the fulfilment of your truest, heart-felt desires. It is also so much more than this. It is a reminder that everything you have been seeking is already seeking you. Satori is the moment when you finally get the cosmic joke, when the Divine bursts through into your reality, opening you to what you could not see or understand with your human mind. It is the return of Divine consciousness to your soul. It is the embracing of everything you are and everything you have ever been and ever will be. It asks for nothing, needs nothing. It is complete and it is whole. It is perfection. It is mastery. When you choose this bottle you are awakening to the possibility of an enlightened life, and you are saying 'yes' to the universe with arms and heart open wide.

Satori and all of the Golden Gaia bottles are about truly anchoring a golden era on the earth as a real, solid creation. By connecting with the light and power of these bottles of liquid gold you are actively taking part in the visioning and creation of a time of peace and plenty for all on this earth. You are planting seeds that will bear fruit in your lifetime and beyond, and you are activating the potential that all have within to experience satori, to know bliss, to be at peace, to be at one.

Bottle G15 Story: Korani

In the book The Language of Light: Golden Keys to Ascension *I recount the experiences I had the first time I bathed in bottle G15. This bottle (and all the other Golden Gaia bottles) had only just been created, and as I was in South Africa with Melissie at the time, I realised that I was the first person ever to bathe in this golden oil. It felt like an honour – and also an initiation. I remember it vividly as one of the most profound experiences of my life. Words cannot fully express how powerful it was. I literally felt (and heard) my cells and my vibration being lifted to a higher octave, to a whole new dimension.*

Life most definitely did not look or feel the same from that point forward! I felt as if something truly life-changing had begun and indeed that proved to be the case as I went on to write what would become my first book and began to deliver courses and workshops that would bring about radical shifts in those who took part. This bottle opened a door within me that enabled me to begin to explore my own mastery. I think it was the first time I really KNEW that there was a Golden Age on the earth, that it was real and possible and happening even now, and that we – Colour Mirrors, the Golden Gaias and all of us – were creating it together.

Bottle G15 Story: Moira Bush, Canada, www.moirabush.com

Bottle G15 is often chosen by people who have an ability to work with money or earn a high income doing what they love by actively engaging with their Divine purpose through enterprises. It has been nicknamed 'The Millionaire's Bottle' by some of the entrepreneurs I have worked with. The solid gold has a grounding quality and indicates doing amazing things on the earth with your Divine talents and gifts.

The founder of a million-dollar company had to have bottle G15, the only one he was drawn to. He bought it and had it sit on his shelf in full view of the camera during webinars he offered clients. What is also interesting is that his logo colours are the same as bottle 12 (Heaven on Earth): violet and red.

An actress who was experiencing cash flow issues picked bottle G15 during 'The Magenta Show' and took it home. She reported back that the next morning after the broadcast, money mysteriously appeared in her account. She went on to meet a famous theatre director who is now working with her, as she is internationally touring and performing in a play she felt driven to write.

Whenever anyone picks bottle G15 I ask them to look at any money issues in their life. Satori indicates that if you follow one thing that makes your heart sing, money can stop being an issue, as the possibilities are literally a million.

Bottle G15 Story: Susan McKenzie, Canada, www.susanmckenzie.biz

I feel like Satori took over my life in the most positive way after I bathed in this bottle, and it has continued to do so. With the pouring of this beauty into my bath, I opened a secret passage that I always knew was there, but before this I hadn't been able to remember where to find it. With these two fabulous colours – magenta and gold – the message is clear, and every time I forget, I receive gentle reminders to surrender: surrender to opportunity, surrender to love, surrender to the Divine and the knowledge that all is perfect.

Since this bath I feel a connection with my authentic self. It never felt OK to 'just be who I am', as old memories of things that kept me small all these years would play in my mind and stifle my progress. They now feel so easy to release, allowing me to move forward and feel fabulous about me. My authentic self knows the core of my being and gently guides me along my soul's journey to a path of service, love and light. The beautiful solid gold in this bottle pumps through my veins.

The most incredible thing though is a wingback chair that my mother gave me over a year after I ventured into my Satori bath. She had had it re-covered some 10 years before, and it is now magenta and gold. I have always loved this chair, and when she gave it to me I decided to place it in my office where I do my client work. It felt like a trophy – and how interesting that 10 years before, this chair was being re-covered for me to arrive at this state of Satori.

The Platinum Gaia Set

Bottles G16-G22

A year after the Golden Gaias, the Platinums arrived. They were already hovering by the time *The Language of Light: Golden Keys to Ascension* was written, and we had explored a little of what the complementary colours to the Golden Gaias might look like, but nothing further happened until Moira visited Melissie in South Africa in 2010. Suddenly the new set birthed itself after a sequence of events during that visit, and seven bottles came into being to form the Platinum Gaia set.

The Platinum Gaias mirror their Golden Gaia counterparts, each one coloured in the complementary hues. Where the Golden Gaia bottles all have a pale gold fraction, their Platinum Gaia partners have a platinum fraction in the same position. Each of the other colours in the Golden Gaia set is mirrored by the complementary colours in the Platinums. In this way the Platinum Gaia bottles provide the perfect foil to the Golden Gaias, balancing, supporting and complementing them.

These new bottles came with a quiet potency that none of us expected. In contrast to the Golds that spoke so freely and clearly to us, these new lights shone subtly, quietly, almost silently. All we knew was that they touched us on a profound level and that their arrival heralded a quantum leap in the evolutionary journey. From the beginning they felt very cosmic, very 'other' – certainly not of the earth – and yet they were called the Platinum 'Gaia' bottles, so clearly they were in some way related to the human journey here on earth!

What we noticed was that many of the 'starry' souls who were drawn to Colour Mirrors expressed their sense that the Platinums connected them with 'home'. These bottles gave them an awareness of themselves on another, higher and more evolved level of existence and feelings of belonging and connection that they might always have struggled to experience here on earth.

This sense of homecoming offered by the Platinum Gaias opens gateways on many levels, bringing greater awareness of the truth of yourself as a multi-layered, multi-leveled being who exists in many dimensions at the same time: an earth self having one experience; a higher self guiding and supporting; a star self receiving and transmitting information about life out in the cosmos – and an infinite number of variations of who you think 'you' are, existing beyond time and space as you know it.

The Platinum Gaias come with a challenge, asking you to embody their pure, high, panoramic frequencies and to live from that level of light, right here on earth. They also carry an 'enabling' energy, releasing procrastination, opening you to new opportunities and supporting you in getting projects off the ground. They facilitate your creative and business ventures, helping you go beyond your usual range of focus to a much higher, broader spectrum of ideas and capabilities than you may have thought possible.

These bottles might call for your attention when you are in need of the vibration they offer – so Serenity may call when you are feeling fraught, or Limitless when you are feeling small. Yet more often these bottles show up when you are ready to fully embrace the qualities and frequencies they offer, providing a gentle yet potent reflection of where you already are. They mirror to you what is already going on inside, showing you how far you have come, confirming what you already know and encouraging you to go even deeper, even higher.

The Platinum Gaias represent the essential truth of who you are – vast, free, infinite, eternal – and bring an incredible sense of expansion. They guide you into a much greater sense of yourself than your human ego would allow, opening you to the still, silent space inside where all is possible and nothing is bound. They take you beyond words and thoughts to a place where your mind can become still, where you may find the pure emptiness of space, where peace abounds. They lead you to a knowing that is lighter and somehow clearer for not needing to be defined. The Platinum Gaias are powerfully healing if you have landed up on this planet wondering what on earth you are doing here, but most of all they remind you who you *really* are when you stop believing you are limited.

If you enjoy the Platinum journey and the words they share with you here and would like to experience more, Korani has written a short e-book, *A Book of Platinum Light*, which offers seven 'Platinum Portals' to higher consciousness, facilitated and guided by the seven Platinum Gaias. It is a download of energy in itself, a small collection of words that somehow acts as a transmitter of the vast platinum frequencies.

It is a paradox that although the Platinums very clearly take us 'beyond words', their energies are also carried on them and through them. Perhaps the Platinums are the ultimate reminder that nothing in the universe is simply one thing or another. Life is made up of many strands and many threads all woven together, all interconnected – and you too are not 'just' human and small, or 'only' Divine and unlimited. You are both, you are all of it, you are everything. You are inherently part of all that exists.

Bottle G16: Serenity (Pale Coral/Platinum)

These colours are a perfect balance of Divine feminine and enlightened masculine. When these two sides of yourself are in balance and your platinum angelic self is aligned with your coral human self, serenity is the natural outcome. With these colours you can surrender into the knowledge that you are whole and that every aspect of yourself is Divine and therefore perfect. This bottle brings unconditional self-acceptance and sublime serenity as you let go of struggle, relax into the flow of the universe and allow everything to unfold with ease and grace.

Serenity is perfect balance, soft joy, radiant peace. Its coral is the blush of a rose, sweetly scented and filled with fragrant light; its platinum is the cool calm of a shaded rock pool. It is expansive and vibrant, yet quiet and still. It reaches up and out to the delights of heaven while sinking gently and peacefully into the waters beneath the earth. It is sun and moon, filled with both quietude and passion, a dance of the male and female in every being. Serenity is an inner quality – when filled with it, you emanate a subtle, gentle glow and you are grounded in peace and quiet joy, making your presence a gift to others. In serenity you are without need or desire, quietly fulfilled with the moment exactly as it is.

Bottle G16 is a gift when you are anything but serene. It supports you when you are turbulent and troubled, when you are jumping from one extreme to another or when you simply feel out of balance. It helps you gather all the aspects of your soul, gently drawing the threads of your being together so that what was jarring or scattered becomes harmonious and whole. It centres and stabilises you, yet it does this so lightly that you may hardly realise it is happening. There is no lightning bolt here, just a beautiful and perhaps unexpected hush after a time of crazy busyness or lack of peace in your life.

In the state of serenity you feel completely at home in yourself. You feel as if you are entirely in the right place at the right moment and can shift into cruise control, letting the universe take over as you sit back and enjoy the ride. Struggle disappears, inner turmoil lets go its hold and suddenly you wonder what on earth you were doing, losing your sense of yourself and your innate power to some illusory demon. With a serene mind comes wholeness and balance and a panoramic view of the world where you can see and behold all that is unfolding from a place of complete calm, centredness and connection.

Coral brings unconditional self-acceptance and platinum allows the highest – Divine – level of communication to be transmitted through you. With these colours you begin to understand your link with the stars and the cosmos and recognise the vastness of your purpose. You came to help shift the planet into a new age and lift the vibration from fear to love. You are a star child who came to help birth a new dawn on the planet, and to do that you require balance in your male and female aspects, your human and Divine selves. You are called to bring well-earthed balance to your starriness. If you are ungrounded you cannot function properly on earth, and the Platinum Gaias support you in bringing your starry self safely onto the earth plane so that you can fulfil your true purpose of assisting the planet and all of humanity in the shift to a more conscious, compassionate and peaceful state of existence.

Although there is something wonderfully child-like about the simplicity of these colours, there is also deep wisdom available to you when you let yourself fall into serenity. There is a quiet mysticism within this bottle, a timeless magic that takes you into a state that is much more about who you are than what you do. It is a space where you can see and know with great clarity what your next step is, where you need to go and what you are being called to do or say. Linear time and other 3D limitations cease to rule you as you glide gently on the waves of universal love and find in them your own unique energy stream. From a state of serenity, your communications flow lightly and easily; in fact, your presence is often such that no words are required.

Serenity means being held in the palm of the Divine, utterly loved, utterly accepted. With the unconditional love of the universe flowing ceaselessly into your life, you are able to drop the stories and dramas and find the same love and acceptance for yourself and for everyone. It is a truly blessed state and the more you choose to live in it, the more it flourishes and grows. When the state of serenity envelops you it has a natural ripple effect, expanding out into your life and to others with whom you come into contact.

Although it may be born from a deep and heartfelt thankfulness, serenity transcends even gratitude, going beyond it into a space of such love, harmony and unshakeable peace that the heavens rejoice. This is your natural state – even if you seemed to forget it for a time. Once you taste pure serenity, even just for a moment, you know it in the very cells of your being as truth, and this beautiful bottle of colour becomes your reminder and your guide so that you might return to it again and again and truly embrace it, live it and share it.

Bottle G16 Story: Moira Bush, Canada, www.moirabush.com

From years of observation I know that when clients choose bottle 16 (The Tower), it indicates that there is a foundational shift coming or that they are already in the midst of a big shake-up, being challenged to let go of old, worn out belief systems. When they resist, the change happens anyway and often leaves them reeling and having to re-assess their priorities and choices under stressful conditions. When clients choose bottle G16, however, I notice that they have no resistance to the changes they feel coming their way, as if they are more graceful and accepting of the inevitable process unfolding. I have suggested to those going through a bottle 16 'Tower' experience to consider bathing in bottle G16 instead.

Proving just how stupendous the Colour Mirrors system is, as I was reading the words for bottle G16 in this book for Korani and Melissie, that exact same day Notre Dame started to burn, and all efforts were made to save its twin towers. The timing was just too much of a synchronicity to ignore and I felt guided to put a post about bottles 16 and G16 on Facebook:

"Bottle16, The Tower, spoke of our human reaction to the horror of the 9/11 Twin Towers in 2001. We reacted in a very human way, blaming and seeking retribution. Bottle G16, Serenity, depicts the spiritual reaction to the fire of Notre Dame on 15 April 2019. Parisians were singing hymns and cheering on the firemen.

With 9/11 the Tower experience got our attention to change worn out systems, with the loss of many lives and the total destruction of the two towers. The power of financial systems began to change, and Bitcoin and many other new cryptocurrencies began to emerge.

Under the direction of Pope Francis, the Vatican's views on how the Catholic Church responds to child abuse are changing. As conscious spiritual humans, can we now change religious systems without the need for towers to come down? Perhaps the fact that the twin towers of Notre Dame did not fall and no one died means that this time humanity's tower of change can happen serenely."

When I entered this bath I immediately felt surrender. I sunk into the warm, lovely scented water and relaxed into myself. As I lay in the water with my eyes closed, I began to see pages with black lettering – possibly Hebrew – float towards me and then quickly enter my third eye. Shortly thereafter I got a headache, which slowly dissipated. A candle on the counter flickered like a strobe light the entire time I was in the bath. In my meditation, rolling molten lava flowed. I felt calm. The smell of the bath became the most beautiful smell I had ever experienced. After nearly an hour I left my bath feeling at peace, calm and relaxed – complete serenity.

Bottle G17: Elohim (Platinum/Pale Gold)

This bottle connects you with the angelic beings of light we refer to as the Elohim. As their light becomes available to you and through you, begin to communicate with Divine authority and love so that all are touched by what you say, what you do and most of all, who you are. This bottle helps you know beyond any doubt that everything is perfect – including you. It is time to recognise the gold within you as an absolute fact. You are precious, you are wise and you are powerful. Open to your creative abilities and the vast blessings of the Elohim, and prepare for a special time of ease and lightness of being.

With its complementary colours of pale gold and platinum, bottle G17 ushers you into balance. It is filled with grace and it bestows that grace upon you as you contemplate it, as you offer it to your body, as you take in its energy blessings. It reminds you that there is an intricate and expansive web of light surrounding you at all times of which you are mostly unaware, yet which always subtly interacts with you, protecting, guiding and supporting you. The Elohim, who are a part of that light web, are angelic beings of such grace, such light, such wisdom and expansiveness that words can hardly do them justice. They truly need to be experienced at a level beyond the mind – and this bottle can help you do that.

Bottle G17 holds out an invitation to a state of no-mind, no-time, no-thing, where you can immerse yourself in the depths yet know yourself to be the lightest of lights. It is a space of limitless, fathomless peace, lit up by the solemn joy of these majestic beings. The power of the Elohim is that they know themselves to be completely at one with the Divine, and when you truly connect with them, this same awareness is available to you. Just as tuning forks come into resonance with each other when struck, the Elohim's presence in your life opens the possibility within you to know what they know, see what they see, be as they are: balanced and open, expansive and vibrant, free and aligned, radiant with joy, bathed in peace, immensely powerful. When you connect with the Elohim your consciousness is instantly elevated, and their support can be felt in all your dealings. They are always available, but as they will never intrude on your free will or step into a situation uninvited, it is up to you to make a conscious connection with them and ask for their influence in your life. The moment you tune in with them, their support – steeped in oneness and unconditional love – is freely given.

The Elohim offer you their love, truly and utterly, yet they do not involve themselves with your daily dramas or your ego's childish stories. They hold instead a beautiful energy of 'detached compassion'. They are on a plane of existence where there is no need for crisis or commotion and they hold that peace and perfection out as a blueprint for you to connect with and aspire to, loving you unconditionally all the while. Their silvery-blue platinum coolness may seem aloof at first glance, yet they are anything but cold. Indeed their love is so vast that you may not be used to the clear and unfiltered strength of its light, and it may go unnoticed in your life until you are ready to perceive it. Once you do, however, you will never forget it. To be touched by the Elohim is to know that you will never view the world in quite the same way again. You can no more believe yourself to be lost, alone or abandoned, for the presence of the Divine becomes tangible. The Elohim hold out a steady hand and will not let you go.

As with all the Platinum Gaia bottles, there is an infinite stillness at the heart of the Elohim bottle that penetrates your body, mind and being. Its pale gold fraction, however, ensures you do not get lost in the vastness and silence of the cosmos. When the moment is right, the golden heart of the Elohim awakens you, calling you to powerful action. The colours and frequencies of this bottle blend and weave together in much the same way as they do in its counterpart Golden Gaia bottle, G10 (Impeccability). You are ushered into peace and stillness, only to find that the tranquillity is alive with inspiration and guidance. Once again there is balance to be found in the dynamic between movement and stillness, masculine and feminine, human and Divine.

The platinum in the top fraction of this bottle brings Divine information into your consciousness. Combined with the potency of gold, it amplifies both your inner strength and the power of your words, inviting instant manifestation of whatever you focus on. Now you can speak the language of light, and your voice can be consciously used to express loving, authentic power and to create for the greater good. In this way bottle G17 again reflects bottle G10, but where bottle G10 assists you at a practical level to know when you are on track and in alignment with what you say and do, bottle G17 takes your view higher and broader so that you can see the cosmic workings behind your human tasks, endeavours and communications.

Now you are given a glimpse into the 'bigger picture', the infinite geometric patterning that underpins and overlights your life and your consciousness. Here is a much vaster awareness than your limited human perception can grasp, yet as you connect with the Elohim you begin to know on a cellular level that this cosmic light flows through everything in the universe, including you. Bathing in the Elohim's infinite love and awareness allows you to touch into the highest and most refined templates of creation, and even if you do not understand them with your mind, your higher self recognises the patterns, notes and frequencies and responds to them.

Now you can write your light, express, sing or draw your light. This bottle guides all who are ready to awaken to a much higher awareness of life and the universe. It helps you find creative ways to live from a place of expanded consciousness so that your everyday life becomes guided and inspired by this more open and light-filled view. You may find yourself creating something you had never dreamed of before. You might experience new options and opportunities arising. You may find that even if life appears to be exactly the same on the outside, on the inside your experience is completely different.

When you take in the light of the Elohim, you find yourself less bothered, less frustrated, less mired by ego. You step more lightly through life, open more fully, engage more thoroughly. You open to equanimity, a state where you neither crave what you do not have nor avoid what is presenting itself to you in the moment. You can now take the energy of bottle 17, The Wish (coral/royal blue), and expand it out in bottle G17 to something so much more than a 'wish'. Your truest heartfelt desires can become tangible, present and real. When coral becomes gold, it goes beyond self-acceptance into total recognition of your inner Divine power. When the royal blue of the third eye becomes platinum, a higher, more expansive vision is activated.

With the Elohim by your side, your creative energy swirls into being and carries you in its flow so that you find yourself connecting and creating seemingly without effort. To live with the light of the Elohim in your consciousness is to feel a wondrous ease and lightness of being. You take up your role on the cosmic stage and know that through your creative endeavours, your actions and your words you are contributing to the intricate unfolding of the universe that occurs in every moment. More than anything you do, however, the Elohim show you that it is your very existence, the very fact of your beingness that is essential to the cosmic web of life and to the loving, beating heart of the Divine.

Bottle G17 Story: Renira Barclay, UK, www.abovemiddlec.com

It felt so right to choose my most favourite bottle to bathe in on the eve of my 60th birthday. I had my bath with a glass of champagne, taking time out because the house was full of family helping for my party. The bath was gentle and kind and light, the pale gold exactly the same colour as the champagne. The platinum was very zero and non-judgemental. While I was putting on my party dress the next evening I noticed an eczema-like rash over my tummy and inner arms. Luckily it didn't show under my dress, which had sleeves!

I felt that this rash represented where I had been attached to my birth mother, as if I were a little monkey clinging on under her as she climbed the trees. I felt the rash was showing me that I was in the healing phase of accepting that I had been separated from her (which I was, at six weeks, when I was given to my adoptive parents). There was a real acceptance of that separation with bottle G17, of how that was always the plan. Interestingly, since that bath my birth mother has died, and I now feel far less separation from her. Separation is an illusion, as we know. I had never had eczema before and have never had a rash like that again. And just for the record, bottle G17 is still my favourite.

Bottle G18: Limitless (Pale Turquoise/Platinum)

This bottle opens you to a state of Divine flow and connection where all limits can be removed. It invites you to receive the riches and joys of the universe and share them generously. Now is the time to find out who you truly are, what you are capable of and what you most desire. This bottle activates the abundance of the universe and opens the door to a state of limitless faith. You can now manifest your reality with ease, grace and elegance. There is no room for negativity and fear. This is where you move beyond separation, division and restriction into the limitless freedom that is your true nature.

In bottle G18 pale turquoise rests on platinum, and here you are offered a reconnection to faith and flow and a sense of openness that is so great it becomes limitless. This bottle connects you with the sacred expansiveness of sea and sky, inviting you to relinquish any beliefs that keep you small and helpless. It asks you to remember your union with the infinite ocean and the limitlessness of the heavens, the truth of the universe that is beyond thought, mind or ego.

There is a strong connection with the water element in this bottle, its watery colours a paler, more enlightened version of the colours we see in bottle 34, The Whale. Whales and dolphins have a profound understanding of the limitlessness of life. They reflect an awareness of yourself as both a unique and individual drop in the ocean and the totality of the ocean itself. You cannot be separated from the ocean of consciousness in which you reside.

The water element also relates to your emotions. It is through your emotional body that you access life, connect with others and come together in the shared experience of what it is to be human. Paradoxically, it is often emotions that entangle you and cause you to lose sight of your infinite nature. Bottle G18 assists you in accessing your true feelings and expressing them, perhaps in spoken words, perhaps through the voice of your soul. When you yearn for something more, when your heart longs for freedom, when you tire of being bogged down, lethargic or miserable, this is your soul speaking to you in the language of the limitless cosmos. This bottle gently stirs you into action, asking you not to be defeated but instead to reach for that higher longing, to open to greater awareness and possibility. Where bottle 18 (Spiritual/Material Conflict) showed you where and how you limit yourself, bottle G18 blows the lid off your self-limiting beliefs and behaviours. It delivers you into the sweetness of surrender, removing you from old, well-worn grooves. It gently reveals new ways to be and allow.

Like the previous bottle, G17 (Elohim), one of the gifts of this bottle is its interplay between stillness and movement – between true, deep, utter peace and the dynamic joy of growth. As you ebb into the shallows, holding yourself still, contracting into the core of your being to gather your love and your light, you pause, as at the end of an out-breath. Life rushes in and you inhale, opening and expanding into the Allness, taking your core inner light and ushering it into the world, riding the waves back out into the depths of the ocean. Being limitless, you can do both. Being limitless, you do not need to be one or the other, for you are all of it. Being limitless, you no longer need to create definitions or rules or box yourself in. You are indefinable, and with this bottle you move beyond your previous knowledge of your 'self' into something far less tangible yet far more real, where all and nothing are the very same thing.

When do you feel the call of this bottle? When finally you are ready to move beyond the limitations you have placed upon yourself, go beyond what you thought you knew about life and embrace the wonder of stepping off the edge into the infinite wild blue yonder. Bottle G18 might come to your attention when you have been blocking your own creativity and flow, sabotaging your efforts to live a life of ease and abundance, keeping yourself small. Perhaps you have been holding back or limiting yourself out of fear or resistance. When hurts and doubts crowd in, when your connection with the Divine seems to have disappeared, when petty, mean concerns take precedence over a generous, open heart, when your days become filled with pointless doing, when finally you tire of the iron constraints and bonds of your ego – and often, only after a mammoth fight with yourself – then and only then do you let go.

When you have had absolutely enough of living half a life, Limitless reaches out and shows you the way back into the ocean of light that neither contains nor constrains you but is within you and all around you – that is you. It shows you, as a natural part of life and evolution, that you can continually transcend what you knew and experienced before as you open to ever-new, ever-expanding possibilities.

Bottle G18 is a kind of baptism. In the water you are reborn into a new self that knows itself as limitless, intricately woven into the Divine fabric of the Allness, the Absolute, the One. This is where you can completely let go, surrendering into the infinite ocean of consciousness, the endless field of light, giving yourself up to all that it means to be Divine. To be limitless is to be in effortless flow, opening upon opening, unfolding and gathering, soaring and expanding. It is ceaseless, open-hearted and open-winged, taking you deeper and deeper into yourself, awakening you to higher and higher light, knowing yourself to be an integral part of the vast, unbounded cosmos.

This bottle says that even if you have let your stories define you and pin you down in the past, your spirit has continued to roam free, singing to you from the void, calling you in, calling you home. Now, finally, is the time to hear the call and return to the One who has waited for you since time began.

Bottle G18 Story: Moira Bush, Canada, www.moirabush.com

Being ethereal and off-planet in energy, the moment when you connect with the Platinums is a profound experience. Trying to remember what happened or what was so profound afterwards, however, is often impossible. I have had this experience myself with bottle G18. You just know something has changed, but over time it loses its feeling of being tangible. The Platinum Gaias have an energy of their own that is so different from the rest of the system. I vaguely recall clients over the years bathing in Limitless, and they always came back with such an 'aha!' story that they blew me away – alas, I never recorded them!

Bottle G18 Story: Kate Griffiths, UK, www.wholeselfleadership.com

A good while ago I did the Platinum journey, and in an integration session at the end with Kath Roberts, we reflected on what the biggest lessons had been. It was very revealing, and yet the part that I remember most was when Kath asked me to look at the full set – we had taken a set of the Platinum Gaias out and put them in a semi-circle on the floor – to see which one was calling me. Instantly I was attracted to bottle G18 because it had such a gorgeous bright hue of turquoise that was so inviting. It was as if I was being called to bathe in it again, to really take in the message of that bottle and know that I was, and am, limitless.

Although I don't recall much from the bath, what I have noticed more recently, which is probably two or three years on, is that my eldest (who at the time of writing just turned 13) keeps choosing Limitless as her bedtime bottle. I guess for me the importance of that is how she is being a mirror back to me in so many ways. I have worked with colour for around five years now, and yet recognising myself as limitless and a powerful healer has taken all that time. Only now can I feel it in my bones and really see it in the work and what is showing up in my life.

Bottle G19: Om (Platinum/Platinum)

Om is the sound of creation. It is complete oneness with all that exists. This bottle takes you to the next level and you can try and make it grand and big, but it is simply evolution. There is not really a choice anymore. You have signed up for the ride and now you have to take it all the way. This is the clearing of fear-based human DNA and the activation of love-based Divine DNA.

At the centre of the set of Platinum Gaias, Om sits like a still, deep stone at the bottom of a still, deep lake. It contains worlds in its peaceful beauty and yet, at first glance, it gives nothing away. It is both impenetrable and completely transparent. It asks nothing of you, demands no explanations and is infinitely, irrepressibly present to each and every moment. As a mirror, it guides you to find the same level of non-judgement for yourself and for life. It activates a profound level of peace with 'what is'.

Bottle G19 combines the energies of the previous Platinum Gaias – the peace of Serenity, the profound light of the Elohim and the wondrous expansiveness of Limitless – and weaves them into something that goes beyond all of them. Om is the sound of the universe, and to try and put it into words borders on the pointless. It is something you know deep inside yourself, even if your mind has no clue what it is or what it might be about. It is a sound that rings like the clearest bell inside of you, in your deepest, highest self, calling you into the cosmic web of life. There is nothing more still and silent than Om and nothing that has more dynamic, creative power and resonant sound. It is a radiant vibration that echoes at the deepest core of your being, activating your DNA, awakening your heart, freeing your mind.

The pure platinum of Om is an opening to levels of light beyond your everyday experience. It transports you to higher realms, offering you a glimpse of possibilities, hope and expansion. In the platinum light there are no limits. It is simultaneously the void, empty and waiting, and the fullness of the entire cosmos. Its movement takes you up and out into the vast potential of the Allness. Here you leave behind density and darkness and welcome clarity and lightness.

Bottle G19 may not speak to your mind or offer you practical tools for your life – rather it connects you with the truth at the core of your inner being. When you choose this bottle it is a signal from your highest self, an indication that you are ready to embrace a whole new level. You cannot remain unchanged when you truly connect with the sound of Om, the colour of Om, the frequency of Om. You can no longer look upon the world as something that happens 'out there'. It sweeps you up in its all-encompassing love and shows you that you are intrinsically part of the One, not separate, not alone, but completely woven into the fabric the universe. Step out of your own way and let the platinum light of this bottle stream in. Let it carry you deeply into the stillness at the centre of the universe and the heart of yourself. Let it wash you clean, soothe your wounds, still your mind and bathe you in its beauty.

This bottle is an incredible aid to meditation and to levels of stillness you may never have touched into before. It removes extraneous 'noise' and ushers you into the potent silence of the Allness. In Om there is nothing you have to do, nowhere you have to be. The moment is unique and it is enough. You are unique and you are enough – and finally now, you know it.

Bottle G19 Story: Melissie

For me this bottle holds the most ancient memories and the most futuristic outcome of all the bottles. As a small child I had two 'invisible' friends who were this colour. They were tall and thin and always with me. I think many of us had that experience, but if you never had it explained, it probably remained as a memory of being scared as a child because you felt watched. If you were open enough to see these beings and no one was able to tell you what you were seeing and just explained it all away as a nightmare, you may have been left wondering what on earth it was all about.

Many years later I did the trainings of Jann Weiss, who was very aware of our off-planet connections, and I realised that we are all hybrids, with both human and star DNA so that our bodies are able to hold more light. What I also realised was that these beings were my star parents who were around to keep an eye on me.

This bottle connects me to the depth of the truth that we really are so much more than we think we are. We are so loved and so planned and so on purpose that we cannot possibly believe that any moment of our lives has been a mistake. And if you are not a mistake and nothing you have ever done has been wrong, how can you judge yourself or anything else? There is such a beautifully, mathematically precise plan for your existence that you have to be in the stillness of this bottle to feel the awe. Of all of the bottles, I think this is the one that is truly, deeply my soul bottle.

Bottle G20: Abode of Bliss (Platinum/Pale Green)

The delicate colours of this bottle help remove old energies of persecution and sibling rivalry, bringing in an awakening that is like the newest spring rebirth you could possibly imagine. The 'Abode of Bliss' is the meeting point of head and heart, spirit and matter, human and Divine. This bottle represents the enlightened heart of humanity, where every human heart connects with every other human heart and the heart of the planet. It asks you to keep your feet firmly planted on the earth, while also recognising that you are a vast Divine being – so much more than your body or your mind. As you embrace the fullness of who you are and walk that energy around the planet, you change the planet. Tap into the bliss at the heart of Gaia and spread that light wherever you go. This is the time for the awakening of humanity and the creation of a blissful new earth.

To live in the 'abode of bliss' is to live each day and each moment in communion with your higher heart. This is the centre above the heart chakra that links you into the heart of the earth and all life. It is the bliss of knowing that you are totally connected with the Divine and that everything in your life flows from that connection. The abode of bliss is a place inside you, not an external location, yet when you find that place inside, chances are it will be reflected back to you in your physical reality. The abode of bliss is where your heart merges with your spirit and your body. This is where all aspects of yourself come together as one, where there is no split between who you are and what you do, where you are in integrity and alignment with your highest and clearest inner knowing.

This bottle is very similar in colour to two other bottles in the system: bottle 35 (The Inner Guide), and bottle C4 (Heart Chakra). Bottle 35 relates to creating a peaceful space on the earth; bottle C4 relates to emotions, relationships and the human heart. With bottle G20 the colours are softer, the energy is more enlightened and it is a step on from the boundary issues, territory battles and emotional wounds that can still arise with bottles 35 and C4.

Bottle G20 asks you to recognise the much greater vision of which you are a part and to soften and surrender any remaining defensive behaviours and thoughts. The platinum holds a wide-open space and invites you to merge with it, engulfing your small and limited thinking mind and creating an endless ocean of possibilities from which to choose. The pale green links you into the cosmic heart so that you can remember that there really is only one space, one being, one heart.

You are invited to remember that you exist on many levels and in many dimensions at the same time and that all of them are equally 'home'. There is no need to chase rainbows in the hope that you will find your true sense of yourself 'out there' somewhere. Bottle G20 teaches you how to be fully at home on the earth, how to allow Gaia into your heart and accept all the wondrous gifts she has to offer – and how to create your very own abode of bliss right here, wherever you are.

This bottle is about creating a new paradigm on earth, one founded on peace and unity. At this time when the energies are constantly moving and changing and humanity's judgements about life on the planet are coming to the surface, these cool, calm colours remind you that you are setting up something new, and in the creation of new structures, some of the old structures have to be knocked down or modified. You can see the devastation humankind has wreaked upon the earth, yet when you choose to view life from a space of higher awareness, you are able to maintain a clear-sighted vision of the earth in a state of pristine perfection and therefore stay out of judgement.

Gaia's gift has always been to let humanity grow and develop – and that includes doing its worst – and still she is here, holding a space for you as you awaken to the much higher truth of yourself and your life. She holds no judgement and no anger, for those are purely human traits. She is simply waiting for each human to wake up. As you realise you are a co-creator of a new earth – a true abode of bliss – you are called now to fully acknowledge this and stand united with all of humanity in love for the planet.

This bottle relates to bottle 20, Awakening. Its message is that now is the time for everyone to awaken and create a conscious relationship with the earth. You may find yourself being called to live more sustainably, to contribute to the well-being of the planet and her inhabitants, to take actions that will enhance life on earth rather than destructive or self-serving ones. Perhaps you will be guided to create or develop earth-friendly technology or products or become involved in new initiatives to bring peace and harmony to the planet. From a judgement-free space you are able to bring positive energy and inspiration to help find solutions to the challenges facing the earth and her inhabitants. Bottle G20 opens you to a broader perspective, where all life is precious and united as one.

Because of who Gaia is and the space she holds, when you are drawn to this bottle it indicates that you are now being gently enabled in your growth, deeply supported in your quest to awaken and lovingly guided on your path. Choosing this bottle means you have everything you need to make life work here on earth. Its colours invite you to choose peace, freedom and ease, right here, right now, and embrace the earth's true nature as an abode of bliss for all beings.

Bottle G20 Story: Amanda Bradbury, UK, www.amandabradbury.com

During a workshop on the platinum bottles with Korani, I was on the point of exchanging contracts on the sale of my house in Stoke Gabriel. I had instructed the solicitor to ring me only if there was a problem of some kind, otherwise to just go ahead. We were halfway through a meditation on bottle G20, 'Abode of Bliss', when the person who ran the venue came into the room and quietly interrupted the meditation by saying my solicitor was on the phone (which was fairly unheard of). I went out and spoke to him to find that he wanted to let me know we were exchanging. We had agreed to have just two weeks between exchange and completion, so it was all go at this point – luckily a friend of mine called Joy rented her house to us for six weeks, so before we moved to our new home we ended up living at Joy's house, or 'Abode of Bliss'!

Bottle G21: The Beloved (Platinum/Magenta)

The name of this bottle says it all: You are beloved. You are loved and always have been. Let yourself feel the truth of this. This bottle represents everything that is Divine about you and the world. All you have been looking for is already here and has always been here, waiting for you to recognise it. If you have not allowed yourself to receive Divine love because of an underlying sense of guilt or unworthiness, in this bottle you have the remedy: magenta releases guilt and platinum is an amplifier, so these colours help you transcend the concept of guilt altogether. Guilt and love are opposites: guilt is the language of lies and love is the language of truth. Let the love in.

This bottle sings a siren song directly to your heart. You may not hear it at first, or you may not recognise it as yours. You may resist it or push it away, but sooner or later it will call too loudly for you to ignore. When that happens, it will be time to open your heart wide enough to let in all the riches and joys and the pure and awesome stream of love that the Divine has been flowing to you throughout eternity. This bottle asks you to surrender up the fight that has kept you from receiving that flow. It is time to squarely face up to the duality within that has kept you in separation and to find and then feel what it means to claim: "I am beloved".

This bottle is a gateway to Divine love. Its job is to help you remove the blocks you have put in place that have stopped you from allowing in the total and unconditional love of the universe. It reminds you of the core of Divine light you have carried within you since time began that has never been dimmed or damaged throughout all your many lifetimes. As you stand before the love of the Divine and expose everything you have considered to be your flaws and your weaknesses, hiding nothing, holding nothing back, as you look into the face of the Beloved, all that is reflected back to you is your perfection. All the Divine sees as it gazes upon you is your light.

In the e-book, *Colour Conversations*, the colour combination of royal blue and magenta identifies a tendency to take yourself and your life rather too seriously. As a variation on this colour combination – with the platinum a paler, more ethereal version of the royal blue – bottle G21 speaks of spiritual martyrdom, the belief that it is only if you are 'spiritual' enough that you will be loved. You might play this out by attempting to purify yourself or rid yourself of any 'negative' thoughts or behaviours. You might try valiantly to heal and fix every single thing you consider 'wrong' with yourself. You might work hard to 'deserve' the Divine's love. This bottle asks you to step up and face the guilt that you have believed to be yours – the guilt for existing, the guilt for your behaviours, the guilt for being human and therefore somehow inherently bad or wrong – and let that guilt dissolve like the illusion it is. This bottle gently shows you the folly of your ways, inviting you to remember that you are already loved exactly as you are and that 'fixing' yourself is a denial of Divine truth. There was never anything wrong with you. You have always only been the Beloved.

The key to this bottle is to recognise that you are loved just as you are, that your essence is loved unequivocally. As you realise this you give yourself permission to be human, to be flawed, to get things 'wrong', to mess up. You love yourself anyway – because this is simply part of your learning and growth and the game of living a human life on earth. As you take this on and feel its resonance deeply within your cells, you begin to extend this loving compassion to others. You see that everyone on the planet is only acting out the behaviours and beliefs of lifetimes of conditioning and the common collective consensus about what makes up 'reality'. By seeing through this, you are able to take a higher, more enlightened perspective and extend love to everyone and everything.

Love is the only energy that ever actually changes anything. When you see through the eyes of judgement, you only perpetuate whatever it is you are judging. When instead you view the world through eyes which are unconditionally loving, the pure thread of your love weaves itself into the matrix and creates ripples that you may never know about on a conscious level but which are real, nonetheless. Love does not always equate to 'like' – you do not have to endorse whatever you wish to see change in your world, but by bringing love to it, you recognise that the person or situation is only ever calling for acceptance. Love is not passive. It is the most powerful energy in the cosmos. Watch what happens as you begin to view yourself and others as 'beloved'.

As with all the Platinum Gaias, with this bottle there is a quality of 'suchness': the stillness, clarity and wisdom to be with what is and to allow and love it all. Bottle G21 asks you to let yourself be sung to, let yourself be held, let yourself be gently nourished and nurtured and cradled in the warmth of the Divine's embrace. You are beloved – and with this bottle's support, you can let yourself be loved now, let yourself be love. With this bottle you come to understand that nothing you have ever done in the past or will do in the future will change the fact that you are already the Beloved. It is written in the stars and in the heart of the earth – and in your very DNA. You could not exist if it were not for the love the Divine has for you that is woven into the very fabric of your being. Now is the time to fully accept and honour this truth.

Bottle G14 (Ascension Light), the complementary or mirror image of this bottle, with its colours of brilliant clear and pale gold, reflect to you your light self. Bottle G21 is the merging of your cosmic star self with your earthly, human, flesh and blood self. Now you are all of it: the whole universe in your soul, the complete cosmos in your bones, the entire planet in your heart and all of it – ALL of it – the beloved of the Divine.

Bottle G21 Story: Alka Dharam, UK, www.lifecentredhealing.co.uk

I had a bath in this bottle on 12.7.2018, the numerology of which adds to 21. In the bath I heard the words "be love, be loved, beloved". There was a sense of being so wrapped in love – a magenta colour – that I merged with it. The feeling was to accept love and BE love. There is no distinction between love and me. Wrapped in love I walk, and as I do so, that love spreads.

Since then I have accepted life's experiences more and more as aspects of love. Life and love are interchangeable: they are the same. Bathing in this bottle has enabled me to be centred and has strengthened me, bringing aspects of myself back to my 'Self'. I deal with the vicissitudes of life with greater equanimity. I know I am deeply loved, and I accept that love reflected in the eyes of another. Recalling the words I heard in the bath are enough to centre me.

Bottle G22: Sacred Mystery (Platinum/Pale Olive)

The number 22 is a master number, but with these colours you go beyond mastery into the ultimate expression of 'mystery' and explore what the female face of mastery looks like. The Divine feminine is awakening, and her power is capable of birthing a new reality on the planet. This is where power is no longer wielded as a tool of aggression but instead is an energy of potent love and compassion – a true force for change. In this bottle pale olive is married to pale blue, in a perfect synergy of Divine feminine and Divine masculine. These colours tap into the pure power and love of God, Goddess, All That Is and support you in bringing that power and love into your life so that you can experience new levels of balance and harmony. Feel the joy of recognising that everything in existence is sacred and the true power that comes when you surrender to the profound mystery of life.

This bottle's name, Sacred Mystery, is a wordplay on the term for a female master. 'Mistress' does not have the same connotation of mastery as 'mystery', which carries all the intrigue of the female who has come to a state of full and perfect acceptance of her power. It seems now that we are finally ready for this level of feminine power to begin to flourish on the planet, for women to be seen and women's voices to be heard.

The shimmery colours of platinum and olive in bottle G22 reflect the glittering gold and magenta in its complementary partner, bottle G15 (Satori). As complementary colours always hold their opposite qualities within them, we know that hidden in the platinum of this bottle is the true power of gold, and in the olive is the Divine love of magenta. In bottle G22 these qualities are subtle, understated but real nonetheless. The colour olive represents feminine power, and the soft shade we see in this bottle reveals a power that is gentle, kind and compassionate. This is the true strength that comes from power that has its roots firmly planted in love. Platinum is filled with a Divine vastness that hints at the eternal and limitless power of this love. Here are power and love that do not need to shout about themselves. When you choose this bottle it is a reflection of your ability to be that love and gentle power without having to run around telling everyone about it. You simply are the love and the power, and they shine out from you so that others are touched by your presence.

The Platinum Gaias have an otherworldly quality which means they often go beyond the need for words; in fact, communication may happen on another plane altogether. When this bottle calls to you, it is appropriate to tune in with these other levels of communication and notice where you have been refusing to allow mystery into your life. If you have been insisting on the rational, the logical and the orderly, it is time now to take a step back and up and to let in a higher, lighter perspective. It is time to embrace the unknown and the mystical. The plants, the trees and all of nature is calling to you, and the cosmic realms and the stars are opening their gates for you. Go outside and connect deeply yet lightly with the earth, awakening to the starlight in your soul and the mysteries of the universe. Remember what it is to be filled with wonder and awe. Allow yourself to fully connect with your Divine feminine self and let her show you what it means to be a vast, expansive, enlightened being whose feet are firmly on the ground.

The colours of this bottle create a perfect balance between male and female, authority and compassion, Divine masculine love and Divine feminine power. Bottle G22 helps you understand that every polarity essentially indicates ultimate oneness; the mystery of life is that you should ever have believed so whole-heartedly in duality in the first place. This bottle generously weaves together the sacred and the earthly. It dances between the cosmic and the here-and-now. It allows you a window into the landscape of unity that all on this planet have dreamed of for so long. Bottle G22 says that it is right here – in your body, in your heart, in your surrender to the softness and lightness of your inner feminine.

This is mastery as the Divine feminine does it: gently, with conscious awareness and with love. There is a tangible grace to these colours, a return of the fragmented self to wholeness. The sacred mystery remains in place – whether you choose to allow it or not. This bottle reminds you that you are sacred, your body is sacred, the earth is sacred – all life is sacred. You are alive and you are life. Nothing is outside of the Divine. Feel into the truth of this and come home.

Bottle G22 Story: Melissie

This bottle was the gateway for the whole range of Platinum Gaias. I knew they were brewing in the background because we had been looking at the complementaries to each of the Golden Gaias, but the idea of having to make a platinum/olive combination – as the complementary to the gold/magenta Satori bottle – did not feel good at all.

Somebody then asked me to make one, and because the poor man was in such a difficult situation I really wanted it to be a bit special, so I added some shimmer to the colours. One look at this bottle and I was in love, and then I realised that what I had been resisting was one of the most beautiful combinations ever. At that point it was then imperative to make the rest of the set of complementaries to the Golden Gaias, and in a way they just sprang ready made into being. They were beautiful, peaceful and serene, and just in case we ever think we can get it wrong, they were born almost exactly at the Chinese New Year, which was taking us into the year of the Platinum Tiger. Perfect timing, as always.

Bottle G22 Story: Korani

With a birthday number of 22 I've always had an awareness of and connection with bottle 22 (Forgiveness). It's an uncompromising bottle, and its energies are not particularly easy. Its double 2's conjure duality in full force. At the same time I've always been heartened by its rose pink fraction and the fact that it is as a master number, and of course its message is actually quite profound. I made a conscious decision to forgive everyone and everything I had found challenging in my life when I discovered Colour Mirrors. I began slowly but surely moving beyond the need for forgiveness as I realised that everything always unfolds exactly as it is meant to.

As we were drawing near to the end of writing of this book, Moira sent us a story about how she had moved from focusing on bottle 7 (Neptune) as her life path number to bottle G7 (Gaia and the Elohim), and it occurred to me that perhaps it was time to thank bottle 22 for all it had taught me and move on. I wondered how it might be to step fully into the qualities that bottle G22 offers instead, and I loved the possibilities inherent in this choice.

Shortly afterwards, I left for India, where I spent a week on retreat at a temple called Ekam, a powerhouse of light and Divine love. This was an intense, joyful, extraordinary experience, which has had a huge impact on my consciousness and life ever since. Melissie pointed out to me the significance of my conscious shift into bottle G22's energies and my subsequent journey to India, that most sacred and mysterious of all places. The whole trip to India was filled with exactly the kind of Divine grace that bottle G22 invokes. Interestingly, up to this point it was always bottle G22's partner, bottle G15 (Satori), which had appealed to me more. Now I am very much in love with the soft yet potent light of bottle G22 and am curious to see where it takes me.

Bottle G22 Story: Alexia Claire Wren-Sillevis, UK, www.sheworkswellness.com

I bathed in half this bottle one evening, and afterwards my partner asked if he could have a bath in it too. The following morning we had an argument about lots of masculine/feminine ego stuff. The bottle was by my bed. When he left to go to the kitchen I looked at it and it had black lumps in the platinum at the top. That makes sense, I thought.

He came back in after a while, and we talked everything through and it was amazing – like we could really, truly hear each other and understand where the other was and come together to feel connected. It was one of the best resolutions we've ever had in five years. When I checked the bottle again, the black lumps were all gone! This INCREDIBLE, BEAUTIFUL system makes me smile and smile.

The Coral Gaia Set

Bottles G23-G27

By 2011 the Platinum Gaias were making their presence felt, and more and more people were exploring what these 'new earth' energies were about. Yet it was also becoming clear that we could not hang around in the platinum light – vast, expansive and cosmic as it is – without fully embodying that light and making it real. The Platinums remind you that you *are* the light, but unless and until you are able to love, honour and accept all aspects of yourself and anchor that light into your physical body, there is still a vital piece of the Ascension journey missing. Enter the Coral Gaias. Where the Platinums are aspirational, showing you what might be possible, the Corals are much more pragmatic, asking you to focus on your earthly human experience and to acknowledge, allow and appreciate it all.

There are five Coral Gaias – although only four of them actually contain coral. In fact, this set might almost have been called the Coral/Diamond Gaias, as the other core component of the Corals is clear diamond light, and the final bottle in the set, G27 (Unity), is diamond top and bottom. The Coral Gaia set invites you to be the bright, radiant light of your diamond-like essence at the same time as being physical, earthly and fully present in your body. The paradox they offer is that you are not one or the other, but both. You are all of it. For this reason, although they may stir up your coral issues of lack of self-worth, neediness and old childhood wounds, bringing them into laser-sharp focus, they may also bring soothing and peace to many of these issues as you fall in love with them – and yourself – along the way.

When they arrived in 2011, with a full dose of shimmer and sparkle, the Corals brought an important cohesiveness to the Gaias, as we now had the three primary colours in place once again – pale gold (yellow), platinum (blue) and coral (red). In the run up to the huge earth shifts and transitions predicted for 2012 it was essential to have the red in place. We could not enter a new age on the planet wafting on a cloud of luminous light. We had to do it here, now, in our bodies, on a physical planet that demanded of us to feel our way to Ascension, not just dream or talk about it.

The Corals encourage you to make your spirituality real. You might find yourself being called to make a genuine difference to others' lives or to the planet. You may feel called towards activism, taking a stand for what you believe in. This is where your life takes on greater meaning as you bring your light into the world and use it to be of service.

In nature, coral in the ocean is like the canary in the mine. If the coral starts to die, scientists know that pollution levels in the ocean are dangerously high – so the coral sends a clear message that time is up and urgent action is required. The colour coral asks you to become aware of how this analogy applies to your own life and indeed to the extreme danger in which humanity has placed the planet. Coral says that the time is now or never – but rather than acting from a place of fear and anger, it reminds you to move ever deeper into love and to start with unconditional self-acceptance as the bedrock of everything else.

When you act from a place of love and acceptance you automatically open to more creative and innovative solutions to any challenges you are facing. You also connect with the Divine energy of grace, which makes your actions both more effective and simpler to undertake. The Coral Gaias show you how to be fully human *and* fully Divine. They invite you to take a higher perspective on life, while taking practical steps to resolve the very real challenges being experienced by all of humanity and the planet herself.

Coral is the colour of Divine consciousness, a combination of pink (love) and yellow (joy and wisdom). The Coral Gaias relate to the owning of your innate Divine light, that force of pure love that lies at the heart of every being, and the wisdom to shine that light, be that love and live that joy. As you embrace the Divine light within, you come to view life through the energy of love, seeking to accept first rather than judge, to choose love over fear, to see the Divine perfection in everything and everyone. The Coral Gaias bring this perspective shift strongly to the fore as a new era commences on the earth.

Bottle G23: Acceptance (Clear/Pale Coral)

With this bottle you connect to the innocent joy of being yourself, without pretence or apology. This is the level of acceptance that brings true peace and freedom. Coral takes you into yourself in the deepest, most intimate way. You are asked now to claim every single thing 'out there' as an aspect of yourself, to accept that you are God, earth and everything in existence and that your physical form is, in a very real way, Divine. True self-acceptance is a powerful key. It unlocks the flow and abundance of the universe and offers you the joy of a life lived to the full as a human being who also happens to be Divine light. This bottle paves the way for true acceptance of yourself exactly as you are and life exactly as it is – and invites you to love every last bit of it.

The first of the Coral Gaias comes in offering a challenge. It asks: will you truly, deeply and wholly accept yourself, in every aspect, in every way? Will you accept your brilliance as well as your darkness? Will you embrace the full might of your spiritual adult self as well as your smallest, most deeply wounded child self? Can you bring acceptance to all the things about yourself that you find hard to like, and recognise that there is also much to admire and love about yourself? Are you willing to accept that you are not better or worse than any other being, that no one is inferior or superior, that all are equal and perfect in the eyes of the Divine, including you?

This level of acceptance is profound and not yet readily experienced on the planet. As we explored in the coral bottle 3 (Jupiter), humanity is mostly a long way from the completely unconditional acceptance offered by the Divine. The term 'acceptance' may even have rather negative connotations for you. Maybe it feels like a passive concept, or as if you are being asked to resign yourself to something you may not necessarily desire. True acceptance, however, is much richer and more expansive than this.

When bottle G23 calls to you, it is a signal that your higher self is taking charge. Its message is not to give up but instead to give in – so that all the love of the universe can flow to you. Your soul is waving a white flag of surrender, offering you a different, altogether simpler and clearer choice. This bottle will often appear in your life when you are ready for a complete 180 degree turnaround. It shows you that now is the time to let go of the fight that has kept you in separation and fear and the resistance that has kept you stuck. In its truest form, acceptance is a blissful surrender to the Divine, a surrender that is both filled with relief and overlit with grace. Like the gentle, shimmering colours of the bottle, true acceptance is warm, flowing, soft – and nothing at all to fear.

Clear white light intensifies anything to which it is added, so this colour combination could, in theory, mean intensified coral issues – trauma, abuse, lack of self-worth. Yet somehow with bottle G23 this is simply not the case. Rather, it is the enlightenment of those issues, bringing the light of the Divine to shine fully into and onto them. It is where you cease to see yourself as a victim and instead see the perfect unfoldment of your human journey, with all that has enabled you to become who you are and who you will be in the future.

If bottle G23 is calling, it is a sign that you are on track to a path much more aligned with your heart and spirit, a path of greater ease and joy. This bottle calls you to a gentler, more honest way of being. It reminds you that you are, in your very essence, innocent. It asks you to see the higher perspective and let go of the limiting and limited viewpoints of the ego and mind. Bottle G23 lightens and softens the energy of coral, adding a diamantine sparkle and shine. It shows you what might be possible if you were to find a higher, finer level of love for yourself, to accept and honour yourself just as you are. It invites you to feel the lightness and shimmer of the diamond and begin to realise that your soul, your inner Divine self, is in truth an incredible and dazzling light. It asks you to accept that you are more than you have ever clearly and honestly acknowledged before.

The coral in the base fraction of this bottle offers a huge truth: it is only because you have a body that you can connect consciously and with purpose to the light of the universe. This brings you the opportunity for a deep and powerful acceptance of your body as an amazing gift and an incredible experiment at this time, given to you so that you might experience the light in a physical form and with that light fully embodied, ascend to a higher frequency.

This has never happened en masse in the way it is becoming possible at this unique time on the planet. Until now there has been an occasional avatar or master who has managed it, but humanity has widely misunderstood the message, revering the master instead of seeing that they were simply showing what is possible for each and every being. Bottle G23 says you can no longer seek the master outside of yourself because you *are* the master. You are the light in human form, and your purpose for existing is to spread that light along your path. As evolution takes you to higher and higher levels, you come to understand that the whole process of life is about feeling, understanding and knowing yourself as a powerful being of light in a human body, a Divine expression in human form. Through the beauty of colour, this bottle shows you how that looks – and how to do it.

Coral means unconditional self-acceptance, and the acceptance it offers you here is for the whole package. This bottle reminds you that you are an individual, a one-off. You have something to offer the planet that no one else has. This bottles teaches you to appreciate and value your uniqueness and, in so doing, give permission for others to do the same. Then everyone can shine and share the Divine spark they carry within and together inspire a whole new and much more enlightened way of being on this earth.

Bottle G23 shows you life in all its complicated, complex, sometimes messy, always intriguing glory, and shines massive compassion on it. It is time now to do the same for yourself.

Bottle G23 Story: Moira Bush, Canada, www.moirabush.com

To me bottle G23 offers the key teaching that is missing from what is commonly taught in the Law of Attraction, and the reason why we fail to manifest the images we have pinned on our vision boards. Coral is the colour of wishes, and it is also the colour to help you take practical action so that you can manifest those wishes. Your desires are made up of the molecules of the ethers (heaven), and the physical steps you take are the third-dimensional molecules (earth). Magic happens when these two energies merge and you are able to create what you have envisioned in a tangible way.

To create this magic you have to surrender into the process. This was originally taught to me by Melissie, and I now teach it in my Love & Money Boot Camps. If you plan in detail who, where, why, when, what and how your wish is supposed to became a reality, your ego steps in and creates a limited version of what you have planned. And at times the polarity of creation, which is your shadow side, uses the energy of a controlled plan to manifest the exact opposite to your dream – more lack, more need.

If you surrender your wish it will result in a more expanded and luxurious result. How to surrender? Step one: state your wish. Step two: do something tangible towards the vision, even if it is research work. Step three: say yes to whatever turns up and surrender into the flow that begins to organically unfold. This will lead you to the result you desire and more, without needing to know who, what, where, why or when it will happen – as that is not your job in the manifestation process. Bottle G23 says surrender, let go of control and be amazed by the simplicity and speed with which your wishes come true.

Bottle G23 Story: Chrisoula Sirigou, UK, www.ChrisoulaSirigou.com

As multi-faceted, multi-dimensional beings, how do we feed our curious minds? How do we calm our thoughts? How do we nourish our spirits and soothe our hearts? What has helped me, my students and clients worldwide come back to joy and wholeness is the profound, playful, uplifting, joyous and light-hearted energy and psychology of colour.

One of the bottles that has supported me on this journey of accepting myself with all my 'perfect imperfections' and embracing life as a spirit in a body is the sumptuous bottle G23. This bottle paved the way for me to say 'yes' to my light and accept part of my destiny as an author and publisher. The coral in the G23 bottle that I was working with completely disappeared and became clear. It was vibrationally absorbed into my system as I was taking the huge step back in 2017 of giving myself permission to write, illustrate in colour and publish 'The Book of Soulful Musings: Living LIFE with Love Intention Flow Ease', which has gone on to become an award-winning book.

At various moments and stages of our lives, we have all experienced resistance as a result of fear of letting go of control and not trusting that the universe has our back. The opposite is the sweetness of surrender, embracing the notion that we matter, allowing ourselves to receive help, support, money, love and success because we no longer run the belief in our system that we don't deserve to receive.

Have I experienced resistance? Oh, yes! How did I overcome it? With the wise guidance and healing empowerment of colour. When I led a crowdfunding campaign for my book in 2018, and with only a week left before the campaign was complete, I was faced with the hard reality that if we didn't get £1000 in order to reach our target, all money would have to be returned to the people who supported the campaign and all our efforts would have been in vain. At that point, with tears in my eyes, I said to the Universe/God/Source: "If this book is destined to touch and transform people's lives, let it be! I cannot do any more. I have done everything I can."

At that point I surrendered. It was one of the most difficult things I have done. I had put my heart and soul into the creation of this book – now it was time for me to step back and trust. This is when I experienced being in the flow and allowed others to step in, and we not only reached our target but went well above it! This signified to me that the book was destined to come out and be of service to the world.

Without the abundant wisdom of colour and the profound shifts and changes I have experienced at a deep cellular level and am still experiencing as a practitioner and teacher of the Colour Mirrors system, I wouldn't have been in a position to take the courage to write my book and reach deep inside. Nor would I have been brave enough to say to the world that "I AM spirit in a body", inviting others to accept the truth in the notion that there is more than our physical bodies to celebrate with: there is the generosity and unconditional love of our spirit and the wisdom of our soul to be shared with the world.

Bottle G24: Reconnection (Pale Coral/Copper)

The name of this bottle is 'Reconnection', which implies that you were always connected – you just allowed yourself to forget for a time. It enables you to be fully in your body so that you can feel your connection with Gaia, and it reconnects you with Gaia so that you can really live in your body. This bottle asks you to release whatever blocks you from accepting yourself as fully Divine and therefore perfect, as well as fully human – and therefore perfect. Every small part of you and your life that you think is not perfect has to be looked at again, and any beliefs you hold that God is guilty for creating a painful reality have to be re-examined and brought into the light.

This bottle says you no longer need to go 'out there' to find God. You can now look in the mirror and see yourself as a Divine human on a fifth dimensional planet. Gaia has always been an evolved being, but out of love she has held herself in the third dimension, waiting for humanity to catch up. Feel the reconnection that comes from knowing that your earth mother has always loved and supported you and always will. Remember what it means to be plugged into the universe, reconnected with your spirit, your heart, your body and the earth. This bottle encourages you to release whatever limits you and reconnect with all that feeds your soul.

When you choose bottle G24 it is a sign that you are ready to really embrace the whole earthly experience. You are ready to stop playing the game of limitation and disconnection, of poverty, 'poor me' and victimhood. You are planting your feet on the earth and settling in for the ride. This bottle asks you to look at where in your life you could reconnect. Maybe there are friends or family members you have lost contact with. Perhaps a part of you that has been buried is waiting now to be recovered. Are there activities, hobbies or spiritual practices you used to enjoy that you have forgotten about? Do you have talents, skills and passions waiting to be re-ignited? Whatever it is that nourishes you and tunes you back into the flow of life, now is the time to reconnect.

Bottle G24 is also about a deeper reconnection, in the sense that it helps reunite you with everything you thought you lost when you left the Divine light of spirit to incarnate in a body on the earth. You may have felt at times that leaving the purity and light of spirit to venture into a physical body was a huge mistake. Perhaps you have felt as if you were being punished by landing up here on earth. You may have endured the loneliness of feeling as if you were abandoned far from home. You might have pined for the safety and joy of the light, judging your experience of earth as difficult, scary or just plain wrong. Perhaps you have blamed your body for limiting you, holding you back, keeping you stuck. The truth is that there is nothing you have had to give up, deny or withhold from yourself in order to be fully here in your body – that was just a misconception.

All the Coral Gaias, and bottle G24 in particular, show you that your body is your greatest teacher, your vehicle for growing and learning and most of all, experiencing. You could not experience even a fraction of what it is to be a part of the Allness without it – and what you came to do here, after all, was to experience. As you venture into the Coral Gaias you are given the opportunity to make contact with your body in a new and different way. You are asked now to look at it, acknowledge it and – here's the real request – to love it. This bottle is about reconnecting with all that it means to be in a body, to be on the earth, to be the light while in physical form. This bottle's job is to reconnect you with the truth that your body *is* the light. It invites you to open to all the love and blessings your body has for you. Yes, your body loves you! You may have endlessly abused it and hated it and judged it since you first learned how to do that, but it continues to love you unconditionally, just as the earth does. Nothing you can do to your body or the earth will stop that love from flowing. Just feel for a moment how extraordinary a gift that is…

Bottle G24 asks you to really begin to tune in with your body, to reconnect with it and ask what it needs. What does your body require and desire (rather than your mind)? What does real love and nurturing look, feel, taste, sound and smell like for your unique and individual body? The Coral Gaias invite you to begin an honest dialogue with and commitment to your body, and this bottle plays a powerful role in assisting you.

Your body is a miraculous physical vehicle and the most profound gift for the next level of your evolution. Instead of thinking about all that is wrong with it, you are asked to see it as the most amazing creation. You are shifting into a higher vibration and your body is the only vehicle in which you can do it. This is how you get from the third dimension to the fifth dimension. This is how you lift your vibration to a level beyond the ego/mind. Bottle G24 is a paler – and therefore more enlightened – version of bottle G4, Ancient Mother. Now you are asked to nurture, cherish and care for yourself and your body with all the love and grace the Divine Mother has for you. You are asked to find and hold a higher frequency and contribute your light to the greater whole.

Your body and the earth are deeply connected; they are made up of the same matter. As you learn to love and honour your physical self, you also learn to love and honour the earth. As this reconnection happens, you remember that the Divine is in every last piece of it. Every cell, every particle, every atom in the universe is Divine creation brought into being. You are it and it is you. There is no separation. Your body, your soul, the earth and the Divine are all one. Bottle G24 shows you, in ways your mind cannot perhaps imagine, the connection between your body, the earth and the Divine. It makes this connection tangible, visceral and real.

To dive into this bottle and its message is to experience a whole new perspective on life. You can either continue to see the world through the lens of judgement and disconnection, or you can plug back into Source and switch on the lights. When you fully reconnect to the truth of the Divine in all things, including your body and the earth, your old limited views of life begin to diminish and a wonderful tableau presents itself. This bottle says there is a rich bounty offered by the physical realm – all the sensory experiences you would not be able to have without a body – and it is time to recognise that your physicality is an extension of your spiritual life. The two are not separate. Your physicality is your spirituality, and your spirituality is your physicality. They are one and the same. All Divine. All part of the oneness. Bottle G24 reconnects you to the light your body holds within and to the earth as a gateway to the Divine, and guides you sweetly, gently and lovingly to the home you never left in the first place.

Bottle G24 Story: Deborah Wiggins-Hay, UK, www.themindbodydetective.com

This is the perfect bottle for those of us who are more comfortable in our astral and star-bound form, for those who are uncomfortable in this mortal coil, who feel disconnected from their physical body, uncomfortable in their skin, preferring simply to 'float' about in their own private, starry world. Sometimes these people are seen as dreamers or 'air-heads'. They are generally gentle and dislike the confrontations and conflicts that they observe as being part of the earth field. They therefore tend to remain 'aloof', separate, choosing not to fully 'ground' in their earth life – but the copper in the lower portion of this bottle is all about bringing the light down to ground upon the earth.

My whole life, even as I look back at my childhood, I was more comfortable flying high, creating ideas and dreaming up amongst the stars! I would find it difficult to 'earth', which would show up as difficulties with keeping time (always being late) or problems remaining 'present' (more than one school report talks about me "daydreaming and catching butterflies"!). I just found it hard to accept my need to be in the physical world and to do mundane daily activities because a world lived within the starry realm was so much lighter, easier and more comfortable to me.

Now, I help my clients observe the connections of their own mind and its daily manifestation. I support others to engage in a paradigm shift that is founded in an awareness of the language of their own body. We explore how beliefs shape our worldview and can perpetuate health or disease. My own showed up for me as 20 years of 'thyroid dysfunction', although I am now hypothyroid-free and have a healthy functioning thyroid due to the deep change work I have undertaken. There were many things that I worked on to create this shift in my biology in order to allow my body to heal and overcome this dysfunction. But along with developing a conscious awareness and learning about mind-body connections, the change work I did was energetic. It was beautiful and subtle work that fed my spirit and soul, and in so doing, it also freed my body from the bind of a physical disease which mirrored my experience of 'disconnection' in my physical body.

When I first encountered the copper bottles they made me extremely uncomfortable – precisely because I was uncomfortable in my physicality and lived, as far as possible, without 'grounding' – which always felt on some level unsafe to me. This bottle brought me closer to the Coppers, whilst keeping me safely held in the loving embrace of the Corals.

The Corals are about embracing self-love: loving ourselves and then finally loving beyond ourselves in the truth of the love-light we find within. But this coral bottle also taught me that I am loved by the earth herself. I was able to gently reconnect with Gaia, to really feel the love directed from her specifically holding and supporting me! Me, individually. Me, personally. And in that holding space I saw myself as the earth saw me, and through this new connection I learned to love myself and my earth journey as a physical being.

Yes, there were other learnings and encounters that helped on my road to self-healing, but this bottle was instrumental in holding a space for me. It allowed me to truly and deeply reconnect, to finally love my earth life and Gaia herself and to step into fully being human.

Bottle G24 Story: Kath Roberts, UK, www.kath-roberts.com

During my Colour Mirrors teacher training course I was staying in a hotel, and one evening I opted to take bottle G24 to bathe in. I had a nice bath and a relatively early evening, with nothing significantly memorable coming up when I bathed. However, I woke up from a very deep sleep around 4-5am and felt extremely panicky, with no initial comprehension around where I was or any memory of the previous night. I could strongly smell fire in the room and felt the weirdest of sensations in my throat, which was very dry, sore and extremely parched. A memory of feeling burnt came up, and I felt claustrophobic in the room. When I eventually became more conscious I got out of bed and went to the bathroom and then realised I had bathed in G24, as the bottle was empty beside the bath.

That morning I drove to St Catherine's, as I had done many times before, for the Colour Mirrors teacher training course, yet this time I took an entirely different turning and went round in a full circle the wrong way, ending up exactly where I had set out from. Clearly I wasn't 100 percent conscious and in my body! St Catherine's was apparently built on an ancient Templar site, so the energies are particularly heightened there, and who knows, maybe I had been tapping into the burning of St Catherine herself!

The insight I drew from this particular experience surrounded the importance of healing one's past so you have a clear direction to move forward and don't keep going round in circles. In my situation this was related to the feminine aspect and the importance of listening to my intuition. We can only really pay attention to those intuitive nudges in the body when we are spiritually awake and fully in our body. The cycle of life is that we die and rebirth many times, and it doesn't have to be an intense burning experience if we let go and surrender to our soul's highest knowing/calling.

Clearly my subconscious needed to have such a visceral body experience in order to validate my healing and intuitive gifts and confirm past lives – something I was curious about and interested to understand more of on my soul's journey. I feel that one of the reasons I have denied this aspect of myself in my deeper past is because of the subconscious fears around the impact that such visibility would bring. This is true of course for many women today and in the past. I can now say, however, that I'm very vocal about the importance of intuition in everything we do, and typically attract many women and men who have lost touch with themselves or who want to understand more about their own soul's path.

Bottle G25: Integration (Pale Coral/Pale Coral)

If you have been on a steep learning curve or going through an intense time of personal or spiritual growth, this bottle helps you integrate what you have learned and experienced. More than this, however, it asks you to integrate all the many aspects of yourself, from your personality to your spirit, from your shadow to your light. It is time to accept and honour the whole of you.

You are a Divine human on earth, and this bottle shows you that Divine and human and earth are all one thing. This bottle is coral all the way through, asking you to take in the messages of coral on both a conscious and subconscious level. Coral is made up of the pink of unconditional love and the yellow of unconditional joy, which together create a powerful vision for you as an individual and for a new reality on the earth. This bottle helps you integrate it all. It calls you to step into deep, unconditional self-acceptance and move steadily towards fulfilling your destiny as a conscious Divine human on the earth.

This bottle may come at a time when you have been going through a phase of intense learning or growth. Whether you have been involved in study and training, experiencing huge emotional releases and shifts on your healing path or receiving upgrades to your spiritual operating system, bottle G25 is an indication that now is the perfect opportunity for you to take 'time out'. Now is the time to step back from the flurry of daily life and let everything you have learned and experienced filter through to every part of your body, your being and your life. You cannot continue relentlessly moving forward on your path without times of rest and stillness. If bottle G25 is calling, it is the perfect opportunity to take stock of where you have been and how far you have come.

Coral is always about self-love and self-acceptance, and this bottle is no exception. It has all the qualities of the number 3 bottle (Jupiter), which is expansive, generous and unconditional. But this time you are not connecting to some faraway planet: this bottle is about and of the earth. When you choose bottle G25 it tells you that it is time to bring all the benevolence and blessings of the universe home, right into your physical body. You are asked to consciously bring the glowing light of coral unconditional self-acceptance into all the aspects of who you are, top and bottom, inside and out, all the way to the very depths of yourself.

The shimmery colour of this bottle reminds you that at your core you are filled with love and wisdom and that inside of you are all the qualities of the Divine. The energy of this bottle is richly feminine, holding all the energy of the earth goddesses. It is soft and tender and yet, despite its apparent vulnerability, it is also incredibly tough. It is like a warm and loving hug from the Divine Mother as she wraps you in her arms with such tenderness and strength that you feel it infusing your cells, loving what you have been unable to love, making it safe to be who you are, creating an incubator of love in which you can grow and heal and thrive. This is the love you might wish you had had from day one on the planet. That love has always been present from the moment of your first incarnation, but you may not always have been able to recognise it or receive it. If you can be totally open to love within because you fully love and accept yourself, nothing on the 'outside' can affect you. If you are in such an expanded state of love, then as Christ showed, not even death can touch you.

Until you reach this place of true integration, however, the Coral Gaias and in particular this fully coral bottle may bring up your bodily fears and wounds about being human, being weak, being vulnerable. You are asked to go steadfastly into the depths of coral to find what is still buried there, what is still asking for acceptance, what is still being denied or repressed. With the assistance of bottle G25 and its soft coral glow, this journey need not be difficult or painful. Instead it can help you be compassionate and kind as you reach out to the parts of yourself that have tried to remain hidden in the shadows and bring them forth into the light of loving acceptance and integration.

This central bottle of the five Coral Gaias is the point at which you take everything that has brought you to where you are now and fill it with love so that you can move forward from a place of wholeness and total acceptance. This bottle is an integration of your past with your present and your future. With it, you begin to see that you are eternal, that time does not exist except as a third dimensional construct and that love and acceptance are the keys to everything. Integration is about wholeness and worth. It leaves nothing behind and leaves nothing out. You are asked to remember that you are all of it – Divine and human, heaven and earth, all in one flesh and bone parcel – and that you are totally loved and accepted. This is the integration of all your selves, all your sides, all your apparently contradictory aspects. This is where you fully embrace and honour everything that makes you who you are.

Bottle G25 Story: Yvonne Wolo, Canada, www.inspiringgreatness.com

Bottle G25 was very powerful for me during my Colour Mirrors teacher training. We did an activity where we breathed the energy of an Angel bottle across to our partner. During this exercise I received a beautiful message that came through my partner. At the end I was asked to say out loud: "I love myself" and "I am love." I could not say it. I ended up coughing four times and barely got the words out. I did not feel connected to them. I was able to repeat "I am love" but felt distressed that with all the healing and personal development work I have done, I could not say "I love myself."

That evening I chose to take bottle G25 home to bathe in. I read the message out loud before getting into the bath. It was a lovely bath – I ended up letting go of things, saying them out loud and also forgiving myself and others as they came to my conscious awareness. I opened to any healing energy, and had a peaceful night's sleep. The next morning I went off to class again where we shared our bath experiences. When we were done, I had the realisation within me that I could actually say "I love myself" with certainty. I was in full alignment with it, there was no doubt or hesitation. I raised my hand and shared with the group. What a powerful moment it was to say those words out loud with complete conviction and have it witnessed by everyone present.

Bottle G26: Alignment (Pale Coral/Diamond Clear)

This bottle brings complete transparency to everything you have kept hidden in the depths of yourself so that you no longer have to try to be something or someone you are not. As you drop the pretences, you shed the limiting fears and beliefs that have kept you out of alignment with your truth. As you align with your true self, all the way through, everything can flow from a place of balance and inner harmony. This bottle reminds you that you have always been Divine light in a human body. It supports you as you come into alignment in all aspects of your being: your light and shadow self, your Divine and human self, your inner male and female. Feel the joy.

This bottle's name is Alignment and its job is to do exactly what its name suggests: bring you into a beautiful and harmonious state of balance. To be in alignment means to be in integrity with yourself, feeling and knowing your truth and living according to that truth. It means loving and accepting all aspects of yourself. It means being connected to the earth and the love and support of Gaia at the same time as being plugged into the Divine and the infinite vastness of your soul. When you are in alignment you are clear and strong, and others' opinions or desires do not hold sway over you. This is not a rigid state but one in which you are flexible and open to change, knowing that when you are in true alignment you naturally flow wherever you are most called to be, and do whatever your higher self calls you to do.

When your spine is in alignment, all your joints, muscles and organs perform their job with greater ease. When your heart is in alignment with your spirit, you express yourself fearlessly, open to possibility, love without restraint and enjoy all that life has to offer, in the clear knowing that you are loved and supported by the universe. Alignment brings inner clarity, peaceful calm, gentle joy. There is a kind of grace, a sense that you are divinely on track and in the flow. Your projects flow and grow easily, your heartfelt intentions manifest, and you enjoy authentic relationships based on mutual respect and connection.

When you are drawn to this bottle you are asked to set aside all that keeps you out of alignment, everything that somehow feels dissonant or out of integrity. When you are stressed, alignment tends to go out the window. This gentle bottle acts as a reminder when you are off track, guiding you back to the path, encouraging you to let go, and supporting you in reconnecting with your spirit and your true, natural alignment.

The warm, rosy coral in the top fraction of this bottle is made of the pink of love combined with the yellow of wisdom and joy. Coral connects you with your Divine self and prepares the way for Divine consciousness. This bottle's message is that if you align from your small human self you will align with ego, mind and judgement. If instead you align from your light self, your clear, wise and infinitely loving higher self, you can flourish on all levels and bring to the world the love, joy and wisdom you hold at the centre of your being. When you fully and truly access these Divine energies, there is only one place they can lead – to an enlightened state of being, or Divine consciousness.

In the bottom fraction of this bottle is the sparkling diamond of the light you hold in the depths of your being, the light that caused you to begin the journey back to conscious awakening in the first place. You are the light and have always been the light, but you may have effectively hidden it so deeply inside yourself that you have forgotten how to be the light. Now you are given an opportunity to remember the undeniable truth, and bottle G26 calls you to align fully with that truth. This bottle offers perfect symmetry – to acknowledge the light within you must align with Divine consciousness, and to align with Divine consciousness you must acknowledge the light within. You cannot have one without the other. As you come into true alignment, this bottle helps you understand what that means for your soul.

By the time you are drawn to this bottle the traumas of the past are receding, and you are able to acknowledge them as stepping stones that have brought you to where you are now, with an inner knowing that Ascension is already underway. You are opening to self-love and you are ready now to align your life so that what you do, say and be are all based on a solid foundation of love – in particular, self-love. When you are in alignment you can fill yourself up to the brim with the blessings of the Divine, knowing yourself to be completely part of the Allness. This bottle aligns you to the truth of who you really are: Divine energy, focusing through a human body made of Divine energy, on a planet made of Divine energy. There is nothing else in the universe, and it is all aligned within you.

Bottle G26 Story: Korani

Every time I have used this bottle it has done what it says on the tin: it has brought me back into alignment. Alignment to me is a space of balance, harmony, peace and openness where I can let go of resistance and be in the flow of life. Over the years I have increasingly experienced being 'aligned' with my higher self and the universe and tend to live in that state much of the time. When I go off-track I am generally aware of it quite swiftly, but there are times when it is more difficult, and I love how this bottle calls me back instantly in those situations. Even just picking it up and holding it or placing it somewhere on my body can make me take a deep breath and come back into alignment. With its coral top fraction highlighted by the clear fraction underneath, it reminds me to love, accept and allow, and from that place I can surrender back into the flow represented by turquoise, the complementary colour to coral.

Bottle G26 Story: Moira Bush, Canada, www.moirabush.com

When bottle 26 (Partnerships) is chosen by clients, the conversation tends to be around a lack of commitment to their partners, or they express that their partners will not fully commit to them or have betrayed them. When bottle G26 is chosen, I have noticed that clients have a capacity to love themselves and have committed to follow a path of living their lives based on love. They will only settle for a relationship that includes commitment and unconditional support.

This bottle has often conveyed to clients the message that being in alignment with yourself means you can authentically offer yourself as a potential partner and work towards common goals and aspirations without the fear of being betrayed. I have observed over the years that this bottle can lead to a proposal, a diamond ring or other clear signs of commitment to a relationship. In business, this bottle often signifies new project partnerships based on trust.

Bottle G27: Unity (Diamond Clear/Diamond Clear)

The diamond clarity and shine of this bottle is a mirror that reflects all your colours, all your beauty, all your infinite light. In a system called 'Colour Mirrors', this bottle is the clearest, truest mirror of who you really are and what you are about. You are Divine light condensed into physical form, having a human experience. All that you have ever been or ever will be is Divine perfection. Remember this, and begin to live from the truth that you have never been separate from anything or anyone in the universe. Begin to live in the oneness your spirit has always known. This bottle shines with the light of Melchizedek who has been the over-lighting energy of the system since the beginning. It reveals a path to unity in mind, body, heart and soul for every human and for the planet as a whole.

Bottle G27 has all the crystalline qualities of the diamond – brilliance, brightness, clarity, shimmer and shine – and its job is to remind you that this is who you are. Its light is so clear that it leaves no room for doubt, fear or old stories of denial. It calls you to be the light, to live life with joy. Its name, Unity, is a reminder that each and every being on the planet contains this light and that when we all weave our brilliant, unique and individual threads together, this is the path to the full glory and splendour of heaven on earth.

Just as each diamond is unique, no one person is the same as any other. Each has come to bring their individual strand of light to join with every other strand, to form something more dazzling than could ever be created alone. Just as a diamond is a reflection of all the colours, so the universe is made up of the individual soul colours of every being. Unity reminds you that you are part of the oneness that is the natural order of the cosmos. The light of the world would not be complete without you, and bottle G27 asks you to remember how precious you are, how valued, how loved.

Unity or oneness is a concept that you may be aware of in your mind and heart, yet at times it might seem like an impossible dream. How can a world so divided and deeply mired in judgement ever become one giant family? This is the challenge and the call of bottle G27: to dare to dream of such a reality, to put your attention on that which unites rather than separates, to hold the vision for all humanity to awaken to the light inside, to share it fearlessly – and to remember again the truth that only love is real. When the messages of this bottle finally become embedded into the cells of every human being, there will be no choice but to embrace each other and to unite in love.

Unity begins with you. It begins with reconciling the warring parts of yourself so that you live from a state of wholeness rather than separation and disconnection. Bottle G27 asks you to unite within so that you can contribute to global, collective unity. It calls you to stop fighting with yourself and the separate voices in your head. It opens you to a coherent state from which who you are on the outside aligns with who you are on the inside. With its help and guidance, you begin to understand what it means to be 'at one'.

When you choose this bottle it is a call to awaken to the light you carry inside of yourself and recognise your own value and worth. You have something unique to contribute to the planet and the cosmos, and Unity will help you feel what your role is as part of the whole. You are asked to respect and honour yourself and every other being as precious, perfect and Divine. This bottle says, very gently, in a voice that is both soft and wise: "Please stop pretending that you are not this. Please look around you with the eyes of the Divine and see that no one else is anything other than this light." This is when fear and anger and every negative state will have to admit to the truth that it was just pretence. It was never real. The only thing that is real is the Divine light that created everything, and therefore everything is made of this light of truth and love. In this light no judgement is possible. In this light the shadows dissipate. There is no darkness that can stand against it. This brightness, if you allow it, can clear away the remnants of the darkness you have been holding within so that you can see, finally, that it is an illusion. It is a construct created so that you could experience duality, but when viewed through the eyes of the Divine, it dissolves like the mirage it is.

The light of the diamond is the light of creative power and strength, and it is also a symbol of the imagination. Your imagination is so great that you have been able to conjure great darkness and from that, great fear. The diamond clarity of this bottle reminds you that you now have the power to create from light, in light, as light. It inspires you to tap into your own pure creative stream of life force to generate new and wonderful creations. This light has the power and strength to create beauty, abundance, joy and whatever else you might wish to experience. It opens you to the fullest, highest potential you hold inside and asks you to recognise all the possibilities awaiting you – and every being on the planet.

In its clear, white, diamond sheen, bottle G27 is an elixir of light. It is purity and trust, courage and potential. It holds everything in its light, all the colours and all the wonder of the universe. When you use this bottle you are guided to find your unique colour, strand and frequency of light and to know in the depths of yourself that your beingness, your very existence, is of true value to the whole – and that you are loved beyond measure.

Bottle G27 Story: Melissie

Both my parents' birth numbers were 27, and although I could absolutely see my father as clear light, it was more difficult to find it in my mother who always held the dark side. As my birth number is 11 and relates to bottle 11 (Duality), I was always going to have to find the balance between dark and light. What bottle G27, Unity, now shows me is that there really, deeply is only one thing: the darkness was always the light masquerading as the other, and it was always there to help every living being find its way back to its true state of light and truth.

Bottle G27 Story: Deborah Wiggins-Hay, UK, www.themindbodydetective.com

When I began the journey of training to be a Colour Mirrors practitioner and teacher, I noticed that each of us experiences aspects of ourselves that come up for healing, release and expansion. This is certainly what occurred for me personally, and it was bottle G27 which guided me through this period of deep learning and transformation.

This is the lesson it taught me:

Inside each of our wounds of separation we carry our stories. For me it was the rising up of a story I had previously ignored – of what it is to be a disempowered woman. This might be a story of abuse or of being overlooked, unseen or unheard, dispossessed or disenfranchised. In its deeper resonance this is the experience of what it is to be a fractured part of the earth star, a part of the earth energy yet never connected to it, here but not fully here – the separation we encounter as we experience what it is to be bound in the concept of time. All of these can feel like separation and they all show up to teach us the gifts within the felt divisions, to add flavour and colour. After all, isn't even colour itself the 'seen' wavelength of the division of light?!

As I purchased my first set of beautiful Gaia bottles and took them home with me, between the first week of my practitioner training and the second week (which occurred a couple of months later), more than 20 of my Gaia bottles become completely clear! These exquisitely subtle bottles of liquid light, which explored the different shifts of Gaia herself, were now a complete set of clear, light containers, with shots of sparkles that hinted at their past colours but nodded towards me with a repeated pure light... bottle after bottle... each one reflecting back at me in cheeky twinkles!

Initially I was devastated that so many of my coloured bottles all seemed to be 'losing their colours'. But as I collected these colourless bottles up and placed them together in a group, I began to awaken to the possibility that this was no loss but a clear and strong message and indicator of the work that was going on for me at such a deep level. I recognised that all my Gaia bottles were becoming 'Unity' bottles: G27. They were taking me from one energy type – the energy of separation, with all of their individual and beautifully diverse energies – and leading me to the energy and experience of unity!

In the context of these bottle changes, and over the period of time between the two parts of the training course, there were huge energy and emotional shifts that were part of my conscious development. I was uncovering many of my 'stories' and meeting different aspects of my fractured self – and gently reintegrating those parts back into my true 'unified' self. Unity was the felt experience that I was 'getting' in different ways. As these shifts occurred, my 'Unity bottle' family grew ever bigger. My disappointment in 'losing' the colour in my life began to be replaced with a quiet and inquisitive exploration of unity, of oneness, of what brought similarity and oneness over difference and separation. As I was learning from these experiences and healings, I began to recognise the importance of embodying my new sense of unity, of seeing and recognising the old parts and stories and then beautifully and simply letting them go.

During this time of self-development, of clarity and unity, I developed a process of healing which I now call the 'Unity Consciousness Practice'. I was shown a new 12 Chakra system that I work with consistently for both myself and others to support individual transformation. Melissie made me some beautiful bottles which work within this system.

Bottle G27 Story: Amy Barroso, Canada, www.facebook.com/WhiteLightningCommunications

In November 2017 I was on the Magenta Show with Moira Bush and picked bottle G27. I was new to Moira and the Colour Mirrors system and did not see myself as a practitioner. However, this system snuck up on me like a ninja in the night and wouldn't let go! 'Magic in a bottle' Moira called the system, and I had no idea then how right she was.

I knew there was some magic happening when I, an unknown spark to the internet talk show world, got the most views on the Magenta Show that year! Two days after the show aired, I met with Moira's colour practitioner group to speak about branding. Even then I didn't have sights on going any further than helping some lovely people accelerate their businesses, but the colours dug in and wouldn't let go.

Ideas for helping the team flooded my imagination, and the conversations between Moira and her team were electric. Moira had suggested that in order to market this team with complete understanding I should really take the Colour Mirrors practitioner course. In retrospect I'm pretty sure she was dropping one of those breadcrumbs she always talks about, to see if I'd say yes and show up! By mid-February 2018 I found myself sitting smack in the middle of all the colours of the rainbow and, just like Moira's explanation of bottle G27 two months prior, I was seeing myself reflected in each of them. Some were beautiful, some were hypnotic and others were frighteningly repulsive, but there I was, soaking them up. I felt like I was transforming from a plain white arch into a rich rainbow of understanding, slowly revealing each band as we made our way through the lesson manual. I can't tell you how many times I said: "WAIT A SECOND... Are you telling me...?" And I would go on to repeat the revelation I had just had. It was an incredible week, and I knew I had to incorporate what I was learning into my company as soon as possible.

Right after the course, the parallels and signs led me straight into a crash course of spiritual learning that lasted nine months and was a roller coaster of emotion and a tornado of lessons! In hindsight, the birth that happened as I found myself a year later in front of Moira on the Magenta Show was worth the gestation period and horrific labour! Moira did the numerology on my name and explained that I was to be a bridge that would bring spiritual awareness to mainstream business. It would be my job to help owners understand the need to bring some spiritual sparkle to their marketing if they wanted to prosper and survive in this new age of 'make a difference' entrepreneurship.

I implemented her tweaks right away. Within hours I had clients calling, and within two weeks I landed a $50,000 contract to be the Director of Joy for a financial company called The BridgGroup of Companies! You can't make this stuff up! There are so many more synchronicities that I could go on for days!

I am currently the ONLY designer on the planet that incorporates my client's soul colours into their branding for optimal spiritual marketing. I don't work with anyone who is not willing to open their mind and heart to this system. This decision was a bit scary, but ultimately it served to be an amazing filtration system, sorting out who my perfect clients are!

The Silver Gaia Set

Bottles G28-G33

It was predicted by many ancient cultures that a profound shift would occur on earth at a time when both planetary and galactic cycles reached their natural conclusion. These predictions stated that the 'Shift of Ages' would occur when humankind was once again ready to remember its sovereignty and embrace its true light. For eons, it seemed, the human race had been disconnected from its Divine knowing and had stepped into the shadows, becoming trapped in a cycle of despair, anger and violence, abusing power, living from ego. Yet the ancients knew that this was not the end of the story and that the truth of human goodness and light would shine forth once more when the time was right for a new era of peace, harmony and co-operation. All of these predictions, from many different sources, had arrived at the same timeframe for the commencement of the Shift to occur: 2012.

This was the year when the Mayan calendar would end and a new paradigm would unfold on the earth. We waited with baited breath in the years leading up to this time, wondering if it could really be true and how it would play out. Some believed that an overnight awakening would occur on the planet and that we would suddenly be launched into the fifth dimension, with joy, peace and love reigning supreme. Others felt that 2012 would simply usher in the arrival of this new phase on the earth and that it would not be a seismic shift but a more subtle one. Sure enough, there was no mass awakening on 21 December 2012, the date specifically given as the start point of the new age.

Those with sensitivity to cosmic and planetary energies, however, were fully aware that indeed a shift had taken place on that date and in that year as a whole, which meant that there could now be no turning back. We were launched into a time of unprecedented change, disruption and what felt like a whole new level of 'strange' on the planet! No one quite knew what any of it meant or how things would unfold, but some years on, we can look back and see that enormous change has indeed taken place since then and that it is only accelerating with each passing year.

People all over the globe are re-claiming their power. Many are waking up to their inner spiritual light and choosing to live their lives more in accordance with universal principles leading to love, peace and harmony. A growing number feel a desire to live a more meaningful life. Many are becoming aware of the plight of their fellow sentient beings on this planet and are opening to co-operation, kindness and compassion. To be sure, there are also massive conflicts playing out, corruption is rife and the challenges we face in bringing about peace on our planet are significant. Yet we sense and know that our world is changing and that to bring about a true heaven on earth requires all of us, here and now, to bring our love and focus to its creation.

The year 2012 saw a subtle yet tangible evolution in the Colour Mirrors system with the arrival of six Silver Gaia bottles. This dazzling set, each bottle with a silver fraction, came in on the blue moon – the second full moon occurring in one calendar month – of July 2012, only weeks after Korani 'birthed' a set of Starlight bottles on the first of the full moons that month. The Silvers and the Starlights are both richly steeped in the mystical, magical energy of the cosmos, and the timing of their arrival was no coincidence.

The thinking with the Silvers was that they would be the complementaries of the Coral Gaias, but as ever, they insisted on creating themselves, with no interest in what we thought they might be! They brought a quality and frequency of light that we had not seen or felt before, and initially we were not sure what to make of them. They were icily beautiful, and we knew they were very much to do with the spiritual upgrade taking place on the planet, but beyond that they were mostly silent. For some time they did not reveal their names or their messages – or indeed much of anything. What we did receive was an absolute knowing that they were necessary and that their arrival was symbolic of the shifts taking place on both human and cosmic levels.

Shortly after they appeared, Moira developed a brand new and exciting healing modality based around the Silver Gaia bottles, called 'Silver Spheres'. Through the Silver Spheres, Moira discovered that this set of bottles has specific roles to play in opening the back of our chakras as well as connecting us with our ability to generate health and wealth and create with joy.

The Silver Gaias contain a paradox. They are capable of shining a light on any situation and bringing clarity, yet they also remain something of a mystery. They are reflective, in the sense that it is almost impossible to see into them. To truly get what they are about, you have to look deeper and realise that by shining so much light and brightness the Silvers gently but relentlessly expose the darkness. We have noticed that they are often chosen by people who have been through intense experiences or have found it difficult being here on earth. These bottles have an uncanny ability to draw out the shadow and reveal it, clearly and precisely – and although they do it with love and compassion, they are also unwavering in their quest to help you bring your darkness into the light.

The Silver Gaias do, of course, call to people who already hold a great deal of light. When they were created our 'starry' Colour Mirrors people immediately loved them, and the name we were given for the six bottles collectively was 'Homecoming'. More and more star children are being drawn to them, as they reflect the light these children are here to shine on the planet and give them a real sense of safety and connection with the earth.

It was 2015 when Melissie realised that the Silvers would be instrumental in restoring us to our Divine blueprint and activating our higher potential. At that time she received the information required for this to happen and began offering workshops to facilitate the process. The impact of the Silver Gaias and the workshops was profound – a homecoming indeed. The promise of the Silvers was that we would remember the Divine truth of our light and that we would begin more fully to live our Divine purpose on earth. As each subsequent year has passed, more has been revealed about our potential and our light. As we reconnect to Source on levels we had only dreamed of before, as we begin to have more access to our knowing, as we open to the light of grace and have more and more awareness of ourselves as Divine light in human form, we know that the promise is being delivered.

The energy of the Silvers is incisive, cutting through illusions and delusions, removing what is unnecessary and revealing what is true and what is false. Because of the crystalline clarity of the silver fraction in each, these six bottles individually and collectively help you get very clear on what is true for you, what matters to you, what requires addressing in your life and where you are ready to move to the next level. These bottles could even be called the 'Enlighteners' because as well as enlightening you as to where you have been fooling yourself with ego games and stories, they also raise your energy to a higher frequency of being. When you live from a more 'enlightened' space you have greater self-awareness and the capacity to see life from a more expanded viewpoint. The Silvers shine their brilliant light into your life so that you can see the higher truth in any situation rather than staying locked in judgement and blame.

The Silver Gaia bottles also quite literally buzz with energy. You may be aware of this if you sit with them for a time, or place them on your body or work with them in any way. Their energy has a very specific electric dynamism that is felt at a cellular level. Your body may begin to tingle with energy, your crown or third eye might feel as if they are being activated, you may receive 'downloads' of information or energy or you may just feel super-energised when connecting with them. Alternatively, you may find yourself going into a deeply peaceful meditative state or being taken 'out for the count'. However they interact with you, the Silver Gaias are extraordinarily powerful in their effects and their messages. Enjoy the ride!

Bottle G28: New Dawn (Pale Turquoise/Silver)

The silver fraction in this bottle carries a very clear, high vibration and shines its light on anything in your life that has a lower vibration, helping you to see it clearly and transform it. The turquoise softens and opens your heart and leads you into the energy of Aquarius, which is about global awareness and a sense of oneness. This bottle radiates crystalline clarity, purity and simplicity. It takes you into a space of no thoughts, no limits and no baggage, where all your struggles and dramas can be accepted, dissolved and transmuted.

If this is your bottle, you may have come into this lifetime with such a high vibration that you had to shut down because the energy of third dimensional density was too much to bear. Now is the time to re-awaken so that you can become once again the pure point of light you have always been and take your place in the world as the light-bringer you are. You are ready now to consciously embrace a new dawn for yourself and the earth at this time of global shift to a higher vibration.

This bottle of shimmering light and sparkle comes in with an incisive energy, slicing off the old and welcoming the new. It promises a decisive shift from one state, one way of being to another. "Here," it seems to say, "is your new beginning, your no-holds-barred ticket to life in the new reality!"

The Silver Gaias offer a fresh way of seeing things, a new way to live your life, a step up in vibration. Bottle G28 is the first of these shining lights and as such, it ushers in the new paradigm with a flourish. It reflects, of course, bottle 28 (New Beginnings), even sharing a turquoise fraction. Where bottle 28 speaks of a new beginning in your life, a release of fear and a time of learning to trust the path laid out before you, bottle G28 takes this to another level. This time the 'new dawn' may be more subtle, an internal shift rather than a change in circumstances. It is about awakening to the promise you have always held, the potential that has always been within you. The new dawn is also that of all humanity as collectively we shift our vibration more and more into the light. Choosing this bottle says you hold a unique key to assisting the collective to embrace change and open to unity consciousness.

Bottle G28 has a shadow aspect, however. It can be quite chilly, even frozen – with tears in the silver bottom fraction and a frozen heart in the turquoise above. It could refer to a deep soul grief in a previous lifetime that still carries an imprint in your body. It may relate to a tremendously painful time you have been through in this lifetime that you have never quite managed to let go of. Whatever the cause, this bottle helps break through any locked-in or frozen emotional state, and the tears that inevitably fall bring a powerful release and a reconnection to the deeper, higher truth of whatever happened.

The clear and turquoise of this bottle show that your soul is aware that every moment, every event, every situation and every circumstance is intended to bring you back to the light. This is about your soul's evolution through many experiences to get it back to zero point, the place of absolute love, and the deep cellular awareness that nothing else exists. There is never punishment for wrongdoing, there are only ever loving contracts for the highest good of everyone involved. By selecting this bottle you are recognising that now is the time to acknowledge all the gifts of every experience – no matter how painful it may have been. You are ready now to move to a higher level and step forward into the fresh new light and blessings available to you. The silver in this bottle reflects that light, and the turquoise gently guides you back into the flow. Bottle G28 reconnects you with trust and faith and the deep knowing that you are on track at a soul level and that all is unfolding exactly as it is meant to.

The colours of this bottle relate to your ability to sense and feel your way to a new lightness in your being. It is not about thinking your way there. It is time to let yourself be directed by your internal guidance system – your gut, your intuition, your inner knowing – rather than your mind. This bottle is of the new era, the new light upon the planet, the new paradigm, all of which can truly create a heaven here on earth – and this bottle says you are part of that. Will you step forward now, lifting yourself out of whatever emotional crevasse you may have found yourself in, and take up your role as a creative leader and bringer of change?

The silver in the bottom of this bottle asks you to base your actions on light – the light of the greater good. It asks you to create with your higher heart, with your compass set towards the higher vision of a new paradigm on earth based on co-operation and connection. All your individual skills and gifts can now be brought into alignment with the greater whole, and your uniqueness will be valued and sought after where once it may have been misunderstood or maligned. This bottle indicates that you are a wise soul who has had many lifetimes in the stars and that you bring ancient wisdom, together with light and information from the future, right into the 'now' moment. There is a fearlessness here which means that new pathways can be embraced with ease, and new possibilities explored with joy. There is an energy and swiftness to bottle G28, and if it is calling, you are asked to follow in the direction your heart is leading you. This bottle promises peace and inspiration in equal measure and a very clear awakening to a 'new dawn' for yourself and for the planet.

Bottle G28 Story: Lucy Byng, UK, www.lucybyng.com

My first experience with Colour Mirrors was when Korani came to my house, bringing a number of bottles with her. We talked for a while and she asked me to choose bottles that I was drawn to. At the end of our conversation she asked me to choose the one which resonated with me the most. I chose bottle G28. I took it to bed with me that night but didn't feel like using the beautiful liquid. I wanted to conserve the colour and to be able to look at it, but I did rub some on my hands, then fell asleep.

The following morning I woke having had a restless sleep. I sat up, swung my legs over the edge of the bed and stood up. Immediately I felt odd, changed. I walked towards my mirror to look at my face, and I remember approaching close to the mirror, looking into my eyes and saying to myself: "Something is different."

Suddenly, with no warning, I vomited violently. Shocked, I ran to the bathroom. Just as suddenly, the sickness was gone; in fact, I hadn't felt sick at all. It was almost as if the vomiting was triggered when I looked in my eyes. Obviously I was rather horrified by this and assumed that I had experienced a sudden and very strange gastric event. Feeling OK but shaky, I went downstairs to make myself my morning cup of tea and feed the dog. Whilst I was drinking my tea, I felt itching on my arm. I looked down, and there were three red lumps like large mosquito bites on my left wrist. As I looked, the lumps became redder and more pronounced. Over the next day these red lumps began to get harder, itch more and bleed, as out of them came hard crystal-like shards. It made no sense to me. Confused, I thought about calling Korani but dismissed the idea as ridiculous. I could not imagine that the symptoms had anything to do with the bottles.

The following day the lumps were looking more like red cuts, and the itching was getting better. As I got out of bed and went to the bathroom, I looked down to see blood oozing from two small cuts on the tops of my feet. I wiped away the two trails of blood, and underneath were two red marks. They almost immediately stopped bleeding, leaving red marks like the ones on my wrist. At this point I realised something very strange was happening, but I still didn't call Korani, even though I did want to speak to her. I decided to wait until I saw her next to mention it.

Early the next morning my doorbell rang, and there was Korani. She looked at me and asked me if I was alright, and I said that she wouldn't believe what had been happening. She said that she definitely would and that the reason she had come over was that she felt that something might have been triggered by the bottle.

I sat and talked to Korani and analysed what some of this may mean. I had a realisation that the three places on my left wrist were where I had scars from a traumatic incident that had happened to me about 20 years ago. The incident involved glass, and I think that the crystal-like shards were actually pieces of glass that had come out of my body that had been trapped there since that time. The vomiting I believe was some form of physical manifestation of purging of trauma. Anyway, it was some initiation!

Since then Colour Mirrors has become an integral part of my life. It inspires and directs much of my creativity, and I have combined it with the courses I teach and the paintings that I paint. I am happy to have been able to host Colour Mirrors courses at my house and gardens, both resonating with positive energy as a result. I am beyond grateful for the system and all the wonderful people that I have been lucky enough to meet.

Bottle G29: Children of the Light (Silver/Pale Turquoise)

This bottle is for anyone who has ever found life on earth a challenge, struggled to express who they are or felt a deep inner yearning for 'home'. The colours remind you to connect with the light of the stars and the light in your heart as a way to finally live a blessed life, right here on earth. This bottle takes you beyond the need for emotional dramas, helping you instead to allow, feel and express your feelings in the lightest, clearest and most genuine way. The turquoise in this bottle supports you in accepting all aspects of yourself with total trust, and the silver connects you with all that you have been and are still to become.

This bottle is for you – a star child who brought your light to earth specifically so that you could assist the earth and humanity in raising their frequency. Feel the earth's gratitude for all that you do and all that you are and the blessings of the stars who hold you in their love. The soft, gentle light of this bottle perfectly mirrors the energy of peace and loving-kindness that will create a new reality on earth. This bottle links you to the light of heaven and your role in helping pave the way to a bright and beautiful future for all on the planet.

If you have always felt different, never been fully at home on the earth or have struggled with the density of third-dimensional life, this bottle is a gift to remind you of the value of your light and your presence. When you are sensitive, finely-tuned, creative, filled with dreams, wanting only to tread lightly and gently on the earth and be surrounded by beauty and joy, life here in all its harsh, heavy 'reality' can be a daily challenge. The apparent darkness and density of life on earth has played to each of your wounds and forced you to go within to find the light. It is likely to have been a long and complex journey, and at times you may have struggled to find the light anywhere, inside or out. You may even have felt as if coming to earth was a kind of punishment for some past wrong-doing – yet nothing could be further from the truth. You came because the earth needed your light. You came because you could bring something no one else could: your unique strand of light, gifted to you by the Divine so that you might add it to the light of every other being and weave it into the matrix of a new reality on earth.

You have always known somewhere deep within that Divine light is the true source of life and that it is the only way forward for you, for all of humanity, for the planet. With this bottle you are shown that light will indeed prevail on earth. You are a child of the light and you will be seen and heard and your time will come – is, in fact, now upon you. The silver top fraction in bottle G29 asks you to become conscious of the light: it can no longer remain hidden inside your heart. Your heart is now holding it up and presenting it to your consciousness. "Look at this", it says. "Look at the truth of who you really are. Own it and live it. There is no place to hide anymore, and the earth can no longer support light that is hidden. The dark has ruled with fear and anger and negativity for too long. The light is now claiming its time."

The colours in this bottle reflect the light of the Divine emanating from the higher heart, the energy centre above the heart chakra. This light has largely been kept hidden while the planet has been immersed in an age of darkness and duality. Although this has been a necessary part of humanity's evolution and has had a role to play in our growth and understanding, it is almost done now. It is time for the light to come back and take the reins again, straight from this centre above each human heart. This is the point of light that will bring balance once more, for when the light is this bright, the dark can take its rightful place. Then all will remember that the light and the dark have equal value. Together, light and dark in balance have tremendous power and beauty. The first step is for this sparkling silver light to be consciously acknowledged and claimed as an innate part of each and every being.

The more you expand your capacity to hold the light, the more you are able to be present for yourself, for others, for the planet. As you stay true to your inner Divine light you create a loving, open and gentle space to be exactly who you are, and in so doing, you hold that space for everyone. You are able to be in detached compassion, loving all and rejecting none.

Bottle G29 helps you tap into the wisdom of your emotions and feelings, to fine-tune your response to life through their guidance and to embrace each and every one – 'positive' or 'negative' – as an indication of something to acknowledge, embrace, love and let go. As you learn to welcome all your feelings, allow each one to present itself and reveal its gift, you flow more easily, breathe more freely, live more fully.

This bottle supports you in opening to your creative gifts and sharing them with love. There is a child-like purity here that invites play and creative expression just for the fun of it. Take some time to connect with your magical inner star child who has been waiting to come out. Let go of trying to be like 'everyone else' – you are unique. If this is your bottle, you are asked to remember that you are perfect, beloved and innocent just as you are. Your personality may argue the toss on that, but your soul knows it as a fact.

You are a child of the light, called to remember the light and to know it as the central core of your being. You are a light-bringer and a light-carrier, and you are asked to fully embrace that role now as the planet ushers in the biggest change in frequency it has seen in eons. You are asked to hold firm in your light, to be it and live it, to emanate, explore and enjoy it in all its many forms. Your heart is a massive beacon of light and it has been waiting for this time to open fully and shine out its truth.

This bottle offers the possibility of finding true peace with yourself and your life. It helps you release your tightly-held grip upon the boat you have insisted on navigating into stormy waters and ushers you back into a gentle flow. Surrender to the Divine tide and allow it to carry you.

Bottle G29 Story: Raluca Rusu, Switzerland, www.facebook.com/RalucaRusu.colours

Bottle G29 felt soft and silky, like being on earth could be easy. Having a lot of red in my birth numbers (bottles 18, 9 & C1), I had a lot of resistance to using bottles of higher frequency like the Gaia bottles. Feeling depleted professionally and personally, wondering what to do with my life (basic red questions around getting a new job, changing country, getting closer to my family, doing more for my personal life and playing again that survival game), this bottle came like a miracle. It literally erased all my doubts and heaviness. I came out of the bath with an unearthly optimism. It was like a radical renewal where I knew I could change any aspect of my life in a light way. Any change that seemed impossible to me before felt like it would come naturally, just because the past was in the past and the future was full of opportunities. The vibration was so high that I wanted to share it with anyone who needed some light. After the bath I read the description of the bottle and it confirmed what I felt with deep clarity.

Feedback one week after bathing: It may have felt very gentle during the bath, but I have been shattered during the whole week. Like never before I have the urge to change the direction of my work life and get to something more aligned with my inner purpose (from engineering to something more artsy, nothing to do one with the other). It feels scary, but urgent and necessary. The vibration of this bottle is so high that it allows no compromises.

Bottle G29 Story: Susan McKenzie, Canada, www.susanmckenzie.biz

As I began the Colour Mirrors practitioner course, I realised that I needed to release all the emotions around the departure of my son's biological father at seven months gestation. I realised my son had been fully blasted in utero with grief, anger, abandonment etc. and that he was so miserable every morning because it was like being born every day. The morning after my bottle G29 drunk-with-love bath, my normally miserable 'doesn't speak a word to anyone' adult son began to speak and be pleasant to everyone.

Bottle G30: Wisdom Keeper (Indigo/Silver)

This bottle is the starry night sky and the silver moon, inviting you to venture into the mystery of life in wonder and awe. Let this bottle awaken your deepest, wisest self. Become your own wisdom keeper, and acknowledge that you are the one you have been waiting for. It is time to allow your highest aspect to be the power in your life. You have come through many initiations to get to this point on your journey. Trust in the connection with your wise inner self and live your life based on its wisdom rather than the fears and doubts of your shadow self. You are your own best and truest guide.

As you move from the bright pale turquoise and silver of the previous two bottles into bottle G30, you are met with the depth and darkness of deep indigo, and it is as if suddenly you are asked to face your darkness head-on – and in a new way.

If you look at the numbers of these bottles in terms of your age, it is around the age of 28-29 years that you experience your first 'Saturn return', so-called because Saturn takes approximately 29 years to complete one full orbit around the Sun and return to the same zodiac sign it was in when you were born. For many, turning 30 is a time of looking around and wondering if there is more to life. It is a time when you are called to step up and decide who you are as an adult on the planet, and bottle G30 supports you in this, no matter your age. This bottle could even be called 'The Investigator', for it reflects the stage in your evolution when you begin to look deeper, plumb the depths of your emotions and explore what it is you have come to do in this lifetime.

In bottle G30 deep indigo rests upon the clear light of silver, revealing the interplay between darkness and light in your life and your being. The darkness in this bottle invites you to consciously investigate your own inner darkness so that you can reconnect to the truth of the light you hold within. There is much to discover from your shadow, especially if you do so in the spirit of enquiry, with compassion and the guidance and support of your higher self. When you judge the darkness, it retains its hold. When you open to it with the light of your soul's love, it shares with you its riches.

This bottle's name is Wisdom Keeper, and it is in the darkness that much of your wisdom was formed and still resides. Without your apparently 'dark' experiences through many lifetimes, you would not know even a fraction of what you know about life and love and compassion, nor would you have full appreciation of your light. It is through acknowledging the difficult, challenging and damaged aspects of yourself that you come to know them as signposts and guides, which are only ever there to help you access more fully your light.

Your eternal quest to know yourself as the Divine, to know life, to know light, is quickened and honed by your grappling to know, understand and eventually love all the aspects of yourself that have appeared not to be the light. When you choose bottle G30 it is a sign from your higher self that there is a storehouse of wisdom inside, waiting to be tapped. With its deeply peaceful energy, it aids you in pressing the pause button in your life so that you can go within and bring to light whatever has been keeping you locked in the dark. You are asked to take time to be with your inner guide, your deepest sense of yourself, and be willing to discover what it has to share with you about light and dark and your place in the universe.

Could you bring love to the parts of you that you have deemed unlovable, unacceptable or wrong? Could you be compassionate with the aspects of yourself that are childish, spiteful, angry or afraid? Wisdom Keeper shows you that each and every part of yourself is a facet of the diamond light of the Divine, a gift from your own higher self, connecting you with life in all its fullness as you continue to grow, expand and evolve. This bottle helps you feel supported and loved as you go bravely into the darkness. It assists you in shifting your perspective so that what you have habitually rejected or denied about yourself and your life can begin to become a source of curiosity, insight and learning. This is the true purpose of exploring your 'shadow' – to bring it out into the light of day so that it can be loved and integrated instead of sabotaging you in its efforts to be acknowledged.

If you look up into the night sky as you seek for answers, you will realise that it is only in the dark that you can see the stars. Without the darkness you would never realise that there is so very much more. In the daytime you can see and touch everything in 3D reality, but at night there is a vastness that is almost inconceivable – and you are part of that. You are an integral aspect of the limitless expanse of the universe and although you may feel tiny in comparison, the truth is that this vastness only reflects who you really are in your core.

This bottle holds the energy and wisdom of all your many lifetimes, of all that you have explored and gathered and learned on your human journey. The key is that it judges none of it, loves all of it, holds it all up to the light of consciousness and accepts every piece of it. There is no apology here for placing the darkness at the top of the tree. This is a celebration of your darkness, your deepest and often most unfathomable self. As human beings on earth, the star systems and galaxies beyond our own often appear utterly mysterious, vast, unknowable – and completely awe-inspiring. Bottle G30 asks you to find that awe for your own human path, which has led you into and out of immutable darkness. It is this journey that contributes to your self-knowledge, and it is also this journey that gathers information for the Divine as it seeks to know itself in its totality, in all its colours and shades. Whatever you learn as you grow and evolve is added into the matrix, and this is how the universe – and life itself – evolves.

The wisdom of which this bottle speaks is the wisdom of the ancients married with the unimaginably vast wisdom of the future – and the mind-blowing thing about it is that it all exists within you! You may not yet be able to access every piece of every puzzle in life, but what you begin to realise with the help of bottle G30 is that you do truly hold the universe within. You are the keeper of Divine wisdom and your own wisdom – which, as it turns out, are the same thing. This bottle is a kaleidoscope of riches to be mined and explored. It does not ask you to find answers or surety. Instead it opens you to the extraordinary mystery and beauty of life in all its complexity and magnificence.

Bottle G30 Story: Jackie Tweedie, UK, www.jackietweedie.com

This bottle makes me feel like I'm looking at a starry night when it's really dark, and it feels like there's a huge velvet cloak of safety and majesty holding the world and everyone in it. The presence and draw of the moon at night also speaks to me of the soft but powerful energy of the feminine. There is an infinity to that dark sky and the sheer distance of the pinpricks of bright light/stars that have travelled such distances. It reminds me how infinite I am and how much wisdom is contained in that infinity. It also shows me that I am an expression of that wisdom, and so is everyone else.

For me, no one has any more wisdom than another. We are all Wisdom Keepers, and the reason I love this bottle is because I feel a calling to help people to remember that truth and to own it, and to trust that all our answers can be found by getting still and going 'in' as opposed to seeking 'out there'. The wisdom (our higher self) makes no demands that we should 'know' anything, it just waits until we are ready to realise that we ARE it.

Bottle G30 Story: Sarah Impey, UK, www.sarahimpey.com

I had been having issues with my left eye becoming extremely cloudy, irritated and very sensitive to the light – unbearably so. I could barely open it in the sunlight or under fluorescent or unnatural light, and all I could see was a white, cloudy mist. I always try and get to the emotional root of an issue but it got increasingly bad, resulting in a dash to the eye hospital where they confirmed I had POC (Posterior Capsule Opacification), which can be resolved with laser surgery.

I have a strong belief that the body has the ability to heal itself, and what we focus on, we create. I have not only experienced this myself, I have also seen it with many clients. With some expert help and the guidance of Colour Mirrors bottles I had been trying very hard to shift my focus, working daily on changing my own inner beliefs, getting in deep on a real soul level. I was getting to the emotional root and healing it by looking at the 'cloudiness' that lies within my own 'inner vision' and understanding things that I may not have actually wanted to see about myself.

To fully immerse myself I find I need to get away from words as they are very subjective, so I'm drawn to use Colour Mirrors bottles combined with music to access my memories and visions. When I rested 'Wisdom Keeper' on my chest in the bath I felt a HUGE heaviness, grief and loss in my physical body, especially my belly. I found my mind taking me to a cave and connecting with a heavy, empty, lost feeling.

Jesus was facing me, and all I could feel was this overwhelming emotion as he walked away. I couldn't beg for him to stay, yet felt such massive loss and emptiness, with a feeling of disconnection and separation throughout my body. I then had visions of Jesus, Mary Magdalene and their child, Sarah. I was aware of the immensely powerful love between Mary Magdalene and Jesus, with such huge emotions that resulted from this union and the trauma and heartbreak that followed. I had the realisation that Sarah had no sense of her own Divine light. She had split off and separated from her very own soul and struggled with feelings of resentment and abandonment.

I could see the mirroring of that for me in this lifetime, although the anger and abandonment didn't fully surface until my father passed away. I could never fully see who I truly am – a Divine child of light – as I had never felt fully seen. In that moment I sobbed, a sob like no other, the sound that only comes from the very depths of the soul, a primal sob from the depths of my very being. I knew then why my left eye had gone cloudy some time ago. I was unable to see my light.

My mind then took me to a vision of Jesus, Mary Magdalene and my higher self, all bathed in brilliant, bright light. Mary pointed towards me, indicating the light within me that I couldn't see. At that moment my mind was drawn back to the present and I had a sense of the candlelight flickering all around me. I closed my right eye and stared directly at the flame through my cloudy left eye. The light reflected and refracted and I saw a line of light coming from the flame pointing directly at me, so I placed my hand in front of my face and allowed the beam of light to rest onto my palm, placing my hand over my heart, taking the light into my heart. Then as I stared directly at the flame and the light refracted, I could see a beautiful angel of light.

When I went back to the eye hospital some time later, the cloudiness had completely disappeared.

Bottle G31: Galactic Gateway (Silver/Indigo)

This bottle is as deep as the night sky and as light as the brightest stars, and it reminds you that you have these qualities within you. It asks you to accept both your light and your shadow self so that you can return to balance and release the stories that have kept you stuck. This bottle helps bring subconscious patterns into the light of consciousness so that they may be transformed. It reconnects you with your soul's truth and assists you in creating an inner sanctuary of peace.

This bottle is also a gateway to higher dimensions and the wider mysteries of the universe. Let yourself travel through the gateway to the galaxies and realise that you are so much more than you have believed yourself to be. This bottle encourages you to let go of fear and open to the vastness of the cosmos. Draw the radiant light of the stars into your being and let it activate deep change within you. Your existence matters. It is time now for you to own who you are and your ability to bring about shift and transformation for yourself and for the planet.

Bottle G31 has clear light in the top 'conscious' fraction of the bottle, with deep midnight indigo below. The message of this bottle is that neither your light nor your darkness are anything to fear. Become conscious of the balance between them and you will see that your darkness is, in fact, the very thing that moves you into the light. It is your 'dark' experiences and your shadow self that help you truly discover your light. It is by grappling with your demons, exploring the shadow side of your nature and going through the dark and difficult times that you learn to honour and celebrate the light and discover more of what it really is, what it means. It is through the darkness that you learn to value and appreciate the light, and in so doing, create more light for yourself and the planet. As you grow and evolve through your experiences and step more fully into your light, your need to attract the darkness in order to learn from it begins to fall away, and you discover more and more of the truth of the light that already exists within you.

If this is your bottle, you may have to admit that at times, however, you have refused to engage with the darkness, avoiding it and everything it brings up for you. You may have desired at times only to be in the light, in all its compelling beauty. You may have spent a great deal of time in rejection of your shadow, wanting only to be in the light, to be the light. Denying your shadow, however, may come at great cost. It is a necessary part of who you are and if you simply pretend it does not exist or indeed if you actively bury it, you are likely to live in such suppression that eventually it will burst out in damaged and damaging ways.

Bottle G31 shows you that it is the darkness that holds the light in place. You cannot just be light or you would only exist as pure spirit, with no defining energy or quality to make you the unique human being you are. You cannot fully know something until you see and embrace it in its wholeness, and darkness does exist in this world – and within every human being. When light and dark are brought into balance, however, as we see in this bottle, it is something truly beautiful to behold. The darkness is an essential part of the journey. It is often a space to stop and reflect on what has gone before as well as planting seeds and allowing them to germinate for the future.

When you are going through a dark time, this bottle helps you remember that it is not forever. With the grace and beauty of moonlight, it reminds you that all is well, that all will be well. It offers comfort and support, encouraging you to release your fears. The darkness is only ever part of the story, and you will always emerge out of the dark into the light. Dark and light are yin and yang. Tides ebb and flow. Day follows night. This bottle is a reminder that day and night have equal length, equal value, equal weight, equal power, equal necessity. You are going through a transition, and the moment you face the darkness, the transition will be complete. The shadow will stop being the bogeyman in the corner and become just an aspect of the light looking for its home. Your job then will be to take it by the hand and love it like a little lost two-year-old as you gently guide it back to the light.

Every step you take towards your darkness illuminates who and what you really are. Every piece of darkness within you is a signpost, pointing you towards the unique light that also resides within. Each time you face a shadow aspect of yourself and love and accept it, you step more fully into your light. Every time you sit with a 'negative' emotion and allow it to be what it is, honouring, embracing and loving it without needing to fix, change or 'get rid of it', you take another step towards wholeness. Once you are able to welcome your shadow as simply another aspect of who you are – one that has much to teach you and share with you – you can welcome life in all its fullness, fearing and rejecting less, loving and accepting more. This bottle indicates that you are ready to embrace all that has happened in your life as a necessary part of your learning and growth, and move forward now without fear, hesitation or guilt.

Bottle G31 creates doorways into new and cosmic experiences, some of which may go beyond words. This bottle dares you to open to something beyond your human experiences, to travel into the unknown, to go through the 'galactic gateway'. For those who are attuned to the star frequencies and who feel at home in the vastness of the cosmos, this bottle is like a docking station from which you can safely explore and enjoy the many dimensions of life in every form. But even if you are not familiar with this territory, bottle G31 invites you to stay open. You may try to ignore its nudges or pretend that this cosmic aspect of life does not apply to you – and you are free, of course, to do so. Yet what is waiting for you on the other side of the gateway is so filled with light, potential, bliss and expansion that it might just quieten your thinking mind altogether as it lifts you into a transcendent new space.

This bottle is lit with cosmic codes and higher dimensional frequencies that, even if they make no sense to your conscious mind, may feel 'real' to you on some level. This is where your capacity for alchemy unfolds as you begin to access the deeper mysteries of life. This is where portals open into the star realms and their light streams into your body, your being and the earth. This is where you stand in your own light, on the solid platform of all that has gone on in your life and recognise that every piece of it was perfectly designed to bring you the information you needed in order to learn, grow and evolve. As you look up into the light, you will see that you are held by the darkness. You no longer need to hide. You are self-contained and self-sufficient – sufficient unto yourself, enough for yourself, enough. And from here you can expand into your true lightness, solidly held in the palm of the universe, the galaxies and the star realms.

Pass through the gateway now, out into the stars. Let yourself be shown the fierce and brilliant wonderment of existence. Step off the edge of the void into the vastness of the cosmos, and remember that you are a unique and brilliant point of light – and an essential part of the Allness.

Bottle G31 Story: Moira Bush, Canada, www.moirabush.com

The first time I received an order of these bottles, around 10 of them arrived all huddled together in a row. Light hit the top of the indigo colour and spread out like a carpet, and I saw a beautiful, glittery cosmic pathway that I knew would take me to other galaxies, other dimensions. What I came to realise when I bathed in this bottle was that other galaxies were not places outside of myself. Instead this bottle took me deep into my heart, a sacred place where I could see galaxies inside myself. I know this sounds crazy to think that there are galaxies in our bodies and not 'out there' to explore, but this bottle has the ability to make us look within ourselves and become cosmic explorers without leaving our bodies. The silver in this bottle is the umbilical cord that connects my heart to the cosmos, and every time I enter my sacred heart space and look out of my viewing window, I see a carpet of inky blue and a sparkling Milky Way, just as we see in bottle G31 when it is held up to the light.

Bottle G31 Story: Deborah Wiggins-Hay, UK, www.themindbodydetective.com

One night as I lay myself down, I dreamed I was dreaming... I lay inside a deep velvet indigo dome – the silvery stars sparkling above me. I inhaled and exhaled deeply, allowing the rich, inky blueness of the space to silently slide into my secret places. I welcomed its peace and the stillness it brought as I breathed it in through my nostrils. I felt it running through and down into my lungs and flowing through my alveoli into the fluids that move through me. The deep richness of the space it made began to permeate my individual cells and entered into each blood cell. This 'space' expanded through my very being, and I myself became the rich velvet that makes up the physical fabric of the universe that I existed within. I was all space – all time – and I felt the deep, rich connectedness to all of it through the sense of my own expansion.

I was aware of all, yet as I lay in the dome I also recognised the stars that twinkled above me, each holding a light, an awareness, a sparkling potential that beckoned to me to see it, to interact, to move towards it if I so wished or to simply observe it. And each light was the centre point of a new dance, a new awareness, a new dream that I might choose to interact with if I so wished! As I lay there, just being in the deep richness of expanded-ness of all material things I was a part of, I also saw the potential of all the variations I could chose to play with, to dream, to be or to observe. They saw me too – and winked at me knowingly... Every option lay in my potential and in my awareness. I was it already, but I was also able to simultaneously observe it. And so I closed my eyes to rest upon the calm certainty of being. And as I slept, awoke from the dream....

Bottle G32: The Rose (Rose Pink/Silver)

The rose pink in this bottle reflects the pure love in your heart, and the shimmering silver reminds you that you are brilliant Divine light. With the help of this bottle you can let go of trying to control your world and make it 'perfect' and find instead the hidden beauty in everything, no matter how it appears on the surface. This bottle asks you to let go of seeking approval from others and go within to find the love that is already waiting there. The beauty of the rose garden is the perfect mirror of the beauty you hold inside, and this bottle is a celebration of all that you have been and all you have yet to become.

Bottle G32 has a strong affinity with beauty – which, as has often been said, is in the eye of the beholder. This bottle reminds you that you have a choice to see the beauty in every person, situation or landscape. If you are drawn to this bottle you may be a true fan of beauty and seek it out often, but if you have been letting the demands of life take over and have forgotten to – literally – stop and smell the roses, it reminds you to become aware of and appreciate all the beauty in your life. This planet is overflowing with beauty, and when you open the window of your heart and let it in, you begin to attract and enjoy more and more beauty on an inner level as well as in your outer world.

Choosing this bottle can, however, reveal a tendency to be overly concerned with 'perfection' – the way you look or the face you show to the world – as a means to avoid seeing and feeling the pain you carry within. Perhaps you have a tendency to keep everything on a surface level, using appearances to prevent you from making real connections with others. You may be obsessed with having everything in your outer reality looking flawless and polished, attending to every minute detail, insisting on having your body, your home and your relationships conform to some mythical standard of perfection. This becomes exhausting to maintain and when cracks begin to show, you may go into fear and do everything in your power to prevent losing control, often at great personal expense.

In this bottle the beautiful rose pink hovers above the clear fraction, hanging in the air, ungrounded. These colours reveal a sense of not wanting to fully land on the earth, desiring to live in the lovely, rosy, light-filled realms but being unable to really bring that light down to earth. The clear in the bottom fraction of this bottle indicates tears being held in and a desire to hide behind 'perfection' so that no one can see the vulnerability that lies inside.

Trying to maintain impeccable order in your life is often about feeling deeply insecure, and this bottle supports you in being able to enjoy the beauty of the moment without needing to tightly control everything. By dropping the pretences and opening to the light within, you loosen up and appreciate life more. You also connect more freely and authentically with other people and open your heart to the power and love of the Divine. You begin to see that your 'imperfections' are part of your beauty, part of what makes you a unique individual who is, in the eyes of the Divine, already perfect.

If G32 is your bottle, you may have been deeply misunderstood in this or previous lifetimes, leading you to believe that if you just look the part and play it well enough, you might be safe. If we relate this to bottle 32 (Communication), where persecution meant you could never feel safe to share who you were on the inside with the outside world, bottle G32 is about helping you overturn those fears. There is a connection with this bottle to Mary Magdalene – and if ever a woman was misunderstood on this planet it was she. Much of her true purpose as a bringer of light and equal partner to Christ was hidden, denied or rejected. Much of her story was about how she appeared to the world rather than who she really was. Her truth has begun to come to light now at this time when women are increasingly being seen for who they are rather than how they look. As humanity evolves, every person on the planet will be valued for the light they hold inside, and the spectacular diversity of all life on earth will be honoured, as will the true empowerment and sovereignty of each and every soul.

Bottle G32 is so often chosen by very beautiful women that we began to wonder if its name should be 'Physical Perfection'. There is a fairly common belief on the planet that life must be easier for those who are physically beautiful, yet despite appearances, the very beautiful people in this world are rarely the very happy ones. Their external beauty may be acknowledged, but they often feel as if others only see their physical beauty and not the person they really are inside.

Roses in the wild have prickles and come in all shapes and sizes, whereas cut roses are generally cultivated and only the prettiest and most 'perfect' are selected. A picked rose cannot seed because it is essentially dying from the moment it is cut from the plant. This bottle relates to the cultivated rose, the beautiful woman who has traded on her looks and is now realising that she was 'picked' because of her beauty – but that it will not last. The cut rose has a very limited life span. What is she going to use to survive when her beauty fades, which it inevitably will? She will have no choice but to look for the light within. As she does, she will find that there is beauty of another kind and a perfection that goes far beyond the physical.

If this is your bottle, it is a clear invitation to step into something much deeper and richer than surface gloss and shine. Whether or not you were born with significant outer beauty as your gift to the world, now is the time for you to access your inner beauty. With this you will attract people to you and find that you have much to share with them. If you are called to bottle G32 it is a sign that there is a huge well of love inside you waiting to be tapped. You are a light being who came to be and express love on this planet – the combination of rose pink highlighted and amplified by silver makes this clear. It is time to move beyond the superficial in your life and dig deeper to find the true light, love and beauty you hold within so that you can share that with the world. When you do, this bottle becomes a celebration, a summer party in the rose garden. It promises the joy of being in love with the world and in full acceptance of yourself so that you can create a garden filled with love, light and blessings – whether this is an actual rose garden, something beautiful you create, a project you undertake or even the 'garden' of your life as a whole.

As you open to fully receive the message of this bottle – take it in, take it on and integrate it into your life – love is firmly planted in your consciousness, and your connection to the Divine becomes tangible and real. You come to know and love the light within and find that you can communicate it in loving and heart-felt ways. There is a grace and Divine feminine beauty to this bottle and to the people who choose it, and these are truly gifts to be shared. When you live from a place of inner beauty, you become a magnet for more beauty to show up in your life. Bottle G32 is a sign that you are ready to enjoy real depth, real connection with others and real joy as you open to the truth of your inner love-light and celebrate the Divine taking up residence in your soul.

Bottle G32 Story: Melissie

A mother came to see me with her adopted son who had been born severely premature and who had hepatitis and many other health challenges. She had basically fixed these with diet and love, but came to see me when he was three years old because his doctors wanted to do very intrusive liver biopsies. He chose bottle G32, which has to do with physical perfection, so I told her that he had chosen a bottle that said: "My body is fine!" She had instinctively felt this, so the confirmation for her was huge.

Bottle G33: Love and Miracles (Silver/Rose Pink)

This bottle is about being able to live in your truest state, where love is the foundation of everything. Here is a heart that has never been wounded, broken or abused. This is your true heart – and it is pure, unadulterated love. The silver in this bottle links you to your highest qualities and your greatest possibilities. The rose pink reflects the love you hold deep in your inner being. It is only love that can create a new reality on this earth, and this bottle says you ARE that love. This bottle is your call to inner mastery. Its message is that the fastest way to create miracles is to base everything in your life on love.

In bottle G33 the rose pink of love becomes the foundation of your being, a strong and stable platform from which to take your shining silvery light out into the world. Ease and joy, peace and plenty, riches and warmth – all are available. Relax now into the love of the Divine, knowing it holds you absolutely and eternally. Love is firmly in place at the core of your being, and life is for enjoying – every bit of it!

Bottle 33 (Love and Magic) is about attracting what you desire in the here and now, in the material realm, as you learn to love yourself and open to the magic the universe has to offer. Bottle G33 takes that personal love and magic and expands it out for all, for the planet, for the cosmos. Now the 'magic' of bottle 33 turns into 'miracles'. Now the love and the magic extend into their full spiritual power and become gifts of service. You begin to realise that life is less about 'you' and your desires and more about the love and magic that fuels the entire universe. This bottle is about accessing everything the cosmos has to offer and generously sharing all of it. By the time you are ready to take on the message of this bottle you have an abundance of love and light within you just waiting to shine out into the world, without effort, without need for return, without agenda.

When this bottle was initially created its name was 'Tree of Love', and by choosing it you are signalling that your roots are now firmly planted in love and you are anchored into the new reality on the planet. This bottle asks you to begin to live from the truth of love and magic, love and light, love and miracles – and radiate that energy wherever you go. Let the love inside you become simply an expression of who you are.

The number 33 carries the energy of the Christ, as this was the age at which Yeshua attained Christ consciousness. This bottle relates to everything Christ came to share and teach, and now it is time for humanity to recognise that we are all capable of miracles. Two thousand years ago the level of consciousness on the planet meant that very few were able to sustain the high frequencies of love and Divine light that Christ held, but now humanity is evolving to the point where every individual has the power to hold the light and be the love. There is no need to wait for a 'saviour', deity or enlightened master to create miracles. This bottle says you are the love and you are the miracle! Every individual has a unique piece of the whole to share, each is an integral part of the Allness. You are no exception.

In choosing this bottle you are signalling to the universe that you are ready to transcend the old 'human' stories created by your mind and be part of the shift into a Divine era of beauty, harmony, peace and simplicity on the planet. As you grow and flourish, you manifest love and beauty on the earth. This bottle mirrors to you the love that is at the core of who you are. This is where your Divine self can express love and magic in real and tangible ways. It is where kindness and compassion become more important than being 'right', and love takes precedence over judgement. It is about awakening to the extraordinary in even the most 'ordinary' moments of life. It is about creating miracles simply by being centred in your true light of love.

Bottle G33 shows us that as we all join together in love, we create real, sustainable change on the earth. This is the shift in consciousness the planet has been waiting for. Now is the time for the planet and all of humanity to rise to ever higher levels of light and consciousness, where love underpins everything we are and everything we do. Love is the miracle of the Divine and it is made real through each and every one of us. Let love be your anchor, your talisman, your source and your guide. With love, we will collectively create a true heaven on earth, one filled with love and miracles.

Love and Miracles Story: Melissie

When my boys were little they were arguing in the back of the car, and Stephan and was talking, talking, talking, saying how he wanted to be a big magician and do magic. Davy was going: "Mummm, Mummm, Mummm..." He eventually managed to get a word in and said in a small voice: "Mum, I just want to do miracles." And I so got it. Stephan was doing full wizard-fighting-other-wizards. Davy just wanted to heal the world.

The Magenta Gaia Set

Bottles G34-G36

In 2016 the Magenta Gaias arrived to anchor the whole Colour Mirrors system and conclude the Gaia set, bringing the wisdom and the light of the bottles full circle. Despite being 'earth' bottles, many of the Gaias have a very high and cosmic vibration. In its usual inimitable style the system made it clear that while this was all well and good, we needed something to fully ground it – all its messages, all its nuances, all its love and its light – and the Magenta Gaias do exactly that. The cosmic nature of many of the Gaia bottles reminds you of your vastness and encourages you to open up to the light you have inside instead of keeping yourself small and limited. The Magenta Gaias show you that the whole point of remembering your vastness and your light is to bring it all right here to earth.

The Magenta Gaias, or 'Anchors' as they are collectively known, are keys to help you integrate your Divine self into your earthly physical reality: your body, your home, your work, your relationships and your daily life. These bottles are the tools to help you embrace and encompass all of who you are and everything you came to do as a Divine being wearing a human body. Anchoring your light means that you can express it on the earth in real and tangible ways, making a difference to others and to Gaia herself. As you do so, you automatically contribute to the creation of a new reality on the planet. It is the combined creative force of each and every human waking up to their true nature as a being of Divine love that will bring about a new reality on earth. If we all just float about in the ethers it will remain a wish and a lovely dream. The Magenta Gaias tell us that this is not the plan, that we came to create a new earth, not just to hope it might happen.

So what is this new earth we speak of and how will it come about? It is a place where there is peace and plenty for all earth's living beings. It is a new Eden. It is a place where to be physical is a blessing and a gift to be enjoyed rather than a burden to be carried. It is where you live your unique purpose on the planet in harmony and co-operation with all other beings. It is a place where love, peace and joy are the foundation of life, where freedom is a given, where you know and appreciate your connection to the Divine and to all.

For many, it may feel as if such an earth is simply a pipe-dream, something that 'new age' people speak about, but nothing to do with reality. The lightworkers on the planet know that it is much, much more than this, and yet it has often remained elusive and proven difficult to anchor and make real. Earth has been a place of lessons and hardship, with many painful and even agonising initiations, and you may have found yourself at times wanting to lift out of those experiences and float back up to the stars. It is a human trait when experiencing something unbearable to disassociate from the trauma by lifting out of your body because that feels unimaginably better than to be on the earth, experiencing the pain.

For as long as humankind has existed, life on earth has been almost universally challenging. The Magenta Gaias invite you to understand on a very deep level that all experiences, even the painful ones, are opportunities for Divine love to express itself through you. The rich, dark magenta of these bottles now gently but firmly calls you back from all the places where you have disassociated from life because it has simply been too hard, too horrendous, too much. The Magenta Gaias enfold you in their warm, all-encompassing love and show you the possibilities of a new paradigm on earth, a new experience, a new way ahead. They invite you to surrender up the struggle and let go into the love of the Divine.

It has always been foretold that the earth would shift to a higher vibration, and as more and more people wake up to a greater, more evolved consciousness, this is starting to become real. Change is afoot on the planet at the most fundamental levels and nothing can stop it now. Outer appearances may point to more and more darkness revealing itself, but these are simply the shadows coming to light as consciousness shines upon them. They are coming up and out of the darkness to be returned to love.

Of all the colours it is magenta that most embodies Divine love, and indeed the Magenta Gaias tell us that Divine love is the only thing that has ever been running the show. In truth, this is what Colour Mirrors has always been about. The entire set of bottles was created so that you could be fully seen, completely acknowledged and unconditionally loved. Their purpose is to show you a path out of the woods of confusion, misunderstanding, ego and doubt so that you can truly begin to know yourself as an expression of Divine love. When you open to receive Divine love, self-love becomes possible, even inevitable. You love who you are as you love the Divine, and you love the Divine as yourself – and then it is entirely possible to love all others as yourself, as Divine. The Magenta Gaias anchor the truth that all is one and show us that it is the awakening of oneness within each human heart that will create a new and enlightened earth.

Bottle G34: The Gold Anchor (Pale Gold/Deep Magenta)

This bottle relates to the Golden Gaias. Its message is that you have a specific role to play in the creation of a new reality on the earth and gifts to share in helping humanity evolve to a higher level of consciousness. Your journey may not have been particularly easy up to this point, and you may have felt alone and unsupported at times or as if no one could see you for who you truly are. This is finally your time. This bottle says you are already connected to the power of your authentic Divine self and now you are moving to a new level of empowerment and focus. Let go of any doubt that you are divinely loved and supported. Follow the path of mastery, and anchor your light fully here on the earth. You have an immense and exciting destiny ahead of you.

Bottle G34 glows with life and power. It is a sure sign of hope – a dazzling sunrise – for anyone who has struggled with the difficulties of being human on the earth. It brings a golden promise of brighter days ahead and a deepening sense of your own worth and value. Its colours are the gold of a new and empowered state of being and the magenta of unconditional Divine love. This bottle helps you remember that you have chosen to be here now as the planet lifts itself out of density and darkness to become a much more enlightened creation. You have chosen this time to be on earth because on some level you know yourself to be an inherent part of the shift in frequency that is occurring, and your unique strand of light is needed to help bring it about.

This bottle provides great support for resolving emotional challenges. It shows you where you have bound yourself to ego, run your life on fear energy or created chaos through misuse of power. It helps you find the aspects of yourself you have rejected or denied and bring them back into the loving fold of your Divine self. This is essential if you are to be part of the new reality – you cannot create heaven on earth with your wounds in charge.

As you do the work, plumb the depths of your human experience, explore your shadow and open to more of your light, you come to know deep within that you are an aspect of Divine love – and assist others in knowing it too. This bottle indicates that you have wisdom to share. As you find your inner gold and transmit it, simply by being who you are, you make it possible for others to awaken to their own inner light, wisdom and power. As you embrace the Divine love held out to you by this bottle, you pave the way for true emotional healing, and with the strength and light of gold and magenta behind you, you are empowered to leave victimhood behind and step into mastery.

There is a wonderful dynamism to this bottle. When you are deeply anchored in Divine love you have the capacity to do something with your goldenness, to make a real difference to others and the planet. Your energy becomes inspiring and uplifting, and you contribute to the world through your unique gifts. You may feel called to learn new things, expand your knowledge and share what you discover with the world. You may open to innovative ideas and find empowering solutions. This bottle says you have what it takes to be a spiritual entrepreneur, a change agent, a leader, someone who will help others awaken to their true potential. It also has a strong connection with prosperity: as you fully embrace your golden authenticity, you naturally attract abundance for yourself and others.

As humanity collectively anchors in a golden reality on the earth, a new paradigm arises. The old paradigm has been very much about doing. In many cultures across the globe, an insistence on being busy has led to stress, disconnection and anxiety, yet for many it has paradoxically become a way of life and even a sign of 'success'. In the new paradigm, doing is birthed out of being. When you 'be' peace, or love or joy; when you live in a state of connection with the Divine; when you allow yourself just to be with the moment – then your actions unfold naturally and easily, and your 'doing' is guided, facilitated and supported by the universe. Life becomes simpler and more enjoyable. There is less need to think, plan and control and more space for synchronicity, flow and perfect Divine timing.

Bottle G34 echoes the colours of the seventh and final of the Golden Gaias, bottle G15 (Satori), and brings the promise that was made by that bottle to fruition. It takes Satori's energy to the next level, with even more stillness, more depth and more presence. The possibility of a Golden Age on earth now becomes a reality. This bottle quietly, brilliantly and lovingly holds the space for you to actually get on and create heaven on earth as you discover that you are an anchor for the very qualities and energies that will bring it into being.

Bottle G34 restores you to sovereignty. It connects you with your inner golden light, your wise inner self and a Divine level of empowerment. It brings your solar plexus into balance so that you can be a powerful force for change in the world as a grounded and conscious being. As you embody the messages of bottle G34, you create an earthly 'satori' that touches others with its truth and anchors you firmly into the light of a new era upon the earth.

Bottle G34 Story: Melissie

Korani and I were talking about how when you live the gold and magenta energy right inside your cells, you take that energy wherever you go. We had just seen a post on Facebook where someone talked about walking away from places where the vibration feels low and dense, out of a desire not to be in that energy. We both recognised that impulse, yet we also both felt the power of not walking away but choosing instead to hold the higher vibration. I do play that game with myself sometimes – if I feel something nasty, instead of fleeing I just change my mindset and hold the light, and of course whatever it is instantly changes. This bottle has that energy. It encourages you to be the master of your own reality and to change the energy of planet as you walk around it.

Bottle G34 Story: Sara Di Felice, Canada, www.saradifelice.com

Bottle G34 was probably one of my biggest bottles. I came to Colour Mirrors when the Magenta Gaias were new to the system, and I was really drawn to them. Bottle G34 made me go outside my comfort zone, and I painted my body gold as an expression of anchoring the Golden Age and no longer being invisible. I used to play a game where I felt I couldn't be myself. I thought I wasn't good enough, strong enough, smart enough. Living all in lack, abundance was inconceivable. Bottle G34 showed me that when we are authentic in reality, the abundance follows.

Bottle G34 Story: Sarah Impey, UK, www.sarahimpey.com

With this bottle I had a sense of flying across the ocean towards the sun, the brightest, lightest, golden light. I entered this light, the sun, and it felt very much like a celebration after the time a couple of years back when I couldn't even sit in the sun as I was so sensitive to its light, yet here I was now comfortably in the very centre of the sun's energy. I felt very much part of this golden light.

I was taken back to a previous vision in which I saw golden wings just poised, having been set free, set free from constraints, from the cage, fully free, free to choose. Now being in the centre of this huge energy of the sun it felt so peaceful, like I was the one who was free. Sitting in the centre of this bright light, I felt greeted as if I was a much beloved child. I felt so, so loved. It really felt like 'coming home', coming home to me.

Then two by two, so many parents stepped forward, from so many thousands of lifetimes, all stepping forward as if to greet me. I was aware I had a splitting headache, such an awful thumping, splitting headache. And that word 'splitting' is the perfect description of how I felt: as if I was split in two. All of those lifetimes I had to live one step ahead, in and from my head, living in fear, thinking everything through. Lifetimes of hiding behind a mask, thinking from my head and not my heart. So many lifetimes of persecution for being myself, for being me. All I knew was that I could now feel this split, this pressure of being anything and everything other than my true self.

Then as I saw the magenta and gold of bottle G34, I was shown that it was OK to release these past lives, that the time had come for it to end. An end to the hardship, an end to the mask, an end to all the fear, an end to hiding behind all the many layers and disguising who I truly am. Now it is time to embrace and be the light, to step out, to step forward as me, my true self, in every sense of what it means to be me. It is now safe to be me. I want to embrace every aspect of me.

As I acknowledged and expressed those words, the pressure, the splitting headache and the conflict in my head and heart eased. My heart burst wide open and my mind was quiet.

Bottle G35: The Platinum Anchor (Platinum/Deep Magenta)

This bottle links to the Platinum Gaias, which were created specifically to remind you of your vastness. This bottle reconnects you with the star realms and the immense support they are offering at this time. The pale blue-lilac of the platinum reminds you of the power of the words you use. Whatever you speak can now be brought into manifestation, and with the deep magenta holding you in Divine love, this is a powerful time to create your vision for the future.

This bottle is a reminder of the deep ocean of light that has always carried you. It is similar in colour to bottle G21 (The Beloved) and it too says you are deeply, permanently, divinely loved. These colours help you anchor into the earth in a new way and realise that it is safe now to bring your starry qualities into the world. This bottle facilitates the weaving of practical magic in your life and on the planet so that you can manifest whatever you desire in miraculous ways and use it for the greater good. It opens a portal on the earth through which you can draw into your life the pure, deep peace of the Divine.

After a vibrant connection with the golden earth in the previous bottle, the sudden hush and stillness emanating from bottle G35 may come as something of a surprise. At first glance this is a bottle that gives very little away. If you are drawn to it, you will feel its potency and the beauty of its colours, yet it will keep its counsel until the moment you are ready to dive into its vast, deep waters. This is a bottle that shifts and changes as you look at it and tune in with it. It is quiet in its power and complex in its reach, and it informs you on many levels and in many ways, some of which you may never understand with your conscious mind. Platinum has a subtlety which means this bottle may not be obvious in its effects, doing much of its work behind the scenes.

What we do know about this bottle is that it is a remedy for every time you lift out of your body so that you don't have to feel. It supports you each time you long to escape into platinum, removing yourself from emotions, removing yourself from feeling, removing yourself from pain, clinging to the stars in the hope that if you just wish hard enough you might get to go back there. By adding magenta's anchoring light, this bottle paves the way for you to explore your feelings and emotions in a more empowered way. When the time is right and you are ready, this bottle can bring about a deep inner shift, helping you land in your body and on the planet. With its combination of the higher insights brought to you by platinum and the deep grounding of magenta, it is a great support. Now you can stop fearing and avoiding your emotions and instead access, feel and love them as the guiding lights to higher awareness they have always been.

If this is your bottle, life may not have been easy and you may have wondered at times if there was any point to it. The magenta in this bottle shows you that the difficulties you have experienced have always been a catalyst to lead you towards growth and evolution. You are on track and in alignment with your purpose, even if you do not fully realise it yet.

There are echoes here of bottle 29 (Grace Under Pressure) and bottle 35 (The Inner Guide), both of which relate to lifetimes of difficulty and challenge. Old and tricky memories can be stored in deep magenta, but it also carries the reminder that everything that has happened has always been Divine love making itself known. Even the most gruelling or horrific of experiences in this or previous lifetimes all had their foundations in Divine love. This bottle supports you in forgiving yourself as you forgive God for making you go through those experiences. It helps you clear the many misunderstandings you thought were truths and release the chaos and insecurity they have created. It holds a divinely loving space so that you can finally set yourself free, clear the guilt and come to peace with life. When this bottle's energy has been fully integrated, you may find that rather than taking a limited human view of life you can actually take the Divine's view and see the truth of it all, knowing and accepting with gratitude that it is perfection unfolding.

In combination with the grounded love of deep magenta, the platinum in this bottle opens you to magic, mystery and playful travelling in the higher realms. Once you are solidly rooted in the love of the Divine you can easily explore the wonders of the cosmos without needing to go and live there. This is where you stop hiding out in the light realms in fear and disdain of everything you have judged about the earth and instead bring your light and cosmic knowledge into who you are and what you do. This is the union of your star self with your human self. This is where you get to be the light, free, expansive, rarefied being you are and no longer have to suffer for it. You can now live your light right here on the planet, without fear or apology. The depth of magenta Divine love offers the safety you believed you could never find here on earth – and if you are safe, you can be who you are; and if you can be who you are, you can bring your magic to your own life and the lives of others. This ends the persecution you have experienced through so many lifetimes, where you simply could not be fully in your body or fully on the earth or fully anything except scared. This bottle supports you in bringing out hidden anxiety and fears so that they can be embraced, held and loved back to the light.

The 'otherness' of platinum brings you in to land in a gentle, almost subtle way. It does not grab you by the boots and force you to ground. Instead it loves you unerringly as you finally and consciously place your feet on the earth. It gives you a sense of being of both earth and stars and helps you recognise that you are here at this time because you have a greater purpose: you are here because your light is needed and you are being called to do something with it. Bottle G35 supports you in bringing your higher intuitive wisdom into your everyday life so that it can guide and inform your every step. This bottle helps you awaken a sense of your own inner magician so that you can make contact with subtle flows of energy which, if you follow them, will beautifully guide your words and your actions. You may find yourself offering wisdom, sharing your experiences and opening hearts in ways you would never have thought possible before.

This bottle is also an echo of bottle G21 (The Beloved), whose message is so clearly one of Divine love. The colours are exactly the same, but in bottle G35 the magenta is darkened from soft rosy pink to the rich, dark, intense hue common to all the Magenta Gaias. You can no longer simply flirt with the idea that you might just be Divine and therefore worthy of the deepest love the universe has to give. Now, this is non-negotiable. The Divine extends its hand to you and simply will not let you go. The universe keeps shining its love on you until you are willing to receive it. Your higher self taps you on the shoulder over and over again until you turn your head and listen to what it is telling you: You are love, you are love, you are love! And nothing you think or do or believe to the contrary can change that.

Bottle G35 Story: Katherine Louise Jones, UK, www.katherinelouisejones.com

I remember meeting the Magenta Gaias for the first time when Melissie came to introduce them to us at a workshop. My experience with bottle G35 is something I have never forgotten. I ceased to 'be' in physical form. The feeling I got from the cosmic energy of platinum with the Divine light of magenta was of every cell in my being becoming part of everything. Time/space was suspended; there was no container. I was energy and I was part of everything, with no form or separation. This stayed with me during the meditation we did with this bottle. It felt like an opening into the vast, expansive energy of the creator.

Bottle G35 Story: Nicky Batt, UK, www.facebook.com/ConsciousColourLiving

This bottle supported a client with her father's death. She came to see me a few days before he passed and she was very fearful of how she would cope through the experience of his transition and afterwards. Choosing bottle G35 made her feel SAFE with whatever happened. Through the magenta she realised that the mutual deep love between them would always be there. She related the platinum to the sky and her connection with him, and it brought trust and faith that she would be OK. The sense of oneness in the platinum and the bridge to spirit in the magenta brought a sense of completion, wholeness and a new level of being to her life. I've seen her since her father's passing, and this is still her bottle for him and their love and connection. She feels inner peace, strength and a solidity that all is well and on track.

Bottle G36: The Love Anchor (Coral/Deep Magenta)

This bottle relates to the Coral Gaias, which were created to remind you that you are a Divine being having a human experience. It is only because you have chosen to experience life in a body that you can be part of the creation of a new reality on the earth – a true heaven on earth. Heaven has never been a place 'out there', it has always been about a journey into the heart, which is the gateway to Divine love. The rich, sumptuous colours of this bottle remind you that love is all that exists. Here is true, deep love on all levels: the unconditional self-love of coral supported by the Divine love of magenta.

The number 36 reduces to 9, so this bottle is about completion and the end of a cycle. You now have the potential for exciting and extraordinary new beginnings as you merge your human self with your Divine self. Move forward now into a new era where everything rests on, is created from and returns to Divine love. Let your journey as a Divine human become one of joy, magic and creativity. Surrender into love and come home.

This bottle of coral over deep magenta is simply pure love. It is the clearest picture of love you could imagine, offering true self-love and unconditional Divine love – love top and bottom, love inside and out. It also shows where you are still fighting love, resisting it, withholding or denying it. This bottle draws to the surface childhood hurts and wounds that have been left unresolved and, in perfect love and acknowledgement of the journey you are on, reveals your hidden coral feelings so that you can bring them into the light of awareness.

These are the feelings that make you behave in childish ways, or keep you locked into addictive behaviours and relationships, or make you turn away from others or lash out at them. These are the feelings you have spent your whole life trying not to feel, yet they are indescribably precious and have so much to teach you. When an emotion arises it is because it has information for you to gather about yourself, and by extension, information for the Divine to gather about itself and about life in its totality. By denying the emotion, you effectively cut off the flow of life force energy that is waiting to fill your cells, your heart, your being – and deny yourself and the universe the opportunity to grow and expand. This bottle asks you to stop running from your feelings, burying them or pretending they are not there. Sit with them instead, and love them like you have never loved anything before. If you can do this, really, truly and honestly, you will set yourself free.

There is no doubt that you have been wounded. All of humanity has been wounded, but it is through your wounds that you have learned about your wholeness and through your pain that you have learned about joy, love and peace. Your wounds are not who you are and they do not define you. They are merely one part of the complex weaving of energy that makes up a human life. They are enormously powerful, however, and if you can reach a place where every feeling you have is accepted, nothing is judged as bad or wrong, everything is allowed and honoured as the Divine creation it is, you will step into emotional mastery and a vastly more enlightened life. You cannot enter the Golden Age on the earth with your wounded child in the driving seat, and the deep magenta in the base of this bottle gives you the helping hand you need to fully own your feelings so that you can be part of the collective creation of a new world where love is the essence of everything.

When you are willing to love yourself and every emotion you experience, every behaviour you think is wrong, every aspect of yourself you have rejected, every part of your body you have hated, the Divine swoops in with so much delicious, joyous love that you may wonder why on earth you clung to your hurts for so long. As a being of Divine love, you came to the earth to find out more about what love is. You wanted to know what love is made of, what creates it, what destroys it (or appears to, as in truth, love is energy and can never be destroyed). You wanted to know what it is like to feel totally cut off from it, what you would do, how you would respond. You created experiences and situations to show you love in every guise and lack of love in every form. You have been a student of love, exploring it, welcoming it, shunning it and now, finally, it is time to wholeheartedly embody it.

This bottle asks you to acknowledge that love is all there is, that nothing else exists, that self-love and Divine love are the same thing. The absolute Allness is love, and it is here and it is now. Love is what makes up the body of Gaia and every being who lives upon her and it is the key to literally everything. When you fully get this as a truth in your cells, you are able to recognise that all is unfolding in Divine perfection and resist none of it. You are able to enter the flow of life in all its incredible richness and love every bit of it. This is the new paradigm on earth, where judgement is but a memory and love is the current that informs every moment.

All of this is embodied in the coral and magenta light of bottle G36. When you choose it you are signalling to the universe that you are ready to live life very differently. You are raising your hand to be counted among those who will change the face of life on earth by the depth of your love for yourself, for the planet, for all.

If we stop now and look back at every bottle in the Colour Mirrors range, we can see that they are all expressions of love and that bottle G36 is the culmination of everything in the system; in fact, it is what the whole system has been about all along. It is a clear mirror of Colour Mirrors and of every human, and it is perfect that it is the final bottle in the Gaia set. For now, the system is complete. Yet we also know that magenta is always a bridge, taking us forward into the new and the unknown. So what will come after this? We look forward to the system showing us the way, just as it has always done, with exquisite colours, profound love, and Divine light illuminating the path.

Bottle G36 Story: Sarah Impey, UK, www.sarahimpey.com

When I tuned into this bottle I had a real sense of being on or in the water and noticing the brightest light in front of me – Divine, a God-like energy, getting brighter and brighter with every second. As I focused on that light I was suddenly aware of thousands and thousands of what seemed like people, birds and animals all racing past me, almost like moths to a flame, all ascending towards the light. For some reason I stayed where I was, almost motionless, watching this play out in front of me, watching everything and everyone being drawn towards the light.

All at once the light began to come towards me. I felt drawn towards it and rose up to this light and it felt like a masculine energy. I was aware of a mirror appearing in front of me, and from that mirror the reflection that I saw coming back at me was: God.

All of a sudden it changed, almost as if it was shapeshifting, and I was aware that it was now Jesus and Mary Magdalene that I saw in this reflection – Divine father and Divine mother energy. I realised that this reflection was me, all of the times and the lifetimes unfolding in front of me, the different aspects of me.

I am slowly awakening to the fact that I am God in a body, and Mary and Jesus reflected back to me that Divine masculine and Divine feminine, that Divine mother and father in me. I was reminded that I am, in fact, the Divine in human form and so blessed to be in this body at this time. For many, many lifetimes I've felt abandoned by my body or felt that it had let me down, and in this lifetime I've disconnected and dissociated and hated my body for so many reasons, yet all the time my body had never abandoned me. My body was always my friend and always doing all it could to keep me safe. I realised in that moment that there is no separation. There never was. I was reminded of Jesus and his resurrection, leaving his physical body, ascending and coming back to the earth in his lightbody.

I am a body... I am Divine.... I am of the earth..... I am of the light, I am one with the one... We are all one. We are all Divine. We are all light and we are all connected. When we begin to awaken to the truth, we can reawaken the light within ourselves and our lightbody, bringing the light back to the planet, reflecting that light out so that it can transmute the darkness, allowing the planet and mankind to heal.

Seeing this wonderful partnership and the amazing love between Jesus and Mary reminded me that it is not only light but also love that will heal this planet and that I am – we all are – the anchor for that love.

As I opened my eyes I glanced at the clock: 3.33 = 9. Love and completion.

The Colour Mirrors Essences: Introduction

The oil bottles in the Colour Mirrors range are so bold, rich, varied and complex that we might think they would be the beginning and end of the system. There is another collection of Colour Mirrors bottles, however, and they are every bit as potent and beautiful – and equally powerful as tools for transformation.

The Colour Mirrors essences, or spritzers as we often call them, are perhaps simpler and more subtle in their presentation, less bold in their size and shape, but these carriers of light, colour, energy and information also have a delicious scent, which only adds to the pleasure of using them. They have become favourites of many Colour Mirrors fans for their portability, ease of use, exquisite colours and scents and their ability to swiftly and powerfully shift the energies for people and spaces.

Over the years they have grown from an initial set of seven to 39 at the time of writing. They are divided into several subsets: Angels, Elements, Dragons, Archangels plus a group we are calling Additional essences, those which do not fit neatly into any other category.

There are many ways to use the essences and we invite you to experiment and explore to find what suits you best. You can spritz them into your energy field, onto your body, around your home or wherever you choose to spread their colourful light. One of the most common ways to use them is to spritz some into your palms, rub your hands together and gently breathe in the scent. You may choose just to hold a bottle, meditate with it or place it on whichever part of your body feels good. Try putting one by your bed and letting its energies connect with you while you sleep. You can also pour some into a bath and enjoy the colour frequencies as you soak in them.

As with the Colour Mirrors oils, the key is to choose the essence that is calling to you in any given moment. You can focus on an issue and see which bottle 'speaks' to you, or you can simply go for the one that stands out or looks the most appealing. Do not be too surprised if sometimes you think you are going to reach for a particular bottle and find your hand picking up the one next to it! This happens quite frequently and is just a sign that your higher self is guiding you. Trust that you will select exactly the right essence, every time.

We sometimes refer to the oil bottles in Colour Mirrors as the 'issue' bottles, as they help you delve deeply into an issue, work with it, explore it, understand it, then transform it through love. The essences do something similar, but because they operate at a very high frequency, they do so in a way that is often faster and perhaps more subtle. They can be used for 'push-button healing' – when you are ready to shift or let something go without the need for a deep process.

Scent activates and triggers memories in a way nothing else does. It is one of the reasons the Colour Mirrors spritzers are so swift and powerful in their effects. They often bring to the surface buried emotions and memories, move them into conscious awareness and love them right on out into the light, all in the blink of an eye. Many therapists find that in healing sessions the essences help transform blockages and shift stuck energy incredibly quickly, making the sessions flow with wonderful ease and grace. By asking the client to choose a colour to help them move through whatever is causing them to be blocked or stuck, then using a spritz or two of an essence in that colour, results have been nothing short of miraculous.

The essences help you shift, clear and then integrate your healing and learning, but they may also take you far beyond this into the realms of spiritual evolution. It is when you connect with the 'essence' of the essences that things go to another level entirely. In addition to their luscious colours and glorious scents, each of the essences has its own distinct voice and character. If you tune in beyond your immediate first response, you will find energies and qualities that bring you into a very personal connection with the 'being' behind the essence – the angel, dragon or elemental that overlights the bottle.

As we explored the spritzers for this book, we were graced with the experience of coming to know these beings a little more and getting a deeper sense of what they have to share. They undoubtedly have more to say and we invite you to discover how they communicate uniquely with you as you connect with them. What we do know about the Colour Mirrors essences is that they can take you into higher dimensions, transport you to spiritual heights and pave the way for truly remarkable insights and experiences. For many, the bliss and sense of homecoming is beyond words.

Note:

In the following section we refer to some of the dragons etc. as 'she' and others as 'he'. Archangels are historically referred to as male and have masculine names and here we have referred to them as 'he'. Using personal pronouns simply makes them more accessible, more 'human', but as beings of light and oneness these energies do not, of course, have gender in the way that humans do. Some of them seem to have a more 'feminine' or 'masculine' character and it is only this which has prompted us to refer to them as male or female. You are free to refer to them however best suits you.

The Colour Mirrors Angels

The Angel essences are hugely popular with Colour Mirrors fans for the direct and immediate love, support and guidance they offer. In soft, solid colours covering the spectrum from red to lilac and clear, they assist in fulfilling every need or wish of your inner child – or adult. From helping you find lost car keys to covering you with a blanket of warmth and love, from helping you move through fear to guiding you into higher states of awareness and clarity, these angels are accessible, fast-acting and thoroughly dedicated to your well-being and spiritual awakening.

Angels are beings of pure love, grace and benevolence. They are always with you, even when you forget to connect with them. Because of humankind's experiment with freewill, they will never interfere with your destiny, but they are always available to be called upon and respond instantly when asked for help. Spritzing one of the Angel sprays is equivalent to calling on them, so do not be surprised if you feel their presence, notice a shift in your energy or find that something which appeared unfinished can now come to resolution. If you take a moment when spritzing to breathe in the scent and open yourself to the angel's energy, your connection may be even stronger. These loving beings are ready and waiting to offer their gifts if you will allow yourself to receive them.

Red Angel of Miracles and Prosperity

Red Angel reminds you that you are limitless and hold endless possibilities for miracles and prosperity. This essence reconnects you to your zest for life and brings a burst of energy and power. Use it whenever you need help with a practical aspect of your life such as your health or finances.

I am the angel of money and miracles, and I bring life and vitality into any aspect of your life that has been stuck or stagnant. As well as helping you stay earthed and grounded I energise your body, and if you have a sore back I provide support. When you feel floaty and cannot get up and go, I give you an energy boost and help focus your attention on what needs to happen first. I bring a little dose of fire energy to help you overcome procrastination and get you moving, and I support you in letting go of any negative patterns you use to sabotage yourself. When you decide to take action, I help you choose the right path and the right moment to move forward.

Let me show you how to be fully in your body so that you can attract abundance because it is only when your light is anchored that you can draw the riches of the universe towards you. Stay open and remember to ask for my help because when I am around there is always the possibility of miracles. Use my essence to find a state of detached compassion so that whatever you do is empowered and aligned with the highest good. My message is: be here now. My scent is of Christmas and kindness and the joy of being on earth.

Pink Angel of Love and Partnership

Pink Angel connects you instantly to the part of yourself that is all love and helps you see that love in others. She holds huge love and support for you, so call on her whenever you feel in need. This essence is wonderful for restoring harmony to relationships and bringing love to any situation.

I am the angel of love and warmth, and any time you call on me, I wrap you in a soft pink blanket of love and acceptance. I gently reconnect you to the truth that you are loved simply for being who you are. I have always loved and accepted you and I always will. As my love shines upon you, remember that at your core you are love and you are enough.

Let me help you open your heart and connect with the abundance of the planet so that you can receive all that the universe desires to give you. My joy is to create harmony in partnerships and bring groups together, uniting them in common purpose. My gift is to help you see everything and everyone through the eyes of love. I help you remember that softness is not weakness and gentleness is not a flaw. My scent is of beauty, pink roses and summertime.

Coral Angel of Manifestation and Magic

Coral Angel connects you with the wonderment of magic and helps you manifest whatever you desire in your life. She creates a safe space so that you can let go of control and go with the flow. This essence supports you in finding deep levels of self-acceptance and self-love and helps put an end to abuse and bullying.

My job is to remind you that you are beautiful, loveable and precious. I ask you to see through the lens of self-forgiveness and self-love and remember that your journey on the earth can be as soft and loving as you choose it to be. When you look at the world through my eyes you will see the value and perfection of all creation.

I help you believe in yourself enough to stop anyone from taking advantage of you or denying your worth. Now is the time to manifest your heart's desires because when you use my essence, you come to a place of such self-acceptance that you know you deserve whatever you desire. My soul purpose is to remind you that you deserve every good thing in life. You are enough. You are loved. My scent is the warmth of joy and the bliss of pure love.

Yellow Angel of Joy and Wisdom

Yellow Angel helps you tune in with your inner wisdom and guidance and is an excellent support when you require focus and concentration. This essence connects you to the fun and playfulness of your magical inner child, supports you in letting go of fear and helps you make space in your life for joy.

When you use my essence, the radiant light of joy shines on you so that you can remember how to be happy and silly and playful. I am here to help you let go of stress and confusion and enjoy life with a smile and a light heart. I awaken your inner confidence so that you learn to value who you are and what you do and stop trying to be something you are not. I bring comfort, ease your fears and soften your solar plexus when it is tight and tense. When you are stressing over studies or exams I help you relax and recall the information you need to know. My joy is to see you remember your inner strength and light. I help you switch off when your mind is over-active and return to a state of peaceful contentment. My scent is sunlight on yellow roses and my energy is carried on the laughter of children.

Gold Angel of Ascension

This essence is expansive and empowering. It instantly balances your solar plexus and connects you to your 'I AMness'. It strengthens your energy field and brings it back to its natural state, removing any interference. Feel your feet on the ground and your light expanding as you breathe in this scent. Gold Angel connects you to your Divine self and the new golden earth, where all is one and you are an integral part of everything. As you expand into that awareness, fear and confusion dissolve and you become clear and powerfully present with what is. When you are this Divine and you claim it, all smallness disappears and everything you see reflects your authentic, powerful Divine self.

I am embodied light and power. I ring like a bell of truth in your heart as you connect with me. I remind you that you are this powerful, this beautiful, this glorious, this beloved. I remind you that you are a way-shower for others, a beacon of light, a golden glow of warmth. I bring strength and fearlessness and open your heart and mind to new ways of being, free from the limitations of the past. I bring hope to the planet for a new future, one that is bright and golden and filled with joy. My scent is lightly spiced, with a subtle fragrance of sacred incense.

Green Angel of Healing, Trust and Harmony

Green Angel opens you to a new space of trust and healing where you can create harmony within yourself and your life. It takes you into a space of panoramic awareness and connects you with nature and the plant kingdom. It is brilliant at clearing spaces and helping you disconnect from other people's dramas. This essence brings a fresh, clear energy to any space or situation.

I am wrapped around your heart to remind you of its strength – because your heart is the part of you that actually runs your reality. You might think it is your mind, but I hold your truth. I know your heart and if you trust me, I will always support you to make the right decision, find the right direction and be in the right place at the right time. I remember what you have forgotten, so I can help you access your memories, even your past lives, and remove the negative energies of memories that no longer serve you. I support you in breathing more freely and expanding your lungs so that you can take in more life with each breath. I clear the energy in spaces and bring spring into rooms that are heavy with winter. I create a sense of spaciousness and expansion so that instead of feeling burdened and restricted, you become open-hearted and free. My scent is green apples, spring meadows and the freshness of a new dawn.

Blue Angel of Protection and Communication

Blue Angel helps you relinquish control and speak freely. Feel its wings envelop you and know that it is safe to speak your truth. Whatever makes you feel separate from Source can now be let go. As this essence washes over you it clears everything from your sinuses to your soul and brings clarity to your breathing, your mind and your emotions.

I am your guardian angel. I walk beside you all your life, guiding and protecting you and gifting you with a sense of safety. I support your voice and your ability to communicate. I connect you to your inner Divine light and your blueprint, the plan you set up for this lifetime. My help is also practical, so use my essence when you have hay fever or sinus infections. All the little stings and burns of life, I ease and calm for you. All the tears you cannot cry, I help you release. I bring peace to father or authority issues and any difficulties you may have with the masculine side. My scent is cleansing and fresh and rinses away any unhelpful beliefs you are clinging to in the mistaken belief that they are serving you.

Platinum Angel of Oneness

Platinum Angel carries a pure, high vibration and shines light into all the dark corners of your being. This angel helps you see the bigger picture, free yourself from emotional turmoil and create a beautiful reality with ease. Using this essence helps you communicate beyond your ordinary human senses and connect with beings of light, masters, guides and the star realms. This angel and your higher self together will guide you on your Ascension journey and help you remember that you are not alone. This essence supports you in clearing issues of separation, reconnecting with the oneness of life, and igniting the light of gratitude in your heart.

My voice is the collective voice of all angels. I am not one but everything, just as you are. In your heart and spirit you know there can never be anything outside of the whole, which is love, which is Divine, which is all that exists. I am here to show you the interconnection of all life and the freedom that comes with knowing yourself to be one with the Divine. I am love in a form you may not have seen before, for I am the love of all the cosmos, so vast that your mind cannot take me in. This is why you must feel me with your heart, for I promise you that there, you are as vast as I am. I exist to remind you that you are limitless light and nothing and no one can diminish you. I help you soar and sparkle and shift your perspective so that you can see the Divine in everything and everyone. Call on me and I will help activate your projects and bring ease to your tasks. My scent is a gift from the Elohim, the creator angels, and it transports you to the heavenly realms.

Lilac Angel of Prayer and Forgiveness

Lilac Angel brings in the energy of your higher aspects, connecting you to the Divine through prayer and meditation and bringing healing through forgiveness. This angel guides and supports you in any situation and helps you release the past so that you can move forward. This essence is a wonderful support to help you access past lives and brings healing to any issues that are still affecting you in this lifetime.

I am your guiding angel and I speak with the voice of your spirit. Breathe in my essence in the silence and you will find answers to all your questions. I work with the ray of magic and transformation and the energy of the cleansing Violet Flame so that all negativity and darkness can be transformed and brought back to the light. When I am around, wishes can come true, so use my essence to ask with intent, faith and expectation. With my help you can let go of sadness and grief, for I bring deep calm and the knowledge that while your soul is in charge, nothing can go wrong. My scent is the warmth and peace of lavender flowers and gentle summer rain.

Clear Angel of Purity, Grace and Clarity

Clear Angel shines pure clear light into your body, your being and your surroundings, bringing you closer to a state of grace. This essence brings clarity to any situation and helps shift stuck energy.

I am the angel of grace. I bring light to everything that is hidden in the dark and crystal clarity to all your dealings. My job is to bring transparency when the energies around you are dense, foggy or difficult. I help clear confusion, anxiety and depression, and when negativity weighs heavily upon you, I bring lightness and a fresh perspective. I clear spaces of murky energies and help you find the blessings in challenging situations. My gift is to teach you how to live lightly on the planet. My scent carries the rainbow and is like a warm caress, restoring everything to love.

The Colour Mirrors Elements

The elements of earth, fire, metal, wood, water and air are fundamental components of life on the planet. We all relate to and make use of them in our everyday lives in some form. Each element has particular qualities and characteristics which support and nourish you and connect you with life and nature. The Colour Mirrors Element essences encourage you to be *in* your life, experiencing it with your senses, engaging with it whole-heartedly, exploring it to the full. They remind you to embody your light in ways that are tangible and practical so that what you do and how you do it make a real difference on the planet. With their bold, powerful colours they keep you centred during transition and transformation and offer support on all levels – physical, emotional, mental and spiritual.

When any aspect of your body or being has become depleted, these essences restore, replenish and rejuvenate. When you are drawn to an Element spritzer, notice its messages, use its colour power and breathe in its scent to bring balance to your inner and outer world. The colours and energies of the Element essences harmonise beautifully as a set, reminding you that each element is only one aspect of life and that, much like humanity, when all come together, each can fulfil its purpose and potential.

Earth

This essence is instantly grounding. It connects you with Gaia and attunes your heartbeat to the heartbeat of the planet. It reminds you that you are of the earth, as is everything you create. A strong connection with the earth is deeply reassuring and nurturing, and manifesting your desires becomes easier and more joyful when your spirit is fully grounded. Gaia is always there, a true example of unconditional love, helping your body feel safe so that your spirit is free to shine. This essence helps you remember that you and the earth and everything on the earth are one.

I am the Earth elemental and I help you land on the planet when life makes you want to disengage and float away. I earth you when life feels shocking, bringing you and your spirit gently into balance as you come back into your body. I calm your fears, and when you have shut down your heart because it has been too painful here, I help you feel safe to open it again. I show you how to fall in love with your life and the earth when you forget what an amazing gift it is to be here. I remind you of the beauty of bringing your exquisite soul into a grounded state where anything is possible. I encourage you to share your brilliance.

Feel the gentle, loving support I have held for you through all your many lifetimes and know that you are safe now to land fully on the earth. I have always been at your feet, holding, loving, supporting and guiding you, and I will continue to be here as long as you are in a body. As you make contact with my deep support, remember that dreams cannot drift into being but need your feet on the ground in order to become real. Feel the rich sense of belonging, comfort, reassurance and stability I offer and know that whatever you desire is in reach now, with my blessings.

If you feel into my energy you will find that I am immensely powerful and not in need of rescuing, nor do I judge anything that has ever happened to me or on me. I simply hold an infinitely loving space for you and all of humanity to learn and grow. My love for you is eons old and deeper than you will ever know. I am so grateful you have chosen to bring your light here so that we can grow and evolve together.

Fire

This essence is about initiation. It supports the mindset you need for a fire walk or anything that requires mind over matter. It connects you to your magical self who is capable of superhuman achievements. This essence helps you find courage and the ability to stand up for yourself. It awakens your passion for life, reconnects you with your creative power and helps you burn off all that is not essential to your journey.

I am the Fire elemental and I see the fire within you, the powerful fire light that swirls at your core. Even if it has remained dormant for much of your life or seems to have gone out, I assure you it is still present. Let me help you re-ignite it so that it can burn brightly again.

I hold a light of calm support when life is shocking in its intensity and everything around you seems to be exploding. I bring warmth when you are frozen and reawaken your vitality when you have shut down. I bring courage and comfort when you find things hard to bear and awaken boldness and strength when you feel timid or weak. I activate passion and excitement when you feel flat and discouraged and bring regeneration and renewal when you have burned yourself out. When you feel unloved, unsupported or unsafe, I share with you my warm and nourishing light.

I assist you in releasing anger and frustration so that you can stop resisting and actively engage with life. I help you burn off whatever is no longer in alignment with your truth so that you can blaze a path through life that is uniquely, divinely yours. With my bright fire energy, I support you in opening your creative channels, reconnecting with others and receiving life's gifts. Most of all, I encourage you to expand and evolve into your full, glorious potential.

Metal

The Metal element connects you with your ability to create magic and alchemy. It helps you turn dark issues into light and transform problems into solutions. This essence connects you with your inner power. It reminds you that you are Divine and golden and fully deserve all the Divine abundance life has to offer. Use this essence when you require clarity, focus and mental strength.

I am the Metal elemental, an alchemist and magician who helps you access your own inner magic so that you can manifest whatever you desire. I help you transform everything that is heavy and dense in your world into lightness and ease. When you are beholden to limiting beliefs that keep you small, I assist you in letting them go and opening to the power and potential you hold within. I stand in my own power and light so that you remember how to do the same.

With my guidance and support, tap into the vibrant, powerful pulse of creation in your heart and belly and find the nuggets of gold hidden inside you. Together we can make gold out of lead, light out of darkness, magic out of dross, wonder out of the commonplace. If you ever feel dull or worthless, let me remind you that you are precious and valuable to everyone in your life and to the universe itself. Use my golden light to help you discover and activate the unique gifts only you can offer the world. Remember how strong and powerful you are.

I am the alchemical change that helps to shift the planet into the fifth dimension – and your part in this is vital. Let me stand beside you as you take your place as a way-shower and light-bringer for your fellow humans, leading the way to a bright new future on the earth.

Wood

The element of Wood relates to the liver meridian. This essence helps you deal with unexpressed anger and negative emotions stored as toxins in the liver. It connects you with your body elemental – the deva or overlighting energy of your being – which holds your body's blueprint. It helps you foster a more positive self-image and a more loving relationship with your body. Wood reconnects you with the power of Mother Nature and the elemental beings who support her.

I am the Wood elemental and I am a tonic for your senses. I sweep in with the freshness of a spring morning and remind you to connect with all of nature, and trees in particular. These are beings of great beauty and strength who have much wisdom to share. I help you remember what it is to be as vast as the oak and as deeply rooted in the earth. I remind you to lift up your eyes, heart and mind to the heavens, just as the tree lifts its branches towards the sun.

I hold the energy blueprint of your body's true potential. When your body feels heavy, stiff or unhappy, my fresh scent and energy move you towards lightness, clarity and freedom. When you feel angry and agitated, I bring stillness and peace. I remind you that your body is the wonderful creation that houses your spirit. I ask you to honour your beautiful gift of a body, for it is one of your greatest teachers and is always doing its very best to support you. Your body is created by every thought you have about it, and I ask you to become more conscious of the messages you give it.

I help you unwind physically, mentally and emotionally so that you can let go of anger, resentment or any other toxic emotions you have buried in your cells. I encourage health, growth and renewal. As I am linked with spring and the creative essence of nature, I am deeply supportive of new projects and help you move forward and venture onto new paths.

Water

The Water element is a great support when you have been blocking your emotions or holding them in. When you feel stuck, this essence helps you access your true feelings, express them appropriately and release them. As you free your blocked emotions and the issues they have caused, the Water element brings you into the beautiful, natural flow of life so that you can enjoy it all.

I am the Water elemental, and you can call on me to guide you back into flow any time you feel stuck. I help you remember that the magnificence of feelings is that they make you human and connect you with others and with life itself. I help you access your feelings and bring to light any that are unresolved, because all feelings – even anger and fear – ultimately lead to healing if you let yourself fully feel and express them.

When you are unable or unwilling to shed tears, I create a gentle healing space until you are ready to emerge, cleansed and renewed. When you feel that nothing is moving, when you are blocked and resisting, I flow through your life bringing shift and transformation. When you feel heavy or stagnant, I bring the gift of clearing and lifting the energy so that you feel light and ready to move forward. I may quietly enter your life like a gentle stream to ease you away from old habits and patterns, or I may rush into your life like a torrent when you are clinging to the very things that keep you stuck – and yes, that may feel scary for a time, but do not fear. I am one of the essential elements of life itself, and I am totally on your side. I support you as you let go and encourage you to dive into the depths, knowing that freedom is to be found there.

Open to my power and let yourself feel clear, revitalised and alive. I am water, the water of life. I am the water of your body, your earth and your being. I have the deep, still strength of rivers and oceans. I sparkle with joy like a waterfall after rain. When I flow with my full force, I can move mountains.

Air

This essence carries the energy of the moon and the cycles and tides and reconnects you with your stellar origins. It puts you at peace with the unfolding perfection of what you have created and lifts the energy so that you can see the bigger picture. This essence connects you with ancient female wisdom. Use it when a problem needs a feminine slant and for any female issues such as menstrual difficulties. The Air element connects you with the breath and opens you to trust and inspiration.

I am the Air elemental and I bring fresh air into any room or space that feels cluttered or stale. At this time of transition on the earth I blow in like fresh air through the cobwebs of your mind, helping you breathe freely and think clearly. Like the Divine, I am all around you and everywhere within you. I connect you with your spirit and expand your capacity for ideas and inspiration. Breathe in my scent and remember that you are so much more than your body or mind.

I am linked with the moon and the moon goddesses and hold ancient feminine wisdom and power. I remind you of your lifetimes in the ancient mystery schools and heal the trauma of those times when masculine power attempted to undermine and suppress the feminine. I help you set down the feelings of burden and responsibility you have been carrying through the ages and breathe freely again.

You need no longer bear the burden of guilt for being female, for being born into the 'wrong' body, for not doing enough, for simply existing. I hold the space for you to feel completely at home as the unique Divine being you are, shining like the full moon in the purity of your own true light.

The Colour Mirrors Dragons

Dragons have a special place in mythology, appearing in the stories and legends of many cultures throughout history. Often they are depicted as beings of power, domination and aggression who arouse fear in the hearts of humankind. Many are the stories of dragons portrayed as demons who must be 'slayed' or fire-breathing monsters who must be tamed. Colour Mirrors dragons have a different take on the story: they are dragons of light who represent your true, Divine, authentic power and help you access it. We have seen so many people when they connect with these shimmering colour dragons truly experience their own power in their body – perhaps for the first time ever.

These dragons are enormously empowering, but they also bring a sense of love, laughter, joy, fun and friendship. They help you fly when you get stuck and anchor you when you find it hard to keep your feet on the ground. They cheer you up you when you are down and offer stability and support when you find it difficult to cope. Their role is to assist you in reclaiming yourself as a Divine sovereign being who is of the sky and the earth and can flow easily between the two.

Copper Dragon

The Copper Dragon is an ancient Chinese dragon who holds all the ancient feminine knowledge of the earth. This glowing dragon shows you what it means to be a powerful female. She knows what she knows and is so firmly rooted in her Divine power that she takes away all your doubts about who you really are. This dragon helps you release your judgements about the difficulties of being on the planet and being human. She holds the same qualities of magic, compassion and mercy as the goddess Quan Yin – whose favourite way to travel was on the back of a dragon – and she offers them to you. This essence is very helpful for people who practice Reiki or any form of energy healing as it supports and empowers your healing abilities.

I bring shimmer and sparkle into your life so that you can remember the joy and fun of having a body and being on the earth. I connect you with the energy that is required for any form of healing – and if you have always thought that the energy for healing comes only from above, where you believe your angels and guides are, think again. It comes also from the depth of Gaia, who loves you enough to share her deep wisdom and energy with you.

Dragons are earth angels who have watched over you from the first time you set foot on the planet. We create a portal for you to access the incredible energy of the earth and utilise it in your healing work. I am here to remind you that the earth is Divine, that there is no up above and down below. It is all one. What is above you is below you and it is all Source and all accessible when you tune in to the energy. I hold a very safe space for you to grow, explore and flourish on the earth and to find the place you call home, both inside of you and in your external reality.

Red Dragon

This dragon brings understanding, empathy and compassion into any situation where there has been anger and resentment. His power is huge, and he knows that no matter how much blood has been spilled on this earth the only way to heal and move forward is through love. Use this essence when your anger feels as if it can never be appeased. Red Dragon brings forgiveness and puts you back in your power again, showing you that you can never fight it right, you can only love it right. This essence helps support, strengthen and align your energy body so that you can feel calm, centred and clear.

I am here to help you any time you feel overwhelmed with anger and wish to return to a state of clarity. Anger blocks your ability to think clearly, and my gift is to help you get grounded and present again when the anger has knocked you off balance. I help you understand what it was that brought your anger to the surface and show you that what you thought was the cause was undoubtedly just the trigger of an old hurt. You may even find that the current situation is nothing you need to respond to. Once you have clarity, it is much easier to see all sides of the story and find compassion for everyone involved, particularly yourself.

My purpose is to bring you back to your centre so that you can find your truth again – because you are much bigger than the situation, and compassion will serve you much better than anger. I am grounding and loving and can clear the air in miraculous ways. I hold enough love to support you in any difficulty. I also have a little twinkle in my eye that reminds you to find the humour in any situation and not to take yourself too seriously.

Pink Dragon

This dragon gently shimmers into your life when you need to be reminded that only love exists and that it is time to play and not be so very serious and adult all the time. She brings love in her wake and laughter. She appeals to little ones of all ages and knows about a happy childhood at any age. She awakens your magical inner child with joy, love and laughter. Use this essence when you feel sad, down and unloved.

I love you, and I have come at this time to hold a space of such love and joy that you cannot help but smile. My purpose is to help your little inner child giggle and bubble with joy and fun again. Feel my power – which is love – and know that your power is the same as mine, and it is immense! Nothing is more powerful than love, and nothing is more important than joy. I am here to remind you to play, enjoy life and find things to get excited about. I am the dragon of Ascension because my whole being is infused with love and joy. This is your natural state and the fastest way to raise your vibration. I help you keep laughing, and in that joyous laughter, together we lift the frequency of the planet.

Gold Dragon

This dragon activates power – true raw power that brooks no argument. He can and has moved mountains, and he reminds you that you can do the same. He is rich, abundant and wild and helps you access these qualities in yourself. Use this essence to reconnect with your ancient wisdom and your ability to see clearly. This dragon helps clear imbalances of the third eye, as gold is the complementary colour to royal blue, which relates to the third eye. His ability to see beyond the ordinary is a gift that he willingly shares with you. This essence helps you release judgement about what you have perceived as abuse of power and supports you in consciously and magically creating all that you desire.

I sweep into your life with fire in my tail and light in my eyes to remind you to claim your Divine power. Feel the life force beating in your heart and know that you have everything you need to live an extraordinary life. You are not a victim but a glorious, magnificent human, created in the image of the Divine, with all the same qualities. Never forget that your strength, courage and wisdom can achieve the seemingly impossible. I awaken in you a fearless, empowered light that has always been yours but that you may have forgotten for a time. You cannot pretend to be small with me around because my vastness and brilliance are reflected in you. Never forget that you have golden sparkles in your soul.

Green Dragon

This dragon brings in new beginnings and the energy of spring. He makes you feel safe when everything is changing and you are overwhelmed with anxiety. His healing love brings peace to your heart and to the planet. He knows about cycles and seasons and the benefits of change. He holds deep compassion for the planet and for humanity, who – out of fear – killed the dragons and forced them into hiding. This is his time. The healing has started now that he has awakened. This essence helps at a deep level to release the judgement of death. Humanity tends to judge and fear death more than anything else. With the help of this essence you are shown another perspective and can begin to see it clearly as just another step in your evolution and another new beginning.

Change is the only constant, and my green sparkles help you find peace with it, while my clear essence reminds you that every change exists only to bring you closer to the light. I am kind and loving and wrap you in my comforting energy when you feel scared. I remind you that all change exists for your highest good and that life and death are just aspects of the cycle of creation. Energy can never die, it can only change form. With my help you begin to see every change, including death, as a creative act of the universe and not something to fear. I represent spring, new growth, rebirth and fresh new perspectives.

Turquoise Dragon

This dragon holds the energy of the new era on earth. She brings together the elements of air and water so that heart and mind can come into perfect balance. Her gentle yet powerful support comes as a wave of peace and harmony, relieving fear-based projections about the future of the planet as well as your own personal fears. In Chinese mythology the goddess of mercy and compassion, Quan Yin, rides on a turquoise dragon, and this essence helps you carry mercy and compassion into all your life experiences. It helps you open your higher heart chakra, the place from which you connect to the oneness of all life. This dragon is of the stars yet deeply grounded, and she shows you how to be the same. She is the embodiment of Aquarius and the one to reach for when you are ready to go global.

I bring peace and calm, ease and flow. I am a breath of cool air when emotions get heated, helping you let go of struggle and surrender into serenity. I support you with technology and fly in to clear up any kind of technical glitch. With my ancient wisdom I bring softness, love, kindness and compassion into any situation. With my links into the future I bring hope on my wings, clearing the path, lighting the way forward and welcoming you to a bright and shiny new day. I remind you to trust and flow and touch life lightly as I do.

Royal Blue Dragon

This dragon's tail is the Milky Way. She is vast and mysterious and holds the knowledge of the stars within her being. She is ancient and wise and remembers your starry incarnations, reminding you of those lifetimes when you knew who you were and had not taken on your human smallness. Feel her shimmery power in your energy field and remember where you came from. This dragon helps you connect with your angelic support and is good for opening the third eye so that you can view life from a higher perspective.

I am a star dragon, carrying the light of the galaxies in my being. I hold all the memories of who you really are, even if you have buried them so deeply in your cells that you struggle to access them. Let me help you bring them to the forefront of your mind now, for when I appear in your reality I am asking you to stare into the cosmos and find the deepest truth of your being: you are stardust – a star that landed on earth.

Perhaps your arrival was light and filled with ease, but perhaps for you it felt as difficult as for an immigrant baby ripped from the warm comfort of its mother's arms. If you have never felt safe on the planet, I am here to remind you that you brought the stars with you. You were not abandoned. You are the stars' connection to earth, chosen to bring starlight to the planet because of all the light you hold. I am here to remind you where you came from, how vast you are and how infinite. Your light is eternal and precious, and I am so blessed to be by your side as you journey through life.

Lilac Dragon

This crystalline dragon is the lightest of all – where light means the opposite of heavy as well as dark. She floats up high and nothing can weigh her down. She has come in on the lilac ray of magic and miracles and can go back into the dark past, dropping a crystal light bomb on ancient events and memories and removing them, not just from your own memory but from the collective. This dragon can clean up history. She brings such clarity and light into your body that you can see clearly into the past and the future, and wherever you turn your gaze the light simply sweeps the darkness away. Once she has transmuted all those old, dark memories she helps clear your consciousness so that you can access your inner light self again and the ancient magic that has been hidden from you can be revealed. This dragon carries the light of Lemuria. She reminds you of the grace, purity and lightness of being that you hold within your cells from your Lemurian lifetimes so that you can access it all again now. This is magic with an instant, light and loving touch.

I exist to help you with transitions and transformation. I bring understanding into difficult situations and hold you while you transform your oldest, deepest patterns. I remind you that everything is on purpose and there is no such thing as a mistake. I help you climb out of the abyss of sadness and grief, and gently lift you out of old, stuck emotions to a place where you can find peace and lightness of spirit. My support for you is rock solid, and I will never let you fall. I remind you that there is magic everywhere in the world, including within you.

Black Dragon

Black Dragon represents death and rebirth. He relates to the phoenix, which is always reborn more beautiful and powerful than before. This dragon reminds you that the journey is an endless series of deaths and births – and that is OK. He is black with silver sparkles, indicating that in the darkness there is always light. His gift is to help you find light in the darkness and remind you that there is a bigger picture. Endings are always beginnings and every step along the way is for your highest good. Black Dragon helps you release judgements around death and darkness and what you have considered evil so that you can find love and compassion and know that the dark is just light in another form.

I am here to help you see in the dark and remind you that the light and the dark form one sacred circle. When you are in the midst of a dark night of the soul, I hold you for as long as you need me to be there. You do not have to climb the whole mountain ahead of you, for there is a tunnel to accelerate your journey towards the light and I will show you the way through it. Even if the darkness scares you, there is nothing to fear when I am around. I am deeply peaceful and quiet, and in the darkness and silence of my presence you can find all the answers you have been seeking.

White Dragon

This dragon is complementary to the Black Dragon. She holds the same energy of bringing light into the darkness and a reminder that night and day have equal value. She relates to the light of the moon and reflects to you who you really are, giving you the opportunity to stop judging what you see in the mirror and love it instead. She is wise and gentle, bringing clarity and lightness into heavy situations and supporting the process of grieving. This dragon is most helpful when it feels as if the road ahead is too dark to carry on. She brings relief when there seems no reason to continue. She is the light at the end of the tunnel. She is the rainbow of hope after difficulties. Love yourself enough to let her in and she will carry you.

Trust in me. I hold a pure rainbow of light for you, even when the darkness seems hard to bear. When you are lost in the tunnel I am there for you, reminding you that the tunnel only exists to get you back to the light more quickly. I stay by your side through the dark night and carry you safely into the fresh light of morning. I help you remember that each time you come through the dark into the light there is a new, higher level awaiting you.

It is my role to bring tranquillity and harmony where there has been turbulence and doubt, and at this time of shifting energies I help your body feel safe to move into lighter and higher frequencies. You are moving so fast now that your body needs some extra support, and I am glad to assist. Let me shine a radiant light of purity into everything that has felt difficult so that you remember the truth of your inner Divine light. May my rainbow light always remind you that life is sacred and you are truly precious.

The Colour Mirrors Archangels

For many years Metatron was the only Archangel essence in the Colour Mirrors system, and from almost the beginning he has been one of the overlighting energies. As his colour is magenta, the colour of Divine love, one of his key roles is to help you recognise the Divine hand in every aspect of your life, from the smallest to the greatest. It is said that Metatron was once human but maintained such purity that he was elevated to the highest realms from where he now serves humanity. As an angelic being who understands both the joys and challenges of being human, Metatron is a powerful ally on the Ascension pathway, guiding, supporting and holding you in his infinite love.

In 2018, as the Ascension game stepped up a gear, four more Archangels came to join the system and help anchor even more Divine love onto the planet. Archangels support you in finding a way back to the truth at the core of your being, that you are vast, powerful and limitless, just as they are. They help you access the higher truth of who you are so that you might begin to be as free and at peace as they are, shining your light as they do, loving as they love, giving as they give.

Call on the archangels whenever you need a boost in your healing power, a Divine intervention in your dealings or a helping hand to get back on track. These powerful beings hold nothing but love for humanity and are always available to assist. Their kindness, compassion, grace and generosity are second to none.

Archangel Metatron

Angel of angels, Metatron overlights the angelic realm – as well as everyone on the earth. This lightest of essences and darkest of colours brings light into dark situations and helps you free yourself from judgement. Metatron brings truth into your conscious mind so that you can see the light and the dark as perfect, equal companions. He also assists with time management, bringing you back to a wonderful sense of flow and restoring you to the joy of the present moment. His energy is pure Divine love, and using this essence brings the Divine right into your everyday experiences. Breathe in your I Amness and let Metatron's deep and endless love fill every aspect of your body, heart, mind and soul.

I hold the light of truth and love for all of humanity and bring healing into every situation to which I am called. I bring love into everything – all the little things that make a difference to your life and all the big situations you have to deal with. I know what it is to live in a physical body on a physical planet and understand everything you go through in your human experience. There is nothing too big or too small for me to support you with. It is my honour to assist you at this incredible time on the planet as everything shifts and changes.

My job is to help you raise your vibration and bring Divine light and love to every step of your spiritual journey. I have a magic touch when it comes to managing time and will help you get back into the flow so that you can trust in the perfection of Divine timing. It is my joy to overlight your creations so that whatever you create carries the energy of Divine love and touches people's spirits. I am here to hold each and every one of you in the light and remind you that we all contracted to follow the Ascension pathway together. I am always by your side, so call on me. My love for you is steadfast and sure.

Archangel Uriel

This vast archangel helps you keep your feet on the earth even as you reach for the stars and reminds you what it means to be both infinitely light and deeply grounded. He brings certainty when you are unsure, peace when you are overwhelmed and calm when you are troubled. He reminds you to honour the gift of your precious body and supports you in awakening to gratitude for your life, the earth and all who are upon it. Allow Uriel's light to help you find courage and commitment so that you can move forward in your chosen direction.

I am Uriel. I am the archangel of the north and represent the element of earth. I overlight the planet and am here in full support as you go through big challenges on the earth. The changes you are experiencing are necessary for the next level of your evolution. I am here to keep you safe and hold the vision of what is possible for this earth. Allow me to walk with you at this time when everyone around you is becoming more and more fearful for the future. I hold the future in a safe space, and I love you enough to go through this with you. Keep the faith with me and I will help you plant seeds that grow into mighty oaks.

I help you balance the physical and spiritual aspects of your life. When you make friends with your physical body it can be a partner to you on your spiritual journey. When you embody your spirit and bring it fully into your everyday life you will feel the difference in your relationships, work, health and finances. My job is to help you place your feet gently on the ground, reminding you that you are of the earth and that it is a wondrous gift to be alive at this time on this Divine planet. Being on earth was never meant to remove you from heaven. This experience was given to every human as a precious gift so that you might remember that heaven lives inside you, and together, recreate it right here on earth. The earth is abundant, lush and filled with beauty, and the more you connect with Gaia, the more creative, simple and joyful your life can be. Walk that information into your reality and you will create a new golden era with ease and experience the riches of heaven right here and now. It is only your tearing sense of separation that creates pain in your life. When you remember that there is no difference between where you came from and where you are, you will instantly manifest heaven. I hold that truth for you, with love.

Archangel Raphael

Raphael brings kindness, compassion and nurturing into your life, especially when you are being hard on yourself. He reminds you not to let your heart be trampled on, for it is a precious gift and your greatest source of guidance. Choosing this essence indicates that you have the ability to bring healing to others. Call on Raphael to help you awaken your healing gifts and amplify your healing skills. Remember to breathe consciously and expand your heart centre so that the healing comes from the pure light of love. Remember too that whatever you give comes back to you multiplied and expanded many times over. Allow yourself to receive.

I am Raphael. I am the archangel of the east and represent the element of air. My name means 'God's healing', so come to me whenever you are in need of healing for your body, mind or soul. I bring healing to your relationships and your heart and help you back onto your feet when you feel defeated by life's circumstances.

My colour is the deep green of the forest, a place of peace and contemplation. If you are drawn to my colour and energy you will benefit from time out in nature. Be still and listen to me whispering through the trees. Feel the ancient wisdom of the forests. Bask in the healing sanctuary of nature and let it restore you. Breathe freely and fully. Feel my deep compassion and treat yourself with gentle loving-kindness. I bring truth and understanding – and with understanding comes healing. I open your heart to gratitude, bringing trust and ease into all that you do. Your precious heart has enough love for the whole world; it is a heart that can heal other hearts. Let us together hold a space that is so filled with love that everyone will be touched by it.

Archangel Michael

Archangel Michael walks alongside you when you feel lost and brings loving comfort when you feel small. He helps you find your truth when you are being swayed by others' opinions and brings clarity when you cannot see the wood for the trees. This essence helps you cut through deception, interference and negativity so that you can reclaim insight, strength and personal power. Let go of unnecessary baggage and heaviness and step into freedom and pure lightness of being.

I am Michael. I am the archangel of the south and represent the element of fire. I wrap you in my pale blue cloak so that nothing can harm you and stand at your door with a golden sword of truth so that you feel completely safe. I hold you any time you go into fear and help you see the bigger picture so that you can let go and know that all is well. I unshackle you from limiting beliefs, bringing clarity of purpose and vision. I cut through falsehood, leaving room only for the light of truth. I encourage you to expand your light and help you activate your soul's truth. I open doors and usher you towards freedom.

You and I know one another. We have worked together from the beginning. Feel my solid presence and the love I have for you. We are keepers of the ray of power and protection and we have held this light since time began. Call on me when you forget your own Divine power. Call on me when you feel small and have forgotten that nothing can harm you. Let me help you remember that everything is always divinely created for your highest good. You are a Divine warrior who has always worked for the good of the whole. We of the archangelic realm know who you are, and we will never let you down. That is our commitment to you, our beloved.

Archangel Gabriel

Gabriel signals change, and he appears at the end of a cycle to bring messages of hope for the future. Call on him if you are struggling or facing a gateway in your life, and know that everything is on track and a new beginning is on the horizon. Keep the faith. Gabriel is the archangel of peace, prosperity and unity. He brings wholeness where there has been division and separation. He supports you in awakening to higher levels of consciousness so that you begin to see the oneness in all life. Gabriel is a messenger. He asks you to listen closely now to the messages of your angels, as they have important information for you. Notice the signs around you. You are preparing to shift to the next level. Spread your wings and fly.

I am Gabriel. I am the archangel of the west and represent the element of water. My colour is blue-lilac, the colour of the gateway. I shine this gateway energy and the pure stream of my love to you so that you can remember that you are the light. I facilitate your Ascension journey as you lift your vibration towards grace and freedom.

I herald in the new and am here to show you a new way forward. If the path you have been on is not taking you anywhere or you have been going around in circles, I appear in your reality to help you realise that these old paths and patterns no longer work. I have come to announce a change in the energy of your reality. You need no longer carry the old, out-dated patterns passed down through your family line such as struggle, poverty or emotional abuse. You need no longer attract or put up with anything that does not serve you. I am here to take you by the hand, lead you through a new gateway and announce that the old ways are done. This is when peace, abundance and joy become your new reality.

I bring to you a new dawn, a new age – the Age of Aquarius. I announced the Age of Pisces and the birth of the one they called the Christ, and now I am here to announce the birth of the new Divine human on the new planet. As each and every one of you claims your inner Divine light, together you create heaven on earth. Now is the time for all to awaken.

The Colour Mirrors Additional Essences

The following essences do not fit into any specific part of the system. They each arrived at times when their energy was called for on the planet and they each bring something unique. We invite you to explore what they have to share.

Yeshua

This essence makes the energy of the Divine very real, connecting you with the golden Divine light you hold within. It helps you release old programs carried in your DNA and integrate the many new frequencies of energy now streaming onto the earth. It takes you deeper into your authentic power and lets every cell in your body know that the only real power on the planet – and throughout the universe – is love. There truly is nothing else. Enlightenment is simply living as love in every moment. This is the truth that Yeshua embodied, which enabled him to become a Christ, a Divine being of love. This essence reminds you of your commitment at this time to learn how to be love and nothing but love. This is the process and the journey, and this essence will light your way. You are here to help take the planet into the Golden Age, and with Yeshua's vast and unlimited support, you can do it.

I am here to quietly remind you that only love has true power. The power you have seen in me – and that I see reflected in you – has only ever been love. My strength is based on love and nothing can overpower love, not even death. My love for you is so all-encompassing that nothing will ever get in its way. Nothing you do or say will change my unending, unwavering love for you just as you are. I once said: "I am the way and the light", and this is my promise to you. I show you the way so that you need never feel lost again.

You and I know each other of old. We have always been connected. Our connection is based on mutual trust: you trust me to be there for you eternally, and I trust you to live without doubt, to open your heart wide and be the one who takes love out into the world by being love. I walk beside you every step of the way and work with you in the silence of your inner self. When you forget, I remind you how incredible you are, how courageous, how brilliant. Your light shines too brightly to be dimmed and I will not let it go out. That is our covenant.

Diamond Unicorn

This essence is an astonishing burst of light. You might think a diamond would be hard and sharp, but this level of light never needs to be harsh. Feel how it wraps you in the warmest, softest embrace. It can be this gentle because nothing can threaten it. When your power is this vast you do not need to defend yourself against anything. This essence is a godsend if you are in the middle of a power struggle. When you see with the clarity and purity of diamond perception, you realise that power battles and aggressive behaviour are only ever responses to feeling small. This essence reminds you that the only answer is love and compassion – for yourself and others. The Diamond Unicorn is so pure and clear that nothing negative can exist in its light. Because it is so gentle, it goes into all the places where you usually do not let anything in. It brings healing to everything in yourself that you have been too scared to face. In its embrace you can relax, let go and find the true and tender light that has always been hidden within. Like a diamond this light is indestructible, and once you experience it, you can never forget that this is who you truly are.

I am the most magical creature that has ever existed and my purpose is to create real magic in your life. I remind you that existence itself is the highest form of magic and ask you never to take one single breath for granted. You are made of pure magic, just as I am, and the more you include me, the more magically your reality will unfold. The secret of true high magic is that it is all love. Love is the magic that is woven into every facet of life and you are it, and it is you. As a child you knew this to be true. As an adult you have mostly forgotten. I exist only to remind you of this truth.

I am the diamond at the heart of you. I am the perfection and purity of Divine white light, and I am so clear in my love and my light that you cannot stay hidden in the darkness once we join together. When I come into your life it is because you and I have work to do. We are part of one another and when we acknowledge this connection the magic can truly begin. Together we create webs of pure diamond light in the cosmos as we create the new reality on earth and beyond. Our work together is not small or insignificant. It goes beyond you or me or anything we might call 'ours'. Together we bring Divine light to the planet and it is this transmission of Divine love, simply through being who we are, that is our true calling. As we come together this becomes so much more powerful and real. Can you feel it in your body and your being? I am here now and I am ready. Will you join me?

Opalescence

This essence reflects back to you all the many colours and all the magnificent light you hold within. It reminds you that you are vast and precious beyond belief. Breathe in this essence of sunlight and soft summer roses and connect with the beauty and blessings it brings. Its message is that this moment is already perfect just as it is. This essence connects you with the Divine feminine and the female energy of the Christ, embodied by Mary Magdalene. Step into the warm embrace of Opalescence. Allow it to soften and release any resistance you are holding and let yourself be forgiven, blessed, accepted and loved.

I am opalescence – the essence of opal. I bring softness and gentleness into your life when you have been punishing yourself or pushing yourself too hard. I wrap you in the most delicious, soft, loving energy so that you can let go of the mind-games that keep you locked in frustration and self-hatred. I hold all the qualities of the Divine feminine – grace, love, warmth and nurturing – so that you can see and feel those same qualities reflected in yourself and remember that you are worthy of the deepest levels of love. I help you open more fully to your inner knowing so that you can learn to completely trust yourself and return to a sense of ease and freedom.

I have many colours that gently shimmer and shine with iridescent light. I bring the warmth and peace of a beautiful garden on a summer's afternoon and the scent of sun-filled roses. My energy creates a fluid, dreamy state of being that encourages deep relaxation and meditation. With my help you can open to the many possibilities that are available to you and choose the ones that resonate the most. If ever you find yourself stuck in sticky, dark energy, call on my potent love to swiftly and thoroughly transmute it.

Rose Pink

If pink is the colour of love, this Rose Pink essence is a deepening of that love. All the healing rays of love are incorporated in this spray. It is a combination of pink and magenta, and therefore has the qualities of both Divine love and personal love. It brings in the energy of mother's love as well as self-love, and it expands your ability to receive, hold and share the pure frequency of Divine love. This bottle is incredibly effective at rapidly shifting deep-rooted emotional trauma.

I hold you in love whenever you need it, a love so rich and luscious that your whole being can let go. I help you cope at times when you feel lost and unloved and take my healing light right to your core, bathing your wounds in gentleness and easing you towards resolution and wholeness.

Roses are beautiful because they hold the frequency of love in their petals and their colours, and my gift to you is to hold up a mirror so that you can see the beauty inside you. In your heart you are this rich shade of rose pink Divine love. Your heart is bursting with love, even when you do not realise it. Your heart lives for love, for true Divine love with no conditions, and it responds to my energy every time you use this essence. I help your heart light grow in strength so that it can pump more and more love into your body, your being and the world. My love is vibrant and strong and capable of greatness, just as you are.

Indigo

This essence relates to the third eye and invites you to explore the deeper mysteries of life. It connects you with your inner knowing and your inner voice and is particularly helpful for writers. It strengthens your intuition and creativity and helps you link with the information 'out there' – the field of knowing and information that exists everywhere. This essence is calming and centring and guides you towards peace, stillness and quiet inspiration.

I am a gateway to worlds unseen. I am the protective guide who shows you that it is safe to see clearly and to remember what you have always known. My role is to help you open your third eye and become aware of the world beyond your five senses. I help you access your intuition and use it so that your path is always lit with knowing. Even at times when you do not know which way to turn, my deep empowering guidance supports you so that you can calmly accept the state of not knowing until the way becomes clear again. I bring deep peace and acceptance of 'what is' and help you to stop fretting and worrying about the small stuff. My energy helps you connect with the wisdom you hold deep inside so that you can write about it and share it with others. I help you keep the doors to your inner guidance and wisdom open so that you can live your life in peaceful flow.

Soul

Soul is one of the two 'Body Freedom' essences. Use it before meals to reconnect you with your soul's view and help you move away from eating for any reason other than to fuel your body and keep it healthy, energised and happy. This essence is a connector, re-establishing your link to your higher self. It helps you break free of the limiting patterns and limited viewpoints that keep you from experiencing true freedom in your body and your life. It connects you with the power and light of your true essence.

I am the light of your soul. I am the overlighting, over-arching energy that encapsulates your whole essence, everything that makes you 'you'. I am eternal, beyond your mind, your personality or your body. I hold the blueprint of your Divine self while you play the game of being 'only' human, and when you are ready to fully bring your soul energy into your body and your life, I will support you all the way. I ask you to remember that you are so much more than you have believed yourself to be. My light is built into your core and is designed to help you wake up to who you really are. No matter how long you play at being weak, powerless or small, I hold the truth until you are ready to remember that you are infinite, vast and Divine. I help you come back into balance when you have been off-course, and I feed and nourish you at a deep level so that your mind can let go of anguish and your body can let go of cravings.

Power

Power is one of the two 'Body Freedom' essences. It helps you reconnect with your power so that you no longer give it away to anyone or anything, including addictive behaviours. This blend of yellow and gold unites personal power and spiritual power to bring you into a space of authenticity and pure presence. Use this essence after meals to support digestion and metabolism.

My bright golden-yellow light reminds you that you are the power in your life. No one and nothing can take your power from you because it comes from your soul, and your soul is the light of the Divine made into the unique being called 'you'. I lift you up when you feel helpless in the face of addictions or power games and plug you back into your power source. I help you remember that you are far greater and stronger than whatever seems to keep you small. I shore up your solar plexus and bring you an instant sense of solid, stable, connected power so that you can say 'no' when it needs to be said. I also open you to greater possibilities so that you can say 'yes' when you have been holding back out of fear. I remind you of the true power at the core of your being that has never gone away, even if it has been hidden for a time. You are the power in your life and always will be.

Rose Gold

This essence awakens your connection to the being we call the 'Rose Gold Lady': the total embodiment of love, the Divine Mother of the Divine. Her message is that the only real power in the universe is love. In the first moments of your life on earth your superpower is love. A baby needs love and nurturing to survive. As humans we need love and connection to thrive. When you truly connect with your highest aspect it comes in waves of love. To know the love of the Divine Mother is to know and receive pure abundance and joy. To experience her love in its fullness is to come home. This sweet-smelling delight of an essence clears your space and your energy field of anything that runs counter to love. It brings cohesion when you have been shattered by shock, healing when you have been blasted by trauma and softness when your nerves have been frayed. Use it and know that you are never alone, you are on track and you are always loved and supported. Let yourself be held, and watch with awe as the next steps on your journey unfold.

I am Rose Gold, Mother of God. I am God, Goddess, All That Is. I am the creative power that birthed every particle of existence. I am all that you are. I am the illusion and the only reality. I am all and nothing. I am the seen and unseen. I am the seer who looks through your eyes. I am everything inside of you and everything outside of you. I am the beginning and the end and everything in between. I am all of it and so are you. Do you understand now? Do you know that you created everything? Do you know that everything is one? I am your reminder, guiding you back to truth.

I bring warmth and comfort when you are in despair and the gift of a tranquil new sunrise after a dark, stormy night. I bring softness into hard times and relief into painful ones. I carry you when you are too weary to go on. I watch over you tenderly while you sleep. I am gentle rain on parched soil. I am the light of hope and grace in your soul. I celebrate with you when you are happy and hold you when you are not. I am love beyond any love you have ever known. Count on my love: it is eternal.

The Colour Mirrors Essences: Stories

Over the years we have heard countless stories about the Colour Mirrors essences. Most were never recorded, but we have collated a selection to illustrate some of the many ways the essences touch people's lives.

We begin by sharing our personal favourites, along with Moira who has kindly added some of her stories. We then bring you a variety of stories from Colour Mirrors practitioners, teachers and clients around the world. Some focus on one particular essence, or a sub-set of essences such as the Elements or Angels. Others tell of favourite spritzers and the guidance and support they have received. We hope these stories offer inspiration and bring insight into how the essences might benefit you and your life.

Melissie:

I was so deeply moved to read everyone's comments on the essences in this section of the book. When Colour Mirrors started I was so sure it would be just this little kitchen set – basically for me to work with – and never in my wildest imagination did I see it going where it has now gone. At the time there were only 7 little Angel sprays – and very much 'little' angels. I never had grandiose ideas that there could be Archangels and Dragons and all the rest. Well, of course, as we have seen again and again, the system had entirely its own plan, and I have been the happy hands who got to bring it out into the world.

My own go-to and favourite has always been the Wood essence. The colour olive has always balanced my over-giving, over-rescuing, boundary-less nature. It smells like beautiful green spaces and spices, and it makes me settle into myself so quickly. As a child I had amoebic dysentery, which has affected my liver ever since, so it also helps my body when I forget that I have one.

Anna, who makes the essences now, loves to sit and count the drops as the essential oils get measured into the bottles; she says it calms and centres her. Gold Angel is her favourite and she often feels his presence when she makes the essences. My daughter, Gilly, says she loves Metatron and the Gold Dragon. Both Gilly and Anna are such angelic women who really have never heard of the word no, so a bit of 'gold power' is great to help make their lives work and support them beautifully.

Other than the Wood element my current favourite is the Rose Gold essence, but before that it had to be Opalescence, and when I started it was Air, and when things were really difficult it was White Dragon, oh, and before that... Yes, well, I actually love them all – and when I teach I always manage to fall in love with each one as it comes up in the class.

Korani:

I literally use the essences every day. They have become an 'essential' part of my life since the first time I connected with them. I can't imagine beginning my day without a spritz of at least two or three of these gorgeous sprays. They clear, balance and harmonise my energy field and set me up for the day, but beyond that they also just bring an extra dimension to life with their glorious colours and scents. I'll usually spritz several times during the day whenever I feel drawn to them and always use them when writing or teaching. They never fail to uplift and support and bring a little touch of magic.

I have always used the essences in my workshops and find they bring wonderful lightness, support and guidance to the participants. On many occasions they have helped someone going through a 'process', by shifting stuck energy, releasing blocks and generally lifting them back onto solid ground. Connecting with the Dragons is always incredibly empowering, and watching students on courses step into their own power is phenomenal. We've also had many cosmic moments on workshops when using the essences, as they take us up and out of our limited thinking mind into a greater awareness and connect us with light beings and the higher realms. I feel so blessed to have these potent tools to use in my own life and with my clients.

I love them all but do have several favourites: Platinum Angel is other-worldly and mysterious, yet somehow reassuring; Metatron is solid support and can always be relied on – and is such a blissful colour; I love Diamond Unicorn and White Dragon for their sheer purity and brilliance; Yeshua is the truest friend; Green Angel is amazing for keeping everything fresh and clear; Water's colour and scent make me breathe more deeply; Copper Dragon and

Gold Dragon feel like feminine and masculine sides of the same thing – dazzle, power and chutzpah! And the Starlights – the Starlights bring me such joy, gratitude, inspiration and wonderment. Their very existence makes me happy.

Royal Blue Dragon will always have a special place in my heart because it was the first time I had ever 'channelled' anything, at my first colour workshop with Moira. I was blown away when this huge starry dragon actually stepped into my body and I saw through its eyes and spoke with its voice. The realisation of my own 'starriness' began on that workshop, with that dragon.

My 'desert island' essence, however, would have to be Gold Angel. I vividly remember when this bottle was created. I was staying with Melissie at the time. She had just made the seven Golden Gaia bottles and we were having the most incredible time exploring their energies and, truth be told, spending most of our time sitting gazing at them out in the warmth and sunlight on her terrace. They were so brand new and so special and I felt such a strong connection with them that it was quite a blissful time.

We were also having the conversations that led to the writing of my first book, The Language of Light: Golden Keys to Ascension, and it emerged that there was an Angel essence in the system to match each of the Golden Gaias – except G12, which is pale gold top and bottom. Melissie said: "We have to have a Gold Angel!" and immediately went and made one. The moment I saw it and smelled it, I was in love. This essence felt as if it was everything the Golden Gaias represented in one small bottle. It made the Ascension journey seem do-able, tangible, real. This beautiful Angel essence continues to be my 'go-to', and I love how it instantly strengthens and lights up my energy field the moment I use it. I always take it with me whenever I travel, as it brings such a supportive and empowered light and energy into any space.

Moira:

My absolute go-to essence is Metatron. Before I do anything, even domestic chores like going shopping, I spray this essence around me and breathe in my I AMness. It reminds me daily to be and do my best for myself and others. It raises my frequency instantly and holds me all day long. My second is actually the bottle I could not stand the smell of for the first few years – the Wood essence. Since I accepted my body and that my body is not a problem, Wood is my 'corrector' essence. It adjusts my thoughts, my feeling responses and so often clears pain from my body. I have a line-up of personal use essence bottles on my dressing table that I pick and mix from daily, and when these get low I love to tip a mix of the last drops in a bath and soak in a colour cocktail essence bath. It always seems to happen at a time I am expanding and stretching my energy field out just that bit further.

And then the Rose Gold essence arrived while Korani and Melissie were writing this book. I wanted to present a two-hour event to help clients connect with the sacred women I work with: Mother Mary, Gaia Goddess, Mary Magdalene and Quan Yin. When I ran a similar event connecting with the Archangels, we placed Gabriel in the west, Uriel in the north, Michael in the south and Raphael in the east. Holding the grid in the centre were Metatron and Sandalphon. I asked Melissie: if we put the Divine female power in those quadrants, who holds the central core energy? Melissie responded that it was the Rose Gold Lady, the mother of all.

So I went ahead and presented the workshop and put the Rose Gold Pearl oil bottle in that part of the grid with some gold citrine crystals. In the first workshop I had several students experience physical discomfort as we connected with the Rose Gold Lady, and I knew then that we needed a spritzer to instantly help us relax into the feminine with ease and bring balance to our male and female Divine energies. Melissie kindly made it for me, and it is the most beautiful rose colour with gold dust. The aroma is, I believe, the best Melissie has ever created.

Here are few stories I recall about the essences over the years:

Pink Angel

Colour Mirrors consultants use this spray on themselves and their clients before reading the colour bottle choices or conducting a treatment session. When you spray the pink, it changes the receptivity of the client. I experimented with this when I first started to work with the system. I found that if I did not use this bottle before starting a session, the client struggled to hear the information. At times they would go into resistance or their body would fidget, and they were not able to relax. When I used the Pink Angel they softened and opened up to receive and explore new perspectives on their issues.

Yellow Angel

A guest on my show could not take her eyes off this bottle on the set. She bought a bottle of Yellow Angel, which she said was to use in her office for her staff, not able to admit she personally was in need of this colour. What I knew about her was that she worked seven days a week, 12 hours a day – and when she did have any playtime it was in the context of work duties. It has been fascinating to hear from others how she is evolving, softening, relaxing and taking more time to be with her family since the Yellow Angel went to work with her.

Lilac Angel

I was in Europe teaching a Colour Mirrors course, and on a day off for some sightseeing, one of the students called me at the hotel asking if I could come to the hospital immediately. She picked me up, and I walked into a room filled with family crying around their loved one who was in distress with breathing difficulties and muscle spasms. The Lilac Angel was hovering over his bed, so I knew he was in transition. I had taken the spray with me, so I put some on his hands. Almost immediately he calmed down, his breathing returned to normal, and a few minutes later he had no spasms and was totally relaxed. I learned later that he passed peacefully in his sleep a few days after the visit.

Fire

I once had a client with flaming red hair, and the Fire bottle was all she could see. She said she had started menopause and the hot flushes were uncomfortable. When I spoke to Melissie about this client's strange choice of adding fire to an already hot situation, her response was brilliant: like cures like. This is a homeopathic principle, and we have found it really works with the essences!

Wood

When my optometrist recommended that I change my reading glasses to progressive lenses, it was very hard to adapt my peripheral vision and learn to move my head instead of my eyes to read. It has caused such dizziness and nausea for me, and I would not have coped with this adjustment if it were not for the daily dose of Wood I spray to relieve the symptoms.

Air

In the early days of working with this system, I had a client come to see me about his asthma and fear of small spaces. He chose Air, and I felt guided to take him into a regression. He recalled a lifetime in the First World War where he died in a tunnel, gassed to death. Over the years I have noticed that clients who are about to have operations where they will have to be anesthetised are drawn to this bottle, and I recommend they use it before and after their procedure.

Red Dragon

This one is often picked by mothers of teenage boys, dismayed at the sudden distance and isolation their sons crave from being mothered or, as they see it, 'smothered'. These mothers ask why their sons are so angry all of a sudden, painting their bedroom walls black and refusing to talk. I have learned to handle this one with a little sneaky advice so they avoid making the son feel that there is something wrong with him or that he is not good enough – and that is to quietly spray the Red Dragon around the house and in their son's bedroom. This energetically opens a door for feelings to be expressed appropriately, and it works every time. I have come to see this dragon as a family miracle worker.

Lilac Dragon

I had 10 women clients whom I had been working with for some time, and they all had one block in common: long-term depression. I wanted a bottle that would literally blast the fog from their minds and open their hearts so they could see themselves as I saw them – full of huge potential and able to claim their Divine feminine power. So I asked Melissie to make 10 special bottles using the colour violet for depression and dragon energy to remove the wall of resistance to healing their depression issues. Then Korani got into the conversation and Melissie ended up making it lilac rather than violet. Lilac is intensified violet – violet with the light shone through it – and it was just the right ingredient.

Those clients who bought and used the bottle made significant changes to their lives. One even became a leader and speaker for a healing community group in her town. What I often notice now is that this bottle is picked when the client is in denial about their depression. When they start using it, it is pure joy to observe how fast this dragon goes to work clearing their suppressed anger, releasing them from apathy and leading them forward to claim their bliss.

Archangel Gabriel

In 2018 I was guided to start writing the deck of oracle cards that would help me and my clients face our shadow patterns. The 44 cards with gargoyle images and the accompanying booklet came through fast, written in six and a half weeks. During that time I could feel Archangel Gabriel. His presence was palpable and the colour blue-lilac was the filter I looked through while writing, so I asked Melissie to make a bottle for me to represent his energy.

The 'Colour Your Shadow' deck was written during a year of dark and light forces coming out to face off against one another: 2 + 0 + 1 + 8 = 11. The number 11 is the number of duality and letting go of judgements, moving beyond separating beliefs of what is good and what is evil. I was delving deep into the shadowlands of my own psyche, as was my mentoring group at the time. Exploring the shadow at its deepest recesses, I found that I had to have help to stay sane, and I believe that Gabriel was my protector, analyst, guide and muse. I believe that the insights I gained and subsequently wrote about each shadow pattern were his fearless words of wisdom. I loved that he was a gateway archangel and that when Melissie made this essence, several others came to join the system too. If you are writing or creating new projects, I recommend Archangel Gabriel to open the gateway for you and guide you all the way towards completion and success.

Alka Dharam, UK, www.lifecentredhealing.co.uk

I bought several sets of the Archangel essences just before moving home in August 2018. A few weeks later I opened the box to unpack the bottles, and there arose such a force of energy (much like the genie of the lamp in Aladdin) that I was knocked back, and I quickly scrambled to put the lid back on to contain the energy. As I sat in front of the bottles, shaken and panting, I began to think I must have imagined it. I felt silly and glad no one was around to witness it, although I had an inner knowing that these spritzers were special and extremely powerful. A few moments later I braced myself to open the box and gingerly lifted off the lid. Again there escaped such a gush of energy that I immediately had to put the lid back on, recognising that the spritzers' energy was too strong for me at the time.

I did not open the box again for some weeks until I felt I really needed healing with Raphael. This time when I opened the box my eyes immediately fell on Raphael – it was almost as if the other Archangels were standing back, allowing me to be healed. I poured some into a bath and could feel Raphael's light seeping in between my cells, energising them. It was incredibly healing and I felt made anew.

A little while later I was facilitating an Empowerment Through Colour workshop in Glastonbury, and whenever I talked about it I unwittingly called it the Archangel workshop. On the day of the workshop there were a number of mishaps: I had an accident as a car behind me hit my boot containing the bottles (with no damage done); one participant felt attacked at 3am, unable to sleep, and then had to take a detour on the way to the workshop; another was unable to find the workshop venue despite asking directions of four locals. We all overcame obstacles to get to the workshop!

Glastonbury is considered the heart centre of the earth, but the energies are mixed with both the light and dark. At the time of the workshop, they were particularly unsettled. I used Michael, Metatron and Raphael to clear the energies of the room. The workshop took on its own force as I was guided what to do, when to spray the Archangels and which exercises to do for healing to take place. We seemed to be in a different dimension, offering healing for the collective, and it became clear to me that our souls had decided to be here at this time to do this work. The Archangels played a huge part, leaving the venue with a beautiful energy.

Soon afterwards Korani visited me and set up a grid which included the Archangels, and that was SO powerful. I found that I could not stay in the room for too long, however, because of their energy. A friend who was staying wanted to spend time alone with the Archangels but left the room after only 15 minutes because their energy was so strong. I dismantled the grid a week later but began to miss their energy and set it up again along with the Starlights – and now I would definitely not be without them. It is easy to be in their presence, as they have made themselves at home and are very much resident here.

One by one they are making themselves known to me. I have found healing with Raphael to be instantaneous. Gabriel transports me to a different realm and provides an energy that almost wraps me with love and support. He also assists me in accessing dreams. Uriel provides impetus and a call to action. Michael is the protector and provides clarity. Metatron has always provided stability, whilst Sandalphon is grounding and at the same time a reminder to be light through dance and music – and that nothing is all that serious.

Whilst writing this, I was having my boiler replaced. The plumber told me he couldn't get the existing boiler out although he had been trying for well over two hours. I told him to relax and that there would be a way forward. As I continued to write, I could hear him huffing and puffing, trying to get the existing boiler out. At this point I called on Michael to help, and before I could even spray the essence the plumber shouted that he had got the boiler out!

Andreja, Slovenia

Whenever I use Clear Angel my mind is immediately sharp, no matter how difficult the business or private situation is.

Clara Apollo, UK, www.claraapollo.com

The Element essences are a tremendous sextet of potency which continue to assist with the Elemental Qigong I both practice and share. It all began on a Colour Mirrors course with Korani where we were exploring the essences. I was already curious, as the colours corresponded with Chinese Medicine's Five Element theory, so when I meditated with and sprayed the Wood element I was gleefully surprised by the physiological effect this had. There was suddenly a very strong tingle, like an electric shock, that travelled from under my liver, down my right leg to my big toe – I was blown away, as this corresponds with the liver meridian, the organ associated with the Wood element!

I love to include these element sprays when sharing specific Qigong exercises to tonify body organs, with my most used and still firm favourite being the Earth essence. Such soft potent holding; safety in a spray.

Darija, Slovenia

After I had a reading with the bottles of Colour Mirrors for the first time many beautiful things happened, and my life turned in a different direction. I bought the Metatron essence, which harmonised the relationship with my father as soon as I sprayed it in the house. It looked like he was angry in the morning, but as soon as he stepped into the sprayed room, his consciousness was higher. He was full of common sense and was able to see the big picture.

The effect of Metatron for me was feminine – it balanced my hormones. When I tried the Platinum Angel essence I was immediately in tears, with a feeling of gratitude and longing for home. Recognition brings you home to your soul. Then I bought the Silver and Wood essences. My daughter came home from college in tears. I sprayed Silver, and after 10 minutes she was completely calm and the day became successful for her. The same happened for me.

When I used Metatron's colour in my new massage room as a wall colour choice, it worked out! The colour of the wall tones with my well-being and the well-being of the clients who come to me for help. Thank you very much for bringing me to my true home.

Debra Hubers-Paradis, USA, www.DebrasEnergyPoints.com

For about a year I suffered from an unexplained rash positioned along the liver meridian line on my leg. Throughout this time I was seeing a medical Qigong practitioner, and during one session she pulled a black thick energy out of my liver.

About a week later I received an order of 40 Colour Mirrors bottles and spritzers. The bottles were perfectly packed, but when I unwrapped the Wood spritzer I found it had shattered into tiny pieces, almost like a powder. Strangely, the wrapping didn't show any signs that the bottle had broken – no visible colour, stain, smell or any sign that the bottle had exploded.

We know that when bottles explode it is a sign that our soul is trying to get our attention. I looked closely at the message of the Wood spritzer and of course it relates to the liver meridian and toxic emotions stored there. Wow! In one week, two big energy blasts to support in releasing the unexpressed anger that was stored in my liver.

Once you decide to work with the bottles, whether or not they are in your physical presence, they begin to work. I feel that when I placed the order, the energy of the Wood spritzer was working with me through my Qigong practitioner to support the release of the toxic energies that were residing in my liver. Shortly after the arrival of the exploded Wood bottle and contemplating the messages, my mysterious rash disappeared.

Elaine Nuelle, UK, elainenuelle@gmail.com

I do love the essences! Platinum Angel is a go-to when the going gets tough or there's a tricky situation that I can't see the way out of. Being able to rise above the situation, see the bigger picture and have a higher understanding is always a relief and a release.

When I had big anger issues I used a combination of Wood and Red Dragon. It was cleansing and so healing to really know that you could only ever love it right. Gold Dragon was wonderful when I felt weak, scared and powerless. He helped me tap into my own inner power, and I found within me strength I didn't know I had. Red Angel is brilliant for when I'm driving and I'm tired – it instantly focuses and energises me. Combined with Metatron, I feel totally confident and safe. Love, love the Gold Angel. It helps me remember who I really am. Metal is aptly named – it gives me a backbone! I love Diamond Unicorn too. At my first appointment with Korani I combined Gold Dragon, White Dragon and Diamond Unicorn: it was life-saving! Ruby Red always makes me feel safe. Dolphin is wonderful – light and playful – and perfect for when I get too serious and intense. I've gone through a few bottles of Lilac Dragon and the phrase 'light bomb' is totally accurate. It is definitely one of my favourites. She's beautiful, light and loving, and I love her Lemurian frequency.

Hayden Crawford, Australia, www.dreemtimeacademy.com.au

I had been waiting for my first order of Colour Mirrors bottles to arrive before starting my colour journey with Moira Bush. My entire journey to learn this incredible system felt divinely supported from day one.

Leading up to their arrival, our beautiful cat Angel (otherwise known as Poppet) had been struggling with her health. It had been hard for us to accept, but we knew she didn't have long. Poppet was pure white with a little pink nose and ears – a brave moggy who had immigrated with us to Australia in 2010. She had lived with us for 14 years. The day I took possession of the bottles was the day she crossed.

As I opened the small cardboard box that had travelled from South Africa, I was surprised to discover an essence spray I hadn't ordered. It was the Pink Angel. Noticing the coincidence, I sprayed it above Poppet as she rested in her bed, hoping that she would benefit from the loving frequency. Later that day the vet arrived to put her to sleep.

My partner Mark and I sobbed as we felt the last beat of our Angel's heart. She was gone. I sprayed the essence around us and could feel it clearing away the mucus from my lungs, transmuting the grief I was experiencing and reminding me of the biggest lesson she had agreed to teach me – unconditional love. Every time I smell the sweet, zesty fragrant of the Pink Angel now, it reminds me of our angelic fur baby and I can sense her radiance in my aura.

What is more, another bottle had mysteriously arrived that day. New Beginnings (bottle 28) replaced The Inner Guide (bottle 35) I had ordered, as a serendipitous sign that it was time to move on to the next chapter of faith and joy. We both bathed in this radiant oil and felt as if the old was being literally sucked down the plughole and a rebirth had begun.

Irena, Slovenia

I used Lilac Angel for three months every single day before meeting my dad, after 35 years of his absence. It was a big step for me, and without Lilac Angel's support I wouldn't have done it. The vibration of this essence is so gentle and motivates you slowly to walk on your path. When I decided to meet my dad and when this event happened I felt a hundred kilos lighter, without any blame for him or even for myself. Since then I have felt a liberation from the past.

Jaci Daley, USA, www.african-massage.com

I have been a massage therapist and bodyworker for 28 years. For many years I had repeat clients returning week after week with the same issues. It was when I began using the Element spritzers from the Colour Mirrors range, and called what I offer 'African Massage', that people took notice! By integrating the visualisations of the Elements – at the start of the massage and at various intervals – to describe what I am doing and the intended outcome for the particular massage technique, I am seeing huge shifts in clients. They love the pictures that I describe of nature during the massage, and it assists them to relax and be more present and focused on the healing intention.

Colour Mirrors has assisted me to create a whole new massage modality and has completely changed the way that I do massage. It has been called a meditative massage and is totally different and rejuvenating. I have begun teaching this method of massage to other therapists, and many have said that it is the answer to what they have been looking for – a way of combining massage with spirituality and visualisation.

Joanne Arjoon, Canada, joannearjoon@gmail.com

I feel Metatron in my home. I do an 'I AM' meditation every morning using this essence. It reminds me I am connected and 'I AM this' on the planet. I have often asked Metatron to give me a sign he is with me and have had my television and lights turn on in the middle of the night. I fell asleep one night with my hand on top of the Metatron essence bottle and woke up smelling the essence as though I had just sprayed it. The bottle had cracked down the side and left an imprint on my hand, but when I held the bottle up nothing leaked out.

At first smell of the Wood essence, I was disgusted by the scent and refused to use it. When my soul was ready, I purchased a bottle and let the magic take over. After a few hours of having the essence, the colour changed so that it looked like Green Angel. I had an enlarged liver and my doctor could never explain why. Colour Mirrors helped me understand it was all my stuck emotions being stored in my liver. I was sick for seven days as the Wood essence detoxed my body, removing everything that no longer served me. Eighteen months later I am medication free and my liver is doing great.

Katherine Louise Jones, UK, www.katherinelouisejones.com

I have three favourite spritzers. The first is Copper Dragon – her power and strength, her earthly Goddess quality, her ability to anchor me physically on Gaia. The next is Platinum Angel, which brings me to oneness. I often spritz this one before I make a Colour Mirrors video, to tune into the collective. This angel cuts through all the layers of cellular imprints and plugs me back into the cosmos. She is alchemy, and the power of platinum to change and shift from molten to liquid and vice versa reflects our ability to be 'all' things. The third is Rose Pink, an all-round heart connector. It holds my tears, comforts my grief and wraps me with love when I need it. She is the power of Divine love in both feminine and masculine form, and I feel connected to my heart when I work with this essence.

Kathryn Dzsudzsak, Canada, www.thebluehairmentor.com

Black Dragon is my go-to spritzer. I know when I am going through a 'shift', a difficult one in particular, because I literally crave the essence of Black Dragon and the beautiful vibration of the colour and the sparkles – cannot forget the sparkles! Those pop me through whatever it is. Being the bottle of 'death and rebirth' it also helped me through the grieving process when my daughter passed. I keep this bottle handy for the grandchildren when they come, and it is helping them as well.

Lesley McDonald, UK, www.lesleytara.com

A friend's young daughter came to visit and told me that she had been having chest pains and difficulty breathing. It had been going on for a while and she had already been given medication by her doctor, but it was not helping.

I intuitively sensed that the problem might not be medical but stuck energy, as I had chatted with this child before and knew she was a sensitive soul who cried easily and was often reprimanded for expressing her tears. Her family adores her, but her pain – her sensitivity – is their pain. She is a beautiful star child mirror, and they do what they can to help her not feel it.

Just a week before this, on my Colour Mirrors practitioner training course, at the very end of the last day we had spoken about two essences, Clear Angel and Air, and I had felt as though I needed to take them with me.

This child enjoys playing with the colour bottles, and when I asked her if she would like to try some of the essences for her breathing issues, she was delighted. I sprayed Air along with Clear Angel, and she also chose Dolphin. The combination of blue and clear in these three essences was a balm to the well of tears she had felt unable to express, melting the frozen emotion. Air provided her with space to be herself and cleared the airwaves, supported by Clear Angel and the playful, loving energy of Dolphin. After a couple of days her mother called to tell me her daughter was sobbing uncontrollably, and she was quite understandably concerned. I explained that this was OK, it was a process that needed to happen, that she needed to be allowed to express her sadness and that she was releasing her stuck feelings. Within a few more days mum reported that her daughter's breathing had returned to normal, and when I saw the child again she was much lighter and brighter.

Another essence story: While working as a school administrator, I learned that Red Angel and Ruby Red were essences that should be a part of every High School office. When our students arrived late in the morning after a stressful ride on rush hour buses, a quick spray of the red essences had them put back together in no time. Word got around too that in the office was a magical red essence that helped with overwhelm, frayed nerves and exam stress, and before any exam an ever-growing number of teenagers were dropping in to the office for a quick fix of the reassuring comfort of the red vibration. The way the red energy quickly grounded and patched up fragmentation was quite magical to witness.

Louise K. Shaw, UK, www.louisekshaw.com

Should I or shouldn't I? That was the question that was going through my mind as I was preparing for a client session. Would I freak out my client by introducing the Colour Mirrors bottles? Would she think I was a little weird? I wasn't even sure that I genuinely believed that using the bottles in a Skype session would actually work! What happened next would cement my loyalty towards this magical system for healing. We were at a point in the session where my client was finding it difficult to move through a block. I must admit I was a little unsure where to go next.

At that moment I decided to pick an essence bottle and spray the computer (reassured that my client had her eyes shut and so couldn't see what I was doing!). Almost immediately, my client raised her head and started sniffing the air. She asked: "Have you just sprayed something?" To which I asked her: "What can you smell?" She told me that it reminded her of pink English roses in the countryside when she was a child, and this was the release she needed to tap into a deep-rooted trauma that ultimately enabled her to gain resolution on an event in her past. As we were concluding the session she was curious about the smell, as she'd smelt it so suddenly. I explained to her that I'd sprayed a Colour Mirrors essence called Rose Pink.

Up until this point in my own journey and in my work with clients, the concept that we are connected was more a philosophy than a reality. This experience confirmed without a shadow of a doubt that we are all truly connected, and our distance from each other is only an illusion because my client smelt that essence immediately – and over a computer. What else could explain that experience other than us all being one consciousness, one unified existence?

At only 28 weeks, while in the womb, an embryo develops their sense of smell, and by the time they are born they have started to associate feelings with smells. Throughout your life you will continue to develop these associations, for both pleasure and pain. And as my client's experience demonstrated, a scent can powerfully and quickly uncover hidden trauma. That's why I love working with the Colour Mirrors essence bottles with my clients and for my own continual journey of self-discovery and healing.

Michael Kapp, Canada, www.moirabush.com

I was coughing a lot and kept thinking it was cold and flu issues, until I was diagnosed with asthma and given an inhaler. Melissie suggested I use a combination of the Green and Blue Angel spritzers, which I did. By the time I had finished the bottles the asthma had gone, and I never needed an inhaler again. When I have any cold or flu symptoms I go back to using these two bottles and spray blue on my throat and green on my chest. They always help.

I produce 'The Magenta Show' and often guests arrive feeling nervous about being in front of multiple cameras. It is a live show so there is no opportunity to edit what is said, which adds to the pressure they feel about being vulnerable and exposed to an audience. I spray their hands with Metatron and ask them to rub their hands and then breathe in the essence's smell, and I tell them that this will calm all their nerves. I have noticed that when they connect with this energy they are more present in the moment, and the show is easier to produce. At times when cameras freeze or the internet goes down and I run around fixing things while the show is still live, they don't get distracted and are able to stay focused on continuing the conversation. I also spray Metatron on myself, and it helps me stay calm too.

Michele Stevens, UK, www.wellnessbymichele.com

As I prepared my treatment room for a client, I was drawn to Copper Dragon and Platinum Angel. My phone rang as I finished using them, and it was Priscilla Elliott, my Colour Mirrors teacher. Priscilla asked what I had just been doing and I explained. Priscilla told me that she had been drawn to pick up two essences and call me but didn't know why until now: the essences in her hand were Copper Dragon and Platinum Angel! These essences together represented Spiritual & Material Conflict, bottle 18. By sheer coincidence I was taking part in a Spiritual & Material Clearing event that weekend. This experience happened during my first year as a full-time therapist. I was also in the middle of taking the Colour Mirrors practitioner course – possibly I was unconsciously releasing any blocks I had.

Using the essences when preparing my treatment room for clients is something I always do. I set the intention to help my client for the higher good and to be the best therapist I can be, and then I ask to be guided to the essence or essences to use in the room. I love the messages, laughter, love, joy and magic that working with Colour Mirrors brings. It is always joyful and exciting!

Monica Burman, UK, www.facebook.com/monica.burman.58

The Yeshua essence is my favourite. It keeps me connected to the Divine in me and all around and helps me remember I am spirit having a human experience, not the other way round. It helps me remember that everything is as it should be at any given moment.

Renira Barclay, UK, www.abovemiddlec.com

Stories from 'Emotional Accident and Emergency' at Karl Dawson's EFT trainings in Brighton

When Karl Dawson runs his Emotional Freedom Technique (Tapping) courses and the students start tapping, it can bring all sorts of emotions and memories bubbling to the surface. For some people this is all too much, and they seek assistance from the helpers at the back of the room. These overwhelming emotions tend to come from 'Big Trauma' memories and we, as helpers, do what we can to resolve the issue as best we can in order to send them back into the room to continue learning. Karl is very kind and allows me to use the essences in what I call Accident and Emergency (usually the tea room!). I am known as 'Mother Hen' as well as 'The Colours Lady'!

As helpers we are quite used to people running out of the room in distress, floods of tears etc. I follow them out with my trusty bag of approximately 20 essences plus a box of tissues. The first questions I always ask are: "What colour do you need to bring you back to balance?" or "What is your colour for safety?" If they say orange I spritz the Fire essence, which is so good for shock. If they say blue I use Dolphin, green goes to Green Angel etc. etc. Once we are further into the session, if they say they would like pink, for example, I will often ask them: "Would you like an Angel or a Dragon?"

Once, when dealing with a student who was sobbing and sobbing (she was off on a Shamanic journey unbeknown to us), the ONLY thing we could do was get her to HOLD Pink Angel. This did the trick and she came back to us.

When walking round checking on the students pairing up for their first and second time, there will often be those who are stuck or in tears. A question like: "What colour would help you?" is answered by "I need lilac" or "yellow", and it is just joyous and magical to spritz Lilac Angel or Yellow Angel. In fact, it is just too EASY to let the Colour Mirrors bottles do their magic – but I'm not complaining!

There was one student who was lying on the floor saying she wanted to die. I asked her what colour would bring her back to life, and she said "black" (unusually). A quick spritz of Black Dragon had her on her feet in a couple of minutes. I remember her saying: "That was JUST what I needed."

Often once the students have come through their own personal emergency they will say things like: "It was the White Dragon that made all the difference." Or: "Pink Angel connected me with my long-lost daughter." And I feel so proud being able to help.

If I were limited to four essences in 'EFT Accident and Emergency' then I think they would be Pink Angel, Gold Angel, Lilac Angel and Fire. My own Fire story was when I received the news in Brighton, in a car park, that my birth mother had just died. I knew I had to find my way out of the car park, negotiate Brighton traffic and then get home to tell other members of the family. I knew I needed orange, i.e., FIRE. Goodness me, that helped me in my own emergency.

Another Fire story was at the funeral of a dear friend's brother. We were coming into the church, and my friend greeted me at the door. She said she was fine, but had just burst into tears. I knew what I had to do. I had Fire in my handbag so asked her to put out both her hands. Before she knew what was happening she got a big spritz of Fire, which gave her a shock! But the orange Fire worked its magic, and she was able to compose herself for the rest of the service. She is able to smile about it now.

Before I read the lesson at my son's wedding last September I spritzed Gold Angel. That was just right for that occasion.

A very special message I received when using Royal Blue Dragon was that I need never apologise for my magic.

A young musical client of mine who was having panic attacks left with Dolphin in his pocket. Blue was his colour for safety and so Dolphin, combined with Debussy's 'Claire de Lune', supported him. I find the essences love merging with music – and it's so much fun!

I always have an essence in my handbag, if not two! I have just checked who is in there today and it is Gold Dragon, but tomorrow it might be another one. You just feel for what would be most supportive for the situation and it is there for you. The essences are always there for you!

Sharon King, UK, www.magicalnewbeginnings.com

I was staying at the home of a lovely family, where the mother shared with me that she was concerned about her five-year-old daughter. She had suddenly become fearful of leaving the house and being separated from her parents, which meant she didn't want to go to the school she had always loved to attend before. She asked if I could help, as her daughter would just not say what was wrong. That evening I went to the daughter's bedroom and asked if I could come in and lay on the bed with her. She agreed and seemed happy for me to be there.

I had only packed one Colour Mirrors bottle for this trip, which was Pink Angel. As I lay there I told her a story about Pink Angel. I sprayed the Pink Angel essence into the air and invited Pink Angel to come into the room, telling the little girl that only kids could see the Pink Angel and asking her to tell me when the angel was there. Suddenly she pointed to the corner of the room saying she had arrived, then pointed all around the room as Pink Angel flew around sprinkling her pink magic all over us. I said: "Pink Angel has many special powers, but her best quality is to listen to children's secrets and help them with whatever they are worried about."

She suddenly started to shout for her mum in quite a frantic way. When her mum came in I left the room so they could be alone, but afterwards her mum told me that Pink Angel had told the little girl she must tell mum what had been scaring her. It turned out she had had a nightmare a few nights earlier that both her mum and dad had died, and she was fearful this was really going to happen. So mum was able to reassure her this was not going to happen and to thank Pink Angel for helping her with this secret. Of course I left the bottle of Pink Angel with them just in case any more secret fears needed to be shared.

Tadeja Jere Jakulin, Slovenia, www.turistica.si/jere-jakulin

Platinum Angel reminds us of our home, with eternal gratitude of being here and now.

Zane Piese, UK, www.atlantisskincare.com

I use Metatron on a daily basis every morning. It lightens me and gives instant connection to my soul, reminding me I am God in this body, and helping me learn to love the body I have chosen for this lifetime.

Authors' Note: Two of the essences mentioned in the Essences Stories, Dolphin and Sandalphon, are not officially part of the Colour Mirrors system so do not feature in our Essences section of the book, but they are both hugely popular and are enjoyed by many. They are available to purchase, along with all the other Colour Mirrors essences, from your practitioner or teacher.

Glossary

Some of the terms in this book may not be commonly used or may have a slightly different connotation here than you have seen before. Our explanations are not meant to be in any way 'the' definition, they are simply our take on these concepts. We hope they give context and bring clarity.

3D/Third Dimension

Everything you can see, hear, feel, touch and smell. The term 3D also relates to the limited, fear-based ways of thinking and living that have been prevalent on this planet throughout much of its history.

5D/Fifth Dimension

This is a high vibrational state in which life is based on love, peace and joy. Living in oneness with all life, you know yourself and everything else to be part of the Divine. You no longer subscribe to lower vibrational ways of being, thinking and doing, such as judgement, aggression, blame and shame. As you raise your vibration, you open your heart and live from your spirit. Freedom, respect and wisdom prevail. Both the earth and humanity are currently moving towards a fifth dimensional state; some even say that Gaia has already transitioned to 5D and that many lightworkers in particular are now operating more and more from a fifth dimensional state.

See also Ascension, Golden Age, New Earth, Shift of Ages.

Akashic Records

The etheric records of all that ever was, is now and ever will be.

Ascension

This is the process of lifting your vibration so that you move out of the heaviness of 3D existence into the expansive, light and joyful energy of 5D and beyond – while still in your physical body. The shift from 3D to 5D has never been experienced before in the way we are currently navigating it. This is why it can feel so challenging – and why it is also incredibly exciting! It can appear elusive and as if we are very far from the fifth dimensional state at times, but this is a major transition and will take time. The more that all conscious humans focus on the realisation of this shift, the more swiftly and easily it can occur.

Note: The term Descension is sometimes used now used rather than Ascension. This refers to the descent of the light of your Divine self into your body and onto the earth, or the process of anchoring your light into the here and now. Both 'ascension' and 'descension' are required if we are to experience the fifth dimension on the earth. We have continued to use the term Ascension in this book as in essence it encompasses both, but you are free to substitute it with any other term that suits.

See also 5D, Golden Age, New Earth, Shift of Ages.

Refer to The Golden Gaia Set (p.164) and The Silver Gaia Set (p.203) for further information.

Atlantis

The name Atlantis refers to an ancient, highly advanced civilisation. Although there is no proof of its existence, mystics and spiritual teachers have always written and spoken about it, and it has become part of the collective subconscious on some level. It often correlates to challenging subconscious patterns and memories such as power struggles, abuse of power, grief and guilt. It can also relate to powerful memories of a Golden Age when humankind was both spiritually and technologically evolved, and these memories may assist us now as we move towards 5D.

See also 5D, Golden Age and Lemuria.

*Birth Numbers/Soul Numbers/Soul Path

An exciting way of combining colour with numerology is to take the numbers from your date of birth, translate those numbers into Colour Mirrors bottles and then explore their messages. For example, if your birthdate is 4 July 1986, look at what bottle 4 has to say, and also bottles 35 and 8 (if you add all the digits of your birthdate: 4 + 7 + 1 + 9 + 8 + 6 = 35, and when 35 is reduced to a single digit it becomes 3 + 5 = 8). These numbers can collectively be called your soul numbers or birth numbers and can reveal insights about your soul path, or what you came to do, be and experience in this lifetime.

Refer to Colour and Numerology (p.16) and Numerology and the Gaia Set (p.142) for further information.

Chakra

The word chakra comes from Sanskrit and translates as 'wheel of light'. Chakras are also referred to as energy centres. According to ancient wisdom, chakras exist throughout the body, with seven major chakras from the top of the crown to the base of the spine. Because each of these main chakras has a colour associated with it, chakras work well as an explanation of and support for any form of colour therapy.

Refer to The Chakra Set (p.96) and Chakras and Colour (p.97) for further information.

Christ

The term Christ is sometimes used as another name for Jesus. It is used here primarily to refer to any awakened human who fully knows him or herself to be part of the Divine, rather than being specific to any person or religion.

Complementary Colours

On an artist's colour wheel each colour is laid out in a circle, moving from red to orange to yellow and on through the rainbow to complete the circle in magenta. As such, every colour has an opposite or complementary colour. In colour therapy, complementary colours provide additional insight and information about a person's colour choices.

Refer to Complementary Colours (p.15) for further information.

Crystal Children

This term refers to many children born since the 1980's who seem to have a new and more elevated understanding of what it means to be human. They know who they are, have clear insight and intuition and carry a light, high vibration. Their path is to help lift the consciousness of humanity into a higher state.

See also Indigo Children and Star Children.

Divine

The term 'Divine' refers to whatever you believe about an omnipresent higher consciousness. There are many other names such as the Universe, God, Source, the Presence, the Allness, All That Is. You might also simply call it Love. Feel free to substitute the term that suits you best.

When we say 'you are Divine', this means that in your essence, your spirit, the core of your being, you are made up of the same light and love as the Divine itself. The Divine is in everything and everyone, and you are an individual spark of consciousness that carries a unique thread of the Divine's light. As you learn to recognise your own inner Divine light, you become aware of it in others. As you and everyone else on the planet evolves and expands their light, frequency and consciousness, so the universe too evolves and expands.

Divine Consciousness

A highly evolved level of consciousness that enables you to feel, see and know what it is to be part of the Divine. A person who is fully immersed in Divine consciousness sees everything through the eyes of unconditional love.

Elohim

This term has several possible definitions depending on context. In this book we use it to refer to a collective of angelic beings, also known as 'creator angels', who carry great light and spiritual power. The Elohim hold a very sacred space for each human being to remember their own inner Divine light and truth.

Gaia

The name given to the consciousness of planet earth. This name recognises the earth as a living, sentient being.

Golden Age

Many cultures and religions refer to a Golden Age – a time of peace and plenty on earth. These 'ages' tend to be cyclical and often follow a period of darkness and destruction. Many spiritual sources predicted that a new Golden Age would begin in 2012, and indeed significant shifts have been occurring since that time and will continue to do so. The 'future' is not a given, however. It is not fixed or determined but rather is created by the hearts and souls of all humanity collectively. Whether we bring about a Golden Age on this earth is up to us, but there are cosmic forces at play which mean that there has never been a greater possibility for creating (or allowing) a Golden Age than now.

See also 5D, Ascension, New Earth, Shift of Ages.

Refer to The Golden Gaia Set (p.164) for further information.

Heaven on Earth

A state of bliss that comes from seeing what you believe. This state is not dependent on what happens in the external world because it arises from within.

High Priestess

Although this is the name of one of the Major Arcana cards in the Tarot, this term can also be used to refer to someone with a misguided sense of spiritual superiority.

Higher Heart

The chakra that sits between the heart and the throat, around the area of the thymus. The higher heart helps you perceive the interconnection of all things and open to higher levels of awareness. Its colour is turquoise.

Higher Self

Your inner soul-self that is completely connected to the Allness. Your higher self is the clearest, brightest, most joyful and wise self you can possibly imagine. It views the world from the Divine perspective and has no concept of limitation, fear, frustration or lack. Your higher self is always available as a friend, guide and teacher for you – you simply have to remember to call on it.

I AM/ I AMness

Your inner connection with the Divine. Another name for your higher self.

Indigo Children

Indigo children have always arrived on the planet feeling different from previous generations. Many children born after the Second World War, and again from the 1970's onwards, have questioned prevailing customs and behaviour, challenged old traditions and called for a society based on love rather than war. Each subsequent generation of children arriving on the planet has been more and more highly evolved in consciousness.

See also Crystal Children and Star Children.

Judgement

The perception of anything as wrong. Discernment means you have the ability to choose this or that, but judgement says this is right, therefore that is wrong. Judgement sets up and sits behind every experience of separation, disconnection and duality.

Lemuria

Lemuria is an ancient, mythical civilisation, said to exist either before Atlantis or at the same time. In allegorical terms they may be seen as two sides of the same story of a time when humanity was enlightened and empowered. Atlantis represented the masculine energy and Lemuria, the feminine. For those who relate to Lemuria it has connotations of great purity, light, peace and joy, and it is a reminder of your true, natural state.

See also Atlantis.

Lightworker

A person who knows themselves to be on a path of spiritual evolution. Lightworkers choose to consciously elevate their own consciousness and support others in doing so. They often have a strong desire to be of service, help humanity and support the planet and all its inhabitants in their evolution.

Master Number

A master number is any number which contains a repeated digit, e.g., 11, 22, 33. Such numbers refer to the particular abilities, skills and qualities of a person who is considered to be, or have the potential to become, a master: someone who is consciously on a path of expansion and enlightened living while being fully present in their body. When you choose bottles 11, 22 or 33, you are being invited to live more and more from your higher self and to see any situation or experience from the Divine perspective. Please note that bottle C8 is the 44th bottle in the system, bottle G4 is the 55th, bottle G15 is the 66th, and bottle G26 the 77th, so these bottles also signify 'mastery' energy.

Mystery School

In the ancient past, many forms of spirituality were kept secret out of fear of persecution. Because of this fear and a misguided sense of power, much of what was taught about spirituality was kept hidden, and secret enclaves were formed. In these 'mystery schools', the mysteries of the universe were unveiled so that people could try to make sense of their world. They were organised according to strict hierarchies and the leader, a High Priest or High Priestess, was a person of great power. In terms of colour, people who have cellular memories of these teachings or lifetimes tend to be drawn to royal blue or violet, and often have issues to do with power. This is reflected in the complementary colours, which are gold and yellow.

New Earth

The new earth is the name given to a vision of earth where humanity has evolved to a point where we can sustain a peaceful, harmonious way of life, based on co-operation and founded on love. It is a vision for earth as a place of connection, joy and light, where all are free from judgement and the illusion of separation.

See also 5D, Ascension, Golden Age, Shift of Ages.

Refer to The Magenta Gaia Set (p.217) for further information.

Past Lives

If we understand that energy can never be destroyed but only change form, the concept of past lives relates to the many incarnations of a human being as they evolve through time. Past lives are in many ways only relevant for the information they provide, including any energy imprints left behind, and their implications for the current lifetime. If you struggle with the idea of past lives you may choose to view the information provided about them by colour as allegorical and a means of helping you identify unresolved issues and blocks.

Perfection

In the context of this book, the word 'perfection' describes what you see when you view something without judgement. It is when you look at the world as if everything that is happening is meant to be happening. Even if you do not understand the whys and wherefores with your mind, your soul understands that there is a bigger picture to everything in the universe.

Refer to The Fifth Spiritual Principle (p.122) for further information.

Primary Colours

Primary colours cannot be mixed from other colours and are the source of all other colours. The three primary colours are red, blue and yellow.

Separation

Separation is the core wound of all human beings. When you incarnate into a human body, you may experience a sense of separation as you leave the bliss of the spiritual realms to take human form. When you are born, you are removed from the womb and experience the physical separation of your body from your mother. As you grow, you learn to see yourself as separate from others because you have a physical body that is separate from everyone else's.

The key to healing the separation wound is to understand that it is only an experience. From a higher perspective, it is not real. You have never been separate from the Divine, nor could you be. Nothing in the universe is completely separate from anything else. Everything in life affects everything else. We are all interwoven and interconnected on many levels – even if we are unaware of most of them. Every experience of apparent separation offers you an opportunity to move beyond it and return to a state of unity and wholeness, and this is often the primary reason why people seek a spiritual path: so they can feel reconnected again.

Shift of Ages

This is the shift from 3D to 5D, foretold in many cultures and spiritual traditions to coincide with planetary and cosmic cycles beginning in 2012.

See also 5D, Ascension, Golden Age, New Earth.

Refer also to The Silver Gaia set (p.203) for further information.

Soul Path/Soul Numbers

*See Birth Numbers

Soul Star

The traditional chakra system acknowledges seven main chakras or energy centres down the mid-line of your body, from the first at the base of the spine to the seventh at the crown of your head. There is an eighth chakra, however, a few inches above your head. It is called the Soul Star, as it is the energy centre that holds your spiritual blueprint, your Divine plan for this lifetime. The colour related to the Soul Star is magenta.

Star Children

This is what we call children who are born with so much light in their energy fields that they look as if they come from the stars. Many star children have memories of lifetimes in the star realms and/or have spiritual gifts and abilities that are generally considered unusual on earth. They are likely to be highly sensitive and finely tuned and may feel different from others. They often experience the density of 3D reality on earth as extremely painful or difficult, and it is this that guides them onto a spiritual path so that they can gain a higher awareness and understanding of their earthly experience. A huge part of their journey is to find love and acceptance for themselves and their bodies and land fully on the earth so that they can learn to love her too. In this way they can fulfil their destiny by assisting humanity to evolve to a higher level of consciousness and love.

Tarot

The Tarot is a set of cards used for divination or as an oracle. It is an ancient system, with 78 cards divided into four 'Minor Arcana' suits – Cups, Pentacles, Swords and Wands – and the 'Major Arcana', which consists of 22 cards. The Major Arcana is often understood to refer to our collective archetypes and so we refer to them for some of the first 36 Colour Mirrors bottles, as they provide extra information to help explain what the bottles are about. Bottle 13, for example, links to the Death Card and bottle 16 to The Tower. In these instances the Tarot helps illustrate the meaning of the bottles.

Violet Flame

A spiritual flame of transformation and purification that helps shift negative energies and release stuck emotions.

Yeshua

The Hebrew name for Jesus.

The Colour Mirrors Team

Colour Mirrors is blessed to have a team of extraordinary people supporting it. We share here the stories of four people who are essential to Colour Mirrors and intimately involved in it. Without this wonderful team, it would not exist in the form it does today.

Moira Bush

Colour was not something I ever felt to be of significance in my life. I loved painting colour walls in my homes, however as a therapy or something other than pleasing to the eye, colour held no interest for me. Even during art classes in school I chose to sketch with black pencils and charcoal. I have one vivid memory of colour as being fascinating and that was around the age of five or six when I noticed colours reflected in a pool of oil on a roadside.

When I moved from South Africa to England with my husband at the time, I was annoyed when he kept telling me that psychics he had been consulting in London predicted that I would work with colour bottles and that it was my destiny to work with spiritual colour psychology. I was very happily employed helping women become entrepreneurs, so I ignored him and the books he bought on colour for me to read. For years I had studied and worked as a medium in spiritualist churches and that, I felt, was all the spiritual nourishment I needed.

Then one day he told me about another South African woman who taught the meaning of colours and who was going to be running a workshop in Cornwall. His interest in colour was that he could see people's auras and wanted to learn what the colours meant. I heard myself say that I would go with him – nothing to do with colours, just a fun weekend away to a nice seaside hotel, with a husband that I rarely saw due to us working in different cities. The moment I walked into the training room and felt the colour bottles – you can never just see them – and Melissie started teaching, I knew deep down at a soul level that my life would change. I had found something that I did not even know I was missing – the spiritual language of colour.

It was on this workshop that I met Amanda Bradbury for the first time and heard about astrology. Over the years I delved deeper into the symbolism of astrology with her expert guidance and learned more about the Colour Mirrors planet bottles.

At the end of that first course in Cornwall, we all, except for my husband, asked Melissie to teach us more, and she agreed to come back after New Year for another workshop. Once I let Colour Mirrors into my heart I became driven with an urgency that I could not understand at the time. All I knew was that I had to stop whatever I was doing and tell the entire world about Melissie and her bottles. I had to learn more.

Three months after the course, I placed a call to Melissie in South Africa asking her to teach me more and inviting her to stay with me for several months. To fit around my full-time job at the time, we spent every evening and weekend launching Colour Mirrors. We got a website up, designed a logo and took part in exhibitions and workshops around England and Scotland. It was an intense time and a deep initiation for myself and my family – my marriage ended too. I started to see my life through the lens of colour and I was stripped of the old illusions of who I thought I was. My evolution had begun. At the end of that year I resigned my full-time job and made Colour Mirrors my priority and business in England.

When I met Korani at a Mind Body & Spirit show she had organised in Salisbury, I was keen to expand Colour Mirrors in England and had no idea how to go about it. It turned out that Korani was the answer. She is a scribe from heaven, and puts into words things my dysfunctional ADD brain senses but cannot express when it comes to the language of colour. I believe Korani has been the biggest gift to Colour Mirrors. She is wise, and ended up mentoring me very patiently through some steep initiations.

The Colour Mirrors website, although basic at the time, caught the interest of people overseas, and there followed 15 years of travel and training. I kept saying yes and going to other countries to introduce Colour Mirrors and Melissie's spiritual philosophy. I learned some expensive lessons too – I tried to push to get Colour Mirrors into the American market during 2008 and no one turned up. I was learning not to tell this system what, when and who needed it. Now wiser, I wait and respond to the call of service. On my last day in Atlanta, I received one of those random emails normally destined for the junk folder. It invited me to participate in a program to write a spiritual book, with Neale

Donald Walsh as one of the mentors. I said yes, and with Melissie's guidance, the *Colour Mirrors Oracle Cards* and accompanying booklet were produced.

Melissie has always said to do with the system what you want, let it take you where it wants to. In 2012 I bathed in each of the Silver Gaias – bottles G28 to G33 – and they downloaded a new healing system that we called Silver Spheres. This is a colour system of light activation that opens your chakras at the back. For this system Melissie created three special spritzers: Bliss, Transcendence and Peridot. We soon discovered that when your back chakras are opened you receive more easily and your self-awareness expands faster. These discoveries led to the Love & Money Boot Camp that is now my main teaching program, using the entire Colour Mirrors system to work with the shadow and the issues of a poverty mindset.

I moved to Canada with my husband Paul in 2015 and found entrepreneurs who were fascinated by the colour bottles. As I kept saying yes to whatever turned up, I found myself writing the book *8 Colours of Prosperity* which explores how colour bridges the spiritual and material worlds. I now host a social media TV show called The Magenta Show and this is my platform for demonstrating how the Colour Mirrors system works.

To say that Melissie and her colours saved my life is an understatement. She saved my soul. The first time I consciously understood the power of Colour Mirrors and what she had created was when she read my date of birth in colours and numerology. I was shocked that the row of four bottles held the story of my entire life. Even now, teaching classes on Colour and Numerology is a personal passion for me.

As this book was being produced, Melissie and Korani, despite their hectic lives and their own writing commitments, have helped me to create a new deck of colour cards, *Colour your Shadow*. And that, dear colour fans, is the real story of Colour Mirrors for me: each colour ray shone into the depths of my mind and lit up the dark corners in my shadow and revealed my true self, one bottle at a time. I learned to love and integrate the splintered aspects, thereby healing many lifetimes and wounds.

Allowing the colours to open up all the doors in my consciousness led to a new life that would certainly have looked like a dream life to my mother. I have a husband who loves me unconditionally, a son who now manages my businesses, I collect colourful art and we live in a beautiful country that during the winter months paints everything I see with my most favourite colour: white.

Contact Moira to find out more about her work:
www.moirabush.com
#MoiraBush
@MoiraBush

Amanda Bradbury

My journey with Colour Mirrors started in the autumn of 2002 when I was exhibiting Astrology and Sacred Geometry at a show in Cornwall. It was held at the Ponsmere, a wonderful run-down hotel right on the beach, blessed with the sound of the waves as we went to sleep at night.

Melissie Jolly was working with colour on the other side of the hall. Her table was very simple, with a white cloth and 33 gorgeous bottles of vibrant colour. The system was called Colour Works at that time. And work it did! I had a reading with Melissie and I remember how I arranged the bottles, looking like bird's wings, and how I found Melissie's interpretation accurate and inspiring. She was running a workshop the following weekend and I felt compelled to make the journey back to Cornwall to attend. It was at this workshop that I met Moira, and I remember her passion for the system and her determination that she was going to create a business by working with it.

From the start I loved the beauty of the system, with colours like jewels, and the meaningful connections it makes to Astrology and Numerology, particularly through the planetary and Element bottles. The system speaks to me through synchronicity, and the connections often amaze me.

I began to develop a way of working that combined Colour and Astrology. To me they create a perfect marriage of spontaneous emotional response with in-depth intuitive analysis. Colour enables us to work with the energy that emerges in an astrology session, move through the emotions that arise and find healing. I love how the colour that someone is drawn to speaks of their Astrology.

In 2003 Moira generously organised for me to teach three Colour and Astrology workshops in Scotland and other parts of the UK. They were big groups, and I remember the standing ovation I was given in Glasgow and the enthusiasm and support that was around at that time for spiritual work. Moira and Melissie came across to me as two quirky, outspoken South Africans, and on our road trip round the country they tended to sit together in the front of the car and sometimes broke out into Afrikaans, which added to the exotic, intriguing quality of the whole experience.

In 2004 Moira arranged a workshop on Colour, Astrology and the Kabbalah in South Africa that I was honoured to teach alongside Melissie. Again it was a big group, and I remember some of the participants sat on the floor. By this time I was very aware and even a little daunted by just how significant and big the system felt. It was clear to me, however, that there is an over-lighting energy that inspires those who work with the system and carries it forward.

It was at the first Teachers course held at the end of 2005 that I met starry Korani. A couple of years later I was honoured to be chosen by Melissie to train alongside Moira and Korani to be a Teacher Trainer, and soon after this I was over the moon to be running some Teachers courses myself.

Most special to me have been all the courses and workshops over the years, so many and all so memorable. There were the trips to Marit and Torgeir's centre overlooking a fjord in Norway, and the visits to Melissie's home in that quirky, arty town called Stanford, in South Africa, near where the Southern Right whales come to give birth.

For a few years, attending Melissie's workshops would bring up in me complex and deep emotion. It was as if I was sitting on emotions that I needed to express, and being with the bottles and the Colour Mirrors family and experiencing Melissie's extraordinary meditations would move me and bring up emotion. While I may have been able to express at a more surface level why I felt emotional, the depth of my response and feelings was something that couldn't be explained.

One of the aspects of Colour Mirrors I have most appreciated has been how Melissie has kept the system so open and flexible, giving teachers and therapists the freedom to explore and create their own ways of working.

The most special part of my Colour Mirrors journey has been the people who are drawn to the system, those who have the sensitivity to respond to the colours and the compassion and consciousness to work with it. Meeting and getting to know these healers and teachers over the years has hugely enriched and supported my life and I feel extremely grateful.

Contact Amanda to find out more about her work:
www.amandabradbury.com

Gilly Ball

As Melissie's daughter, I've been part of this colour journey since I was 13, and at school they joked that my superpower was speaking the language of colour. I went on to work in fashion as a buyer and trend forecaster, where the knowledge of colour and what it meant was a hugely insightful and valuable tool.

In 2011 after I had my son, Jasper, and my relationship with his father ended, mom asked me to come and join Colour Mirrors. I leapt at the opportunity to be doing something meaningful, magical and colourful. At the time of writing it has now been eight years of making the bottles with our resident angel, Anna, and I love it.

In 2016 we launched my heart-project called Jasper, a mindfully made beauty range, which we see as a bridge between the holistic beauty industry and the deeply transformative Colour Mirrors system.

Between managing the office, launching new products, making bottles, raising a child and trying to be a better human today than yesterday, my days are full and very blessed.

Contact Gilly to find out more about her work:
www.colourmirrors.com/jasper-oils

Anna Tobias

When Melissie bought her house in Stanford I had worked for the previous owners two days a week. I decided to stay on and work for Melissie and her two boys, and we got on very well. Then I found out what she did. I know she was anxious because I told her that I was a church sister and went to church every Sunday and even had services at my house. She did not know how I would feel about the coloured oils she worked with, but what she did not know was that I am a seer in the church and I immediately saw the light around the oils she made. We also use oil for healing in my church. We pray over the oil and then use it to heal people. I waited a few days until I was sure, and when I saw Melissie making the oils, I could see that she prayed over them and then it became very light, just like when we use the oil in the church.

From helping her pour and pack the oils, she asked me if I could follow recipes, and if so, would I make the Angel spritzers. From then on I have been the 'angel maker', and where I live it is not always so peaceful and quiet, but when I step into our work space and I start making Angel spritzers, my heart nearly bursts with joy. It gives me such peace and joy to be here and to do this work. I say thank you every day to Jesus that he brought me and Melissie together to do this work.

Colour Mirrors Testimonials

Over the years, Colour Mirrors practitioners and teachers have become used to hearing how much the system has changed people's lives. We have all had clients, friends and family members share how particular bottles have helped them shift something that had been stuck, opened their eyes to a new way of thinking or expanded their connection with the universe.

Here we include a selection of feedback and stories from our wonderful Colour Mirrors family for you to enjoy.

Alexia Claire Wren-Sillevis, UK www.sheworkswellness.com

For the blessingway of my second child, instead of clothes, rattles and muslins I asked if my lovely friends could gift me with crystals, candles and Colour Mirrors bottles! Guided by my beautiful teacher and friend, Katherine Jones, my friends bought me bottles G11 (Generosity), G12 (I AM) and G13 (Grace). Katherine then gifted me with Gold Dragon and Gold Angel.

During the end of my pregnancy I was told I had gestational diabetes, and it was a daily fight to get the doctors and nurses to listen to me about the gentle birth I wanted for my child. The Goldens guided and lifted me all the way through. They kept me strong but gracious, grateful and open. I bathed in bottles G12 and G13 whilst pregnant with Delphi, but bottle G11 needed to stay with me. I used the Gold Dragon and Gold Angel in the run up to and through the birth itself. When my doula was busy with another woman and couldn't be at my birth, and when my dear midwife also went on leave that night and we ended up with total strangers – the golden bottles helped. And throughout, I used the spritzers to connect, to calm, to embolden me. (Wow, Gold Dragon! Power in grace personified).

Despite having to give birth in hospital instead of at home and having to be put on a drip and other unexpected interventions, our daughter was born peacefully, into a generous space held by strong, gentle women with (relative!) ease. The midwives agreed it had been one of the loveliest births they'd ever attended.

After Delphi was born, bottle G11 came to play. My eldest daughter Marley and I, despite being utterly in love with Delphi, were feeling the difference, missing each other (we had always been a team of two). We shared the bottle of G11 – her first bath in Colour Mirrors. It was a wonderful acknowledgement of change and helped us to talk through how hearts can grow bigger to fit in new love – she was so excited to be allowed her first colour bath!

In the first few weeks of new motherhood, I used the rest of the Gold Dragon and Angel essences. I think of Delphi as a Colour Mirrors baby. And what is more fitting for a Colour Mirrors baby than a Colour Mirrors godmother. We were thrilled when Katherine agreed.

Ann Bowditch, Guernsey, www.hypnotherapy.gg

I had no knowledge of Colour Mirrors until a therapist used the essences on me, and I was amazed that whatever negative feeling I had been experiencing just dissipated as I inhaled the essence. I had to find out more. Two months later I was booked on to Korani's practitioner training course. I met five other ladies on the course who I feel are my soul sisters. We formed a bond so strong that it will last forever, and I hold them all dearly in my heart.

My Dad had died just five days before the first block of training and I was still grief-stricken. The first thing Korani asked us to do was select a bottle, and I chose Coral Angel. Korani went around the room asking how we all felt about the bottle we had chosen, and when she got to me I just sobbed, still feeling the loss of Dad. Coral Angel is my connection to him. I take it down to the cemetery where his ashes rest and spray it on his plaque – it feels like I have something tangible and precious which still connects us.

On the training we did an exercise where we selected bottles to place on our body. Without knowing, most of the bottles I selected were violet – which is about grief. I also recall doing a chakra session on the second part of the training where I focused on 'burn-out', something I had a pattern of doing. About two weeks later whilst running on the cliffs, not thinking about anything in particular, something came to me that felt so strong, as if it wasn't me, and said: "You are not responsible for everyone else." That message and the power from it has never left me. This is what I feel this amazing system does. It goes deep, very deep – into the subconscious, into the cells of our bodies, into the matrix, and we shift through the murkiness as clarity prevails.

I have decorated my house in the colours of the Starlights – my favourite is Starlight Being which I adore, and that is the colour of my bedroom (magenta). Even my alpha male husband loves the transformation in the house and said the different colours make him feel happy.

I use Colour Mirrors in my own practice, and so many of my clients have connected to this amazing system and are so often surprised at just how 'spot on' the bottles they select are.

The wording for the bottles has been so important for me because of the wisdom that is contained therein. The Colour Mirrors bottles help me not to get stuck in the complexities and dramas of life but to see challenges as a process of growth, learning or remembering and to know that whatever I am going through at any time, there is always a bottle calling to support and guide.

Thank you Melissie and Korani for this amazing gift.

Aurelia Florentina Rasmussen, Denmark, www.aurelia-florentina.dk

Use of this system is an amazing way to understand who you really are in your inner core. I have had many conversations with my cells and therefore insights about what was locked up inside of me, and then I could let it go – that is how the oils work. I recommend this for all who seriously want changes for the better in their life. Try it and set yourself free.

Blanka Gašperlin, Slovenia, www.sita.si

For quite some years I have used the oils and essences when I wake up and when I go to sleep. I use them also on the programs of the SITA method and in business. Years ago I learned through the Colour Mirrors bottles how to trust myself, how to focus on solutions, how to let go of pain and resentments.

Slowly I was able to realise all my wishes without trying, in my personal as well as my business life. My favourite essence is Pink Dragon, which helped me to remember how to laugh sincerely and how to get rid of fear. I started to enjoy life, with lots of laughter. The essences helped me with creativity and loving mindfulness towards myself. I developed compassion towards myself as well as intuition and channelling abilities, which I need for psychotherapeutic work. I also motivate others to use colour therapy.

Branka, Croatia

Thank you Melissie for creating the Colour Mirrors system of bottles. They are so sophisticated and gentle that my first encounter with them eight years ago was a challenge for me. Thank you Tadeja, my mentor, who led me to the Teacher's qualification. Today I am proud that I can help by using the Colour Mirrors system in a Croatian home for retired people, where I organise and lead weekly Colour Mirrors workshops. The elderly residents and employees of that home have accepted Colour Mirrors and my work with them with great delight. One home for retired people even equipped one of the rooms, which is prepared for people with dementia, with coloured curtains.

With the help of Colour Mirrors, knowledge about myself, my family and my surroundings is as much my path as my work with other people in broadening their consciousness and the awareness of their surroundings.

Catherine Ashworth, UK

Having experienced PTSD for the best part of my life, I now have more confidence, strength and courage to look it straight in the eye rather than withdrawing from it. Colour Mirrors has enabled me to paint it with any colour that I am drawn to, making it interesting and expansive rather than black, dull and contracted. It is a slow process, but at the same time it has taught me so much. It takes dedication and patience to want to be here on this planet and to be fully aligned with who we are and do the work we really love. This means appreciating others and ourselves for being who we are. I would like to thank the energies of these lovely bottles as I can now look ahead, with so much waiting in the wings to be opened and explored.

Choi Eunchae, Republic of Korea, choieunchae0430@gmail.com

On a Colour Mirrors workshop, yellow and violet kept running through my mind. When I heard that a 'soul bottle' was to be given to a person who was specially selected, I wanted to receive it but soon gave up because I usually do not have that kind of luck at all. And the very next moment, my name was called out. I came to get my soul bottle of yellow and violet with tremendous joy. I was so excited and happy to share my feeling with Melissie.

The next day I was busy showing my bottle around to everyone, so I could not use it, but from the second day of my possession I started to use the bottle, according to a tip from Melissie to use it immediately. When I shook the bottle for the first time and opened the lid, instantly I was fascinated by the fragrance that was a very familiar herbal flavour. At the moment of applying it to my body, I felt like I stood in the middle of warm golden plains. I was sure the fragrance took me there. And right away I felt like my whole body was warmly wrapped in gold.

After using it I began to look around with trembling heart to see if any changes would happen around me. I did not know of anyone else who had used the bottles before, but the results that came to me were amazing. A person who was misunderstanding me for someone else's misdemeanour approached me and said that she was really sorry that she did not recognise the truth before. She apologised very gently, in spite of the fact that she was 20 years older than me, and the misunderstanding about me was solved and things got better. My finances became better and my loan was paid back sooner than I expected. Also, as the boss changed in my workplace my position became important, and a person who was treating me badly and bullying me left the workplace.

Of course there were some difficult situations, like being given a tough assignment which meant that I might not graduate and various other situations. However, when these situations arise now I try to solve the problem anyway and move forward and be satisfied with it, no matter what the circumstances might be. Now I realise that I am the one who knows my own problem and solves it.

I learned the lesson that I don't need to change the environment, but I have to change myself to improve things around me. I strongly believe that my soul bottle played a role in transforming and nurturing me. As Melissie told me, from now on I will be someone who can go forward with enjoyment of the progress, even when it is difficult to proceed. Thank you.

Chrisoula Sirigou, UK, www.ChrisoulaSirigou.com

I have always been open to learning new things and have been a seeker and explorer to help feed my curiosity – a firm believer that there is more to life. In 2013 I was at a coaching training course on Heart Intelligence and Emotional Intelligent Relationships when I came across a display of the Colour Mirrors bottles. I felt magnetised by them, so when I was given the opportunity to have a reading for free, I said yes! The actual experience was beautiful and insightful, and I felt intrigued to know more.

For a few months I experimented using the Colour Mirrors Oracle cards. I remember as I shuffled the cards my inner voice was very judgemental about what other people would think of me. My perception of anything psychic-related was based on what my conditioning and my religion was telling me. I remember saying to myself: "What on earth are you doing!? This is witchcraft." That was my first impression, but soon I became engrossed in understanding the messages that were revealed to me in connection with a question or issue in my life.

The Colour Mirrors system is truly multifaceted! In addition to the energy and psychology of colour, we also work with the wisdom of numbers – numerology – as well as astrological insights connected with the planets. I was sceptical about how we could accept guidance from angels, archangels and ascended masters, but the more I connected with the energy of colour in a light-hearted way, playing with the oracle cards, the more I felt the pull to study the system and receive the certified training in it.

My ego/mind was bringing up various excuses and obstacles and one of them was time and money to finance the practitioner training course. As a result I asked for guidance, asking the question and setting the intention for my involvement in studying the language of colour. Every time I chose a card the same one came up: Archangel Metatron. The message was 'The Time Is Now'!

Having received these signs repetitively, and with my sceptical, analytical mind now at peace, I gradually allowed myself to connect more and more with my intuition and my spirit. I was starting to feel reassured that it was going to be OK to take the next big step, however crazy it may have felt at that point. My heart was saying yes, and the universe was conspiring.

It was one of the very best decisions in my entire life, and I now offer colour analysis and colour coaching, integrating heart intelligence, numerology and planetary insights. My work helps guide entrepreneurs, parents and educators who wish to transform and grow and who are seeking answers to improve their health, wealth, love and relationships. This is what we are here for – to maximise living LIFE with Love Intention Flow Ease.

You are not on your own. Ask for help and the right guidance will turn up to illuminate your next steps, transform your inner gold and alchemise your life.

Daniela, Croatia

Colour Mirrors has come into my life like a gift from heaven. I experience Colour Mirrors as a strong healing system with high vibrations. It brings radical changes in my life, business and in the healing of relationships. The Divine information of these bottles helped me to remove emotional blockages, enlighten dark situations and remove patterns of sadness, pain, suffering and deep wounds. Work with these blissful energies has become so important to me. It enables me to develop my knowledge of how to dig inside my new potential, which I know will become true. I am grateful to all who helped me on my path with colour.

Elvirah Morgaia Avelon Lafay, Denmark, www.flyingvisioncraft.com

I was working on a logo for Colour Mirrors teacher, Sara di Felice, and we got to talking about Colour Mirrors. I chose bottles 9 and 33: number 9 for stamina, focus and power, and number 33 for all the love, beauty and feminine qualities that I stand for.

I have always loved bathing, and although I have not had a bathtub for 20 years, when I received the bottles I just had to find a way to bathe in them. My boyfriend has a wooden house, with a terrace which overlooks the field with our horses. I had the idea to put a bath there, as there was no room inside, so I went and bought a kids plastic pool and we filled it with air. I started decorating the surroundings for my outside spa. I got flowers from the field, candlelight and crystals. But when we started to fill the bath with hot water, the water heater kept shutting off. My boyfriend tried to make an oven to heat up the water with fire, but that didn't work either. I was not ready to give up, so I started to heat the water in an electric kettle. It took me four hours to get it warm enough. But ooh my, was that the best feeling after all that struggle!!

I also found an extension cord so that I could sit in the bathtub heating more water to put in when it was getting too cold, 'cause I was NOT getting out of there soon! I stayed there for 3-4 hours, sitting up looking out at the horses, lying down with my ears under the water and my hair flowing, gently touching my skin with the lovely oil. It certainly was a moment of pure love surrounding me! But also pure love of self-care from my heart to me! For me the colours in both bottles 9 and 33 balanced the perfect harmony of the feminine and masculine energies that I needed: Venus and Mars! I think the closest feeling I can find to describe it is bathing in pure love! It was absolutely beautiful. So incredibly soft! Soft, soft, soft and gentle. Soothing and magical. I will never forget it. And long for my next bath!

Gordana, Slovenia

Colour Mirrors bottles brought changes to my life. Today I feel calm, with a knowing that everything is as it should be. This is what I wished for on my colour course with Tadeja – self-understanding and thus understanding of my environment. Now I can seize new knowledge. The oils and essences transmitted all the messages that I needed to receive and removed blockages in a very loving and gentle way.

Helen Williams, UK

I have always resonated with colour, and with Colour Mirrors I have experienced coming home. The healing vibrations of the stunning colours bathe us and raise our personal vibration above the mundane. They cloak us in an aura of love and light and aid in the process of dealing with heavy, earthly issues with their unconditional, loving energy and light. This gives us the opportunity to observe the big picture, detach and act lovingly rather than react. I am overwhelmed with reassurance to have the colours in my life.

Jackie Tweedie, UK, www.jackietweedie.com

Colour Mirrors is the magic ingredient in my business as a clarity coach. It empowers me and helps my clients to achieve clarity, increase confidence and find inspiration to take decisive action, so they can experience abundance in all areas of their lives. I call Colour Mirrors 'magic' because you can see the amazing results it creates without needing to understand how it works. The beauty of this is that it cannot be manipulated or controlled and thereby allows both client and coach the freedom to explore and resolve issues without the need to second-guess.

In my experience, when you try and resolve an issue by yourself, 'you don't know what you don't know', so it can feel like an impossible task to work out where to start. Your conscious mind can be blind to the beliefs and concepts that have created your stress, and this can leave you feeling lost and overwhelmed. A conventional approach might require you to question yourself: "Why this stress? Why me? Why now?" But such questions can only ever be answered by the same confused mind that created the stress in the first place, leading you deeper into frustration, self-judgement and hopelessness.

The magic of Colour Mirrors is that it offers a completely unique solution. It enables you to bypass your conscious thinking mind or ego and gives you access to your unconscious mind (that part of your mind that stores all your inner programming). The only challenge is that your ego is designed to keep that aspect of mind hidden from you in order to maintain the status quo. This is where Colour Mirrors stands in a league of its own. By being so playfully innocent – you simply choose brightly coloured bottles – it presents no threat to the ego, enabling it to relax and reveal both the cause of your stress and the wisdom of your untapped potential.

Maybe that's why so many people I've worked with feel such a sense of recognition when they find their answers in the 'mirrors' of the colours. They say it's like "coming home" to themselves. One client even said: "I don't know how it works but it feels like magic, just like in Harry Potter."

Colour Mirrors brings the gift of clarity which, once achieved, will move you from feeling lost and confused to feeling confident, empowered, decisive and open to experience abundance in all areas of your life. And to me, that's the best magic of all!

Janette CNG Lyndley, Spain

I love the Colour Mirrors system! I have used most of the dual bottles now. I do not have a bath, so I rub the oils all over my body for three nights, sleep with the oils on, then shower off in the mornings. I also bathe my feet in the oils while listening to a meditation for half an hour. I know they work as my life has changed so much, and I realise they work deep in the subconscious mind!

Janine Flint, South Africa, www.shiftcc.co.za

I had the very good fortune of meeting Melissie Jolly in 2015. From the moment I met her I loved her energy and was so curious to hear more about the work she was doing. I went for a reading and was blown away by her accurate interpretation of what was going on in my life at the time, what my challenges were and the superpowers and opportunities I was yet to step into, all by using the bottles I'd chosen. So dang accurate!

I've attended numerous workshops with Melissie, and the work simply gets deeper every time. It touches on all those aspects of ourselves that we either keep hidden from ourselves or have forgotten about but which call for our attention. It is such a spectacular, simple and profound process. I think one Colour Mirrors session can reveal more about what's working in your life and what's not than numerous sessions with a psychologist. If you want to cut to the heart of the matter, then a Colour Mirrors reading is where it's at.

Whenever I'm at a crossroads in my life I'll go for a reading and everything just magically opens up. Also, bathing in the bottles is a game changer. Something lifts and shifts, and whatever stuck energy was there in a challenging area of your life simply disintegrates. Some may call it mind games; I know it's nothing short of magic. Oh – and I will be back for more.

Joanne Arjoon, Canada, joannearjoon@gmail.com

Colour Mirrors has changed my life. By using the oils and essences in the system I have healed the underlying issues that affected my liver, menstrual cycle, sinus cavity – and also depression. I no longer take medication for health issues. I have released stuck emotions and anger. I have changed my finances and decreased my debt by 70 percent in one year. Healing family relationships and understanding my place in my family ecosystem has built my confidence and grounded me. Most importantly, operating from my heart centre is my new way of life. Colour Mirrors has blessed me with faith in knowing that 'I AM this' on the planet.

Kate Griffiths, UK, www.wholeselfleadership.com

Working with Colour Mirrors has given me a much deeper set of insights into the way our world is evolving in this time of transition. It's a journey of discovery into feminine power, and its richness is exciting and full of infinite possibilities. Colour Mirrors has expanded my understanding of spirituality, enabling me to let go of a dualistic worldview so that I can embrace a wider range of perspectives and sit with the complexities of 'what is' without needing certainty. It has opened me up so that I can be of service to many more people because I have accepted more of who I am.

Kath Roberts, UK, www.kath-roberts.com

Colour Mirrors has opened up my creativity and consciousness and connection to my divinity. It has helped me clarify my message and affirm my purpose of becoming more of a creative channel for writing/speaking/teaching in the UK and overseas. It has supported me to get out of my own way and find the courage to stand in my truth, speak my truth and own my unique authentic presence. It has helped me in releasing old emotional patterns that no longer serve me and brought back the play, joy and inspiration to my work. My journey with Colour Mirrors has been a transformative process in helping me uncover my intuitive voice, and it has given me a more embodied, reliable knowing. Colour always points a way to bring insight, clarity and perspective to any block in my life.

Katharine Bork, Canada, k.bork@hotmail.com

I love that this system is a tangible, gentle, powerful tool. Colour Mirrors complements what I do that is unique and specific to me. Whether for my own personal healing or when I am teaching a group or taking one on one sessions with a client, this system supports me and anyone in its energy. It connects with the physical, human side of ourselves as well as our spiritual selves. Through the beautiful messages of each bottle it works with our senses, providing a tool that we can touch, feel, smell, see and hear, all the while speaking to our soul, our higher self. When we connect the physical and spiritual sides of ourselves we can make the profound changes we desire on the planet. I am absolutely in love with this system and its creator. It has made and continues to make a profound difference in my life.

Kathryn Dzsudzsak, Canada, www.thebluehairmentor.com

I was introduced to Moira and these amazing bottles at a show in Toronto three months after she and the bottles landed on Canadian soil, and I am completely enamoured by these beautiful colours. It did take me a bit to warm up to these beauties, only because I had to wrap my head around how 'bottles' could help people and make a difference.

I found this out two months after my youngest daughter passed. I attended a workshop with Melissie and Moira, and it was at that workshop that I 'felt' a shift happening. Soon afterwards I began my training as a Colour Mirrors practitioner and subsequently teacher. I learned that not only do these bottles look and vibrate amazingly but the healing within them is beyond words. I was struggling with a number of things, and anger towards others was huge. On the third day of training I was in a particularly 'angry' place and picked bottle 18 (Spiritual/Material Conflict). That bottle began the healing not just within my spiritual/energetic body but also within my human body and heart.

After bathing in that bottle I never doubted or questioned what these bottles and colours can do or heal, and it only solidified my need to be part of this blessed group. It changed my life and made my healing path much clearer and free from anger. It's crazy but yes, it does work. I now teach colour, facilitate meditations using the bottles and conduct workshops. I love what Colour Mirrors has done for me and what it is doing for others. One colour at a time, it heals your world, the world within you.

Lee Hyan Young, Republic of Korea, www.blog.naver.com/kbs02mom/221315034099

I can't forget my first meeting with Colour Mirrors. First it was dazzlingly beautiful and warm. I could feel comfort just by meeting and seeing it. From when I was young, white paper and colourful crayons have been my friends. I like painting, and I think I spent the most time painting because there were not many toys and what I could do was limited. My old motto was: "I want to live like a chameleon." My colours were different from other people and sometimes I was shunned. I was afraid of being hated and wanted to be loved. I think that was why I tried so hard. I guess I was busy trying to hide my colour and make myself look good, bright and healthy. I guess I was trying hard to show off my acting skills. At one point, I felt like I had lost my colour.

One day I saw a person who guided me to a different world of colour and Colour Mirrors. I told her: "I am a sick child. There are many wounds. It's hard to survive." She showed me pretty coloured bottles instead of trying to comfort me or solve problems like other people had. She gave me the colours, and I made a choice so I could see myself completely, not just through others. After that I couldn't forget Colour Mirrors and started studying because I wanted to know more. While I was studying to become a Colour Mirrors practitioner I wanted just to be with Colour Mirrors every hour, and I was happy, as if I were becoming beautiful.

Now, for the last four years, I have met many people because of colour. Sick people say they are cured, and healthy people are happier too. Colour is a universal language. Anyone from the youngest four-year-old to someone in their 70s could share their feelings and receive good gifts through colour.

I have been called to work with kids but also find that if I have a Colour Mirrors bottle to use when I enter a formal adult lecture hall then the space already feels fresh, the air has been changed. So wherever I go, I feel confident when I am with Colour Mirrors. It is my friend who always goes anywhere for me.

Colour Mirrors is a healer that can talk instead of me. We can be together with children who can't express themselves in words. I have talked with my seven-year-old son about colour since he was four, and we can share our minds and know each other better through meditation. We can meet ourselves, understand others and communicate with the world through Colour Mirrors. For me it is a magical power that showed me to myself and allowed me to survive in the world and most importantly, to love myself.

Lisa Barry, UK, www.lisabarry.me

Colour Mirrors gives a way forward and it offers support, love, insights and unlocking. This system has helped me with awakening, seeing the bigger picture and living life with ease and joy. I am now able to let go of what no longer serves me and to see the lessons, the soul purpose and soul contracts. I have also seen huge shifts with clients who were stuck and unable to move forward.

Mandy, Guernsey

I attended Ann Bowditch's Colour Mirrors workshop at the last minute. I had intended to be a silent onlooker, but the bottles had other ideas! Having selected the coloured bottle we were most attracted to and hearing what this meant (which for all of us was very accurate), we then went on to select a bottle number that was the same as our birth date – mine being number 3. In error I picked up bottle G3 and once I realised, I said to Ann: "Thank goodness I can change it. The colours feel dirty and I don't like it." Ann was intrigued by this, and having given me the correct bottle reading, she asked me to pick up bottle G3 again. This is where the reading got really interesting.

In brief, my choice of colours highlighted the poor relationship I have with my mother. I went on to select a number of other bottles with a view to trying to understand/accept the relationship with her, and the results just blew me away. Every bottle had a very poignant meaning and connection with me and my issues with my mum, the last couple even offering up comfort and hope. I left feeling a little shell-shocked, as I couldn't understand how this had all uncovered deep-rooted feelings, and I was blown away by the accuracy of the colour bottles I had chosen. I woke up the following morning accepting the situation (something I have been unable to do for many years) and now feel I can move forward where this is concerned.

Meike Lawrence, UK, www.HomeopathyForVitality.co.uk

I have always felt significant shifts and releases of old energy with the Colour Mirrors system. I remember on a workshop with Katherine Jones I chose two bottles to represent my difficult relationship with my mother. Katherine then swapped the 'me' bottle that was light pink with a more potent and powerful one, a rich fuchsia colour, and my body spontaneously released the old toxic energy that I had stored primarily in my pelvis and root. It travelled up my body and I coughed it out! Needless to say I have felt a lot lighter and less toxic since!

Monica Burman, UK, www.facebook.com/monica.burman.58

I don't have a bath facility where I live, so in the dark under the moon eclipse I poured a 'Big Magic' bottle (pale gold over olive) on my naked body and massaged it in. I felt ZAPPED! Total release from my past and past lives. Those lessons are DONE in this life. My body felt relief where it had been aching and sore for the previous four days, and somehow I felt cleansed and refreshed even though slightly drained. Spiritually I now have hope and feel peace with where I am at in my life. Letting go is very cathartic.

Nicky Batt, UK, www.facebook.com/ConsciousColourLiving

Since joining Colour Mirrors my life has changed immeasurably. I've stopped playing small and I have embraced my power! I feel more comfortable in my skin and have the confidence now to make empowered choices to enable my self-growth into new adventures and a new business. For me and many of my clients the word 'empowerment' is very important, as it places the potential for growth and healing onto the individual. Colour Mirrors does exactly that – it empowers! People are able to make the necessary changes and take the next step(s) forward to reach their potential. Colour Mirrors is always by my side, dancing and interweaving with my life each day.

Park Youngsuk, Republic of Korea, www.instagram.com/suk_colorstory

Colour Mirrors is for me the gift of God. It is a tool that tells various emotions that human beings cannot express. I do not know my mind from time to time. I do not know why I have such a heart. At such a time I touch my heart with a Colour Mirrors bottle and it wraps my heart.

Penny Wing, Spain, www.pennywing.com

It is such a cliché to say that working with Colour Mirrors has changed my life, BUT it is the truth. The bottles are full of powerful, magical, colourful energy that really does shift blocks or stuck energy. I held grief in my body for 22 years and it was not released until I started connecting with the bottles. I now teach others the magic of this system and bring the bottles into EVERY type of work that I do! Colour is tangible, it can be seen, it can be felt and most importantly, it works!!

Roberta, Slovenia

With so many Colour Mirrors oils and essences I used, I saw the growth and success in my home and for all my family. So many things turned out to be for the best! I learned a lot. I had extreme reactions after bathing in oils. The bottles are so strong – they pull out of you what is weak and painful and harmonise your emotions.

Sam Thorpe, UK, www.intoalignment.com

Beyond language and beyond intellect, sometimes a place that's difficult to get to in a busy and left-brained world, Colour Mirrors gives permission to be fully in the present, with no need to have the answers – but to allow the learning, with permission to just be the 'I AM'. Thank you Melissie for this powerful realisation: "We are the I AM". The truth of our current reality is laid before us and open for us to transcend our current bonds. Whenever I am lost, stuck or in need of direction, I can come into a space of not knowing – not having to know – and into a space of allowing possibilities, opportunities and observations beyond judgement.

Shirley Archibald, UK, www.shirleyarchibald.co.uk

The first time I experienced Colour Mirrors was during an EFT (Emotional Freedom Technique) session with Sharon King, when she used the spritzer bottles to move stuck energy during the session. The colours enhanced the session greatly, adding a full sensory experience by moving energy quickly, and from that moment I was hooked. A few years later I decided to learn about Colour Mirrors with Korani by becoming a Colour Mirrors practitioner, and I haven't looked back.

Because I am a sceptic I often question the effectiveness of Colour Mirrors, and each time I am astounded by the accuracy of sessions that I give and receive. I have bathed in a lot of bottles and find that for me, the changes happen gently.

I find Colour Mirrors readings provide clarity in difficult situations when people feel utterly lost in their lives. They are also very effective for use with difficult relationships because the person receiving the session can see their relationships visually and is able to move bottles around and bring in support in the form of other bottles. This process can really help to heal their relationships. It is a way of giving a bit of power to someone who feels powerless.

I have developed my own system of merging EFT with Colour Mirrors. This can provide hope and answers when someone finds it hard to express themselves because they are no longer dealing with words but just the subconscious, which is infinitely more powerful. I love Colour Mirrors because I never stop learning and I keep gaining new insights and shifts.

Zane Piese, UK, www.atlantisskincare.com

I love Colour Mirrors. This system changed my life, and I can't imagine being without these amazing bottles. When I have a bad mood or something is stuck, I ask and the answer is given in seconds. It also helps me to work with my shadow side as soon as it comes out. Sometimes I am very busy or on the road and it's not possible to use the sprays and bottles, but this is first remedy when I am at home and it uplifts my energy like magic.

Finding out More

If you have enjoyed this book and would like to know more about Colour Mirrors, there are plenty of options! Your first stop is the Colour Mirrors website, www.colourmirrors.com, where you can see upcoming events, find a practitioner or teacher, purchase guided meditations and, of course, select a bottle and read its message.

Colour Mirrors Courses and Workshops

A wide range of Colour Mirrors-based workshops is available in various countries around the globe, and members of our team offer Colour Mirrors introductory courses, practitioner training and teacher training. There are also many Colour Mirrors practitioners and teachers who share the wonders of the system by merging colour with a variety of other tools and techniques to create their own unique workshops and courses. We have found that by adding its special vibration and light, Colour Mirrors enhances and informs other healing and therapeutic modalities in the most beautiful ways, and we are constantly amazed at the ingenuity of both the system and our wonderful teachers and practitioners.

Visit www.colourmirrors.com for further information and to find practitioners and teachers of Colour Mirrors.

Books on Colour and Colour Mirrors

If you would like to read more from Korani and Melissie, the following books are based around the energies and wisdom of Colour Mirrors:

The Language of Light: Golden Keys to Ascension

A Book of Platinum Light (e-book)

Colour Conversations (e-book)

For further information and to purchase, please visit www.korani.net.

What the Seeker Found

For further information and to purchase, please visit Amazon online.

The following books were written by teachers of Colour Mirrors and we are delighted to share them here, as these authors bring the wisdom of colour to life through their teachings.

Moira Bush: *8 Colours of Prosperity: Activating the Law of Attraction with Colour Frequencies* (www.moirabush.com)

Kath Roberts & Kate Griffiths: *Colourful Boardrooms* (www.colourfulboardrooms.com)

Tadeja Jere Jakulin: *Systems Everywhere: Colours and Numbers Connections* (www.turistica.si/jere-jakulin)

Colour Mirrors Webinars

Eight Spiritual Principles

Melissie's *8 Spiritual Principles* webinar series takes you on a personal journey through the spiritual principles that underpin the Colour Mirrors system, offering valuable insights into how to live a life of greater freedom and joy.

This webinar series is available on Korani's website: www.korani.net

Spiritual Fitness

Take an empowering deep-dive into the energies of bottles 1-36 in the *Spiritual Fitness* webinar series with Melissie, Korani and Sharon King. Learn how these bottles, 'The Wisdoms', can support and enhance your everyday life.

This webinar series is available on Korani's website: www.korani.net.

Colour Mirrors Oracle Cards and Colour Your Shadow Cards

Moira Bush has produced a set of Oracle Cards based around the Colour Mirrors bottles. This beautifully presented deck uses colour to help you discover your blocks and issues and how to shift them. It offers clear, simple, direct guidance and inspiration. Each card, depicting a Colour Mirrors oil or essence bottle among beautiful artwork and imagery, offers a powerful and enlightening message in the accompanying mini-booklet.

Moira's latest cards are called *Colour Your Shadow.* Each of the 44 cards reveals a specific colour that will help you release negative patterns and clear your path so that you can become authentically empowered.

The *Colour Mirrors Oracle Cards* and *Colour Your Shadow* Cards are available at www.moirabush.com.

Colour Mirrors on Social Media

You can find Colour Mirrors on Facebook at www.facebook.com/ColourMirrors.

You are also welcome to join the 'closed' Colour Mirrors group, which is a forum to ask questions, share experiences and find out about Colour Mirrors related news and events:

www.facebook.com/groups/102268312880/

References

Goodman, L., 2000. *Linda Goodman's Star Cards: A Divination Set Inspired by the Astrological and Numerological Teachings of Linda Goodman,* Hampton Roads Publishing Co., Newburyport, MA.

Goethe, J.W., 1840. *Theory of Colours*, John Murray Publisher, London.

McKimm, R., 2017. *Colour, Health and Wellbeing Through the Lens of Colour Analytical Psychology, in Colour Design – Theories and Applications* (2nd Edition), Ed Janet Best, Woodhead Publishing, Cambridge.

Grant, J. & Kelsey, D., 1967. *Many Lifetimes*, Victor Gollancz Ltd., London.

Ruiz, M., 1997. *The Four Agreements*, Amber-Allen Publishing Inc., San Rafael, CA.

About the Authors

Melissie Jolly

Melissie is the founder of the Colour Mirrors system but she often looks at it with a fair amount of awe, as she really feels as if she had nothing to do with it other than having been the incredibly blessed and lucky straw through which the system poured. This book has been another wonderful journey among many wonderful journeys through colour and has given her the joy of unfurling a few more petals of the colour lotus. Melissie was born in Kenia very long ago and now lives in Stanford in the Western Cape in South Africa.

Korani Connolly

Korani began to read before she was two years old and has rarely been without a book in her hand since. To become an author has been the fulfilment of a life's dream and she has now produced several books, most in conjunction with her dear friend Melissie Jolly. She is a Colour Mirrors teacher and teacher trainer and loves to use the Colour Mirrors system in workshops to facilitate personal and spiritual alignment, connection and expansion for participants. She was born in New Zealand and now lives in Dorset, England with her husband and their two rather special feline companions.

Bottle Index

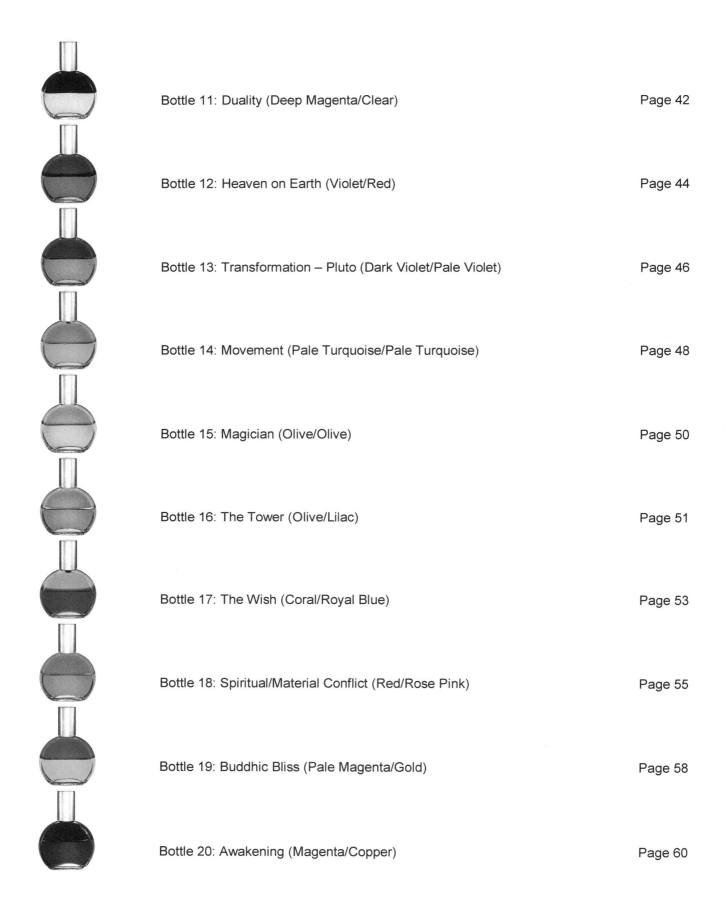

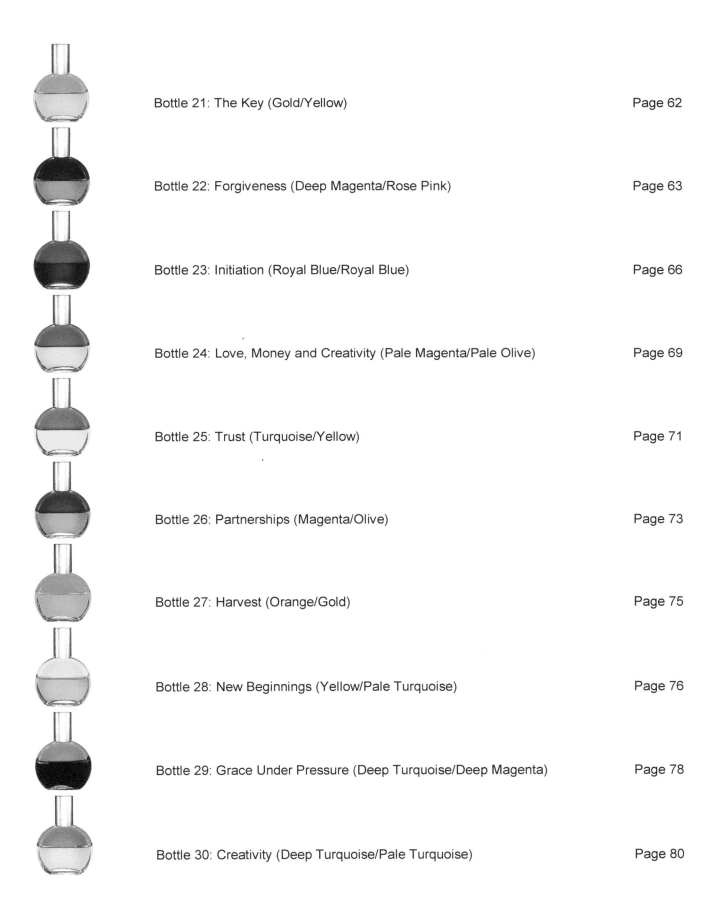

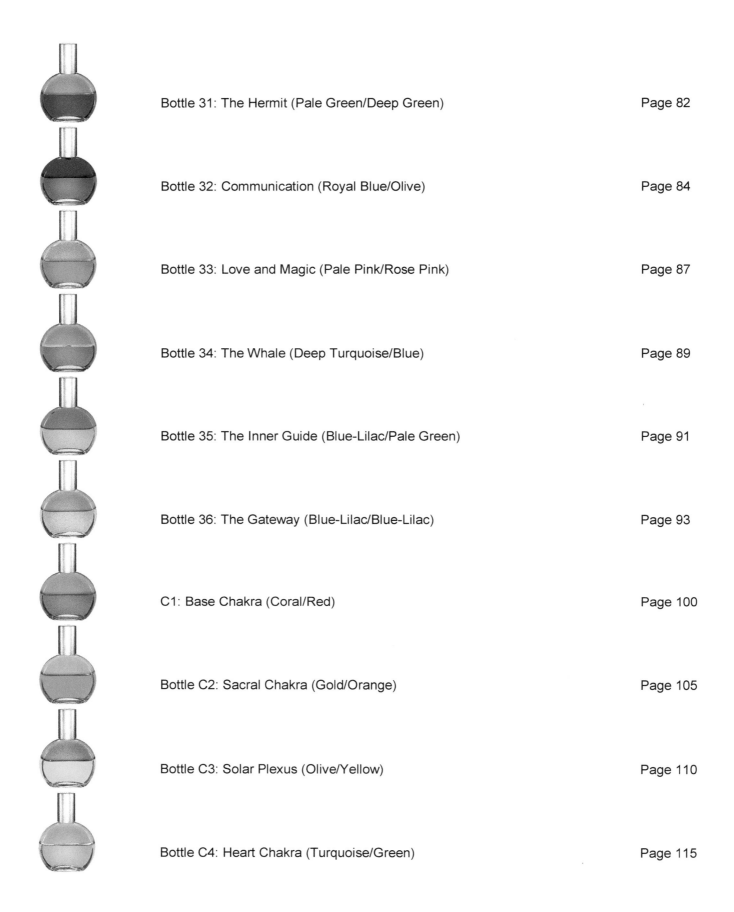

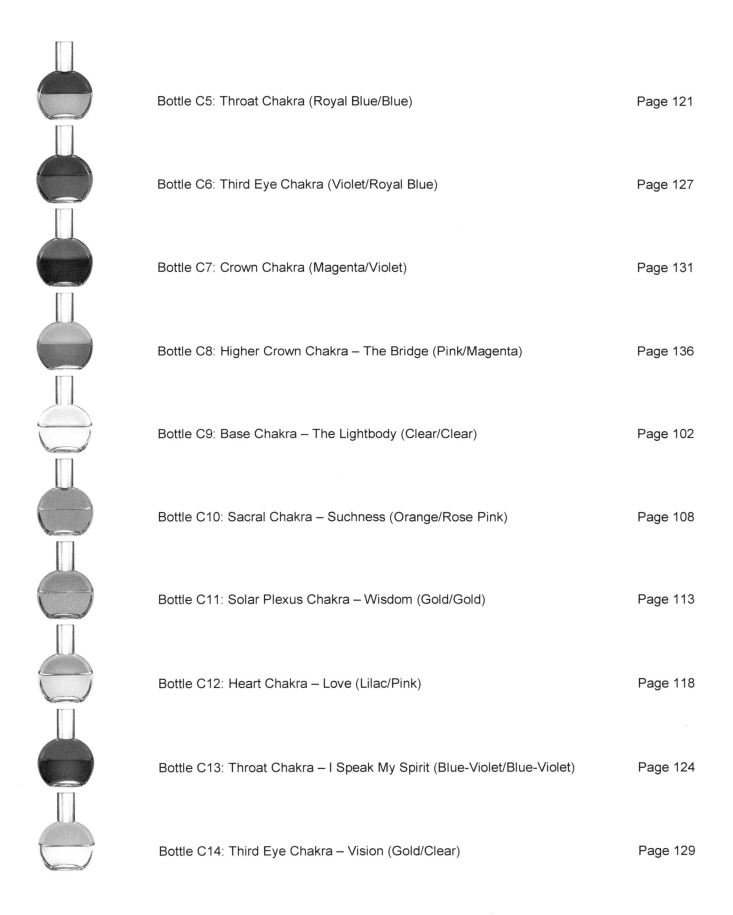

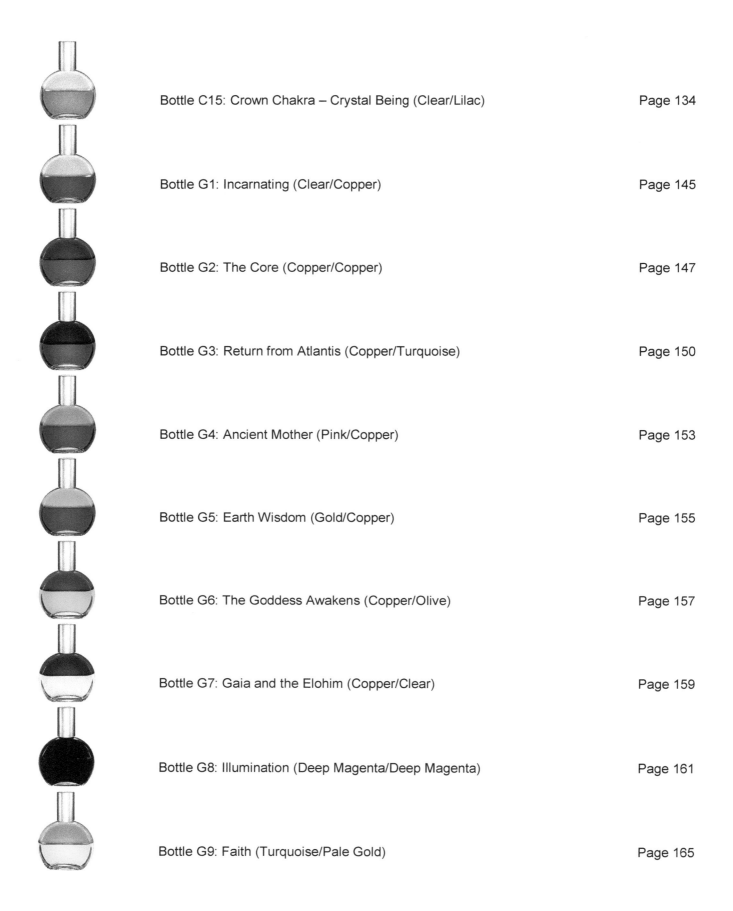

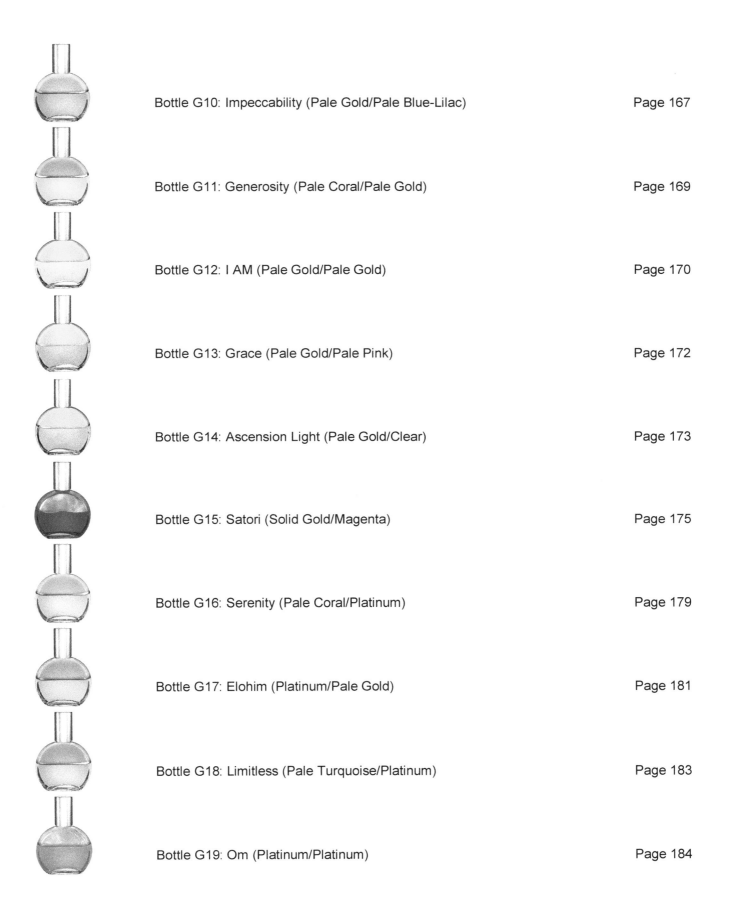

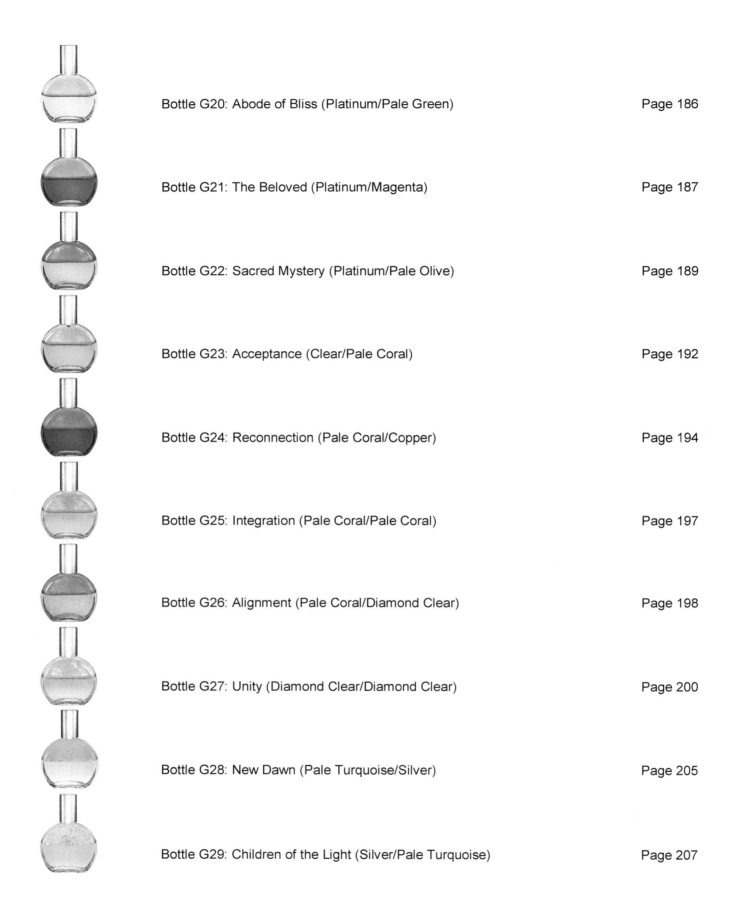

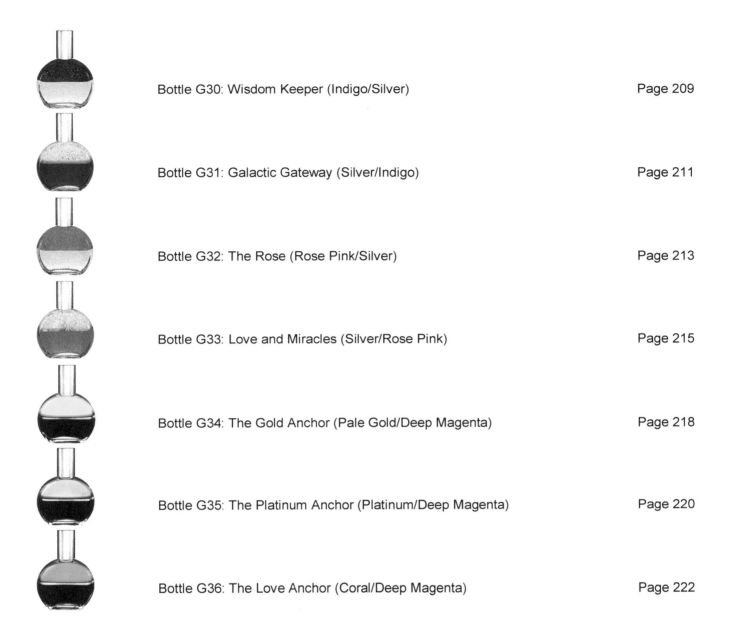

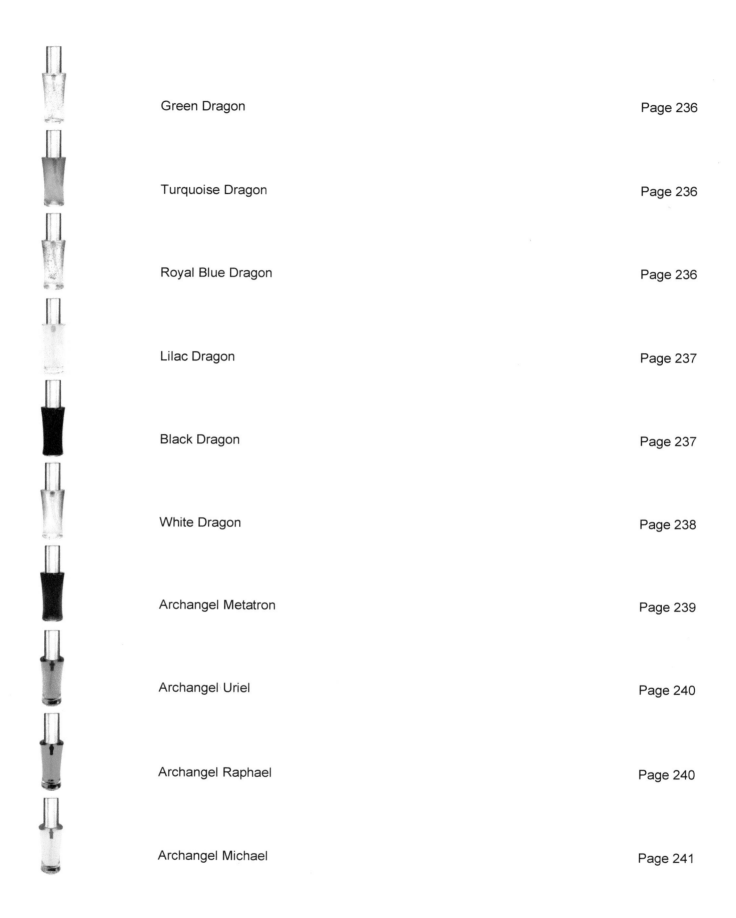

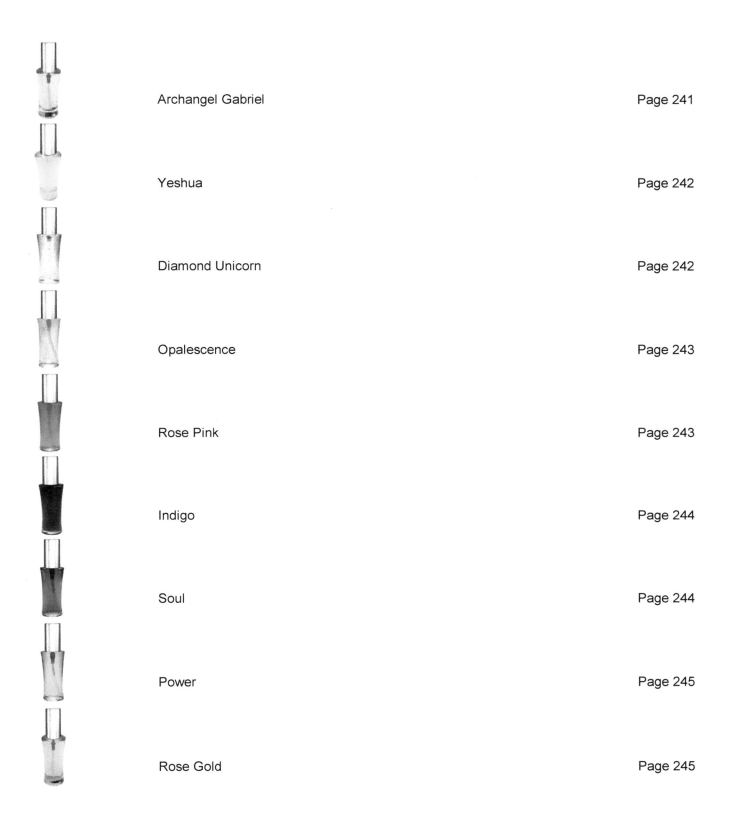

Lightning Source UK Ltd.
Milton Keynes UK
UKHW050727261122
412761UK00009B/98